THE PENGUIN BUSINESS DICTIONARY

Michael Greener was born in Barry, Glamorgan, in 1931. He was educated, *inter alia*, at Douai School and graduated in economics, law and accountancy at the University of Wales, Cardiff, in 1953. Articled with Deloitte, Plender, Griffiths – chartered accountants – he became an Associate Member of the Institute of Chartered Accountants in England and Wales in 1956 and a Fellow in 1966. He was personal assistant to the secretary of the *Western Mail and Echo*, Cardiff, where he was mostly responsible for the reorganization of accounting systems (1957–60). He was then assistant lecturer, later lecturer in accounting at the College of Commerce, Wednesbury, Staffordshire, until forced to resign due to ill-health in 1963. After a period in hospital he gradually assumed control of the family retail jewellery business and, in due course, became chairman and managing director. In 1973 he opened, in a personal capacity, the Barry Art & Book Centre. This closed in 1983 and the bookselling section was merged with the jewellery business. In the later years of that decade the jewellery trade was discontinued and the business is now solely devoted to retail bookselling. Married in 1964, he is divorced and has one son, Matthew Dominic, who is married and working in greater London. He has contributed many articles to professional journals, both at home and overseas, and still devotes much of his time to writing. His books include *Between the Lines of the Balance Sheet* (1968: revised and expanded edition 1980), *Problems for Discussion in Mercantile Law* (1968), and a children's fantasy *The Red Bus* (1973). In 1991 he gained a BA degree in the humanities from the Open University.

THE PENGUIN
BUSINESS
DICTIONARY

Revised Edition

Michael Greener

PENGUIN BOOKS

PENGUIN BOOKS

Published by the Penguin Group
Penguin Books Ltd, 27 Wrights Lane, London w8 5tz, England
Penguin Books USA Inc., 375 Hudson Street, New York, New York 10014, USA
Penguin Books Australia Ltd, Ringwood, Victoria, Australia
Penguin Books Canada Ltd, 10 Alcorn Avenue, Toronto, Ontario, Canada m4v 3b2
Penguin Books (NZ) Ltd, 182–190 Wairau Road, Auckland 10, New Zealand

Penguin Books Ltd, Registered Offices: Harmondsworth, Middlesex, England

First published by Penguin Books as *The Penguin Dictionary of Commerce* 1970
Reprinted with revisions 1971
Second edition 1980
New edition published as *The Penguin Business Dictionary* 1987
and simultaneously by Viking
Revised edition 1994
5 7 9 10 8 6 4

Copyright © Michael Greener, 1970, 1971, 1980, 1987, 1994
All rights reserved

Set in 8.25/10 pt Monophoto Bembo
Set by Datix International Limited, Bungay, Suffolk
Printed in England by Clays Ltd, St Ives plc

for Max

PREFACE TO THE THIRD EDITION

This is the third, and extensively revised, edition of a book which first appeared in 1970 as *The Penguin Dictionary of Commerce*.

In the preface of the second edition attention was drawn to the difficulties that necessarily attend the codification of a topic which is in a continual state of change. These problems have been exacerbated by the many and various shifts in both law and practice which have occurred in the intervening period, and although many of the entries remain essentially unchanged, a considerable amount of new material has been added which it is hoped will aid and inform the non-specialist in the contemporary business world. In an attempt to indicate more exactly the area covered and to keep the content within manageable limits, the book has been given a change of title.

Irrespective of this change, the objective remains the same. It is to provide a key to the multifarious rules and regulations which surround and attach to man's behaviour in the market place, whether that market place be the City of London, the local shopping precinct or the country fair.

These constraints have been developed progressively through the centuries. In so far as they were enshrined in statute or imposed by judicial precedent, they comprised what for many years was known as the law merchant, or, more commonly, mercantile law. Because so great a part of British trade was connected with the sea, much of that law was similarly orientated, and a tendency developed to equate mercantile law with that body of legislation appertaining to the mercantile marine, or Merchant Navy. With the object of dispersing such confusion the adjective 'mercantile' gradually gave way to the more neutral 'commercial' and the parameters within which both national and international trade were conducted came to be described as commercial law, or, more laconically, as commerce.

Recently, a further shift in nomenclature has taken place. The term 'commerce', with its slightly Dickensian overtones, has itself fallen into disfavour as being somewhat inappropriate in an age of advancing technology and the phrase 'business studies' has taken its place. Students who once studied the methodology of commerce now tend to pursue increasingly specialized courses in business studies at colleges of advanced technology.

The relaunching of an old product under a new label can often be dismissed as a cheap gimmick to boost flagging demand. On the other hand, a similar technique may be employed to call attention to changes in both design and substance which will render that product more relevant to the genuine needs of the market. The contribution of the service industries to the British economy is increasing at an extraordinary rate and the present financial services revolution looks certain to reinforce that trend considerably. It is in the light of these changes that the redesignation of this book as *The Penguin Business Dictionary* should be seen.

The context does not claim to be exhaustive and the balance must inevitably be open to criticism, but, in attempting to give a general insight to the casual inquirer, the needs of those seeking in-depth knowledge within particular areas must inevitably be sacrificed.

The aim has been twofold. It is, first, to provide a guide to those, whether they be students or inquisitive laymen, who wish to obtain some familiarity with the language and practices common to those who inhabit the corridors of national or international trade and finance, and, second, to supply those who may be experienced in certain specialized areas with rudimentary facts concerning matters outside their immediate remit.

Needless to say, one cannot hope to provide within limited space a comprehensive guide to the complex structure of the contemporary business world, nor a reliable key to the singular languages spoken therein. This is particularly so when that structure is expanding at a hitherto unprecedented rate and the jargon becoming daily more esoteric. The most that one can usefully do is attempt to give a broad overview of the paraphernalia of laws and practices as they exist at one selected point in time whilst, at the same time, highlighting areas and directions of change in a subject-matter which is as amorphous as it is immense.

In compiling a book of this nature it is inevitable that books written by specialists in various fields are combed for relevant material. These books number so many that it would be neither feasible nor practical to list them and a general acknowledgement of the help that their authors provided must suffice. Wherever possible, source material has been used. Various organizations and institutes were approached with the object of obtaining their own assessment of the role they occupied in, and the services they offered to, the business world. Most provided information in abundance and in expressing thanks I must apologize for the omission of so much of the material so generously supplied. I can only trust that in abstracting what seemed to be the salient facts I have done these bodies no disservice.

It only remains to acknowledge the debt owed to all those who assisted with the practical problems of putting the book together, not the least the editorial staff of Penguin Books, who curbed my wildest impulses and laid down necessary guidelines.

All the additional typing was elegantly effected by Ann Mabey, who showed considerable cryptographical expertise, not to mention immense patience, in making some sense out of my untidy and much annotated scripts. In the laborious business of proofreading, help was received from various sources. The principal burden was carried by my son Matthew, but other sufferers included Lorna Palmer and my nephew and niece, Peter and Kate Harvey. To all these I can only say – thank you. I hope that the end product is not totally unworthy of the time and effort they most generously gave.

PREFACE TO THE 1994 EDITION

As in industrial technology so also in the business world, it is not so much the velocity of change which astonishes but the very acceleration that appears to underlie that process. New terms, abbreviations and acronyms are continually springing forth within the lexicon of trade and monetary affairs and nowhere do they emerge with more unrelenting frequency than in the areas of financial instruments and derivatives which, although they may be constant in intent, are as variable in both description and presentation as are the products of *haute couture*.

Such circumstances make the updating of a reference book such as this an unenviable task. In this revised edition the aim has been to present a summary of the state of affairs within the world of business which is as true and fair as can be achieved, but in the almost certain knowledge that the time between the finalization of revisions and the publication of the revised text will provide a gap through which both new terms, and modifications of old, may make their way into what might be termed business-speak without affording opportunity for apprehension and definition. It can but be hoped that such novelties prove to be few and of no great moment.

One such change of usage that has occurred between manuscript and proof is that flowing from the general adoption of the Maastricht Treaty which has led to the European Community becoming known, albeit prematurely, as the European Union. This alteration in nomenclature has, as far as possible, been admitted by changes in the text wherein references to the European Community have been supplanted by the newly adopted term 'European Union' and EC has become EU. In putting EU where once was either EC or EEC the object has been to reflect change of usage rather than any fundamental revision of meaning.

In preparing this revised edition thanks must be given to Pamela Gibbons who struggled most effectively with typing the manuscript pages, not to mention my friend Matthew Griffiths who rescheduled the list of abbreviations. The very arduous task of proofreading was facilitated by the freely given time of Kay Mitchell with the additional help of Ann Mabey, Philippa Keen and Sarah Rafique, while support and refreshments in the early stages were ever supplied by Tony and Audrey Mullen and family. It should be emphasized that any remaining errors or omissions are mine alone.

LIST OF ABBREVIATIONS

3i	Investors in Industry
aa	always afloat
AAAI	Associate of the Institute of Administrative Accounting and Data Processing
AAIA	Associate of the Association of International Accountants
aar	against all risks
AB	able-bodied seaman
ABAA	Associate of the British Association of Accountants and Auditors
ABI	Association of British Insurers
ABP	Associated British Ports
a/c	account
ACA	Associate of the Institute of Chartered Accountants in England and Wales
ACAS	Advisory Conciliation and Arbitration Service
ACCA	Associate of the Chartered Association of Certified Accountants
ACEA	Associate of the Association of Cost and Executive Accountants
ACIB	Associate of the Chartered Institute of Bankers
ACIS	Associate of the Chartered Institute of Secretaries and Administrators
ACMA	Associate of the Institute of Chartered Management Accountants
ACT	advance corporation tax
ADP	automatic data processing
ADR	American depositary receipt
AEA	Atomic Energy Authority
AEU	Amalgamated Engineering Union
AFBD	Association of Futures Brokers and Dealers
AFRC	Agricultural and Food Research Council
AG	Aktiengesellschaft (type of German company)
AGM	annual general meeting

AHC	Accepting Houses Committee
AIA	Associate of the Institute of Actuaries
AICS	Associate of the Institute of Chartered Shipbrokers
AID	Agency for International Development
AIMTA	Associate of the Institute of Municipal Treasurers and Accountants
AIQS	Associate of the Institute of Quantity Surveyors
AMA	American Management Association
APACS	Association for Payment Clearing Services
APEX	Association of Professional, Executive, Clerical and Computer Staff
APR	annual percentage rate
APT	Advanced Passenger Train/Automated Pit Trading
AQL	acceptable quality level
ARC	Agricultural Research Council
ARCA	Associate of the Royal College of Art
ARCUK	Architects' Registration Council of the United Kingdom
ARIBA	Associate of the Royal Institution of British Architects
ARICS	Associate of the Royal Institution of Chartered Surveyors
A/S	designation for a Scandinavian company: *Aksjeselskap* (Norway), *Aktieselskab* (Denmark)
ASA	Advertising Standards Authority
ASB	Accounting Standards Board
ASCA	Associate of the Society of Company and Commercial Accountants
ASLEF	Associated Society of Locomotive Engineers and Firemen
ASSC	Accounting Standards Steering Committee
ASTMS	Association of Scientific, Technical and Managerial Staffs
ASVA	Associate of the Incorporated Society of Valuers and Auctioneers
ATII	Associate of the Institute of Taxation
AUEW	Amalgamated Union of Engineering Workers
AUT	Association of University Teachers
BA	British Airways plc
BAA	British Airports Authority plc
BACS	Bankers Automated Clearance Services
BASIC	Beginners' All-purpose Symbolic Instruction Code
BAT	British American Tobacco
BBA	British Bankers' Association

List of Abbreviations

BCCI	Bank of Credit and Commerce International
b/d	brought down
BEd	Bachelor of Education
BEHA	British Export Houses Association
BES	Business Expansion Scheme
b/f	brought forward
BFPO	British Forces Post Office
BIIBA	British Insurance and Investment Brokers Association
BIM	British Institute of Management
BIS	Bank for International Settlements
bit	binary digit
B/L, bl	bill of lading
BOTB	British Overseas Trade Board
BP	British Petroleum plc
BPC	British Productivity Council
BR	British Rail
BRS	British Road Services
BSC	British Steel Corporation
BSI	British Standards Institution
BST	British Standard Time; British Summer Time
BT	British Telecom plc
BTC	British Transport Commission
BTDB	British Transport Docks Board
BTEC	Business and Technical Education Council
BTG	British Transport Group
BTR	British Tyre and Rubber Group
BUPA	British United Provident Association
BVCA	British Venture Capital Association
BWD	British Waterways Board
CA	Chartered Accountant (Scottish Institute)
CAA	Civil Aviation Authority
CAMRA	Campaign for Real Ale
CAP	Common Agricultural Policy
Caricom	Caribbean Community and Common Market
CBI	Confederation of British Industry
cc	cubic centimetres
CCA	current cost accounting
CCT	Common Customs Tariff
CD	Certificate of Deposit

c/d	carried down
CDC	Commonwealth Development Corporation
CE	Civil Engineer
CEng	Chartered Engineer
CEO	Chief Executive Officer
CET	Central European Time; Common External Tariff
C&E	Customs and Excise
c/f	carried forward
c&f	cost and freight
CFC	chloroflurocarbon
CGT	Capital Gains Tax
CHAPS	Clearing House Automated Payment System
cif	cost, insurance and freight
cifi	cost, insurance, freight and interest
CIPFA	Chartered Institute of Public Finance and Accountancy
CIR	Commissioners of Inland Revenue
c/o	care of
COBOL	Common Business Oriented Language
cod	cash on delivery
COHSE	Confederation of Health Service Employees (now part of UNISON)
COI	Central Office of Information
COMECON	Council for Mutual Economic Aid
COMEX	New York Commodity Exchange
CPA	critical path analysis; Certified Public Accountant
CPP	current purchasing power (accounting)
CPRE	Council for the Protection of Rural England
CPSA	Civil and Public Services Association
CPU	Central Processing Unit
Cr	creditor
CSCE	Conference on Security and Co-operation in Europe
CSE	Certificate of Secondary Education
CSO	Central Statistical Office
CTT	capital transfer tax
D/A	deposit account
DBST	Double British Summer Time
DCF	discounted cash flow
DD	direct debit; demand draft
DE	Department of Employment

List of Abbreviations

DEP	Department of Employment and Productivity
DG	Director General
DHS	Department of Health
DipEd	Diploma in Education
DipHE	Diploma in Higher Education
DMS	Diploma in Management Studies
DNA	deoxyribonucleic acid
DoE	Department of the Environment
dpt	department
Dr	debtor
DSS	Department of Social Security
DTI	Department of Trade and Industry
DTP	desk-top publishing
d.w.t.	dead weight tonnage
dwt	pennyweight
EBRD	European Bank of Reconstruction and Development
EC	European Community
ECGD	Export Credits Guarantee Department
ECSC	European Coal and Steel Community
ecu	European Currency Unit
EDP	electronic data processing
EEC	European Economic Community
EETPU	Electrical, Electronic, Telecommunication and Plumbing Union
EFTA	European Free Trade Area
EFTPOS	Electronic Funds Transfer at Point of Sale
EGM	Extraordinary General Meeting
EIB	European Investment Bank
EMA	European Monetary Agreement
EMI	Electrical and Musical Industries Ltd
EMIP	equivalent mean investment period
EMS	European Monetary System
encl	enclosures
E&OE	errors and omissions excepted
EPOS	Electronic Point of Sale
EPU	European Payments Union
ERM	Exchange Rate Mechanism
ESA	European Space Agency
ETA	estimated time of arrival

EU	European Union
Euratom	European Atomic Energy Community
faa	free of all average
FAIA	Fellow of the Association of International Accountants
FAO	Food and Agriculture Organization
fas	free alongside ship
Fax	facsimile
FBAA	Fellow of the British Association of Accountants and Auditors
FBI	Federation of British Industries
FBIM	Fellow of the British Institute of Management
FCA	Fellow of the Institute of Chartered Accountants in England and Wales
FCCA	Fellow of the Chartered Association of Certified Accountants
FCEA	Fellow of the Association of Cost and Executive Accountants
FCIA	Fellow of the Corporation of Insurance Agents
FCIB	Fellow of the Chartered Institute of Bankers
FCII	Fellow of the Chartered Insurance Institute
FCIS	Fellow of the Chartered Institute of Secretaries and Administrators
FCMA	Fellow of the Chartered Institute of Management Accountants
FFA	Fellow of the Faculty of Actuaries (Scotland)
FHA	Finance Houses Association
FIA	Fellow of the Institute of Actuaries
FICE	Fellow of the Institute of Civil Engineers
FICS	Fellow of the Institute of Chartered Shipbrokers
FIEE	Fellow of the Institution of Electrical Engineers
FIERE	Fellow of the Institutions of Electronic and Radio Engineers
FIFO	first in first out
FIMBRA	Financial Intermediaries, Managers and Brokers Regulatory Authority
FIMTA	Fellow of the Institute of Municipal Treasurers and Accountants
FIQS	Fellow of the Institute of Quantity Surveyors
FIS	Family Income Supplement
FIS	Fellow of the Institute of Statisticians
fob	free on board
FORTRAN	FORmula TRANslation
FOX	Futures and Options Exchange
fpa	free from particular average
FRC	Financial Reporting Council

List of Abbreviations

FRIBA	Fellow of the Royal Institute of British Architects
FRICS	Fellow of the Royal Institution of Chartered Surveyors
FRS	Financial Reporting Standards
FRS	Fellow of the Royal Society
FRSA	Fellow of the Royal Society of Arts
FSA	Financial Services Act
FSS	Fellow of the Statistical Society
FSVA	Fellow of the Incorporated Society of Valuers and Accountants
FT	*Financial Times*
FTII	Fellow of the Institute of Taxation
G7	Group of Seven
G10	Group of Ten (Paris Club)
GAFTA	Grain and Free Trade Association
GATT	General Agreement on Tariffs and Trade
GCE	General Certificate of Education
GCSE	General Certificate of Secondary Education
GDP	Gross Domestic Product
GEC	General Electric Company
GEMMS	Gilt-Edged Market-Makers
GMB	General, Municipal, Boilermakers and Allied Trades Union
GmbH	Gesellschaft mit beschränkter Haftung (type of German company)
GMT	Greenwich Mean Time
GNP	gross national product
GSS	Government Statistical Service
HCF	highest common factor
HGV	heavy goods vehicle
HMI	Her Majesty's Inspector
HMS	Her Majesty's Ship
HMSO	Her Majesty's Stationery Office
HNC	Higher National Certificate
HND	Higher National Diploma
HP	hire purchase
hp	horse power
HWM	high water mark
IAAS	Incorporated Association of Architects and Surveyors
IAEA	International Atomic Energy Authority

IATA	International Air Transport Association
IBA	Independent Broadcasting Authority
IBA	International Bankers Association
IBM	International Business Machines
IBRC	Insurance Brokers Registration Council
IBRD	International Bank for Reconstruction and Development
ICA	Institute of Chartered Accountants
ICAB	International Cargo Advisory Body
ICAO	International Civil Aviation Organization
ICAS	Institute of Chartered Accountants of Scotland
ICCH	International Commodities Clearing House
ICFC	Industrial and Commercial Finance Corporation
ICFTU	International Confederation of Free Trade Unions
ICI	Imperial Chemical Industries
ICJ	International Court of Justice
ICT	International Computers and Tabulators
IDB	inter-dealer broker
IEA	International Energy Agency
IFC	International Finance Corporation
IHA	Issuing Houses Association
ILO	International Labour Organization
IM	Institute of Marketing
IMF	International Monetary Fund
IMRO	Investment Management Regulatory Organization
Inmarsat	International Maritime Satellite Organization
Intelsat	International Telecommunications Satellite Consortium
IOM	Institute of Office Management
IPA	Institute of Practitioners in Advertising
IPM	Institute of Personnel Management
IQS	Institute of Quantity Surveyors
IR	Inland Revenue
IRC	International Reorganization Corporation
ISBN	International Standard Book Number
ISFA	Institute of Shipping and Forwarding Agents
ISRO	International Securities Regulatory Organization
IST	Institute of Science and Technology
ISTC	Iron and Steel Trades Confederation
ITA	Independent Television Authority
ITO	International Trade Organization
ITU	International Telecommunications Union

List of Abbreviations

IWA	Inland Waterways Association
IWSP	Institute of Work Study Practitioners
JCB	Joseph C. Bamford
JDipMA	Joint Diploma in Management Studies
JIC	Joint Industrial Council
KG	Kommanditgesellschaft (German limited partnership)
kW	kilowatt
kWh	kilowatt hour
LAFTA	Latin American Free Trade Association
LAUTRO	Life Assurance and Unit Trust Regulatory Organization
LCD	lowest common denominator
LCE	London Commodity Exchange
LCH	London Clearing House
LCM	least common multiple
LDT	Licensed Deposit Taker
LEA	Local Education Authority
LIBID	London Inter-Bank Bid Rate
LIBOR	London Inter-Bank Offered Rate
LIFFE	London International Financial Futures and Options Exchange
LIFO	last in first out
LME	London Metal Exchange
LRIBA	Licenciate of the Royal Institute of British Architects
LSD	*librae, solidi, denarii* (pounds, shillings and pence)
LSE	London School of Economics and Political Science
Ltd	Limited
LTOM	London Traded Options Market
LWM	low water mark
MAFF	Ministry of Agriculture, Fisheries and Food
MBIM	Member of the British Institute of Management
MEd	Master of Education
mega	one million times
MEP	Member of the European Parliament
MICE	Member of the Institution of Civil Engineers
micro	one millionth part
MIEE	Member of the Institution of Electrical Engineers
milli	one thousandth part

MIMechE	Member of the Institution of Mechanical Engineers
MIOM	Member of the Institute of Office Management
MIPE	Member of the Institution of Production Engineers
MIRAS	Mortgage Interest Relief at Source
MIT	Massachusetts Institute of Technology
MIWM	Member of the Institution of Works Management
MLR	minimum lending rate
MOT	Ministry of Transport (now the Department of Transport)
MS	manuscript
MTFS	Medium Term Financial Strategy
MV	Merchant Vessel
NAFTA	North American Free Trade Agreement
NALGO	National and Local Government Officers Association (now part of UNISON)
NASDAQ	National Association of Securities Dealers' Automated Quotations
NASDIM	National Association of Securities Dealers and Investment Managers
NASUWT	National Association of Schoolmasters/Union of Women Teachers
NATS	National Air Traffic Services
NBA	Net Book Agreement
NCB	National Coal Board (now British Coal)
NDPS	National Data Processing Service
NEDC	National Economic Development Council
NEDO	National Economic Development Office
NERC	National Environmental Research Council
NGA '82	National Graphical Association 1982
NHS	National Health Service
NIC	National Insurance Commissioners; National Insurance Contribution
NMS	normal market size
NP	notary public
NPV	no par value; net present value
NRDC	National Research Development Corporation
NSB	National Savings Bank
NUCPS	National Union of Civil and Public Servants
NUJ	National Union of Journalists
NUM	National Union of Miners

List of Abbreviations

NUPE	National Union of Public Employers (now part of UNISON)
NUR	National Union of Railwaymen (now part of RMT)
NUS	National Union of Seamen (now part of RMT); National Union of Students
NUT	National Union of Teachers
NV	Naamloze Vennootschap (type of Dutch Company)
NVQ	National Vocational Qualification
OAPEC	Organization of Arab Petroleum Exporting Countries
OAS	Organization of American States
ODA	Overseas Development Administration
OECD	Organization for European Cooperation and Development
OEEC	Organization for European Economic Cooperation
OFFER	Office of Electricity Regulation
OFGAS	Office of Gas Supply
OFTEL	Office of Telecommunications
OFWAT	Office of Water Services
OHG	Offene Handelsgesellschaft (German unlimited company)
OHMS	On Her Majesty's Service
O&M	organization and method
ONC	Ordinary National Certificate
OND	Ordinary National Diploma
OPEC	Organization of Petroleum Exporting Countries
OR	operational research
OTC	over-the-counter market
PAYE	Pay As You Earn
PC	personal computer, Price Commission
PE	price earnings
PEP	Personal Equity Plan
PERT	Programme Evaluation and Review Techniques
PIB	Prices and Incomes Board
PLA	Port of London Authority
PLC, plc	public limited company
PLR	public lending right
PO	Post Office; postal order
POP	Post Office Preferred
POWU	Post Office Workers Union
pp	*per procurationem* (on behalf of)
PPI	policy proof of interest

PR	public relations
PRO	public relations officer
Prox	*proximo* (next month)
PSBR	Public Sector Borrowing Requirement
PSV	public service vehicle
Pty	proprietary company
QANTAS	Queensland and Northern Territories Aerial Services
Quango	quasi-autonomous non-governmental organization
R&D	research and development
RAM	Random Access Memory
RHA	Road Haulage Association
RIBA	Royal Institute of British Architects
RIE	Recognized Investment Exchange
RMS	Royal Mail Steamer
RMSD	Royal Mail Special Delivery
RMT	Rail and Maritime Transport Union
ROM	read-only memory
RPB	Recognized Professional Body
RPM	resale price maintenance
rpm	revolutions per minute
RSA	Royal Society of Arts
SA	Société Anonyme (type of French company)
sae	stamped addressed envelope
SAYE	Save As You Earn
SDR	special drawing rights
SE	Stock Exchange
SEAF	Stock Exchange Automatic Exchange Facility
SEAQ	Stock Exchange Automated Quotation System
SEAQI	Stock Exchange Automated Quotation System International
SEC	Securities and Exchange Commission (USA)
Sepon	Stock Exchange Pool Nominees
SERC	Science and Engineering Research Council
SERPS	State Earnings-Related Pension Scheme
SET	selective employment tax
SFA	Securities and Futures Association
SFO	Serious Fraud Office
SFS	Summary Financial Statements

List of Abbreviations

SI	Statutory Instrument; Système Internationale d'Unités (international measurement system)
SIB	Securities and Investments Board
SIC	Standard Industrial Classification
SOGAT	Society of Graphical and Allied Trades
SRL	Société à Responsabilité Limitée (type of French company)
SRO	self-regulating organization
SSAP	Statement of Standard Accounting Practice
SSP	Statutory Sick Pay
STAGS	Sterling Transferable Accruing Government Securities
STD	subscriber trunk dialling
stet	let it stand, reinstate
SVQ	Scottish Vocational Qualification
TALISMAN	Transfer Accounting Lodgement for Investors and Stock Management
TAURUS	Transfer and Automated Registration of Uncertified Stock
TEC	Training and Enterprise Council
TESSA	Tax Exempt Special Savings Account
TDC	Technical Development Corporation
TDR	Treasury Deposit Receipt
TGV	Train à Grande Vitesse (high-speed French train)
TGWU	Transport and General Workers' Union
TMA	Terminal Market Associations
TOPIC	Teletext Output Price Information Computer
TSA	The Securities Association
TSB	Trustee Savings Bank plc
TSSA	Transport and Salaried Staffs Association
TUC	Trades Union Congress
TVEI	Technical and Vocational Education Initiative
UCATT	Union of Construction, Allied Trades and Technicians
UCCA	Universities Central Council on Admissions
UDM	Union of Democratic Mineworkers
UITF	Urgent Issues Task Force
UKAEA	United Kingdom Atomic Energy Authority
UNCTAD	United Nations Conference on Trade and Development
UNESCO	United Nations Educational, Scientific and Cultural Organization
UNISON	Amalgam of NALGO, NUPE and COHSE

UNRRA	United Nations Relief and Rehabilitation Association
UPU	Universal Postal Union
USM	Unlisted Securities Market
VAT	value added tax
VCR	video cassette recorder
VDU	visual display unit
VSO	Voluntary Service Overseas
WCL	World Confederation of Labour
WEA	Workers' Educational Association
WEU	Western European Union
WFTU	World Federation of Trade Unions
WIP	work in progress
WIPO	World Intellectual Property Organization
xd	ex dividend

NOTES ON USING THE DICTIONARY

Words and phrases printed in **bold type** are separately defined elsewhere in the dictionary. Those at the end of an entry and preceded by ◊ should be followed up to obtain a better understanding of the subject.

a.a. 'Always afloat' relates to marine chartering. The charterer agrees that the ship will remain afloat whether at port or at sea during the time of the charter. This is to avoid damage to the hull, which is more vulnerable out of the water.

'A' list of contributories ♢ **Contributory**.

'A' ordinary shares The prefix 'A' or 'B' to shares normally denotes some curtailments of the rights customarily or legally attaching to those shares. In the majority of cases 'A' shares are non-voting shares. They are frequently issued when the majority shareholders of a company wish to raise additional risk capital without either committing themselves to a fixed annual dividend or diluting their real control. For this reason they are frowned upon officially by the Stock Exchange but, to date, no unequivocal move has been made to eliminate them from the official listings of share dealings or prices.

There are fewer new issues of these shares now than in the past since the institutional investors, who make up an increasingly high proportion of the shareholding public, are not prepared to take up risk capital where there is no corresponding element of control. ♢ **Shares: ordinary**.

AI A term particularly applicable to shipping. When applied to a ship, the letter indicates the condition of the hull and the number the condition of the trappings. To be AI is therefore to be in perfect condition.

To be more precise, 100 AI after a Maltese Cross indicates that the ship was built completely under Lloyd's survey. Without the cross, it indicates that it was built to Lloyd's specifications.

The term is now also used in a more general sense.

Abacus A piece of equipment, as opposed to a machine proper, still used in Eastern countries by skilled operators for making arithmetical calculations. Based on a system of beads on wires, it can, when used by the expert, often match the speed of Western adding machines in arriving at the correct answers to quite complex problems, particularly those involving the addition of a multitude of figures.

Abandonment A **marine insurance** term for abandoning a ship as dangerous or unseaworthy. This would normally be a total loss and the insurer would have a right to claim the subject matter. Notice of abandonment should be given to the insurer immediately.

Able-bodied seaman Strictly, one who has served three years before the mast, at least one of them in a trading vessel.

Above par A **Stock Exchange** term: **shares** are said to be above par when their **price** is above the shares' **nominal value**.

Accelerated depreciation Effectively a synonym for taxation deferred through anticipating **capital allowances** on plant, machinery, etc. In recent years, the Treasury offered aid to industry in combating the ravages of inflation and subsequent cash shortages by allowing fixed assets to be completely written off for tax purposes within the first year or few years of acquisition. By being able to increase, often substantially, capital allowances available for setting off against profits, the businesses concerned could lower their immediate tax liability and thereby make more monies available for reinvestment. This privilege was abolished in March 1984.

Acceptance When a **contract** is made there must be both **offer** and acceptance, unless it is a **contract by deed**. If one person offers to do something for another, the contract is not complete until the offer is accepted. Acceptance must be in the same terms as the offer and must be communicated to the offeror. A conditional acceptance is equivalent to an offer and is not an acceptance.

Acceptance for honour ◊ **Acceptance supra protest**.

Acceptance supra protest If a **bill of exchange** is protested and then accepted by another party to save the name of the drawer, this is known as acceptance supra protest, or acceptance for honour.

Acceptilation A term used in Scottish law: it means formal release from debt.

Accepting house or Acceptance house A financial enterprise whose principal function lies in facilitating the negotiation of **bills of exchange** either by accepting them or guaranteeing them. The main offices of these houses are situated near the central bank and other institutions concerned with the smooth running of the country's financial system. They have in modern times become very much like merchant banks and usually operate as such. Most are members of the **Accepting Houses Committee**, which was established to ensure maximum collaboration between them and generally to oversee their business. Today, these houses also hold a large portion of the country's **sterling balances**.

The signature of an established accepting house on a bill of exchange is a sign of the reliability of that bill and will enable the holder to discount it at the most favourable rates. In their modern role of **merchant banks** they also add speed to international trade by lending money to an exporter on a **trade bill**, thus bridging the gap between the release of goods and payment by the foreign buyer. Such a loan is sometimes referred to as an 'acceptance credit'.

Accepting Houses Committee Comprised of leading accepting houses and the major merchant banks, it was set up originally to supervise accepting houses and dealings in **fine bills** generally. Membership is normally reserved for merchant banks and accepting houses whose bills are freely taken by the Bank of England and are of the highest quality. ◊ **Accepting house**.

Acceptor The person drawing a **bill of exchange** is the drawer and the person on whom the bill is drawn is the drawee. When the drawee has accepted the bill, i.e. has accepted liability, he is known as the acceptor. The normal form of acceptance is by signature on the face of the bill. He cannot deny the existence and capacity of the drawer or payee or the signature of the drawer – he can, however, question an **Endorsement** (he would not be obliged to pay on a forged endorsement). Delivery is necessary for complete acceptance: this means the acceptor willingly parts with possession or gives notice of acceptance. If the bill is in the hands of a **holder in due course**, delivery is presumed.

It is possible for a bill to be negotiated before acceptance. It is then up to the holder of the bill to present it for acceptance before or at the time of payment. Presentation for acceptance is not obligatory except where the bill so stipulates or where it is payable after sight, or payable elsewhere than at the residence or place of business of the drawee.

Access ◊ **Credit card**.

Accommodation bill A bill of exchange signed by one person to accommodate another. The person signing is a **guarantor** and receives no **consideration**. Once value has been given for the bill, he is liable should the **acceptor** fail to pay at the proper time.

Accord and satisfaction When one party has completed his obligations in a **contract** he may agree to release the other party from that party's obligations. This may be by a document under seal, or by receiving some new **consideration**. Release in return for new consideration is known as accord and satisfaction.

Account, credit A term normally reserved for credit arrangements made by a purchaser with a particular trader. The purchaser is permitted to buy goods up to a certain value without paying for them on acquisition – the value is set as a maximum for a specific time period, often one month. He receives a summary of his transactions at agreed intervals and pays on a basis specified when the account

is opened. There is an increasing tendency to use this method, but with certain variations that protect the vendor, e.g. it is not uncommon for a person to open a credit account at a store and to pay fixed monthly amounts from the date of commencement. He may then obtain goods when needed up to a limit fixed at the time of the original agreement. ◊ **Credit** ◊ **Credit card**.

Account, current This refers to the cheque account opened by an individual or an organization with a bank or building society. It is an account into which monies are paid or from which sums are withdrawn either in cash or by cheque in the course of everyday affairs. Most individuals keep a current account on which to draw cheques in settlement of debts. Banks, or building societies, nowadays issue a cheque guarantee card to regular customers enabling the bank's guarantee to be attached to cheques issued by the customer provided certain conditions are followed.

Customers receive regular statements from the bank, or building society, giving details of all transactions and the outstanding balance. While normally this should be a credit balance certain banks do allow accounts to be overdrawn up to a stated maximum without charge. This, however, is the exception rather than the rule and unless overdraft facilities have been arranged beforehand the bank is entitled to refuse to allow the account to be overdrawn and may decline to honour any cheque which would cause this to happen. ◊ **Bank overdraft**. At one time charges were made on personal as well as business accounts, the level of which depended on the number of transactions effected. Competition has persuaded banks to drop such charges for personal customers but they have been retained for business accounts and are governed by the tariff published by the bank. Most banks and building societies execute **standing orders** and **direct debits** on behalf of their customers.

Account days A **stock exchange** term for the days set aside for the settlement of accounts (deals between members). They are also called 'settling days'. Transactions in **gilt-edged securities** are accounted for daily, other transactions are settled fortnightly on alternate Mondays. Clients receive statements on preceeding Thursdays to give them time to send in the necessary money. Accounts may be carried over from one period of account to another – a payment is made for this privilege, known as contango, or the contango rate. (Strictly speaking, this applies to transactions where the buyer does not wish to take up the **shares** at the particular time, i.e. **bull** transactions.) Where it is a question of the non-delivery of shares, e.g. where the client has not yet obtained them and does not wish to at prevailing prices, the rate is known as **backwardation**.

The present system of fortnightly accounts and prescribed 'settling days' was due to be abolished and replaced by a three-day rolling settlement once the share transfer system had been transformed by the introduction of automated share transfers through **Taurus**. Problems and disagreements within the City have led to the abandonment of the Taurus programme and in consequence the projected abolition of the fortnightly account has been indefinitely postponed.

Account executive A term used to describe an employee of an **advertising agency** who carries full responsibility for looking after the affairs of one or more of the agency's clients, i.e. has complete responsibility for particular advertising contracts and their fulfilment.

Account payee This is one of various **cheque crossings**. When a cheque is crossed with the words 'account payee' or 'account payee only' written between the crossed lines the intention of the drawer is that the monies should be paid only into the account of the drawee. Until recently this instruction had no legal force and if the cheque bearing such a crossing had been endorsed and paid into another person's account the bank would have been under no liability to reimburse the drawer unless negligence could be proven. Defiance of the crossing might have been construed as negligence on the part of the accepting bank. The law has now been changed giving legal effect to such a crossing and banks are bound to respect it as allowing the cheque to be paid only into the stated payee's account. This has the drawback of creating problems for persons without bank accounts. If they receive a cheque crossed 'account payee' they cannot endorse it over to another person for collection on their behalf.

Account, sales A term used when **goods** are consigned for sale to an **agent** in another country. The agent submits an account of sales to the **consignor** of the goods, giving details of the goods sold, together with the selling price, **commission**, expenses and the **net profit**. It usually accompanies the amount due.

Account, savings and deposit Bank customers frequently open interest-earning accounts in which to place funds surplus to everyday requirements and against which they do not need the facility to write cheques. The High Street Banks offer a variety of such accounts with rates of interest which vary according to both the size of the sum to be kept in the account and the time for which it is to remain deposited. Similar savings-type accounts are offered by Building Societies, again with rates of interest dependent on the size of the deposit and the frequency of access. In the present competitive environment the names and conditions of such accounts are continually changing in the attempt to attract customers. As a general rule it can be said that the closer to instant access that the customer requires his savings to be, then the lower the likely rate of interest will be – though there are exceptions where the customer agrees to keep the balance above a certain minimum level. Overdrafts are not available on savings or deposit accounts. In most banks where a customer keeps both a current and a savings account it is possible to arrange with the bank that a certain sum will be transferred from the savings account into the current account when the balance on the latter falls below an agreed level. This enables the customer to maximize the interest earned on his savings by keeping the minimum necessary on current account. This practice has been partly anticipated by the banks offering interest-bearing current accounts.

Account stated An account showing a **balance** agreed on by two parties as due from one to another. It is legally binding unless it can be shown to be untrue.

Account, trading This shows income from **sales** and deductions from them, together with the cost of buying the **goods** and/or putting them into a condition for sale. The final figure is the **gross** **profit** on trading which is transferred to the **profit and loss account**.

Accountant Generally speaking the term accountant refers to a person who is responsible for preparing and keeping the accounts of an organization. In a more specific sense it is used, with a prefix such as 'Chief' or 'Assistant' or 'Cost', to denote a post of financial responsibility in industry or commerce, e.g. the chief accountant of a business is the person appointed to control the financial running of the concern and, with his staff, to keep all books and records demanded by law or by the proprietor(s). His position is one of considerable responsibility.

The term is also used in a generic sense much as the term 'lawyer'. Any unqualified person may set up business as an 'accountant' and take in work – usually tax work. He may advertise himself as such but must not, by the use of a prefix or suffix, suggest that he is a member of a professional association. ◊ **Auditor** ◊ **Certified Accountants, Chartered Association of** ◊ **Chartered accountant** ◊ **Cost accountant** ◊ **Management accountant**.

Accounting for inflation Published accounts are commonly prepared on **historical cost accounting** principles. In times of inflation such accounts do not give an accurate picture of real profits or the real present value of **capital employed**. In order to give both the public and the investor a proper appreciation of business results it is thought desirable to eliminate, as far as possible, variations that result from, and only from, changes in the value of money, e.g. if the price level has doubled over five years or, which is to state the same point, the value of money has halved over that period, then a profit of £200,000 this year is not worth the same amount as that sum five years ago. Over such a period a business would need to have doubled its profits just to remain on an even keel.

In order to reflect the effect of inflation on published figures various accounting measures have been proposed. However, none has yet found sufficient support in financial circles to be enshrined in law, particularly in company law inasmuch as most of the nation's business is conducted by companies of one kind or another. Each proposed system has been attacked for a different reason and one of the more common objections relates to the fact that in times of inflation not all prices increase at the same rate and, even if they do, it is necessary to make the almost impossible distinction between increases due to inflation and increases due to improvement in the asset purchased.

Despite the many differences of opinion, however, there is fairly general agreement about the need for change in accounting techniques, and although no final steps have been taken to alter the method of providing annual accounts, many companies append statements to the filed copies of their accounts which show the existing figures adjusted for changes in relevant price levels.

In 1980 after much heart-searching the major accounting bodies agreed that a form of **current cost accounting** should be introduced and that larger public companies should include with their annual accounts an additional set of accounts based on current cost accounting principles, which, as set out in SSAP 16, are a modified version of those recommended by the Sandilands Committee. Whilst there were no statutory requirements for such additional accounts to be prepared, members of the accountancy

bodies were expected to conform to the proposals and auditors were to give reasons if current cost information was excluded. The majority of the public companies concerned did, in fact, supply the additional accounts, though not always with enthusiasm or conviction. The experiment was initially for a three-year period. There were, however, reservations within the accounting profession as to the efficacy of the system and this, together with the failure of many major companies to comply with the recommendations, led to the proposals being temporarily aborted. The need to establish a reliable method of accounting for inflation is still, none the less, seen by the professional bodies as of considerable importance.

That the present position is not accepted as ideal is evidenced by provisions in recent legislation for alternatives to historical cost. The Companies Act 1989 supplies what are referred to as 'alternative' accounting rules which allow most assets to be shown in the accounts at current cost or at a value which the directors deem more a true and fair view. If this option is taken the company must, however, give details in those accounts of the corresponding value at historical cost for each item so revalued or the difference between the value shown and the historical cost equivalent. The same applies to depreciation figures relating to assets revalued which have been restated in the accounts so that they relate to the new asset values.

Accounting period This is the regular period to which the accounts of a business or an organization are made up. When accounts are published, the period to which they refer must be stated and the beginning of one period should follow immediately upon the end of the preceding one. For a limited company, the period is normally one year, with certain exceptions, such as when the year end needs to be changed to bring trading periods of various members of a group of companies into line. Again, it is becoming common to use a 52- or 53-week year rather than a calendar year.

As far as limited companies governed by the Companies Acts are concerned, the period of accounting is known as the '**accounting reference period**', and the date to which this period runs in each year must be notified to the Registrar of Companies. If no contrary notification is made, then the relevant date will be 31 March of each year. There are also various provisions concerning notification of any change in the date of the end of the accounting reference period. Penalties may be incurred by directors where these provisions are not observed. ◊ **Accounting reference date**. ◊ **Annual accounts** ◊ **Annual report** ◊ **Annual return.**

Accounting principles The principles according to which accounts are prepared. The term does not relate to the mundane processes of double-entry book-keeping but to the concepts adopted in defining and calculating individual items of income, expenditure, assets and liabilities. Generally speaking, these concepts and processes have been agreed over the years within the accounting profession and in more recent times have been the subject of various Statements of Standard Accounting Practice (SSAPs), to which members of the major accounting bodies are expected to conform. These principles have particular reference to the accounts of limited companies, which must by law be filed and distributed to members, but they are also intended as fairly com-prehensive guidelines in the preparation of any sets of accounts, whether of trading organizations or non-profit-making bodies.

In more recent years the law itself has begun to concern itself with accounting principles and a number of these which should be observed were listed in the Companies Acts from 1981 onwards. In the Companies Act 1989, there has been an attempt to lay down general principles to be applied in producing annual accounts which must be adhered to unless the directors can show good reasons for departing from them. If they do depart from them then a note to the accounts must give details of such departure, the reasons for it and the effect such a departure has on the accounts provided.

The statutory principles can be summarized as (1) the accounts must be prepared on a going-concern basis; (2) accounting policies must be consistent both within the accounts and from one year to another; (3) stated profits must include only those actually realized at Balance Sheet date; (4) all losses and liabilities relating to the period of account must be brought into reckoning whether they occurred before or after balance sheet date, as must all income and expenses regardless of the date actually incurred; and (5) in determining aggregates each component must be determined separately. It may be that such rules are already part of normal good accounting practice but they have now been given the force of law.

Accounting ratios In assessing the viability or performances of a business, certain ratios are often considered to be of particular importance. In so far as these ratios are calculated from the figures appearing in the accounts of the business they are known as accounting ratios. There are many such ratios and their relative importance varies with both the priorities of the person using them and the purpose for which they are used, e.g. in looking to see if the business is solvent the immediate ratios to consider are the **liquid ratio** and the **current ratio**. ◊ **Insolvency**.

Many analysts see the ratio of **return on capital** as the most important of all in any serious investigation and will be interested more in the movement, or trend, of that ratio than in its absolute value at a particular time. Generally speaking, trends are always of greater relevance than absolute values.

Accounting records Generically speaking, accounting records are all those books of account kept by a business, together with the various invoices, receipts and other documentary evidence relating to them.

Companies enjoying the privileges accorded them by the Companies Acts have certain defined legal obligations concerning both the records that must be kept and the length of time for which they are to be kept.

Basically these requirements are such as to ensure that proper annual accounts can be prepared, i.e. a profit and loss account and a balance sheet. There are, however, specific regulations which require the records to show: (1) details of all monies received or spent and the reasons therefor; (2) details of all **assets** and **liabilities**; (3) proper stocktaking lists from which the stock figure is derived; (4) with the exception of everyday transactions in the retail trade, details of all goods bought and sold with the names of the vendors or purchasers.

These records must be kept at the **reg-**

istered office of the company or another such place specified by the directors, and must be available for inspection by all officers of the company at all times. Special provisions relate to overseas subsidiaries, etc., and there are heavy penalties for default.

Accounting reference date This is defined by the 1989 Companies Act as the date on which its accounting reference period, that being its financial year, ends in each calendar year. Every company must notify the Registrar of Companies of its accounting reference date within nine months of incorporation. If no date is chosen, or notice is not given, then the reference date will be 31 March for companies incorporated prior to April 1990 or, for other companies, the last date of the month in which the anniversary of its incorporation falls.

A company may change its accounting reference date by giving notice to the Registrar in the specified form. If the notice shortens the accounting period there are no restrictions on the frequency of change. If the effect is to lengthen the period then a company cannot make such a change more frequently than at five-year intervals unless special circumstances exist, e.g. a subsidiary company wishing to align its accounting reference period to that of its holding company.

Accounting staff ◊ **Institute of Accounting Staff**.

Accounting standards In view of the diversity of available principles which at one time could be legally applied in the preparation of the published accounts of limited companies and by extension to accounts generally, certain professional accounting bodies have attempted for some years to define standards which should be adopted by their members when preparing such accounts. These statements of recommended practice had no force in law, though should a court case arise the fact that they had not been followed might prejudice the position of the accountant if his good faith were questioned.

For many years standards were produced, after consultation within the profession, by the **Accounting Standards Steering Committee** which published a series of Statements of Standard Accounting Practice, known as SSAPs, which were accepted by members of the various professional bodies as practices which were, if not mandatory, not lightly to be ignored.

A radical change came about when the 1985 Companies Act provided that accounts not prepared according to applicable accounting standards might be ordered by the court to be prepared anew and at the personal expense of those directors who approved them. The 1989 Companies Act took the matter further by defining accounting standards as those issued by the professional accounting bodies and relevant to the company's circumstances and to the accounts. These standards now have the force of law in company accounts.

Since 1990 a new standard-setting body, known as the **Accounting Standards Board**, has taken over from the Accounting Standards Steering Committee. It immediately adopted the extant SSAPS issued by the committee and stated that these would form the base on which new standards, henceforth to be known as Financial Reporting Standards (FRSs), would be built.

Accounting Standards Board This new body, set up in 1990 under the auspices of the **Financial Reporting Council,** was charged with the task of devising a comprehensive and effective system of accounting standards.

Such standards will be issued on the Board's own authority which will require agreement by two thirds of its members. The standards are to be supported by statements of the principles on which they are founded and reasons are to be given why alternatives were studied and rejected. The object is to produce standards of maximum quality with the minimum opportunities afforded for prospective users to disregard or override them.

The ASB has taken over the role of the **Accounting Standards Steering Committee** but has adopted all the extant Statements of Standard Accounting Practice (SSAPs) issued by that committee. Future standards published will be known as Financial Reporting Standards (FRSs).

Accounting Standards Committee (ASC) This body, which preceded the **Accounting Standards Board**, was responsible for developing standards of good accounting practice. It was formed in 1970 by the Institute of Chartered Accountants in England and Wales and immediately joined by the Institutes for Scotland and Ireland. In 1971 the Chartered Association of Certified Accountants and the Chartered Institute of Management Accountants were admitted, as was, in 1976, the Chartered Institute of Public Finance and Accountancy. In 1976, the committee was reconstituted as a joint committee of the six member bodies acting collectively as the CCAB. The recommendations of the Accounting Standards Committee, as it then became known, were from thenceforth issued with the imprimatur of all six major

accountancy bodies in Great Britain and
Ireland. In 1990 the role of the ASC was
taken over by the newly constituted
Accounting Standards Board.

Accounting system The particular
methodology of record-keeping employed within an organization. There are
many systems, the most elementary being
the single-entry system employed by the
small businessman who is unskilled in
accounting techniques. The more complex systems, often restricted to the largest companies because of cost, are the
increasingly sophisticated electronic data-
processing systems. The choice is dictated
by the needs of the business, the demands
of the law and the ever-present question
of cost. Ideally the answer will lie in the
cheapest system consistent with the information that must be produced.

Manual and electronic systems obviously differ considerably in form as well
as in cost and most organizations opt for
an admixture of both. Electronic systems
themselves also differ according to manufacturer, but are essentially varieties of
basic electronic data-processing techniques.

**Accounts, nominal, real and per-
sonal** Terms used in bookkeeping.
Ledger accounts are divided into these
three broad categories, though the distinction is of no particular value. Personal
accounts are those of debtors and **creditors**, real accounts are those giving details
of **assets** and **capital** of the business,
nominal accounts deal with expenditure
and revenue. ◊ **Impersonal accounts**.

Accounts, receivable An alternative
and increasingly popular term for **debtors**. ◊ **Factoring** ◊ **Hire purchase**.

Accounts, variance ◊ **Standard
costing**.

Accrued charges An accrued charge is
the measure of an expense incurred for
which no charge has yet been made by
the creditor. The fees chargeable for an
audit may appear under this heading
where the accounts are printed before
the auditor had submitted his account.
Rent, rates, electricity charges, etc., may
also fall under this heading when demands therefor are made in arrears, e.g.
the charge for electricity used can only
be assessed when the meter is read, which
must be after the expense has legally
been incurred.

Accrued charges should be distinguished from **provisions** for anticipated liabilities, the amount of which
cannot be determined at the time an
account is being drawn up, and from
payments in advance, which refer to
monies paid for future benefits. Telephone bills are a useful instance of the
application of both accrued charges and
payments in advance. They contain both
a bill for calls made in the past and a
rental charge for the future.

Accrued interest Interest due but
not yet received or paid. ◊ **Accrued
charges**.

Accumulated depreciation A term
used in published accounts for the total
depreciation written off to date on a
fixed asset, or group of fixed assets.

Acre An area of land (4,840 square
yards). One square mile is 640 acres. Irish
and Scottish acres are larger than English
ones. 100 Irish acres = 162 English; 48
Scottish = 61 English. The United States
acre is equal to the English one.

Accumulating ordinary shares Shares
issued in lieu of dividend on ordinary
share capital. Tax is deducted from the
dividend payable on ordinary shares and

the net amount is then used to subscribe additional ordinary shares, known as accumulating shares, in the name of the investor. These may be held 'on trust' for those investors and allowed to accumulate. Though this procedure can avoid income tax, any profits would be treated as capital gains. The appeal of these shares lies in the substitution of compound growth of capital for annual income.

Act of God A loss to be caused by an act of God is one arising from a direct, irresistible, unpreventable act of nature. **Contracts** often exclude liability from damages arising from an act of God.

Actionnaires The name given to the shareholders of a type of French public company known as a **Société Anonyme**. Liability is limited as in a UK public company. There is, however, no fixed minimum number of action-naires, but in certain circumstances any interested person may petition the court for a winding-up if there are not at least two members. Another point of difference is that in a Société Anonyme at least one quarter of the nominal value of shares issued for cash must be paid on application. Again, fully paid shares are almost always in the form of warrants or bearer shares, thus making transfer very simple.

Active stock This term is normally used with reference to the Stock Exchange and its dealings. Any stocks or shares in which there are frequent or continual dealings are referred to as active stocks to distinguish them from 'dead stocks' or stocks in which dealings are rare. Most shares of leading industries would be termed active, particularly those where sudden price movements are common,

i.e. where the market is particularly sensitive to change or rumours of change.

Actual total loss A term used in **insurance**, particularly **marine insurance**, where the subject-matter is completely destroyed, or in effect destroyed in so far as the owner can no longer make use of it. If a ship is missing for a long time, an actual total loss can be presumed. No notice of **abandonment** need be given to the insurer.

Actuary A person who, on the basis of available statistical information, assesses probabilities. Actuaries are of particular importance within the insurance industry, where they make the original appraisal of the risk involved on which the **premiums** are based. Again, where **assurance** is involved, it is the actuary who, by research into matters such as life expectancy, will determine the amount that the insured will pay for the cover required. Qualified actuaries normally belong to the Institute of Actuaries and, particularly since the introduction of strict rules governing the behaviour of insurance companies (e.g. the Insurance Company Amendment Act 1973 and the Insurance Companies Act 1982), have responsibilities not dissimilar to those of the auditor of a public company in certifying reports of the liabilities on the policies issued by such companies.

Ad referendum When applied to a **contract**, this term means that although the contract has been signed, certain matters have been left over for consideration.

Ad valorem From the Latin 'according to the value'. An adjective applied to tax, duties, etc., where the amount payable to the Inland Revenue, Excise Authority or whoever receives it is directly related to the size of the chargeable transaction and is not a fixed amount, e.g. duty on **share capital** is payable on an ad valorem basis by the company, whereas a driving licence fee is of a fixed amount. ◊ **Stamp duty**.

Added value A concept that has become of particular importance since the introduction of **value added tax**; it refers to the value of the improvement made to goods or services at any particular and separate stage in their production, i.e. it is the difference between the price of a product or service taken in as the basis for improvement and the price at which the improved or finished product or service is sold either to the next operative in line or to the consumer. The term is synonymous with value added.

Adding machines A generic term for machines which facilitate the addition of a series of figures, particularly those in columnar form in business analysis or summary books. The type of equipment available ranges from the **abacus** to the most sophisticated electronic **computer**. In so far as the reliability of the answer given is totally dependent on the accuracy of the input, it is usual for all machines, however complex, to incorporate some form of double-check to guard against human errors. In the absence of a built-in verification device, the most common manner of checking is for the operation to be completed twice and the answer accepted only if identical on each occasion. For routine matters, the most familiar of adding machines available are the **add-lister** and the pocket or desk calculator.

Additional personal allowance At one time a married man could obtain an additional personal allowance in respect of his wife's earned income. This was abolished when **independent taxation** was introduced in 1990 and husbands and wives became separately taxable with each entitled to the scheduled personal allowance.

An additional personal allowance is now only available to a single person having a 'qualified' child resident with them. A qualified child is one under sixteen years old at the beginning of the tax year, or over sixteen in full-time education. The claimant must be legally responsible for the upkeep of the child. An allowance may also be claimed by a married man whose wife is totally incapacitated, physically or mentally, throughout the year in question.

Add-lister An adding machine which also records the figures added, on a roll of paper. It fulfils the functions of an **adding machine** and it is often used in retail business, for recording takings and listing goods, normally in a **self-service store** or supermarket. The more complex machines enable the operator to include a reference alongside each figure, these reference numbers, which may be used for **stock control**, not being added unless required. They may also have two or more registers, enabling figures to be tabulated in more than one column, and may give separate totals for each column.

Address commission A **Commission** paid to the **chartering agent** for arranging the loading of a vessel.

Adjusted selling price ◊ **Stock valuation**.

Adjustment Settling the amount due by an insurer, particularly by one of a number of insurers involved in, say, a **marine insurance** claim. ◊ **Slip**.

Administration expenses Although this term has a particular meaning when applied to the costs of the administrator of the estate of a deceased person (◊ **Administration, letters of**) it is also used in a more general sense in the printed accounts of companies or other organizations. Here it refers to expense headings which cannot be related directly to a stated department but which are attributable, in an imprecise sense, to the overall running of that company or organization.

Administration, letters of These are granted, on application to the court, to the person whom the court appoints to settle the affairs of a deceased person in accordance with that person's proven will or on his intestacy. The provisions of the law regarding the duties of the testator to provide for certain classes of dependants and the rules applicable on an intestacy must be observed. They are only granted when no executor has been appointed or when an appointed executor is unable or refuses to act, or is debarred from acting.

Administration order The Insolvency Act 1985 introduced the concept of an administration order as an alternative to the commencement of winding up in the case of insolvent companies. If a company is insolvent or seems likely to become unable to pay its debts then the members, directors or creditors may apply to the court for an administration order. This will be granted provided that the court is of the opinion that there seems a likelihood (a) that the company could be rehabilitated in part or in whole; (b) that creditors would be better served by such an order than if liquidation proceedings were to be instigated; (c) that it would further the chances of a compromise or arrangement with creditors as provided for by the 1985 Companies Act.

Once an administration order has been made (1) any petition for winding up must be waived; (2) any previously appointed Receiver for all or part of the company must vacate office; (3) no security over company property may be enforced without permission of the court; (4) no proceedings may be taken against the company, or continued if already commenced, without the leave of the court. The Administrator will be appointed by the court when the administration order is made and will be a qualified insolvency practitioner as defined by the Insolvency Act.

Administrator, powers and duties An Administrator appointed by the court under an **administration order** must do all that is necessary for the management of the company's affairs. His powers are extensive and include the right to dismiss or appoint directors, to call meetings of members or creditors and to dispose of such company property as is consistent with fulfilling the purposes set out in the order by which he was appointed. This includes the power to dispose of secured assets though the proceeds must be applied to paying the secured debt.

On appointment he takes charge of all assets of the company together with any rights of action then existing and must manage the affairs of the company according to the instructions contained in the order, or once he has submitted proposals to creditors and received their assent to such, then in accordance with those proposals.

He must send to the company, and to all known creditors, a copy of the order by which he has been appointed. He must cause a full statement of the company's affairs to be submitted to him by the company and in the form prescribed. This statement must be accompanied by a sworn affidavit. Within three months of his appointment he must prepare a statement of his proposals and send copies of these proposals to the Registrar of Companies, to all creditors and to members whose addresses he possesses. He must then call a meeting of creditors at which they consider his proposals and accept or reject them. They may ask for modifications but each such is subject to the administrator's approval. If the proposals are rejected then the court may either rescind the administration order or take such other steps as it deems necessary.

Admiralty measured mile 6,080 feet. It is distinguished from a nautical mile, which varies from 6,045·93 feet on the equator to almost 6,107·98 feet in latitude 90°. The mean nautical mile is 6,076·91 feet.

Advance corporation tax (ACT)
When the rules regarding **corporation tax** were changed in 1973 by the changeover to the imputation system, that part of the tax imputed to the persons in receipt of dividends from a company was deemed to be deducted at source when those dividends were paid. The amount so imputed was equal to the prevailing standard rate of income tax, but from April 1993 the rate has been set at 20 per cent. No further income tax, is therefore payable, as it was previously when profits were distributed, though recipients liable to higher rates must account to the Revenue for the difference between amount due and amount deducted at source.

Because part of the corporation tax

liability has been imputed to dividends, that tax has effectively become payable in two parts, the part so deducted and the balance, which is any excess of corporation tax over standard rate income tax plus the full amount payable on undistributed profits, known as **mainstream corporation tax**. Because the ACT and the mainstream tax will be payable at different times, then different rates of corporation tax could apply to each.

The introduction of ACT was intended to encourage distributions at the expense of retention of profits by companies. It did this by doing away with the old system under which distributed profits were effectively taxed twice, once by the corporation tax assessed on total profits and secondly by the deduction of income tax at source on profits distributed as dividends.

Under the new system companies must, however, be careful not to lose capital allowances, which by their nature can only be deducted from undistributed profits, i.e. the balance of profit remaining after dividends have been paid. If 90 per cent of profits are distributed only 10 per cent remain against which to set capital allowances. These cannot be used to reclaim tax imputed to the dividends paid, that tax being suffered by the members not by the company.

A further development since the introduction of the imputation system has been the much increased equity investment by pension funds, which, being tax exempt, may reclaim the tax deducted from the dividends they receive. The fact that this deprives the Treasury of a large amount of tax revenue has been a factor in the lobbying for the removal of tax exemption privileges enjoyed by pension funds.

Advance freight **Freight** paid in advance. A shipper may pay the freight, enabling the ship-owner to endorse the **bill of lading** with a freight release, and the importer to take immediate delivery. It may be payable even though the ship is lost, provided the voyage was actually commenced.

Advanced notes Drafts on ship-owners given by captains to their crews before sailing but payable, say, three days after sailing. They help the sailor to provide for his family.

Adverse balance In general business this term refers to a balance on an account indicating a revenue loss or a liability. It has a more particular meaning in the accounts of a nation; where it indicates that the balance of payments is such that amounts payable exceed those receivable. ◊ **Balance of payments**.

Advertisements (Hire Purchase) Act 1957 Any advertisement offering **goods** on **hire purchase**, **credit sale**, or **conditional sale**, and stating details of **deposits**, **interest** and hire purchase price, must comply with the provisions of this Act and the Consumer Credit Act 1974. Certain information must be given, in particular and *inter alia*: (1) details of the deposit; (2) the amounts and number of instalments; (3) the frequency of the instalments, and whether any are payable before delivery; (4) the cash price and the hire purchase price; (5) the true rate of interest. ◊ **Annual percentage rate**.

Advertising The publication of facts or opinions re **goods** or services, to awaken the public's interest and persuade them to purchase. There are various forms: ◊ **Advertising, competitive** ◊ **Advertising, informative** ◊ **Advertising, persuasive** ◊ **Advertising, subliminal**.

Advertising agency An organization concerned with **marketing**. It considers the **goods** and services that clients wish to offer to the public and advises on the best method of advertising them in order to maximize profit or goodwill. The agency is therefore interested in the product itself, in alternative methods of promotion, in presentation, and in effective copywriting. It may wish to study the product, and the persons to whom it is hoped to sell it, and will wish to consider the pattern and areas of distribution. It will need to be conversant with all methods of advertising, with appropriate magazines, journals, newspapers, TV, etc.

Advertising agencies are necessarily independent but, in order to preserve standards and prevent abuse, an Institute was formed as long ago as 1917, becoming known in 1954 as the Institute of Incorporated Practitioners in Advertising. There is a British Code of Advertising Practice which attempts to establish legal, clean, honest and truthful advertising. The practice and interpretation of this code is supervised by a Code of Advertising Practice Committee. The Institute helped to form the code of practice and is represented on the Committee. It also took part in forming the **Advertising Standards Authority**.

Advertising, competitive **Advertising** designed to sell one's own products at the expense of those of others. It is sometimes advantageous to advertise against oneself, for instance by bringing out a new product that competes with one already made, provided the amount of business taken from competitors exceeds the loss on sales of one's own first product. ◊ **Advertising, informative** ◊ **Advertising, persuasive** ◊ **Advertising, subliminal**.

Advertising, informative This refers to that branch of advertising which aims to advise producers or consumers of new products, changes in old ones, recent inventions or innovations, etc., of which they might otherwise be ignorant, in such a way that although primarily for the reader's benefit it is also to the advantage of advertisers themselves. ◊ **Advertising, competitive** ◊ **Advertising, persuasive** ◊ **Advertising, subliminal**.

Advertising, Institute of Practitioners in This is the trade association and professional institute for advertising agencies operating within the UK. The IPA has a Governing Council made up from elected representatives of member companies and headed by a Director General. Members of the IPA handle over 80 per cent of all advertising placed in the UK. The day-to-day running of the Institute is in the hands of professionals specializing in various fields from research to public relations. Professional competence and financial viability are prerequisites of membership which is open to all those concerned with the creation or placement of advertising whether they be individuals or companies.

The IPA represents members' interests in connection with prospective legislation and provides a collective view in dealing with the Press, the trade unions and consumer organizations. It has a separate management group to handle matters arising from Britain's entry into the European Union and to act as a bridge between UK advertisers and their European counterparts.

Advertising, persuasive This form of advertising comes into the 'no holds barred' category. The aim is to sell the product or service without reference to the need of the consumer or the economic or public good. One common ploy is to create artificial markets by promoting a product in such a way that consumers are encouraged to satisfy needs which have arisen solely from the insinuation of advertisers. Advertisers succeed when they can sell something of no intrinsic value to consumers who neither want nor need it – consumers may rush out to buy a product which they cannot afford, just to fulfil a desire created in them by the manufacturer and advertiser. ◊ **Advertising, competitive** ◊ **Advertising, informative** ◊ **Advertising, subliminal**.

Advertising Standards Authority An independent organization composed of five persons connected with **advertising**, five with no connection and an independent chairman. The objects are 'to promote and enforce throughout the United Kingdom the highest standards of advertising in all media and to ensure in cooperation with all concerned that no advertising contravenes or offends against these standards'.

Advertising, subliminal A particularly insidious form of advertising aimed at the consumer's subconscious. A message or blurb is flashed across a visual screen at such a speed that it does not register in the conscious mind. The idea, which has been proved effective, is that the message is registered subconsciously and will influence the recipient to buy the goods promoted. This form of advertising is illegal in the UK. ◊ **Advertising, competitive** ◊ **Advertising, informative** ◊ **Advertising, persuasive**.

Advice note A document sent by a supplier to the customer prior to the **invoice**. Sometimes it precedes the **goods** and sometimes accompanies them; it states the nature and quantity of the goods but not their **price**. Essentially just an indication that the goods are on the way, it is sometimes confused with a **delivery note**.

Advisory Conciliation and Arbitration Service (ACAS). This was set up in 1974 by the Secretary of State for Employment. It consists of ten persons, three each appointed respectively by the TUC and the CBI after consultation with those bodies, three academics with experience of industrial relations and an independent chairman. It offers free mediation in industrial disputes within both the public and private sectors, and will also arbitrate in matters relating to such diverse subjects as trade union recognition and collective bargaining. If asked by the parties concerned it will also appoint specialist arbitrators to handle specific disputes. It also publishes Codes of Practice concerning the conduct of industrial negotiations generally. Although ACAS decisions or findings are not in any way binding, they carry considerable weight in influencing both governmental attitudes and public opinion. ◊ **Arbitration**.

Advocate A term used in Scotland to describe a person admitted to plead at the Bar (corresponding to the English **barrister**).

Affidavit A declaration in writing made on oath before a person entitled to administer oaths (a commissioner for oaths, normally a **solicitor**). It is a criminal offence deliberately to make a false statement in an affidavit.

Affirmation of contract A person induced to enter a **contract** by a **misrepresentation** may be bound by the contract, and lose his right to rescission and/or

damages, if he expressly or implicitly affirms the contract with full knowledge of the facts. This he may do by verbal affirmation or simply by failing to take action within a reasonable time.

Affreightment, contracts of These are **contracts** for the carriage of **goods** by sea. They may be part of a **charter party**, or the terms may be set out in a **bill of lading**. ◊ **Freight**.

After-sales service A vendor of goods often offers additional inducements to prospective purchasers in the form of after-sales service. This varies considerably according to custom of trade but can be of particular importance in the selling of branded capital goods where replacement of parts or normal maintenance and repair require the specialized knowledge of the manufacturer or his agent. The service comes in two stages. Initially there is the period of guarantee during which faults must be put right by the vendor without charge. Subsequently, when the guarantee has expired, the manufacturer or vendor agrees to inform the customer of centres where there is a qualified staff who can take on repairs and supply new parts. This is of particular relevance in the automobile industry, where exporters of cars need to provide for repair and replacement facilities in the country of import. ◊ **Sale of goods**.

After sight A **bill of exchange** drawn after sight is payable when it has been accepted and the **acceptor** has written a date of acceptance on the bill.

AG ◊ **German companies**.

Against all risks (aar) A marine insurance term which legally means 'insured against all generally accepted risks'.

Age, misrepresentation of by infants If a **minor** misrepresents his age to bring about a **contract** he will not be bound by the contract but **equity** will not normally allow him to take full advantage of his fraud and may force him to restore any gains he has made and release the other party from any obligation. It will not, however, enforce the contract. ◊ **Contract, infant's**.

Age relief Generally speaking, anyone over the age of 65 is entitled to 'age relief'. At present, this takes the form of a higher **personal allowance** on income up to a fixed amount, after which the allowance is progressively reduced to the normal. ◊ **Allowance, personal**.

Agency bills Bills of exchange drawn on, and accepted by, the London branches of foreign **banks**.

Agency, creation of An agency is a contractual arrangement, either express or implied, written or verbal, whereby one person may act on behalf of another and bind that other as if he or she had acted personally.

The law relating to agency is generally related to the law of contract, as it is for the purpose of making legally binding contracts that an agent is normally appointed.

The most extreme kind of agency, in the eyes of the law, is created by giving the agent a **power of attorney** to act for the donor. Other common forms are categorized as **agent, special** and **agent, general**. Appointment may be in writing and must be so in instances where the contracts themselves are bound to be in writing; it may also be by verbal request, by implication or may arise from circumstantial necessity. Examples of the latter are the implied authority of a wife

to pledge her husband's credit for necessaries (but ◊ **Necessaries**), or the **agency of necessity**.

Contracts improperly made by an agent (being outside his ostensible authority) may be ratified by the appointor, in which case the ratification dates back to the time that the contract was made. This is only possible where the principal himself could, had he so wished, have made the contract himself at that time and, in addition, the other party must have believed that he was dealing with an agent even if the name of the principal was not disclosed.

Agency might also arise where circumstances prevent the principal from denying the agency, i.e. he is 'estopped' from disclaiming acts done in his name. This often happens in **partnerships** where notice of termination has not been properly given or, again, in any situation where failure to disclaim liability after the facts have become known is taken to imply ratification. ◊ **Agency, determination of** ◊ **Holding out**.

Agency, determination of An agency may be determined by express agreement. A special agent will cease to be an **agent** when he has completed the task for which he was employed. A universal agency will be terminated by agreement. The principal must remember that if a person has acted for him for some time or has been looked upon as his agent, then it may be necessary to give express notice to persons with whom the agent has dealt and perhaps general notice to the public, before the agency can be considered terminated ◊ **Estoppel**. The principal may otherwise continue to be responsible for debts incurred by the agent. Agency is automatically terminated by the death or bankruptcy of the principal or the agent (except that if the agent is bankrupt the agency may continue where he is still capable of acting as agent). ◊ **Agent, special** ◊ **Agent, universal**.

Agency, fiduciary nature of A **contract** of agency is a contract that creates a special relationship between the parties. The agent must act in good faith, and even though there is no express agreement he must not make any private or secret profit out of the agency. He must always act in his principal's interest, and if he professes any skill he must use this to the best of his ability.

Agency of necessity This occurs where one person acts on behalf of another without that other's express permission, in order to safeguard the interests of the other party. The other party will be bound by the agency. Agency of necessity cannot arise, and there would be no legal agency unless: (1) it is impossible to communicate with the principal; (2) a **contract** of agency already exists; and (3) immediate action is necessary.

Agency: undisclosed principal Where an **agent** contracts without disclosing that he is an agent, many problems arise. Generally the principal or the agent may sue or be sued. However, if the third party had reason to believe that he was dealing with the agent as principal and that this was a relevant fact, only the agent may sue on the contract: if A will not contract with B, B cannot evade this by contracting through C, an undisclosed agent. Where the third party may sue principal or agent, he must make a decision and cannot sue both.

Agency: un-named principal A term used in a **contract** of agency where the agent discloses that he is contracting as

agent but does not give the name of his principal. There is little difference from a normal contract made by an agent, though it must not be used to persuade third parties to contract where they would not had they known the identity of the principal.

If the agent subsequently refuses to disclose the name of the principal he becomes personally liable.

Agenda Details of business to be transacted at a meeting, made out by the person calling the meeting or the secretary appointed to do so. The agenda paper is frequently sent out to those invited to attend and is sometimes accompanied by an invitation to appoint a representative to act or vote for the recipient if he cannot attend personally – as frequently happens in meetings held by companies. ◊ **Proxy**. Certain company meetings called to discuss matters affecting the rights of members require special notice. These matters must be detailed, as required by the 1985 Companies Act, in the agenda accompanying the notice of the meeting.

Agent A person with express or implied authority to act for another person (the principal), the object being to establish a contractual relationship between the principal and third parties. ◊ **Agency, creation of** ◊ **Agency, fiduciary nature of** ◊ **Agency, determination of** ◊ **Agent: duties to principal** ◊ **Agent, special** ◊ **Agent, universal**.

Agent de change The French equivalent of a **stockbroker**. ◊ **Bourse**.

Agent: duties to principal These are generally a matter of common sense, but in particular an **Agent** must: (1) observe the agency agreement; (2) follow his principal's instructions when not illegal; (3)

always act in the interest of his principal; (4) use the skill that he is supposed to have; (5) not in any way compete with his principal or take on any other work which competes with his duties to his principal; (6) respect the confidence of his principal, even after the end of the agency; (7) not make any secret profit or take a bribe; (8) compensate his principal for any loss arising from breach of duty; (9) account properly to his principal.

Agent, general An **agent** with authority to act for his principal in all matters concerning a particular trade or profession, or in some specified field. A travelling representative is one example.

Agent: misrepresentation Misrepresentation by an **agent** is equal to misrepresentation by his principal, whether fraudulent or innocent. However, if an agent makes an innocent misrepresentation it does not become fraudulent by reason of the principal's knowledge of the true facts: e.g. A contracts with B through agent C; B is aware of faults in goods being sold to A; C is not; A relies on C's representation; A cannot then claim damages for fraudulent misrepresentation unless B has deliberately misled C.

Agent, special An **agent** with authority to do one particular act, or to represent his principal in one specific transaction.

Agent, universal One with unrestricted authority to **contract** on behalf of his principal, e.g. a person holding **power of attorney**.

Agent's lien A lien is a right to retain the property of another against non-payment of a debt from that other. ◊ **Lien, general** ◊ **Lien, particular**. An agent can claim a lien on property belonging to his principal which is legally in the possession of the agent when the right arises, provided that there is no agreement with the principal that precludes such a lien. The lien may be general or particular. The rules are similar to those applicable to liens under other contracts. One special case that could apply relates to bankruptcy and the **order and disposition** clause, where the goods which are in the possession of the agent could be claimed by his trustee in bankruptcy as a general lien against all of the bankrupt agent's property. This supposes that those goods appeared to belong to him and no agency could genuinely be assumed to exist with relation to the goods in the eyes of an innocent creditor of that agent.

Agent's torts The principal is jointly and severally liable for his agent's torts if the **agent** is acting in the normal course of his agency or on the instruction of his principal. The agent must indemnify the principal where the principal has not expressly or implicitly condoned the tort.

Agricultural Mortgage Corporation Ltd This was established in 1928. **Share capital** was subscribed by the **Bank of England** and other **banks**; the bulk of the funds, however, comes from **debentures** (over £100,000,000 outstanding) plus grants and loans from the Ministry of Agriculture, Fisheries and Food. Its primary purpose is to grant long-term loans against first **mortgages** of agricultural land and buildings. It has power to grant sixty-year loans, but forty-year loans are more common. Its secondary purpose is to make loans to landowners, to help carry out improvements to agricultural land and buildings.

Borrowers apply through bankers or

directly to the Corporation. Advances are limited to two-thirds of the estimated value of the property. **Rates of interest** vary from loan to loan, depending on market conditions. Repayments are made by half-yearly instalments. Loans for improvements depend on the **annual value** of the land being increased by at least the annual amount of the loan charges.

The Corporation confines its activities to England and Wales. There is, however, a Scottish Agricultural Securities Corporation Ltd, subscribed by three Scottish banks.

Agricultural and Food Research Council This was established by royal charter in 1931. There are eighteen members, including representatives of the Agricultural Departments of the Government, distinguished scientists, and men with practical farming experience. The Council may be directed by the Secretary of State for Education and Science, but is otherwise autonomous. It takes advice from the Ministry of Agriculture, Fisheries and Food, and the Department of Agriculture and Fish for Scotland. It is responsible for fourteen independent state-aided Agricultural Research Institutes, controls ten others and has established fifteen more (this is in addition to the eight in Scotland). It also makes grants to further university research, whose purpose is to help farmers increase efficiency and produce better and cheaper food and agricultural products. This involves the study of soils, plants, animals and food. It publishes annual reports and an Index of Agricultural Research.

Air freight Although initially airlines saw their principal function as passenger vehicles offering swift travel services between different countries or parts of countries, and considered the carrying of freight as a side-line or a means of filling empty space, the idea of operating an airline for carrying cargo has gained increasing favour.

The first type of air freight was mail, which took up relatively little space. As time progressed producers of goods saw the competitive advantages of being able to fulfil orders, particularly those for lightweight goods, in a far shorter time by using air transport. The attraction is still greater where the weight-related charges are small or very competitive. Now, far from seeing cargo as an 'extra', airlines are becoming increasingly conscious of its economic benefits and aircraft have been designed and flown on a 'cargo only' basis. ◊ **Air transport load factor**.

Airline Users Committee Established in 1973 and consisting of persons representing various consumer interests. The job of the committee is to assist the **Civil Aviation Authority** in fulfilling the fourth point of its objectives, i.e. looking after and furthering the interests of air transport users. It also investigates particular complaints where the plaintiff has not been able to obtain satisfaction from the airline concerned.

Airmail letters Letters sent to Europe from the UK normally go by air unless another means will secure earlier delivery. For countries outside Europe, a letter will only travel by air if the appropriate fee is paid and either a label is attached, or words denoting the intention to send it by air are written on the top left-hand corner of the envelope. Needless to say, mail sent by air to such countries will bear a much higher charge than if sent surface mail, i.e. by sea. To combat such expense the Post Office sells specially light airletters, and publishers of newspapers often use particularly light paper for copies intended for overseas sale. Airmail letter rates vary from one destination to another and are classified according to 'zones', which depend on distance. Rates can be found in the **Post Office Guide**.

Air traffic control This is a service provided on a joint military/civil basis by the organization known as N A T S (National Air Traffic Services) to ensure safety within stated geographical limits for aircraft while in flight, taking off or landing. It seeks, by various devices including radar, direct radio communication and other navigational aids, to expedite a safe and orderly flow of air traffic by monitoring all movements, and to prevent collisions both between aircraft in the air and between aircraft and obstacles on taking off or landing. The area of responsibility is dictated by international agreement and the British liability for aircraft 'en route' normally extends to the agreed point at which it is handed over to the control body of a neighbouring state.

Control extends not only outwards but upwards, and various control centres are allocated responsibility for safety in the three principal agreed levels, i.e. upper air space, middle air space and lower air space. ◊ **Air transport insurance**.

Air transport insurance This is a complex subject governed by many national and international agreements, particularly regarding injury to persons and damage to goods in transit. In view of the continual changes in legal requirements and measures of liability it is not possible to give a precise list of available remedies.

Generally speaking, the liabilities of airlines are set out in a series of statutes, beginning with the Carriage by Air Act 1952, and by international law or agree-

ments. The latter imposes limits to claims. These are stated in terms of gold francs per kilo and are, in the absence of evidence to the contrary, maximum limits. The carrier can only escape liability if he can establish that the damage was caused by the negligence of the plaintiff, and can mitigate liability if he can show contributory negligence on the part of the claimant.

As far as damage to the persons or property of third parties is concerned, whether on land or water or arising in the flight or on take-off or landing, the plaintiff is covered by the fact that airlines are legally obliged to take out **third party insurance**, which applies whether the airline is negligent or not.

It is quite common nowadays for passengers to take out personal insurance before flying. This will cover the particular trip and the rates are usually very low. The life cover can often be obtained from a slot machine at the departure terminal.

Air transport licensing For a British airline to operate a scheduled or charter flight service it must first apply for, and obtain, an air transport licence. These licences are at present only obtainable from the **Civil Aviation Authority**, which will hear any objections raised and which is bound by law to satisfy itself that the airline is British-controlled and that it is financially stable and efficiently run. Considerable attention is given to the safety standards incorporated in the structure of the applicant airline and it is presumed that such standards can only be maintained by a financially sound company. ◊ **Airworthiness**.

Air transport, load factor This is the ratio of cargo or passenger capacity to actual load carried on an aircraft. Airways offer a service and not a storable product. Consequently the profitability of any particular airline is determined by the maximization of the use of available space, i.e. by the load factor ratios.

Air waybill A term used to describe the document made out on behalf of the consignor of goods by air as evidence of the contract of carriage. It, or a copy thereof, accompanies the goods throughout their journey. ◊ **International Air Transport Association** ◊ **Air freight**.

Airways letters Until relatively recently the Post Office had an agreement with British Airways whereby first-class mail would be carried on internal flights by British Airways and then would either be collected or transferred to the postal system at the airport of destination. This has now been discontinued because of the increasingly stringent security provisions now in force at airports. This makes such a service incompatible with the necessary privacy attached to letters and packets entrusted to the Royal Mail.

Airworthiness A current certificate of airworthiness, obtainable from the **Civil Aviation Authority**, must be held in respect of every aircraft operated for public transport. There is also a British Airworthiness Code to which all such aircraft must conform and which lays down certain absolute minimum levels of airworthiness. These are known as the BCAR (British Civil Airworthiness Requirements). The Civil Aviation Authority has power to carry out any such tests as it deems necessary in enforcing these requirements.

Alarm call Any person may ask the telephone exchange to ring a specified number at a specified time. This service is useful as an alternative to relying on an alarm clock in the morning to ensure that one is awake in time for an appointment. There is a fixed charge for the call, which is much higher than that for a normal dialled call. The service is an inland service only and may not be available at remote country exchanges. ◊ **Telephone**.

Aliens, contracts with Distinguish between alien friends and alien enemies. Alien enemies are those who reside in a hostile country or in a country occupied by a hostile power (the nationality of the alien is not relevant). The subject of a foreign power would also be an enemy if resident here at the outbreak of hostilities with his country. Alien friends may normally **contract** in the ordinary manner. Resident enemies cannot enter into contracts during hostilities; nor can non-resident enemies without permission from the proper authorities. Contracts in force at the time of hostilities are not cancelled unless this would be in the public interest, but they are unenforceable until the cessation of hostilities, when rights are reinstated. Sovereigns and official representatives of foreign states are immune from liability on contracts unless they choose otherwise. However, they may bring an action themselves. The protection extends to diplomatic staff and certain other foreign nationals but normally only while they are acting in an official capacity.

Allocatur When costs are ordered to be taxed by a taxing master, i.e. when costs incurred in an action, **liquidation**, etc., must be approved, the certificate given by the taxing master is known as an allocatur.

Allonge A slip attached to a **bill of**

exchange to allow for extra **endorsements**. It does not need a stamp.

Allotment note This is a note signed by a sailor authorizing the master of his ship to pay all or part of his wages earned at sea directly to his wife, his family, or to his bank. It should not be confused with a letter of allotment, which is issued by a company in connection with the allocation of shares.

Allotment of shares When a company receives an **application for shares** issued by means of a **prospectus**, it proceeds to allot the **shares** on a predetermined basis (which is set out in the prospectus). Where applications exceed the shares available, allotment is made proportionately, though often applications for shares up to a stated number are accepted in full. The allotment of shares is made by means of a letter of allotment. This entitles the recipient to a certificate for the number of shares stated in the letter. His title may, however, depend on his paying the sum previously stated as due on allotment. The same procedure would apply to shares issued through an **issuing house**.

A public company cannot, since the 1980 Companies Act, allot shares until at least 25 per cent of the nominal value has been paid up plus the whole of any premium. This does not apply to shares allotted under an employee share scheme.

Allowances, child These were deductions allowed against income in respect of each child supported by a taxpayer. They existed up to the tax year 1979–80, when they were abolished in favour of direct payments to families through **child benefit** and **family income supplement** schemes.

Allowance, life assurance This was a measure of income tax relief given to those paying life assurance premiums up to a fixed limit. It was abolished in 1979–80 in favour of a system whereby the relief would be given by the life assurance companies themselves by way of a reduction in premium. Although this relief still exists for old policies, it has been abolished in respect of life assurance policies taken out after March 1984.

Allowance, mortgage interest At one time each taxpayer could claim relief from income tax to the extent of interest paid on a mortgage obtained for the purchase of his own dwelling house. The relief was reflected in his PAYE coding or allowed in his Schedule D tax computation. From 1983–4 the system changed and the MIRAS scheme was adopted. The effect on the taxpayer remains the same, but instead of claiming his relief from the Inland Revenue directly he claims it through the mortgagee who deducts the tax from each payment of interest. The relief so claimed is at the basic rate only. If the taxpayer is entitled to relief at higher rates of tax, this must be claimed from the Revenue as previously.

Allowance, personal ▷ **Personal allowance**.

Allowances, sundry In addition to personal, age and life assurance allowances, there are other tax reliefs obtainable in special circumstances. The current tax legislation should be consulted to identify these but they include allowances for dependants other than children, the services of an unmarried daughter, housekeeper allowances and special allowances for blind persons and widows.

Other allowances are available, usually on agreement with the Inland Revenue, for certain expenses necessarily attaching to one's job, e.g. fees payable for membership of professional organizations, special clothing needing to be provided by the employee, books or other 'tools of trade' not supplied by the employer.

Alternate director The **articles of association** of a company sometimes give a director power to appoint another person, known as an alternate director, to act for him at a specified meeting of the board of directors which he is unable to attend. The extent of the authority of the alternate director and his entitlement, if any, to remuneration will be determined by the relevant paragraph in the articles. The approval of the other directors is a common requirement. Alternate directors should not be confused with 'associate directors', nominal appointees to the board representing, say, employees' interests, nor should the concept be confused with the rotation of board membership, whereby directors take it in turn to resign each year and apply for reappointment. Alternate directors are peculiar to the UK ◊ **Rotation of directors**.

Alternative accounting rules The 1981 Companies Act provided that as the overriding obligation upon companies and their auditors is to give a true and fair view, then a certain flexibility should be permitted in the accounting conventions employed in the preparation of annual accounts. It is now permissible to prepare accounts on either (1) a **historical cost** basis or (2) a **current cost** basis or (3) a historical cost basis but subject to the revaluation of certain selected assets. The overriding obligation is for the basis chosen to be indicated and to be applied consistently. However, the Act provides that where a basis other than historical cost is selected, the historical figures, or

the amount by which these differ from the revised figures, must also be given either in the accounts or by way of note.

Amalgamation Within the world of companies an amalgamation refers to the coming together by arrangement of two or more individually registered companies for the purpose of maximizing potential trading opportunities to the mutual benefit of the companies concerned.

This is the ideal form of true amalgamation but the term is also used of takeovers by one company of another, often for the principal benefit of the first, and again for shotgun company 'marriages' brought about by outside interests with the ostensible purpose of benefiting the community at large. The State has, in the past, had occasion to make aid to ailing companies conditional on their agreeing to be amalgamated into one unit. The term 'merger' is commonly used as an alternative to amalgamation.

American depository receipt (**ADR**) American depositary receipts are securities, in the name of nominees, issued by United States banking houses in exchange for shares in UK companies deposited with them. This makes trading in the shares of these companies possible on the New York and other US stock exchanges, whether or not the shares are actually listed on those exchanges.

As an ADR is itself evidence of ownership of the underlying shares deposited with the bank which issued it, the ADR can be traded and share ownership changed without recourse to the company whose shares are involved. This effectively makes ADRs similar to bearer securities, and makes trading free from UK stamp duty which is payable only on the original transfer to the bank issuing the ADRs. It also increases the popularity of ADRs with American investors, both individual and institutional, particularly as ADRs are exempt from any prohibition that might exist in the US against holding shares of foreign countries.

American Express A credit card company which operates on an international basis. As the advertisements tell you, by becoming an American Express Cardmember, you 'have a worldwide charge account'. There are American Express Travel Centres in most countries to help and advise cardholders with personal and business travel problems and to provide cash in an emergency. Unlike most credit cards, American Express Cards do not impose pre-set spending limits for particular transactions but, needless to say, applications are carefully vetted and there is an annual membership charge. The membership fee covers a high automatic Travel Accident Insurance. ◊ **Access** ◊ **Barclaycard** ◊ **Diners Club**.

Amortization In commercial parlance this has particular reference to the writing off of assets – the lives of which are determined not by deterioration or obsolescence but by the expiry of the tenure of ownership. The principal instance would be a leasehold property. A business with a fixed lease of an asset, particularly a building or land, would wish to provide for the renewal of the lease or its replacement with another type of tenure by writing off the cost of the asset over its fixed life and, in addition, probably putting an equal amount each year into a **sinking fund** which would be invested to provide monies for the eventual replacement or renewal. This manner of writing off an asset is referred to as amor-

tization and is distinguished from **depreciation** in that there is generally no deterioration in the performance of the asset during its life.

Anchorage Dues paid for anchoring in certain ports or harbours.

And reduced Words appended to the name of a **company** where, after reorganization, the **capital** is reduced, with court approval. The court may order these words to be added to the name. ◊ **Companies: reduction of capital**.

Annual Abstract of Statistics A comprehensive collection and collation of statistics relating to every field of endeavour within the UK and published annually by the **Central Statistical Office**. It is supplemented by the more succinct Monthly Digest of Statistics, which traces the pattern of economic progress, or regress, throughout the year – with additional figures relating to such matters as population, licence registrations, weather patterns, etc. Each issue contains comparative information for a number of previous years.

Annual accounts Financial statements showing the state of affairs of a business or other organization at a particular date and the results of operations during the period, usually one year, which ends on that date. The nature of these accounts will vary according to the entity to which they apply and with the various regulations and provisions, legal or otherwise, relating thereto.

The annual accounts of limited companies are governed by the Companies Acts, particularly the Companies Act 1985 as ammended by the Companies Act 1989. The directors of every company are responsible for preparing and filing the individual accounts of that company for each financial year that the company exists. Those accounts must take the form of a **balance sheet** as at the end of the year and a **profit and loss account** for that year. These must be prepared in accordance with the provisions of the fourth schedule to the 1985 Act as to both form and content. They must be prepared on the **accounting principles** laid down in the 1989 Act taking into account the overriding imperative that the accounts published shall give a 'true and fair' view both of the state of the company's affairs at the close of the financial period and of the profit or loss made during that year. The 1985 Act gives alternative formats which may be used for both the balance sheet and the profit and loss account and also indicates what categories of information may take the form of notes to the accounts rather than be embodied in the accounts themselves. There are particular rules laid down in the Acts attached to the preparation of the accounts of certain special categories of company, e.g. banking companies, insurance companies and overseas companies. There are also less onerous provisions relating to the accounts of **small** and **medium-sized companies**.

In addition to individual accounts, **holding companies** are bound by law to present **group accounts** for each financial year which must also conform to the provisions set out in the fourth schedule to the 1985 Companies Act as amended by the Act of 1989.

Copies of the annual accounts of companies and of groups must be filed with the Registrar of Companies each year and must have attached to them a **director's report** and an **auditor's report**. These accounts must also be laid before the members at an **annual general meeting** and copies must be sent to all members. This does not apply if those members have agreed to accept **Summary Financial Statements** in place of the account and if the conditions attached to the issue of such, as laid down in Companies (Summary Financial Statements) Regulations 1990, have been satisfied in every respect by the Directors of the company concerned.

Annual accounts are not, of course, the preserve of limited companies. They are needed, for tax assessment purposes if for no other, by the proprietors of virtually all trading organizations. Non-company accounts, though not bound by the demands of the Companies Acts, tend to appear in a very similar form to those of limited companies, particularly when prepared by independent accountants. Non-trading organizations also produce annual accounts though these usually substitute an **income and expenditure account** for the profit and loss account.

The 1976 Companies Act attempted to speed up preparation and filing of the accounts of limited companies by making it obligatory for such accounts to be submitted to the Registrar within seven or ten months (depending on whether the company is a public or a private company) of the end of the financial year unless extenuating circumstances can be shown to apply.

Annual allowances ◊ **Capital allowances**.

Annual charges These are payments made by a person or corporation from which tax has been deducted by the payer, who must account for it to the Inland Revenue. They are mostly interest payments and amounts paid by way of **covenant**. In the latter instance the deduction is deemed to have been made even though the taxpayer does not officially do so. The amount that he covenants to pay is treated as a 'net' payment and the payee, if not subject to tax for one reason or another, e.g. because of charity status, then obtains repayment of the tax notionally paid by the payer. In preparing a tax computation the annual payments are deducted from income and then later brought back into account and tax collected from them at the standard rate. For that reason, entering into covenants is not recommended for the low income earner if the tax applicable to his net income is nil – or less than the tax on the covenant – for he will be paying not only the covenant but also the tax that he has been deemed to have deducted from it. In order to minimize his liability it is important that the tax due on his income – after adding back the gross equivalent of the annual charges – is greater than the tax on the annual charge itself.

Annual general meeting (AGM) It is common practice, even where not legally imperative, for all organizations to hold an annual general meeting of members, specified as such, where those members are given the opportunity to meet and talk with each other and with those who run the organization on their behalf. The latter will, at such a meeting, be asked to give an account of their stewardship since the previous meeting.

In the case of a limited company a meeting must be held in each calendar year, and in the notice summoning the meeting it must be specifically designated as the annual general meeting of the company. Additionally, not more than fifteen months may elapse between successive AGMs though, in the case of the first meeting, this may be held at any time within eighteen months of incorporation. The business to be conducted at a company's AGM is not defined by statute, apart from the requirement to appoint directors, but it is normal for the agenda to cover, *inter alia*, the **auditor's remuneration** and appointment, the consideration of the **annual report**, the payment of dividends, etc.

All members must receive notice, as prescribed in the Companies Act, and that notice must be accompanied by forms allowing the member to appoint a **proxy** to attend and/or vote in his stead. Provided the statutory rules are followed, any business may be transacted at an AGM and **special** or **extraordinary resolutions** are not excluded (but see the requirements regarding these).

The 1989 Companies Act permits a **private company** to dispense with holding an annual general meeting provided an **elective resolution** is passed to this effect.

Annual percentage rate (APR) When the rate of interest payable under a loan or other agreement is stated in terms of a rate per week, month, quarter etc., or any period less than one year, then the annual percentage rate that is being charged is the equivalent of the annual interest rate – a figure which will be much higher than the rate quoted for the shorter period and perhaps representing a greater burden than the payer may be led to believe. Because of the misleading nature of rates stated for short periods, whether in hire purchase contracts or other credit or loan transactions, e.g. for charge cards, the true annual percentage rate, the APR, must be stated in the initial agreement between the parties. ◊ **Hire purchase** ◊ **Consumer Credit Act 1974**.

Annual report A report under the

names of the directors of a company sent each year to the members of the company and to other persons who are entitled to receive it either by right or by request. The report contains those documents which are required by law together with such other information regarding the company's affairs, e.g. simplified charts for the benefit of the layman, as the directors see fit to provide.

The law demands the inclusion of an audited copy of the company's **balance sheet**, the **profit and loss account**, any other explanatory papers required by statute, the **auditor's report** and the **directors' report** for the relevant year. These documents must conform with the various provisions of the Companies Act. Where the company is a **holding company** then the report must also include the audited consolidated balance sheet and profit and loss account or such other form of group accounts as are applicable in the particular case. ◊ **Consolidated accounts**.

Other information that may be included voluntarily and as an aid to the uninformed member or investor might include pictorial diagrams showing how income is derived from various sources and how it is expended. The inclusion of **cash flow statement** charts is also becoming more and more common.

Another document often, though not always, incorporated into the annual report is the **chairman's report** or review, which is a personalized message to members from the chairman of the board in which the fortunes, past and future, of the enterprise are surveyed – not always without a degree of poetic licence.

Annual return All companies are bound by the Companies Acts to submit successive annual returns to the Registrar of Companies. The form and frequency of such a return has been altered from 1 October 1990. Each return must be made up to a date within twelve months of the previous return or, in the case of new companies, twelve months from incorporation. It must be submitted, with the prescribed filing fee, within twenty-eight days of the date to which it is made up and must be signed either by the Secretary of the company or by a director. Companies House will automatically send either a blank or a partly completed return to each company shortly before the date it is due to be filed. The part completion will have been from details already on record. The filed return must contain certain information including (1) address of the registered office; (2) principal business of the company as per VAT trade classification code; (3) type of company as defined by the Memorandum of Association, e.g. 'public limited company', 'private unlimited company with share capital' etc; (4) personal details of the secretary and all directors, including other directorships held; (5) where the Register of Members and/or Debenture Holders is kept, if not at the Registered Office; and (6) in the case of a private company which has elected to dispense with holding an AGM, and with placing accounts before such a meeting, a statement to this effect.

Additionally, where the company has a share capital the return must contain certain information relating to that share capital including (a) total number of shares issued and their nominal value; (b) details regarding each class of shares; (c) names and addresses of all members including those whose membership has ceased since the last return, details of shares held by each, distinguishing between classes of shares, and any transfers of those shares since the previous return. If the list of members is not in alphabetical order an index must be attached. With regard to (c) these lists may be omitted if they were provided in either of the two previous returns.

Failure to submit a return as demanded by the Act can involve both the secretary and directors in substantial financial penalties.

Annual value The annual value of an asset, whether it be real property such as a house or land, etc., or personal property such as a business interest or a share portfolio, is the amount that accrues annually by right of ownership. A distinction is normally made between gross annual value and net annual value, the former being before, and the latter after, deduction of expenses incurred by ownership. Generally speaking, no asset has a fixed annual value in so far as both income and expenditure must obviously fluctuate, so the term is normally only used with reference to the notional benefit from possessing property which is kept for personal, rather than for commercial, purposes.

At one time tax was levied, under the now defunct Schedule A, on the annual value to the occupier of the house in which he lived. Business rates are still calculated on a similarly notional value, referred to as the rateable value of commercial premises. The value is calculated by reference to the rack rent, i.e. the amount of rent that the premises would be expected to fetch in the open market, assuming vacant possession and no encumbrances, and that the landlord is responsible for fixtures and outside repairs and the tenant for the maintenance of the inside of the property.

Annuity A fixed sum payable each year

for a number of years, either following a certain event or else for a definite period of time. Annuities may be purchased, e.g. an **assurance** company might be approached and asked how much it would be necessary to pay now to guarantee the payment of £1,000 per year, either for the next, say, twenty years or for life, starting at a given age. A person receiving an annuity is known as an annuitant.

Ante-date To ante-date a document is to put a date on it earlier than that on which it was issued.

Anti-trust laws A system of laws in the USA aimed at preventing the formation of large **cartels**, **monopolies**, etc., and similar in purpose to the **Monopolies and Mergers Act** of this country.

Application for shares When a person wishes to purchase **shares** on a new issue, he sends in a formal letter of application stating the number of shares he requires, and enclosing the sum of money payable on application. The form of application is usually published with the **prospectus**. The company will then proceed to allot the shares, though not necessarily the number applied for. ◊ **Allotment of shares**.

Appreciation In general commercial usage this is an accounting term relating to the increase in value of an asset, particularly a **fixed asset**. In this sense it is the reverse of depreciation, which measures the fall in value of fixed assets over their normal lifetime.

In times of high inflation appreciation will be common to all balance sheet assets. Even current assets, such as stock, will increase in **nominal value** whilst held in store. Generally, the term is reserved for property or, more specifically, land and buildings. In any viable modern economy, such property tends to increase in value over the years – if only because the scarcity of usable land forces up its price in a competitive situation. Needless to say there are considerable difficulties in assessing the increase in value of any particular asset. This is principally because of the variety of interpretations that can be attached to the word 'value' itself. For reasons of expedience rather than logic, the valuation to be put on land and buildings belonging to a company is normally left to the discretion of the directors of the company – subject to the watchful eye of the auditors. The necessity of such an exercise in valuation, though dictated by common sense, was first underlined by the Companies Act 1967. This Act imposed on the directors the duty of expressing an opinion on the present **market value** of any land or interest in land contained in the fixed assets shown in the balance sheet, and of drawing attention to any significant increase (despite the fact that no specific figure could be honestly supplied regarding the extent of such increment). The purpose of this provision in the Act was partly to protect members against the unscrupulous entrepreneur, who, with private knowledge of the high **asset value** of companies which is not, however, reflected in current share prices, might seek to buy their shares to indulge in **asset stripping**. ◊ **Capital allowances** ◊ **Capital gains tax** ◊ **Depreciation**.

Apprentice One who signs a **contract** or **indenture**, agreeing to serve for a definite period with one employer or master. The apprentice's intention is to learn a trade, and although he may receive only a nominal wage, he expects to gain valuable experience. The master

agrees to teach his trade to the apprentice. ◊ **Articled clerk**.

Appropriation account An accounting term referring to that part of the annual accounts of a business wherein the net profit, having been determined, is allocated to various claimants as the directors so determine. It will disclose, *inter alia*, amounts declared as dividends and amounts transferred to named reserves. ◊ **Annual accounts** ◊ **Profit and loss account**.

Appropriation of payments When a creditor receives money from a debtor he can, in the absence of instruction to the contrary by the debtor, appropriate the payment to any debt outstanding on that debtor's account. This can be very important, as the creditor could set the monies against a debt that was **statute-barred** as far as legal recovery was concerned, and sue the debtor on the other non-barred debts. It has also been held, in court, that a banker may appropriate a payment to an unsecured debt where the debtor does not indicate that it was intended to apply to a secured debt. The bank may then claim the security as a lien on the unsecured debts in a subsequent **liquidation** or **bankruptcy**.

The right of appropriation does not, of course, apply where the debtor makes known the purpose of the payment, nor does it apply when there is a running credit account between the parties. In the latter instance it is assumed that debts are being settled in the date order in which they were incurred. Appropriation can never lawfully be made to an illegal debt.

Arbitrage This relates to the deliberate switching of funds between markets in order to maximize net gains on short-term investments. Dealings may be in currencies, commodities or **bills of exchange**. A person acting in this specialized business field may buy, say, a quantity of rice or deutschmarks three months forward and then invest the due purchase price payable in another commodity or currency. He will do so where he will receive a higher return on that investment than he will need to cover his forward transaction. Arbitrage is not considered to rank with pure speculation, though the line of demarcation is somewhat indistinct, when it is conducted on a genuine business basis. It can serve the smooth running of international, or national, trade and commerce, if only by making funds available in the right place at the right time. ◊ **Forward purchases**.

Arbitration The reference for settlement of a dispute normally arising out of **contract**, to one or more independent persons, rather than to a court of law. The arbitration must be agreed initially, it cannot be imposed afterwards. Some advantages are: simplicity, speed, economy and the avoidance of publicity. There is, of course, no guarantee of justice or impartiality on the part of the arbitrator. Contracts of arbitration may be oral or may be in writing in accordance with the principal Act, the Arbitration Act 1950. This Act rules that the arbitrator need not be named but the parties must sign, though signatures may be dispensed with where the contract is obvious from the behaviour of the parties. An agreement to refer a matter to arbitration does not prevent either party taking legal proceedings instead. This right to take proceedings cannot be denied by the contract. A court may, however, insist on the arbitration. Costs

of arbitration will be apportioned by the arbitrator. Where there is more than one arbitrator, an umpire is appointed. His decision is final if the arbitrators fail to agree (known as umpirage). The decision of the arbitrator is called the award. In order to be binding, it must be final, certain, possible and consistent. It must also take all matters submitted into account. The arbitrator must not act outside his jurisdiction. He may, and if required to do so must, state a case for a court to decide where a point of law is at stake. The award may be set aside, referred back or enforced by the court but only on points of law. Certain awards made in foreign countries may be enforced in England. ◊ **Advisory Conciliation and Arbitration Service** ◊ **Central Arbitration Committee**.

Architect A person qualified to design buildings and to supervise their erection. In Britain the title is restricted to those on the register of the **Architects' Registration Council of the United Kingdom**.

Architects' Registration Council of the United Kingdom This was formed in 1938 and has three main duties: (1) the maintenance and annual publication of the Register of Architects; (2) the maintenance of correct standards of professional conduct; and (3) the award of scholarships and grants to needy students. The Council has disciplinary powers over members who have committed criminal offences or been guilty of disgraceful conduct in a professional respect. Public complaints are referred to the disciplinary committee; less serious complaints are dealt with by the professional services committee. There is a code of professional conduct, similar to that of the Royal Institute of British Architects.

Architects, Royal Institute of British
This was formed in 1834, received a royal charter in 1837 and now has over 21,000 members. It imposes a code of professional conduct, and controls a Board of Architectural Education to supervise the teaching of architecture in schools and colleges and to help with educational guidance. The Architects' Registration Acts 1931 and 1938 restricted the use of the name 'architect' to persons who had passed the necessary examinations. There are various bodies of architects, the RIBA being the most important. All members of these bodies must have their names entered in the Register of the **Architects' Registration Council of the United Kingdom**.

Arithmetic mean A statistical term used for the figure obtained by totalling a series of values and dividing that total by the number of items in that series, e.g. the arithmetic mean age of a family of five, the ages of each being 45, 40, 11, 5 and 9 would be $45 + 40 + 11 + 5 + 9$ divided by five, i.e. $110/5 = 22$. ◊ **Average** ◊ **Geometric mean** ◊ **Mean**.

Arithmetic progression A mathematical term often connected with statistics. It refers to a numerical series within which the difference between consecutive items is constant. It should be contrasted with a geometrical progression, where this difference increases by a given factor as the series continues; e.g. x, 2x, 3x, 4x, 5x, 6x ... is arithmetic whereas, x, x^2, x^3, x^4, x^5, x^6 ... is geometric.

Arrears Monies due but unpaid.

Arrears of dividends Where **dividends** are in **arrears** and are payable,

the amount due should be shown in the **annual accounts**, or in a note to the accounts. The amount shown should be the gross amount, distinguishing between classes of **shares**.

Arrestment Scottish equivalent of **attachment**.

Arrived ship A vessel that has arrived at the agreed port of discharge or loading, proper notice having been given that it is ready to start discharging or loading.

Articled clerk A sophisticated name for an **apprentice**, usually applied to a person apprenticed in a professional firm, e.g. of **accountants** or **solicitors**.

Articles of association These are the internal regulations on the running of a **Company**. They are registered when the company is formed. They bind the company to the members as if each member had signed them, but do not bind the company or the members to outside persons. The articles are subject to the **memorandum of association** and must not contain anything illegal or **ultra vires**. They can be altered by the company by **special resolution** at a general meeting. The effect of registration is to give general notice to the public – any person may inspect the memorandum or articles of any company at the Companies Registration Office, on payment of a fee. A specimen form of articles, **Table A**, is provided by Section 8 of the 1985 Companies Act. This may be adopted in part or in whole.

Articles of association, alteration of The articles may be altered by a **special resolution** at a general meeting. The alteration must be within the powers given by the **memorandum of association**. It must concern legal acts and must not be a fraud on a minority of shareholders: that is, it must be for the good of the **company** and must not be an attempt by the majority to take advantage of their position. Where alteration of the rights of any class of shareholders is concerned, the articles often provide that special class meetings must be held and that the consent of the class must be obtained. Where the rights are fixed by the memorandum, then if the method of alteration is not specified it may be necessary to appeal to the court.

As per advice If these words are written on a **bill of exchange** it is an indication that the drawee has been notified that the bill has been drawn on him.

Assay The testing, or trying, of an alloy to determine the content of a precious metal. This has particular reference to coinage and to gold and silver products. There are a number of Official Assay Offices in the United Kingdom and each has its special distinguishing mark which is stamped on the article assayed (though not on coins of the realm) in addition to the **hallmark** proper. In this way the assay office responsible for hallmarking an article can be distinguished.

Assay master An official responsible for **assay**.

Asset Anything owned, whether in possession or by right to take possession, by a person or group of persons acting together, e.g. a **company**, the value of which can be expressed in monetary terms. Assets may be classified in many ways. The principal distinction normally made for business purposes is between **fixed assets** and **current assets**. Other business sub-divisions include **intangible assets**, that is, those assets which, though not visible, add to the

earning power of the business, e.g. **goodwill**, **patents**, **copyrights**, etc. (sometimes referred to as **invisible assets**); **liquid assets**, which are a subdivision of current assets; and also categories labelled **trade investments**, **quoted investments** etc.

In the **balance sheet** of a company certain divisions are required by law and are to be found listed in the **fourth schedule** to the Companies Act 1985. All balance sheets consist basically of total assets set against total liabilities. The two figures, in keeping with the principle of double-entry book-keeping, must be equal. A quick way of calculating the profit for a given period is to find the difference between the net asset figures at the beginning and end of that period.

Asset stripping A colourful term for somewhat nefarious dealings which were particularly common in the decades following the Second World War and which led to the acquisition of fortunes by the less scrupulous operators. The opportunities arose from the escalation of property values, coupled with the innate inaccuracies of **historical cost accounting**. The shrewd operator would look for a company possessing large **reserves** hidden in undervalued properties which were not being run to the cash advantage of the shareholders. He would gradually, or by a quick take-over, acquire a controlling interest in the company. The properties would then be revalued to create a substantial reserve, which would feature in the annual accounts. The **assets** of the company, particularly the more valuable properties, would then be sold for cash, which would be distributed – the operator taking the bulk consistent with his majority shareholding. If possible, by use of some of the cash generated and assuming many assets were sold and leased back, he would put the company into a profit-making position, declare dividends to bump up the price of the shares and then make a second killing by unloading his holdings or shares on to a more eager market – a market that by this time placed a higher value on them than when he bought them.

Asset value The asset value of shares, or, more correctly, the net asset value, is obtained by estimating the realizable value of the company's assets, deducting known liabilities and dividing the result among the equity shares. ◊ **Equity capital**. This manner of valuing shares was used in calculating death duties due on the death of the virtual owner of a company. Where the shares were not quoted it was the only manner in which the value could be ascertained. However, even when a **quotation** was available, this technique was often used where the authorities considered that a more realistic valuation would emerge from it. The fact that death duties are now referred to as **capital transfer tax** in no way affects the eventual outcome.

There is an even more drastic step that can be taken by the taxman to obtain an asset value for a majority shareholder's shares. This is not as frequently used but involves calculating the proportion of the company's income received by the shareholder, by dint of his shareholding and in whatever manner paid over by the company, and applying that percentage to the total **net assets** of the company. ◊ **Value** ◊ **Market value**.

Assets, circulating An alternative term for **current assets** which came into use because of their constant change in composition as business proceeds, e.g. stocks

are turned over and debtors change from month to month both as to name and amount. In a sense, current assets circulate within the fixed asset structure as oil does in a machine, helping to increase output. ◊ **Current ratio** ◊ **Overtrading** ◊ **Working capital**.

Assets, liquid An accounting term referring to those assets of a business concern which are represented by cash or near cash (e.g. **money at call and at short notice**), trade debtors, short-term bills, etc. Liquid assets are important in the calculation of **liquid ratios** and should be distinguished from **current assets**, which are a combination of liquid assets and stock in hand, **work-in-progress**, etc. ◊ **Current ratio**.

Assignment The transfer of rights and/or obligations by one person to another particularly with reference to a **contract**, so that under certain strictly defined conditions the second person takes over those rights and obligations and can enforce them, or have them enforced against him. For certain types of assignment the permission of a third party must be obtained. A building contractor can assign work to a subcontractor without the permission of his employer but an artist employed to paint a portrait cannot assign the work to another artist without permission. Generally speaking, a person cannot assign a duty to another when it is of a personal nature. The owner of a business who sells cannot assign to the purchaser the various contracts of employment which he has made. Assignment falls into three categories. Where there is an agreement that A shall do something for B, A may wish to assign his obligation to C; similarly B may wish to assign the benefit to D: (1) Basically A may assign with the permission of B. This then becomes in effect a new agreement between B and C, and A is no longer concerned. ◊ **Contract of novation**. (2) A may assign to C by custom of trade, e.g. subcontracting. B cannot complain but has a remedy both against A and against C. (3) A may assign without consulting B and without having any implied right by trade to do so. B may ignore the assignment and treat A as wholly responsible and as having breached the original agreement.

Where B is assigning the benefit much the same rules apply. ◊ **Assignment, legal** ◊ **Assignment, equitable**.

Assignment, equitable A term referring to assignments of debts or choses-in-action which are not proper **legal assignments**. The assignee takes the assignor's rights subject to equities. **Consideration** is not necessary provided the assignment is complete and is not conditional. The assignment is valid between assignor and assignee, even if notice is not given to the debtor. If the debtor does not receive notice, he may pay the assignor, leaving the assignee no rights against him. If he has received notice, he should pay the assignee. Assignees rank, not according to date of assignment, but according to the date of notice to the debtor.

The disadvantage of an equitable assignment is that the assignee must sue in the name of the assignor. This only applies to the assignment of legal rights. If the rights are equitable he can sue in his own name.

Assignment, legal It is possible legally to assign a debt or other legal **chose-in-action** so that the assignee acquires all rights and remedies, legal and equitable, provided that the assignment is absolute, in writing, and signed by the assignor.

Notice in writing must also be given to the party to be charged, usually the debtor. If these conditions are not fulfilled the assignment may still be enforceable as an **equitable assignment**. Legal assignments are governed by the Law of Property Act 1925.

Assignment of copyright ◊ **Copyright**.

Assignment of leases Where a lease is wholly assigned, the original lessee remains liable to the lessor but may have redress against the sub-lessee. The lessor may also sue the sub-lessee directly. Where only part of the term of a lease is assigned, the lessor's rights are only against the original lessee.

Assisted areas Certain areas of the UK are designated as assisted areas. They are further divided into 'development areas' and 'intermediate areas'. The designation is made by the Department of Trade and Industry and, in so far as the exact geographical locations might vary, individual firms should inquire at regional offices of the Department to ascertain whether or not they qualify for the assistance available in these areas.

The aid is generally directed towards new business ventures, and in order to qualify it is usually necessary to demonstrate not only that the venture is one which will create employment opportunities but that, whilst being a viable project, it could not be established in the absence of such aid. Grants available will vary with the projected fixed capital costs of establishing the business and the number of jobs likely to be created over the first three years. If approved, the venture may also attract substantial grants towards in-plant training.

In addition to funds made available by

the UK government, grants may also be forthcoming from the European Investment Bank and/or from the European Union. The **exchange risk guarantee scheme** will also cover any exchange risks flowing from borrowings in foreign currency.

Associated British Ports The ownership and administration of the major ports in the UK has seen many changes since the Second World War. The nationalization policies of the post-war Labour government brought many of the existing ports into public ownership, principally through the nationalization of the railway companies, which had long been the principal port-owners.

Initially, the state-owned ports were put under the control of the Docks and Inland Waterways Executive, but in 1953 this was abolished when docks and waterways were each put under separate management within the overall care of the British Transport Commission. The Transport Act 1962 dispensed with the BTC and ports became the responsibility of the British Transport Docks Board set up by that Act. This board was to gradually increase the number of ports and also its own role as the ultimate port authority. In the following years it transferred twelve of the thirty-one ports it controlled to regional authorities. This trend was reversed by the 1981 Transport Act, which, in an attempt to provide more scope for private initiative, set up Associated British Ports as a statutory corporation. This corporation took over the nineteen ports remaining with the BTDB and was itself controlled by Associated British Ports Holdings PLC, a company quoted on the Stock Exchange. Since 1981 ABP has been free to diversify its operations, though it is still primarily a port operator with its head office in London and its ports mainly in four groups – Southampton, Humber, South Wales and Small Ports.

Associated company Often a company has a substantial interest in another to the extent that they might be *de facto*, if not *de jure*, partners in some venture. Whilst the holding of the former company is not such as to render the latter a **subsidiary company** as legally defined, the relationship needs to be drawn attention to and the latter is referred to, in the accounts of the former, as an 'associated company'.

Prior to 1967 an associated company was treated virtually as a **trade investment** of the principal company, and real control could often be operated without the legal requirements imposed upon a **holding company** proper. The Companies Act 1985 now makes it necessary for details of any holding in another company, in excess of 10 per cent of any class of share, to be disclosed in the accounts of the investing company. ◊ **Equity capital** ◊ **Substantial shareholdings**.

Associated undertakings A term introduced by the Companies Act 1989 to describe business entities which, although not companies under the provisions of the various Companies Acts, might be legally considered as part of a **group** for the purposes of the compilation of **group accounts**.

Association for Payment Clearing Services (APACS) This was set up in 1985 as the umbrella body to oversee the major payment clearing systems of England and Wales, to ensure their continued operational efficiency, and to consider possible improvements in those systems in the light of new technology and needs.

It also acts as a forum for the discussion of matters relating to money transmission, and monitors the development of plastic payment cards and whatever anti-fraud measures might be deemed necessary.

It is an unincorporated association whose members consist of most of the leading UK banks and building societies. It also has associate members which, while not being full settlement members in any clearing, act as agents providing payment services to their customers. APACS has replaced the old Bankers Clearing House usually known as the London Bankers Clearing House. Membership of APACS is restricted to financial institutions which can demonstrate their ability to meet the technical and operational requirements of membership, are adequately supervised, and maintain settlement account facilities at the Bank of England.

APACS operates through three distinct clearing companies limited by shares, each of which is responsible for a particular area of clearing. These are (1) the **Cheque and Credit Clearing** which handles bulk paper clearings; (2) **Chaps & Town Clearing** which deals with high-value clearings; and (3) **BACS Limited** which is responsible for bulk electronic clearing.

In addition to the three clearing companies, operational groupings have been set up by APACS to cover currency clearings, cheque card and eurocheque schemes.

Association of British Insurers (ABI)
A major trade association for UK insurance companies, established in July 1985. It replaced the British Insurance Association, which was for many years the primary governing body for the insurance industry. The new body also takes in both the Life Offices Association and the Industrial Life Offices Association together with other smaller organizations, and, in doing so, it becomes the parent body for companies transacting over 90 per cent of worldwide insurance business. It is hoped that by concentrating the older associations into one single body not only will the interests of the general public be better served but the insurance industry will have a more powerful voice in dealing both with government and the EU.

Association of Futures Brokers and Dealers (AFBD) This was one of the initial **self-regulating organizations** set up under the terms of the Financial Services Act and acting beneath the umbrella of the **Securities and Investments Board**. It represented Futures and Options Dealers who were not traders on the Stock Exchange. It subsequently merged with the Securities Association to become part of the **Securities and Futures Association**.

Assurance Distinguished from **insurance** in that assurance does not depend upon a possibility. It is a payment of premium at regular intervals in return for a fixed sum which will become payable at a stated time. The obvious examples are life and endowment assurance. With **life assurance**, payment becomes due on the death of the life assured. With endowment assurance, payment becomes due at a stated date. It is common to combine both in a life and endowment policy. Certain companies deal only with life assurance. As an assurance contract is one of the category known as **uberrimae fidei**, all facts relevant to the risk taken by the company must be stated. Some companies often insist on a medical examination. If not, this does not always prevent them disclaiming liability if the claimant was suffering from some serious complaint (unknown to them) at the time the policy was taken out. Policies often contain long and complex clauses limiting liability. Care should be taken to read these before the **contract** is signed.

Assurance policies may be with or without profits. A policy with profits entitles the holder to a share in the profits of the company during the term of the policy. This can amount to a considerable sum. Premiums on these policies are of course higher. In comparing one company with another it should be remembered that those who offer the higher profits possibly charge the higher premium. It is usually a question of whether one wishes to pay more now for a higher sum in the future.

There is an increasing tendency for assurance companies to offer what are known as equity-linked policies. The premiums are then invested in what is equivalent to a **unit trust**. The idea is to combat inflation and compete with unit trusts offering assurance policies.

Assurance policies are often used in connection with house purchase. As with most contracts of assurance, the assured must have an 'insurable interest', e.g. it is not possible for A to take out a policy on the life of B unless A stands to suffer loss. His claim will be restricted to the amount of the loss. The interest need only exist at the time the policy is taken out. A **creditor** can insure his debtor and a wife has an interest in the life of her husband and *vice versa*, but a parent has not normally an interest in the life of a child nor a child in the parent (save where a parent is supporting a child). ◊ **Insurable interest**.

If a man takes out a policy for the benefit of his dependents the money will be treated as a separate estate for tax purposes. This could be a considerable advantage. The advantage, however, was modified considerably by the Finance Act 1968. In order to avoid aggregation, the policy must have been irrevocably taken out in the name of another and the premium should have been part of normal expenditure. The **gifts** *inter vivos* rule may also apply.

Assurance companies offer variously named policies of an endowment nature for, e.g., educational purposes.

Profits of assurance companies are determined by quinquennial valuations. The profit is the difference between the value of the **assets** and an estimate of the probable liability to the policy holders. ◊ **Paid-up policies** ◊ **Actuary**.

At and from A marine insurance term for policies covering a ship in port as well as at sea.

At call ◊ **Money at call and at short notice**.

At par ◊ **Par value**.

At sight A term used for **bills of exchange** payable on presentation, as opposed to on a particular date.

Attachment Prevention of a debtor from disposing of specific money or **goods** in the hands of third parties, until the debt has been settled. ◊ **Charging order** ◊ **Garnishee order** ◊ **Notice in lieu of distringas**.

Attorney In England, a person practising at the Bar. It may also mean someone who holds a **power of attorney**.

Attorney, power of ◊ **Power of attorney**.

Auction This occurs when **goods** are offered for **sale** in public by an **auctioneer**. The conduct of an auction varies according to custom. Normally goods are sold to the highest bidder. The auctioneer acts as **agent** for the seller. **Sale of goods** at an auction may be subject to a **reserve price** stated by the seller (this fact should be known to those persons attending the auction though the price need not be disclosed). If the hammer is brought down before the price is reached the sale can be avoided. This does not apply when the **contract** is one to be evidenced in writing and the auctioneer has signed the memorandum.

It is illegal for a dealer to offer a person a reward not to bid at the sale: penalities can be levied on both parties. A dealer is a person who buys for resale.

Auctioneer A person authorized to sell **goods** or land at a public **auction** or sale. Initially the **agent** of the seller, he becomes also the agent of the buyer after the item has been knocked down; he can therefore bind both parties where writing is necessary. Sale is normally only for cash where the custom is not otherwise; the auctioneer has a **lien** on goods for his charges provided he has the goods; he has no implied authority to warrant the goods sold, nor the owner's right to sell; he must act in good faith.

Advertisement of an auction does not bind the auctioneer as it is not an **offer** but an invitation.

Audio typist A person who types out work dictated to a machine with a recording device, so that messages can be recorded at the dictator's convenience, stored until the typist is available, and then taken down exactly. The obvious advantages of this system have made it increasingly popular. ◊ **Copy typist**.

Audit Inspection of a set of books and/or accounts by a person other than the one who prepared them (with the object of ascertaining whether or not the books are properly kept and/or the accounts show a **true and fair** view of the state of affairs of the organization at the date stated) followed by a report to the persons by whom the **auditor** was appointed.

Auditor A person appointed by the members of an organization to inspect accounting, and other, records, and report on the manner in which those conducting the affairs of that organization on behalf of the members have accounted for their stewardship.

Particular legal requirements apply to the auditor of certain businesses under the protection of various statutes. The most important in this context are the Companies Acts of 1985 and 1989.

Every company registered under the Companies Act is obliged to appoint an official auditor. ◊ **Auditor, appointment of** ◊ **Auditor's remuneration** ◊ **Auditor, removal of** ◊ **Auditor's report** ◊ **Auditors and third parties**.

The company auditor is essentially independent and is employed by, and must report to, the shareholders. He must belong to one of certain named professional bodies specified by the Department of Trade and Industry. At present these bodies are the Institute of Chartered Accountants in England and Wales; the Institute of Chartered Accountants of Scotland; the Institute of Chartered Accountants in Ireland; the Chartered Association of Certified Accountants. Prior to the coming into effect of the Companies Act 1976, the Department of Trade and Industry could approve the appointment of other suitable but unqualified persons if they were satisfied that such persons had the requisite knowledge and skill. At one time it was possible for any person to be appointed as auditor of what was known as an 'exempt private company'. Such companies were abolished by the Companies Act 1967, which decided that limited companies would be divided into two categories only: public companies and private companies, categories redefined by the Companies Act 1985. ◊ **Company, private** ◊ **Company, public** ◊ **Company, exempt private**.

Auditor, appointment of The **auditor** of any company registered under the Companies Act 1985 is appointed by the members of that company acting in concert at the **annual general meeting** and holds office only from the end of that meeting until the conclusion of the next – though he may be reappointed by a resolution of members. Prior to the coming into force of the 1976 Act existing auditors were automatically reappointed if no resolution to the contrary was passed at the annual general meeting.

The **directors** may appoint the first auditor(s) and fill any casual vacancy, but the appointment must be confirmed at the next annual general meeting. If not so confirmed then the office of auditor falls vacant. Any failure to appoint an auditor must be reported to the Secretary of State at the Department of Trade and Industry within one week and the Secretary will then make the appointment himself. The remuneration of auditors is fixed by the company in general meeting, except where the appointment is made by the directors or the Secretary of State, when the remuneration will be fixed by the appointers. Remuneration as auditor should be distinguished, in the accounts, from amounts paid for purely accounting work or the computation of tax liabilities, etc.

In company accounts the latter will be included in an expense heading and must never be included in the audit fees required to be shown by the **fourth schedule**.

Auditors of organizations other than companies are appointed as the constitution of the organization directs.

Auditor, removal of Auditors may generally be removed at any time by the persons appointing them, subject to any suit for breach of contract. In the case of a limited company the auditor can be removed from office by an ordinary resolution passed by the members at a general meeting. Notification of such a resolution must be given to the Registrar of Companies within fourteen days of its being passed.

If an auditor is to be removed prior to the expiry of his term of office or, if it is intended to pass a resolution appointing someone other than the retiring auditor at a general meeting, then special notice must be given to the company of an intention to put such a resolution. The company must then notify the auditor who then has the right to make such representations as he sees fit and ask that these be circulated to members prior to the meeting at which the resolution is to be moved. If the representations are not sent out then the auditor may require them to be read out at the meeting. There are provisions in the Act which negate the requirement to circulate or read out such representations where a court is satisfied that to do so would merely afford undue publicity to defamatory matter.

Auditor's remuneration ◊ **Auditor, appointment of**.

Auditor's report The report made by

an **auditor** appointed to examine and report on the accounts of any organization. The term has particular reference to the books and accounts of limited companies in so far as the Companies Acts require that the accounts of limited companies must be audited annually by an approved auditor. These requirements now extend to the **directors' report**. Eligibility is determined by law and the Department of Trade and Industry. A copy of the auditor's report must be appended to every **balance sheet**, and documents that the law requires must be attached thereto and laid before members in general meeting. The auditor's report must also accompany the accounts that are filed with the company's **annual return**.

An auditor's report normally takes one of the forms approved by the professional organizations – such a form having been adjudged to cover all requirements imposed by law on the auditor.

Reports may be 'clean' or 'qualified'. A report is qualified if it contains any indication that the auditor has failed to satisfy himself on any of the points on which the law demands that he report. The qualification may be notional, as when the report adds a rider stating that because of geographical difficulties the appointed auditor has had to rely on information supplied by other auditors in the countries where certain subsidiaries are located and where the size of the subsidiary company does not justify an expensive visit by the official auditor in person. More serious qualifications do however arise and, with the growing concern in the public mind as to the reliability of published accounts, are becoming more frequent. Such qualifications may refer to the inadequacy of information or explanations supplied, or

the fact that the auditor is not satisfied that proper books, or other records, are being kept.

Naturally, no company likes to publish its accounts with a **qualified report** and it is customary for every effort to be made by directors and management to fill gaps, give adequate answers to inquiries and allay any doubts that the auditor may have as to the fairness of the accounts. In the past there has been the danger that an auditor might be willing to lean a little too far backwards to safeguard his appointment, but both the law and the accounting profession are now taking steps to minimize such a possibility, if only by emphasizing that the first loyalty of the auditor is not to the **directors** of a company but to its **members**. It is to them that he makes his report. What is more, should he fail to disclose irregularities, or to qualify his report when facts show that this is necessary, then he may be sued for negligence by members of the company and, in some instances, by third parties who have lost money as a result of relying on wrong information in the accounts to which the report relates. ◊ **Auditors and third parties**.

Auditors and third parties Auditors have no duty normally to persons relying on accounts audited by them. The **contract** is between the **company** or other organization and the auditor. The auditor has a duty to the organization and can be sued in the normal way for negligence. He is not generally liable to persons who might rely on the accounts in, say, lending money. However, there is a tendency for the law to take the attitude that where the auditor knows the purpose for which the accounts are wanted (i.e. to persuade someone to lend money) then if he is negligent he may incur liability.

Authority to negotiate A term used with reference to **bills of exchange**, and the finance of overseas trade, particularly with the Far East. The London branch of a foreign **bank** discounts bills drawn on overseas buyers, which are then sent to the other country for collection. The bills are not popular in the London money market–collection must be made in the other country. If payment is not forthcoming the exporter himself will be liable as drawer. These bills are therefore not easy to negotiate.

Authorized capital The amount of **capital** stated in the **memorandum of association** of a company. A company cannot issue more unless the amount is first increased by the methods prescribed in the Companies Act 1985. The authorized capital is usually stated in the company's **balance sheet** and is distinguished from **issued capital**. Authorized capital as stated in the memorandum must be divided into **shares** of a certain amount. It does not necessarily have to be divided into **ordinary shares**, **preference shares**, etc. This can be done at a later date. ◊ **capital clause** ◊ **Nominal capital**.

Authorized depository The Exchange Control Act 1947 disallowed the circulation of **bearer securities**, e.g. bearer bonds. It ordered that all such **securities** should be deposited with specified institutions, which would then be responsible for collecting and paying the dividend. These were known as authorized depositories and were **banks**, members of recognized stock exchanges, **solicitors** and certain specialized financial institutions. Although the issue of bearer securities was

prohibited in 1947 the ban on the issue was removed in 1963.

Automated Pit Trading (APT) This trading system was introduced by LIFFE to supplement rather than replace the traditional Open Outcry Market. It is based on a high-resolution colour screen which uses a colour-coded system to pinpoint various pits and traders in the LIFFE market. Orders are transmitted directly to selected traders by moving a computer mouse to the particular location, where the trader executes the deal immediately. The system is used for trading after the floor market closes at 1620 hours until 1800 hours, enabling dealers to cover the end of the European and most of the US trading day. APT is a relatively new development which has opened the door to a variety of enhanced trading methods that will become available to LIFFE.

Average A single number taken to be typical of a series of numbers or, alternatively, that central number in a series around which others revolve or on which they tend to converge. There are various kinds of average. The most common is the **arithmetic mean**, e.g. to find the average age of a group of people, total the age of each and divide by the number in the group. Other averages are the **geometric mean**, the **mode** and the **Median**, all of which have particular uses in statistical analysis.

In insurance the word average has a specialized meaning as used in the **average clause**. In marine insurance further applications are found in **general average loss** and **particular average loss**. ◊ **Average adjustor**.

Average adjustor When an insurer has to meet a claim under a policy, he frequently employs an average adjustor to inspect the property which is the subject of the claim and to ascertain the extent of the liability of the insurer under the operative policy. This can be very important where the policy contains an **average clause** and in marine insurance, where a claim may be for **general average loss** or for a **particular average loss**.

Average bond A bond given by a person receiving cargo, stating that he will contribute to any **general average** claim. ◊ **Average adjustor**.

Average clause That clause in a policy of insurance that protects the insurer from under-insurance by the policy holder. It states that the amount of a claim to be paid will be reduced to that proportion of the claim that the insured value bears to the true value of the property insured. Particular rules apply in marine insurance. ◊ **Particular average loss** ◊ **General average loss** ◊ **Marine insurance**.

Average cost The **average** cost of producing goods, sometimes referred to as the **unit cost**. It is customary, in the accounting world, to distinguish average fixed cost from average variable cost. ◊ **Fixed costs** ◊ **Variable costs**. There is also an important difference between the short-term average and the long-term average. The average cost of producing a single batch of goods, or of one month's production, may be very different from the average taken over a long period. This distinction is important in fixing prices especially under free competition, for although a company cannot fix prices below the long-term average on a permanent basis it can bring them down to the short-term average and below, where

there is a competitive advantage to be gained. But ◊ **Marginal cost**.

Average cost is also used with reference to **Stock-in-trade**, and the valuation thereof. ◊ **Stock valuation**.

Average due date The date on which a number of payments all due at different times may legally be paid together, thus discharging the whole debt.

Averaging A term used in connection with dealings on the **Stock Exchange** where additions are made to a block of shares owned, at a time when the price has fallen, in order to reduce the average cost of the shares held. The term is occasionally used in the reverse situation where advantage is taken of a sudden upsurge in the price of shares to increase the average selling price of a block partly disposed of earlier.

Avoirdupois The system of weights used in England and America consisting of, *inter alia*, ounces, pounds, quarters, hundredweights and tons. An ounce contains $437\frac{1}{2}$ grains, and the value of the grain was defined by Act of Parliament in the reign of George IV. ◊ **Metric system**.

Award The decision of an arbitrator. ◊ **Arbitration**. The term has increasing relevance to wage negotiations by trade unions, where differences between the amount asked and that offered may sometimes be taken to arbitration. An award may be made by a tribunal after hearing the arguments of both sides and also noting the declared policy of the government in power. That government can, and does, where circumstances deem it necessary, negate the award made. ◊ **Advisory Conciliation and Arbitration Service**.

'B' list of contributaries ◊
Contributaries.

Back duty Tax payable on income un-disclosed at the time earned. The attitude of the Inland Revenue to tax evasion is severe – particularly when indulged in over a long period and where large amounts of tax are involved. In reclaim-ing tax the Revenue can go back as far as it wishes and has powers to demand con-siderable documentation and explana-tions. The law varies from time to time but normally, in back duty cases, defend-ants become liable for payments far in excess of the amount originally evaded and interest well above that normally payable on overdue tax. This is by way of a penalty for their offence. In extreme cases they may also be imprisoned. ◊ **Direct taxation** ◊ **Indirect taxation** ◊ **Tax avoidance** ◊ **Tax evasion**.

Back freight Freight payable when delivery is not taken within a reasonable time at the port of discharge and the master, who has implied power to do so, deals with the **goods** at the owner's expense, perhaps by transferring them to another port or by returning them to the consignor.

Back-to-back credit A term used in finance. It is a credit given by a British **finance house** acting as go-between for a foreign buyer and a foreign seller. The foreign seller delivers the relevant documents to the finance house, the finance house then issues its own documents in place of them, and the seller's name is not mentioned.

Backed note A receiving note endorsed by a **shipbroker** and authorizing the master of a ship to take on board water-borne **goods**. It is evidence that **freight** has been or will be paid.

Backwardation Backwardation is the obverse of the contango coin. Where, at the end of a Stock Exchange account period, on **account day**, a person who has sold shares or bonds short wishes to defer buying the necessary stock until the price has fallen, he may apply to have settlement carried over into the next account. In doing so he will pay interest known as backwardation to the prospec-tive purchaser. Backwardation, therefore, is the price paid by a **bear** speculator for the privilege of carrying over a trans-action into the next settlement period. It is also a term used with reference to commodity markets where the cash price exceeds the three months price, or in market-making when a temporary situ-ation arises where one market maker is offering to buy at a price higher than that at which another is selling.

BACS Limited This is the name given to Bankers Automated Clearing Services Limited when that company was made part of APACS in 1987. BACS provides an automated clearing house service in the UK for transactions either originated by members themselves or by those who members sponsor in order that they may

45

use the service. BACS has more members than either of the other two main clearing companies. Of these, some 25 per cent are Building Societies.

Bad debts Debts due to a person or business are either good, doubtful or bad. Bad debts are those which appear irrecoverable, or where the estimated cost of recovery is greater than the value of the debt. In preparing accounts they are treated as a loss and written off in the **profit and loss account**. Bad debts should be carefully distinguished from those which are merely doubtful. The former are known losses and are treated as such; the latter are merely a possible future loss which should be provided against. ◊ **Doubtful debts, provision for**.

Bailee ◊ Bailment.

Bailment Possession of the **goods** of another without ownership. This may be voluntary, e.g. borrowing an article, or involuntary, e.g. having an item left on one's premises by accident. A **bailee** is, if voluntary, expected to take care of the goods. The degree of care depends on circumstances. Problems appear frequently in **contracts** for repair. Generally speaking the repairer is a voluntary bailee until time for collection. After this he is an involuntary bailee. As involuntary bailee he is not bound to take particular care but in most instances is nevertheless bound by statute law. This insists that he retain the goods for a period at the bailor's expense. He may then, after advertising the sale in open market, sell, and after deducting costs must retain the net proceeds for a specified period. ◊ **Uncollected goods, disposal of**. Another common form of involuntary bailment occurs when goods

are sent to a third party in the hope that he may purchase them. In such a case the recipient need take no care of the goods provided he does not indicate acceptance of the **offer**. It is sufficient that he redirects the goods to the sender at the latter's expense, or notifies him that the goods are not required and are to be removed forthwith. If they are perishable the bailee may be forced to dispose of them. He would then retain the net proceeds until the bailor collected them. ◊ **Order and disposition**.

Balance Apart from its non-commercial meanings and its application to the concept of symmetry in matters of weight, the term 'balance' has a particular significance in the world of accounting or, more precisely, in **double-entry book-keeping**. The balance on an account is the sum shown as owed or owing, or in ultimate debit or credit, after the difference between the total of the entries on each side of the account has been determined. It is, in fact, the amount that must be inserted on one side or the other to ensure that the total debits equal the total credits. This balancing figure is then shown as the opening item in that account for the ensuing period. In double-entry book-keeping it is axiomatic that if all balances in the ledgers are extracted and listed, each on its proper side of a summary account, called a **trial balance**, then the totals of each side of this account must agree. ◊ **Balance sheet**.

Balance of payments This is, effectively, the income and expenditure account of a nation over a given period. In the UK the most important account is that prepared at the end of a fiscal year on which after necessary updates the Chancellor of the Exchequer, guided by the permanent secretaries at the Treasury, bases his official annual budget. Monthly balance of payments accounts are, however, also published, in two principal parts – the balance of external trade and the movements of capital to and from other countries.

The balance of trade deals with exports and imports, which may be visible or invisible. Visible trade is that concerned with buying and selling goods. Invisible trade consists of services provided to (or by) other nations, e.g. by insurance companies, **discount houses**, currency dealers, shipping firms issuing charters or handling cargoes, etc. It also covers interest charged on foreign loans and income earned or expenditure incurred in expediting foreign trade generally, e.g. in the provision of financial services. In recent years the tourist industry has been an important factor in invisible trade when it involves the transfer of foreign currencies.

Movement of capital, the second ingredient of the balance of payments, relates to the volume of international investment either by or in other countries. The amount of such investment is influenced by many factors, not least of which is the level of interest rates. In the absence of express government interference, and other things being equal, money is attracted to the place where interest rates on low-risk capital are greatest. Any government can attempt to regulate the inflow of foreign currencies by the manipulation of the central bank's base rate, which will, in turn, have a parallel influence on interest rates generally. Naturally, the fact that interest paid will itself have a detrimental effect on the balance of payments must be taken into account in any long-term planning by the State and puts a restraining hand on any tend-

ency to push up too far the rates offered. Additionally, where exchange rates are volatile, the attraction of high interest rates may be counterbalanced by the possibility of losses brought about by depreciation of the capital invested. ⟡ **Minimum lending rate**.

There are limits to the power of any government to balance its national accounts by playing with interest rates – at least in the long run. Nevertheless, in that long run, a balance on international payments must be achieved and this is at the root of many currency **devaluations**. Short- or medium-term imbalances can be covered either in the traditional way by the transfer of gold or foreign exchange reserves or, more commonly nowadays, by loans – either direct from one country to another or, indirectly, through one of the international financial bodies, e.g. the **International Monetary Fund**.

A healthy economy will have little trouble in balancing its payments and a prosperous economy will budget for surpluses on its balance of trade in successive years, thereby building up both its reputation and its reserves. There is a parallel here with the successful public company which, by good management and perhaps a run of good fortune, is able continually to increase its capital by adding annually to its reserves, provided that such additions are real and not merely a reflection of inflationary costs and prices.

Balance of trade ⟡ **Balance of payments**.

Balance sheet A statement produced by an organization, whether run for profit or not, showing the financial position of that organization at a particular date. This date is normally at the termination of an **accounting period**, which, in the case

47

of companies, will almost always be at the end of a financial year. It is a kind of statement of affairs, which lists and distinguishes between the various assets and liabilities of the organization at that date.

The traditional balance sheet is two-sided, the liabilities being shown on the left-hand side and the assets on the right. There is, however, an increasing tendency to adopt the vertical form of presentation which, among other things, avoids the confusion engendered in the layman's mind by the appearance of the owner's capital as a 'liability'. The vertical form lists the **fixed assets** and adds the net **current assets** to them. The total is described as 'net capital employed'. There follows a summary of what this capital consists of, distinguishing between loans and the capital subscribed by the proprietor(s), to which retained profits or surpluses are added. This list of contributors of capital may also include long-term creditors and reserves for taxation (or other defined purposes).

The balance sheets of limited companies are governed by, and must conform to, the various provisions contained in company law and, in particular, must be prepared in accordance with the **fourth schedule** to the 1985 Companies Act which has replaced the **eighth schedule** to the 1948 Act. The new Schedule contains a choice of two formats, one of which, subject to the notes also contained in the Schedule, must be selected as the form in which the balance sheet is to be shown. There is, however, an overriding provision in the 1985 Act which effectively allows the formats to be varied if, and only if, such a variation is essential to the presentation of a **true and fair** view of the state of affairs of the company. The balance sheet is the principal docu-

ment to be attached to a company's **annual return**.

Balance ticket ◊ **Certification of transfer**.

Balancing charge or allowance ◊ **Capital allowances**.

Ballast Material used in lieu of, or in addition to, cargo to stabilize a ship.

Baltic Exchange Located in a purpose-built building in St Mary Axe, London, the Baltic Exchange is one of the oldest and best-known centres for freight chartering in the world both by sea and air. Its members, over 700 companies, are concerned principally with the movement of goods by ship between the various nations and its brokers act for ship-owners on the one hand and those wishing to charter for the dispatch of cargoes on the other, matching the service of the former to the needs of the latter. Specialist members perform a like service for those wishing to charter aircraft for both passengers and freight. The Exchange building was blown up by the IRA on 10 April 1992. After a temporary move to Lloyd's the business is now back in the restored building.

Baltic International Freight Futures Exchange (BIFFEX) This respresented an additional facility offered by the Baltic Exchange for the purchase and sale of freight futures as well as those in certain agricultural products. In 1991 this business was transferred to **London Fox**.

Bank An institution which handles other people's money both to their advantage and to its own profit.

Historically, the bank has grown out of basic community needs. Firstly, it provided a safe place to store valuables, secondly, a source from which to borrow money for specific purposes and/or periods and, thirdly, the means of settling debts without having to carry large amounts of money from place to place.

At one time these needs were met by goldsmiths, with whom people would leave their gold and other valuables for safekeeping. Gradually, these trustees began to realize that the quantity of gold, etc., left with them would not all be recalled at once and that they could safely lend part of it to others for short periods at a profit. Conversely, the depositors came to realize that the receipt given by a reputable goldsmith was increasingly becoming as good as the gold itself and that a debt to another person could be satisfied merely by handing over the receipt. Loans began to be issued in the form of receipts, and hence we have, in embryo, the emergence of the modern banking system.

Although such a practice was *prima facie* both illegal and immoral, it did provide a very valuable spur to the growth of trade by substituting credit for cash and, by thus increasing the rate at which business was transacted, it certainly speeded up the rate of economic growth.

In time, and after much legislation, the present banking system emerged. It was none the less true that until relatively recently, when the obligation to give gold to the face value of a pound note was abolished, the country's economic wealth rested on a needle-point of faith. Should all notes have been presented at the banks for conversion into gold at the same time then the nation would have been totally bankrupted and the banks barely able to pay a fraction of the face value of their debts represented by the notes in issue. ◊ **Bank, commercial** ◊ **Bank of England** ◊ **Banks: big four** ◊ **Merchant bank**.

Bank advance An amount lent by a bank to its customer either as a **bank loan** or an **overdraft**.

Bank bill A **bill of exchange** issued or accepted by a **bank**. A bank bill is more acceptable than a normal **trade bill**, as the risk is less; **discounts** therefore tend to be less also.

Bank charges These are the charges made by a bank to the customer who maintains a current account at that bank. They are payable by both business and personal customers. Business customers are usually charged a sum which bears a direct relation to the number of transactions on the account, though where the average balance is large the bank may forgo the charges partly out of a wish to keep the particular account and partly because of the reward accruing to the bank from the use of the balance retained. At one time personal customers were always expected to bear bank charges which varied according to bank and customer. In recent times, however, competition, both between banks themselves, and more importantly between the banks and the newly agressive building societies seeking customers, has brought about a change in attitude towards charging personal customers. It is now common for High Street banks to forgo charges for personal accounts kept in credit, and for some banks to allow accounts to remain charge-free up to a fixed sum overdrawn. If the customer exceeds the charge-free limits, however, the bank may either impose a lump-sum charge or penalize the customer by re-imposing charges for the whole quarter in which the transgression occurred.

Bank, commercial A modern term for the joint stock bank, though the latter is still officially the name of those banking companies that deal with the general public and have branches in High Streets everywhere. At one time there were many joint stock banks, but their number has been reduced considerably through amalgamation and there are now four major banking companies – Lloyds, Barclays, Midland and NatWest. Others not quite so prominent, though enjoying a sizeable portion of the banking business, include the Royal Bank of Scotland, Coutts (a subsidiary of NatWest), the **Trustee Savings Bank**, Girobank, the Co-op in England and Wales and certain Scottish and Irish banks. Branches of major foreign banks also operate in Britain as commercial banks.

The developing banking world gradually divided into two major parts, the public and the private (◊ **Bank**). The former category, which now comprises the commercial banks, became limited companies, and concerned itself with offering a deposit and transfer service to the general public (which could include both individuals and trading or industrial entities). The latter tended to retain the format of partnerships and grew into the many merchant banks and/or discount houses that deal almost exclusively with industrial finance and foreign trade. ◊ **Accepting houses** ◊ **Discount houses** ◊ **Merchant bank**.

At one time many, or most, of the commercial banks issued their own bank notes, but since the Bank Charter Act 1844 this privilege has been gradually restricted to the Bank of England and to a lesser extent (◊ **Legal tender**) the Scottish and Irish banks. **Cheques** are particularly associated with the commercial banks and are the means by which they conduct most of their dealings, though the increasing adaptation of computer technology by the banks indicates rapid movement towards even swifter methods of transferring money. At present the results of daily cheque transactions by the public are settled through inter-bank transfers, most of which are handled through the auspices of APPCS, which arranges settlement by transfer between the accounts kept by individual banks at the Bank of England. ◊ **Bank notes** ◊ **Bank of England** ◊ **Clearing banks** ◊ **Cash dispenser**.

Bank draft This has the same relation to a cheque as a **bank bill** has to a **trade bill**. Bank drafts are basically cheques drawn on a particular bank and obtained from that bank by a debtor for the payment of a debt where the creditor will not accept the debtor's personal cheque or the debtor does not have a bank account.

Bank for International settlements (BIS) Originally established to coordinate the activities of various Western European central banks in settling First World War reparations, and intended to become a central organization of world trade. Its headquarters are in Basle.

Most of its intended functions have been taken over by the **International Monetary Fund**, though it still acts as a clearing bank for the central banks of the participating nations. Even though it is technically subservient to other institutions it holds regular meetings of the representatives of the member nations, who attend as directors, providing an important forum for the exchange of opinions and current information, and thereby facilitating the coordination of the monetary policies of the various nations. It also takes careful note of, and intervenes where necessary in, international monetary speculations and acts as an agent for such other bodies as the **Organization for Economic Cooperation and Development,** the **European Union,** the **European Monetary System** and even the International Monetary Fund itself.

Members of the BIS are the UK, France, Germany, Italy, Switzerland, Sweden, Belgium and the Netherlands. The USA, Japan and Canada also send representatives.

Bank holidays Public holidays prescribed under the various Bank Holidays Acts. Banks are not required to open on these days and legally binding payments falling due on such days are deferred until the working day following. Persons required to work on these public holidays are entitled to additional remuneration or, if they so agree, to a day off in lieu. Bank holidays in England, Wales, Northern Ireland and the Channel Islands are New Year's Day, Easter Monday, May Day (first Monday in May), Spring Bank Holiday (last Monday in May), August Bank Holiday (last Monday in August) and Boxing Day. In the Channel Islands 9 May, Liberation Day, is added and in Northern Ireland so is 17 March, St Patrick's Day. Good Friday and Christmas Day are also public holidays, though they differ from the others in that bills, or other payments falling due thereon, are payable on the preceding day. In Scotland the public holidays correspond to those of England except that 2 January is substituted for Easter Monday and the August Bank Holiday is taken on the first, rather than the last, Monday in August.

When a bank holiday falls on a Sunday the following day becomes the holiday in its stead. Commercially, bank holidays enjoy a similar status to Sundays inasmuch as not only are bills of exchange payable on that day postponed to the following day but such holidays are not counted in reckoning **days of grace.**

Bank, joint stock ◊ **Bank, commercial**.

Bank loan A fixed amount lent by a bank to a customer for an agreed time and on specified terms. Contrast with a **bank overdraft**, which is a permit to overdraw on an account up to a stated limit.

Loans are made by banks as part of their normal business. Interest is payable by the borrower at a rate agreed at the time that the loan is negotiated. Where, in the case of business customers, there are provisions for renewing the loan at the end of the period for which it was initially granted, there will usually be a clause in the agreement which allows for renegotiation of the interest rate. ◊ **Revolving credit**.

The bank will generally require security for a loan, which may comprise such assets as title deeds, insurance policies and **bills of sale**. It will normally be of greater face value than the amount of the loan and may need to be accompanied by a guarantee, in writing, from a third party. It is within the bank manager's discretion to decide on the security and, on occasion, a guarantee on its own will be accepted, where the guarantor is considered to be absolutely reliable.

In fairly recent years a new category of bank loan, known as a **personal loan**, has emerged. This is a relatively short-term loan to a specific person and in many instances no security is asked for – the bank manager relies on experience and a knowledge of the borrower. These loans tend to carry a higher interest rate than do secured commercial loans and the amount lent plus the total interest for the period is paid back in fixed, weekly or monthly, instalments.

The willingness of a bank to lend money, and the interest rate it will demand, depends on the current state of the economy and the degree of governmental interference. The latter may be operated by directives to the banks generally or by the manipulation of **special deposits**. If banks are required to increase their deposits with the central bank then the consequent reduction in money available for lending may seriously curtail the number of new loans, and the fall in liquidity might result in the premature calling in of old loans, where no fixed date applies, or the reluctance to renew expiring credits.

Bank loans and overdrafts, disclosure of Bank loans and overdrafts must be disclosed in the **balance sheet** of a limited company. Only one figure need be given.

Bank note A piece of paper purporting to pay the bearer on demand a specified sum of money in gold or silver coin. Bank notes originated in the old receipts given by goldsmiths. ◊ **Bank**. The issue of bank notes is now restricted to the **Bank of England** and the requirement to pay coin on demand has, since 1931, been abolished. The issue of bank notes by other banks was curtailed by the Bank Charter Act 1844 which stated that no bank could be formed with the power to issue notes and that any bank that amalgamated with another or became a limited company would automatically relinquish the right to issue notes. These provisions resulted in the gradual extinction of all note-issuing banks except the Bank of England, although the last of them did

not disappear until 1921. The Scottish and Irish banks still retain a limited right to issue notes, but this power is rather weakened by the provisions regarding **legal tender** and by the need to support note issues by balances held at the Bank of England.

Bank of England notes were originally required to be backed by gold. In 1844 the Bank Charter Act provided for the notes available to be supplemented by a **fiduciary issue** of notes backed not by gold but by government securities held by the Bank of England. Though initially small, this fiduciary issue grew considerably over the years until it came to comprise the greater part of notes in circulation. With the abolition of the Gold Standard the concept of a note issue, even in part backed by gold, was abandoned and the UK note issue is now entirely fiduciary and effectively controlled by the government through the Bank of England. The currency of the UK is now to all intents and purposes a non-convertible paper currency controlled by the State.

Bank of England The central bank of the country, nationalized in 1946 by the Labour government. It was originally a **finance company** founded by a Whig government. The goldsmiths of the City of London deposited their gold by tradition with the Treasury. Charles II, being rather hard up, shut the Treasury and confiscated the gold. The credit of the government was ruined from then on. The depositors devised a new scheme for banking their gold: they formed a **company**. To induce subscriptions, the subscribers were to be known as the Governor and Company of the Bank of England. £1,200,000 was raised at 8 per cent. The Bank came to work hand in hand with the government, lending it money and helping it to raise a **national debt**. In return, it received from the government three important privileges: (1) it was the government's banker; (2) for some time it had a monopoly of **limited liability**; (3) it was the sole **joint stock company** allowed to issue bank notes in England. At one time private bankers could issue notes, but today the Bank has a complete monopoly. ⟡ **Bank of England, functions of** ⟡ **Lender of last resort** ⟡ **Note circulation**.

Bank of England, functions of (1) It acts as a **bank** in the normal sense of the word, though its customers are for the most part the government, the commercial banks, overseas central banks and international organizations. There are some private accounts: these are kept for sentimental reasons and also to keep the Bank in touch with everyday banking problems.

(2) The government keeps all its main accounts at the Bank, though subsidiary accounts are kept at commercial banks outside London. Monies paid into these accounts, however, would normally find their way to the Exchequer Account at the Bank of England. The Bank does not make short-term loans to the government on a large scale – these needs are satisfied by borrowing in the market by means of **treasury bills**, etc. The Bank, however, may act as the government's agent in these matters.

(3) The Bank is also known as the bankers' bank. It is banker to the commercial banks and also to **discount houses** and **accepting houses**. It acts thus as **lender of last resort** to these institutions. The most important accounts are those of the London clearing banks, and because of this the Bank can, by market operations and calls for **special depos-**

its, control the amount of money in circulation in accordance with government policy (the ability of the clearing banks to lend being geared to their balances at the Bank of England).

(4) The Bank acts as banker to other central banks and has accounts for overseas central banks and organizations such as the **International Monetary Fund** and the **International Bank for Reconstruction and Development**. Many central banks, particularly those in the **sterling area**, hold the bulk of their external reserves in London – others keep large working balances in **sterling**.

(5) The Bank is the central note-issuing authority (⟡ **Note circulation**). Bank of England notes have been legal tender since 1833.

(6) The Bank acts as registrar of government **stocks**, stocks issued by nationalized industries, and stocks of some local authorities, public boards and Commonwealth governments. This involves over 5,000,000 **dividend** payments annually.

(7) The Bank is the government's agent in administering **exchange control**. It also supervises the operations of the money market generally and, manages on behalf of the Treasury, the **exchange equalization account**.

Bank: open credit facilities These are granted by a bank to a customer to enable him to draw money, or cash cheques, at other branches of that bank, or other specified banks, up to a prearranged limit. Such facilities are valuable to people who are obliged to travel widely in the course of their work or who, for some other reason, may need to spend some time in another part of the country or abroad. Short-term problems are now more frequently solved by the **cheque card** or the **cash dispenser card**, but business customers may often want to make greater withdrawals than these cards make possible. Alternatives to such facilities are **letters of credit** or, for foreign travel, **traveller's cheques**, though it is possible to arrange for credit facilities at a specified foreign bank. This would be arranged between banks and might be preferable for extended business travel abroad. ◊ **American Express** ◊ **Credit card**.

Bank overdraft Common sense dictates that the amount that can be withdrawn from a bank account is limited to the amount put in. However, particularly in the business world, the wheels of trade need to be oiled by a certain flexibility in banking policy. Constant movements of cash often call for short-term facilities to take more money out of a bank account than it contains, which are referred to as 'overdraft facilities'. This enables customers to overdraw within agreed limits and at any time. The bank will charge interest on excess drawings but it will be charged on a day-to-day basis and will not, as with a **bank loan**, be a fixed sum for a stated period. The fundamental difference between a loan and an overdraft is that in the former case the bank actually puts the amount lent into the customer's account, whereas in the latter it merely suffers the account to go into the red.

Overdrafts are subject to the threat of governmental interference of the kind that affects loans but, as they are not normally for a predetermined time, the effect on them is greater and more immediate. Whether or not security will be demanded for the granting of overdraft facilities will depend on the particular bank manager and customer. ◊ **Bank charge** ◊ **Personal loan**.

Bank rate This was the official rate of interest charged by the **Bank of England** in its role as lender of last resort. Since 1972 the term bank rate has been discontinued and has been replaced by the term **minimum lending rate** (MLR). The principal effects remain much the same, though the rates charged by the commercial banks to their customers are now not directly tied to the rate charged by the Bank of England. The idea behind this change was to foster competitive rates in the general **money market** but for the major commercial banks, movements in rates charged tend to remain concerted. ◊ **Bank, commercial** ◊ **Bank loan** ◊ **Bank overdraft** ◊ **Banks: big four**.

Bank reconciliation As at any particular time **Cheques**, etc., issued or received, may not be banked, the **balance** shown on a **bank statement** at a particular date will not necessarily agree with the balance shown at that date in the **cash book**. It is therefore necessary, in order to prove that the records have been properly kept, to prepare a bank reconciliation. This begins with the balance in the cash book and then details the cheques issued but not banked, and the monies received but not banked. The former will be added and the latter deducted. After any other necessary adjustment for direct bank debits or credits the resultant balance should be the same as that on the bank statement.

Bank statement A statement issued in debit and credit form to the customers of a **bank**, detailing the transactions and showing the **balance** outstanding on their accounts at the date stated. Statements are issued to individuals whenever a page is complete, on demand or by arrangement. The frequency with which they are issued to business depends on the size and requirements of the business.

Banker, disclosure of information by A banker must not normally disclose information on acustomer's account. He may do so: (1) if a court orders him to do so; (2) if it is a matter of public duty; (3) if it is to protect his own interests; (4) if the customer has given express or implied authority to do so (this could be by giving the **bank** as a referee); (5) if the **auditors** request details of a client's account(s) in the course of an audit and the client has agreed to it. ◊ **Numbered account**.

Banker's cheque A cheque drawn by one **bank** on another either for clearing purposes or for transferring customers' money. ◊ **Association for Payment Clearing Services**.

Banker's draft A bill of exchange drawn by a banker on himself. It is often used in international trade. A foreign exporter receiving a banker's draft may cash it at the local branch of that bank.

Banker's guarantee In international trade, loans are sometimes made by British banks to overseas buyers to support the purchase of high-value capital goods from suppliers in the UK. The supplier is paid by the bank as if the transaction had been for cash. The loan is guaranteed by the **Export Credits Guarantee Department** to cover instances where the overseas party fails to repay the bank loan. These guarantees are normally only available for transactions where the cost is over £5m and are referred to as banker's guarantees.

Bankers, Chartered Institute of This was founded in 1879 to afford opportunities to acquire knowledge of banking

theory, and to facilitate consideration and discussion of matters of interest to bankers. It is also intended 'to help our members to educate themselves not only for banking but also for responsible citizenship' (Sir E. A. Carpenter). The Institute has a series of examinations leading to a Banking Diploma. Holders of a Diploma may use the letters ACIB (Associate of the Chartered Institute of Bankers). They may also be elected Fellows (FCIB). Syllabuses may be obtained from the Institute without charge. Exemption from certain papers is given to persons with other recognized professional qualifications. There is a journal available to members, published in alternate months.

Banker's order ◊ **Standing order**.

Banker's revocation of authority to pay cheques A banker may refuse to pay a **cheque** when: (1) payment is countermanded by the customer; (2) he receives notice that the customer is drawing **cheques** unlawfully or for unlawful purposes (e.g. in breach of trust); (3) he receives notice that the customer is dead, insane or an undischarged bankrupt; (4) he receives a **garnishee order** attaching to the customer's balance; or (5) he receives an instruction or court order restraining him from making any payment.

Bankrupt, disabilities of No undischarged bankrupt may: (1) act as a **director** or take part in the management of a **company**; (2) sit or vote in the House of Lords or any committee of it; (3) be elected as a peer of Scotland or Ireland to sit and vote in the House of Lords; (4) be elected to sit and vote in the House of Commons or any committee of it; (5) be appointed or act as a justice of the peace; (6) be elected to or hold the office of mayor, alderman, councillor or county councillor.

Bankrupt shareholder If a shareholder is bankrupt, the **trustee** in **bankruptcy** may sell or disclaim his **shares**.

Bankruptcy Bankruptcy occurs when a debtor is not only insolvent (i.e. unable to pay his debts as and when they become due) but has also demonstrated that he will be unable to pay such debts in full at any foreseeable time in the near future. A creditor may alone, or in company of other creditors, apply to the court under the provisions of the **Insolvency Act** 1986 which has replaced the Bankruptcy Act 1914. On hearing a petition, which may be brought before it by persons other than creditors (◊ **Bankruptcy, petition**), the court may choose between various options. It may make an Interim Order with the object of ascertaining the possibility of a **voluntary arrangement**, it may make a bankruptcy order in which case the bankrupt's estate will vest in the Official Receiver pending the appointment of a Trustee in Bankruptcy, or it may reject the petition.

Bankruptcy: creditors' committee The creditors of a bankrupt may appoint a committee, known as a creditors' committee, to act as their representative during the administration of the estate by the Trustee in Bankruptcy. The role of the creditors' committee is similar to that of the **liquidation committee** in a company winding-up.

The creditors' committee cannot be appointed while the Official Receiver is administering the estate, except at the meeting of creditors at which a Trustee in Bankruptcy is appointed in place of the Official Receiver.

Bankruptcy: debtor's property There is some difficulty in deciding what property is available to **creditors** in a **bankruptcy**. Certain property is not available – this includes trust property where the bankrupt is a **trustee**, tools of trade, clothing, etc., certain personal rights of action, property settled on protective trusts, and **goods** subject to a **lien**. State benefits and certain property are available only where the court orders them to be so. These are: (1) Army, Navy, Air Force and Civil Service pay; (2) the salary or income of the bankrupt (the court will normally allow the debtor to keep enough of his salary to maintain himself, his wife and his family); (3) property situated abroad, where the law of the foreign country does not allow the trustee to take possession.

Apart from these three categories all property in the possession of the debtor at the commencement of the bankruptcy will be available to creditors. The trustee's title relates back to the commencement of the bankruptcy – this is known as the doctrine of relation back. The bankruptcy commences with the granting of the Bankruptcy Order. To avoid the hardships that could be caused by the application of the doctrine of relation back, certain transactions are protected. Which types of transaction are protected is normally just a matter of common sense: they include payments to creditors, **contracts**, etc., by the bankrupt for valuable **consideration**.

Property acquired by the bankrupt after adjudication vests in the trustee. Property in the possession of the debtor with the consent of the true owner may also be vested in the trustees for the benefit of creditors where the true owner has allowed the debtor to give the impression of ownership. The property must have been acquired for the purposes of trade or business. The trustee may also obtain property by avoiding fraudulent preferences, fraudulent conveyances and certain voluntary settlements. The trustee is given protection where without negligence he seizes and disposes of property that does not really belong to the debtor.

Bankruptcy: discharge A person declared bankrupt may apply for his discharge after the expiration of a period of three years (two years in the case of a **summary administration**) after commencement of the bankruptcy, being the day on which the Bankruptcy Order is made. There is an exception in the case of a criminal bankruptcy or where the applicant has been an undischarged bankrupt within the previous fifteen years. In such cases five years must elapse after the Bankruptcy Order.

On hearing the application the court may (a) refuse a discharge; (b) make an order granting absolute discharge; or (c) make an order of discharge conditional with respect to subsequently acquired income or property which must be applied in the manner dictated by the court. In deciding what action to take in regard to the application for discharge the court will ask for a report from the Official Receiver and/or the Trustee in Bankruptcy. An absolute discharge releases the debtor from all bankruptcy debts barring certain categories of debt enumerated in the Act.

Bankruptcy, disclaimer in By becoming the owner of the debtor's goods, a Trustee may be saddled with onerous liabilities and contracts *re* property in the debtor's possession. He is therefore given power to disclaim, i.e. wash his hands of, these items. The items include land where

there are onerous covenants, unprofitable contracts, **stocks** and **shares**, etc. Disclaimer is by notice to the other party normally within twelve months of the trustee becoming aware of the property. The permission of the court is not generally necessary, but may be so where a lease is to be disclaimed. Where property is disclaimed the Trustee loses the benefits as well as the obligations. The relevant **creditor**, if any, may of course prove his debts in the **bankruptcy**.

Bankruptcy: duties of debtor It is the duty of the debtor to cooperate in every possible way with the court, and the trustee. Failure to do so could be contempt of court. He must: (1) give a full list of his property and **creditors**; (2) attend meetings when required to do so; (3) submit to an examination (either a public examination or an examination by the creditors); (4) generally, when adjudicated bankrupt, go to more than ordinary trouble to help realize his property and distribute it among his creditors.

Bankruptcy: effect of discharge Discharge releases the bankrupt from all provable debts in the **bankruptcy**. The debts he is not released from, apart from non-provable debts, are certain debts due to the revenue authorities, debts incurred by fraud, and debts incurred by seduction, matrimonial offences and the **common law** liability to support a wife. Where the discharge is conditional the debtor, after two years, may apply to have the terms modified, but such a discharge may also be rescinded if the debtor fails to observe the conditions. An order of discharge may be accompanied by what is known as a certificate of misfortune. This states, more or less, that it was not the debtor's fault he became bankrupt.

Bankruptcy offences Should a person against whom a Bankruptcy Order has been made be guilty of any of a number of listed offences prior to his discharge, then he may be liable to imprisonment, or a fine, or both. Most of the offences detailed relate to failure by the bankrupt to disclose the whole of his available estate to the Trustee or Official Receiver, or attempts by him to delay realization of his property or mislead its extent. In this context, property includes all such books or records relating to his state of affairs and it is an offence to attempt to conceal, destroy or mutilate such papers. Furthermore he must account for any substantial loss of property within a twelve-month period prior to the presentation of the petition. Failure to do so constitutes an offence, as does any attempt to transfer to another party any property within the preceding five years, with the intention of keeping it from creditors. Other offences include gambling, hazardous speculation, leaving, or attempting to leave, the country with any property which should rightfully be handed over to the Trustee or Official Receiver, and seeking to obtain credit from a third party without disclosing the existence of the Bankruptcy Order.

Bankruptcy: partners Many difficult problems arise when a **partner** is responsible for the debts of his firm. Distinction must be made between joint **creditors** and separate creditors: joint creditors are creditors of the partnership firm, separate creditors are creditors of the individual partners. The firm may be made bankrupt, or partners made bankrupt separately. Where the firm is made bankrupt on the petition of a joint creditor, a receiving order *re* the firm applies to all partners, but each partner must be adjudi-

cated separately. Generally speaking the **bankruptcy** of a firm does not necessarily involve the **insolvency** of all partners. However, if a firm is made bankrupt, all partners are fully liable for all debts and as this is so, the separate creditors may also wish to prove lest one partner be called upon to pay the debts of the others. In fact, the bankruptcy of a firm will normally involve the bankruptcy of all partners though the bankruptcy of a partner would not necessarily involve the bankruptcy of the firm. Where the firm is made bankrupt problems arise with reference to the priority to be given to joint or separate creditors. There will be a number of separate bankruptcies, separately administered: the bankruptcy of the firm and the separate bankruptcy of each partner. Generally speaking the trustee should apply the joint estate first to satisfy joint creditors, and the separate estates should be applied primarily to the settlement of claims of separate creditors. This means that the joint creditors have first pick of the **assets** of the firm but that separate creditors have first pick of the assets of each separate partner. There are certain exceptions: (1) where joint creditors pay off all separate creditors; (2) where a breach of trust is involved on the part of a partner (in this case the creditor may prove his debts in either joint or separate estate but not both); (3) where there is no joint estate and no solvent partner (if the creditor petitioning against a separate partner is also a joint creditor he can prove in the separate bankruptcy for both debts). Joint and separate **dividends** are usually declared simultaneously. There will be one trustee for all bankruptcies but various creditors' committees. Where the bankruptcy is a separate bankruptcy and not a joint one, the creditors of the firm may prove for their debts but only after separate creditors have been paid in full. These bankruptcies normally dissolve the partnership.

Bankruptcy, petition A petition to the court for a Bankruptcy Order against any person is usually made by one creditor acting alone or by a number of creditors acting jointly. In order to succeed the applicant must demonstrate that (a) the debt is a liquidated debt and above the 'Bankruptcy Level' (this is at present set at £750); (b) a statutory demand has been served upon the debtor requiring that he settle, secure or compound the sum due; and (c) that the debtor has made no attempt to meet the demand during a period of three weeks since it was served upon him. It must be additionally established that the debtor is domiciled in England or Wales and present there at the time the petition is presented, or else that he is ordinarily resident in England or Wales, or has carried on a business there during the preceding three years.

On hearing the petition the court may grant a bankruptcy order but will not however do so if it considers, on the advice of an **insolvency practitioner** appointed to enquire into the debtor's affairs, that the interests of the creditor(s) would be better served by a **voluntary arrangement** proposed by the debtor and supervised by the practitioner.

Apart from a creditor a petition may be made by (1) the debtor himself; or (2) an individual appointed to supervise the debtor's estate under a **voluntary arrangement**, or (3) the **official petitioner** in the circumstances of a criminal bankruptcy.

Bankruptcy: preferential debts ◊ Preferential debts.

Bankruptcy: proof of debts A **creditor** wishing to share in the proceeds of a bankrupt estate must prove his debt. He does this by submitting to the **Official Receiver** or trustee an **affidavit** giving a statement of account. This statement must be detailed and give means of verification. If the creditor has any **security** he must say so; if he does not he may be deemed to have surrendered it. Trade discounts are deducted and also agreed cash discounts but not exceeding 5 per cent. (Special rules apply to **moneylenders**.) The cost of the proof must be borne by the creditor. Double proof is not allowed, i.e. two creditors cannot prove for the same debt (both **guarantor** and creditor cannot prove, for instance). However, one creditor could prove in two bankruptcies. Proofs must be dealt with within a specified period. Proofs may be admitted, rejected or held over for consideration. It is not necessary for each employee to prove separately for wages.

Bankruptcy: protected transaction ◊ **Bankruptcy: debtor's property**.

Bankruptcy: provable debts These include debts or liabilities, certain or **contingent**, present or future, that exist either at the time of the receiving order or are likely to be incurred thereafter because of circumstances that arose before the receiving order. In particular: (1) a wife may prove for **arrears** of maintenance and the capitalized value of future payments; (2) where the liability is contingent the debt may be proved for where the court is of the opinion that it is capable of being estimated; (3) there are special rules with reference to rates and taxes; (4) a **guarantor** can prove where he has paid the debt but no two persons can prove *re* the same debt (therefore the **creditor** and the guarantor cannot both prove *re* the same debt); (5) with reference to a **fraudulent conveyance** that has been avoided, the injured party may claim for the amounts paid; (6) **statute-barred debts** are not provable; (7) calls on **shares** may be proved for even before they are made; (8) the capitalized value of **annuities** may be proved for; (9) with reference to **bills of exchange**, the holder can prove even though the bill is not matured; so might an endorsee where the liability is contingent; (10) liquidated damages can be claimed; (11) unliquidated damages may be estimated and proved for when they arise from **contract** or breach of trust but not when they arise from tort. Certain debts are not provable, *inter alia* illegal debts, e.g. gaming debts.

Bankruptcy: public examination
After issuing a receiving order and receiving a **statement of affairs**, the court may hold a public examination of the debtor's conduct, dealings and property. Notice of the examination is given to creditors, advertised and published in the **London Gazette**. **Creditors** who have proved debts may question the debtor. The debtor is examined on oath and must answer even incriminating questions. However, if criminal proceedings are likely, the examination may be postponed to prevent the debtor incriminating himself.

Bankruptcy: result of Bankruptcy Order When a Bankruptcy Order has been made then the Official Receiver becomes receiver and manager of all the bankrupt's property pending the vesting of that property in the Trustee in Bankruptcy, whether he be the Trustee appointed by creditors or the Official Receiver himself. Not only does the bankrupt's property vest in his Trustee, but also any rights of action accruing to the bankrupt. The Trustee must take all necessary action to protect the property that vests in him and may sell, and give a good title to, any part of the property which would diminish in value if retained.

Bankruptcy: set-off A **Creditor** can set off a debt owed to him by the bankrupt against a debt owed by him to the bankrupt. This right only arises with reference to mutual credits, mutual debts and other mutual dealings between the bankrupt and the creditor. The creditor cannot set off a debt owed to him in one capacity against a debt owed by him in another.

Bankruptcy: small bankruptcy Where from the statement of affairs obtained by the Official Receiver it appears that the aggregate of debts falls below the 'small bankruptcy' level or that the debtor's assets are below a specified minimum, such levels or minimums being those then in force, the court may direct that the bankruptcy shall henceforth be conducted as a summary administration. The point of such a proceeding is to minimize the costs of the bankruptcy in order to maximize the funds available for creditors. To this end the Official Receivers will usually seek first a **voluntary arrangement** and if this is not possible will assume the role of Trustee. He will then follow the normal course of realizing the debtor's assets and, having established a list of creditors, will hope to conclude the administration by paying one final dividend to creditors. In conducting the bankruptcy he may be relieved of the necessity of giving prescribed notices to creditors for less than a certain amount and will not normally call for a creditors' committee to be appointed.

When a summary administration is in progress a creditors' meeting may call for a full Bankruptcy Order to be made and may bring this about by proceeding to appoint a trustee in bankruptcy. The Official Receiver will then cease to act.

Bankruptcy: statement of affairs

When a Bankruptcy Order has been made other than on a debtor's petition, the bankrupt must, within twenty-one days, submit a statement of affairs to the Official Receiver. This statement must contain prescribed details of creditors, debts and assets together with any other information which the Official Receiver shall require. Except in the instance of a summary administration, the Official Receiver has a duty to investigate the conduct of affairs of the debtor and report back to the court. He may also either of his own volition, or on being requested to do so by over 50 per cent in value of creditors, apply to the court for a public examination of the bankrupt.

Bankruptcy: Trustee in

The Trustee in Bankruptcy is usually the person appointed to that position at a meeting of the bankrupt's creditors. If no such person is appointed, then the Official Receiver becomes the Trustee.

The Trustee must be an authorized Insolvency Practitioner, and if the person appointed is not the Official Receiver then he must furnish the latter with all the necessary information for him to carry out his duties.

Once appointed, all property of the bankrupt, save tools of trade, household effects etc., vests in the Trustee as do any rights of action accruing to the bankrupt. The Trustee has various powers to disclaim any onerous property, including unprofitable contracts and assets not readily saleable, provided proper notice is given to the parties affected. Such a disclaimer relieves the Trustee from any liability concerning the property disclaimed dating back to the commencement of his trusteeship. Any person suffering genuine loss as a result of such a disclaimer is at liberty to prove for that loss in the bankruptcy.

Other powers of the Trustee are (1) to carry on the business of the bankrupt; (2) to bring or defend actions relating to the estate; (3) to mortgage property in order to raise money with which to pay creditors; (4) to make payments or incur liabilities which are necessary to obtain monies or property for the benefit of creditors; (5) to make compromises or arrangements with creditors; (6) to sell and give good title to any of the property comprised in the bankrupt's estate and to give receipts for monies received; (7) to make contracts or enter into engagements binding on himself and successors; (8) to employ an agent; (9) to execute deeds, powers of attorney or any other instruments and do any other thing necessary to the proper exercise of these powers.

The Trustee also has power to apply to the court for a **special manager** to be appointed where it seems necessary that an additional person be available to manage some part of the bankrupt's estate, e.g. a business. If appointed the special manager will usually be required to give security, will be obliged to keep such accounts as may be necessary, and will be bound to act according to the powers and responsibilities set down by the court.

The duties of the Trustee cease when he (a) resigns his office; (b) is removed from office by a resolution of creditors; (c) is released from office on the completion of the administration of the bankrupt's estate. The latter will occur when he is satisfied that all availble assets have been realized, or as great a part as can be realized without needlessly prolonging the administration, and has declared a final dividend and called a meeting of creditors to which his report of the administration is presented.

Bankruptcy: unclaimed dividends and undistributed funds Any unclaimed dividends or monies which, for certain reasons cannot be distributed, are paid into the Insolvency Services Account at the Bank of England. The Secretary of State for Trade and Industry may at intervals transfer balances from this account to the Consolidated Fund.

Banks: big four A term used with reference to the four major British commercial and **clearing banks**. These are Barclays, Lloyds, Midland and NatWest – the latter being an abbreviation of National Westminster, which was formed by the merger in 1968 of the two large banking companies previously known as the Westminster and the National Provincial.

Barclaycard ◊ **Credit card**.

Bareboat charter The charter of a ship where the charterer pays all expenses during the time of hire. ◊ **Chartering, marine**.

Bargain (1) The official **Stock Exchange** jargon for deals involving the buying and selling of shares.

(2) The obtaining of more than value for money in a transaction, without **fraud** or **misrepresentation** on the part of the party making the gain. In some cases both parties to a transaction may claim to have made a bargain – particularly where the seller unloads unwanted goods on a buyer who happens to have a specialist interest in the particular items. Perhaps one of the more spectacular bargains on the international scene was the purchase of Alaska from the Tsar of Russia by the USA for the sum of 7.2 million dollars in 1867. Gold discoveries alone in Alaska during the succeeding twenty-five years were worth more than forty times this sum.

These two definitions have nothing in common.

Barge A flat-bottomed **freight** boat commonly used on canals. ◊ **Inland waterways** ◊ **Lighter**.

Barratry This refers to improper acts of the master or a seaman of a ship which, apart from being wilful, cause damage to the ship or cargo.

Barrel A container, and also a measure of liquids: in the UK, 36 gallons; in the USA, 42 gallons. The word is also used for solids, e.g. a barrel of butter = 224 lb.

Barrister One who pleads cases in court. One who is instructed by a **solicitor** to handle direct court proceedings on behalf of a person who wishes to bring a legal action against another or who needs to defend himself against proceedings taken by another. The barrister may also be called 'counsel'.

Barristers are often confused with solicitors, particularly as the term 'lawyer' is commonly applied to both. The professions are, however, quite distinct, although in minor cases brought in the lower courts the solicitor will also act as counsel. The barrister earns his wage by his ability and skill in presenting a case in court and, to this extent, may be less academically qualified than the solicitor who provides him with the case, i.e. 'briefs' him. It is easier to become a barrister than to qualify as a solicitor, but a really successful barrister will find far more fame and fortune than his more hard-working and less glamorous counterpart in the solicitor's trade. The barrister is, by custom rather than the nature of his role, never approached directly by the person he will represent but by that person's solicitor: this is peculiar to the English legal system. Another, equally archaic custom is that a barrister cannot sue for money earned in the course of his profession. The solicitor can, however, pay the barrister's charges and sue his client for the total costs of the case. Judges are more often chosen from the ranks of barristers than from any other branch of the legal profession.

Barter The direct exchange of commodities or services by way of trade, without the use of an intermediate and neutral currency such as coin, **promissory notes**, or **bills of exchange**. Barter is the most primitive manner of trading, but, in certain circumstances, the most satisfactory. It could, by eliminating the need for the keeping of records, be a useful way of avoiding taxation – which can only be applied to stated profits – and so, such transactions, when undertaken in the course of business, must under law be recorded in monetary terms for the calculation of tax. ◊ **Black economy**.

Base date In calculating an **index**, e.g. the **retail price index** or the **Financial Times Ordinary Share Index**, the various figures are related to a chosen base date. The value of the index at any particular time is expressed as a percentage rise over, or decrease from, the value at the date chosen as the base, usually represented as 100, e.g. if an index of prices is stated to be 164 then that figure is only meaningful if related to the date on which it is based and should properly be stated as, say, 164 (base 6 January 1962) or 164 (6 January 1962 = 100).

Base rate The minimum rate of interest that a bank will demand on money loaned, rather than the actual rate, which will be fixed according to normal market pressures and the element of risk involved. Changes in base rates will tend to flow from changes in the **minimum lending rate** of the Bank of England and will, in turn, be reflected in the many other branches of the **money market**, particularly rates on **bills of exchange** discounted, mortgage rates, interest charged or allowed by finance houses and the cost of money generally. ◊ **Bank loan** ◊ **Bank rate** ◊ **Minimum lending rate**.

Base stock ◊ **Stock valuation**.

Bear A Stock Exchange term derived, by tradition, from bear-hunting, where the trapper would make sure of his market for the skins before setting out to shoot the bears. It refers to a speculator who sells shares forward, that is, to be delivered at a fixed future date – usually the official **account day**. The bear anticipates that the price will fall and that the shares promised, which at the time of the 'sale' he does not possess, can be acquired at a price lower than the selling price when the time for completion of the contract arrives. The bear may 'carry over' the contract to the following Stock Exchange account period by paying a form of interest known in the market as **backwardation**. Bear activities are not confined to share dealings, though that is where they originated, but are also to be found in other areas of speculation such as the buying and selling of commodities and foreign exchange.

A market situation which favours bear operations is known as a bear market. ◊ **Bull** ◊ **Forward dealings** ◊ **Selling short**.

Bear market ◊ **Bear**.

Bear slide A term often used in the more sophisticated financial papers to indicate a general movement of stocks and shares quoted on the **Stock Exchange** towards the conditions obtaining in a **Bear** market.

Bearer bonds Another name for **bearer securities**.

Bearer securities Documents of **title**, to **stocks**, **shares**, **debentures**, etc., transferable by hand, being made out to bearer and not to a named person. ◊ **Share warrants**. These should now be deposited with **authorized depositories** but are nevertheless dealt with on the **Stock Exchange**.

Bed and Breakfasting This term refers to the practice of selling shares one day and buying them back the next, and is associated with attempts to minimize taxation liability in a particular financial year. ◊ **Tax avoidance**.

Bells A complicated system of announcing time on board ship. Starting at midnight, a bell is sounded at each half hour, the number of strokes increasing by one every thirty minutes up to eight bells, after which the whole process begins again. Therefore eight bells is sounded at 4 am, 8 am, 12 noon, 4 pm, 8 pm and 12 midnight. A bell is also sounded fifteen minutes before each watch. Watches are of four hours' duration, coinciding with eight bells. The one difference is that the period 4 to 8 pm is divided into two dog watches, 4 to 6 pm, and 6 to 8 pm.

Below the line A term at one time frequently used in the national accounts to describe dealings concerned with capital, as opposed to revenue. The National Exchequer has two distinct sources of funds: those raised by taxes and duties, and those borrowed through the **money market** either through the sale of government stock or by loans from other nations or neutral bodies such as the **International Monetary Fund**. Traditionally, money raised by direct and indirect taxation or by **Customs and Excise** duties is to be used for non-recoverable public expenditure, i.e. the day-to-day costs of running the country. Money raised by borrowing, i.e. on capital account, is intended to be used for long-term investment. The former transactions are referred to as 'above the line', the latter as 'below the line'. There is always a certain overlap, however, inasmuch as capital funds may be needed to cover a loss on the revenue account. If the overall national budget is to be balanced then this necessarily means that the amount taken from 'below the line' funds must be compensated by an identical reduction in capital investment. Similarly, if capital investment 'below the line' exceeds the capital flowing in, this must be balanced by additional taxation or a cut in expenditure 'above the line'. This annual movement of funds from one category to another is known colloquially as balancing the national budget. ◊ **Balance of payments**.

Balancing the annual budget has now ceased to be of prime importance and deliberate budgeting for deficits or surpluses has become acceptable, so the distinction between above and below the line transactions is of academic interest only in contemporary society – though, in the long term, the principles involved cannot be safely ignored.

In everyday commercial, particularly company, accounts 'below the line' entries are concerned with the distribution, rather than the determination, of profit, e.g. transfers to or from reserve accounts or declarations of dividends are technically below the line adjustments in this context. ◊ **Profit and loss account** ◊ **Appropriation account**.

In advertising, promotional methods other than the usual visual and oral ones, i.e. free samples and special offers, are described as 'below the line'.

Beneficial interest Where a person is not the official holder of property, i.e. does not have legal **title** to it, but by reason of a trust or private agreement enjoys all or part of the benefits of it, he is said to have a beneficial interest. ◊ **Nominee shareholder** ◊ **Trustee**.

Beneficial owner The person who is the true owner of property and the rights attaching thereto may, for various reasons, including the wish to remain anonymous, allow some other person to be registered as owner or, where applicable, hold the title deeds on the express or implied understanding that that other person is owner in name only and is acting as a trustee for the true owner. The latter is referred to as the beneficial owner. This frequently occurs in share transactions where the registered holder of the shares is acting as a nominee for the true shareholder, who is not disclosed in the register as a company need take no notice of trusts regarding title. The Companies Acts 1985 and 1989, however, require that any person who, directly or through nominees, holds more than 3 per cent of the 'relevant share capital' of a company must make this fact known to the company immediately and in writing. 'Relevant share capital' refers to issued capital carrying full voting rights, and the 3 per cent is the ratio of the holding to the nominal value of that capital. Cessation of such notifiable interests must also be made known to the company. ◊ **Nominee shareholders**.

Benefit in kind Benefits other than money received by employees, by reason of their employment. Generally speaking, employers cannot force employees to take wages in kind. ◊ **Tommy shops** ◊ **Truck**. However, benefits (e.g. use of car, cost-price purchase, etc.) may be given in addition to wages and used as incentives. Benefits in kind may be taxable, particularly those received by **directors**, and also where the recipient has a right to forgo the benefit and receive additional income. Certain minor benefits, sometimes appropriated rather than given, are known as 'perks' or 'perquisites'. ◊ **Company cars; directors and highly paid employees**.

Benelux The group of countries comprising Belgium, the Netherlands and Luxembourg, which as long ago as 1932 agreed to band together for trading purposes in the manner that the **European Union** has adopted. Their efforts did not obtain a definitive form until after the Second World War, in 1948, when a customs union was officially formed. In 1960 the three countries merged their monetary and fiscal systems after having each joined the European Union in 1958.

Betterment levy A tax innovation introduced by the Land Commission Act 1967. It took the form of a levy on the development value of land when sold. It was short-lived and its principal purpose has now been swallowed up in the system of **capital gains tax**.

Bid price A term now associated with **unit trusts**. Units are quoted at two prices: the bid price, which is the sum that the management company will pay for units held by third parties; and the **offer price**, which is the figure at which they will sell. The offer price is higher than the bid price so that when people buy units they must, if they are not to lose on the investment, retain them until they have risen to a point above the bid price. For this reason (among others) unit trusts are seen as a long-term rather than a short-term investment.

Bidding rings It is a criminal offence for a dealer to give or receive **consideration** (i.e. a **bribe**) with the aim of preventing a person, or himself, from bidding. A third party, i.e. a seller of **goods**, can avoid the **contract** unless the sale is to a **bona fide** person; even then he can claim **damages** from the guilty parties.

Big Bang This term was coined to describe the major changes in the securities market within Great Britain, and particularly in the conduct of business on the Stock Exchange, which took place in October 1986. That date saw the Stock Exchange's traditional methods of operation completely transformed. The changes were triggered by the agreement of the then government not to investigate the methods by which dealings were conducted under the provisions of the Restrictive Trade Practices Act, provided that the Stock Exchange agreed to restructure those methods itself. The results of the changes then effected have been to remove virtually all dealings from the Stock Exchange floor and replace them with dealings by electronic means. The old distinction between jobbers and brokers has been abandoned in favour of a system whereby the greater part of security trading is effected through **market-makers**. These are dual capacity firms which agree to make a continuous market in those shares in which they opt to deal. Whereas previously the broker acted for the investor by buying or selling through a jobber who held shares on his own account, both functions are now combined under one roof by the market-maker. He quotes buying and selling prices on a continuous basis through **SEAQ**, the automated price information system whereby all market-makers' prices are electronically available on screens accessible to all dealers.

Those members of the Exchange who did not wish to become market-makers had the option of acting in single capacity as broker-dealers, or in firms which, although they could supply clients with shares held on their own account, had no obligation to make a continuous market. Both market-makers and dealer-brokers could also act as agency brokers buying and selling on behalf of clients and charging a negotiated commission, the old system of fixed commissions having been abandoned as a restrictive practice.

A further change brought about by the 1986 restructuring was that restrictions on ownership of Stock Exchange firms were relaxed. This allowed outside ownership of such institutions and the bringing in of new sources of finance, which enhanced both the size and the overall liquidity of the Exchange. Again, in 1986, the Stock Exchange merged with the International Securities Market Association to become officially the International Stock Exchange of the United Kingdom and the Republic of Ireland. In 1991 this cumbersome title was abandoned and the Exchange reverted to the old title of the London Stock Exchange.

Bill broker A bill broker is similar to a **Discount house**, though there is a difference in that brokers do not always buy and sell on their own account, but may merely act as intermediaries in return for a commission. ◊ **Bill of exchange** ◊ **Trade bills** ◊ **Treasury bills**.

Bill of entry ◊ **Customs: final clearance inwards and entry outwards**.

Bill of exchange This is defined officially as 'an unconditional order in writing, addressed by one person to another, signed by the person giving it, requiring the person to whom it is addressed to pay on demand, or at a fixed or determinable future time, a sum certain in money, to, or to the order of, a specified person, or to the bearer'. Bills of exchange involve the payment of money only. The time of payment must be definite in the sense that it is bound to occur, even though the actual date may not be known. One payable x days after an event which may never happen will be invalid. If the words and figures do not agree the words take precedence (though if it is a **cheque** the bank will probably send it back). The sum stated on the bill may be subject to **interest**. The payee must be specified, e.g. a cheque 'pay cash' would not be a bill of exchange and therefore would not be negotiable. The person drawing the bill is called the drawer, the person to whom the bill is addressed is called the drawee, the person to whom it is payable is called the payee and anyone signing the bill on the reverse is called the endorser. If the endorser endorses the bill to a specified person that person is known as the endorsee. The drawee becomes the **acceptor** when he has accepted the bill. A bill is not invalid because it is ante-dated, post-dated, or dated on a Sunday, nor is it invalid if it is not dated at all, nor need it state the place where it is drawn or where payment is to be made. If a bill is not dated the holder could date it himself. Bills are either 'inland' or 'foreign': an inland bill is defined by statute as 'both drawn and payable within the British Islands or drawn within the British Islands upon some person resident therein'. Any other bills are foreign. Generally speaking, inchoate bills, i.e. bills in any way incomplete, can be completed by the holder – this does not of course give him authority to forge another's signature.

Bill of exchange: dishonour Bills are dishonoured by: (1) non-acceptance, i.e. having been presented for acceptance and not accepted (allowing for the normal time lag, e.g. twenty-four hours); (2) non-payment, e.g. when payment is refused or the payer cannot be traced, or when presentation is not necessary and no payment has been made; (3) where a receiving order in **bankruptcy** has been made against the **acceptor** before payment is due.

Notice of dishonour must be given to all parties whom it is intended to charge: drawer, acceptor and all endorsers. Notice need not be in writing but it is advisable to make it so. Notice should be given promptly but unavoidable delay will be excused. It need not be given where the relevant party cannot be found or is a fictitious person, or where it has been waived expressly or by implication.

Bill of exchange: stamping The **stamp duty** payable on the majority of **bills of exchange** was abolished as from 1 February 1971. The abolition of this duty was of considerable significance as applied to **cheques**, as, before the abolition, bank customers were obliged to pay the stamp duty applicable to a cheque book when they obtained it from a bank.

Bill of lading A document used in foreign trade similar in some respects to a **delivery note**. It sets out the name and address of the customer, the nature of the **goods**, etc. In carriage by sea there are three copies: one retained by the seller, one given to the master of the ship, one forwarded to the buyer or his **agent**. The buyer obtains the goods by presenting his copy to the master of the ship. The bill is usually accompanied by a **bill of exchange** drawn upon the purchaser. Though not legally a document of **title** it is effective as such inasmuch as a person who has possession of it with the consent of the true owner of the goods can give a good title to an innocent purchaser for value. ◊ **Title** ◊ **Marine insurance** ◊ **Stoppage in transitu**.

Bill of quantities ◊ **Quantity surveyor**.

Bill of sale A document transferring **title** to **goods** (other than real property) absolutely or conditionally to another person, possession remaining with the person making the transfer. It is often used to raise money – the borrower retakes the title when he repays the money. Bills of sale must be registered and are subject to the Bills of Sale Acts 1878 and 1882. ◊ **Bill of sale, absolute** ◊ **Bill of sale, conditional**.

Bill of sale, absolute This occurs when the **title** to the **goods** is transferred absolutely: the transferor cannot retake the title and the transferee may take possession at a specified time. An absolute bill of sale must be witnessed by a **solicitor**.

Bill of sale, conditional This is a bill where the transferor reserves the right to retake the **title**. It must be witnessed but not necessarily by a **solicitor**. It must be in the form stated in the Bills of Sale (1878) Amendment Act 1882 and must show the **consideration, rate of interest**, date of repayment and any conditions. The **value** must be more than £30 and a list of the **goods** must be attached. The transferee can only take possession if (1) the conditions are not observed, (2) the transferor becomes bankrupt or allows the goods to become distrained for **rent**, rates or taxes, (3) the transferor attempts to dispose of the goods, (4) the transferor loses possession by a judgment at law. After taking possession, the transferee cannot move or sell the goods for five days.

Bill of sight A shipping term used where an importer is not able to give full details of his cargo. He completes a bill of sight. The cargo is then inspected by customs authorities. The importer subsequently completes the entry, and the completion is known as perfecting the sight.

Bill of sufferance A shipping term for a bill giving coastal vessels authority to trade from port to port with dutiable **goods** on board. The goods must be placed in a bonded **warehouse** when landed.

Bills in a set One bill of exchange issued in duplicate or triplicate. Payment of one discharges the whole. The same reference number appears on each bill – only one must be accepted. If the drawee accepts more than one, he will be liable on more than one.

Bills payable An accounting term for **bills of exchange** due for payment at some time in the future. They will be included with **current liabilities**.

Bills receivable An accounting term for **bills of exchange** held and due to be paid to the holder at some time in the future. They will be included with **current assets**.

Bin card A card kept in a storehouse recording the actual quantity of material in a bin or other receptacle. The card is marked each time items are purchased or requisitioned.

Black economy Unofficial economic activity which, although technically contributing to the gross national product, is not contained within national statistics. It is for the most part conducted on a cash or barter basis and, although generating a substantial portion of the unofficial national income, the fact that it is not formally recorded in any accounting records takes it out of the tax net. It is the very fact that income earned within the black economy escapes taxation that renders it attractive to those working within it. ♢ **Moonlighting**.

Blank bill A **bill of exchange** where the name of the payee is not stated.

Blank cheque A **cheque** where no sum of money is stated. The holder can fill in the amount himself. Blank cheques are often used in letter transactions where the price of the **goods** to be purchased is not known. The buyer may send a blank cheque but writes, e.g., 'Not to exceed £2' on it. The bank will usually respect this instruction.

Blank credit **Letter of credit** where the amount of credit is not recorded.

Blank endorsement ♢ **Endorsement**.

Blank transfer A blank transfer of **shares**. Shares are transferred by completion of a transfer form. Where the name of the transferee is left blank, this is known as a blank transfer. It may be used when shares are **mortgaged**, the mortgagee having a right to fill in his own name if the money is not repaid by a certain date. It is also used when persons hold shares as nominees for others, the registered owner giving the **beneficial owner** a blank transfer.

Blanket policy An **insurance** term for a policy which covers many different types of risk. For instance property may be insured against fire, theft, etc.

Blocked account A bank account from which monies cannot be drawn except in defined circumstances. An account may be blocked for a variety of reasons, for instance if the holder's affairs are in the hands of a trustee in bankruptcy or liquidator, and the court wishes to prevent misuse of the funds by the holder. ♢ **Bankruptcy: trustee in.**

Blocked accounts appear more frequently in international trade. When a government is overthrown it is common for accounts in the names of foreigners, or undesirable residents, to be blocked by edict of the new rulers. Many accounts in countries where revolutions have occurred remain blocked almost indefinitely – more particularly where the revolutionary government considers that the monies in those accounts were accumulated by exploitation or, alternatively, where withdrawal of the monies would put a strain on the holding country's foreign currency reserves.

In wartime the accounts of enemy aliens are invariably blocked pending cessation of hostilities – the monies may even be summarily confiscated with little redress available to the owner in later years due to political agreements made subsequently or merely effected one-sidedly by *force majeure*.

In other circumstances accounts may be partially blocked for political or other reasons and these may oblige the account holder to use the contents of the account solely for transactions within the holding State and stop him taking any part of the monies out of that country.

Blue Book An unofficial term for the annual 'National Income and Expenditure' publication issued by the **Central Statistical Office** and available to the public through HMSO bookshops. ◊ **Stationery Office**. It is a sort of annual report and accounts of the State's stewardship of national resources, and also contains a great number of statistical tables and other figures relevant to the particular economic year.

Blue chip investment A colourful term for that type of investment which, though not gilt-edged, is considered to be safe, so that there is little likelihood of losing **capital** or income. They are usually the **shares** of particularly well-known and sound companies.

Board meetings ◊ Meetings of directors.

Board of directors The effective management committee of a company limited by shares. In theory the members of the board represent the interests of the shareholders and are appointed by them for that purpose. In fact they tend to be appointed initially by the company **promoter** and thenceforward they become a sort of self-elected oligarchy, filling its own vacancies as they arise and unlikely to be upset except as a result of a major revolt among members. ◊ **Director** ◊ **Directors, removal of**.

Board of Trade Founded in 1786, the Board was a committee of the Privy Council; the last recorded full meeting of the committee took place on 23 December 1850. The functions of the committee were taken over by the President of the Board of Trade – a political appointment, with a parliamentary secretary responsible for the textile industry, and three ministers of state, one for home industry and commerce, one for overseas trade and the third for shipping, the shipbuilding industry and tourism. The main functions of the Board concerned: (1) commercial relations with other countries including the promotion of exports and dealing with the **General Agreement on Tariffs and Trade**; (2) providing a link between home industry and the government and supervising regional development and redistribution of employment; (3) supervising all aspects of the shipping industry; (4) collecting, evaluating and publishing statistics relating to trade and industry regarding the United Kingdom and the Commonwealth, and also preparing censuses of production and distribution; (5) administrating long-term legislation on, for instance, **patents**, **trademarks**, **copyright**, **insurance** companies, **bankruptcy**, and weights and measures; (6) various other activities with reference to new or temporary legislation concerning the country's commerce. In 1972 the Board of Trade ceased to exist under that name, though its functions were taken over by the newly created Department of **Trade and Industry**. The Secretary of State for Trade and Industry retains the title of President of the Board of Trade.

Boarding Preventive Officer The person responsible for boarding an incoming ship to check against infectious diseases.

Body corporate ◊ Corporation.

Bona fide 'In good faith'. The phrase is used frequently in the law of **contract** e.g. 'a *bona fide* purchaser for value'. To gain the full protection of the law, persons are expected to contract in good faith, i.e. they must not feign ignorance of facts which are material to the contract. The *bona fide* provision is particularly relevant in contracts of **insurance** where the failure to disclose, whether expressly or by implication, facts that have any bearing on the risk can invalidate the whole contract, thus making the policy void. *Mala fide* means 'in bad faith'. ◊ **Uberrimae fidei**.

Bona vacantia This refers to property where there is no apparent owner and no claimant. This could be property remaining in the hands of a **liquidator** when a company has been dissolved. Such property passes automatically to the Crown or the Royal Duchies of Lancaster or Cornwall. They could also disclaim it, and then its ultimate destination would depend on the nature of the property: **shares** would be surrendered to the company; land would probably be compulsorily acquired by a local authority. A liquidator may need to apply to a court for direction.

Bond A term widely used in the UK to describe fixed-interest securities issued by the State or by local authorities. Bonds may fall into various categories named for convenience 'long', 'medium' or 'short', reflecting the date at which they are redeemable. Irredeemable bonds such as **consols** are also issued, but these are normally the prerogative of the central government and are incorporated into the **national debt**.

In recent years the bond market in the UK has grown as other countries have issued sterling bonds in London. Another phenomenon has been the emergence of the index-linked bond where both the rate of interest and the capital value of the bond are linked to the Retail Price Index and, in times of inflation, will be revalued upwards at stated intervals.

New issues of government bonds are managed through the Bank of England and are made in one of three quite different ways: (1) By offer for sale by tender. The Bank offers a stated total amount of new stock at or above a certain price and invites tenders from the market. The bonds are then sold to those who put in the highest bids; (2) By offer for sale by Auction. As in the first case a total amount available is specified but no minimum price. Again the stock will go to the highest bidders; (3) The Bank of England takes the new stock on to its own books and disposes of it over a period in day-to-day dealings with **Gilt-Edged Market-Makers**.

Not all bonds are sterling bonds. There are also bonds issued by other countries in their own currencies. The price and attractiveness of these will depend both upon the respect in which the issuing nation is held and the volatility of its currency. ◊ **Euro-bonds**.

Bond and disposition in security ◊ **Scotland: company law**.

Bond note A term used in shipping with reference to export of goods. Dutiable goods must be put in bond. A bond note is issued indicating that the necessary formalities have been observed. The note acts as authority for recovering the goods from the **warehouse** and exporting them.

Bond-washing A rather ignoble practice whereby the rich essayed to become richer at the expense of others and, at the same time, avoid paying taxes by juggling with stocks and shares or **Bonds** – hence the name – and taking advantage of certain loopholes in the tax laws. These gaps have now been effectively closed and the term is of little more than historic interest. The bond-washer was the person who, not being a dealer in shares, sold them **'cum–div'** with a prearranged agreement to buy them back, almost immediately after they became 'ex-div'. The selling price would necessarily include the accrued **dividend** but the buying price would be lower as a result of the dividend having been paid. The resultant profit would be of a non-taxable capital nature. Since the introduction of **capital gains tax** such a gain is now treated as if it were a normal profit on trading. In a sense 'bond-washing' was a rather sophisticated instance of normal **bear** operations. ◊ **Asset stripping**.

Bonded carmen ◊ **Bonded lighterman**.

Bonded goods Imported **goods** on which duty, either customs or excise, has not been paid. They are put in a bonded **warehouse** pending either payment of the duty or re-export. The owner of the warehouse **guarantees** that duty will be paid if the goods are released. If he does otherwise he is subject to stringent penalties, stated in the bond itself. Bonded goods may be moved from one bonded warehouse to another. Goods may be released in any quantity in the presence of a customs official. The document authorizing removal is called a warehouse

warrant. This describes the goods and the duty and is also a delivery order. If goods are re-exported the customs authorities issue a bond note on one side of which is an order authorizing release of the goods and on the other a statement that the warehouse owner will pay twice the duty if any irregularities occur.

Bonded lighterman A person responsible, with bonded carmen, for moving **goods** from one bonded **warehouse** to another.

Bonded stores Similar to **bonded goods**, these are stores to be used on board ship and so placed in bond, duty not being payable.

Bonded vaults These are bonded **warehouses** for wines and spirits.

Bonded warehouse ◊ **Bonded goods**.

Boodle Money obtained by corrupt dealing in public affairs, and also counterfeit money.

Book-keeping The formal processes of accounting – the keeping of records concerning the everyday activities and transactions of a business or non-profit-making organization. The 'books' normally kept generally categorized as books of prime entry on the one hand and **ledgers** on the other. Books of prime entry are those which contain the preliminary and detailed record of transactions. They consist of (1) the **cash book**; (2) the 'day books' for purchases and sales – which, as the name suggests, carry day-to-day details of goods or services bought and sold; and (3) the 'journal' which records details of the more unusual transactions or transfers which are not purchases or sales in the normal course of business or which do not involve cash.

Ledgers contain detailed accounts for both **assets** and **liabilities** and income and expenditure on the one hand, and debtors and creditors on the other. The former comprise what are known as 'real' and 'nominal' accounts and the latter comprise 'personal' accounts. ◊ **Accounts, nominal, real and personal**. Specialized books of account may be used in certain business ventures, e.g. the solicitors' rules, which apply to accounts kept by solicitors, require two distinct ledgers for clients – the one recording dealings in the clients' own funds held on trust and the other recording expenditure incurred on the clients' behalf and chargeable to them – to be set against payment of bills rendered.

Other books of record which may be included among those involved under the general heading of book-keeping include stock-books and asset registers. On a lower plane subsidiary books such as the petty cash book and the postage book may also be numbered among permanent records. The degree of training or experience required by a person entrusted with the job of book-keeping will vary considerably with the size and complexity of the organization. ◊ **Books of account**.

Book tokens A type of **gift token** scheme within the bookselling trade and geared to the specific purchase of books. The scheme is operated through Book Tokens Ltd, a company set up by the Booksellers Association for the benefit of its members, all of whom are primarily booksellers and do not, like newsagents, sell books as a sideline. Booksellers buy the tokens from Book Tokens Ltd, who also provide the cards to which the tokens are attached when purchased by the general public. The tokens can be exchanged for books at any bookshop throughout the UK. The bookseller accepting the token then returns it to Book Tokens Ltd and receives cash in its place. The book token has become one of the most popular forms of gift token; they are widely used as gifts and prizes, their appeal being considerably enhanced by the style and variety of the cards to which they are affixed. Book tokens can only be used for the purchase of books and cannot be exchanged by a customer in part or in whole for cash, though such rules are not always observed by booksellers who carry other types of merchandise.

Book value An accounting term describing the recorded value of an asset in the books of a business. This may be the original cost (known as **historical cost**) of the asset or, where periodic revaluations are made, the last decided value. Book value should be carefully distinguished from **net book value**, which is the book value less amounts written off by way of **depreciation** or other wastage.

Books of account Those books in which the transactions of a business are recorded. The term is often prefaced by the word 'proper'. Proper books of account are those that the law demands shall be kept by certain categories of businesses. For limited companies, proper books of account are defined in the Companies Act 1985 and consist of records kept manually, mechanically or electronically that enable the **annual accounts** to be prepared, and contain details of all receipts and payments, assets and liabilities and sales and purchases. The need for proper books of account is most apparent in a **liquidation**, when **directors** and other officers of a company may be liable in **tort**

for not keeping sufficient records to identify various transactions and parties thereto.

Proper books are also required to be kept by any trader for the same reason, should he become bankrupt. ◊ **Bankruptcy.**

The law also requires that the books and records kept shall be retained for a certain period. The period varies with the type of business, but it is well to remember that the tax authorities have power, in circumstances where failure to disclose is suspected, to go back many years and, if proper records are not available to prove otherwise, to make arbitrary assessments of taxable income with the onus on the person charged to provide evidence that such assessments are not correct. ◊ **Back duty.**

In the case of companies the 1989 Companies Act specifically states that the accounting records required by the 1985 Act shall be kept for three years, in the case of a private company, and six years in the case of a public company. This is quite apart from the need to maintain records for longer periods to cover enquiries raised by the Inland Revenue or, in the case of VAT, by Customs and Excise.

Boom The point in the trade cycle where the upward movement is complete, **prices** and employment being at their maximum. A boom tends to break suddenly, when government action is not sufficiently strong. This can result in a sudden depression and quite severe economic hardships. ◊ **Slump** ◊ **Trade cycle**. The term 'boom' is also applied generally to periods when business is particularly good from the proprietor's point of view.

Bottom In mercantile language, an-

other name for a ship – hence **bottomry bond**.

Bottomry bond A master of a ship may need money quickly during a voyage. He may then borrow it on the **security** of the ship and cargo by means of a bottomry bond. He only does so when money is necessary to complete the voyage and when communication with the owner is impossible. If money can be obtained on the shipowner's credit, this must be done. A bottomry bond holder loses all his money if the ship is lost. If there are several bond holders, the last is paid first. The ship cannot be disposed of until the bond is paid.

Bought notes ◊ **Contract notes**.

Bourse The French equivalent of the London **Stock Exchange**. A member of the Bourse is known as an *agent de change*. He must put up a very large sum of money to obtain membership, and is usually the head of a group of sleeping partners. It is almost unheard of for a member to fail: if he did so his brother members would be liable for his debts.

Bradburys A slang term for £1 and 10s. notes issued by the Treasury in place of **gold coin** in 1914. The name derives from the then Secretary of the Treasury, John Bradbury. In 1928 the **Bank of England** took over the issue of these notes from the Treasury.

Branded goods Goods marketed as proprietary brands, pre-packed by manufacturers, with the name of the product displayed. In law a **retailer** has some additional protection when selling branded goods. The Sale of Goods Act 1893 states that when goods are sold under a **patent** or trade name, there is no implied condition as to their fitness for any particular purpose. Most branded goods were once subject to **resale price maintenance**. They are all still subject to the Trade Descriptions Act.

Brand values A variety of **intangible asset** which has become of increasing relevance to company balance sheets in recent years. Businesses which develop products bearing a brand name which has become synonymous with the product itself are apt to attribute substantial monetary value to the brand name – on the grounds that when the business is sold the value of the brand name is a significant component of any purchase price. Obvious examples lie in the malt whisky business and also in household names such as Guinness, Coca-Cola, and various soap powders and cosmetics. The argument in favour of attaching a monetary value to such names is not dissimilar from that which justifies the practice of attributing particular values to newspaper and magazine titles in the balance sheets of companies which own them. However, perhaps a more immediate attraction attaching to the inclusion of brands as valuable intangible assets lies in the potential for substantially increasing the net asset value of company shares – frequently a formidable first line of defence against possible take-over bids.

One of the problems attached to brand valuation is its necessarily subjective nature. For this reason a considerable degree of scepticism has been generated within the accountancy profession. While the practice has not been outlawed in the field of published accounts and no specific **accounting standards** have been issued on the matter, there is a general requirement that brand values should be treated with the same degree of careful scrutiny required by other intangible assets, that the method of valuation should be examined carefully by the auditor, that the amount allocated should be regularly reviewed and subject to strict amortization over the predicted useful life of the asset in question.

Breach of warranty of authority Where an **agent** acts outside his actual and apparent authority, the principal is not liable and a third party can sue the agent for breach of warranty of authority.

Break-even chart A chart used to give information about the viability of an enterprise and effective in warning of approaching disaster. In its simplest form the figures charted are those of total costs and total revenue. When these totals are equal, a 'break-even' point has been reached, i.e. the business is neither making money nor losing it.

More elaborate charts will differentiate between various categories of cost, e.g. **fixed costs** and **variable costs**. The difference between revenue and variable costs will represent **gross profit** and, other things being equal, will rise with output. The point at which this difference equals fixed costs will be the break-even point. This can be illustrated on a graph where the x axis denotes levels of output, revenue is shown as a curve beginning where the two axes intersect and variable costs as another curve commencing at a point on the y axis, $y = C$, where C represents fixed costs. The point of intersection of the two curves is the break-even point. More sophisticated graphs can be drawn to illustrate the rate of increase in profits with rising output, both before and after the break-even point is reached.

Break-up value An alternative to

selling a business as a going concern is to sell it piecemeal, each asset separately. The value put on a business or a group of related assets sold in this manner is referred to as the break-up value and, in most instances, this will be the maximum amount realizable on disposal of those assets.

The term is also used in the context of valuing ordinary shares in a company. If there is no known value for shares, i.e. if they are not quoted on the Stock Exchange or on the Unlisted Securities Market and there is no figure at which they have recently changed hands, then they can only be valued either on the basis of estimated minimum earnings or on the break-up value of the assets they represent. This break-up value can only be an approximation and will be calculated by estimating the likely net realizable value of all assets, assuming they are disposed of individually in a free market, deducting from the total thus ascertained external liabilities and dividing the result by the number of shares. If there are shares which have priority of repayment over the ordinary shares, an adjustment must be made for the amount applicable to those shares. The share value thus calculated is also sometimes known as the net asset value. ◊ **Value** ◊ **Asset value** ◊ **Market value** ◊ **Net book value** ◊ **Nominal value** ◊ **Value in use** ◊ **List price**.

Bretton Woods Agreement An international agreement entered into at Bretton Woods, New Hampshire, by the UK and its western allies towards the end of, and as a direct result of, the Second World War. It was signed in 1944 and was to give birth to various international agencies aimed at establishing peaceful trade between nations and keeping a watchful eye on the conduct of that trade. The principal remaining legacies of the Agreement are the **International Monetary Fund** and the **International Bank for Reconstruction and Development**.

Bribe A bribe is a payment by which the payer obtains some right, benefit or preference to which he has no legal entitlement and which he would not have obtained but for the payment of the money. It is a criminal offence to accept a bribe. Any bribe taken by an **agent** must be handed over to the principal. It is an offence, punishable by imprisonment and/or a fine, for an agent to accept a bribe, or for a person to offer a bribe to an agent.

Bridging loan A temporary loan made to 'bridge' the gap between receipt of funds from the buyer and handing them over to the seller. It is particularly common in house or property purchase, where a bank may lend, in the short term, the monies needed by the purchaser to complete the transaction before the main source of funds arrives, e.g. while waiting for the completion of negotiations with a **building society**.

British Airports Authority Set up in 1966 to own and manage the main state-owned international airports. Its functions, apart from freely cooperating with such bodies as the **Civil Aviation Authority**, were to provide and maintain services and facilities at the airports under its control consistent with the smooth and safe operation of the airports, and to ensure their continual development in providing an efficient air service. It was also required to conduct its business in such a manner as would provide sufficient income – e.g. from landing fees – to cover expenditure.

In 1987 the British Airports Authority passed into the private sector and became British Airports Authority plc. Its functions, however, remain much the same though it has lost many of the powers that accrued to a public undertaking, such as the ability to pass by-laws and compulsorily to acquire land and rights over land. ◊ **Air Traffic Control** ◊ **Air transport licensing** ◊ **Airline Users Committee** ◊ **Airworthiness**.

British Airways A public limited company formed in 1984 to acquire all assets and liabilities of the state-owned British Airways Corporation in exchange for shares initially issued to the Secretary of State for Transport for subsequent sale to members of the public.

The public corporation had been established in 1972 by the Civil Aviation Authority, which had been set up to acquire the existing UK airline services operated by British Overseas Airways Corporation and British European Airways. ◊ **British Airports Authority** ◊ **Air transport load factor** ◊ **Airline Users Committee** ◊ **Air waybill**.

British Bankers Association This was founded originally in 1920. In 1972, when Britain joined the EU, the Association became the major representative body for recognized UK banks. Banks established under British law and with head offices in the UK are full members, as are British branches of other EU banks. Foreign banks with offices in the UK may be admitted to associate membership.

The BBA is active in voicing the opinions of its members and making their views known to the Bank of England and governmental departments and other bodies whose actions or attitudes are relevant to banking affairs. Its field of refer-ence is not restricted to the UK but will include the whole EU.

British Coal ◊ **National Coal Board**.

British Export Houses Association The Association formed by British **export houses** to give free advice to exporters on finding an export house and/or **confirming house** suitable to their needs.

British Gas Until relatively recently all supplies of UK gas, for both industrial and domestic use, were manufactured, principally from coal, in various gasworks throughout the country. Once manufactured, the gas was stored in local gas-holders pending distribution.

During the 1960s the gas industry was transformed by the discovery and marketing of natural gas obtained from massive subterranean fields located for the greater part under the North Sea. These were developed both by the gas industry itself and by independent oil companies, which then sold their output to the national gas suppliers. Needless to say, the recovery of natural gas requires considerable capital expenditure both for exploration of fields and for their exploitation.

The gas industry was nationalized in 1949. In 1972 the Gas Council, set up after nationalization, was replaced by the British Gas Corporation. In 1986 this Corporation was privatized and became British Gas plc, responsible for the supply of gas in Great Britain. British Gas obtains supplies of natural gas from fields on mainland Britain and in the North Sea. It also imports gas from other countries. It supplies consumers through a network of regional organizations, though it must allow competitor suppliers to enter into contracts to use its distribution channels.

The industry is overseen by the Director-General of OFGAS who monitors the supply and price of gas to customers and generally protects their interests.

British Institute of Management ◊ Management, British Institute of.

British Insurance and Investment Brokers Association (BIIBA) With the passing of the Insurance Brokers (Registration) Act 1977, both the Corporation of Insurance Brokers and the Association of Insurance Brokers were dissolved and a new professional association, known as the British Insurance Brokers Association, was established in their place to be the representative and governing body for all members of the insurance broking profession. Intended to complement the statutory **Insurance Brokers Registration Council** set up at the same time, the Association is essentially a representative body controlled by its members but intended to set and supervise standards within the profession for the benefit of members and general public alike. As a national association it also seeks to protect the interests of its members *vis-à-vis* central government and to increase public awareness of the services that responsible brokers can provide. To this latter end it has established regional offices and an informal conciliation service which deals with customer complaints which are insufficiently serious to rate reference to the IBRC.

With the advent of the Financial Services Act it became clear that BIBA would need to broaden its scope if it was to remain the principal representative body for insurance brokers. Accordingly in 1987 it changed its name to the British Insurance and Investment Brokers Association (BIIBA) to indicate that it was duly representative not only of registered brokers but also of those brokers who carried on investment business and were members of FIMBRA.

British Overseas Airways Corporation (BOAC) Formally established in 1939, with British European Airways, to be responsible for the greater part of air transport, passenger and cargo, to and from the United Kingdom. It was absorbed by **British Airways** after the reorganization brought about under the auspices of the **Civil Aviation Authority** created in 1971.

British Overseas Trade Board An official organization headed by the Secretary of State for Trade and Industry but with members drawn from the private sector, set up to promote UK exports and to advise exporters concerning the multifarious aspects and complexities of marketing goods and services overseas. As a government-sponsored organization, part of its mandate is to liaise effectively between government and private industry with the aim of maximizing existing opportunities for the development of overseas trade, and in so doing to advise government as to the most effective strategies available in this context.

It publishes a range of booklets – some available free, others on sale at HMSO – dealing with both the technicalities of exporting goods and the problems associated with selling in individual countries. It will advise on the suitability of particular agents and distributors overseas by means of confidential 'status reports'. It arranges assistance for displaying products in trade fairs and in-store promotions abroad and even provides financial aid for companies wishing to join trade missions to overseas markets. Additionally, it guides new exporters through the maze of foreign tariffs and regulations and will even provide conditional financial assistance for gaining a foothold in new markets.

The BOTB has offices in various parts of the UK and exporters should contact their nearest regional office. ◊ **Export assistance register** ◊ **Export Credits Guarantee Department** ◊ **Export incentives** ◊ **Exports** ◊ **Export house**.

British Productivity Council This was formed in 1952. Its members are normally nominated by sponsoring bodies, i.e. the Confederation of British Industry, the Trades Union Congress, the Association of British Chambers of Commerce and the nationalized industries. Its statement of policy runs: 'the British Productivity Council represents management and workers in every type of industrial sector. It is non-political, free of government control and concerned only to stimulate the improvement of productivity in every section of the national economy by every possible means.' The chairmanship alternates between employers and trade unionists. It publishes *Target*, taken over from the Central Office of Information. It encourages inter-firm relationships and cooperation, and team visits abroad. It has local committees, holds study groups, seminars and work-study groups. It services the National Association for Quality and Reliability and releases many publications.

British Rail British Rail runs two basic services, passenger and freight. Attempts have been made to streamline both. Passenger services have been divided into sub-groups, the principal being Intercity and Regional railways though there are various sub-divisions within these groups. Travellers are offered incentives ranging from special services for business people

◊ **Business travel** (**British Rail**) to a variety of reduced-rate fares in off-peak periods for rail travellers generally. Freight services have been similarly subdivided into Trainload Freight and **freightliners**. It is not feasible to give detailed information on freight transport as much depends on the nature of the goods and the speed with which delivery is required.

At present various moves are being made with a view to returning the railways to the private sector. To this end a decision has been made to separate the provision of train services from the need to provide and maintain the railroads themselves and that part of the infrastructure which naturally attaches thereto. The responsibility for the latter has been passed to a newly formed organization known as Railtrack. The next stage will be to pre-package the various passenger and freight services and sell them off as self-contained units paying a rental to Railtrack for the use of the system.

British Road Services Group Originally an independent company, British Road Services became part of the National Freight Corporation and was subsequently acquired by the **National Freight Consortium**. It is the largest road transport and distribution company in the UK and is a market leader in contract hire and fleet management, over half of its fleet being in the livery of its customers.

British Savings Bonds Government-backed securities for the small investor, issued only on the National Savings Stock Register and therefore not listed on the Stock Exchange. They were available for purchase at banks and post offices. The interest paid was at competitive rates and tax was not deducted at source.

These bonds were withdrawn from sale on 31 December 1979 and all those issued have now matured. ◊ **National Savings Bonds** ◊ **Premium savings bonds** ◊ **National Savings Bank** ◊ **Index-linked savings certificates**.

British Standards Institution This originated in 1901, received a royal charter in 1929 and became the British Standards Institution in 1931.

An independent body, government-assisted but not government-controlled, its objects include: (1) the cooperation of producers and users in the improvement, standardization and simplification of engineering and industrial materials in order to avoid production of an unnecessary variety of patterns and sizes for one purpose; (2) the setting of standards of quality and dimension and promoting adoption of British Standards specifications; (3) registering in the name of the institution marks of all descriptions and licensing the affixing of these marks. Some products must be marked with British Standard numbers. It is also possible, if the standard is sufficiently comprehensive, to apply to have compliance with British Standards Institution's standards certified by use of the Kite Mark. This is used under licence from the British Standards Institution on terms requiring regular inspection and testing and the observance of an agreed scheme of supervision and control. The use of this mark can be very valuable to a manufacturer. Attempts are made to promote the adoption of international standards, particularly within the Commonwealth. The British Standards Institution plays an active part in the International Electrotechnical Commission.

British Technology Group A public authority brought into being in 1981 to coordinate the activities of what were originally established as the National Enterprise Board and the **National Research Development Corporation**.

British Telecom The UK telecommunications system was for many years the responsibility of the Post Office. The latter became a public corporation in 1969 and in 1981 this corporation was split into two distinct parts. The postal services remained under the control of a new Post Office Corporation and the telecommunications service was taken over by British Telecommunications Corporation. In August 1984, as a result of a governmental decision to bring competition into play, the assets of the Corporation were transferred to British Telecommunications PLC, of which in November 1984 51 per cent of the shares were sold to members of the general public. British Telecom then became a listed public liability company within the private sector.

BT is the major supplier of telecommunications throughout the UK. It receives a licence for this purpose which commits it both to supply a comprehensive service throughout the country and to provide certain special services such as call box facilities, 999 emergency calls and a directory inquiry number. It is also expected to cooperate with other licence holders, both those which already exist, such as the Hull City Telephone Service and Mercury Communications Ltd, and those which might emerge in the future.

For particular services ◊ **Telephone** ◊ **Telex** ◊ **Freefone** ◊ **Telemessage** ◊ **Payphone** ◊ **Telephone directories** ◊ **Yellow Pages** ◊ **Prestel** ◊ **Subscriber trunk dialling** ◊ **Radio telephone** ◊ **Datel services** ◊ **Confravision** ◊ **Facsimile**.

British Waterways Board ◊ **Inland waterways**.

Broken stowage A shipping term for cargo space lost due to packages of uneven shape.

Broker A mercantile **agent** who, in the nature of his business, makes **contracts** *re* **goods** or property, where he has neither the goods nor the documents of **title** but brings together buyer and seller for a commission. There are specialized brokers, e.g. **insurance brokers** and **stockbrokers**, dealing in services rather than goods. A broker is not bound by the Factor's Act. If acting as broker he does not have any personal liability unless custom dictates. He has implied authority to sell on normal credit terms, receive payment, and do other things consonant with his trade.

Brokerage – Commission charged by **brokers**.

Bubble A 'nine-day-wonder' in the business world. A term used derogatively of a trading venture the initial and often exciting promise of which is belied by results – often with much heart-searching and financial ruin to innocent investors. The most notorious catastrophe of this sort was the **South Sea Bubble** of the early eighteenth century, bursting with a terrible finality and on a national scale in 1720.

Bubble company A **company** that has never had any real business or intended to trade honestly, or a company formed with the intention of defrauding the public. ◊ **South Sea Bubble**.

Bucket shop Slang expression used to describe an unlawful institution for doubtful dealing or **gambling** in commodities, or **stocks** and **shares**, etc.

Budget account A scheme developed by many of the major commercial banks which can benefit both bank and customer. It is based upon the fact that most people are faced with large payments, e.g. for rates, electricity, gas, telephone, etc., which, though they cover an extended period, have to be made at one specific time. A budget account is a separate account at the bank, with a separate cheque book, into which monthly fixed sums are paid which will, when added together, produce the total of the various payments anticipated. The load is thereby spread evenly over the year, to avoid the necessity of finding large amounts of money at particular, and perhaps inconvenient, dates.

Many businesses, although not specifically operating budget accounts, do much the same thing, and arrange for the payment of rates or electricity charges, etc., in monthly parts by **standing orders** or direct debit mandates given to the bank – but only with the agreement of the creditor.

Budget controller The head of the committee responsible for **budgetary control** in an organization.

Budgetary control A system of controlling expenditure and income used by the management of a business. Each department in the business forecasts its probable expenditure or income for the coming financial period. These forecasts or budgets are scrutinized and approved at top management level, so that a provisional **profit and loss account** for the coming year can be drawn up and, if necessary, expenses pruned or sales policies revised. The system varies from firm to firm. Generally speaking budgets must be adhered to and any deviations during the relevant period are reported so that action can be taken if necessary. The major benefits that should arise from an effective budgetary control system include: (1) the availability of cash to fund a foreseen capital expenditure programme; (2) the minimization of the risk of **overtrading**.

Buffer stock In common parlance this is a stock, usually of raw materials, created and kept in reserve against hard times or unexpected hold-ups in normal supplies.

The term also has a more specific meaning in commodity markets where stocks of raw materials are bought, hoarded, and sold in order to stabilize market prices. Though such a practice smacks of speculation against the public good it is accepted, and even promoted, by governments, on the grounds that it can, where properly controlled, prevent the cornering of markets and ensure a steady supply of the commodities concerned without too much disturbance of prices – to the advantage of the average consumer.

Building, Institute of Founded in 1834, this is a professional institution for people involved in building practice in a managerial, technical, commercial or administrative capacity, or engaged in teaching building or building research. The object is to establish and maintain standards of competence and professional conduct. Membership is personal and open to all nationalities. Various publications are issued, and there are also conferences, seminars, etc. Disciplinary powers are the responsibility of a Professional Conduct Committee. It collaborates with the **Royal Institute of British Architects** and the **Royal Institution of Chartered Surveyors**.

Building societies Building societies were born of thrift and self-help. The cost of housing has always been a substantial multiple of average annual earnings. For this reason, back in the earlier days of the industrial revolution, groups of artisans combined their funds in order to acquire land and build houses thereon. For this purpose they formed mutual or friendly societies, non-profit-making in structure, by means of which they used pooled resources to house each member in turn. When this end was accomplished many were wound up, but some expanded into providing a service to the general working public. They accepted the savings of a large part of the nation, paying good interest rates thereon, and used the funds so acquired to lend to persons wishing to buy houses in return for a mortgage on those houses until repayment was made in full. The tendency was to remain non-profit-making and to balance the interest received from borrowers against the interest paid out plus the costs of administration.

Because of the immense amounts of money involved in house purchase, the successful building societies became very large institutions and in time, through the processes of amalgamation and survival of the fittest, were reduced in number to the relatively few major societies that exist today, most with assets amounting to many millions of pounds. Again, as they grew in size and responsibility, they became subject to regulations by the State for the greater protection of the public. The Building Societies Act 1986, replacing the Acts of 1962 and 1967, put such societies into a new legal context and created a new body, the Building Societies Commission, to oversee the application of the regulatory system which the Act brought into being. Building societies can now become corporate bodies with the depositors as principal shareholders or even companies in the full sense of the term (as Abbey National has done) and can engage in a wide range of activities which were once outside their remit. This includes the provision of various financial services which will bring them within the provisions of the Financial Services Act with a requirement to be registered with one of the major SROs.

Despite their new image, however, building societies are still regarded by the public in their traditional role of accepting savings on the one hand and lending for house-purchase on the other. Interest rates on monies lodged with them vary considerably according to the nature of the account opened, but as a general rule it is necessary for an investor to commit his savings for a longer period if he wishes to obtain the high rates of interest – though frequently it will suffice to retain a stated minimum in an account to obtain such rates. The fact that money has been committed for a long period does not prevent the investor withdrawing it. Should he do so, however, without the prescribed notice, he will forfeit the interest he would otherwise have earned.

The contemporary building society is continuing to extend its area of activity and, as the clearing banks have moved into the mortgage arena, so the Building Societies are now encroaching on what was once the preserve of those banks. Most building societies now offer cheque accounts, handle standing orders, provide cash-point facilities and deal with travellers cheques and foreign exchange. However, as they move into the territory of the High Street banks, so also do they attract a greater degree of State regulation.

Built-in obsolescence The price of consumer goods, particularly consumer durables, is often kept down by the adoption of mass-production methods. This can and does lead to the situation where the supply of those goods vastly exceeds normal demand. To counter this, the manufacturer will frequently seek to create artificial levels of demand by the employment of what are known as techniques of built-in obsolescence.

This is effected by deliberately limiting the life-span of goods produced. It can be done by the choice of more perishable materials in the manufacturing process, materials which are often cheaper than the more costly but harder-wearing alternatives. The goods will then need to be replaced more quickly than would otherwise have been necessary, thus increasing public demand. Other methods of inflating demand are to be found in the careful manipulation of public tastes, either by changes in the design of popular durables or by appealing to fashion-consciousness which has been purposely induced by the supplier. Well-prepared advertising campaigns are a common adjunct to these other ploys. ◊ **Advertising, persuasive**.

The morality of built-in obsolescence techniques is frequently challenged, but it is argued that the end effect of ensuring the continuity of supply at competitive prices and in doing so providing employment justifies the system – an extension of the adage 'what is good for General Motors is good for the country'. Although the concept of built-in obsolescence originated in the USA, it was soon adopted in the UK.

Bulk cargo A shipping term meaning cargo which is all of one commodity.

Bulk posting Special rebates are allowed

by the **Post Office** for pre-paid second-class posting of very large quantities of letter-post items. The saving can be quite considerable but the number of letters or packets must be in excess of 4,250 before any rebate is applicable. ◊ **Inland post**.

Bull On the Stock Exchange the obverse of the **bear**. Bull speculators buy shares, commodities, currencies, etc., forward; i.e. they contract to buy at a price fixed in advance at a future date in the anticipation that when the contract matures the price in the market will have risen. In a period of rising prices they will therefore have the advantage of buying at a price lower than that prevailing at the time the contract falls due for completion, and will profit accordingly. They must therefore act on careful anticipation, which may or may not be realized. Like bears they may, if circumstances permit, carry over the contract to another account period (◊ **carry-over day**); the cost of doing so is known as **contango**. Bulls do not necessarily buy forward; they may buy now and hold the stock in the expectation of a future price rise which will earn a profit. Bull markets generally refer to **forward purchasing** in a period of rising prices. Perhaps the most notorious of all bull markets was the **South Sea Bubble**, which burst in 1720 and, in addition to leaving a wake of financial ruin and freak fortunes, set the growth of a credit economy in the UK back some 200 years.

Bulldog bonds A colloquial term for sterling bonds and financial instruments issued by companies and public bodies of other countries on the UK market.

Bull market ◊ **Bull**.

Bullion Gold and silver of a recognized degree of purity. It may be in various forms, normally gold or silver bars.

Bullion market At one time London had the pre-eminent gold bullion market. It was closed in 1939 and when it re-opened in 1954 a major part of gold dealings had passed to New York and Zurich. Zurich has become even more important since Russia and South Africa, the world's primary gold producers, recently decided to route all sales through the Zurich market. Nevertheless, London still maintains an active gold bullion market, respected both for its standards and the highly competitive prices which its near perfect market provides. Dealings are in dollars and each day two fixed meetings of dealers are held at which official prices are set. As such a great deal of business is now conducted by telephone and telex outside the fixed meetings, prices will tend to fluctuate considerably during one day's trading.

Bunkering A shipping term for taking on coal as fuel for the voyage.

Buoy dues Dues claimed by **Trinity House** from ships using ports where there are buoys.

Burden The carrying capacity of a ship. This is not the same as the **tonnage**.

Burglary insurance A specialized form of **insurance**. Claims will normally be made for damage done by genuine burglars – uninvited persons breaking into a premises between the hours of 6 pm and 6 am. This type of insurance does not normally cover loss through pilfering by members of staff or persons invited on to the premises. Persons forcing an entry between 6 am and 6 pm are included as burglars for insurance purposes, even though technically, by law, they are guilty of house-breaking as opposed to burglary.

Business Expansion Scheme (BES)

This was introduced by the government in 1981 to serve two purposes. Firstly to assist smaller unlisted companies to expand by providing a means of raising the necessary capital, and secondly to offer an incentive to high earners to invest in the smaller companies which had potential for growth but lacked the funding to back it. To this end individuals who put money into the purchase of shares in qualifying companies could obtain tax relief in full on the amount so invested – provided the shares were not sold within five years of purchase.

To qualify for investment through BES schemes the company's shares must not have been quoted on a recognized stock exchange at the time of investment and for three years afterwards. The investment had to be in new shares issued for that purpose and there was a limit on the amount any one individual could invest in any one year. Since the inception of the scheme BES funds have been created whereby individuals could band together in making a BES investment and benefit from the expertise of a fund manager without loss of tax reliefs available. Directors and paid employers could not invest in their own company by way of a BES.

In the November 1993 Budget an Enterprise Investment Scheme was established to replace the BES as from 1 January 1995. This new scheme will be similar to the supplanted BES but will not include investment in private rented housing. There is a limit (initially £40,000) on an individual's combined investment under BES and IES and tax relief will be available at 20 per cent on qualifying investments.

Business names Until it was repealed in 1981 the Registration of Business Names Act 1916 required business names which were not solely those of the propri-

etor(s) to be registered. The Act was originally intended as a means of identifying enemy aliens who might be trading under other names within the UK, though, by accident rather than design, it did serve other purposes such as providing a public source of information concerning true ownership of various types of business and indirectly protecting registered names by preventing the same name being registered maliciously by another person.

In order to cushion the impact of repeal and maintain a degree of protection for both traders and the general public, the 1985 Business Names Act contains certain provisions, first introduced by the 1981 Companies Act, relating to the use of business names generally, i.e. applicable to all trading organizations and not only those which have been registered as limited companies.

Broadly speaking, the Act requires that all businesses other than companies trading in their corporate name which bear a name not being solely the surname of the proprietor (plus given name or initial if desired) or where there are more than one, e.g. in a partnership, then the surnames of all proprietors or partners, must abide by the following conditions. These also apply to a company which trades other than in its registered corporate name.

The rules are briefly that organizations not exempted as in the above paragraph must include on all formal business letters and documents the name of the proprietor or partners (unless there are more than twelve, when a notice stating the principal place of business and that a list is available will suffice) and the address at which any legal notice may be properly served. This information must also be displayed at any place at which business is done and be given to any third party doing or discussing business or asking for the information.

Additionally, there is a provision forbidding names which might suggest that the business is connected with the government or local authority or which contain expressions specified by the Secretary of State as undesirable, unless in either instance proper approval by the government department concerned has been obtained.

Business reply service A Post Office service enabling the sender of a letter to receive a reply from the addressee without the latter incurring any postal charge.

Any organization wishing to make use of this service must first obtain a licence from the local head postmaster. It will also be required to deposit a sum of money which will approximate to the anticipated debt that will be incurred by him over the period of one month. The pre-paid cards, letters, forms incorporated in advertisements, etc., must conform with various conditions imposed by the Post Office and listed in the **Post Office Guide**. An international reply service is also available.

Business schools These are colleges of higher education that offer graduate and post-graduate courses in the various skills and strategies pertinent to effective business management in the contemporary world. In addition to research facilities, these schools offer in-depth study of a wide range of business-orientated disciplines. These include resource management, corporate financial strategy, performance evaluation and the effective use of all available technological and electronic management-orientated equipment. The extensive range of courses available is geared to current industrial and commercial requirements and leads to a variety of qualifications up to and including Master of Business Administration (MBA). These business schools cater not only for full-time students of business management, but also for senior managers already in positions of responsibility within both the private and public sector.

Business studies, Master of ◊ **Business schools**.

Business travel (British Rail) British Rail attempts to afford special help to businessmen by providing fast trains between important centres at convenient times, providing food, de luxe cuisine or light meals, sleeping accommodation if necessary and wash-rooms. There are also facilities for carrying on business on the train: a private compartment with office equipment. Businessmen using British Rail regularly can often obtain reduced rates.

Buyers over A Stock Exchange term for a situation where there are more buyers than there are sellers.

Buying in On the Stock Exchange, when a seller fails to hand over **securities** or **shares**, which he has promised to sell, at the due time, the buyer buys in wherever he can obtain shares, and the seller is responsible for all additional expenses.

By-product A saleable commodity produced in the process of manufacturing a main product: e.g. manufacturing waste which has, initially perhaps only incidentally, a market value in its own right. By-products may be natural, e.g. sawdust from a carpenter's shed, or may be developed from disposable waste, e.g. the various by-products of the coal industry such as tar, gas, soap, etc.

Calculating machine A mechanical device, however powered, intended for use in speedily discovering the answer to complex mathematical calculations from the straightforward addition of numerous figures to problems involving combinations of multiplication, subtraction and division. Also used for finding ratios, percentages, currency conversions, etc. The machines available range from the pocket calculator to the most advanced computer. ◊ **Abacus** ◊ **Adding machine** ◊ **Add-lister** ◊ **Computer**.

Calendar The old style Julian Calendar was arranged by Julius Caesar in 47 BC. The year was to be $365\frac{1}{4}$ days, to provide for which the ordinary year was to be 365 days and every fourth or leap year 366 days. The old style was still used in Russia until 1918.

Because the solar year is less than the lunar year by over eleven minutes, the old style involved a surplus of about three days in four centuries. For this reason, Pope Gregory XIII altered the calendar in 1582, omitting ten days in that year and making only each fourth centurial year a leap year: 1600 was a leap year, 2000 will be a leap year, but not 1700, 1800 or 1900. The new style was adopted in England in 1792, when eleven days had to be cancelled. The difference between the old style and new style is now thirteen days.

Call money ◊ **Money at call and at short notice**.

Called-up capital That proportion of the **issued share capital** of a company that has actually been called up. Shares of one pound may be issued by a new company which does not require the total sum involved immediately but prefers to have the right to raise more funds at a later date without the need to issue further shares. In such an instance it may ask only for half the nominal price of the share when applications are made and shares allotted, leaving the balance to be payable, in total or in separate stated instalments, at later dates. The date of any proposed 'call', i.e. demand for an amount outstanding, may be fixed at the time of issue or may be left open. Anyone taking a partly paid share from a third party would, of course, take it subject to the possibility of a **call** being made and the **market price** would reflect this fact. Called-up capital is therefore the total amount for which a demand has been made on the shares issued by a company. **Uncalled capital** may be immediately payable if winding-up proceedings make it necessary for payment of debts. ◊ **Nominal capital** ◊ **Shares** ◊ **Stock** ◊ **Paid-up capital**.

Calls A term used in **company** law for demands made by a company that **members** should pay certain sums due on the **shares** they hold. ◊ **Called-up capital**. In a **liquidation**, the **liquidator** may make a call immediately irrespective of any agreement the company has made with the shareholders.

Calls in arrears ◊ Paid-up capital.

Canals ◊ Inland waterways.

Capacity to contract ◊ Contract: of married women ◊ Contract, infant's ◊ Contract, drunkard's ◊ Contract, trade union.

Capital The total resources of a person or organization (though normally only tangible items are taken into account). The term is very vague and is usually qualified in some way, e.g. **Share capital**.

Capital allowances These are deductions allowed by the Inland Revenue from the profits of businesses assessed under Schedule D for the **depreciation** of capital assets. The assets against which the allowance may be claimed are those specifically designated by the tax authorities but tend to include most industrial plant and machinery, including road vehicles necessarily employed and industrial, rather than commercial, buildings.

The allowances normally relate to companies, in so far as industrial and manufacturing bodies tend to be companies, and the rules governing the amount and entitlement of allowances are constantly changing. A major change occurred as a result of the provisions contained in the Finance Act 1971. After this date assets ceased to be written down as individual items and became 'pooled' according to category. This meant that an allowance was given in total against the written-down value of all plant in use, after adding acquisitions and deducting items disposed of.

Industrial buildings are given allowances on a **straight line** basis. Plant, machinery and cars are treated by a **diminishing balance** method or, in tax terms, on a written-down basis. As a result assets in the latter category receive large allowances in the first year; this means that the **written-down value** may be much lower than for normal accounting purposes, particularly when initial allowances (an extra percentage in the year of acquisition) are applicable.

To compensate for this it is usual for the relevant difference to be set aside from distributable profits in a deferred tax account. ◊ **Deferred taxation**. The balance on this account is then adjusted each year to correspond with the total difference outstanding. When an asset is disposed of the amount received must be subtracted from the written-down value for tax purposes; the balance, known as a balancing allowance, can be claimed from the Inland Revenue (or deducted from the cost of the replacement asset if the Inland Revenue agrees). On the other hand, if the proceeds exceed the written-down value a balancing charge becomes payable.

Capital clause The clause in the **Memorandum of Association** of a company dealing with its **capital**. It states the amount of the company's nominal capital, and the number and amount of the **shares** it is permitted to have. It need not classify the shares though sometimes does, which makes it more difficult for rights to be altered. ◊ **Authorized capital**.

Capital commitments Capital expenditure contracted for by companies or other organizations, of which nothing has been paid by **balance sheet** date. The Companies Acts provide that these commitments should be shown in the accounts of limited companies, as a note or otherwise, and that a distinction should be made between items contracted for, and those agreed by the **directors** but not yet contracted for.

Capital employed An accounting term difficult to define but frequently used in published accounts. As there is no agreement as to how it should be calculated, the method of arriving at the figure varies considerably. It is generally taken to be the **net assets**.

Capital employed from the point of view of the analyst is the total capital used in a business for the acquisition of profits. It may be thought of as the **ordinary share** capital and reserves or on the other hand as total **assets**, depending on a point of view. ◊ **Return on capital** ◊ **Yield**.

Capital expenditure Expenditure on **fixed assets** rather than assets purchased for resale.

Capital gains tax As the name suggests, this is a tax on profits or gains made in the course of capital transactions, i.e. on the buying and selling of assets other than in the normal course of a taxable business. The tax was introduced in two doses, on short-term gains in the Finance Act 1962 and on long-term gains, calculated by different rules, in the Finance Act 1965. The distinction between long-term and short-term gains, other than where gilt-edged securities are concerned, has now been virtually abolished and all gains are subject to the same rate of tax and are calculated according to one set of rules. These rules are too complex to be enumerated here, but taxpayers normally have an option of either paying tax at the current capital gains rate on the total gain or at their highest income tax rate on one half of that gain.

In determining what are to be included as capital gains for tax purposes certain important exceptions apply. The more important include the sale of the taxpayer's personal dwelling-house, when no tax is charged, and the sale of government securities and other securities and loan stock quoted on the Stock Exchange or USM held for more than twelve months. There are also exceptions in the case of low-value transactions, i.e. sales totalling less than a stated minimum. Rules vary from year to year and, as with business profits, capital losses can be set against capital gains or carried forward to be set against subsequent gains. One further point to note is that a gain arises when an asset is transferred at a profit, whether for cash or not. A benefit need not be a cash benefit. The position was complicated by the introduction in 1975 of capital transfer tax. This applied to all transfers of assets and tended to overlap capital gains legislation. This transfer tax has now been abolished having been superseded in 1986 by **Inheritance tax**. ◊ **Capital profit** ◊ **Appreciation**.

In respect of capital gains some of the sting has been taken out by the introduction of an indexation allowance applying to assets sold after 5 April 1988 where the original cost of the asset, or its value in 1982, can now be increased by an amount representing the increase in the Retail Price Index since 1982, or the date of purchase, whichever is later. There is also substantial relief from the sale of a family business, or shares therein, by the owner or proprietor on reaching retirement age.

Capital gearing This term refers to the various types of capital assembled to fund a business – usually a company. Capital may be in shares or loans with a considerable variety of each category available, e.g. shares may be ordinary, preferential or deferred. They may be entitled to dividend, which is fixed or variable, cumulative or not. So also with loans, which may be long-term, middle-term or short-term and carry varying interest rates. They may also be 'convertible', i.e. lenders have a right to convert their loan into shares.

A business must always be aware of its future commitments and the managers' assessment of the future income flow will determine how they gear their capital, i.e. how it is spread among the various categories mentioned above. A company which anticipates an uneventful career with a fairly constant rate of profit may be content to be low-geared. It may be willing to raise the greater part of its capital by one issue of shares, part fixed dividend and part ordinary. Where the life of the business is unpredictable and depends on a great many unknown factors, it may be better to rely on a variety of fixed-interest short-term loans which can be raised as and when necessary and which will come up for repayment or renewal at frequent intervals, preferably staggered. Such a business would be highly geared. Generally speaking, the greater the spread of capital over various types and at various interest rates the higher the degree of capital gearing there is said to be.

From this it follows that the fortunes of ordinary shareholders are very much determined by the degree of gearing. If a large part of the capital is raised in fixed-interest securities then their dividend will vary quite disproportionately to profitability: nothing will come to them when profits are equal to, or less than, interest payable; however, above this level **dividends** could well rocket unexpectedly and unreservedly. ◊ **Debentures** ◊ **Fixed-interest securities** ◊ **Loan capital** ◊ **Shares**.

Capital-intensive An adjective used to describe those industries where the amount of fixed capital used in production is high, both absolutely and as an amount per person employed. Capital-intensive industries are those which depend more on the machines involved in production than on the people employed to tend them, i.e. industries where the cost of capital constitutes the major cost factor and far outweighs the cost of labour. The ultimate in capital-intensive industry would be a fully automated factory.

Capital issues The issue of shares in a company, by means of **introductions**, **placings**, **offers for sale**, **tenders**, and more commonly by **prospectus**. ◊ **Rights issues** ◊ **Scrip issues**.

Capital levy Effectively another name for wealth tax, this is a special charge on the richer members of society and in addition to tax on income, which varies according to the amount of the payers' capital assets, i.e. their accumulated wealth. People with the greatest 'fortunes' pay the greatest amounts – assessed at a rate of so much in the pound on the value of assets legally owned. Legal ownership would be defined to prevent any evasion of tax by the creation of trusts, etc. At present there is no wealth tax in the UK though successive Labour governments have seriously considered imposing one. In a sense, the old surtax was a form of capital levy in so far as it obliged those with very high incomes to pay an extra portion of their earnings in addition to income tax. The investment income surcharge, introduced in 1968, comes into a similar category, though both this and the prior surtax were defined as taxes on income and were levied on income rather than on the capital from which the income proceeded. The difference is legally real but in practice no more than a semantic exercise as the tax must usually be paid out of capital.

Capital loss The opposite of **capital profit** but calculated for most purposes in the same manner. For tax purposes capital losses can be set off against capital gains. ◊ **Capital gains tax**. A fact often ignored, particularly by the tax collector, is that apparent profits or losses may be quite illusory. This happens frequently in the present-day market where the continuous fall in the value of money causes assets to appreciate in cash price while their value, calculated in terms which ignore the effects of inflation, may have remained constant or even have fallen. Until recently, **stock relief** made some attempt to alleviate this injustice.

Capital market The term used to describe the various sources of long-term capital needed both for the creation of new companies and for the development and expansion of existing ones. The **Stock Exchange** is not a provider of capital, but it is of vital importance to a healthy capital market because it provides a forum for transferring stocks and bonds raised elsewhere. The propensity to supply money in exchange for shares will obviously be influenced by the existence of a market in which they can be sold. There are various institutions, apart from banks, which specialize in engineering supplies of capital to industry – whether the recipient is in the UK or elsewhere and whether the funds are required in gold, dollars or some other currency.

Funds are normally raised by the issue of **shares**, **bonds**, **debentures**, loan stock, etc. The project may be public or private, government-backed or government-sponsored, or it may be quite independent. If the help of state

bodies such as the **National Economic Development Council, Industrial and Commercial Finance Corporation**, etc., is not wanted then the problem of raising capital is normally handed over to an **issuing house** or a **merchant bank** which will decide on the most appropriate way to raise the monies required, often employing the aid of an **underwriter**.

There are too many ways of raising capital to be enumerated here though reference might be made to other terms defined, such as **prospectus; rights issue; placings; offer for sale; bonds**. Much depends on whether the funds are to be raised at home or abroad and on the location of the project in which they are to be invested. In the UK there are State incentives to invest in certain areas. ◊ **Development areas** ◊ **Enterprise zones** ◊ **Business expansion schemes**.

One important point to note is that there is a difference in principle between the capital market, where long-term funds are sought, and the banks and the **money market**, which are more concerned with the provision of short-term finance.

Capital profit A profit arising from the realization, either in cash or in kind, of an asset not bought originally for resale in the course of business. A distinction is necessary between capital profits made by individuals and those made by companies. Although both are assessable to **capital gains tax**, there are additional points to note *re* the capital profits of limited companies governed by the Companies Acts.

At one time capital profits of companies could only be distributed in strictly defined circumstances. The position was changed and clarified by the 1980 Companies Act, which permitted the distribution of capital profits in the manner of revenue profits provided that those profits were both real and realized, had not been previously capitalized and remained after all accumulated realized capital losses had been accounted for. Public companies must also show that the additional conditions appropriate to **distributable reserves** of public companies are satisfied.

The changes introduced by the 1980 Companies Act go some way towards preventing the abuses of **asset stripping** whilst leaving intact the option all companies enjoy of using capital profits, whether realized or unrealized, to fund the issue of **bonus shares**, though not redeemable bonus shares, which would defeat the purpose of the legislation.

Capital redemption reserve fund
When a **company** redeems **preference shares**, a sum equal to the **shares' nominal value** redeemed is transferred to this fund. The fund is treated as part of the **paid-up capital** of the company and cannot be used for **dividends**. The fund can, however, be used to issue paid-up **bonus shares**.

Capital reserves A class of **reserves** generally associated with limited companies, being those reserves which are not available for distribution to members because such distribution is forbidden by law. Until recently they also included reserves which in the opinion of the directors should be retained indefinitely as part of the capital of the company. The 1980 Companies Act virtually abolished the necessity to distinguish capital reserves in company balance sheets by redefining reserves as undistributable and **distributable reserves**. Those that

are undistributable are now generally required to be identified individually, e.g. **share premium** reserve or **capital redemption reserve**, and not grouped into a combined all-embracing figure for capital reserves.

Capital: serious loss The 1980 Companies Act introduced a provision stating that directors of public companies must call an extraordinary general meeting of shareholders at any time when there appears to have been serious loss of capital. The Act does not indicate any specific measures that should be taken at that meeting, which is merely for the purpose of apprising members of the deteriorating financial position.

A serious loss of capital is deemed to have occurred when the net assets of the company have been reduced to a figure of 50 per cent or less of called-up capital. The calculation of net assets in this context will involve valuing the company's fixed and current assets on one of two distinct bases, either on a going concern basis or on a 'break-up' basis. The latter will apply only where it is to be proposed that the company should go into **voluntary liquidation**.

Capital transfer tax (CTT) This was introduced in 1975 as part of a general attempt to tidy up the tax laws. It followed the earlier introduction of the **imputation system** but was concerned with transfers of capital, or capital assets, rather than with the taxation of income from trading or employment. In so far as it dealt with transfers of assets it replaced the system of **estate duty** that had prevailed for so many years and at the same time swallowed the **gift tax** and a great part of **capital gains tax**. As originally enacted, it applied to all gratuitous transfers of property by an individual during his lifetime and to the whole of his estate upon his death. As from 18 March 1986 CTT has been replaced by **inheritance tax**.

Capitalization The term refers to the **reserves** of limited companies which, either because they are not legally distributable or because the company wishes them to become a permanent part of capital, are given capital status by being allocated to members as bonus shares to rank alongside existing shares. The procedure for this is defined in the Companies Acts. ◊ **Capital reserves** ◊ **Scrip issue** ◊ **Capital profits** ◊ **Shares: pre-emptive right of purchase**.

Captain's entry Details of cargo given by the master of a ship when he wishes to unload at a port.

Captain's protest This is made by a captain on any damage suffered by his ship or cargo. It takes the form of an official declaration.

Car hire There are three kinds of car hire business: (1) the **taxi** business; (2) the businesses which hire cars for specified periods at an agreed rate, normally based on time and mileage; (3) a variation of (2), the organizations which put cars at the disposal of customers at particular places and for specified purposes. These customers may then leave the cars at agreed places at the end of their journeys, for example: a businessman arrives at London airport, takes a self-drive car for the remainder of his journey to Glasgow, as planes are grounded. The car is then collected at Glasgow by the owners.

Car hiring in this third sense should be distinguished from car rental, where a person, rather than purchase a car, rents one on a permanent basis. He does not own the car but enjoys all the privileges of ownership. The charges and responsibilities will depend on individual contracts. The car is usually replaced at specified intervals.

Car tax An indirect tax which was payable on cars made in, or imported into, the UK. It was in addition to **value added tax** and was non-reclaimable. It was halved in the 1992 Budget and abolished in the following year. Car tax should not be confused with road tax or vehicle licence duty.

Carat A unit in measurements of gold refinement. Pure gold is twenty-four carat. Gold is theoretically divided into twenty-four parts, so that eighteen carat gold would be eighteen parts gold and six parts alloy. ◊ **Hallmark**.

Carriage by rail ◊ **British Rail** ◊ **Private carrier** ◊ **Common carrier** ◊ **Freight liner** ◊ **Passenger's luggage**.

Carriage by road ◊ **Common carrier** ◊ **Private carrier** ◊ **Road haulage** ◊ **British Road Services Group** ◊ **National Freight Consortium PLC.**

Carry-over day A Stock Exchange term. Accounts are made up at stated intervals, normally of two weeks. The first day of each new account is known as the carry-over day, because those who have not the money, when the time comes for settlement, to take the shares they have asked a **stockbroker** to buy, often wish to carry over payment into the following accounting period. ◊ **Account days**.

Cartel A term to describe a number of companies banded together with the object of monopolizing a particular market and carving it up so that each company has an agreed area of operation.

Cascade tax

Price competition is eliminated as selling prices for the particular products are fixed centrally. Cartels are outlawed by the UK and the USA on the grounds that they are by definition monopolies not in the public interest. They were fairly common in Germany between the two world wars and the term is generally associated with that country. ◊ **Monopoly** ◊ **Monopolies and Mergers Commission**.

Cascade tax A form of turnover tax allied to **valued added tax**. In contemporary international trade it may apply to goods which pass through two or more different countries in the course of production, collecting different rates of tax in each; though storage in **bonded warehouses** may offset its effect by exempting the goods from tax in the country where they are bonded. It follows from this that goods produced in a country where the VAT is low may be cheaper to the ultimate consumer than goods passing through a variety of tax systems. It is also used as a synonym for turnover tax though, as can be seen from the above, it is not an exact synonym.

Case of need When a **bill of exchange** is endorsed 'case of need', a name is given of someone to whom the holder may apply if the bill is not paid.

Cash book In book-keeping, the basic book of account, where all receipts and payments are recorded. Receipts are shown as debits, payments as credits. Each side normally has two columns, one dealing with transactions in cash, the other with bank transactions. The payment side may have many supplementary analysis columns so that an amount paid can be written in the column appropriate to the type of expenditure. The totals of the various analysis columns will be ultimately transferred to the relevant expense accounts in the **nominal ledger**. The cash book is both a book of prime entry and a ledger account. Effectively, it is as if the cash account from the nominal ledger were kept in a separate book because of the multiplicity of entries. Consequently all debits and credits in the cash book are part of the **double-entry** system of book-keeping.

Cash and carry Strictly an epithet applied to a manufacturer's or **wholesaler's** warehouse from which retailers collect goods for resale to the general public – a kind of retailer's **supermarket**. Nowadays there is a tendency, alien to the interests of retailers, to allow the general public to bypass the middleman (the retailer) and buy direct from wholesalers through their cash and carry, thereby obtaining lower prices. However, there is a risk that in putting the retailer out of business the public will lose the benefit of good after-sale service and the reliable advice that the specialist retailer can give.

Cash discount The reduction given by a **creditor** on an account paid before a certain date, to encourage quick payment. It is usually stated as a percentage. Cash discounts may sometimes be quite high. The original price then effectively contains a penalty for late payment.

Cash dispenser A generic term applied to the individually labelled schemes operated by banks and some **building societies** whereby a customer can obtain cash from his account without needing to go into the bank (e.g. after hours). The normal method is to supply a customer with a coded plastic card which, when inserted into the particular machine outside the bank, will, as the result of the customer punching certain digits, cause specific sums in notes to be delivered and, at the same time, retain a record that will automatically result in the customer's account being charged with the amount. These dispensers should not be confused with 'change machines', which merely convert one coin into a number of coins of smaller denomination but of the same total value.

Cash flow statement ◊ **Source and disposition of funds**.

Cash-on-delivery The Royal Mail operates a COD service in connection with addresses within the UK, the Channel Islands and the Isle of Man. Only solicited goods up to the value of £350 may be sent COD and the documentation prescribed by the Post Office must be closely followed. Appropriate labels are obtainable at any post office. All parcels, letters and packets for which COD is required must be handed in at a post office and packets and letters must be sent by first-class registered post. Fees are payable by the sender when the item is accepted at the post office and he will be given a certificate of posting. For amounts exceeding £50 the addressee must pay the sum due at the office of delivery but for smaller amounts it will be collected by the postman. The Post Office will remit the sum collected to the sender by girocheque.

Cash price The **price** at which a **vendor** is prepared to part with **goods**: that is, the money to be tendered at the time when they are required. This is opposed to the **hire purchase** price, which includes **interest** over the period of payment.

Cashier Generically this term is applied

to a person who has the responsibility of accounting for cash transactions and keeping a record thereof. In a narrower sense it denotes a particular job at a **bank** – normally that of handling cash transactions with the public at the bank counter. ◊ **Teller**.

Casting vote The chairman of a meeting's vote, used if the votes cast for and against a particular resolution are the same. The casting vote is not a legal right – the chairman must be given it by, for example, the **articles of association**.

Causa causans The true cause, or the sum of all incidents bringing about a particular situation, as opposed to the *causa proxima*, the final cause or last straw, or the *causa remota*, the most remote cause. The *causa proxima* is normally taken to be the actual cause in legal proceedings.

Caveat emptor Legal expression meaning 'let the buyer beware'. Generally speaking the law presumes that a man uses common sense when buying **goods**, and if he suffers loss through his own fault he will not find the law sympathetic.

Caveat subscriptor A legal maxim meaning 'let the signer beware'. Anyone who signs a **contract** is bound by the terms even though he has not read them or is unaware of their precise legal effect.

This situation has been substantially modified by the Consumer Credit Act 1974 which provides, *inter alia*, that when a person enters into a credit sale agreement, other than on the shop premises, he must be afforded a 'cooling-off period' during which he may reconsider the contract and withdraw from it if he should so wish without incurring any penalty.

Ceefax ◊ Teletext.

Central Arbitration Committee
This was created by the Employment
Protection Act 1975 and began operations
on 1 February 1976. It replaces the Industrial Arbitration Board (Industrial
Court), which dated back to the Industrial Courts Act 1919. Although it works
on behalf of the Crown in parliament it
is an independent body and is not obliged
to heed directives from government ministers. Its task is to settle wage claims,
terms of employment, arbitrations and
disputes regarding equal pay which are
referred to it. Despite the statutory nature
of much of its work the emphasis is, as
far as possible, on informality and the
preservation of good industrial relations.
Claims are dealt with at fixed hearings
after written representations have been
submitted by both sides. The aim is to
adjudicate and also to advise. For this
reason membership of the committee consists of representatives of not only the
government, the employers and the employees but also persons with particular
knowledge in certain fields.

Although it may still act as an industrial court it prefers to settle disputes by
voluntary submission to arbitration and
agreement to accept any award made. In
making an award the committee is not
bound by any governmental pay policy
in operation at the time, though it is
unable to prevent the government setting
aside an award on the grounds that it
conflicts with such a policy. The Central
Arbitration Committee has been somewhat overshadowed in the public eye
by the rather more informed **Advisory
Conciliation and Arbitration Service**,
established in 1974.

Central Office of Information A government department acting as the central
government agency for preparation and
supply of publicity material required by
other government departments.

Central Statistical Office More concerned with economics than with commerce, it is a UK government department which collects and collates information regarding the national economy and
reproduces this information in statistical
form for, *inter alia*, publication in the
annual **Blue Book**.

Centre for inter-firm comparison
This was established by the British Institute of Management and the British Productivity Council in 1959. Membership
is voluntary and information supplied
confidential. The object is to advise businesses whether or not they are above the
average and suggest reasons for any apparent inefficiencies.

Certificate of damage A document
issued by a dock company when it receives damaged **goods**. The damage is
inspected by the docks surveyor, who
states the apparent nature and cause of
the damage.

Certificate of incorporation The
document issued by the Registrar of
Companies to a new **company** once it
has fulfilled the various conditions laid
down in the Companies Act. It gives the
recipient the legal status of 'company',
which affords the right to contract in the
company name as a legal persona. It is
still necessary for other conditions to be
met, however, before a public company
can be given permission to commence
business. ◊ **Trading certificate**.

Certificate of origin In the course
of international trade, and particularly
since the creation of the **European
Union,** any article exported must have

attached to it, or be accompanied by, a certificate of origin. This states the country from which the goods are deemed to have originated – although in the course of production they may have been partly processed in a variety of countries. The identification of the true country of origin is made necessary because tariff laws differ from one country to another and between the EU and the outside world, e.g. **tariffs** payable on goods brought into France are not constant but may vary according to whether they have originated in another EU country or, say, India or Hong Kong. Likewise, in the UK, goods originating in Common Market countries will be loaded with different tariff charges from those entering from Commonwealth countries. This fact has been at the root of many arguments opposing British entry into the **Common Market**. It is felt that the loss of traditional Commonwealth sources could be detrimental. In fact, special arrangements had to be made for certain British Dominions before the final step to membership of the EU was taken.

Certificates of deposit These were introduced into the British banking world in 1968 though they were common in the USA many years prior to then. Sterling certificates of deposit were certificates issued by banks in the UK, including British branches of foreign banks, stating that the sum shown thereon had been deposited in the bank. They were intended as a competitive instrument with which the **merchant banks** could attract funds away from the **clearing banks** by the offer of higher interest rates on up to five-year fixed deposits.

From 1971 the UK clearing banks themselves began issuing certificates of

deposit for large sums deposited with them by companies or other organizations. The deposit is for a fixed term and at a given rate of interest. The bank gains by the knowledge that it has the use of the money for the agreed period. The holder of the CD cannot cash it in before the stated date, but can use it as a negotiable instrument and obtain cash by selling it to a discount house which deals in CDs.

In recent years the CD market has broadened substantially and to the original sterling CDs have been added dollar CDs, Yen CDs and CDs in various other acceptable currencies. Trading in CDs is brisk and widespread and they now occupy an important sector of the London money market, one in which brokers play an active part.

Certification of transfer A shareholder transferring part of his holding hands his **share certificate** plus a transfer form to the **company**. Before the transfer form is handed to the purchaser the company marks on it that a certificate for x **shares** has been lodged at the company's office. This is signed by the **secretary** and is said to be certification of transfer. It is accepted by the **Stock Exchange** as a good delivery of shares. The company then proceeds to make out two new certificates. ◊ **Share transfer** ◊ **Talisman**.

Certified Accountants, Chartered Association of One of the major bodies of accountants, whose members are recognized by the Department of Trade and Industry as properly qualified to audit the accounts of limited companies. ◊ **Auditor**. The Association is an examining body but differs from the Institutes of **Chartered Accountants** in that it derives its membership more from

97

without than from within private practice and does not insist on 'articles' as a prerequisite for membership. ◊ **Articled clerk**. It therefore gains a large part of its members directly from industry, where applicants have studied accountancy whilst continuing full-time employment. Increasingly, selected students are given extended leave on full pay to participate in special **sandwich courses** provided by technical colleges and geared to the examination requirements of the Association. Members may be Fellows (FCCA) or Associates (ACCA). The Association derives from the Corporation of Accountants (founded 1891) and the London Association of Certified Accountants (founded 1904). These were merged into the Association of Certified and Corporate Accountants, which in recent years was given its present title of Chartered Association of Certified Accountants. It is a company incorporated by Royal Charter.

Cesser clause A clause in charter agreements meaning that a charterer's responsibility ends when the cargo is loaded. The shipowner may, however, have a **lien** on the cargo for **freight** charges.

Cesser of action This applies in a **liquidation** where after a winding-up petition, the court may stay proceedings pending against the **company**. When a winding-up order is made actions must be stayed. This also applies in **bankruptcy** after a petition has been presented.

Chain store A shop, or store, one of many in common ownership, each in a different location; not to be confused with a **department store** or **supermarket** though either of these might be a member of a chain-store group. Some of the better-known chain stores are Woolworths (one of the earliest), Boots and Marks & Spencer. They are present in the main shopping area of most towns in the country. Structually, they are organized on a branch basis. There is one main shop, or non-trading head office with a registered name, which operates the other shops over a vast area. One contemporary development which could be against the public interest has been the merging of different chains of shops without altering the name. One can have the disquieting situation where three or four well-known distinct chain shops in the same street are no longer in direct competition but in the hands of a single company. This can help the retailer through retaining goodwill acquired but will not be to the good of consumers, who have effectively lost their range of choice and will, in the extreme case, be shown the same goods in all the shops.

Chairman of a company Normally the senior person in a **company**, and often merely a figurehead who takes no active part but presides as chairman at meetings of **directors** (a chairman is necessary by law on such occasions). An active chairman is often both chairman and **managing director** or **chief executive**. ◊ **Chairman's report**.

Chairman's report A report, generally made annually on the activities of a **company**, and signed by the chairman. It is normally given at the **annual general meeting** and included in the annual report, often accompanied by a photograph of the chairman radiating benevolence. It may contain tributes to staff, and generally discusses the results of the year and the prospects for the future. The tendency is to draw attention to success and away from failure, thus painting a picture of an organization emanating from Utopia. It is not one of the documents that have, by law, to be issued by the company each year. ◊ **Chairman of a company**.

Chamber of commerce In the UK, chambers of commerce are voluntary organizations financed by members' subscriptions. In this manner they are distinguished from chambers in many other countries, where state aid is relied upon. Generally speaking, any group of persons can form an alliance and call it a chamber of commerce, but if they wish to belong to the national and official parent body, the Association of British Chambers of Commerce, they must abide by its rules. To join, they must apply to the Department of Trade and Industry for recognition as an incorporated body under one of the various Companies Acts. The Department of Trade and Industry will not allow the use of the name Chamber of Commerce unless it is satisfied that the association is financially secure and truly representative of trade and industry within its area.

Chambers of commerce should be distinguished from the more casual organizations of retailers often known as **chambers of trade**; the latter have a far more limited membership and a narrower purpose. Chambers of commerce represent all branches of trade and industry, whether manufacturers, distributors, middle-men or those who carry on professional services ancillary to the business community. Their *raison d'être* is to protect and promote the interests of members either by collecting or disseminating information or by making representations to the government where legislation affecting the basic interests of members is in prospect. They are not generally em-

powered to take part in wage negotiations and are strictly non-political.

The Association of British Chambers of Commerce, formed in 1860, represents over 60,000 members in different chambers, of which perhaps 50 per cent are in **manufacturing industry**. The main task of the Association lies in attempting to coordinate the efforts and aspirations of its various members' chambers and, where appropriate and feasible, to represent them at a national level.

In the same way as individual chambers are run by an elected council, so the parent Association has its council and committees. This enables it to link up with national chambers in other countries and has led to the founding of both the Federation of Commonwealth Chambers of Commerce and the larger International Chamber of Commerce. The latter has close contact with the United Nations Economic and Social Council, by which it may be consulted. Through its own International Council, it also has strong and helpful links with both individual governments and intergovernmental agencies.

Chamber of shipping An organization of ship-owners and others interested in the shipping trade, performing functions similar to those of a **chamber of commerce**, i.e. looking after the interests of shippers and ship-owners, and making representations on their behalf.

Chamber of trade Often confused with the **chambers of commerce**, a chamber of trade is an organization set up by retailers in a locality to protect their common interests particularly in such matters as local authority rating policies. Since 1897 it has had a parent body known as the National Chamber of Trade, which, like the Association of

British Chambers of Commerce, represents the genuine interests of its members (the various local chambers) on a national level.

Champerty This occurs when a person pays for a court action in which he is not sufficiently personally involved in return for a share of any damages received. It is illegal and any **contract** concerning champerty is also illegal. ◊ **Maintenance**.

Chandler Originally one who made and sold candles; now any person selling groceries, provisions, etc. ◊ **Ship's chandler**.

Chaps & Town Clearing Company Limited This was established under the APACS umbrella in 1985 and operates the two daily high-value same-day clearings in the UK. CHAPS is an acronym for Clearing House Automated Payment System and provides a same-day guaranteed sterling electronic credit transfer service within the UK. Originally the minimum amount transferable through CHAPS was £1,000, but since 1 January 1993 this has been reduced to zero. Consequently CHAPS now accounts for some 99 per cent of the company's clearings.

Town Clearing is a low-volume generally manual same-day paper clearing for cheques or other items exceeding £500,000 and handles only such items drawn on or paid into banks within a limited area of the City of London.

In both CHAPS and Town Clearing daily settlements are effected through members' accounts at the Bank of England. Members include most of the banks operating within the UK.

Charge A term used in commerce in two major senses: first, as a synonym for price, where sale of goods or services is concerned (though usually one speaks of a *charge* for services and the *price* of goods); second, in the context of **mortgages** and the lending of money on security. The creditor is said to have a 'charge' on the property, real or personal, which is provided as **security** for the loan. The property need not change hands and it is more common for the relevant documents of title or a **bill of sale** to be given as security. In certain instances the creditor must register this charge. ◊ **Register of charges**. Many charges on the property of a company cannot be enforced until they have been registered at the Companies Registration Office and, in a liquidation, they will be honoured not in the order incurred but in the order registered. The company itself is equally bound to register such charges. Although it may not be necessary to have all charges on the assets of a company registered, it is safer for the creditor to do so lest there be any doubt.

Again, charges on land must be registered at the Land Registry if they are to be effective against a subsequent purchaser, though possession of the title deeds on a legal mortgage should make registration unnecessary for the protection of the lender. Charges secured on a **bill of sale** must also be registered under the Bills of Sale Act. Charges by way of securing a debt fall into two main groups: **floating charges** and **fixed charges**. Floating charges are generally associated with loans to businesses and especially to companies; the charge is not on a particular item of property but on the company's assets generally. It remains despite changes in the composition of those assets. A fixed charge, on the other hand, refers to a specified asset, e.g. a defined piece of land or a building, whether freehold or leasehold.

The whole subject of charges and the registration thereof is a complicated one and the subject of much litigation. It is not possible to deal with it comprehensively here and any person confronted with a problem in this field is advised to take professional advice.

Charge account Another name for a **credit account** offered by a retailer, the purpose of which is to attract more trade by giving customers extended credit terms. Such accounts are now controlled by the **Consumer Credit Act 1974**, which not only makes the retailer obtain a licence but generally protects consumers from the consequences of their possibly over-hasty inclination to jump into credit agreements without proper advice. ◊ **Credit** ◊ **Credit card** ◊ **Hire purchase**.

Chargeable gain A capital profit on which tax is payable. ◊ **Capital transfer tax** ◊ **Capital gain** ◊ **Capital gains tax**.

Charges forward The buyer pays for the **goods** and the cost of sending them only when he receives them.

Charging order A court order attaching to a debtor's **goods** for the benefit of a **creditor**. If the debt is not paid within a specified time the creditor may have the right to sell the goods for his own benefit. ◊ **Lien**.

Charter by demise A charter agreement which gives the charterer complete control of the ship. It is navigated by his own men. Such **contracts** are not very common today. ◊ **Chartering, marine**.

Charter party ◊ **Chartering, marine**.

Chartered accountant A member of the Institute of Chartered Accountants in England and Wales (or in Scotland or Ireland). The Institute, being the governing body, establishes certain rules of conduct to which the chartered accountant must conform at his peril. ◊ **Auditor**.

Chartered Accountants, Institutes of There are three in number in the UK: the Institute of Chartered Accountants of Scotland (membership denoted by CA), the Institute of Chartered Accountants in England and Wales and the Institute of Chartered Accountants in Ireland (membership of both denoted by ACA or FCA – the fellowship automatically being granted ten years after becoming a member). The Scottish Institute is the oldest, receiving its royal charter in 1854 although its present name dates only from 1951. The English Institute received its Royal Charter in 1880 and the Irish Institute in 1888. All three institutes are independent of each other, but members of each are recognized by the Department of Trade and Industry as qualified to audit the accounts of public limited companies.

Membership of each institute is attained after serving a required period under articles to an existing member and passing the examinations set by the parent body, with certain exemptions afforded to graduates. All three institutes recognize similar codes of practice and seek to establish a high degree of competence among members. This aim is supported both by the publication of standards of accounting practice and by a disciplinary committee to deal with members who stray from accepted norms of behaviour. It should be noted that the standards referred to have no legal effect and, in addition, are the only part of the 'accepted code of practice' in writing. However, although published 'standards' are not binding on members, they could well be quoted in a court action for negligence where the defending accountant had not observed them. ◊ **Accounting standards** ◊ **Negligence of auditor**.

Each institute publishes its own journal on a monthly basis and issues a report and accounts to members at the time of its annual general meeting, at which members of the governing council of the particular institute are appointed.

Chartered agent A **broker** responsible for finding space for cargo on board ship.

Chartered company A **company** created by royal charter. These were once more common than they are today – they were used for developing international trade. One well-known company still in existence is the Hudson's Bay Company, or more properly the Governor and Company of Adventurers of England trading into Hudson's Bay. This was formed in 1670. Other famous chartered companies include the East India Company and the South Sea Company.

Today charters tend to be reserved for special organizations, such as the governing bodies of certain professions. These companies must observe the rules of their charter. Members have no personal liability unless this is stated in the charter. There is, however, another type of chartered company known as a patented company, formed by letters patent. Here the liability is unlimited unless the terms of the letters patent state otherwise.

Chartered Secretaries and Administrators, Institute of This was founded in 1891, and given a royal charter in 1902. Members are not only **company secretaries**. The Institute's objectives are: (1) to provide examinations to test the capacity of potential administrators in the fields of commerce, industry and the public service; (2) to hold conferences and meetings and publish papers, documents and lists of members; (3) to represent members' interests in dealings with government departments and the public; (4) to provide professional supervision over membership through a disciplinary committee. Members may be Associates (ACIS) or Fellows (FCIS). An Associate must be twenty-one or over, have passed the necessary examinations and have had appropriate experience (which might be as much as six years).

Chartered Surveyor ◊ **Chartered Surveyors, Royal Institution of.**

Chartered Surveyors, Royal Institution of Formed in 1868, and given a royal charter in 1881, this is the oldest and largest professional body of chartered surveyors in the world. It deals with all sections of the surveying profession. Most senior posts are open only to members of the Institution. It has a code of professional conduct. A member is accepted as an authority on building costs, practice and contract procedure. Education is carried on by professional experience and official examinations. To become a Corporate Member a person must pass the final examination and have had five years' experience. Various exemptions are available to candidates with degrees or similar qualifications. Members may use the letters FRICS or ARICS depending on whether they are Fellows or Associates. The members specialize in their examinations in either general surveying, agriculture and land agency, quantity surveying, land surveying, or mining surveying.

Chartering, marine A vessel is chartered when it is, as it were, hired in part or whole for a particular time or a particular purpose. The **contract** is known as a charter party. Where the contract does not otherwise specify it is covered by the Carriage of Goods by Sea Act. There are various forms of charter. ◊ **Voyage charter** ◊ **Time charter** ◊ **Charter by demise**.

The sum paid by the charterer is known as **freight**. Charter conditions vary considerably: the ship may be taken over completely, or with the shipowner's crew.

Chattels Movable as opposed to real property.

Cheap jack A person who specializes in selling **goods** quickly by somewhat unorthodox means. He normally obtains a quantity of goods cheaply (bankrupt stock perhaps) and sells in the manner of an **auctioneer** either in the open air or in empty shop premises. He appears to sell items of value at ridiculously low prices initially in the expectation that this will enable him to sell the remainder of his stock without difficulty. He relies upon the gullibility of his customers, and moves from place to place depending on circumstances and the police. ◊ **Mock auction** ◊ **Street trader**.

Cheap money Money is said to be cheap when credit is easily obtainable and interest rates are reasonably low. Governments sometimes deliberately foster cheap money policy with the intention of promoting a high level of investment. This happened in the UK in the years preceding and immediately following the Second World War, when government interference kept the **bank rate** very low and, by doing so, encouraged heavy borrowing by industry to increase production. Part of the consequent increase in the money supply was swallowed up in government securities, such as 2½ per cent **consols**, which in turn gave the government the funds to forward its own investment projects. This era came to an end in the early 1950s. The policy rebounded with a vengeance in later years when the increase in interest rates impoverished many innocent investors, who saw their **gilt-edged** securities fall catastrophically in capital value. The State suffered rather less as the period of rising prices and falling redemption values of stocks reduced the real value of interest payable on undated securities and lowered the cost of redeeming the dated stocks through the market, before the stocks matured.

Check trading An old system of credit trading which enables people to buy goods on credit without entering into a **hire purchase** agreement or opening a credit account with the supplier. Prospective purchasers 'buy' checks from a company (usually a finance company), which they pay for over an agreed period. These checks can then be used for the purchase of goods at retailers who have 'joined' the scheme. The retailer then redelivers the checks to the financing company, which will give cash for them after making a service charge, i.e. it discounts them much as a **discount house** will buy **bills of exchange**.

The financing company may lose on some defaulting customers but stands to gain on three counts: (1) its discount charge to the retailer; (2) its charge, if any, to the customer; (3) the investment benefits on the monies paid in by the customers (in the same way as a bank can profit from monies held on current accounts), which although individually fluctuating represent a fairly large constant balance in hand.

Chemist Amongst other things, a dealer in medicinal drugs.

Cheque Originally a **bill of exchange**, drawn on a banker and payable on demand, it afforded a straightforward method of settling outstanding debts without incurring the risks attendant to the carrying around of large sums of ready money. Once the preserve of clearing banks, cheques are now also drawn on those building societies which offer their customers accounts for that purpose.

Cheques may be 'open' or 'crossed'. An open cheque is payable on presentation by the holder at the drawee's premises and, consequently, care must be taken to avoid the cheque falling into the wrong hands and leaving the true holder no redress. A crossed cheque can only be paid into the bank account of the person presenting it for payment – not necessarily the account of the original payee as a cheque can be negotiated by proper endorsement even if crossed 'not negotiable' (◊ **Cheque crossings**). Although most crossings have no legal force the law now states that a cheque crossed 'account payee' can only be paid into the account of the original payee and that such a cheque can no longer serve as a negotiable instrument.

The introduction of the **cheque card** has been of considerable help in reducing cheque fraud because a stolen cheque book is only of limited use without the backing of the relevant cheque card.

Cheque, alteration of Bankers are wary of altered **cheques**. Alterations should be initialled by the drawer or customer. When a crossed cheque is opened, the full signature of the drawer should appear. Bankers will even then refuse to pay over the counter unless they know the customer.

Cheque card Often wrongly called a **credit card**, this is a card issued by a bank branch to its customer; it **guarantees** that any **cheque**, up to the amount stated on the card (e.g. £50), issued by a customer will be honoured by the bank. The person taking the cheque must ensure that the cheque card is not out of date, that the account numbers on the card and cheque are the same, and that the specimen signature on the card corresponds with that on the cheque. The number of the card should be written on the reverse of the cheque by the person taking the cheque, not by the person issuing it. Though it is common practice for the latter to do this it should be noted that, if the bank could prove that this was so, then the guarantee would be inoperative. One further important point: in so far as the bank becomes responsible for the cheque immediately the number is entered thereon, the person issuing it cannot stop payment as he can with a normal cheque transaction.

Cheque and Credit Clearing Company Limited This was established in 1985 as part of the structure under the APACS umbrella and operates two bulk clearings, the Cheque Clearing and the Credit Clearing, both in London and covering the whole of England and Wales. Inter-member settlement is effected at the end of a three-day cycle through members' accounts at the Bank of England. Settlement of cheques and credits originating in Scotland and Northern Ireland comes outside the remit of APACS and such business in handled by clearings in Edinburgh and Belfast respectively.

The members of the Cheque and

Credit Clearing Company comprise the major UK banks and certain large building societies.

Cheque crossings Payments of large sums of money are for obvious reasons normally effected by **cheque** rather than by cash and the payer will wish to take the maximum precautions against the possibility of the cheque falling into the wrong hands. A cheque made out as payable on demand could be cashed or negotiated by any person into whose hands it might accidentally fall, whether lost in transit or dishonestly obtained. To minimize such a possible loss it is customary to 'cross' the cheque. Historically the crossing, two parallel lines running transversely across the cheque, struck out the word 'on demand', thus denying the bank on which it was drawn the right to pay out cash across the counter in exchange for it. Although those words no longer appear on cheques the crossing is still effected in the same manner and is accepted as being an express instruction to the receiving banker that the monies are to be paid into an account at that bank – the account being either that of the payee or, where the cheque has been endorsed by the payee, into the account of the person presenting the cheque.

Additional precautions are also often taken. At one time the receiving bank was designated between the crossing, though with the reduction in the number of banks this practice has disappeared. The words '& Co.', written between the lines, are a relic of those days; this allowed the payee to put the name of his bank before '& Co.', thus making the general crossing specific. The most effective modern practice is to write the words 'not negotiable' between the lines. This has the defined legal effect of erasing the negotiability of the cheque. Although it can still lawfully be passed from one person to another, the person taking the cheque, whether or not in good faith, will never obtain a better title to the monies stated thereon than the person from whom he obtained it. This means that if the cheque were to be stolen the thief, having no good title to it, could not legally pass any title on and the true owner would be entitled to recover his loss from any banker who paid out on it. However, the Cheques Acts do give certain protection to bankers acting in good faith and without negligence. ◊ **Cheques: protection of banker**.

Until recently the words 'account payee' or 'account payee only' written between the crossed lines did no more than put the banker on alert. Now, however, they have been given legal force and any cheque so crossed can only be paid into the account of the named payee. ◊ **Crossing, general** ◊ **Crossing, special** ◊ **Negotiable instrument**.

Cheques: endorsement Cheques, being **bills of exchange**, are transferable by **endorsement**. No endorsement however is necessary where they are paid into the account of the payee. A **bank** will however still require an endorsement where the payment is over the counter or to a person other than the payee.

Cheques: protection of banker Where a banker in good faith and in the normal course of business pays a **cheque** drawn on himself and the **endorsement** does not appear to be irregular, he will not normally incur any liability if the cheque is irregularly endorsed. The **bank** is not expected to know the signatures of its customers' **creditors**. This protection does not apply if the cheque is paid outside hours or if crossings or other instructions are not observed. So far as the collecting banker is concerned, if he collects the cheque for a person and that person has in fact no right to the money, he will not be liable to the true owner when he has acted in good faith and without negligence. The person for whom he collects must be a customer, that is a person with an account at the bank. The banker could be liable if he opened an account for a person not known to him and without good references. Negligence is a matter of interpretation: a banker would be negligent in collecting a cheque for an employee when the cheque is made out to the firm, even where it appears to be endorsed.

Cheques: returned to drawer When a **cheque** is incorrectly made out, either innocently or fraudulently, or if it is drawn on an account without sufficient funds to pay it, the bank will return it to the person presenting it, having written on it the words 'return to drawer'. This has made creditors or vendors reluctant to take cheques in payment for debts due or goods sold. The reluctance has been reinforced by the traditional noncooperation of the banks themselves in rectifying errors or disclosing addresses of customers so that the creditor can seek redress.

The growth of credit trading and the continual escalation in the number of **current accounts** at banks has considerably increased the use of cheques in the commercial world and traders stand to lose much business by not accepting them. The banks have helped somewhat by encouraging the use of **cheque cards**, which carry a banker's guarantee, but the position is still far from satisfactory. To facilitate the correction of inno-

cent errors it is usual for the payer to write his address on the back of the cheque – this enables the customer to be contacted without having to ask the bank itself to send the cheque to him. This is no safeguard against fraud, however, and the banks will not follow up 'bad' cheques on behalf of the creditor; nor are they legally obliged to do anything apart from return the cheque to the person who paid it in. However, most banks will, on the strength of personal knowledge of their customers, re-present the cheque on up to three occasions, notifying the creditor that they are so doing and asking for his authority to do so. The only redress available to the creditor, other than taking legal action for payment, is to take advantage of any untoward delay on the part of the bank in returning the cheque and then claim from that bank on the grounds of negligence. Banks make a charge to customers for any cheques paid in and subsequently dishonoured. ◊ **Banker, disclosure of information by** ◊ **Banker's revocation of authority to pay cheques**.

Chief executive Term used to describe the person who has overall responsibility for the day-to-day running of an organization, whether a trading company or some other corporate body. In the case of a limited company the chief executive is normally the **managing director**, appointed by the **board of directors** on the authority of the members.

Child benefit Child benefits paid through the Post Office by the DSS replaced the old family allowances and allowances given for dependent children against income tax. Child benefit is available for each child up to and including the age of sixteen and for children in full-time education up to the age of eighteen.

Chinese Walls Within the financial services industry there is an ongoing tendency for existing organizations to broaden the spectrum of services offered and for smaller suppliers of specific services to merge with suppliers of different but compatible products and thereby become a more competitive force within a rapidly expanding market.

In circumstances such as these difficulties necessarily arise when information received or advice given by one department is of such a sensitive nature that it cannot be shared with other departments within the organization without breaching client confidentiality or even legal obligation. A fair example might be of a merchant bank which, in addition to acting as financial adviser on take-over situations, also operates a market-making department. For a market-maker to be privy to the details or time-table of a proposed take-over bid would be quite contrary to the law regarding **insider dealings**. Where the possibility exists for such conflicts of interest, then a rigid system of compartmentalization must be installed and properly supervised. The internal barriers which are erected – barriers which though invisible must be secure – are known as Chinese Walls. Needless to say, such barriers are by no means invincible. Should they be breached the resultant damage would destroy whatever measure of goodwill that particular multi-service provider once possessed, and goodwill once sacrificed is almost impossible to reinstate.

Consequently efficient Chinese Walls are a *sine qua non* for a successful provider of an extensive range of financial services, whether these be from the High Street branch of a lesser known bank or a city institution of historic integrity and international renown.

Choses-in-action Strictly speaking a chose-in-action is a right to, but not possession of, property or a sum of money; taking possession may be contingent on some event. The right can be enforced in a court of law. Examples of choses-in-action are debts, **negotiable instruments**, **mortgages**, **insurance** policies, **warrants**. A particular quality of a chose-in-action is that it can be assigned to another person, though this may be conditional upon permission being obtained from some other party. ◊ **Choses-in-possession** ◊ **Assignment**.

Choses-in-possession Goods or other rights which a person has in his possession and for his enjoyment. ◊ **Choses-in-action**.

Circuity of action If a **bill of exchange** comes back, in the course of its tenure, to the person who first signed it it may be renegotiated. However, if this happens that person forfeits any right of action against those who put their names to it between the date of first signature and that of renegotiation. ◊ **Endorsement**.

Circulating capital ◊ **Working capital**.

City Code on Take-overs and Mergers A code of conduct concerning **takeover bids** and **merger** agreements. It originated on the initiative of the government and the **Bank of England** as far back as 1959. In its present form it was compiled in 1968. Those compiling it were the City Working Party, that is, the Association of **Investment Trust Companies**, the **British Insurance Association**, the **Issuing Houses Association**, the **Accepting Houses Committee**, the London Clearing Bankers, the **Stock Exchange**, the

Confederation of British Industry and the National Association of Pension Funds. As the code is not legally enforceable, a panel was appointed to supervise its implementation. This Panel, known as the Panel on Take-overs and Mergers, was made up from members of the City Working Party. There has been some discussion recently as to the desirability of introducing legally enforceable rules as it appears that, however good the Panel's intentions, without any ultimate sanction they have no real power, although in certain limited areas they do receive the backing of the SIB through the Financial Services Act. The Stock Exchange can theoretically withdraw permission to deal in the shares of a company breaking the rules but where big names are involved there may naturally be some reluctance to act.

The Panel is always available to give advice to parties involved, that is, to the offeror company or the offeree company, but not to individual shareholders as to whether they should sell their shares. The principles involved and the specific rules on the conduct of take-overs or mergers are contained in a booklet, *City Code on Take-overs and Mergers*, available from the Secretary, The Issuing Houses Association. It is not possible to give these principles or rules in detail here but one or two points of general interest are:

(1) A bid should be fair to all the shareholders of the offeree company. Minorities should be protected and no particular category of shareholders should obtain an advantage. For this reason **directors** are asked to put their personal interests aside, and if private dealings in shares are made after the announcement of a bid at terms more advantageous than the bid price, similar terms should be offered to all the other shareholders.

(2) When a bid is made it should be made to the board of the offeree company. This company should then communicate immediately with shareholders, initially by press advertisement, and secondly by a written communication. Where no definite bid has been made but rumours are leading to speculation in shares, the board should make a statement so that the shareholders of the offeree company and possibly also of the offeror company should be fully aware of what is going on.

(3) There is a fairly general insistence that clandestine dealings in shares prior to a merger and even after the announcement of a prospective bid should be prevented.

(4) The importance of keeping shareholders informed is stressed. At the earliest possible opportunity after a bid a full statement, preferably a joint statement by both companies concerned, should be sent to the shareholders. Where this statement is followed by a further statement giving figures or reasons for accepting or rejecting the bid, the provisions of the Third Schedule of the Companies Act 1985 concerning **prospectuses** should be observed.

(5) When an offer has been made any dealings in the shares of either company by the companies themselves or any other interested parties should be reported to the Stock Exchange.

(6) It is very important to prevent a false market arising in the shares of either offeror or offeree company and both parties should take all possible steps to avoid this.

(7) It is most important that the directors, particularly of the offeree company, should act honestly and in the interests of all shareholders. They should therefore (a) take competent advice if necessary,

(b) refrain from any action aimed at frustrating the bid without consulting the shareholders, (c) make no material changes in the business of the company while the bid is being considered, (d) make all necessary information available to shareholders without giving any one group a particular advantage, (e) where they themselves have a controlling interest, tread carefully, and if possible seek the advice of the Panel.

(8) After a bid is made the true identity of the bidder must be disclosed and also the number of shares already held.

(9) Bids for less than 100 per cent of the shares of a company are not considered desirable.

(10) Unless the Panel agrees otherwise any person acquiring, either alone or in concert with others, shares which bring the holding to a level where 30 per cent or more of voting rights in the company has been reached, then such person or persons must extend an offer to all shareholders in the class of shares where they have such a holding and such an offer must include a cash alternative equal to the highest price paid by the offeror during the preceding twelve months. The only permitted conditions to the offer are that it will lapse if acceptances fail to bring the holding to over 50 per cent or if the offer should be referred either to the Monopolies and Mergers Commission or to the EU.

(11) Again, unless the Panel decrees otherwise, if any person or persons holding alone or in concert between 30 per cent and 50 per cent of the voting rights in a company acquires an additional 2 per cent within a twelve-month period, then an offer as described in (10) must be made.

(12) Where an offer has lapsed or been withdrawn then it cannot be repeated for at least a twelve-month period without the consent of the Panel, nor can the offeror acquire such a quantity of shares which, if this prohibition did not exist, would make such an offer obligatory.

City terminal service An air transport term for the surface carriage of consignments between the carrier's city handling station and the relevant airport.

Civil Aviation Authority (CAA) This body was set up in 1971, to act from 1 April 1972, as a result of the findings of the Edwards Committee, published in a report called 'British Air Transport in the Seventies'. The objects of the CAA, bringing together the responsibilities of various other loosely connected bodies, were prescribed as fourfold: (1) to ensure the sound development of the UK civil air transport industry in providing a safe, financially viable and efficient transport service with the maximum benefit to the public both in frequency of services and reasonableness of charges; (2) to provide for competition with the then **British Airways Board** and now **British Airways** plc in both charter and other services on those routes covered by (1); (3) to encourage the air transport industry to do everything possible to aid the national balance of payments; and (4) subject to the above, to 'further the reasonable interests of users of air transport services'. The CAA is constitutionally independent of the government and its staff are not considered civil servants. It maintains the United Kingdom Register of Civil Aircraft, which establishes the nationality of aircraft registered therein. It also maintains the Register of Aircraft Mortgages.

Civil engineer A person concerned with the design and construction of engineering works. Members of the Institution of **Civil Engineers** are known as chartered civil engineers.

Civil Engineers, Institution of This was established in 1828, and is the governing body for **civil engineers**. To become a member a candidate must obtain an engineering degree or some similar qualification, have had a number of years' practical experience, and pass an oral examination. There are rules of professional conduct and a disciplinary committee.

Classified advertisement The type of advertisement usually contained in newspapers and magazines under a specific column heading or classification common within the newspaper world, e.g. situations vacant; flats to let; births, marriages and deaths; plant for hire, etc. It is normally paid for on a lineage basis, i.e. at so many pence per word.

Classified directories ◊ **Yellow Pages** ◊ **Telephone Directories**.

Claused bill A bill of lading containing **endorsements**. ◊ **Clean bill of lading**.

Clean bill of lading At one time this was a **bill of lading** free from any **endorsement**, now it is one which bears no superimposed clauses expressly declaring a defective condition of the goods or packaging. Bills with endorsements are known as **claused bills** ◊ **Foul bill of lading** ◊ **Received for shipment**.

Clear days When reckoning days in a **contract**, clear days do not include the days when the contract commences or terminates.

Clearance outwards ◊ **Exporters' declarations**.

Clearing banks Commercial banks which are members of APACS, which facilitates the settling of daily balances due between the member banks arising from cheque and cash transactions throughout the country, both by the general public and individual banks themselves. At present the clearing banks are the 'big four' (Lloyds, Midland, Barclays and NatWest) plus Coutts, a subsidiary of NatWest, Royal Bank of Scotland, Co-operative Bank, Abbey National, Clydesdale, Girobank, Yorkshire Bank, Bank of Scotland and Trustee Savings Bank.

Clerk A person concerned with keeping records.

Clock cards Cards used in a factory to record the time worked by employees paid on a time basis. Times are stamped automatically by a clock in an office or entrance to the works when an employee arrives and again when he leaves.

Close company A **company** controlled by the **directors** or by five or fewer participants (for this purpose a director could be a person who is not specifically appointed). It suffers from various disadvantages, the principal one being that it may be liable to a tax direction; that is, if the tax inspector is of the opinion (and there are certain tests) that insufficient profits are being distributed in order to avoid tax, he may make a direction that a certain proportion of the undistributed profits are to be treated as distributed for the purposes of collecting tax (they are theoretically apportioned among the persons who would have received them).

Changes in tax legislation have rendered these powers afforded to the Inspector of Taxes less important. They are now rarely applied except where the income of the company derives from investment income rather than trading profit.

Closed indent ◊ **Open indent**.

Closed shops A restrictive practice, though not a registrable one under the Restrictive Practices Act, whereby trade unions and other associations of employees insist on membership of their union or association as a precondition for employment in the activity which their union or association represents. Originally such practices were intended to maintain standards of craftsmanship and discipline, the standards of which were set and supervised by the governing body, i.e. the trade union or craft guild. In more recent years, however, the closed shop has been used less for the maintenance of standards and more for its value as a power base in negotiating terms of employment and pay. Needless to say, the closed shop is not the prerogative of trade unions but is also operated by professional associations, which generally claim greater justification. ◊ **Employment legislation**.

Closing price The **price** at which shares are quoted at the close of any day's **Stock Exchange** dealings. The prices can be found in the **Official List**, published daily by the Stock Exchange. Two prices are given for any share. This is because a **market-maker** always quotes two prices: one for buying and one for selling. When shares are being valued the **mean price** is usually taken. The closing prices are also given in certain daily newspapers. The list is not necessarily complete as the option of publication lies with the **company**. The price given in the newspaper may be in double form, or may be the middle market price.

Coastguards An organization originally formed to prevent smuggling, but now a general coast police force in the employment of the Admiralty.

Coasters Vessels trading along the coast, dealing only with home trade.

Coasting trade ◊ **Coasters**.

Coemption Buying up the whole supply of any commodity. ◊ **Cornering the market**.

Cohabitation Under the law of **contract**, where a man and a woman are living together the woman has an implied right to pledge the man's credit for **necessaries**, irrespective of whether they are married.

Cold calling Direct and unsolicited approaches to third parties, by mail or by telephone, with the object of obtaining business. Persons to be approached are selected at random or taken from lists prepared by specialist agencies in which names and addresses are arranged according to leisure interests, social groups or employment categories.

There is a long-established tradition of selling consumer goods in this way through what is known as the **mail order firm**, and in that context the visibility of the product, the high level of competition and the facilities for returning substandard items have all contributed to the protection of the consumer.

The success enjoyed by the mail order firms has encouraged those offering services to employ similar direct-selling techniques. In so far as personal contact is often integral to the provision of a service, the methods favoured tend to centre on direct approach by telephone. Unfortunately, because the quality of services provided can usually only be judged in retrospect, this area of commercial activity has provided too many opportunities for the less scrupulous to take advantage of the ill-informed. As a result, the epithet 'cold calling' has become virtually a term of abuse, and restrictions on the use of this method of selling are contained in the Financial Services Act 1986.

Collateral agreement An agreement or **contract** running alongside an existing agreement or contract. If the initial contract is void the collateral agreement is not necessarily void: much depends on whether the second contract restates the void agreement. However, if the initial contract is illegal, the collateral agreement will also be illegal. ◊ **Contract, illegal** ◊ **Contract, void**.

Collateral security Security given for a loan. It is often additional security given over and above assets on which the loan is charged.

Collective bargaining A term normally applied to the process of wage fixing in a free economy. The rates of pay for various categories within the workforce are agreed by direct negotiation between the employers and the trade unions, through agents appointed by each party to act for them. The rates may be fixed on a national scale or merely within one business organization. ◊ **Advisory Conciliation and Arbitration Service** ◊ **Central Arbitration Committee**.

Collision clause ◊ **Running-down clause**.

Colporteur A **hawker** or **pedlar** of books or newspapers, particularly religious ones.

Commencement of business ◊ **Trading certificate**.

Commercial Accountants, Society of This was founded in 1942 as a professional organization for accountants employed in commerce and industry. Membership is open to all employed in accountancy work and is obtained by examination and experience. Members may be Fellows (F Comm A) or Associates (A Comm A).

Commercial credit ◊ **Acceptance credit** ◊ **Bank: open credit facilities** ◊ **Credit** ◊ **Credit rating** ◊ **Export Credits Guarantee Department**.

Commission Payment to a **middleman** for services rendered, often based on the **value** of the **goods** handled. For instance, the commission paid to an **estate agent** varies with the **price** of the house. ◊ **Del credere agent**.

Commission agent An **agent** acting on a **commission** basis.

Committee of inspection This was a committee which could be set up by creditors to supervise the conduct of a company liquidation or the distribution of a bankrupt's estate by the Trustee in Bankruptcy. As a result of the changes brought about by the Insolvency Acts 1985 and 1986 these committees no longer exist. According to the provisions of the 1986 Act a committee of creditors formed during a company winding-up is referred to as a **liquidation committee**, and a similar committee set up to oversee a Trustee in Bankruptcy is known as a creditors' committee.

Commodity exchange A market where dealings in a particular commodity are made or recorded on a national or international scale. Historically, London has long been the home of most commodity exchanges even though, in modern times, the transactions are no longer in the form of the goods themselves but in paper dealing with titles thereto. This process has been greatly facilitated by the introduction over the years of reliable 'grading' services which save the trouble of personal inspection. In fact, commodities can be bought, shipped and sold without the person effecting the transaction ever setting eyes on them. This does not apply to all commodities as some are still auctioned off after inspection, e.g. tea and wool, thus preserving the old personal touch and judgement. The transactions effected at the exchanges may be 'spot' dealings, i.e. at the current prices, or dealings in **futures**. These latter are similar to **forward dealings** on the Stock Exchange in that the contract is made at an agreed price which will not be affected by any movements in the spot price before the date on which the future transaction is to be completed. Perhaps the best known of the commodity exchanges was the Corn Exchange in the City of London. This was formed in 1749 and was reputedly the largest trading centre for cereals, fertilizers and animal feedstuffs in the UK ◊ **Spot transactions** ◊ **Traded options** ◊ **London Fox**.

Common Agricultural Policy One of the conditions of membership of the **Common Market** was acceptance of this policy, which was written into the agreement in order to protect the European farming industry. It is essentially a protectionist policy as far as farm food prices are concerned but need not remain so once the level of efficiency within the member countries rises sufficiently to bring European prices down to those charged by competitors. It was the necessary loss of Commonwealth low-priced farm products which was a strong argument against Britain's membership of the market, but the long-term view prevailed, i.e. the view that the establishment of a self-sufficient European Union was an asset that would outweigh temporary inconvenience. ◊ **European Free Trade Association**.

The operation of the Common Agricultural Policy is too complex to explain in detail and can only be outlined here. Generally speaking, the EU fixes minimum prices for various farm products through the European Commission. Imports from non-member countries must not fall below these prices and where goods are bought below the price then the Commission makes a levy on the importing country to the extent of the difference. On the other hand, where producers in member countries have surplus stocks for sale then the Commission may buy in these stocks at a figure slightly below the minimum price. It will also pay out an amount by way of restitution where members sell products to customers outside the market at world prices below the agreed minimum prices. The option to buy in surplus stocks is referred to as buying at an **intervention price**. As another way of helping the uneconomic farmers within the Community, the Commission is also empowered to aid the modernization of the farms concerned by making cash grants out of the **Common Budget**. ◊ **Green pound** ◊ **Mountain**.

Common Budget This refers to the pool of funds available to the European Commission of the **Common Market**, principally for intervention necessary to support the **Common Agricultural Policy**. It was established by agreement between member countries and was to be funded by money collected through levies raised to enforce the common price structure – particularly in connection with farm prices. It is supplemented by customs duties payable on imported industrial goods plus an agreed proportion of the **value added tax** receipts of the member countries. The money is used almost entirely to run the Common Agricultural Policy.

Common carrier A person offering to transport **goods** for anyone who will employ him. He may specify the type or size of goods, or his area of work, but provided he implies that he is willing to carry goods for anyone he is a common carrier. He is bound to carry a goods when requested to do so, subject to any limitations he has previously made known. This does not apply if his vehicle is already full or there is an extraordinary risk attaching to the goods. He must carry them without unnecessary delay and by his normal route (unless another is agreed upon) and for a reasonable **price**. The price need not be uniform. He has a **lien** at **common law** on the goods. This is usually a **particular lien**, i.e. it only attaches to the charge for the particular job and not to debts previously incurred. At common law he is an insurer of the goods, i.e. he warrants to carry and deliver them safely and securely and is liable irrespective of negligence. He is not, however, liable for damage from an **act of God** or the Queen's enemies, or damage due to the negligence of the **consignor** (e.g. bad packaging) or the **inherent vice** of the goods. These limitations do not apply at a time when he was not fulfilling his contract, or when the loss could have been foreseen and was not avoided. He must provide a proper vehicle. Where bad packing is concerned, the loss will always be attributed to the consignor. He is not liable for loss due to delay if delay would not normally have damaged the goods, and special circumstances should be made known to him. A contract of carriage is not a contract **uberrimae fidei**, therefore the consignor is not expected to make known all facts relating to the goods. He must, however, state if they are of a dangerous character. For details of carrier's liability, it is advisable to consult a standard work on the subject. Generally speaking, he may limit his liability by private notice to the consignor. This might take the form of a printed notice at the depot. If he has been negligent, however, only fraudulent concealment of **real value** would limit his liability.

Common law This is the common law of the land, which has accumulated since time immemorial. It is based almost entirely on what is known as the rule of precedent, whereby decisions are made on the basis of previous decisions: judges are bound to follow rulings made in previous cases, unless they can find some means of distinguishing the case before them, so as to give a new ruling and thus create a new precedent. One commentator, perhaps unkindly, spoke of precedent thus: 'It is a maxim . . . that whatever hath been done before may legally be done again, and therefore they take special care to record all the decisions formerly made against common justice and the general reason of mankind. These, under the name of precedents, they produce as authorities, to justify the most iniquitous opinions, and the judges never fail of directing accordingly.'

Common Market After 1945 Europe, or the greater part of it, was in ruins both politically and economically. Many countries were faced with rebuilding and repairing whole economies. For many reasons, recovery had to be speeded up and a stable market for international trade established, reasonably independent of American aid. It was during these early years that the concept of a federal Europe emerged. The theory was that a larger federated economic body would carry greater bargaining and building powers than a collection of small individual states. It was also thought that a macro-Europe would be a more formidable combatant in the world political and economic arena when faced with the might of the American and Russian superpowers.

These aspirations were never completely fulfilled, due partly to the resurgence of nationalism and partly to the dilution of enthusiasm by the recovery of individual countries. The pre-existing burdens, interests and commitments of various participants, which tended to overlap the planned multi-national Europe, also made fulfilment difficult if not impossible; e.g. both Britain and France had overseas ties which they were not eager to break, particularly Britain, which had long-standing agreements with Commonwealth nations. ◊ **Commonwealth preference** ◊ **Sterling area**.

Nevertheless, the basic concept, once mooted, remained – albeit in a diluted form – and first found shape in the Schuman Plan of 1950, which aimed to unite the coal and steel industries of France and West Germany. A year later came the **Treaty of Paris**, wherein the Coal and Steel Community was enlarged by the official inclusion of four other countries:

Italy, Belgium, Holland and Luxemburg. The founding members of this community had intended it as the first step on the road to federalism but, not long after its creation, France took the first retrogressive step by refusing, in 1954, to ratify the plan for a unified European defence community. Britain had been unwilling to participate in any of the original schemes and her attitude was blamed for the collapse of the federalists' plans. The other countries then decided to abandon the search for political unity and concentrate on strictly economic cooperation. So, in 1957, those six countries put their names to the **Treaty of Rome** to form an economic community which became active from 1 January 1958. The declared aim was, and is, to 'transform the whole complex of their relations into a European Union' with a common economic foreign policy and, it was hoped, a common currency by 1980. The community was known collectively as the Common Market and is now referred to as the European Union (EU). After much debate, deliberation and a referendum, Britain joined the then Common Market as from 1 January 1973, followed by the Irish Republic and Denmark. Greece joined in 1981 and Spain and Portugal were admitted in 1985. Prior to becoming a member of the then Common Market the UK had, with certain other non-EU countries, formed the **European Free Trade Association**. This was more loosely knit than the EU in that although it encouraged the removal of **tariffs** between member states it did not, as the EU aimed to, offer a common tariff to the outside world. The present twelve-member Common Market has a population which in total well exceeds that of either Russia or the USA. Further steps on the road to greater integration were set out in the **Maastricht Treaty**.

Britain's membership was subject to certain provisions contained in the Act of Accession 1972, which preceded full membership. These provisions would be gradually phased out as the need for them disappears. They were principally intended to soften the blow to other multinational and bilateral agreements to which Britain was party, with particular reference to established Commonwealth ties; e.g. it was initially agreed that New Zealand should be treated as a 'special case' as regards dairy products exported to the UK. That country would continue to enjoy benefits in quota and tariff matters for some years, but the preference would gradually be phased out.

For more detailed information on the European Union and its rules and regulations reference should be made to the Treaty of Rome and the Act of Accession. ◊ **Certificate of origin** ◊ **Common Agricultural Policy** ◊ **Common budget** ◊ **European Free Trade Association** ◊ **Value added tax**.

Common ownership An economic principle which states that every person connected with the production of certain goods or services is an equal owner of the means of production. Indirectly it is connected with the cooperative movement and the Cooperative Wholesale and Retail Societies. The latter operate on a 'mutual' basis whereby profits are paid back to member-customers. These profit payments, being profits after management expenses, are known as 'dividends'. Common ownership should not be confused with the specialized property law concept of ownership in common. ◊ **Worker cooperative**.

Common prices system The system operating in the **Common Market** for equalizing and controlling prices under the **Common Agricultural Policy**. ◊ **Intervention price** ◊ **Target price** ◊ **Threshold price**.

Common shares An American equivalent of equity shares, usually of no-par value or of a stated face value of, say, $1 per share, which bears no relation to the true value. ◊ **Common stock**.

Common stock The term used in the USA to describe **ordinary shares** in a company.

Commonwealth Development Corporation A public corporation established in 1948 to assist overseas companies, especially newly independent Commonwealth nations, with problems incurred in developing their economies, particularly but not solely their agricultural industries. It is currently authorized to borrow through the UK Exchequer up to £750m. Priority in aid is always afforded to poorer countries, the finance is directed at projects and is not to prop up specific contracts, and the minimum investment in any one project is in the order of £1m. There are no quotas for individual countries and each investment is assessed on its own merit, whether it be a direct involvement or one entered into in partnership with the government of the receiving country or some other international development agency. The CDC is expected to be self-financing and to show, if possible, a surplus on its activities. Investments are therefore in the form of interest-bearing loans, though at a rate lower than that charged by either the International Finance Corporation or the World Bank.

Commonwealth preference This is

a relic of the old days of the supremacy of Britain. The creation of the British Empire, now known as the Commonwealth, brought in its train very strong economic links between the UK and the various Dominions and colonies which constituted the interests of Britain overseas. These links translated themselves into preferential treatment in the form of greatly reduced customs duties applied to Commonwealth goods entering the UK. As so much of British foodstuffs and raw materials for industry were imported from Commonwealth countries this had the effect of maintaining the prices of food and other goods in Britain at artificially low levels and protecting the UK from the worst effects of world commodity crises. These halcyon days came to an end during the years following the Second World War, firstly by the necessity of observing the rules laid down by the **General Agreement on Tariffs and Trade** and finally by Britain's entry into the **Common Market**, although the harshness of this entry was softened by the agreement of the other members to allow Commonwealth preferences to be phased out slowly. ◊ **Common Agricultural Policy**.

Community programme A scheme established under the auspices of the **Manpower Services Commission** to assist both long-term unemployed and individual communities. The idea is to provide a temporary workforce to undertake projects which will benefit the whole of a particular community by doing jobs that enhance local facilities or generally improve the environment, e.g. clearing and renovating disused sites or buildings. The scheme is open to those of twenty-five and over who have been out of work for a year and those younger

persons unemployed for six out of the previous nine months.

Companies Acts With the collapse of the **South Sea Bubble** the image of the company became tarnished to such a degree that it was not until 1844, when the Joint Stock Companies Act was passed, that any measure of respectability was accorded to such corporations in the eyes of the law.

The first Companies Act in its contemporary sense was the one of 1862. After that date the law relating to companies was modified, extended and restructured in various statutes until it was collected and collated in definitive form in the major piece of legislation known as the Companies Act 1948. This Act was sufficiently comprehensive to serve as the basis for all rules and regulations pertaining to limited companies for the succeeding thirty-seven years. It was amended by the 1967 Companies Act and again by other Companies Acts in 1976, 1980 and 1981. By this time so many changes had been effected that, rather than leave companies at the mercy of several statutes, a consolidating Act was drawn up. This became the 1985 Companies Act and with the enactment of the Companies Consolidation (Consequential Provisions) Act 1985 and the Companies Act 1989, which gave effect to certain European Council Directives, all the law relating to companies was contained in these statutes only. The preceding Acts have been repealed, though for the purposes of this book reference has been directed to those earlier statutes so that the date when various regulations came into force will be apparent.

Companies House The home of the Registrar of Companies and the place where records which must be filed by companies are kept and maintained. By law most of these records are available to the general public, who may inspect them and take copies for their own use. ◊ **Register of companies**.

Companies: index of names The Companies Act 1981 required that the Registrar of Companies should maintain an index of names. Bodies whose names were to appear on this index included all limited companies within the meaning of the Companies Act, overseas companies with places of business in the UK, limited partnerships and certain other corporate bodies and societies specified in the Act. ◊ **Business names**.

Any new company applying for registration will be prevented from using a name which is the same as, or too similar to, that of a body already registered. ◊ **Company, name of**.

Companies: purchase of own shares Until recently companies were prohibited from buying their own shares. The law has now been changed and the 1981 Companies Act gave any company the right to buy in its own shares, provided that the power is contained in its Articles and that certain conditions are observed. These are substantially the same as those applicable to the redemption of shares, ◊ **Companies: redeemable shares**. Additionally, it should be noted that where there exists a class of shares with preferential rights over those of the shares to be purchased, then the consent of members of that class must first be obtained.

Purchase of own shares may be made through a recognized stock exchange or by what are known as 'off market means', e.g. directly from a member or through the over-the-counter market. Stock exchange market purchases require the authorization of an ordinary resolution of the company in general meeting. Off market purchases are permitted only by contract and if passed by a **special resolution**. In both cases, details of the prospective purchase must be approved, e.g. number and price limits. The authorization must contain these details and must also set time limits for purchases. A printed copy of any resolution giving authorization for share purchase must be filed with the Registrar of Companies.

When a company purchases its own shares, certain prescribed information must be filed with the Registrar of Companies within twenty-eight days of purchase. Specified details must also be included in the Directors' Report.

Contingent contracts to purchase its own shares are permissible and are covered by off market purchase procedures. A company cannot, however, assign rights under such contracts and thereby use them to speculate against its own shares by buying and selling rights to purchase.

Companies: redeemable shares Traditionally, companies have been able to issue **redeemable preference shares**. The Companies Act 1981 gave companies power to issue redeemable ordinary shares provided that certain conditions were observed. Briefly, these are: (1) the Articles must give this power and specify the manner in which redemption is to take place; (2) after redemption there must still be in issue shares which are not redeemable. This prevents companies buying in all shares and thereby ceasing to have any members; (3) the shares to be redeemed must be fully paid; (4) redemption must be effected out of profits available for distribution or out of the proceeds of a new issue made for purposes of the redemption; (5) the redemption must be paid for at the time the shares are redeemed, i.e. shares cannot be redeemed on credit; (6) shares redeemed must be cancelled. This reduces nominal capital but not **authorized capital**. If the nominal capital of a public company is reduced by redemption, care must be taken that it does not thereby fall below the minimum required to keep its status as a public company; (7) an amount equal to the nominal value of shares redeemed must be transferred to **capital redemption reserve**. The amount so transferred may be reduced by the nominal value of any new shares issued for purposes of the redemption. The effect of this is to preserve capital intact for protection of creditors; (8) after redemption there must still be at least two members.

If a new issue for purposes of redeeming existing shares is mooted, it will not matter if that issue would exceed authorized capital, provided that after redemption the total shares in issue are within the limit.

Any premium paid on redemption must be paid out of distributable profits. Proceeds from any new issue can be used to pay this premium where the shares to be redeemed were themselves issued at a premium to the extent of that premium or to the balance on the share premium account if lower. The amount so paid by way of premium on redemption must be matched by an equivalent transfer to the share premium account.

Private companies may, if their articles permit, redeem shares out of capital to the extent that the balance of distributable profits plus proceeds of any new issue are insufficient.

Companies: reduction of capital A company can only reduce **capital** if its **articles of association** and **memorandum of association** permit. A **special resolution** is required and the leave of the court must be obtained. Much depends on the reason for the reduction – it may be because the company is over-capitalized, or it may be because the company has lost capital by way of a very large trading loss. Where reduction of capital involves a return to shareholders, or a reduction in **uncalled capital**, the court will insist on an inquiry into the debts and liabilities of the company. It will settle a list of **creditors** and all these must consent or be paid off.

Where there is no return to shareholders or no reduction in liability, there will be no inquiry. This type of situation arises when capital is lost irretrievably: the shares may be nominally of £100 each but represented by **assets** of only £10 each. It may be possible to make a profit on these assets and the company may wish to write off the lost capital by reducing capital from £100 to £10 per share. Creditors may not be affected but the rights of members *inter se* may be altered. The court must approve the scheme but the creditors need not. In all cases of permanent reduction of capital, the court may order the words 'and reduced' to be added to the company's name.

Where capital is diminished by writing off uncalled capital an **ordinary resolution** is sufficient provided the articles do not require some other type of resolution.

A forfeiture of shares is, strictly, a reduction of capital and is in fact the only type for which court sanction is not required.

Other means of reducing capital were introduced in the Companies Act 1981 and restated in the 1985 Act. A company can now redeem equity capital and, within prescribed limits, purchase its own shares. Such shares redeemed or purchased must be cancelled, thus reducing issued share capital.

An additional consequence of the 1981 Companies Act is that where a public company reduces its capital to a figure below the 'authorized minimum', which is at present £50,000, it must, unless a court order is obtained to the contrary, immediately take steps to reregister as a private company. A further point introduced by that Act is that, where net assets represent one half or less of paid-up share capital, then the directors must, within twenty-eight days, convene an extraordinary general meeting. For example, a company with paid up capital of £5,000 and net assets of £3,000 may use £1,000 to redeem shares of that value. The net assets would then be only one half of paid-up capital and an extraordinary general meeting would need to be called. ◊ **Capital: serious loss**.

Company A body corporate created by royal charter or by a specific Act of Parliament or registered with the Registrar of Companies under the Companies Act 1985. ◊ **Chartered companies** ◊ **Statutory companies**.

Certain organizations must be registered under the Building Society Acts 1874, 1894, and 1939, and the Industrial and Provident Society Acts 1893–5 and 1913. These are not strictly companies but are often called such. There are also **cost book mining companies** and there used to be **unincorporated companies**.

In the case of companies dealt with under the 1985 Companies Act, liability of members may be limited by shares, or by guarantee, or may be unlimited. ◊ **Company limited by shares** ◊ **Unlimited company**.

Companies may also be public com-

panies or private companies. ◊ **Company, private** ◊ **Company, public**.

In partnerships the word company is often used to describe the firm, e.g. Bloggs & Company. Where the word 'Limited' does not appear, the organization is not a company in the legal sense. The phrase 'one-man company' is often used to describe a small private company, where control is effectively in the hands of one person. By law there must always be more than one member.

Company, borrowing powers of These are set out in the **memorandum of association** of each **company**. If they are exceeded the loan is **ultra vires**, but third parties acting in good faith are protected by provisions in the 1989 Companies Act.

All trading companies have implied power to borrow and to pledge the property of the company.

Company cars; directors and highly paid employees Directors and certain highly paid employees of companies tend to be heavily taxed on the benefit they are assumed to enjoy from private use of a company car or when the company for which they work provides petrol for private use in a car which they themselves own. It should be noted that driving to and from work is classed as private motoring and if the company pays for the petrol so used it becomes a benefit in kind.

Basically, any director (or employee earning over £8,500 p.a.) who has exclusive use of a company car will be assessed both on the benefit of the car itself and additionally for a similar sum in lieu of petrol known as fuel benefit. The rates of this latter benefit are fixed from year to year and vary with the cylinder capacity of the car.

The car benefit, which is in addition to the fuel benefit, is from 1994/5 to be 35 per cent of the list price of the car. This figure will be for cars over four years old and again where business mileage is high. The effective taxable benefit where mileage exceeds 18,000 will fall to 11.66 per cent. Instead of suffering the fuel benefit, which will be linked to PAYE, the beneficiary may elect to reimburse the cost of private petrol to the company.

Directors of small private companies may find that the benefit rules make it preferable to keep their cars out of the company and merely accept reimbursement of necessary business travel costs. This will avoid assessment on both car and fuel benefit.

Company: change of name A company is not obliged to retain its given name but may change it at any time by **special resolution**. It may also be ordered to change its name by the Secretary of State for Trade and Industry in circumstances outlined in **company, name of**. Needless to say, no company can seek to avoid legal proceedings by changing its name and any such pending will be brought as if no change had been made. Regulations as to registering and displaying the new name will apply as they did for the old name.

Company: commencement of business A private company may commence business immediately upon incorporation. A public company can neither borrow nor commence business until certain conditions, first set out in the 1980 Act, have been fulfilled. It must file a second statutory declaration with the Registrar of Companies stating (1) that the nominal value of alloted shares is not less than the minimum required for a public company, (2) the sum of the **pre-liminary expenses** and who paid them, (3) the amount paid on shares allotted and (4) any payment in cash or kind to a promoter and for what consideration.

Company: disclosure of interest in shares In so far as the **share register** must give details of the shareholding of each member, there was by the 1948 Companies Act a requirement for the number of shares held by any one person to be stated, and as the register was available for inspection by the public, individual shareholdings were known. However, the register did not indicate which members were trustees or nominees, and consequently a third party could not ascertain whether any one person was the beneficial owner of a large block of shares. The 1967 Companies Act went some way towards rectifying this omission, but the 1981 Companies Act repealed the relevant section of the 1967 Act and replaced it with detailed and comprehensive requirements for disclosure of true interests in public companies.

It is now obligatory for any person with an interest in 3 per cent or more of any class of voting share in a public company to expressly notify the company of this fact. For the purposes of this requirement a 'person' includes his close family or a company he controls; 'interest' includes equitable interest (e.g. under a trust) as well as direct beneficial ownership. **Concert party agreements** are also caught by the Act and the parties to such an agreement must disclose their interest as if they were each owners of the collective number of shares.

Persons obliged to give such notification must also inform the company if the percentage of shares held changes or if they cease to hold 3 per cent or more. The company must maintain a register of interests in shares covered by the Act. Additionally, a company may specifically require a member to disclose his interest in its shares, and holders of one-tenth of that class of paid-up capital may call upon the company to exercise this right.

The Register of Members' Interests in shares is quite distinct from the Register of Directors' Interests in shares.

Company, exempt private A form of **private company** abolished by the Companies Act 1967. It observed the following conditions: (1) no **company** or other body corporate could be the holder of any **shares** or **debentures**; (2) no person other than the holder could have any interest in any of the company's shares or debentures; (3) the number of persons holding debentures had to be fifty or less; (4) no company or other body corporate could be a **director** of the company, and there could be no agreement whereby the policy of the company could be determined by persons other than directors, **members**, and debenture holders or **trustees** for debenture holders.

Condition (1) did not apply where the holder was an exempt private company and the total membership of both companies did not exceed fifty, excluding employees, nor did it apply to shares, for example, registered in the name of, say, a **bank** as a nominee. An exempt private company had certain privileges, apart from those of a private company. *Inter alia* (1) it was exempt from filing an annual **balance sheet** and **profit and loss account**, (2) it could make loans to directors, (3) the books might be audited by a partner or employee of a servant or **officer of the company**, or by unqualified persons, (4) it was exempt from filing *printed* copies of certain resolutions or agreements.

Company, formation of A company does not exist until it has received its certificate of incorporation. This will be issued by the Registrar of Companies for England and Wales or the Registrar of Companies for Scotland, depending on the locality of the registered office stated in the memorandum. To obtain a certificate certain documents must be submitted. These are (1) a copy of the **memorandum of association**, (2) a copy of any **articles of association**, (3) a statement signed by the **subscribers** giving details of the first directors and secretary together with their written consent to act, (4) notice of the intended location of the registered office, (5) a statutory declaration that the provisions of the Companies Act have been complied with.

If the company is to be a public company, then it will be necessary for an additional statement to be filed to the effect that the requirements necessary to registration as a public company, e.g. as to minimum capital, etc., have been observed.

Once these various documents have been received by the Registrar he may proceed to issue a certificate of **incorporation**, and in the case of a public company he must gazette the issue of such a certificate. ◊ **Company: commencement of business** ◊ **Company, private** ◊ **Company, public** ◊ **Company, name of** ◊ **Company: registered number**.

Company investigations. ◊ **Investigations, company**.

Company limited by guarantee These are companies the liability of whose members is limited by the amount they guarantee to make available to the company should it be wound up. The guarantee may be instead of, or additional to, share capital. Such companies are normally formed for charitable or educational purposes.

Under the 1948 Companies Act such companies could be public or private. The position was altered by the 1980 Companies Act, which provided that all new guarantee companies must be private companies. Public guarantee companies existing prior to the coming into effect of the 1980 Act are permitted to re-register as public companies only if they have a share capital and fulfil the conditions laid down in that Act. If they have no share capital they must reregister as private companies.

Company limited by shares This is the commonest type of company in existence in this country. It has a **share capital** stated in the **memorandum of association** – not all of this may have been issued. For the formation of such companies ◊ **Company, formation of**. Most large trading organizations are companies limited by shares. They may be public or private companies (there used also to be exempt private companies ◊ **Company, exempt private**).

The principal characteristics of a company limited by shares are (1) that it is a separate 'legal *persona*' (i.e. can **contract** as a person separate from its members) and (2) that the liability of the members is limited to the nominal value of the **shares** they have taken up.

Company, name of Although a company has considerable freedom in its choice of name, there are certain statutory obligations which must be observed. Failure to comply with these may result in refusal by the Registrar of Companies to register the name and therefore delay the date on which the company can commence business.

Generally speaking, a chosen name will be acceptable provided that: (1) it is not the same as, or too similar to, that of another company already listed on the **companies: index of names**; (2) it does not contain words or phrases which the Secretary of State would judge offensive, misleading or liable to constitute a criminal offence. In this context a name would be misleading if it suggested that the company was in some way connected with the government or a local authority; (3) it ends with the words prescribed by statute.

The name of a public company must now, since the 1980 Companies Act, end with the words 'public limited company' in English or Welsh or an accepted abbreviation of these words, e.g. PLC. Other limited companies must include at the end of their names the word 'limited' or an abbreviation thereof. Unlimited companies should add the word 'unlimited', and in that instance it must be at the end of the name.

The Secretary of State has the power to order a company to change its name where it appears that the above conditions have not been met, or where the name is too like an existing name which should have appeared on the index of names but was not included. He may also order a change where the original name was obtained as a result of providing misleading information or by virtue of giving assurances which have not been fulfilled. ◊ **Company: change of name**.

Company, objects of The objects of a **company** must be stated in its **memorandum of association**. Anything inconsistent with these objects would be **ultra vires**. For this reason the powers or objects of the company tend to be stated in very broad terms.

If the main object of the company disappears, the company may be wound up. Objects must not be illegal. Objects or powers may be changed by altering the memorandum by **special resolution**. This alteration must be to enable the company to achieve its objects more effectively, to carry on some other business that can be conveniently combined with its own, to restrict or abandon some of its objects, to sell the business or to amalgamate with another company. Application to the court to have the alteration cancelled may be made by holders of at least 15 per cent of issued **share capital**, or **debentures**, or any class of these. The application must be made within twenty-one days of the resolution. The court may confirm or cancel the alteration or may order the interest of the objectors to be purchased. Whatever the alteration, the court can do nothing if application is not made within the specified time. No alteration can be made which increases the liability of any member.

Company, private The Companies Act 1980 defined a private company as any company not being a public limited company, i.e. which had not satisfied the conditions laid down in that Act as necessary to registration as a public company.

A private company may be limited or unlimited and may be formed specifically as a private company or become one by default. All new unlimited or guarantee companies are *de facto* private companies. The old condition that allowed private companies to have fewer members no longer applies, as the minimum for all companies is now two members. Private limited companies are debarred from offering their shares or debentures to the general public and to do so constitutes a criminal offence. For this purpose offers

to members or to employees, offers under an employee's share scheme or offers to the families of members or employees are not offers to the public.

It is customary for private companies to restrict the right to transfer their shares. This was obligatory under the 1948 Companies Act, as was the limitation of members to fifty persons. Both these conditions have now been repealed, as has Part II of Schedule A of the Companies Act 1948, which gave guidance as to the contents of the Articles of a private company. This custom precludes ownership from being widely dispersed against the interests and wishes of other shareholders and is particularly suited to the usual purpose of small family businesses, which make up by far the greater part of all private companies in existence. Prior to the redefinition of the private company by the 1980 Companies Act, such companies comprised some 97 per cent of all limited companies in the UK. In so far as the new legislation has probably reduced rather than enlarged the number of true public companies, this percentage is unlikely to be lower now.

One other legal privilege enjoyed by private companies is that they need only have one director, whereas the minimum for a public company is two. Other benefits include the freedom to commence business without having to satisfy the detailed requirements demanded of public companies, freedom to appoint a secretary without special qualifications, no restrictions relating to age of directors and longer periods of grace in filing annual financial statements.

Company, public Prior to the Companies Act 1980 public companies, as such, were not defined but were a residual class, and only private companies were identified by definition. The position is now reversed.

The Companies act defined a public company as a company limited either by shares or guarantee which has a share capital and which states in its memorandum of association that it is a public company. It must register or reregister under the Companies Act 1980 as a public company and its name must end with the words 'public limited company'. These words can be abbreviated to PLC. If the memorandum states that the company's registered office is in Wales then the Welsh equivalent of these words or abbreviations may be used. All public companies must have a nominal share capital of the 'authorized minimum' – at present £50,000 – of which at least 25 per cent has been paid in cash plus any premium due. The minimum number of members is two. It must also deliver to the Registrar of Companies a declaration signed by a director or the secretary that the requirements outlined have been complied with, together with a copy of the amended memorandum (where applicable) and an official application signed in the same way as the declaration. The Registrar will issue a certificate and only then may the company style itself a public company.

Any company not satisfying these conditions will be a private company. This latter category will include guarantee companies without a share capital and also unlimited companies. ◊ **Company, private**.

Company: register of interests in shares ◊ **Company: disclosure of interests in shares**.

Company: registered number Every limited company is given a registered number by the Registrar of Companies. This number may or may not include a letter. For new companies it is given with the certificate of incorporation.

Company seal Every limited **company** must have a common seal, which must be affixed to certain documents. The company must keep a seal book recording details of all these documents. A company may also have an additional seal for use on securities issued or documents evidencing securities. This additional seal will be a facsimile of the common seal with the addition of the word 'securities'.

Company secretary The person concerned with keeping the **company's statutory books** and generally supervising the administration of its affairs. *Inter alia*, he keeps the minute books for board and company meetings, maintains the **share register**, sees to payment of **dividends**, **interest**, etc. It is a position of particular responsibility and perhaps one of the senior positions in a company. The company must keep details of the Secretary in the **register of directors**. In some companies the legal duties of the Secretary are performed by an outside organization specializing in this form of work.

The 1980 Companies Act included a requirement that the secretary of a public company must be suitably qualified and must appear to the directors to be capable of properly discharging the functions of his office. To this end any secretary appointed after the Act should either belong to one of the recognized professional associations of secretaries or accountants, or be a barrister or have held a position previously which would have provided him with the requisite experience. These conditions appear imprecise but directors may have to justify any appointment they make.

Company, statutory ⟡ **Statutory companies**.

Company, unincorporated These can no longer be formed. They took the form of large **partnerships** with transferable **shares**. They were governed by Deed of Settlement between shareholders and **trustees**. They had unlimited liability. A **company** formed in such a way can register under the Companies Act as an **unlimited company**, substituting a **memorandum of association** and **articles of association** for the Deed of Settlement.

Company: winding-up A company may be wound up but cannot be made bankrupt. Winding-up may be (1) voluntary, (2) by the court. ⟡ **Winding-up, compulsory** ⟡ **Winding-up, voluntary**.

Company's liquidation account When a **company** is dissolved and monies are left with the **liquidator** (because **dividends** have been unclaimed, etc., for more than six months) these monies must be paid into the Insolvency Services Account at the **Bank of England**.

Compensating errors A bookkeeping term for two separate errors, one on the **Debit** side and one on the **Credit** side, which happen to cancel each other out.

Compensation fee parcel service One of the insurance-type services offered by the **Post Office**. Parcels which contain items that the customer wishes to insure against loss or damage may be sent to any part of the UK, Eire, Isle of Man or Channel Isles. The sender must complete a certificate supplied by the Post Office. This serves as a certificate of posting and also states the compensation limits, which will vary on a sliding scale according to the fee paid. The parcel(s) will not indicate that compensation is payable, but the sender should mark it appropriately if it contains fragile or perishable material or could be damaged by bending as it will receive no special handling treatment. Cash or convertible **bills of exchange** or unused stamps cannot be sent by this method.

Compensation for loss of office A sum of money given to a **director** on his leaving a **company**. It is often given in addition to, or in lieu of, a retirement **pension**, but more frequently is in effect a **redundancy payment** following a change of ownership, when a new **board of directors** is being substituted for the old. These amounts must be shown separately in the accounts of limited companies. They are often very high, particularly if the director was also an important shareholder and is retiring. Because the size of the figure very often seems to bear no relation to the actual loss suffered or work done, these payments have become known as 'golden handshakes'.

Competitive market An **open market** where goods are freely and voluntarily offered for sale by any number of willing sellers to any number of willing buyers at prices agreed by both parties. In the ideal competitive market the price of any article will be fractionally above the cost of producing it by the most efficient producer. The latter will be able to sell the goods at a price with which no other producer can compete and still remain in business. In practice, partly due to the limits set by both the saleable output of any one producer and distribution problems concerned with moving goods from supplier to buyer, the actual price will tend to average above the minimum as the output of the marginally less efficient is brought in to fill total demand. ◊ **Cut-throat competition** ◊ **Marginal cost** ◊ **Monopoly**.

Compound interest Interest calculated not (as with **simple interest**) as a fixed amount per annum based on the capital to which it applies, but on an accumulating balance which consists of both capital invested and the interest already earned, e.g. £100 invested at 6 per cent simple interest for two years would increase by £6 in each year and provide £112 at the end of the two years. If, however, it were invested at compound interest, with interest added annually, it would earn £6 in the first year but 6 per cent of £106 in the second year, i.e. £6.36, and would provide £112.36 after two years. This concept is very relevant to calculations relating to **annuities** and **sinking funds**, etc., as the annual sum put away at compound interest to realize £100,000 in twenty years would be much less than if simple interest only applied. It also relates to **discounting back**, where interest is always assumed to be compound. ◊ **Discounted cash flow** ◊ **Net present value**.

Comprehensive insurance This term has particular relevance to motor insurance. Any person driving a motor vehicle on public highways must have a current **insurance** policy that will cover any damage sustained by a third party, irrespective of negligence. This compulsory element in motor insurance was introduced in the Road Traffic Act 1930. Drivers of vehicles may, however, wish to cover more than the minimum legal requirements as regards damage. Policies available are many and of different kinds, varying from one company to another according to the insurer's assessment of risk. The greatest insurance cover available is known as comprehensive insurance. This entitles the owner or driver to recompense for all known possible losses from accidents incurred whilst the car is in his possession or being driven by someone else with the owner's permission. Most insurance companies attach a **no-claims bonus** which, by affording a substantial deduction from the annual premium payable, discourages the person insured from making minor claims.

The term 'comprehensive' insurance is sometimes loosely applied to any insurance policy taken out on real or personal property which affords protection against all known possible hazards.

Comptometer ◊ **Adding machine**.

Comptroller A term used to glamorize the position of **chief executive** in a company. It adds nothing to the responsibility of the job but contributes considerably to its apparent importance. It is usually reserved for the chief financial executive of a **group** of companies to whom the chief executives of the member companies are ultimately responsible. In American usage it possesses less mystique and is used, with the adjective 'financial', to denote the company official responsible for the disposition of funds and the preparation and supervision of the **budgetary control** system. In the UK this person might be referred to as finance manager or financial director. ◊ **Board of directors** ◊ **Management** ◊ **Line management**.

Compulsory winding-up ◊ **Winding-up, compulsory**.

Computer A generic term for apparatus which processes information by electronic means at very high speeds. The two principal types are the analog computer and the digital computer. The latter is the type normally met with in commerce and can vary considerably in both size and complexity depending upon the purpose for which it is designed.

The digital computer operates by converting all information into binary notation which can then be represented by positive and negative electrical charges. It can retain and compartmentalize information fed into it and will retrieve and process this information according to specific instructions given by means of a **program**.

In so far as it is necessarily dependent on both the accuracy of the information originally provided and the technical correctness of the program devised, then the computer has a capacity for error equal to that of user or programmer. In the absence of such human error, however, the computer is able to perform mathematical and other logical calculations at incredibly high speeds and can in a matter of minutes, or even seconds, solve problems with an exactitude which would not have been achieved manually within any reasonable time or with any acceptable degree of accuracy.

As computer technology becomes more sophisticated so do the number of applications of that technology and there are now few areas of commerce which do not make use of computers, whether it be for controlling stock movements in warehouses, keeping customers' accounts in trading companies or recording and monitoring dealings on the Stock Exchange.

Concert party agreements These are arrangements between two or more persons acting in concert each to obtain shares in a public company with the object of combining their holdings at a suitable date. By acting individually with a private agreement to operate in concert they hope thereby to evade the provisions of the Companies Acts relating to obligatory disclosure of interests in a company's shares.

The 1981 Act provided that such concert party agreements should be subject to similar requirements as to written notification of interests in shares in the target company as if the shares were held by one person only. The company concerned is obliged to maintain a register of material interests in its shares. This latter requirement was introduced in the 1967 Companies Act and substantially reinforced in the 1981 Act. ◊ **Substantial shareholdings: details of**.

Condition A term in a **contract** the non-fulfilment of which will entitle the plaintiff to repudiate the contract and treat it as if it had never existed, i.e. demand return of any payment made. In order to be classified as a condition the term must not be merely incidental to the principal objective of the agreement but must be vital to its proper performance. It should also refer to a matter of fact, not to an opinion given, and should be distinguished from a **warranty**. There are two subdivisions of conditions: the **condition precedent** and the **condition subsequent**.

Condition precedent A condition which must be fulfilled before an obligation shall arise.

Condition subsequent A condition which if not fulfilled cancels an obligation or liability.

Conditional bill of sale ◊ **Bill of sale, conditional**.

Conditional order An order given to a banker to pay a certain amount provided a **receipt** is completed.

Conditional sale agreement Defined in law as 'an agreement for the **sale of goods** under which the purchase price or part of it is payable by instalments, and the property in the goods is to remain in the seller (notwithstanding that the buyer is to be in possession of the goods) until such conditions as to the payment of instalments or otherwise as may be specified in the agreement, are fulfilled'. These agreements are governed by the **Consumer Credit Act 1974**, which replaces the **Hire Purchase Act 1965**, where the purchase price does not exceed a certain stated figure. ◊ **Hire purchase** ◊ **Hire purchase: conditions and warranties**.

Confederation of British Industry This was formed in August 1965 by a **merger** of the National Association of British Manufacturers with the British Employers Confederation and the Federation of British Industry. The aim was to present one face to the public on questions of labour relations, taxation, technical legislation, industrial training, management, education, public purchasing, overseas trade policy, etc. It has regional and local councils, headed by the Confederation of British Industry Council, which has monthly meetings. It is politically neutral, but represents industry in dealings with the government and attempts both to respond to and to stimulate government action, often advising on policy and legislation. It is sometimes called the employers' Trades Union Congress. In its own words it is 'not a sinister pressure group dominated by top tycoons who meet clandestinely to manipulate the reins of power. Essentially a democratic organization, it draws its strength from the grass roots of industry, from firms of all shapes and sizes, in all kinds of manufac-turing enterprise, in consultation with them and with their trade associations, puts forward views and policies not only in their interest, but also in what it feels to be the national interest'. Membership includes manufacturing firms, trade associations, employer organizations and commercial associations – not only large companies. Regional councils deal with local industrial problems. Experts are employed to give free advice to members on all matters connected with industry, including taxation, rating and valuation, company and mercantile law, town and country planning, fuel economy, clean air and noise abatement and trade effluent disposal. Also, in the export field, advice on markets, distribution, agents, customers, **tariffs**, etc.

Membership is open to all companies engaged in productive or manufacturing industry in Great Britain, or in construction and transport, and to national employers' federations, national trade associations, etc. Associate membership is open to nationalized industries and commercial associations. Subscriptions vary according to the number of persons employed in the member firm.

Conference lines Ship-owning lines in the same trade working together to offer a standard charge to shippers.

Confidence trick ◊ **Con-man**.

Confirmed credit ◊ **Confirming house**.

Confirming house A form of **export house** acting for overseas buyers. The buyer uses the confirming house as a UK office. The house places an order with a UK exporter and to all intents and purpose becomes the buyer from the point of view of the exporter. The advantages to the exporter are: (1) that he has a

contract enforceable in his own country; (2) that he is paid promptly in his own currency; (3) that the confirming house **guarantees** payment and often finances the buyer; (4) that dispatch and documentation are facilitated; (5) that advice is obtainable on conditions in overseas markets; and (6) that help is given in finding overseas agents, etc. Advantages to the buyer are: (1) that credit is made available on a flexible basis; (2) that the confirming house will negotiate best prices; (3) that information is supplied on local trade conditions; (4) that the confirming house ensures that goods are supplied promptly; (5) that shipment, insurance etc., of goods is supervised; (6) that the best rates of **freight** are obtained. ◊ **British Export Houses Association**.

Conflict of law In **contract**, difficulties sometimes arise as to which particular law applies, where more than one country is concerned. As a general rule, the law of the country where the contract is to be performed will apply, though the intentions of the parties as expressed in the contract are relevant. There are various supplementary provisons. For instance, one country may not enforce a contract valid according to its own law but illegal in the place where it is to be carried out.

Confravision This is an audio-visual conference service provided by **British Telecom** using special studios whereby participants in various areas can in effect meet and discuss issues on a face-to-face basis. It is available only between specified cities. Charges vary between studios and two or three studios can be connected simultaneously. Calls must at present be booked by giving the requisite notice and are subject to the availability of studios and circuits. Confravision is still in its embryonic stage, but the idea of communication combining visual and audio aids must obviously be due for development on a nationwide scale. ◊ **Datel services** ◊ **Telex**.

Conglomerate A contemporary epithet applied to the very large **public companies** with a considerable diversity of interests in the form of subsidiary or associated companies engaged in a wide variety of activities. Some conglomerates happen almost by accident as a direct result of the falling away of demand for the product originally manufactured. As that demand falls, the principal company will underwrite its own survival by putting capital into other projects, which bear no relation to the first other than the prospect of earning profits for the shareholders. The tobacco industry provides many examples. Before being taken over by Hanson Trust, the Imperial Group, once Imperial Tobacco, obtained around one half of its turnover from such diverse products as Ross frozen foods, Courage ales, HP sauce, farm products, potato crisps, plastic bottles, vinegar, roses and fish. British American Tobacco, now BAT Industries, does not confine its interest to cigarettes but is heavily involved in the retail trade through Argos Distributors, in financial and insurance services by way of Hambro Life and Eagle Star, and in the products of paper milling in Wiggins Teape. Again, J. Arthur Rank may primarily be associated with flour milling, but the **parent company**, Rank, Hovis, MacDougall, is far less limited in its interests. ◊ **Associated company** ◊ **Parent company** ◊ **Subsidiary company** ◊ **Group**.

Conjunction ticket A term used in transport for two tickets issued simultaneously and constituting one contract of carriage.

Con-man An abbreviation of 'confidence-trick man', being the colloquial term for a person whose main objective is to play on the inexperience of others in order to obtain the maximum gain for the minimum cost to himself. He achieves this by creating a quite unjustifiable degree of confidence in his honesty and integrity. The victim of his machinations is known as the 'mark' and each particular profit-making operation is referred to as a 'scam'. Although he is commonly associated with the taproom and the racetrack, his methods are not foreign to the world of high finance.

Consequential loss A term commonly used in the **insurance** world where, in addition to compensation for actual goods lost or destroyed, a business wishes to provide against the loss of profit during the period following the incident, e.g. a fire, after which the business was inactive – partly or in whole. Most trading concerns take out what are called 'consequential loss policies'. The calculation of the amount payable by the insurer will depend on the exact terms of the policy. It will normally be related to the average **net profits** over a stated past period, plus standing charges and an amount to cover **audit** fees, **architects'** fees, etc. The method of calculation is too complex to be described here.

Consideration If a **contract** other than a **contract by deed** is to be binding, the promise of the one party must be supported by the agreement of the other party to do or not do some act, or to pay some money. The agreement by the other party is known as the consideration.

This consideration, to be effective, must have some value, i.e. it must be capable of being valued in monetary terms. Valuable consideration has been defined as 'some right, interest, profit or benefit accruing to one party, or some forbearance, detriment, loss or responsibility given, suffered or undertaken by the other'. Two examples: (1) A agrees to sell X to B in return for £10. Both A and B receive something. (Whether X is worth £10 is not always relevant provided both parties act in good faith.) This can be a good contract. (2) A owes B £10. A is a slow payer. B says that if A will pay him the £10 now he will agree to a discount of 5 per cent. This is not a good contract, for A already owes the money and has done nothing extra in return for B's promise. A discount offered for payment before the agreed date might create a new contract.

Consignee ◊ Consignor.

Consignment note A shipping term for a note accompanying a consignment of **goods**. This is sometimes an alternative to a **bill of lading**.

Consignor A term used to indicate a person who consigns goods to another in a contract of sale. The recipient is known as the consignee. In a restricted sense it can mean the person who consigns goods to an **agent** with a view to his selling the goods. The consignor retains the property in the goods until those goods are sold. ◊ **Sale of goods, title**.

Consolidated accounts Any company which has **subsidiary companies** or in any other way is legally classed as a holding company must, in addition to the normal requirements of the Companies Acts, file **group accounts**. These can take various forms but essentially they are intended to show the results for the relevant financial period, and the state of affairs at the end of that period, of the group as a whole.

The most common form is that of consolidated accounts. The individual final and audited accounts of the various companies in the group are combined into one set of accounts wherein intercompany transactions and indebtedness are eliminated on a self-cancelling basis, and the end product consists of a consolidated balance sheet and a consolidated profit and loss account. It should be emphasized that these accounts do not replace but are in addition to the individually filed accounts of each member of the group. There is one exception, and that is that the published accounts of the **holding company**, although they must contain a group balance sheet and an additional balance sheet of the holding company itself, may include only one profit and loss account, the consolidated one, provided that the account distinguishes, as a separate item, the portion of the consolidated profit attributable to outside interests and, where applicable, to the pre-acquisition period. ◊ **Group accounts: omission of subsidiaries**.

Consolidation of capital This applies to a limited **company. Shares** are consolidated when the **nominal value** of the shares is redesignated by stating that, e.g. thereafter every twenty £1 shares shall be one £20 share. This may be done by an **ordinary resolution** at a general **meeting**, unless the **memorandum of association** requires some other form of resolution. **Share capital** may also be subdivided – the reverse procedure.

Consols Government consolidated **stock**. This stock is irredeemable. It is issued at various times at various rates of **interest**. The **price** varies according to the rate of interest prevailing at the time.

In fact, the price of consols is a good indication of current **gilt-edge** interest rates because there is no question of capital repayment to be taken into account. Consols are quoted per £100. That is, if 2½ per cent consols are quoted at fifty, this means that to obtain £100 worth at 2½ per cent it is necessary to pay £50, and the gilt-edged interest rate is therefore 5 per cent, i.e. 2½ over 50.

Consortium Large contracts are often tendered for by a consortium (i.e. a group) of companies or firms none of which is competent to fulfil the **contract** alone. It is generally a 'once only' combination for the purpose of bringing together a number of quite different operative skills or areas of specialized knowledge.

Construction industry That branch of industry concerned with the building and construction of factories, houses, roads, etc.

Constructive total loss A term used in **insurance**, particularly **marine insurance**, where a ship is not completely lost but has been abandoned because the cost of saving it would exceed its **value** when saved. The insured may treat it as a total loss, or partial loss. In the latter instance he claims for damage done, in the former instance he gives notice of **abandonment** and the insurer takes over all rights. ◊ **Subrogation**.

Consulage ◊ **Consular invoice**.

Consular invoice When **goods** are exported the importing country may insist that they are accompanied by an **invoice** certified by their own consul in the exporting country. This enables import duties to be correctly charged. The consul will charge a fee known as consulage.

Consumer Credit Act 1974 This Act, the various provisions of which came into force at different times, is primarily concerned with the hiring of goods by consumers as individuals, including **sole traders** and **partnerships**, or the sale of goods to those persons on credit terms. It is enforced principally by the **Office of Fair Trading** but also by the Trading Standards Departments and, in Northern Ireland, the Department of Commerce. ◊ **Credit** ◊ **Credit sale agreement**.

The object is to give a greater degree of protection to innocent consumers against the possibility of their committing themselves to onerous and unforeseen obligations to suppliers and to lawful victimization by the more unscrupulous providers of credit, who disguise exorbitant interest rates and **conditions** through carefully convincing advertisements.

The main innovation was the introduction of the need to hold a **licence**. This licence is obtainable from the Director-General appointed under the Act and is only granted where the applicant is considered a suitable person to hold one. A refusal may arise from the past record of the applicant or where he is engaged in improper business practices. There is a right to appeal against such a refusal, initially to the Director and ultimately to the Secretary of State. The licensing requirement was brought into force in stages beginning in February 1976, but the general consumer credit system was not included until later, the closing date from which a licence was legally required being 1 October 1977. It is not possible to cover the legislation relating to licences here, but pamphlets are available from the Consumer Credit Licensing Branch at the Office of Fair Trading or from the nearest **HMSO** bookshop.

Generally speaking, anyone engaged in business where credit is given or hiring arrangements made needs a licence. So also do those concerned with credit reference or debt-collecting. There are specific minor exemptions and a general 'blanket' exemption to cover shopkeepers who allow monthly credit terms or credit purchases to be repaid in fewer than four instalments. Licences issued are recorded in a public register maintained by the Office of Fair Trading and this register is available for inspection. There are heavy penalties for indulging in credit trading of a type covered by the Act without holding a current licence. A licence will normally last for three years but can be revoked if the Director so decides.

The Consumer Credit Act is not only concerned with licensing. It also affords other protective measures, e.g.: (1) **credit sale agreements** will usually need to be in writing and contain details of all rights and obligations of the debtor together with the true cost of the credit, i.e. the true APR. This latter also applies to advertisements, which must disclose the true annual interest rate being charged, ◊ **Hire purchase**; (2) when agreements are made other than on the shop premises the consumer will normally be entitled to change his mind, i.e. the contract will not be enforceable until a certain time has elapsed – the 'cooling-off' period. Even after that the consumer will be able to appeal to the court if the terms are extortionate; (3) the consumer will usually have the right to pay off the debt before the agreed date and have a statutory rebate of charges already made for the additional period; (4) where the credit is given by a company other than the supplier of the goods then, if the credit is arranged by the supplier, both he and the creditor are equally liable under the arrangement; (5) any consumer has the right to a copy of any file on him kept by a credit reference agency and additionally the right to have such a file corrected where it is in error. ◊ **Credit rating**.

Consumer loyalty A rather abstract concept in the sense that it cannot be measured in monetary terms even though it is thought of as an asset. It is an adjunct of **goodwill** and often an integral part thereof. It is based on the idea that habits are never easy to break and that a customer will continue to patronize a shop or a brand of goods once initially 'hooked', irrespective of any change (unless very dramatic) in the quality of the goods or the service offered at the shop, e.g. the reason why a housewife uses Pinks soap-powder or shops at Bloggs is merely because she has always done so.

Consumers' Association An independent, non-profit-making organization established in 1956 to help shoppers by testing **goods** that are on **sale** to the public. The goods are obtained anonymously from **retailers**. It is a **company** limited by **guarantee** and publishes a monthly magazine *Which?* which gives the results of the tests. It also publishes a *Motoring Which?* and various paperbacks including *The Law for Consumers*, *The Legal Side of Buying a House* and *Buying Secondhand*. It makes recommendations to the government and provides information for use in schools. It is also prepared to send speakers.

Contango rate ◊ **Account days**.

Contingent liabilities An accounting term for liabilities that may or may not

arise, i.e. a debt contingent on an uncertain event.

Continuation clause A **marine insurance** clause covering situations where a ship is still at sea when its **insurance** runs out. The insurer agrees to cover risks at a pro rata rate of premium.

Continuous stock-taking ◊ **Perpetual inventory**.

Contract An agreement between two or more persons which is legally enforceable provided certain conditions are observed. It normally takes the form of one person's promise to do something in **consideration** of the other's agreeing to do or suffer something else in return.

Contract, ambiguity in Where a **contract** is in writing, or needs to be evidenced in writing, and there is ambiguity, the court may allow oral evidence to determine the intentions of the parties. In oral contracts ambiguity is more likely to arise from **mistake of misrepresentation**.

Contract, anticipatory breach of This happens when one party to a **contract** announces in advance that he does not intend to perform his part. The other party may then sue immediately for anticipatory breach or he may refrain from taking action and wait until the contract date. If he does this he may fail to recover anything if, by that time, the contract has become impossible through the fault of neither party, i.e. has been frustrated. ◊ **Frustration of contract**.

Contract, breach of The failure of one party to a contract to perform his part constitutes breach of that contract. It may take the form of (1) renunciation, where one party states that he has no intention of performing his part, (2) one party making the contract impossible to perform, e.g. by destroying the subject matter, or (3) straightforward failure of one party to honour his obligations. Whatever form the breach takes, the aggrieved party has various rights of action. He may sue for **damages**, or may apply to the court for **specific performance**. Where a contract is only partially performed then if the plaintiff has accepted the **part performance** he must pay for it though he may be able to claim on any balancedue. Hecannotbemadetoacceptpart performance only. Similarly, when the contract is only partly performed and the part-performance is expressly or implicitly accepted, the part-performer may sue for work done. ◊ **Quantum meruit**.

Contract by deed Certain contracts are not binding unless made by deed. These are: (1) gratuitous promises; (2) transfers of shares in **statutory companies**; (3) transfers of British ships or shares in them; (4) conditional **bills of sale**; (5) legal **mortgages** of land or an interest therein; (6) certain **leases** of land, tenements or hereditaments for more than three years.

Contract, continuous A **contract** where agreement is not restricted to one transaction, but applies to a number of them during a period of time, as in a contract of **partnership**.

Contract, drunkard's A drunkard can avoid **contracts** if the other party knew of his condition. He must, however, pay for **necessaries** supplied to him.

Contract evidenced in writing Certain **contracts** although valid are unenforceable unless evidenced in writing. These are (1) contracts of **guarantee**, and (2) contracts for the **sale** or other

disposition of land or interest in land. The memorandum in writing must state the names of the parties and the subject matter of the contract. It must be signed by the party to be charged. The terms of the contract should be stated. The **consideration** should be shown when the contract is in category (2). Various documents can be put together, e.g. letters and envelopes, to provide the necessary writing in bringing the action and parole evidence may be admitted to connect them.

Contract for differences **Stock Exchange** transactions are controlled by the normal rules of contract. Contracts for differences on the Stock Exchange come into a slightly different category. There is no deliberate intention to take or sell on the same account, receiving or paying the difference. These are known as dealings in differences and are, strictly speaking, wagers governed by the rules relating to **wagering contracts**. They are also known as Dealings for the Account.

Contract, gaming A **contract** where two persons stand to win or lose as the result of a game. These contracts are void, some were even illegal. However, certain forms of gaming have now been made legal by the Betting, Gaming and Lotteries Act 1963. Gaming is not illegal providing the provisions of this Act are followed, though gaming contracts are still void. ◊ **Contract, illegal** ◊ **Contract, void**.

Contract, illegal A **contract** formed for an illegal purpose, or one declared illegal by statute, such as (1) a **gaming contract** which does not fulfil the conditions of the Betting, Gaming, and Lotteries Act 1963 (all gaming contracts are void, if not illegal), (2) agreements to commit an indictable offence or civil wrong, (3) agreements against the national interest, (4) agreements to defraud the Inland Revenue, (5) agreements to pervert the course of justice, (6) agreements involving **maintenance** or **champerty**, (7) agreements of an immoral character.

Illegal contracts are void *ab initio*. If both parties are equally at fault, neither can sue the other. Money or property can be recovered, however, (1) by an innocent party from a guilty party, (2) before performance or on **frustration**, (3) where this can be done without pleading, or relying on, the particular illegality.

Contract in writing Certain **contracts** must be in writing if they are to be valid. These are (1) **bills of exchange** and **promissory notes**, (2) **assignments** of copyright, (3) contracts of **marine insurance**, (4) transfers of company **shares**, (5) **hire purchase, credit sale agreements** and **conditional sale agreements** under the **Consumer Credit Act** 1974. In the last instance the contract is valid but normally unenforceable.

Contract, infant's Generally speaking, an infant, that is, a person under eighteen, cannot make **contracts** enforceable against him, except contracts for necessaries ('**goods** suitable to the infant's condition in life and to his actual requirements at the time of sale or delivery'), or beneficial contracts of service (e.g. contracts for apprenticeship). In addition, the Infant's Relief Act 1874 provides that all contracts made by an infant (1) for repayment of money lent, (2) for goods, other than necessaries supplied or to be supplied, (3) on an **account stated**, are absolutely void. Although an infant cannot be sued on contracts generally, he will find it difficult to bring an action

himself where he has obtained some benefit. Generally speaking, an infant cannot ratify on coming of age a contract made in infancy; there must be a new contract. There may be an exception where the contract is a continuing business contract (e.g. a **partnership**) which the infant does not repudiate within a reasonable time of coming of age. If he continues to act as a party to the contract he may be held liable on it, but only for the period since his coming of age.

A person legally comes of age on the day before his eighteenth birthday.

Contract, married woman A married woman may now **contract** quite freely, as though she were single. At one time in **common law** the husband and wife were one person, the husband being that person. The wife was not allowed to contract on her own account. This was true until the late nineteenth century. ⇩ **Necessaries**.

Contract note A note issued by a **stockbroker** as evidence of a transaction to buy or sell **shares**. It is a legal document setting out details of: (1) the number of **shares** or amount of **stock** bought or sold; (2) the **company** involved; (3) the **price**; (4) the **consideration**; (5) the broker's **commission**. The note must be stamped − $\frac{1}{2}$ per cent of the consideration. This is the transfer stamp. There is also a **contract** stamp at an **ad valorem** rate. The note must also show the amount payable to or from the broker and the date of settlement. It should be retained for **capital gains tax** purposes. Contract notes are often called bought notes or sold notes.

Contract of affreightment A **contract** made by a shipper with a shipowner for the carriage of **goods** by sea.

Contract of Employment Act First passed in 1963, this Act gives an employee the right to demand a proper contract of employment setting out the terms on which he is employed, the duties and obligations of each party and the conditions on which the **contract** may be terminated by either party. The Act at present only applies to full-time employees in permanent employment. In industry the contract is usually a standard one approved by the relevant trade union. In the retail trade written contracts are uncommon, the employee tending to rely on the good faith of his employer and his basic rights in **common law**. The Act applies to basic contracts rather than to **service contracts** taken out with directors and senior employees, though the latter type of contract is no less legally binding.

The 1963 Act was strengthened by the Employment Protection (Consolidation) Act 1978 which further provided that within thirteen weeks of the commencement of employment the employee must be given a written contract stating *inter alia*, hours of work, rate of pay, holiday entitlement, details of any pension scheme run by the employer, and notice required for termination of the contract of employment by each party to that contract. ◊ **Redundancy**.

Contract of novation Rights and liabilities in **contract** may be transferred by the substitution of a new contract for the old (with the consent of all the parties affected). This contract is known as a contract of novation. It is common in **partnerships** where one partner is introduced in place of another.

Contract of personal service Certain types of **contract** of employment are of a personal nature: they can only be performed by the person agreeing to do so. If the person is unable to act the contract becomes impossible and **damages** may accrue depending on whether the responsibility was or was not the fault of the person concerned. Distinguish from contracts where delegation is possible. A builder may subcontract work but an artist generally cannot.

Contract of record This is not a **contract** in the normal sense of the word, but takes the form of e.g. a court order where one person is obliged to perform some act such as payment of maintenance. The obligation is entered in the records of a superior court and is binding for this reason – it does not depend on the consent of the parties.

Contract, parole A simple **contract** which is not in writing, though of course the absence of writing may make it difficult to enforce, because absence of writing may mean absence of evidence.

Contract, privity of Rights and obligations generally attach only to parties to the **contract**. An outsider has no right to claim unless he is, for example, a beneficiary under a trust, a third party in a motor **insurance** policy, or a supplier of **goods** who may enforce prices subject to the Resale Prices Act 1964. ◊ **Negligence of auditor** ◊ **Resale price maintenance**.

Contract, specialty This is a **contract in writing** in the form of a **deed**. To be effective it must be signed, sealed and delivered. The latter word is used in a transitory sense though delivery is usually implied unless the contrary can be proved. No **consideration** is required for such a contract and the absence thereof will mean that **equity** will not afford a decree of **specific performance** should the contract be breached.

Contract: substantial performance Where a **contract** is breached because one party has not completed his part, the court will not allow the plaintiff to consider himself completely discharged from his obligations. Where there is substantial performance, the other party must pay up and sue for damages for the amount by which the work is badly done. For example if A asks B to build him a house and B builds the house but paints one or two walls a colour not in the contract, A cannot say that B has not performed the contract and that therefore he need not pay for the house. The court would say the contract was substantially performed and A can only sue for any damage and the additional cost of changing the colour scheme.

Contract, trade union The position is somewhat anomalous. Where the union is registered under the Trade Union Acts 1871–6, it is governed by certain rules applicable to corporate bodies. It can sue and be sued in its own name despite the fact that it has not yet been decided whether a union is a legal *persona* distinct from its members or an association of individuals who can appear in a collective name. It may be sued for breach of particular contracts both by persons outside the union and by its own members. ◊ **Employment legislation**.

Contract, void A void contract is effectively one that never existed, either because it is not recognized by the law, e.g. a **gaming contract**, or because there is a fundamental mistake common to both parties. This latter may be with regard to the subject matter or with respect to the identity of the subject matter or with respect to the identity of the contracting parties. Because a void contract does not exist in the eyes of the law, it follows that no action can arise from it.

Contract, voidable A **contract** which may be rescinded by one of the parties to it. For example, if A is persuaded to contract with B on the basis of a misrepresentation made by B, then A may avoid the contract while B is bound by it.

Contribution A term used in **insurance** when one insurance company claims a contribution from another in settling a claim. This frequently happens in **marine insurance**, and may also happen in other policies where the insured is dealing with two separate companies for the same property. A person cannot obtain more than the **value** of the property by insuring twice: each company will pay a proportion of the claim. ◊ **Average clause** ◊ **Over-insurance**.

Contributory A person liable to contribute towards the debts of a **company** on **winding-up**. The term includes **members of companies** holding fully paid **shares**, though strictly speaking these cannot be called on to pay anything further.

Lists of contributories distinguish between those liable personally and those liable through representing some other person. There are A and B lists. The A list shows present members; the B list, past members. A past member is not liable: (1) if he ceased to be a member a year or more before the commencement of the winding-up; (2) for debts incurred after he has ceased to be a member. Otherwise he is liable for debts incurred while he was still a member, when the other members fail to pay, up to the nominal value of the shares he held.

Control accounts An accounting term for accounts showing total trade debtors and total **trade creditors**. When **invoices** or cash receipts are posted to individual accounts, the total for the day is entered in the control account. The balance on the control account should therefore always equal the total of the individual balances on the personal accounts.

Controller Usually the person financially in charge of a business.

Convertible bank-note A bank-note which gives the bearer the right to have its face value converted to gold or some other commodity of value equivalent to the amount stated. At one time all UK **bank-notes** were convertible – this is evidenced by the 'promise to pay' words thereon – and could be exchanged for gold. Nowadays all the bearer has the right to demand is another note of the same denomination.

Convertible capital bond An instrument very similar to **convertible loan stock** but structured so that it goes through a two-stage conversion process, firstly into preference shares and then into ordinary shares. It may incorporate the Premium Put feature, introduced during the late 1980s. A Premium Put is an option enabling the investor to sell the bond back to the issuing company at a premium if, after a specified period, its price has not risen sufficiently to make conversion attractive or worthwhile. The option can be a disadvantage to the issuing company which cannot be certain whether any or all of the capital raised by the bond may have to be repaid and at a premium. For that reason bonds carrying a Premium Put option are usually offered at a low interest rate.

Convertible loan stock Occasionally companies issue loan stock with a right to convert this stock into **ordinary shares** or **preference shares** at some stated time in the future. This is known as convertible loan stock. The term is also applied to stock issued by the government, which the holder has the right to convert into new stock instead of obtaining repayment.

Cooperatives ◊ **Worker Cooperative**.

Copyright This refers to an amalgam of statute and **common law** which, within the UK, attempts to protect the work of one writer from being freely copied or in any way reproduced by another. Apart from certain limited exceptions, e.g. short 'quotes' as part of another work, the law does not allow an author's work to be used or reproduced without express permission and will punish all parties to such an offence – including the printer as well as the publisher. The principal statute is the Copyright Act 1956, as amended in 1968 and 1971 (and in 1985 to cover computer programs). The copyright restrictions apply not only to writers but also to artists and others who might contribute some creative work to society, e.g. film-makers, broadcasters, musicians, etc. Protection is not given to 'ideas' or 'plots' and suchlike. It is essential that the idea or plot be put into a recognizable form such as a novel, a play or an operetta. Once this is done, copyright arises automatically and no registration thereof is necessary. Generally speaking, the copyright attaches to the 'work' as a whole rather than to its title; separate copyrights can attach to different editions of the work by divers publishers. The copyright is first vested in the creator of the work but may then be sold to and vested in the publisher. Nowadays there is an increasing tendency for publishers to leave copyright with authors and rely on contractual agreements for protection for themselves.

The law of copyright is very complex and, when the question of reproduction in other countries arises, very dependent on international agreements, which themselves are at the mercy of varied interpretations. So far as the originator is concerned the copyright will last until fifty years from the year of his death. During that time, authors or their dependants will be entitled to all **royalties** arising from their work. Copyright may be assigned by the holder at any time. The only legal requirement is that the assignment shall be in writing and freely signed by the donor.

Copy typist A person trained to use a typewriter, and typing from manuscripts or printed matter but not from **shorthand**.

Cornering the market A person corners a market when he obtains a virtual **monopoly** over the supply of particular **goods** or services. He is then able to name his own price. In the past this sometimes happened to the market in raw materials. Markets may be cornered for a short term or a person may make a fortune by controlling the supply of a particular raw material for an unlimited period. The possibilities are now somewhat restricted by state intervention. ◊ **Monopolies and Mergers Commission** ◊ **Anti-trust laws**.

Corporate raider A term used with reference to individuals with very large resources of ready money who, either personally or through a company which they control, buy heavily in the equity of a target company with a view to

either taking control of that company or, more frequently, forcing the directors of the target company to protect their own position and that of the company itself by taking steps that will enhance the attractiveness of the equity to an extent sufficient to dissuade present holders from selling. These measures will usually cause the share price to escalate and enable the raider to resell the shares acquired at a considerable profit. Although corporate raiders were at one time more common in the USA, the practice has now spread to this side of the Atlantic. ◊ **City Code on Take-overs and Mergers**.

Corporation An association of persons recognized by the law as having a collective personality. The corporation can act as if it were distinct from its members: it has 'perpetual succession' and a common seal. It can therefore contract quite freely – it can also be fined, but it obviously cannot be sent to prison or incur penalties which can only be applied to individuals. A corporation is either a **corporation sole** or a **corporation aggregate**.

Corporation aggregate A corporation consisting of a number of individuals: the opposite of a **corporation sole**. The most common forms of corporation aggregate are local councils and limited companies.

Corporation sole This is the earliest type of corporation as it does not relate to a group of persons acting in concert but to an individual who holds some public office under the Crown or the State. This individual has two faces: a personal one, within the normal restrictions set by the law, and an official one, as a public office-holder with power to bind the office itself and all subsequent holders of that office. When acting properly, i.e. not **ultra vires**, in this official capacity then this person is acting as a corporation sole. These two manners of contracting are quite distinct one from the other and nothing effected in one capacity will affect duties or responsibilities in the other. ◊ **Corporation aggregate**.

Corporation tax Introduced originally in 1965 to replace the then operative methods of taxing companies by **income tax** and **profits tax**, it served a double purpose. Not only were the profits of companies taxed, but additional amounts were payable by way of income tax on that part of profit distributed to shareholders. This 'double taxation' was discontinued after 1 April 1973 as part of the drastic tax changes in the budget of that year. ◊ **Imputation system**. Company profits are now only taxed once and there is a lower rate for small companies, with **marginal relief** for those companies just above the limit set for the definition of a small company.

It is not possible to summarize the whole compass of corporation tax here and the reader should seek specialist advice in particular cases. Points to be remembered as of general application are as follows. Corporation tax, unlike the old income tax, is levied on the basis of the financial year (1 April to 31 March). If the **accounting reference period** of a company straddles two financial years the taxable profit will have to be allocated between the two years and the relevant rate charged on the portion allocated to each year. Company profits are not liable to tax on a preceding year basis but on an actual basis; i.e. profits for the year ending 31 December 1978 are not taxed in the fiscal year 1979–80 (as under previous income tax regulations) but are

taxed in two fiscal years: 1977–8 (from 1 January to 31 March 1978) and 1978–9 (from 1 April to 31 December 1978). The rate of corporation tax is fixed in the Finance Act each year and tends to be higher than the standard rate of income tax.

Corporation tax is levied in two parts, known as **advance corporation tax**, paid when any distribution of profit is made, and mainstream corporation tax on the remainder of the year's earnings. Taxable profit is arrived at after making various adjustments to the figure disclosed in the company's own accounts in order to bring the figure into line with the various regulations of the Inland Revenue as to what is an allowable expense and what income is taxable. There are particular rules regarding deductions for depreciation of assets, which are covered by **capital allowances**. Special regulations also apply to the part of a company's income regarded as **franked investment income**, i.e. generally income from investments, already taxed at source. Capital gains are also subject to corporation tax, though the rate is reduced to bring it in line with **capital gains tax**.

Corresponding figures It is common practice for annual accounts of all organizations to provide, in parentheses or otherwise, corresponding or comparative figures for the previous year. Provision of such comparative figures is obligatory in the case of companies. This was laid down in the 1948 Companies Act and reinforced by the Companies Acts 1981, 1985 and 1989. It applies even where there is no current figure. Where the method of calculating the current amount has changed then the comparative figure should be recalculated on the new basis with the reason for the adjustment being given. The requirement to provide corresponding figures extends to the notes to the accounts, with certain limited exceptions.

Cost accountant. Generically an accountant or accounts clerk whose job concerns the fixing of monies due for work done in manufacturing a product (i.e. reckoning the cost of material and labour consumed but who is increasingly called upon to estimate the probable unit cost of a manufacturing process so that a price can be projected for the purpose of making a tender. In this sense the work is closely allied to that of a **quantity surveyor**.

In present usage the term cost accountant has taken on a far wider meaning. Cost and management accounting concern the everyday running of a business, as opposed to financial accounting, which deals with the problems of obtaining and accounting for the necessary finance. Cost accountants are also closely connected with budgeting and **budgetary control**. It is the cost accountant who is responsible for obtaining many of the figures on which a budgetary control system is based. ◊ **Financial accountant** ◊ **Management accountant**.

Cost and freight (c & f) A kind of foreign trade contract, which is similar to a **cost**, **insurance and freight** contract, except that the importer looks after the **insurance**. The seller must give the buyer sufficient notice to enable him to do this.

Cost benefit analysis The evaluation of the social and/or economic worth of a prospective project. It attempts to measure in monetary terms not only the visible, calculable gains and losses of a project but also the abstract benefits or possible detrimental results. If the total projected 'gain' exceeds the foreseeable 'loss' then the project may be approved. Such analyses are not only applied to future possibilities but also to existing situations to decide whether to maintain or scrap them. Cost benefit analyses are viewed with some cynicism, particularly in situations which require a number of subjective assessments; they are often regarded as no more than academic games.

Cost book mining companies Companies formed for working metalliferous mines, or tinstreaming in Devon and Cornwall. These were originally governed by local custom and subject to the jurisdiction of the Stannaries Court. Jurisdiction is now vested in the county court of Cornwall at Bodmin. The rules governing them are found in the Stannaries Acts 1869 and 1887.

Cost, insurance and freight (**cif**) A term used in foreign trade **contracts** where the exporter, in addition to the **free on board** charges, pays the cost of the **insurance** and the **freight**. His price therefore includes all charges up to the port of delivery. He must supply the buyer with the documents necessary to take delivery of the **goods** on arrival. These documents are normally: a **bill of lading**, an **insurance** policy (not a cover note) and an **invoice**. The seller may not actually pay the freight but is responsible for it and if the buyer is to pay for any part of it this will be shown as a credit on the invoice. The goods are usually at the buyer's **risk** after shipment. He must pay when the documents are tendered whether or not (1) the goods actually arrive, (2) they have been lost en route, (3) he has had any opportunity of examining them. Property will pass when the documents are accepted by the buyer.

Payment is often made by accepting a **bill of exchange**. The buyer can always reject the goods if they are not as described in the **contract**.

Cost, insurance, freight, and interest (**cifi**) A type of foreign trade **contract**. It is similar to **cost, insurance and freight** except that interest is paid on the value of the goods. This may be for the benefit of some **middle-man** acting for the importer.

Cost-plus contract Common in the construction industry this is a contract where it is almost impossible to forecast a precise ultimate cost. In order to keep some control over spending the party who will have to pay makes an agreement with the contractor that the final bill will be based on prices for the materials needed with an estimated additional figure or agreed percentage (added to the cost of materials) to cover probable labour costs. This type of contract is less common in peace-time than in war-time as it gives contractors no incentive to keep costs to a minimum – in fact quite the reverse. The higher the cost of the material the more contractors would be paid for their labour, irrespective of the actual work done.

Council Tax A form of local taxation introduced to replace the Poll Tax launched in 1990, as the Community Charge, but abandoned in 1992 as unpopular and uncollectable. The new Council Tax is similar to the local authority **rates** which the Poll Tax replaced but although, like the rates, keyed to property values, it places more emphasis on the number of people occupying a property. Domestic properties are divided nationally into a defined number of bands depending on value. The tax is levied by local authorities as a centrally fixed rate per pound, a discount being given when there is only one adult occupant. Reductions are also applicable where special circumstances apply, e.g people on Income Support.

Counterclaim The claim by a defendant against a plaintiff whereby he hopes to reduce or wipe out the **damages** he may have to pay, the claim being one which could give right to a cause of action as opposed to a **set-off**.

County court judgments In certain circumstances a county court will make an order that a stated sum of money is to be paid by one person to another. This may arise out of an action in **tort** or may be one of many judgments made in some small **bankruptcies**, which are not the subject of an order in bankruptcy but are dealt with summarily by the county court. The person against whom the order is made is known as the **judgment debtor** and the person to whom the money must be paid is the **judgment creditor**. ◊ **Bankruptcy: summary administration**. Any judgment debt for £10 or over which remains unpaid after one month is entered in a register at the Registry of County Court Judgments. The entry will state the name and address of the debtor and the amount of the debt. Anyone may inspect this register and, on request, an official search will be made giving all unpaid debts applicable to a named debtor. The cost is on a sliding scale. When judgment debts are paid or reversed, debtors may apply to the court for removal of their name – though the cost of an official application often deters them from doing so. ◊ **Credit rating**.

Coupon A slip often attached to **bearer**

bonds, the surrender of which gives right to a **dividend** at a particular date. There are normally a number of coupons. A coupon is torn off the coupon sheet each year, or other period.

Covenants Written agreements to pay a stated sum to a stated person or organization for a stated number of years. If the payment is for charitable purposes, the payee can treat the sum received as paid out of the taxed income of the payer and reclaim the tax suffered in producing that net amount. At one time only standard rate tax could be so recovered, but in recent years the recovery of higher rates of tax up to a fixed ceiling has been permitted where the beneficiary is a registered charity.

Although the covenant system was primarily intended to help registered charities, it became an increasingly common way for parents to provide funds for children in full-time education. The parent covenanted a certain sum in favour of the child who could then reclaim the tax paid by the parent on that sum and thereby obtain a benefit greater than the money actually given by the parent. This loophole was stopped in 1988 when such schemes were no longer accepted by the Inland Revenue. Originally, a covenant had to continue for at least seven years. This rule has been relaxed and it is only necessary for the donor to be prepared to continue the payment, not actually to do so, and the amount paid over can be varied at the option of the donor. Details of covenants must be given on annual income tax returns and the donor must provide a written declaration of tax deducted to the Inland Revenue annually.

Cover A contemporary abbreviation of the phrase 'times covered' with particular reference to company **dividends**. The cover for a dividend is determined by the total **net profit** available for distribution; it is expressed as a multiple of the amount paid out, e.g. a dividend which is three times covered means that only one third of profits available for distribution were paid out by way of dividend. ◊ **Price-earnings ratio** ◊ **Yield** ◊ **Dividend yield**.

Cover note A provisional document issued by an **insurance** company to bide over the time between the acceptance of a risk and the issuing of a policy.

Credit In common usage this word is about as meaningful as the word 'nice'. Although generally used as an adjective (credit card, credit note, etc.), it has a more precise meaning in the business world, where it is the opposite of cash. Transactions are made on a 'credit' basis where no cash changes hands. The introduction and acceptance of credit in business transactions was the principal cause of the immense expansion of trade and industry over the past three hundred years; it was to economics, national and international, what the introduction of the 'zero' symbol was to mathematics. The world, particularly the Western world, has now become so credit-orientated that the point is fast approaching where cash will become completely unnecessary.

Another, rather specialized meaning of the word credit occurs in **double-entry book-keeping**, where, as the opposite of debit, it is one side of a book entry, indicating either a liability for **balance sheet** purposes or income in the **profit and loss account**.

Credit card The credit card is becoming a major instrument in consumer transactions and is replacing the cheque in the payment of everyday debts. It appeared first in the USA and is now spreading throughout the developed countries. In its simplest form it is a method of obtaining credit on hire purchase, i.e. the user can make purchases on credit up to an amount agreed by him with the credit card company merely by presenting his card to the vendor in place of cash. The vendor 'processes' the card by using it to frank a voucher, both voucher and franking machine being supplied gratis to him by the credit card company. The vendor separates the voucher into two parts and presents one to his bank, which credits his account and forwards the slip to the credit card company. The vendor retains the other part as a record of the transaction.

The credit card company accumulates these slips and then sends monthly statements to the cardholders, who pay the balance on the statement either immediately or in a number of instalments, according to their agreement with the credit card company. The latter also sends a monthly statement to individual vendors summarizing transactions and making a charge for services rendered, i.e. a percentage on the total of sales handled by that vendor. In effect, retailers or other vendors who sell on a credit card basis give an automatic discount on the price of the goods or services supplied. The credit card company, in addition to the charge made to the retailer, receives sums by way of interest from its customers who have taken advantage of the offer to stagger repayments.

The principal credit cards in use in the UK are those obtained from the companies set up by the big four banks. These, though strictly independent entities, are associated companies of those banks.

Barclays was the first in the field with the inauguration of the **Barclaycard** Company. The other banks combined and came up with the **Access** card, issued by the Joint Credit Card Company Ltd, the shares of which are totally owned by the banks themselves. There is an acknowledged link in so far as Access cards carry an indication of the particular bank at which holders keep their money.

Access cards and Barclaycards are not the only credit cards in circulation. There are also **Diners Club** cards, **American Express** cards, etc., not to mention the international cards, such as Mastercards, Eurocards, etc., which are becoming more and more common. Credit cards should not be confused with **cheque cards**, which fulfil a quite different function, although certain credit cards can also be used as cheque cards. ◊ **Debit cards**.

Credit insurance A form of insurance against financial loss incurred through default by debtors in a trading situation. This may involve monies due for goods or services provided, and may arise through the insolvency of the debtor or from protracted default due to economic or political circumstances. This frequently occurs in international trade. At one time this risk could be covered by government through the **Export Credits Guarantee Department** of the Department of Trade. This department has recently confined itself to coverage against default involving large sums arising from long-term capital goods transactions and has left the smaller risks, on less substantial trading contracts, to be covered by companies specializing in this form of insurance within the private sector.

Credit note A document issued by a **vendor** giving credit to the debtor for, say, **goods** returned, or overcharges made on an **invoice**.

Credit rating A person's credit rating refers to an assessment of their credit-worthiness, i.e. to what extent (both in time and money) they can be allowed credit for amounts due. Credit ratings were traditionally private affairs and were discussed between banks and potential **vendors** with the knowledge and agreement of the person in question. In recent years a noxious tendency to 'trade' in credit ratings has occured. Firms specialize in establishing the credit ratings of individuals through information gleaned from various sources, e.g. county courts, **bankruptcy** proceedings, lists provided by professional debt collectors, **hire purchase** companies, etc. These ratings are made without the consent or even the knowledge of the subject and can be made available to third parties. Some legal steps have been taken to reverse this trend and redress wrongs done to innocent individuals by inserting a clause in the **Consumer Credit Act 1974**. This states that consumers have a *prima facie* right to a copy of any information about them in the possession of a credit reference agency. They also have the right to have such information corrected if it is incorrect. ◊ **Banker, disclosure of information by** ◊ **Debt collecting**.

Credit rating is applied to companies as well as to individuals, and particularly to bonds and other securities issued by companies. The best-known corporate credit rating agencies are the US agencies, Moody's and Standard and Poor's. In the US investors rely heavily on these agencies for their published ratings of the safety of bonds and other commercial paper, and such ratings have a consider-able influence over investment decisions. The top rating given is known as a Triple A rating. ◊ **Data Protection Act 1984.**

Credit Risk Companies whose business involves selling on credit, often for extended periods, are prone to incur cash-flow problems emanating from the inability of debtors to meet due payment dates or, in extreme cases, totally reneging on amounts owing for goods or services supplied. There are a number of methods of providing against such eventualities, the most common being **invoice discounting** and **factoring**. ◊ **Hire purchase finance**.

Credit sale agreement Defined by law as 'an agreement for the sale of goods under which the purchase price is payable by five or more instalments not being a conditional sale agreement'. Such agreements are now covered by the **Consumer Credit Act 1974.** ◊ **Licence**.

Credit squeeze A popular term for the State's interference with normal market forces in an attempt to lower the level of economic activity by reducing the **money supply**. It is effected by making **credit** more expensive in the following ways: through direct instruction to banks; by raising the **minimum lending rate** or Bank of England base rate so as to force other organizations linked to the **money market** to increase their rates accordingly; by making changes in the **hire purchase** regulations so as to deter prospective purchasers. ◊ **Competitive market** ◊ **Mixed economy** ◊ **Prices and incomes policy**.

Credit transfer A method of settling a debt. It is often used by persons or businesses with a great many debts to settle at any one time. A list of the **creditors**

is given to the **bank**, together with the amounts due, and the name and address of each creditor's bank. The bank then transfers the amounts due and the debtor notifies each creditor that the transfer has been made. The obvious advantage of this method is that it saves writing out and signing a great number of **cheques**, though this saving should be weighed against the charges made by the bank.

Creditors Persons to whom or organizations to which money or some other debt is owed. The accounts of all businesses will include, in the balance sheet, a figure for creditors. Companies must, in their accounts, distinguish between creditors payable within the coming year and those payable after longer periods. Additionally, the 1981 Companies Act required specific indication in the accounts of amounts not due for payment until after five years beginning from the day following the date of the accounts together with terms of repayment in such cases and details of any interest payable.

Creditors' voluntary winding-up ▷ **Winding-up, voluntary**.

Critical path analysis An **operational research** technique used in management. The idea is to examine a project in detail with the objective of (1) breaking it down into component parts and (2) examining each part both in isolation and in its relationship to the other parts. By this means it may be seen how the project can be completed in the best possible way in the shortest possible time.

Cross offer When two parties make an **offer** simultaneously in a manner that, had one followed as an acceptance, it would have comprised a **contract**. As

an example: A writes to B offering to sell a certain horse for £1,000. B writes to A offering to buy the same horse at the same price. The letters cross in the post. There is no contract.

Crossing, general Two parallel transverse lines placed across a cheque with or without the words 'not negotiable' or '& Co.'. This makes it necessary for the holder to pay the cheque into an account at a bank rather than being able to obtain cash for it across the bank counter. ▷ **Cheque crossings** ▷ **Crossing, special**.

Crossing: not negotiable If a **cheque** is crossed 'not negotiable' the holder cannot give a better **title** than that which he possesses. This does not stop the holder from transferring the cheque to another party but that other party cannot get a better title than that possessed by the holder himself. The negotiability of the cheque has in fact ceased – it is no longer a **negotiable instrument**. As an example: A draws a cheque. If it is not crossed 'not negotiable' B may steal it and bank it or pass it on to C – A would have no redress. If it was crossed 'not negotiable' B having no title could not give one to any third party and therefore A could recover the money. A cheque is the only type of **bill of exchange** which can be crossed 'not negotiable'. An ordinary bill, if it is to be not negotiable, must state this on the face of the bill.

Crossing, special A special crossing is one where words are added to a general crossing specifying by name the bank at which the cheque is to be presented. ▷ **Cheque crossings**.

'Cum' dividend and 'ex' dividend When the price of a **share** is quoted it is quoted 'cum div' or 'ex div'. This indicates that the price includes or does not include the right to receive the next **dividend**. Quotations are normally 'cum div', i.e. the buyer receives the next dividend. 'Ex div' prices are generally given only for the period (e.g. one month) immediately before the payment of the dividend. When a share goes 'ex div', the price naturally drops rather suddenly.

Cum new A **Stock Exchange** term applied to **shares** when they are offered for sale with the right to any outstanding **scrip issue** or **rights issue**.

Currency The coins, notes, cheques, etc., accepted within a country as a proper medium of exchange in the conduct of business. ◊ **International currency** ◊ **Bank notes** ◊ **Cheque** ◊ **Mint** ◊ **Money supply** ◊ **Legal tender**.

Currency depreciation The extent to which the value of a currency has fallen in terms of its exchangeable value for other currencies. If the currency of one country is tied to another the extent of its depreciation is reflected in the increase in the cost of the other. If, on the other hand, a country's currency is said to be floating freely in the foreign exchanges then the extent of its depreciation will vary according to with which other currency it is compared. ◊ **Balance of payments** ◊ **Foreign exchange market** ◊ **Free exchange rates**.

Currency of a bill A term used with reference to **bills of exchange**. It relates to the time between the drawing of a bill and the date it becomes payable. If the bill is payable **after sight** then the time only runs from the date of acceptance.

Current accounts ◊ **Accounts, current**. The term is also used in bookkeeping with reference to proprietors' personal accounts which are not their **capital** accounts.

Current assets An accounting term for **assets** continually turned over in the course of business. They should be distinguished from **fixed assets** and other assets bought for permanent use. Examples of current assets are **debtors**, **stock**, **work in progress**, cash and also perhaps investments which are not **trade investments**. The phrase 'net current assets' is often used and refers to the total of current assets less the total of **current liabilities**. Another name for this difference is **working capital**. ◊ **Liquid assets**.

Current cost accounting (**CCA**). The method of accounting for inflation favoured by the Inflation Accounting Committee set up by the government in 1974 under the chairmanship of Mr F. E. Sandilands. The report of the committee, referred to as the Sandilands Report, was presented to Parliament in September 1975.

It considered the claims and theories underlying the current purchasing power method advocated by the **Accounting Standards Steering Committee**, but opted for a much more restricted system which involved the restatement of physical assets only and disregarded the effects of changes in purchasing power on monetary items.

Current cost accounting accepts money as the basic unit of measurement, as opposed to 'purchasing power', which is the basic unit implicit in CPP. The Report did not consider that any particular manner of indexing was called for though it did suggest that various indices could be used in arriving at the value of an asset. This value (the value at which all physical assets featured in the **balance sheet** were to be restated) should be reckoned in terms of 'value to the business' and would be fixed after all relevant factors had been taken into consideration by the directors and other persons concerned. ◊ **Index number**.

The concept of 'value to the business' is not new. It had already featured in the Companies Act 1967, where directors were obliged to state whether in their opinion the values of assets shown in the balance sheet differed materially from **market value**. The principal failing of the concept lies in its subjectivity. The value to the business of any asset depends upon so many unknown factors that an arguable case can often be presented for any **value** which the directors may prefer to show. 'Value to the business' could also be construed as 'value in use', which begs the question: what use? In far too many instances there is a wide divergence between value in present use and value in one of many alternative uses. True, CCA may technically insist on value in present use as being the meaning of 'value to the business', but until that is laid down in statute law the concept must be treated very warily.

Although the Sandilands Report recommended the replacement of traditional historically based accounts by current cost accounts it did suggest that certain information drawn from **historical cost accounting** should be provided as a supplement. ◊ **Accounting for inflation** ◊ **Current purchasing power accounting** ◊ **Replacement cost accounting** ◊ **Alternative accounting rules** ◊ **Paper profit**.

Current liabilities An accounting term for those monies owed in the near future,

usually within the next accounting period. These will include **trade creditors**, current taxation, and **dividends** declared and due. They should be distinguished from long-term liabilities and **share capital** or **loan capital**. ◊ **Creditors**.

Current purchasing power (CPP) accounting A concept introduced and elaborated between 1973 and 1975 by the British **Accounting Standards Steering Committee**. It aims to have published accounts restated in terms of a constant unit of purchasing power by using a general **index** of prices as the basis for adjusting all figures shown, so as to express them in terms of the present value of money. Restatement of liabilities would involve unrealized 'profits' which would be classified as holding gains. It is these which have created the most difficulty in gaining acceptance for the method. ◊ **Accounting for inflation** ◊ **Current cost accounting** ◊ **Paper profit**.

Current ratio The ratio of **current assets** to **current liabilities**. In a healthy business this should be greater than one. A lower level would be indicative of approaching **insolvency** or a tendency towards **overtrading**. Other ratios, such as the **liquid ratio**, are rather more important in this context but the current ratio provides an early warning system. As with all ratios it is the trend rather than the absolute figure at a single moment that is the more significant.

Current taxation An accounting term used to describe amounts due to the Inland Revenue in respect of taxation and payable in the near future.

Custom of trade This phrase generally

refers to terms in a **contract** – which may be implied by usage or custom in particular trades. Words take on different meanings in different trades. Usage of trade will also be relevant to the interpretation of written contract. ◊ **Oral evidence**.

Customs: airports Regulations at airports are similar to those at seaports, particularly in the case of stores. Commanders of aircraft arriving from or leaving for abroad must use, except in emergency, airports' Customs and declare cargo carried inwards and outwards. There are facilities for clearing goods from the airports before the entry of the goods is passed and the duty paid. A 'provisional' entry is made and the importer leaves a sizeable cash deposit with the Customs authorities. Airports often have a duty-free shop for the convenience of departing passengers. Goods are sold here free of duty and are controlled by Customs officials. Now that inauguration of the **single market** has taken place customs clearance within Common Market countries should be less onerous. However it is not cost-effective to identify strictly intra-EU flights and provide separate facilities for them. Although holders of EU passports can be afforded swifter clearance, the handling of cargoes must still be closely supervised since intra-EU items can only be identified by the examination of certificates of origin. Where cargoes are mixed this is not always a speedy process.

Customs and Excise ◊ **Her Majesty's Customs and Excise**.

Customs: crews' effects The preventive officer checks all **goods** obtained abroad or during the voyage: forbidden imports are confiscated. A limited amount of duty-free goods is allowed in, and the remainder is either taxed or put in bond until the ship leaves again. ◊ **Bond note**.

Customs debenture ◊ **Entrepôt trade**.

Customs entry ◊ **Customs: final clearance inwards and entry outwards**.

Customs: final clearance inwards and entry outwards – **Rummaging** continues during the landing of a ship's cargo and again when all cargo is landed. The captain then receives a clearance inward certificate. He will need to present this before his next voyage. If the next voyage is outwards he must enter his ship 'outwards' at the Customs House.

Customs: landing cargo The landing of cargo is supervised. A Customs officer ensures that all cargo landed is declared and that nothing not declared has been landed. Cargo is also examined: this is done on a selective basis. The importer or **agent** opens the cargo on the direction of the Customs officer. Customs officers do not open, unpack or repack any goods.

Customs: ships' stores An incoming ship is boarded by a preventive officer who takes account of all dutiable **goods** in store on board – all such goods are put under Customs seal. There are heavy penalties for breaking such a seal – the goods may not be used while the ship is in port.

Customs tariff The list of **goods**, etc., on which duty is payable. Details can be obtained from Her Majesty's **Stationery Office**.

Customs union An agreement between any number of separate countries to standardize and/or abolish restrictions (either volume limits or duties payable) on mutual trade, i.e. to equalize or dismantle any barriers to trade between the countries concerned. In addition to this, those countries within the union agree to present a common front in respect of quotas and duties to the outside world. In the archetypal customs union there would be completely **free trade** between the participating countries and a single **tariff** wall *vis-à-vis* the outside world, so that any non-member country would face exactly the same restrictions on its exports whichever country within the union it approached.

The **Common Market** is a customs union established in 1957. This union, set up by the Treaty of Rome, had as its objective the acceptance of a common internal scale of customs duties which would be gradually reduced until conditions of completely free trade were established. The member countries also agreed to establish common barriers to trade apropos countries outside the Market. Because of the international commitments, first of France and then of the United Kingdom, the acceptance of completely free trade within and a single tariff without posed various problems which caused the setting up of mutually agreed and 'temporary' exceptions. Special facilities had, for instance, to be given to New Zealand dairy products which had been traditionally exported to the UK for many years. ♢ **Commonwealth preference**. The economy of that country had to be given time to adjust to the cutting off of privileged access to the UK market – either by creating new markets or by developing methods which would enable them to compete with or undercut the non-duty inter-European market. New Zealand was therefore given temporary

relief by clauses especially written into the Treaty of Rome.

Other barriers to completely free trade also arose, and methods had to be found of dealing with them without undermining the principles of the treaty. Most of the problems surrounded agriculture and so the **Common Agricultural Policy** was developed. This involved a complex pattern of inter-country subsidizing and finance. With the establishment of the **single market** within the EU from 1 January 1993, all internal barriers to trade between member countries of the Community have theoretically been removed. In practice, though goods may now move freely, there are still restrictions in operation within service industries. Difficulties are still presented by the variations in both rate and incidence of VAT throughout the Community, and until harmonization of this tax has been achieved truly free competition within the EU will remain elusive.

Without the common external tariff, a customs union would merely be a **free trade area**. Initially this was the form of union favoured by the UK and others and in 1959 the **European Free Trade Association** was formed with the UK as one of the more important members, economically. This area still exists, though the UK and some other members have now withdrawn and committed themselves to the European Union.

Cut-throat competition The process whereby the producers of goods systematically reduce their selling prices and maintain them at the lowest level possible for such time as it takes to drive competitors, who are insufficiently funded or less efficient in producing the same goods, out of business. ♢ **Marginal cost**. Although this practice is often lauded as

Damages An amount awarded by a court to an appellant who has suffered loss as a result of the actions of another party. The action for damages may be in **contract** or in **tort**. Damages are intended as a form of compensation and though not the only remedy for loss that a court can supply, they are the most common. Other remedies lie in **Equity** and include a decree of **specific performance** (in contract) or an **injunction**, though damages may be awarded in addition to such orders.

The assessment of damages is a very complex matter, particularly where the case concerns injury or death to another party or parties. In some instances, damages running into millions of pounds have been awarded where an innocent person has suffered serious permanent disfigurement or disability as the result of carelessness on the part of the person or corporation against which the claim is being made. Such massive sums tend to be awarded more frequently when insurance against loss has been effected, and the monies will be payable by an insurance company rather than by an individual. ◊ **Damages, exemplary** ◊ **Damages, liquidated** ◊ **Damages, nominal** ◊ **Damages, substantial** ◊ **Damages, unliquidated**.

Damages, exemplary These apply in tort but not in **contract**. They are punitive damages as opposed to damages for actual loss suffered.

Damages, liquidated Damages stated in a **contract** to be payable on breach. They must be a fair estimate of the damage likely to be suffered. Round sums which do not appear to be related in any way to possible damage are known as penalties and are not enforceable. Where damages are difficult to assess, what might appear to be a penalty may be adjudged to be liquidated damages, if the court considers that the sum was an attempt to evaluate the possible loss. ◊ **Demurrage** ◊ **Penalty clause**.

Damages, nominal Damages awarded by the court in acknowledgement of an offence either in **contract** or **tort** where no actual loss has occurred, e.g. it is a civil wrong to trespass on another person's private land but, in the absence of special circumstances and if no damage was done to anything on that land, a court would accept an action by the owner against the trespasser but would probably only award nominal damages. Incidentally, the notice 'Trespassers will be Prosecuted' is legally absurd; a prosecution is made by the police, whereas the act of trespass is a civil offence that can only give rise to an action in tort for damages.

Nominal damages may also be given when a contract has been breached but where no real loss has been suffered by either party.

Damages, remoteness of ◊ **Rule in Hadley v. Baxendale**.

Damages, substantial Damages

awarded when loss has actually been incurred. The adjective 'substantial' is descriptive of type not quantity.

Damages, unliquidated Damages not stated in the **contract** but awarded by the court.

Dandy note A document used for obtaining from a **Warehouse officer** goods which are required for exportation, etc. It is issued on the authority of the Customs House.

Data Protection Act 1984 The intention of this Act was to prevent the misuse of personal information held in computer or manually operated data banks. It is an offence to keep such personal data unless the holder is registered as a 'data user' with the Data Protection Registrar. To obtain registration it is necessary to provide full details of the information it is proposed to keep, the reasons for keeping it, and the use to which it is intended to put that information.

Individuals have the statutory right to inspect and examine any information which may be held concerning them. Further, they have the right to compensation in the event of such data being misused.

Datapost A swift courier service operated by the Post Office for the transportation of letters, packets, parcels, documents, etc., within Great Britain. Items sent by Datapost are carried quite separately from ordinary mail by a reliable courier with back-up arrangements.

There are two distinct services. The first is Datapost Sameday. This guarantees collection and delivery on the same day. The second service is on an overnight basis and is subdivided into Datapost 10 and Datapost 12. The former offers delivery before 10 a.m. and the

latter before noon. The different services, charging differing rates, are available between most business centres within the UK and any fee paid is returnable if the specified terms are not met. Payment is in cash or, where applicable, the fee is charged to an account. Parcels or packets are collected by the Royal Mail at the sender's request by ringing a Freefone Datapost Number. Alternatively they may be handed in at a post office.

There is a service to Northern Ireland for account holders and also to Guernsey and Jersey in the Channel Islands. There is also a Datapost International Service to various overseas destinations, the number of which is being constantly increased. Details of this service are obtained by telephoning Freefone Datapost.

Datel services Material in digital form, e.g. computer data for immediate feeding into a computer terminal, can be directly transmitted on telegraph or telephone circuits by arrangement with the Datel Services Department of **British Telecom**. There are a number of alternative services, and improvements and innovations are continually under way. Without giving specific information about facilities, it is sufficient to be aware that the public communications system caters for direct transmission of electronic data in digital form and that British Telecom will provide specific information on the extent and limitations of services on application. The Datel service can be used internationally as well as within the UK.

Dawn raid This term refers to an unannounced attempt to obtain a substantial, if not controlling, interest in a company by instructing brokers to buy up as many shares as possible in the targeted company as soon as the market opens. This tactic is often employed by an individual or a company intending to take over another and as a prelude to a full-scale **take-over bid**. The intention is to take the diretors and shareholders of the company by surprise and hopefully effect a *fait accompli*. Such tactics are likely to attract the unfavourable attention of the Panel on Take-Overs and Mergers established under the **City Code on Take-overs and Mergers**.

Day book A **book-keeping** term. Day books are books of prime entry. They record the details of purchases and **sales** as these take place, or rather contain or consist of lists of **invoices** in and invoices out. The **ledger** is then written up from these books.

Day to day loans ◊ **Overnight loans**.

Days of grace The additional time allowed by custom for payment of a **bill of exchange** or **insurance** premium after the actual date on which the amount was due. In the law merchant, customs can set precedents. With bills of exchange, three days of grace are usually allowed (not including Sundays and **bank holidays**).

Dead freight Payable where the charterer fails to load a complete cargo and the shipowner then charges him **freight** for the space that he otherwise could have sold.

Dead rent A term often found in mining leases, for the **rent** payable whether or not the mine is worked.

Deadweight debt A debt incurred, normally by a government rather than by an individual, as a result of borrowing, not secured by the purchase of an enduring asset, to meet current needs. The most common form of deadweight debt is the **national debt**, which accumulates

over a long period of time by the issue of non-redeemable **bonds** by the state – usually for such thankless purposes as fighting a war.

Dear money Money is said to be dear when loans are difficult to obtain and **interest** rates are very high. ◊ **Cheap money**.

Death duty ◊ **Estate duty** ◊ **Capital gains** ◊ **Capital transfer tax** ◊ **Inheritance tax**.

Debenture Strictly speaking a document setting out the terms of a loan. In the case of a single loan it will be held by the lender. Where the loan is in the form of an issue of debentures, that is to say where many people lend money to a business rather than buy **shares** in it, the debenture deed will be held by **trustees** for those people. The deed will state the terms of the loan, when it becomes repayable, and the powers of the debenture holders. If it is charged on specific property, this will be a fixed charge, if on property of the business generally it will be a **floating charge**. Where it is a fixed charge on land or interest in land, it should be registered as a land charge. Debentures secured on property may be referred to as **mortgage** debentures. Consequently, in accounts one finds, for instance, first- and second-mortgage debentures.

Debenture holders receive a fixed interest annually and this must be paid or provided for before any dividends can be paid to shareholders. On a winding-up of the company debentures secured on a **fixed charge** are paid out of the asset charged. Those secured on a **floating charge** also enjoy a preference and are next in line after fixed debentures and **preferential debts**.

The issue of debentures is one of the popular ways of raising money available to a limited company. It may be particularly favoured for certain projects that require finance for a limited period only, since debentures can be easily redeemed by the company. Another advantage is that debenture interest is generally deductible in computing taxable profits, whereas dividends are not. The debentures are, like shares, freely transferable and the company is required by law to maintain a **register of debentures**. In practice debentures issued by a company are usually issued in the form of debenture stock as this makes the transfer of part of a holding simpler. **Stock** also has the advantage that all holders automatically rank *pari passu* in the event of repayment. Individual debentures would rank for repayment in the date order of issue. Whenever debentures are issued by a company on a floating or fixed charge then, with certain unimportant exceptions, that charge must be registered on the company's file at the Registrar of Companies department. This has the effect of making the existence of the charge known to any person subsequently dealing with the property charged. ◊ **Register of charges**.

Debentures, reissue of Debentures that have been redeemed by a **company** may be reissued provided the **articles of association** do not forbid it and that the company has not contracted to redeem them or shown any intention to cancel them. When reissued they rank **pari passu** with other debentures. Details of debentures available for reissue must be shown in the **balance sheet**.

Debit A term used in **double-entry book-keeping** for an entry made on the left-hand side of an account. A credit is an entry made on the right-hand side.

Debit cards In addition to **cheque cards** and **credit cards** most banks and building societies operating cheque accounts offer debit cards to customers. These are similar in appearance to credit cards and can be used for many of the same purposes, e.g. telephone ordering. The important difference from the user's viewpoint is that whereas credit card purchases involve the granting of credit facilities by the issuer with the customer settling all transactions by means of a monthly account presented by the credit card company, the debit card is merely a substitute for a cheque book and each payment by debit card appears on the user's bank statement as if it had been a cheque payment. Most issuers of debit cards combine them with cheque guarantee cards.

Debit note A term used in accounting. A debit note is sent to a customer when it is intended to charge his account, normally in an unusual situation – say when a person has been insufficiently invoiced for **goods**.

Debt Something owed by one person to another. In commerce a debt is one that can normally be expressed in terms of money or money's worth. It may also carry **interest** covering the period during which it is due but not paid, although common business usage allows an agreed period of interest-free credit before payment is demanded. Creditors often offer inducements by way of attractive discounts for quick settlement of debts. The usual term of credit in the business world is one month. Debts which are not intended to be paid until a longer time has elapsed are sometimes covered by a **bill**

of exchange or some other negotiable paper. Longer-term debts, carrying interest, take the form of **mortgages**, etc. **Debentures** are a common form of long-term debt in the company world. ◊ **Capital gearing** ◊ **Credit insurance** ◊ **Debt collecting** ◊ **Debt servicing**.

Debt collecting Although this term refers literally to the collection from debtors of debts incurred, it has additional reference to a form of business which is concerned with the collection of debts on behalf of other people. Some trading organizations consider it more economical to employ an agency for collecting many small debts rather than set up and manage their own collection department. If such an agency represents a number of traders in similar fields there may indeed be a true saving for the individual creditor, though he must set this against possible loss of **goodwill** between himself and his customers. It is but a short step from hiring a collecting agency to dealing with all debt problems by the use of a **factoring** company.

Businesses which collect their own debts normally work to a rule which, though flexible in the case of a small trader, becomes rigid in a larger organization. The rule will vary according to custom but generally, after the normal credit period has expired, the debtor will receive one or two progressive notices that the debt is overdue and, as a last resort, a letter from the trader's solicitors to the effect that legal action will be taken if the money is not paid within a stated time. If such action becomes necessary then the debtor will also have to pay the costs of the action. ◊ **Credit insurance** ◊ **Credit rating** ◊ **Hire purchase**.

Debt servicing A rather pompous term for the payment of interest on debts due. ◊ **Debt** ◊ **Debt collecting**.

Debtors Persons or organizations owing money or some other debt to a third party. In the accounts of companies a distinction must be made between debts due within the following year and those which are not due until some later date.

Decimal currency This replaced the old duodecimal pounds, shillings and pence system as the official currency of the United Kingdom. On 15 February 1971 the United Kingdom followed most of the world in adopting decimal currency. Long-term benefit was possibly forgone for the sake of short-term expediency by keeping the old pound **sterling** as the basic unit of **currency**. This was divided into 100 new pence and new coins were minted to replace the old, most of which were phased out over a period of a few years. The currency change was accompanied by alterations in the rules of **legal tender**, being amounts of particular coin legally allowable in proper payment of debts. It is worth noting that pre-1947 silver coins are not often found in circulation, as their metallic value exceeds their face value. ◊ **Bank note** ◊ **Penny** ◊ **Pound**.

Decimalization The conversion of a system of counting or reckoning into a system based on the number ten, this being universally recognized as the easiest figure for multiplication or division. The system is best known as the **metric system**. It was adopted by the greater part of the Western world in the time of Napoleon Bonaparte, whose legal and administrative systems were as simple and effective as any since Roman times. The

Deck cargo

metric system has prevailed in Western Europe since that time and also, monetarily, in the United States. The United Kingdom accepted it in 1971 when **decimal currency** was introduced – other Commonwealth countries had already switched to decimalization for **currency**. It is intended that conversion to the metric system for weights and measures, etc., will follow in the near future and a Commission has been established for this purpose in the United Kingdom. At present both metric and **imperial systems** are being used side by side. ◊ **Metrication board**.

Deck cargo Cargo on deck rather than in the hold of the ship. The Carriage of Goods by Sea Act 1924 does not apply to this type of cargo.

Declaration of solvency This has application to company insolvency or **liquidation**. If the **winding-up** of a company is to enjoy the title of a **members' voluntary winding-up** it must be preceded by a Declaration of Solvency by the directors. This is a statutory declaration, in the form laid down in the Companies Act, that the company will be able to pay its debts in full within twelve months. It must be made within the five weeks preceding the resolution by members to wind up the company and must contain, *inter alia*, a statement of all extant **assets** and **liabilities**. If these conditions are not met or are proved to be falsely obtained then the winding-up cannot be a members' voluntary winding-up and must be treated as a creditors' winding-up, either voluntary or involuntary depending on the circumstances. ◊ **Winding-up, compulsory** ◊ **Winding-up, voluntary**.

Decreasing term assurance A form

of assurance policy where the sum assured, i.e. the amount that the policy will realize on completion, decreases year by year. Normally associated with house purchase, it is sometimes referred to as a mortgage protection policy as it is intended to cover the balance due on the mortgage, a balance which, with regular repayments, will fall progressively until the mortgage is fully paid off. The assurance cover is usually taken out by a husband for the protection of his family should his death occur during the currency of the mortgage loan. In this instance it is strictly **insurance** rather than assurance.

Deed ◊ **Contract by deed**.

Deed of assignment This term has particular reference to the law of **bankruptcy** and should not be confused with ordinary **assignment**, whether legal or equitable. It occurs where a debtor, as an alternative to being declared bankrupt, assigns all his property to a trustee for his creditors, with their agreement. Such an assignment could be set aside by the trustee in an ensuing bankruptcy proper.

Deed of covenant ◊ **Covenants**.

Deed of inspectorship When a businessman is insolvent and it is possible that he may become bankrupt, he may hand over his business to the charge of his **creditors** by a deed of inspectorship. The creditors will appoint inspectors to manage the business either as a going concern or with a view to its being wound up. ◊ **Bankruptcy** ◊ **Insolvency Act 1986.**

Deep discount stock Sometimes referred to as zero coupon stock. This is loan stock issued by a company at a greater discount than other stock but

158

carrying lower than average, or even zero, interest entitlement. It may be attractive to higher taxpayers, who will save by not having to pay tax on interest received and gain from the much higher profit on redemption. These stocks are, at present, more common in the USA.

Defence bonds Government **securities** introduced in November 1939, and on sale until May 1964. Bonds were issued in units of £5 and there was a maximum holding. At maturity certain issues had a tax free bonus, free of **capital gains tax**. Holders could always convert into a new issue. They were similar to **national development bonds**.

Deferred annuity An **annuity** that becomes payable at a stated time in the future.

Deferred charges ◊ **Payment in advance**.

Deferred shares ◊ **Shares, deferred ordinary**.

Deferred taxation A term used in company accounts. It may refer to amounts set aside for tax deferred by **capital allowances**. Profits of a business are calculated after **depreciation**. Depreciation allowed for tax purposes may differ from depreciation used in accounts, though the total over a number of years will be the same. As tax will not therefore be related to the actual profits shown in the accounts, adjustments are made by adding to, and subtracting from, a reserve set aside for the equalization of taxation with reference to the profits.

    Corporation tax payable more than a year hence but based on the profits for the relevant year is sometimes also shown as a deferred liability. The difference is that, whereas this amount is a known

liability not payable for some time, the first amount is more like a reserve. **Stock relief** was another type of deferred taxation.

Defunct company A company that has been struck off the official **register of companies** because it has ceased to function. This may arise after a **winding-up** or where, after proper formalities have been completed, the Registrar of Companies concludes that the company is no longer in existence. When the name of the company is removed from the Register of Companies it is entered in another book known as the Register of Defunct Companies, referred to colloquially as the 'dead book'.

Del credere agent An **agent** who **guarantees** that the persons to whom he sells goods on behalf of his principal will pay for them. He normally receives an additional **commission** for this.

Delegatus non potest delegare A legal maxim that states in effect that when an **agent** has contracted to do work for a principal, he has no implied right to delegate the work to a third party. In practice this does not always apply. Subcontracting is customary in many trades. The maxim applies mostly where the personality of the agent is important. ◊ **Contract of personal service**.

Delivered docks A term used in foreign trade where the responsibility of the seller ceases when the **goods** are delivered at the docks and unloaded.

Delivery note May take various forms, including that of a part copy of the relevant **invoice** or **advice note**. It is basically the paper listing and accompanying goods delivered to a customer and is signed by the customer on receipt. When the note is returned to the vendor it is *prima facie* evidence of delivery both as to place and person. The recipient should inspect the goods before signing the delivery note, particularly where the note states that the goods have been received in saleable condition. If in doubt he should indicate that his signature is 'subject to inspection' – otherwise he may be stopped from claiming for any damage in transit. Most delivery notes handled by **common carriers** include a warning that claims for damage will not be entertained unless made to both carrier and vendor within, say, three days. ◊ **Estoppel**.

Demarcation dispute A dispute at a place of work, resulting from friction between or within trade unions, and caused by an inability to agree on the apportionment of work between categories of workpeople. That such problems have long been with us is evidenced by a case in 1623 where it was contended that 'bricklayers should not plaster with lime and hair but with lime and sand only and that plastering with lime and hair should belong unto the plasterers'. ◊ **Advisory Conciliation and Arbitration Service**.

Demise charter ◊ **Charter by demise**.

Demurrage Liquidated damages included in a **contract**, usually a building or shipping contract. Normally takes the form of a payment for each day completion is delayed or ships are kept waiting. The fact that the loss is less than the demurrage is not relevant. ◊ **Damages, liquidated**.

Department store A large retail shop where there are various departments each dealing in a separate type of **goods**. ◊ **Chain store** ◊ **Multiple store**.

Deposit, hire purchase agreement The sum which must first be paid in cash, to secure the purchase, as part of a **hire purchase** agreement. The size of the deposit depends on many factors, including the policy of the vendor and the current attitude of the government. The latter can exercise control over the level of consumer spending by altering hire purchase regulations; for instance, it can often dramatically reduce the level by insisting that the initial deposit be a high proportion of the total cost of the item. ◊ **Consumer Credit Act** ◊ **Hire Purchase Act**.

Deposit, lessee A lessor of property, real or personal, often asks for a deposit, sometimes called a bond, from the lessee to cover possible losses through the latter's negligence. This type of deposit is, in the absence of costs against which it was intended to afford protection, returnable on termination of the agreement. This deposit should not be confused with a payment which is a **premium on a lease**.

Deposit: sale of goods An amount of money paid to a **vendor** as part of the purchase money and to secure the **sale**. The depositor is entitled then to buy the property if he pays the balance within a stated period. Normally, if the balance is not paid, he will lose the deposit, assuming good faith on both sides. ◊ **Deposit, hire purchase agreement**.

Depreciation The amount by which the value of a wasting **fixed asset** is considered diminished for purposes connected with the preparation of the **annual accounts** of a business. The 'charge' for fixed-asset wastage to be set against income can vary enormously according to which of the many acceptable methods of computing depreciation is adopted. The only legal constraints are that the method chosen should be consistent and should be stated – though, strictly, these constraints only apply to companies controlled by the Companies Act. The two most common methods of depreciating fixed assets are known as the **straight line method** and the **diminishing balance method**. The former charges equal portions of cost over the expected life of the asset and the latter applies a fixed percentage to the cost or **written down value**, the percentage being based on the probable life-expectancy of the asset. Both systems are weakened by various factors such as the impossibility of making a reliable forecast of the asset's useful life, the possibility of **obsolescence** brought about by changing technology and the likelihood of continual revaluation of the asset in an attempt to keep pace with price inflation.

The amount written off assets by way of depreciation is unique in as much as it is both a **provision** and a **reserve**. As it is a charge for expenditure incurred in production, it must be included in the **profit and loss account** as an expense which can only be estimated, i.e. a provision. The total **accumulated depreciation**, including that shown as a provision in the current profit and loss account, appears in the **balance sheet**, where it represents an amount held back from profit for use in replacing those fixed assets on which it was originally charged. In this sense it must be seen as a **capital reserve**, particularly when, as frequently happens, it contains additional amounts set aside to take account of rising **replacement costs**. The technically important question of whether depreciation should be classified as a provision or as a reserve is usually evaded by referring to

it as neither – the common accounting practice is to refer to it obliquely as an 'amount set aside for . . .' Though the purpose of each is similar, depreciation should be distinguished from **amortization**.

For purposes of calculating taxable profits the amount written off by the business is added back and **capital allowances** are deducted. Adjustments may also be made for balancing charges and balancing allowances. ⟁ **Accelerated depreciation** ⟁ **Free depreciation**.

Depreciation of currency ⟁ **Currency depreciation**.

Derivatives These are financial instruments which are essentially a by-product of the markets in shares, bonds, commodities etc. They comprise for the most part **futures** and **options** which are known as derivative assets in so far as they derive from a more visible series of underlying assets with volatile prices.

Design Centre This is run by the Council for Industrial Design. It provides a shop window to display examples of well-designed modern British goods, and bring the achievements of British manufacturers and designers to the attention of industry, commerce, and the general public. It keeps a Design Index and issues special black and white triangular labels for fixing on goods in the Index. It is open daily. There is no admission fee. General and special exhibitions are held. The Centre also wishes to be satisfied with the technical efficiency of products, but has no testing facilities; instead it employs other organizations, e.g. the British Electrical Approval Board for domestic appliances, the Coal Utilization Council, the Gas Council and the **British Standards Institution**. Products cannot be purchased at the Centre, but information is given as to manufacturer and probable price.

Detinue An action in tort for the recovery of property.

Devaluation Commercially this term is used with reference to currencies and their value on the international exchange. Strictly speaking it applies only to currencies with a rate of exchange that is fixed in terms either of gold or some other **currency** of international repute. For example, the pound **sterling** was for a long period, before it was allowed to float in 1972, always quoted in terms of dollars; the **rate of exchange** between the pound and the dollar was fixed and tendencies for the rate to change were countered by direct action on the part of relevant monetary authorities, principally the **Bank of England**.

When an exchange rate is fixed it can only be changed by devaluation or revaluation by one of the countries concerned and by mutual agreement. The pound, for instance, was devalued against the dollar in 1949 and 1967, making the dollar more expensive to purchase in the United Kingdom and the pound less expensive in the United States. Imports to Britain were thus discouraged and exports encouraged. The effect of such devaluation, reflected in the international exchanges of the world, should benefit the British **balance of trade**, but in fact in 1967 many other countries trading with the United Kingdom devalued their own currencies and the short-term advantage to Britain was not great. Similarly and more re-

cently, when the UK was briefly part of the **European exchange rate mechanism** (**ERM**), it frequently happened that, when one member of the ERM sought to devalue its rate of exchange *vis-à-vis* other members to a degree which exceeded that allowed by the permissible variations built into the system, such an action tended to trigger compensatory 'adjustments' on the part of other members. ◊ **Currency depreciation** ◊ **European monetary system** ◊ **Foreign exchange market** ◊ **Free exchange rates** ◊ **Free trade**.

The rules of the **International Monetary Fund**, set up under the Bretton Woods Agreement of 1944, required exchange rates to be fixed between member countries and the prior permission of the IMF to be obtained before any change in the rate by devaluation or revaluation could be made. It is not surprising that this rule was not always adhered to as the principal benefits from devaluation depend on the surprise element. The United Kingdom did not seek IMF permission before the 1967 devaluation.

The fact that a currency devaluation tends to depress confidence in the stability of the devaluing country tends to make it a last-ditch measure in handling a nation's finances. It is usually resorted to after every possible alternative has been tried and rarely happens twice in a short space of time; it is, after all, much the same as the admission by a person that he is bankrupt.

Development areas ◊ **Assisted areas**.

Development expenditure ◊ **Research and development expenditure**.

Deviation A **marine insurance** term for the circumstances in which a ship may deviate from its course without prejudice to the policy. These are: (1) where the policy authorizes deviation; (2) where deviation is necessary for the safety of the ship or cargo, provided both are insured; (3) to save human life or help a ship in distress; (4) where necessary to get medical help for someone on board; (5) where necessary to comply with an express or implied **warranty**; (6) when it cannot be helped, e.g. through the mutinous conduct of crew.

Dies non A Latin tag for a day on which no business can be transacted.

Dilapidations This rather antiquated term still has application to property leases of long duration. At the end of a long-term **lease**, the landlord is entitled, subject to various statutory provisions enabling the tenant to request a renewal at a fair rent for a further period, to retake the property and demand that it be returned, at the tenant's expense, to a condition consistent with that when the original lease was granted. Where the lease was of land on which the tenant has built without the express consent of the landlord, the extreme case could arise of the tenant having to demolish the building erected – in any event he would have to forfeit the building with the land. Where the lease was of both land and building, then the tenant must hand back the building in good structural condition and pay any costs incurred in restoring it to such a condition. This liability imposed by law upon the tenant is known as a liability for dilapidations. He can counter-claim for genuine improvements made by him with the consent of the freeholder. ◊ **Freehold land** ◊ **Lease** ◊ **Leasehold land** ◊ **Real property**.

Diminishing balance method A method of calculating **depreciation**. The cost or agreed **value** of the **asset** is written off over its expected life by the application of a percentage to the **written down value**. The percentage is calculated so that the asset will be written down to scrap value after a stated number of years. The annual depreciation is charged against profit. This method means that much higher charges are made in the initial years, thus reducing profit artificially. It may also tend to show the value of assets at an artificially low figure, thus making it difficult to estimate the true **capital employed** for the purpose of calculating certain ratios.

Diners Club An American-based **credit card** company operating on an international basis. ◊ **American Express**.

Direct debit mandate Authority given by a customer to his bank to make **direct debits** to his account on the request of a named creditor.

Direct debiting A system of payment for goods which is used in certain types of trade, particularly where, although the supply is to be constant, the precise amount in volume or price can vary within marginal limits from one period to another. The purchaser arranges for the vendor to be paid by a direct bank transfer, the amount of which is notified to the bank by the vendor at the time of delivery. It is not dissimilar to a **standing order** but differs in so far as the periodic charge might vary from week to week, or month to month, within agreed limits.

Direct debits A form of direct debiting peculiar to banks. Annual payments can usually be met by signing a **standing**

order. However, as certain categories of payment vary from one year/month to another, e.g. subscriptions, the normal standing order gives way to a direct debit mandate. The customer authorizes his bank to pay the particular subscription or demand without stating a fixed sum, which means that any variation in the annual amount due will be automatically paid without the need to refer back to the customer.

Direct expenses Expenses which can be directly associated with the cost of producing a particular article or service, as opposed to **overhead expenses**.

Direct labour Labour which can be directly associated with manufacturing a product or providing a service. ◊ **Indirect labour**.

Direct selling The selling of consumer goods by the manufacturer, or a wholesaler, directly to the public, i.e. bypassing the retailer. Methods of direct selling include: **mail order** through catalogues carried by part-time agents; the insertion of an order form in a newspaper or a magazine advertisement; **cash and carry** warehouses; Sunday markets; door-to-door salesmen; circulation of sectors of the population on the basis of lists of names and addresses, sometimes bought from firms specializing in the preparation of such lists; parties at which goods are displayed and ordered through the party organizer; and soliciting custom by telephone. ◊ **Cold calling**. Bypassing the retailer can sometimes be to the disadvantage of the purchaser; not only may he forgo the protection of the **Sale of Goods Act** but he loses the benefit of a retailer's specialized knowledge and advice; he often cannot inspect goods before purchase; he loses the benefit of

being able to exchange faulty goods easily, and generally forfeits the useful and valuable **after-sales service** offered by a retailer. Prices may be much lower, but tend to fall in proportion to the loss of various benefits and safeguards. It should also be remembered that where the sale is effected through an **agent** on commission, the overheads of the vendor may make greatly reduced prices unlikely unless quality is sacrificed. Nevertheless, despite these various disadvantages, the fact of being able to order goods from an armchair, plus the 'easy-payment' terms often offered, have favoured direct selling and the volume of business transacted in this way continually increases. ◊ **Consumer Credit Act** ◊ **Hawker** ◊ **Market overt** ◊ **Pedlar** ◊ **Street trader** ◊ **Prestel**.

Direct taxation Taxation levied directly on the members of a community and paid directly by them to the revenue authorities either personally or through an employer. This is unlike **indirect taxation**, which is not dependent on a person's wealth, but on the goods that he buys (e.g. **value added tax**, Customs and Excise duty, etc.). Direct taxation has taken many forms other than the present **income tax**, introduced during the Napoleonic Wars. There have been poll taxes (i.e. taxes per head), window taxes (on the number of windows), chimney taxes and taxes on servants, etc.; these applied mostly to the rich and were known as iniquitous. They were abolished and replaced by **licences**, levies, duties, etc., which applied to everybody.

Director A person who is an elected officer of a company. Many people who are not normally called directors are considered directors for purposes of the law. Any person according to whose instructions directors are accustomed to act is to all intents and purposes a director when it comes to **directors' shareholdings, close companies**, etc.

Strictly speaking, directors are persons concerned with managing a **company** on behalf of the shareholders. They are in one sense **agents** of the company. They are not liable personally on **contracts** made in the name of the company even when acting **ultra vires** (though they then might be liable for **breach of warranty of authority**). If they contract *intra vires* but outside their own powers, the company will usually be bound, by virtue of the new provisions contained in the Companies Act 1989. ◊ **Rule in Royal British Bank v. Turquand**.

The first directors are often named in the **articles of association** and often also in the **prospectus**. Mention in the articles does not constitute a valid appointment until each director has: (1) signed and sent to the Registrar of Companies his consent to act; and (2) either signed the memorandum for his **qualification shares**, or taken up and paid for them, or contracted for them, or declared that they are already registered in his name.

If there is no appointment in the articles, the first directors are appointed by the subscribers. The manner of subsequent appointments is normally specified in the articles. It is usually done by the company in general meeting, but directors often have powers to fill vacancies on the board subject to confirmation by general **meeting**. Only one director can can be appointed by one resolution unless all members of the company previously agree otherwise. This does not apply to **private companies**. Private companies may have one director (but he must not also be the **secretary**). **Public companies** must have two. (◊ **Register of**

directors ◊ **Register of director's interests**.) Directors act by resolutions made at directors' meetings. Meetings must be properly convened, and notice given to each director. A **quorum** must be present (the number constituting a quorum is usually stated in the articles). Directors must not make contracts with the company, they must declare any interest in contracts made for the company and the articles normally state that in this instance they have no vote. Directors must hand over **secret profits** arising from any such transactions. Infringement of these rules will probably make the contract void. Generally, **loans to directors** are prohibited. ◊ **Directors, disclosure of transactions with**.

Directors have many responsibilities including: (1) keeping proper books of account and presenting **annual accounts** and a **directors' report**; (2) calling **annual general meetings**; (3) keeping **Registers of directors** and secretaries, **Registers of directors' interests, share registers**, etc.; (4) sending the Registrar all documents he is entitled to receive; (5) submitting a **statement of affairs** on **winding-up**.

Remuneration of directors is a matter of agreement between themselves and the company. If it is stated in the articles it can only be altered by **special resolution** at a general meeting. For rules on disclosure ◊ **Directors' emoluments** ◊ **Compensation for loss of office**.

A director may be disqualified if he goes against the articles or loses his qualification. If he becomes bankrupt he can only remain a director by leave of the court. The powers of directors cease on a winding-up.

Directors, age limits Technically, no

person over seventy years of age can be appointed, or reappointed, as a **director** of a **public company**, or a **private company** which is its subsidiary. However, this prohibition is not common, as the age limit imposed by the Companies Act can be countermanded in the company's articles and, even if this has not been done, an over-age director can be appointed at any time provided special notice is given to shareholders. ◊ **Articles of association**.

Directors, disclosure of transactions with The 1948 Companies Act required companies to give details of certain loans to directors in the **annual accounts** and the 1967 Act added the duty to disclose material interests in contracts. Both these requirements have been incorporated into the much wider duties of disclosure first contained in the 1980 Companies Act and now in the Companies Act 1985.

The published accounts must give details by way of a note to the accounts not only of **loans to directors** but also of a wide range of transactions in which any director, or in certain cases any officer of the company, has a material interest, being transactions between the company and the director or by the company on behalf of or for the benefit of the director. The disclosure requirements are very broad and exempted transactions few, tending to be restricted to those involving very small amounts. Special rules apply to banks.

Directors' emoluments Sums of money and **benefits in kind** received by **directors**. These may include fees, salaries for acting as director (or in some other capacity for the **company**), the use of company property, and certain expense allowances. The Companies Act requires that the **accounts** of a company

shall distinguish, *inter alia*, between amounts received in respect of services as director of the company or any of its subsidiaries, and remunerations received for management of the company's affairs or the affairs of any subsidiary. They also require that directors' emoluments should be distinguished from directors' pensions or **compensation for loss of office**. The 1967 Act required that details be given of the number of directors receiving salaries within certain ranges, for instance up to £5,000, £5,000–£10,000, etc. ◊ **Close company**

Directors' fees Payments made to **directors** by reason only of their position as directors. Directors' fees tend to be fairly nominal, the greater part of payment being by way of salary and other benefits. ◊ **Directors' emoluments**.

Directors, Institute of Founded in 1903, the Institute of Directors, often referred to by the abbreviation IOD, received a royal charter in 1906. Membership was given a considerable boost in 1948 when the Labour government appeared to be threatening the very existence of free enterprise, the concept to which the Institute was dedicated.

It has two major aims. Firstly to promote its members' interests by all available means and, at the same time, maximize the influence that the experienced members can exercise in furthering the common good by bringing weight to bear on the proper conduct of public affairs. Secondly, to give every assistance possible to members that they may prove, and improve, their competence to offer leadership in the business world.

The Institute is non-political though, by its nature, it must oppose any policy that seeks to undermine the system of free enterprise. To this end it will make representations to any government that may be in power and will provide a forum for the airing of views and grievances of members at both local and national levels. Its most important function, however, must lie in its desire to provide a single and powerful voice representing the interests of company directors as the lynchpins of the system in which they evolved, that of a free market economy in which the interests of capital, labour and the general public coincide. ◊ **Competitive market** ◊ **Director**.

Directors, removal of A **director** may be removed at any time by the **company**; an **ordinary resolution** will suffice. This does not apply to the director of a **private company** holding office for life at 18 July 1945. Special notice is always necessary. The director may make representations both in advance and at the meeting, and may ask for these representations to be circulated to **members of the company**. Whether he is entitled to compensation or **damages** depends on circumstances and on the **articles of association**. A director may resign at any time in the manner specified in the articles. If nothing is specified then reasonable notice will suffice. A resignation properly given cannot be withdrawn.

Directors' report When the annual financial statements of a company are produced they normally include a report by the directors on the activities of that company during the period covered by the accounts and their views as to the future prospects of the company. The Companies Act 1948 referred to certain information that should be given in a directors' report and further enacted that such a report must be included among the documents required to be filed with

the Registrar of Companies at the time the **annual return** is submitted. The 1967 Companies Act broadened the extent of the information that had to be contained in the report and, in addition, stated that the report must be included with the published accounts sent to members. The scope of the directors' report was even further widened by the Companies Act 1981.

The contents of the report must now include, *inter alia*: (1) the names of all persons who were directors of the company at any time during the financial year; (2) a summary of business development during the year plus any developments anticipated in the near future; (3) the main activities of the company and its subsidiaries, including any changes in those activities during the year; (4) details of amounts that are to be recommended for payment in dividends or put to reserves; (5) details of research and development activities during the year; (6) details of any acquisitions by the company of its own shares; (7) directors' interests in shares or debentures and options to acquire such interests; (8) events since balance sheet date that might influence in a material sense the picture presented by the accounts; (9) contributions for charitable or political purposes; (10) alterations to fixed assets and, where applicable, amounts by which market value differs substantially from book value of any land or interest in land; (11) provisions for health and safety of employees; (12) various details concerning pay, involvement of, and consultation with, employees where the number exceeds 250 – and also in such instances details of company policy towards disabled employees.

The 1967 Act required the directors' report to contain a breakdown of the turnover and profits of the company between various distinct business activities and also obliged disclosure of numbers employed and aggregate remuneration. The 1981 Companies Act stated that this information must be given in notes to the accounts themselves.

Two further provisions of the new legislation are of particular importance. The first is that companies qualifying as **small companies** are relieved of the obligation to file a directors' report – though not of the obligation to provide one for members. The second is that the directors' report must now be subject to audit as with the annual accounts and the **auditors' report** should indicate that this has been effected. An omission to mention the directors' report will be taken to mean that the auditors have approved it.

Directors' resignation ◊ **Directors, removal of**.

Directors' retirement ◊ **Rotation of directors** ◊ **Directors, age limits**.

Directors' service contracts Companies must keep (in an appropriate place) details of service **contracts** with **directors**. If the contract was in writing, a copy of it must be kept. If not, a memorandum will suffice. The appropriate place is the **registered office**, the place where the **register of members** is kept, or the principal place of business. The place where it is kept must be notified to the Registrar of Companies for inclusion in the **register of companies**; it must be open to inspection on every business day for at least two hours, free of charge to all members of the company. There are certain limited exceptions in the cases of directors working wholly outside the United Kingdom, and of contracts for very short periods.

The Companies Act 1985 reaffirms a provision first introduced in the Companies Act 1980 prohibiting service contracts with directors exceeding a period of five years where such contracts cannot be terminated at will by the company or where they can only be terminated in specific circumstances. The object is to prevent directors abusing their position by arranging long service contracts which would provide substantial compensation for loss of office on the company being taken over or substantially reorganized. Contracts entered into before the Act came into force are protected. ◊ **Golden handcuffs**. ◊ **Golden hellos** ◊ **Golden parachutes**.

Directors' shareholding ◊ **Register of directors' interests**.

Directors' valuation Sometimes **assets** in a **company**'s accounts may be stated to be 'at **directors**' valuation' or alternatively 'as certified by **managing director**'. The relevance of this description of the **value** will depend on the circumstances. Generally speaking the directors are responsible for all the figures shown in the **balance sheet**. Where they are not shown at cost but at valuation, the directors must believe the valuation correct. Where the words 'at valuation' are used, there should be an explanatory note stating the method of valuation and whether it was an expert valuation or not. The directors are not necessarily the best persons to value assets. However, the **auditors** will be expected to verify the valuation and to state whether they consider it to be a fair estimate. Auditors cannot avoid their liability to shareholders by relying on directors' certificates.

Dirty bill of lading ◊ **Foul bill of lading**.

Discharge of contract This means the fulfilment of the obligations imposed by a **contract**, or else an agreement to negate the contract or put one in its place. It can also mean a situation where a party may be released from his obligations by impossibility of performance or by **operation of law**. For example, alteration of a written instrument without the consent of the other party will preclude the party altering the instrument from taking action on it and release the other party from all obligations. ◊ **Waiver** ◊ **Accord and satisfaction** ◊ **Contract, breach of** ◊ **Contract of novation**.

Discount (bills of exchange) A bill of exchange may be discounted. This means that it is purchased by a third party for a sum lower than that party will receive when the bill matures. The person discounting the bill gains by receiving money at an earlier date. The amount of discount will vary according to the risk the purchaser takes. A good bill is one which is backed or countersigned by a well-known **finance house** or **bank**. Bills are normally discounted with banks or on a larger scale with institutions known as **discount houses**.

Discount broker A **broker** who neither buys nor sells **bills of exchange** but acts as intermediary between those who wish to sell and those who wish to buy. If a broker deals on his own account he becomes a **discount house**. The question to be asked is, 'Do they run their own book?'

Discount houses These are oganizations situated in the City of London whose business is discounting **bills of exchange** – **trade bills**, **bank bills** and **Treasury bills**. Business is done on a large scale

and funds are obtained principally from the **clearing banks**. To keep the **interest** rate as low as possible and be able to vary the amount borrowed at short intervals, a great deal of money is borrowed on an **overnight loan**. This suits both bank and discount house. To the bank it is **money at short notice**, earning interest. It is lent on the security of bills of exchange that have not yet matured.

Discount store A term often used to describe a retail establishment which offers goods, usually consumer durable goods, e.g. refrigerators, radios, television sets, etc., at prices well below those normally obtainable in the High Street. Similar to a **supermarket** in operation, it is usually located in an out-of-town or temporary warehouse where rent and rates are low and where the scale of operations is very large. This scale enables the owners to take advantage of bulk buying at high discounts and the emphasis is on fast **turnover** of expensive goods – taking low profit per item sold but, due to the quantity of sales and low handling charges, high total profit on goods turned over. Another factor which contributes to profitability is the practice of concentrating on cash sales and thereby avoiding the cost of setting up credit control systems or **hire purchase** arrangements. Needless to say, such stores are not popular with the small trader. ◊ **Cash and carry** ◊ **Credit trading** ◊ **Hypermarket**.

Discounted cash flow (DCF) Any profitable investment, whether it be the purchase of shares or an income-earning asset, must generate a cash flow. The investment will provide the investor with a cash return over a period, the return being monies earned by the asset after deduction of the costs of making the asset productive. Because this return is spread over a future period whereas the acquisition cost is incurred in the present, the **value** of the investment can only be assessed by setting the purchase price against the present value of its future net earnings. This 'present value' is arrived at by a process known as **discounting back**. The discounted future cash flows are then compared, in total, with the present cost of acquisition. If they show a higher figure then the investment would, *prima facie*, be acceptable but if they showed a lower figure then it would appear the project could, on the evidence available, only be carried out at a loss. ◊ **Net present value** ◊ **Pay-back period**.

Discounting back A process of assessing the present value of an anticipated future sum, e.g. what is the value today of £100 in twenty years' time? The solution is found by establishing a sum of money that, if accumulated at x per cent **compound interest** for twenty years, would produce £100 at the end of that time. The **rate of interest** will correspond with rates of interest ruling at the time the calculation is made. Tables are available for giving the answers to such problems.

Disgorging The removal of sediment from wine. The bottles are stood on end, the sediment settles in the neck of the bottle, the cork is removed and the sediment taken away.

Disposable income This term is used to describe the amount of a person's wage or salary after all compulsory deductions, such as **direct taxation**, pension contributions and **national insurance** contributions, have been made. Published accounts often demonstrate the very small increase in disposable income that may follow an apparently excessive rise in the salary of a highly paid company executive. The reason lies, of course, in high marginal rates of tax on large incomes. ◊ **Income tax**.

Dissentient: purchase of interest Where a company is being reorganized or sold to another company by a **liquidator** and shareholders are to receive **shares** in the second company, a member who has not voted for the **special resolution** may demand that the liquidator purchases his interest at a price to be determined either by agreement or by **arbitration**. The dissentient must decide within seven days of the resolution.

Distraint A remedy open to a **creditor** in certain circumstances (normally a landlord for **rent** due). After observing set procedures the creditor can enter the debtor's premises and seize property, holding this property until the debt is paid.

Distributable reserves Essentially, distributable reserves are accumulations of past profits. At one time it was necessary to distinguish carefully between capital and revenue profits, the former going to capital reserves, distribution of which was possible only under specified conditions, the latter going to revenue reserves, which were by definition always available for distribution.

The situation was changed by the 1980 Companies Act. The emphasis is not now on the title of the reserve but on the manner of its accumulation and its contents. Basically, all realized profits, whether capital or revenue, that remain after provision has been made for realized losses in the same categories, may be distributed, except for such part of this net accumulated profit that has been previously distributed or has been capitalized.

There are, however, additional regulations appertaining to public companies. These must not only satisfy the above conditions but also show that such a distribution as proposed will not reduce their net assets to a figure below the sum of called-up capital and undistributable reserves. For this purpose undistributable reserves include not only **share premium account** and **capital redemption reserve** but also the amount by which unrealized capital profits which have not been capitalized (e.g. by issue of bonus shares) exceed unrealized capital losses. In this context additional depreciation consequent on revaluation of fixed assets may be written back into realized profits, though a surplus arising on a general revaluation would, of course, be an unrealized profit.

The extent of distributable reserves may be further restricted by a company's own memorandum or articles. ◊ **Distributions** ◊ **Dividends**.

Distributions A term used in the context of company law to describe the sharing out of profits among shareholders. Usually this will be by payment of a **dividend** and must be made out of profits which could legally be put to a **distributable reserve**.

Distributive industry That part of a country's industry which is concerned with selling goods and services directly to the consumer, in contrast with the manufacturing sector and the construction sector. Retailers are said to be in the distributive trade.

Distributor A **marketing** term for a **retailer** who deals in the wares of certain specified manufacturers, having perhaps the sole agency for an area. He buys and sells on his own account and is not therefore an **agent** for the manufacturer.

Dividend The share of a company's profit paid to a shareholder. The amount he or she receives will depend on the number of shares held. Unlike **interest**, dividends are optional payments made at the discretion of the directors – though failure to pay dividends will have an adverse effect on the **market value** of the shares as very few will be interested in purchasing a non-earning investment. Dividends may be of various kinds. Those paid to preference shareholders have priority, unless the company's articles dictate otherwise, e.g. dividends on **ordinary shares** cannot be paid until the full entitlement of preference shareholders has been met. If the preference shares are 'cumulative', then arrears of that dividend must also be paid before any monies are distributed to ordinary shareholders. In the case of **deferred shares** dividends can usually only be paid after the demands of preference shares have been met and a stated percentage has been paid to the holders of ordinary shares. ◊ **Shares, preference**.

Dividends are usually expressed as a percentage of the **nominal value** of the shares, whatever the category. The rate for preference shares is normally predetermined, being contained in the title of the shares, e.g. 5% preference shares. The rate paid on ordinary, and deferred, shares will depend on the funds available and the amount of profit that the directors see fit to distribute. Often it is paid in two or more instalments, known as interim and final dividends for a particular year. Dividends payable are declared at the **annual general meeting** of the company, though the directors may pay **interim dividends** on account of the total to be declared subsequently at the AGM. All dividends are subject to tax. This is paid by the company before distribution, leaving the recipient to reclaim or adjust tax where necessary by arrangement with the Inland Revenue. The fact that a shareholder may not be liable to tax is not the concern of the company. ◊ **Advance corporation tax** ◊ **Taxation of profits** ◊ **Taxation schedules**.

The dividends paid by the Co-operative Society are slightly different both in entitlement and method of payment. Basically, they are repayments of a part of the Society's profit to its members, who are also its customers. The amount any member receives will depend on the total of his purchases during the period under review.

Dividend cover ◊ **Cover**.

Dividend equalization account When the annual profit made by a company tends to vary considerably over a number of years, and particularly where this variation is consistent with the nature of the business, the directors may wish to take steps to stabilize **dividend** payments, if only to avoid the impression of business instability. This can be done by opening what is referred to as a dividend equalization account (or reserve). An average profit over a period of years is determined and an average dividend is agreed, based on that figure. This amount is paid out each year in dividends to shareholders and charged to the account. The account is credited with annual and unequal appropriations from the **profit and loss account**. ◊ **Appropriation account**.

Dividend mandate An authority given by a shareholder to a **company** stating that **dividends** are to be paid directly into his bank account.

Dividend restraint This term applies to state policy on **dividend** payments and the manner in which it attempts to limit monies so paid out. This may be by express directive, e.g. that dividends must not exceed those paid in the previous year, or must not be increased by more than a stated percentage. Another method used in the past was to penalize dividend payments by exacting additional taxation; it was thought that in this way companies would be discouraged from declaring dividends and that, if they were not, a very large portion would accrue to the Treasury. ◊ **Distributions** ◊ **Dividend tax**.

Dividend stripping When a **company** has accumulated considerable reserves either of a **capital** or of a general nature, a **financier** or a person with sufficient resources may buy a controlling interest in this company, to sell its **assets**, particularly its property (this may be rented back), and obtain sufficient funds to distribute the **reserves** by way of **dividends** (being mostly to himself). The stripper may then sell his **shares** and go. It is a practice rather frowned upon by those who do not have the resources to do the same, by the **Stock Exchange** and by the Chancellor. A serious objection is that it could leave the company in a difficult position or even facing **insolvency**.

Dividend tax A tax introduced in 1965 at the same time as **corporation tax** but discontinued with the introduction of the **imputation system** in 1973. It was in the form of an **income tax** payable on **dividends** paid by limited **companies**. The tax was paid in addition to corporation tax, deducted from the dividend before payment and accounted for by the company to the Inland Revenue. There were certain complicated provisions with reference to dividends received by a company and then paid over to its **members**. The aim of these was to prevent double taxation.

Dividend warrant A document entitling the recipient to a sum of money which can be obtained from a bank. It is similar to a **cheque**. It states gross amount, tax deducted and net amount paid. The shareholder who is not liable to taxation at **standard rate** will be able to claim a return (in part or whole) of the tax paid by sending the tax voucher, attached to the warrant, to the appropriate tax authorities.

Dividend yield Companies usually declare **dividends** as a percentage on **nominal value** of shares. This value may be far removed from **market value**. A company which has been in business over an extended period will, if only because of inflation, find that the current listed market price of its shares is usually well above the price at which they were originally issued – whether this was at the nominal value or at that value plus a premium. This ratio of the dividend to the current market price is referred to as the dividend yield.

There is nothing particularly significant in the fact that a dividend of, say, 60 per cent is declared. This percentage should be related not to the initial nominal value but to the total **equity** capital, i.e. share capital plus reserves. Again, it will appear in quite a different light when the dividend is expressed as a percentage of the present market value of the shares

at the time the dividend was declared. In an expanding company, 60 per cent may well represent no more than 6 per cent on the current price of the share. ◊ **Shares: market value**.

Where **fixed interest securities** are concerned, much the same pattern emerges except that here, because the dividend does not vary and consists of the total share of earnings that can be claimed, both **earnings yield** and dividend yield will tend to converge – provided the fixed dividend has been regularly paid. The yield figure will then tend to follow the prevailing fixed interest rate and reflect less the state of the company than the state of the economy. However, the yields on preference shares are necessarily always affected by the knowledge that the capital itself is more at risk than with, say, a government bond; therefore although yields on fixed dividend shares and other **risk capital**, like interest rates generally, are a measure of public confidence in the state of the economy, they will usually be slightly higher than that on non-risk securities such as **consols**. One other factor that will also affect the yield occurs when the shares, or other capital concerned, is in the nature of redemption capital, i.e. the capital sum is to be repaid at a future date. ◊ **Debentures** ◊ **Redeemable preference shares** ◊ **Redemption yield**.

Dock dues A toll on all vessels entering or leaving a dock.

Dock warrant This is given to the owner of **goods** stored at a dock **warehouse** as a recognition of his **title** to those goods. It is in fact a document of title.

Document against acceptance A

term used with reference to foreign trade, where documents of **title** to **goods** exported are handed over by the master of the ship or some other person when the importer signs a **bill of exchange**. (The bill would be a **period bill**.)

Document against payment Similar to a **document against acceptance** but the bill is a sight bill and the importer must pay immediately, before receiving the documents of **title**.

Documentary credit Credit facilities opened by foreign importers at UK banks for the benefit of exporters, who can then, provided necessary documentation is presented by them, avail themselves of these facilities to discount bills drawn upon the importer.

Dollar An anglicization of the 'thaler', a silver coin of Germanic origin once widely used in European countries, which has become the unit of currency of the USA. Other countries have also adopted the dollar, but in international currency usage the unit is then usually prefixed with the name of the country to which it applies, e.g. Canadian dollar.

Due to the economic strength of the United States the dollar has long been seen as an attractive currency to hold, and for many years after the Second World War it was almost as acceptable as gold. The UK reserves were referred to as gold and dollar reserves. With the growth of other hard currencies such as the deutschmark and the yen the dollar has lost its absolute domination in the currency market, but it is still much sought after, because of its general acceptability in world trade. Many international commodities are officially quoted in US dollars, e.g. gold, oil, etc.

Dollar premium This was a surcharge

on the price of **dollars** arising from the UK **exchange control** regulations, with particular reference to portfolio investments. After the post-war imposition of exchange control regulations and non-convertibility of **sterling** there still remained a pool of dollar securities which could be dealt in. The proceeds from the realization of these **securities** were available for further investment but in order to obtain such dollars an additional amount, a premium, was payable by the purchaser. The **rate of exchange** for dollars therefore increased according to the quantity of dollars available from the realization of the securities. The object of the premium was to inhibit the purchase of dollars, the one agreed hard and safe currency, by making them more expensive for the potential investor. It was not in the British national interest to buy too much from the United States until, by building up our exports, we had sufficient dollars to spare. With the sudden advent of complete convertibility, the dollar premium disappeared. ◊ **Balance of payments** ◊ **Euro-bonds** ◊ **Euro-dollars** ◊ **Euro-market**.

Donee The recipient of a **gift**.

Donor A person who gives property, or a **title** to property, to another person. This word is usually applied to **gifts**, i.e. where no payment is made.

Dormant companies Not to be confused with **shell companies** or skeleton companies, a dormant company is one which, though it is equipped to function, has no field of present operation and indulges in no accounting transactions which would require entries in its books or records other than the taking up of shares by a subscriber to the memorandum.

Where such a company is involved in no significant accounting transactions in a particular accounting period, the Companies Act 1985, following that of 1981, provides that where it is also entitled to the exemption of a small company ⌑ **Small and medium-sized companies** and is not itself obliged to prepare group accounts, then it need not appoint auditors nor provide an auditors' report when filing its annual accounts. The directors must, however, file a statement with those accounts, to appear under their signatures on the balance sheet, to the effect that the conditions necessary to a dormant company prevailed throughout the financial year.

Double-entry book-keeping A form of book-keeping, devised centuries ago, whereby each transaction is entered twice, a transaction being by its nature two-sided. The purchase of an **asset** necessitates the recording of the asset and also, separately, of the debt incurred or the money paid. The book in which all the accounts are kept is known as the **ledger**, though the cash account is normally kept in a separate book, known as the **cash book**. At any time the total debit balances in the ledger should equal the total credit balances. If this is so, it is an indication that (in the absence of compensating errors) double entries have been properly made. This is because, of the two entries made, one is always a debit and one a credit entry.

Double insurance This occurs where a risk is insured against twice. Generally speaking it is impossible to obtain more than the loss suffered and if a risk is insured against twice, one insurer will claim **contribution** from the other. Double insurance should be distinguished from **reinsurance**.

Double option ⌑ Option.

Double taxation relief This is a very complex subject. It deals with the relief afforded a **company** or other business earning profits abroad, this profit being taxable in the other country. There are two principal forms of relief. (1) The tax payable in the United Kingdom will only be such as to make the total tax payable equivalent to the UK rate. This applies where there is a double taxation agreement with the other country. (2) The tax payable abroad is allowed as a deduction when calculating taxable profits.

When the full United Kingdom tax rate is not paid on profits earned overseas, only the United Kingdom proportion, known as the net United Kingdom rate, can be reclaimed by persons receiving these profits and entitled to make repayment claims. Most companies state 'net United Kingdom rate' when this applies to tax deducted from dividends.

Doubtful debts, provision for An amount set aside out of profits to provide against the possibility of debts being irrecoverable. These may be specific debts and/or a percentage of total debtors (the percentage is learnt by experience).

Douceur An eighteenth-century term for a bribe or **gratuity**.

Dow-Jones Index The American equivalent of the **Financial Times Ordinary Share Index**, it is an **index number** representing typical industrial share prices on the United States Stock Exchange. Dow-Jones is the publisher of the *Wall Street Journal*.

Dozen A set of twelve items. In the bakery trade a dozen is supplied as thirteen. Known as a 'baker's dozen', this is a reminder of the days when the substantial penalties under the law for giving short weight in bread caused bakers to add an extra loaf to a dozen ordered so as to be on the safe side of error. There is also a tradition in the newspaper trade of supplying copies to retailers at thirteen to the dozen invoiced. Where unit costs are very low such a practice can be cost-effective in so far as it minimizes time spent dealing with queries on shortages in the number supplied.

Draper A dealer in cloth.

Drawback A rebate which may be obtained for duty paid on imported materials used in the manufacture of exported **goods**. Drawback is avoided if goods are kept in a bonded **warehouse** for re-export. Goods for repair may be imported free of duty. For details of drawback, apply to **Her Majesty's Customs and Excise**.

Drawee The person on whom a **bill of exchange** is drawn.

Drawer The person who draws a **bill of exchange**.

Drysalter A dealer in drugs, gums, etc., and sometimes also in oils, pickles and sauces.

Dumping A term used in international trade for the unloading of large quantities of a particular product in another country at a low **price**. This may be done where the first country is over-producing and wishes to sell at a low profit rather than at none at all (or even to sell at a loss, so that it may get a foothold in the other market). Again, it can be a rather ruthless way of maximizing the profit of a particular industry. Where there is a **monopoly** at home output is restricted and a high price charged. The bulk of the output is then pushed into another country and

sold at prices which producers in that country cannot afford. Dumping is therefore frowned upon by governments, and steps are often taken to prevent it happening. These may be direct, e.g. by duties, or indirect, e.g. by retaliatory action.

Duplication Business transactions inevitably demand a degree of document duplication, whether these be invoices, receipts or letters - for every one issued it is imperative that at least one copy be retained by the issuer. Traditionally this was effected by producing carbon copies of all such documents, whether typed or handwritten. This is still the case with many documents, for example delivery notes, which tend to be printed in triplicate. The sender then retains a copy of the signature admitting delivery. Nowadays, to obviate the need to insert sheets of carbon paper, specially prepared NCR (no carbon required) paper tends to be used.

In circumstances where multiple copies of a document are required a quite different technique is employed. At one time this involved processes such as rolling off copies from a specially prepared or stencilled original. These various machines have now been made virtually obsolete by the ubiquity of the photocopier in one of its many different forms. There are very many photocopying machines now available ranging from the fairly small to the free-standing cabinet variety, with varying degrees of sophistication, but all require the use of specially treated paper on which the duplicates are produced. Those with the finest standard of resolution tend to use a xerographic process (◊ **Xerography**). Photocopying machines may be purchased or leased. Those leased will normally include a built-in device for counting the number of copies taken – the rental charge being, in part, related to this number. **Facsimile (Fax)** machines, which are now common in the business world, have the additional ability to act as photocopiers.

Durable goods Goods purchased for use over a period, such as washing machines or refrigerators. The consumer's equivalent of a **fixed asset**.

Duress The use of force to procure a **contract**. The force need not be physical but may result from the relationship existing between parties: father and son, for instance.

Dutch auction An unusual form of **auction**, often used with reference to charities, where the **auctioneer** starts the bidding at a very high price and then reduces the price until he receives a bid.

Duty free shop ◊ Customs: airports.

Duty paid contracts Ex ship contracts where the seller also pays import duty, and may also pay the warehousing charges.

Earned income That part of a person's income which is obtained as a result of the application of their own labour, either as an employee or as a **self-employed** person. The distinction between earned and **unearned income** is very important for tax purposes, though since the introduction of the **unified system of taxation** in 1973 the degree of importance has been much reduced. Prior to that date earned income was treated quite separately, two-ninths of it being free of income tax. At present all income is treated together and taxed as one lump sum.

Earned income is subject to income tax under schedule 'E' for employees and schedule 'D' for the self-employed. Persons in the latter category can often minimize their tax liability by charging various expenses incurred in earning their income against the amount earned, before the sum taxable is agreed. Although this is possible under schedule 'E', the categories of expense allowed are more strictly defined and must be individually agreed in advance with the Inspector of Taxes so that the employer can be notified beforehand. This is because schedule 'E' tax is collected through the PAYE system and is deducted according to a code number given by the Inland Revenue to the employer. ◊ **Pay as you earn** ◊ **Tax return, personal** ◊ **Taxation of profits** ◊ **Taxation schedules** ◊ **Investment income surcharge**.

Earnings-related pensions Many pension schemes in both the private and the public sector aim to relate ultimate pension entitlements to wages or salaries previously earned by the recipient. To this end regular contributions made by the employee during his working years are geared to his earnings, increasing as those earnings increase. Such contributory pension schemes are referred to as earnings-related. ◊ **State earnings-related pension scheme**.

Earnings yield This term has, over the past decades, assumed an increasingly important role in everyday **Stock Exchange** jargon, principally because it is far more informative of the true worth of an investment, in immediate terms, than any other alternative. The earnings yield relates that portion of divisible **net profit** or earnings of a company applicable to the particular investment to the present market price of that investment and should be contrasted with the **dividend yield**, which relates the dividend paid to that same market price. It is the reciprocal of the **price-earnings ratio**. ◊ **Mean price**.

A company which has the confidence and support of the investing public, i.e. a company which is thought to be heading for even better times, will often have a low earnings yield and a correspondingly high price-earnings ratio. This is because the future profits have been anticipated by investors, causing the market price of the shares, the denominator of the earnings yield fraction, to rise accordingly.

The converse is also true. The fact that a share has a high earnings yield may make it seem a worthwhile investment, but it may also indicate that the market price is falling away, due to a lack of confidence in the future of the company or its management. Anticipation of **nationalization** can often make buyers wary of particular company shares and this fall away in demand may cause a reduction in the market price of the share. In this case the resultant increase in earnings yield would only attract the uninformed or the investor who does not fear capital loss. The encroaching State may thus be able to acquire the shares of a company on very favourable terms. Of course, any serious follower of the stock market will be more interested in the trend of the earnings yield than in its absolute figure at any one time. ◊ **Rate of return** ◊ **Yield**.

Easement This is defined as 'the right of using another's land in a defined and specific way without taking any substance from the land' (*Stephen's Commentaries*, nineteenth edition). A right of way is a typical easement. Easements may be positive or negative. The right of way is a positive easement, the right not to be deprived of light is a negative one. Easements are normally created by **deed** and may be express or implied. An implied easement may arise when a man sells part only of his property, an implication being that he has a right of way over the part sold to reach the part which is still his.

Economic sanction Despite the adjective this is more of a political matter. When the government of one nation, or of many acting in concert, wishes to make more than just a token objection to the policies advocated by another, whether these be in its political actions or general refusal to respect treaties to which it is a party, e.g. the United Nations Treaty, then a common tactic is to attempt to disrupt the economy of the offending nation by the imposition of boycotts and **embargoes** on trade with that country. Such economic sanctions were employed against Rhodesia by the UK and other countries to try to force it to retract from nationalist policies which followed its unilateral declaration of independence some years before the Lancaster House agreement established Zimbabwe as an independent country.

Edinburgh Gazette An official Scottish publication similar to the **London Gazette**, and containing notices which would in England be required to be in the *London Gazette*.

Eighth schedule The regulations laid down by the 1948 Companies Act for contents and form of every **balance sheet** or **profit and loss account** presented to a company in general meeting or filed with that company's annual return. It has now been replaced by the **fourth schedule** to the 1985 Companies Act.

Ejusdem generis rule A rule of law (the words mean 'of the same kind'). The rule might be applied, in, say, **insurance**: the court might decide that although a policy may cover losses not expressly mentioned in the policy, they must be of the same kind as those which are mentioned, and not of a completely different kind.

Elasticity of demand A term used in economics to refer to the reaction of demand to changes in **price**. Demand for a product is said to be elastic or inelastic according to its sensitivity to marginal price changes (marginal because obviously all demand for any product is ultimately determined by price). In this country, the demand for salt is relatively inelastic. The quantity of salt used is not determined by price, though obviously there would come a point where the public would stop buying and look for an alternative. The demand for a competitive soap powder, on the other hand, is elastic, as there are many substitutes available, and a small price change could have a marked effect on demand for that particular brand.

Elective resolution A resolution available to members of private companies. The 1989 Companies Act provided that a private company in general meeting may pass what are referred to as elective resolutions to dispense with certain specified requirements of the Companies Acts. These are five in number and permit Private Companies to (a) extend the period during which shares are allotted at the discretion of Directors; (b) dispense with the necessity of laying accounts before the company in general meeting; (c) dispense with the need to hold an annual general meeting; (d) alter the majority needed to authorize a meeting called at insufficient notice; and (e) dispense with annual appointment of auditors.

An elective resolution is not effective unless at least twenty-one days' notice of that resolution is given to all members who are entitled to attend and vote at the meeting at which the resolution is tabled and approved by all such members at that meeting. An elective resolution can be revoked at any time by an ordinary resolution in general meeting.

Electricity supply industry Since 1990 the industry has been divided into two distinct parts, both being subsumed into the private sector. On the one hand are

the generating companies and the National Grid; on the other are the supply companies charged with distributing electricity to the user. Both generators and suppliers operate under licences obtained from **OFFER**, the independent regulator set up to oversee the industry.

In England and Wales the generators are PowerGen, National Power and Nuclear Power, all public liability companies, replacing the previous Central Electricity Generating Board. The suppliers are regional companies at present holding franchises for their specific areas from OFFER. These franchises effectively give the supply companies monopoly rights within those areas, but this is intended as a temporary measure only until 1998 when franchises will cease and all companies supplying electricity will be free to compete with one another. OFFER sets maximum prices at which electricity can be sold.

Users of more than a stated minimum of electricity units are free to obtain power directly from generators at negotiated prices. This freedom will apply to all users after the franchise system is discontinued. Although licences from OFFER are required by any organization wishing to generate its own electricity, exceptions are made for those who generate for their own use with any balance being taken up by existing supply companies.

The system operative in England and Wales is paralleled by a similar system in Scotland where the generating companies are Scottish Power plc, Scottish Hydro-Electric plc and Scottish Nuclear plc. In all three countries the nuclear-powered generators have been retained in State control, and revenue for those bodies comes from the proceeds of a levy exacted on supply companies and included in the charges made by them to end users.

Embargo When it is forbidden to export **goods** to certain countries, then goods are said to be subject to embargo. The embargo may be imposed by either side, and prohibits the unloading or loading of certain goods, or else prevents ships entering or leaving certain ports.

Emoluments A term used to refer to the total benefits received by an employee. In addition to money paid as salary it includes goods or services acquired as benefits in kind, e.g. private use of a company car, free holidays abroad, subsidized accommodation and free meals. ◊ **Benefit in kind** ◊ **Luncheon vouchers** ◊ **Directors' emoluments**.

Employee buy-out This refers to the control of a company passing to the employees, who purchase either individually or through an employee trust a controlling interest in a company's equity share capital. Although it could happen by gradual acquisition of shares through employee share schemes and/or market purchases, such a manner of taking control is unlikely and is not what is generally meant by the term employee buy-out. Such a buy-out is frequently inspired by the desire of the workforce to protect employment threatened by the possible closing down of the business by management. The employees acting in concert and with private or public financial backing offer a better price than would be obtained by liquidating the assets, and if their offer is accepted then control passes to them.

An employee buy-out also might occur indirectly on the occasion of the privatization by the government of an industry where the existing employees are given prior right to subscribe for the shares and act in concert to purchase all shares on issue or sufficient to give themselves a controlling interest. This happened when the National Freight Corporation was denationalized. It became an employee-controlled company, the **National Freight Consortium PLC**, now listed as NFC plc ◊ **Worker cooperative**.

Employees, information regarding The limited information regarding numbers and remuneration of employees which the 1967 Companies Act required to be given in the directors' report or in notes to the annual accounts themselves was extended by the 1981 Companies Act, which required the information to be given in the notes to the accounts and not in the directors' report.

The rules were changed by the 1985 Companies Act which required that notes to the accounts should give the average number of persons employed by the company during the financial year to which the accounts relate. The average was determined by a formula contained in the Act, and the aggregate amount of wages/salaries paid to such persons and, as a separate figure, the contributions paid by the company on account of those persons to any pension scheme distinguishing between State schemes and other schemes.

In addition to the average number of persons employed, the notes must give the average number in each category of employees within the company – categories to be determined according to the principal areas of business of the company.

Employees: loans for purchase of shares A company may provide loans to bona fide employees or ex-employees other than directors for the purpose of acquiring fully paid shares in that company, or its holding company, provided that the employee holds them as beneficial owner. Loans may also be made towards the purchase of shares under an employees' share scheme, which is for the benefit of employees or their immediate families.

The amount outstanding on such loans must be disclosed, in total, in a note to the **balance sheet** of the company. ◊ **Loans to directors**.

Employers' liability insurance In much the same way as motorists must protect third parties, employers of labour are bound by law to keep an **insurance** policy that will cover injury, death or industrial disease incurred by employees whilst on the employers' premises. This liability is in no way reduced by the existence of the State **national insurance** scheme, although there is an area of overlap. The relevant statute is the Employers' Liability (Compulsory Insurance) Act 1969. ◊ **Third party insurance**.

Employment agencies These are enterprises established either privately or by the State with the object of bringing prospective employers into contact with job-seekers. Private agencies make a charge for services, though whether this is levied on the applicant for a job or the employer or both will vary according to circumstances. State employment agencies do not normally make any direct charge. ◊ **Job Centre**.

Employment agents are something akin to **brokers** in that they help bring parties to a contract together. They neither buy nor sell personally but bring the buyer into contact with the seller, or vice versa. The agency usually keeps a regular register of situations vacant, dividing them according to type. Another register is kept of persons seeking employment, with records of their skills, achievements and aspirations. Interviews, sometimes in depth, may be necessary before a candidate can be matched to any particular vacancy. This will, of course, be more common in the private sector as the agency, unlike the State, depends on its reliability for its continued existence.

Agencies are becoming increasingly important in the professional world, perhaps because of their vetting processes, and more and more posts are now being handed over to agencies for handling. In the UK the point is often reached where running an employment agency is the safest form of work when unemployment figures run high. State employment agencies, or Job Centres, are distinct from the unemployment exchange, though obviously their areas of work overlap. Persons out of work are obliged to register at the **DSS** if they wish to claim unemployment benefit. ◊ **Development areas** ◊ **Professional and executive recruitment** ◊ **Small firms information centres.**

Employment legislation During the 1980s the government has brought in legislation seeking to curb certain apparent abuses of trade union power in the pursuit of what it sees as the public interest.

The Employment Act 1980 tackled a number of contentious issues. *Inter alia*, it imposed restrictions on secondary picketing and other forms of industrial action not at the place of work of the trade union members engaged in a dispute. Those breaching the provisions of the Act lose their immunity from civil action brought by an injured employer. That action could be against the individual employees or against the union itself. As regards picketing generally, the Act permits peaceful picketing at the place of work but not deliberate or aggressive attempts to prevent other workers exercising their right to work. Flying pickets, being essentially both secondary and aggressive, are *de facto* illegal. A code of practice issued later that year suggested that picketing should reasonably be confined to groups of not more than six persons. The actual control of picketing was left with the law enforcement agencies, notably the police, with the Act and the code of practice to guide them.

The Act also attempted to tidy up the existing law and practice on the matter of closed shops. Closed shops have never been illegal but problems have arisen through rulings by the European Court regarding the right to work given to each individual as a fundamental human right. There are also associated problems of employees being either dismissed from employment on the ground of being non-union or refused membership by the union itself, thereby rendering them ineligible for work.

By the 1980 Act closed shops or, as they are now known, union-management agreements are enforceable only if the consent of 80 per cent of the relevant workforce is first obtained. Failure to obtain this means that an employer is liable for wrongful dismissal on the plea of a sacked employee. The government attempted to ease the cost to unions of balloting members on this, and other issues, by making public funds available for the purpose.

The 1982 Employment Act went further by insisting that such ballots should be secret and listing heavy penalties against unions which disregarded the provisions. The Trade Union Act 1984 extended this requirement for secret ballots

to the election of union officers, to the raising of political levies and to any decision involving industrial action by trade unions.

The extent to which these statutory provisions are relied upon by employers will obviously depend both on their particular labour relations experience and their assessment of how each separate incident can be best settled for the maximum good of all concerned.

Endorsement A term used with particular reference to **bills of exchange**. When a bill is negotiated the person negotiating will write his name on the reverse of the bill. A valid endorsement must be written on the bill itself or on an **allonge**. It must be of the entire bill and must be by all parties to whom the bill is made out unless one has authority to act for the others. If the bill is payable to order and the payee's name is wrongly spelt, the endorser may sign it in the incorrect way and add his correct name if he wishes. Where there are a number of endorsements on a bill, they are presumed to have been made in the order in which they appear. Unless the contrary is stated, a bill is presumed to have been negotiated before it is overdue. Any person endorsing a bill becomes liable on the bill to all subsequent endorsees or holders. He cannot deny the drawer's signature or the signatures of persons previously endorsing the bill if asked to pay by a **holder in due course**.

Endorsements may be of various types: (1) a bill may be endorsed in blank, no endorsee being named; the bill then becomes payable to bearer, (2) there may be a special endorsement when the name of the endorsee is specified; the bill then becomes a bill payable to order, (3) there may be a restrictive endorsement, where the bill is endorsed 'Pay A only'; the bill then ceases to be a negotiable instrument, (4) the endorsement may be limited, e.g. **without recourse**.

If an endorsement is forged, the position is more difficult. Generally speaking **title** cannot pass through a forgery and a holder of the bill can only claim from persons signing the bill subsequent to the forgery.

Sometimes bills are endorsed conditionally, e.g. 'To A provided he cashes the bill in X days'. The payer can please himself whether or not he observes the condition.

Endowment A term used with reference to **assurance** policies. An endowment assurance is one where the holder of the policy, by paying a certain annual premium, is entitled to a fixed sum at a stated date. ◊ **Assurance**.

Enterprise allowance scheme Set up by the Manpower Services Commission in 1983 to assist unemployed persons set up their own businesses. Applicants for aid must fulfil prescribed conditions and can then receive an allowance of up to £40 per week for a year. Advice from business counsellors and the **Small Firms Information Centres** is also available.

Enterprise zones These were established in 1980 with the aim of stimulating economic activity in selected areas, particularly within inner-city wastelands where regeneration was urgently needed.

Industry moving into these zones or new enterprises setting up therein can, during their first ten years, claim certain advantages. These include freedom from development land tax, simplification of planning procedures and exemption from both industrial training levies and local authority commercial or industrial rates. An additional bonus lies in the fact that capital allowances of 100 per cent may be claimed virtually right away.

Entrepôt trade This concerns the re-exporting of imported **goods**. The goods may be sold directly from bonded **warehouses**. If they are not, and duty has been paid, the re-exporter may be entitled to a refund of the duty. This is known as **drawback**. Drawback may also be payable where the re-exports contain imported goods only in part. Entitlement to claim is given by a Customs' debenture. ◊ **Freeport**.

Entrepreneur A term rarely used in the commercial world of today, but more common in books on economic history. The changes brought about by the industrial revolution, particularly the economic theory that defended its *laissez faire* image, required fresh words for the new economic roles that participants in the industrial struggles played. Economic theory accepted the two major factors of production as capital and labour but, as these two factors needed to be brought together and harmonized, a third factor was conceived, i.e. enterprise. This was supplied by the individual who thought up a project and risked his own savings in trying to organize the other two factors into making it succeed. He was given the title of entrepreneur. Theoretically, whilst capital and labour were guaranteed their due reward, the entrepreneur took the gamble of either losing his all or becoming rich beyond the dreams of avarice. ◊ **Competitive market** ◊ **Speculation**.

Equipment leasing There are many opportunities for hiring capital equipment. It has been common practice for many years to rent very expensive equipment to save a large and immediate cash outlay. The rental agreement is usually accompanied by a maintenance agreement.

This principle is being developed by **finance companies** to encourage more widespread leasing of industrial equipment as an alternative to purchase. There are normally three parties: the manufacturer of the equipment, the finance company, or lessor, and the customer. The customer agrees with the lessor a minimum period of lease, probably not more than half the life of the **asset**. (He then may have an option to renew at a lower rental.) When this agreement is signed, the customer orders the equipment from the manufacturer. The equipment is delivered to the customer but invoiced to the lessor. The customer notifies the lessor that the delivery is satisfactory, and the lessor pays the manufacturer. The customer from then on pays a rental to the lessor.

Equity That part of the law which deals with matters not within the province of the **common law** of the land, or of statute law. It operates where a special remedy is sought (e.g the **specific performance** of a **contract**) or where someone has suffered loss, for which the common law or statute law does not provide (e.g. breach of trust). It takes precedence over common law or statute law. It originated in the courts of chancery, i.e. with the Lord Chancellor, to whom appeal was made by persons unable to obtain redress in the courts. If the Chancellor, as 'Keeper of the King's conscience', considered that compensation of some sort was right and proper, then he would act accordingly. Because of the nature of the court, it is essential that any applicant must himself be generally beyond reproach. 'He who comes to Equity must come with clean hands.'

Equity capital Traditionally, this refers to that part of the issued share capital of a company held by those who take the greatest risk and are consequently entitled to all profits and reserves remaining after the contributors of fixed interest or fixed dividend capital have been paid their due. Generally speaking, equity capital is that owned by holders of ordinary shares, though for purposes of certain provisions in the 1980 Companies Act (e.g. pre-emption rights) it also includes holders of participating preference shares and other classes of shareholder with an undetermined stake in company profits.

It is customary for equity shareholders, being the true owners of the company in the sense of being the ultimate risk takers, to make all decisions on company policy through the agency of the **board of directors** which they appoint. Although this is the supposed right of the holders of the equity, it is frequently flaunted by the practice of disenfranchisement contained in the creation of what are usually known as **'A' ordinary shares**, which though fully entitled to profit carry no votes. This type of ordinary share capital is not popular with the Stock Exchange but is often created in situations where control of the company through the board of directors is wanted by the original promoters, who are confident of profitability but wish to keep a tight rein on company policy. It was particularly prevalent among the independent television companies that grew up under the IBA. ◊ **Risk capital**.

Equity dilution ◊ **Equity capital**. Sometimes the true interest of a shareholder in a company, as measured by his holding of **ordinary shares**, may be reduced by the issue of a further quantity of equal ranking shares. Whereas before he may have held shares representing 40 per cent of the equity the new shares may reduce this proportion to, say, 30 per cent. The new shares usually rank **pari passu** with existing shares. This is known as equity dilution. The law now protects such existing equity shareholders. ◊ **Shares: pre-emptive rights of purchase**.

Equity of redemption The right of a mortgagor to redeem his property on the repayment of money borrowed. The law does not approve of clogs on the equity of redemption by way of onerous conditions imposed on the mortgagor, or of conditions aimed at making it difficult for him to redeem his property. ◊ **Mortgage**.

Errors and omissions excepted (E & OE) These initials were often included at the end of an **invoice**. The legal effect is somewhat doubtful. The idea was to absolve the person issuing the invoice from clerical errors.

Escalation clause A clause often included in a contract which may take some time to complete, e.g. the building of a new factory. It allows the contractor to increase the price when the incidence of inflation causes costs to rise. The degree to which such increases are permitted is usually defined in the clause. It should be distinguished from a **cost-plus contract**, which involves a different concept.

Escheat An old legal term for the right of the Lord of the Manor or the grantor of land or interest in land to retake the land when the tenant died leaving no heir. This was abolished by the Law of Property Act 1925.

Escrow A **Contract by deed** delivered

subject to a condition, i.e. not becoming operative until the condition is fulfilled.

Estate agent An **agent** or **broker** who is concerned with the sale, letting, management and valuation of real and leasehold property. The work is often combined with that of an **auctioneer**. The agent works on an **ad valorem commission**. He is a **general agent**. There are three professional bodies representing estate agents: (1) the Royal Institute of Chartered Surveyors; (2) the Incorporated Society of Valuers and Auctioneers; and (3) the National Association of Estate Agents, but there is no obligation for an estate agent to belong to any of these. Estate agents are, however, bound by the Estate Agents Act 1979 and the Property Misdescriptions Act 1993. There is an Ombudsman for Corporate Estate Agents providing consumer protection, but his remit does not cover the independents. The National Association of Estate Agents is considering setting up its own Ombudsman scheme to fill this gap.

Estate duty The amount levied by the State on a deceased person's property. It was, in fact if not in name, a wealth tax. The provisions for assessing the amount payable and the persons who were to pay it were very complex. Wealth chargeable to duty could include sums of money or other assets given away prior to death, which were brought into account by dint of the gifts inter vivos rule, i.e. those **gifts** made within the preceding seven years were taxable though the rate of tax was reduced in accordance with the time elapsed. The amount payable on shareholdings could be crippling to a company where the deceased had more than a 50 per cent interest, for the shares could then be valued on what was known as a 'net asset' basis. This would substantially increase the duty payable. ◊ **Asset value**. Estate duty was replaced, so far as deaths after March 1974 were concerned, by capital transfer tax. This itself was much modified in 1986 when, from 18 March, most gratuitous transfers of property by one person to another during the lifetime of the donor ceased to be taxable, provided that the donor did not die within the succeeding seven years. From March 1986 CTT was replaced by **inheritance tax**. ◊ **Death duty**.

Estoppel A rule of law, whereby a person is prevented (or estopped) from denying a statement he has made either orally or in writing (or possibly implied by conduct). It applies particularly to statements made in a **contract by deed**. It also prevents a principal from denying the authority of his **agent**, or a person denying the existence of a **partnership**, where the conduct of the parties has implied that this exists. ◊ **Holding out**.

Euratom ◊ **European Atomic Energy Community**.

Euro-bonds Like the **euro-dollar**, the euro-bond is of relatively recent origin. Euro-bonds are **bonds** that arose initially from the need of American industry to raise money in Europe for investment there. The first euro-bonds were purchasable only in euro-dollars though they are now issued in other strong European currencies. They are intended as a long-term means of raising funds for the industries of varoius countries on an international level in contrast to, e.g. British government treasury bonds. They are issued and subscribed for on the international market and are often used by British companies wishing to raise money abroad, e.g. ICI may decide to raise

funds in other European markets by making a bonds issue in the international arena, intending to attract investment by countries whose currency they need. Conversely, other nationals may buy bonds issued on the **Euro-market** by ICI as an alternative to investing in British government stock. The necessity of obtaining **sterling** may then be avoided, particularly if ICI sells the bonds in the currency of the country in which it is attempting to raise funds. ◊ **Dollar premium** ◊ **Foreign exchange market** ◊ **International Monetary Fund**.

Euro-currencies A generic term for bank balances within Europe stated in a particular currency but held outside the country of which the particular currency is the monetary unit, e.g. **euro-dollars**, euro-sterling, euro-deutchmarks, euro-yen. Until recently, euro-dollars were the most prominent euro-currency, but strengths of other currencies and instability of the dollar have led to greater demand for other euro-currencies. One of their attractions is that they are subject to far fewer rules and regulations than currencies in domestic markets are, so a company may find it both easier and less costly to float a loan in some euro-currency than in the currency of the country in which it is resident.

Euro-dollars ◊ **Euro-market**. A post-1950s phenomenon, these are the dollar balances in American banks, in the names of various European persons or companies, which are used to finance international trade without ever leaving the banks in which they are held. ◊ **Dollar premium** ◊ **Euro-bonds**. For many years the euro-dollar was the closest thing to an international currency in Europe. Euro-dollars were really only a specific instance of the genus euro-currency, but they assumed far more significance than euro-francs or euro-deutschmarks because of the strength of, and immense demand for, the **dollar** in international trade. Until relatively recently, dollars were almost synonymous with gold and the British national reserves were referred to as the 'gold-and-dollar reserves'. The euro-dollar has now lost much of its old trading value as the strength of other currencies (particularly the deutschmark) increases, while that of the dollar falls. ◊ **Gold and foreign exchange reserves**.

Euro-market After 1945 most of Europe was in urgent need of economic help to rebuild the ravaged cities and re-create a semblance of economic strength – one objective being to reduce the risk of a communist take-over. Various forces, not least the Marshall Plan, were instrumental in persuading various nations of the necessity of cooperation in the collective drive to survive and progress. Out of these forces came the growth of numerous international or trans-European agencies and moves towards permanent economic combinations, leading eventually to the establishment of the **European Union**, the **Common Market**, first conceived in the Schuman plan for a common steel industry. ◊ **European Coal and Steel community**.

On the financial side, stemming from the **Organisation for European Economic Cooperation and Development**, came the **European payments union** (EPU) and then the **European monetary agreement** (EMA). Out of these grew the markets in **euro-dollars** and **euro-bonds**, all part of the overall need to pool available funds in the common aim of European prosperity. Euro-bonds were the means of raising long-term funds, while euro-dollars enabled inter-national trade to move swiftly by basing it on the one hard currency acceptable to all – the American **dollar**. This facility was not just a one-way matter, for it also greatly helped the American economy in its trading relations across the Atlantic and in its desire to open European subsidiaries by reducing the necessity of exporting dollars. ◊ **Dollar premium** ◊ **Euro-bond** ◊ **Euro-dollar** ◊ **European Monetary Agreement** ◊ **European Payments Union** ◊ **European Monetary System** ◊ **European currency unit**.

European Atomic Energy Community (Euratom) In 1957 the **Common Market** countries decided to set up a central and common agency for the development of atomic energy for peaceful purposes. The idea was to pool the skills and knowledge of each member country so as to be better able to compete with the superpowers: the USA and the USSR. The resulting agency became known as Euratom. In its early years it was somewhat hidebound by the international limits set on Germany's powers to develop atomic weapons, which could not easily be isolated from peaceful atomic energy projects, and by France's determination, spearheaded by General de Gaulle, to become a nuclear power in her own right.

European Coal and Steel Community Established by the Treaty of Paris in 1951, the European Coal and Steel Community was formed with the object of pooling the coal, iron ore and steel resources of the six founder members of the **European Union**: France, Germany, Holland, Belgium, Luxemburg and Italy. The treaty was based on the Schuman plan, originally conceived by Jean Monnet, which aimed to unite the coal and steel industries of France and Germany. Britain was invited to join but refused the invitation. The Coal and Steel Community was soon to be followed by the far more comprehensive **Common Market** (the EU) in 1957.

European Commission This is one of the four main EU institutions, the others being the **European Parliament**, the **European Council** and the **European Court of Justice**. The European Commission is the executive arm of the Union consisting of a President and sixteen Commissioners put forward by member countries but expected to act in an impartial manner for the good of the Union as a whole. Each Commissioner has special responsibility for one particular area of economic or political concern in which he, or she, executes decisions taken by the Council of Ministers and supervises the day-to-day running of agreed policies. The Commission has no independent powers of legislation but may propose policy and legislative changes which are then put to the Council for adoption or amendment. Once policy has been decided it is the responsibility of the Commission to ensure that member states comply with it.

European Communities Act The British Act of Parliament which gave effect to the various agreements made in the Treaty of Accession and which made the UK a full member of the European Community. ⟡ **Common Agricultural Policy** ⟡ **Common Market**.

European companies Although at present each member country of the European Union has its own codes of practice and legislation regarding the formation and management of limited companies, the intention is to establish a uniform type of company throughout the EU. It is hoped that the standard form eventually adopted will contain what is best in the present practice of each member country. The need for unification in law and practice is continually emphasized by the emergence and growth of **multinational** European companies. Eventually, perhaps, not only the equalization of company law will be achieved but also standardization of taxation in its corporate form. Until this time comes it will be necessary to be familiar with the separate legislation and customs of each of the European countries regarding corporations which enjoy **limited liability**. Because of the many variations that exist at present, it is not possible here to do more than give a few guidelines. The more comprehensive systems are dealt with under the headings of **French companies** and **German companies**. Those operated in Italy, Belgium, Luxemburg and the Netherlands tend to be variations on the French and German systems, e.g. the Dutch Naamloze Vennootschap (⟡ **NV**) is fairly similar to the French **Société Anonyme** (**SA**), though the rules about the appointment of directors are slightly more generous. Luxemburg follows the French pattern and so does Belgium, except in the sphere of private companies, where the Belgian Société de Personnes à Responsabilité Limitée (SPRL) is different in many respects from the French **Société à Responsabilité Limitée** (SRL).

European Council This exists on two levels involving either occasional meetings of the Heads of State of EU countries for the discussion of broad policy issues, or the more frequent meetings of the Council of Ministers the Union's decision-making body that usually acts on recommendations from the European Commission.

These latter meetings are attended by Ministers from member States whose particular responsibility covers the area to be discussed and also by representatives of the Commission. The latter take part in the discussions but not in the vote. The number of votes that each Minister has is proportional to the population of the country he represents. While many decisions can be taken on a majority vote, those concerning more sensitive matters require unanimous agreement.

European Court of Justice Based in Luxemburg this is the Community Institution responsible for the interpretation and enforcement of EU legislation. It rules on disputes between member countries and has the power to override legal decisions made at a national level, its judgments having a primacy over those of member countries. It is comprised of a panel of judges – one being provided by each member of the Union.

European currency unit (ECU) This was introduced within the EU as a mutually agreed unit of account with which intra-EU settlements could be effected. Originally the unit had been known as the EUA, the European unit of account, which had been tied to the dollar. When exchange rates were allowed to float the EUA became impractical and was replaced by the ECU at the time when the EMS was set up in 1979. The ECU is a weighted average of the various EU currencies, and member countries are expected to keep their currencies stable against the ECU within a fairly strict band of tolerance. Countries in difficulties are permitted to negotiate changes in their ECU exchange rate provided they have exhausted domestic measures

to maintain stability. The relative stability thus given to the ECU has led to the ECU being used as a currency in which loans are frequently denominated, particularly when raised by companies seeking capital not only from within their home country but from the EU at large.

European economic area The movement of the EU towards a single market has been accompanied by increasing efforts on the part of the **European Free Trade Association** (EFTA) nations to obtain a share in the economic benefits of such a market. With this end in view, six of the seven EFTA countries have endorsed an agreement known as the European Economic Area Agreement. Through this EFTA members will adopt almost all the provision of the EU single market legislation. EU competition rules will apply in the EEA and there will be close cooperation between the EU and EFTA in such areas as research and development, environmental protection and education etc. It is hoped within EFTA that such measures will bring them closer to developments within the EU and smooth the way for eventual full membership. At present the EU and EFTA have agreed to forge ahead with the EEA without Switzerland, which so far has not been willing to join.

In the longer term the bringing of the EFTA countries into full membership of the EU will be welcomed by present member countries as their admission will considerably strengthen EU finances. Rich new members are ever welcome!

European Economic Community The original title of the economic grouping, also known as the **Common Market**, which subsequently became more generally referred to as the **European Community** (EC). Recently, if somewhat prematurely, it has restyled itself as the **European Union** suggesting a federalism which does not exist.

European exchange rate mechanism (ERM) Part of the **European monetary system**, this was set up in 1978 to replace the European currency **snake** as part of a procedure for exercising some degree of control over the fluctuations in exchange rates between EU currencies, linking those currencies into a framework known as the ERM. Each currency within the system may fluctuate only within agreed limits against any other currency. The bands are strictly drawn though initially two bands operated, a wide band of 6 per cent for those with less stable currencies and the narrow optimum band of 2.25 per cent to which all members were expected to aim. As a further constraint, each member State was to maintain the exchange rate of its currency against the ECU within similarly defined limits.

Countries in difficulties were to support their exchange rates by the intervention of their own Central Bank or, on a longer term, by making necessary adjustments to economic or financial policies. In the last resort they could apply to the ERM for their currency to be revalued within the mechanism, leading to new rates of exchange against all other currencies. Such revaluations are discouraged insofar as they tend to have the domino effect of other countries seeking compensatory revaluations of their own currencies.

The UK joined the ERM in 1990 but economic and monetary difficulties led to it leaving again in 1992.

In the summer of 1993 further economic problems within member countries, together with the high level of German interest rates, threatened the whole structure of the ERM and brought about a considerable loosening of the system in an attempt to avert its disintegration.

European Free Trade Association (EFTA) This was formed in 1959 by the Stockholm Treaty as an alternative to the **Common Market** but with more limited aims. The emphasis was to be on eliminating **tariff** barriers between members but not, as with the Common Market, presenting a common tariff to the outside world. It has other aims, such as improvements in both productivity and standards of living; these are sought through the friendly exchange of ideas rather than by the enactment of laws. It comprises various European countries which have opted not to join the European Union, and it operates on a low-key formula of mutual cooperation. In recent years most of the tariff barriers between EFTA countries and EU members have been eradicated – at least where industrial products are concerned. Policing is necessary in order to prevent abuse of **free trade** agreements by outsiders, e.g. the importation of goods from the Far East into a high-tariff nation through a low-tariff one – this can arise as the member countries do not have a common external tariff. To provide against such misuse, **certificates of origin** must accompany imported goods.

Before joining the Common Market in 1973, the UK was a member of EFTA, as was Denmark. Both withdrew at the end of 1972. ◊ **Cascade tax** ◊ **Common Agricultural Policy** ◊ **Organization for European Economic Cooperation**.

European monetary agreement (EMA) This was formed in 1958 to replace the **European Payments Union (EPU)**. It served much the same function as the EPU with regard to the clearing of balances, but with the advent of free convertibility, settlements had now to be effected in **gold** or freely convertible currencies. The credit facilities afforded by the old EPU were also abolished in favour of a special European fund, tied in with the IMF to cover temporary **balance of payments** problems of member countries. ◊ **Currency** ◊ **Foreign exchange market** ◊ **Free exchange rates**.

European monetary system (EMS)
This was established in 1979 as a more ambitious replacement of the **snake**. It was hoped that a stable currency zone within the EU could be brought about, and to this end one of the more important parts of the EMS was to be the **European exchange rate mechanism**. The other vital part is the **European currency unit** (ECU) which it is hoped will eventually become an accepted common currency within the Union. This was to lead to a pan-European Central Bank to which the existing central banks of individual member countries would be subservient. Such long-term aims have now been put on hold pending the resolution of outstanding differences between members on the future, both politically and economically, of a more closely structured Europe. One other temporary feature of the EMS is the European Monetary Co-operation Fund. This acts as a clearing house for the separate European Central Banks, and each deposits, with it on a short-term basis, 20 per cent of their gold and foreign exchange reserves in exchange for ECUs.

European Parliament This is a directly elected EC institution though its powers are somewhat less than those of national parliaments. It exists in a consultative rather than a legislative capacity, and serves principally as a forum for discussion of recommendations of the European Commission or proposed decisions of the European Council.

European Payments Union (EPU)
This was established in 1950 as an off-shoot of the **Organization for European Economic Cooperation**. Its primary function was to act as a Clearing House for settlements arising from European trade and thereby hopefully speed up that trade. With the advent of currency convertibility it was superseded in 1958 by the European monetary agreement. ◊ **Bank for International Settlements**.

European Union The name by which the **European Community** is increasingly becoming known. The title stems from the 1958 Treaty of Rome. It was intended to become the name by which the original European Economic Community would be known once the signatory countries had aligned their economic and foreign policies and had agreed on a common currency. These conditions have not yet been met but the euphoria generated by the coming into force of both the single market and the **Maastricht Treaty** has encouraged the more general use of the term somewhat before its time. This unfortunately suggests a political union which is more of a pious hope than a reality and a degree of federalism to which many members of the Community are very much opposed.

Exceptional and extraordinary items In the ascertainment of business profits for a particular period it is customary to deduct from turnover the various expenses, both direct and indirect, incurred in achieving that turnover. Occasionally items of expenditure occur which are of an unusual nature or of a once-only variety and which, in the opinion of those preparing the accounts, could lead to a misleading net-profit figure when comparisons are made with similar periods in the past. The fact that such irregular items of cost have a habit of occurring in a fairly regular manner, if in differing guises, from one period to the next, is frequently overlooked. In the past it became customary to isolate these items and show them as 'extraordinary' or 'exceptional' expenses in the published accounts, and furthermore to show them as deductions from net profit rather than as costs incurred in earning that profit.

So far as the accounts of companies covered by the Companies Acts are concerned there is now a provision that particulars of all such items should be given in the published accounts. What is more, applicable accounting standards have now defined exceptional items as those material amounts which derive from events or transactions that fall within the ordinary activities of the company, and stated that such items must be taken into account in arriving at a figure of profit from ordinary activities. These may be given by way of a note to the accounts. Extraordinary items on the other hand have now been defined as material costs or credits which derive from events or transactions outside the normal activities of the company, which are consequently not expected to recur with any degree of regularity. Such items are to be shown in the accounts after the profit or loss on ordinary activities. Although these rules apply to the accounts of companies, because they arise from statements of stand-ard accounting practice they will apply to the production of accounts generally where these are prepared by members of the accounting profession.

Exchange control Prior to 1979, conservation of the national reserves of gold and foreign exchange was effected by various controls on monies used for payments overseas or transfers of capital abroad. The legal basis for the restrictions imposed was contained in the Exchange Control Act 1947. The purpose of the controls was principally to help keep a healthy **balance of payments** and maintain the value of **sterling**. The restrictions were various and included the **dollar premium**, but applied more to the larger transactions. Many small foreign payments, by way of subscription, etc., were handled without hindrance by the commercial banks – though here again the standard charge made by the bank was itself a deterrent. Restrictions also applied to the amount of money that could be taken out of the country for holidays abroad. These varied from year to year, but their existence was one reason why travel costs were often prepaid in sterling to the specialist holiday firms. These various controls and restrictions did not apply in the **sterling area**. All exchange controls were systematically abolished after May 1979. ◊ **Common Market** ◊ **Customs Union** ◊ **European Free Trade Association** ◊ **Exchange equalization account** ◊ **Foreign exchange market** ◊ **Free exchange rates** ◊ **Gold and foreign exchange reserves** ◊ **Rate of exchange**.

Exchange equalization account An account opened by the government at the **Bank of England**, and managed by the Bank, the main object of which is to control and usually stabilize the value of sterling on the foreign exchange. This is effected by buying and selling sterling as necessary in the exchange market. ◊ **Foreign exchange market**.

Exchange rate ◊ **Rate of exchange**.

Exchange risk guarantee scheme Where loans are obtained in foreign currencies through either the EIB (European Investment Bank) or the ECSC (European Coal and Steel Community) in connection with aid to **assisted areas**, then the government will cover any exchange risk in return for an annual service charge related to the size of the loan.

Exchequer At an earlier period of English history taxes payable to the Crown were collected by the local sheriffs and accounted for at what was known as the Court of the Exchequer, in London. It derived its name from the chequered tablecloth on which dues were placed for easy counting. The head of this court was known as the Chancellor of the Exchequer, a title that has been retained for the use of the principal finance officer of the Crown, acting through parliament.

Excise duty A tax levied on certain **goods** and services produced in this country (principally beer, wine and spirits, but also matches, mechanical lighters, etc.) together with fees for **licences** necessary to produce these things, as opposed to customs duties, which are charged on goods produced outside the UK. The duty is collected by **Her Majesty's Customs and Excise**. There are some instances when goods, such as alcohol, are not subject to duty, for instance when used for medicinal purposes. One of the main reasons for licence fees is to enable the Customs and Excise to keep track of all establishments making goods liable to duty in order to ensure that the

duty payable on those goods is accounted for. Generally speaking, duty is an internal levy on specified goods, made when they cease to be **bonded goods**. Because the levy is internal it does not apply to particular products when they are outside the UK, e.g. wines and spirits, can be purchased duty-free aboard ship, though technically duty is payable on any such goods brought on to British soil by returning travellers ◊ **Single Market** ◊ **Customs**: **Airports**.

Ex dividend (ex div) Company **shares** are referred to as either **cum div** or ex div. This adjective merely indicates whether or not a buyer at the stated price will receive the next **dividend** paid. On the **Stock Exchange** shares will tend to drop suddenly in price when they are no longer carrying dividend entitlement, i.e. when they are marked as ex div, the seller receiving the dividend. ◊ **Share transfer** ◊ **Share**: **market value**.

Executive director A company **director** who is also a working employee of the company in one of a number of executive posts. Sometimes directors are appointed to the board for the sake of the glamour attached to their name or because of certain specialist knowledge that can be used at relevant board meetings. These are known as **non-executive directors**. ◊ **Board of directors**.

Exemption clause A clause put into a **contract**, particularly a contract for the **sale of goods**, excluding the **vendor** from liability for breach of **condition**, or **warranty**, or both. The law is not sympathetic towards exemption clauses, and if they are to be effective they must be carefully worded; e.g. a clause exempting implied conditions will not exempt express conditions; a clause exempting conditions will not apply to warranties.

Ex gratia 'As a matter of favour'. Often used for payments made where, though not legally bound, the payer feels some moral obligation.

Ex new A **Stock Exchange** term. **Shares** are quoted ex new when their **price** does not include the right to take up new shares being offered. ◊ **Cum new**.

Export assistance register An aid to exporting. The register gives details of a great many experienced exporting firms which are prepared to help beginners in the field. In doing so they obviously give away some of their own secrets but normally only to non-competing firms. The founders were the **Federation of British Industries** and the **Institute of Directors**.

Export credit insurance Insurance against the additional risks attendant on foreign trade. Commercial **credit insurance** companies provide normal cover, but the **Export Credits Guarantee Department** (ECGD), attached to the Department of Trade and Industry, is available for giving long-term cover against bad debts and political and exchange risks.

Export Credits Guarantee Department (ECGD) This government department was first established in 1991 to insure UK exporters against some of the risks attendant on overseas trade, particularly non-payment by foreign customers. The ECGD is answerable to the Secretary of State for Trade and Industry and is regulated according to the Export and Investment Guarantee Act 1991.

It provides specifically (1) finance for exports at favourable interest rates, (2) guarantees to banks which agree to pro-

vide export finance, and (3) insurance against non-payment on long-term export contracts. Short-term insurance, which it also provided up until 1991, is now provided by the private insurance sector.

In addition to insuring against normal commercial risks the ECGD also provides valuable cover against political risks which are outside exporters' control, such as war, civil disturbances, expropriation of assets by foreign states, and shortage of hard currency available to the buyer.

The ECGD is expected to run its affairs on customary insurance principles in assessing risks and setting premiums that match those risks. It is also expected to generate reserves that will enable it to break even over the longer term. ◊ **Accepting house** ◊ **Discount houses** ◊ **Documentary credit** ◊ **Credit insurance**.

Exporters' declarations These are made by exporters for Customs purposes. There are various forms available. The Customs check that the necessary **licences** are obtained. There are no export taxes but export control is necessary for various reasons: for example, some exports are prohibited. Duty-paid goods may be eligible for refund when re-exported. It is also necessary to check that goods, which are dutiable if for home use but not if for export, are not re-landed. A Customs officer may attend the loading of a ship to see that no goods are loaded without the necessary licence. Dutiable **bonded goods** are examined to see that they are properly shipped and not relanded. The taking on of ships' stores is also supervised. If dutiable they are put in a sealed store and cannot be used till outside British waters. **Rummaging** continues during the loading of a ship. When loading is complete the captain applies for a clearance outward certificate. This will be given provided all regulations have been observed. The ship may then sail. Within six days the captain or shipping company must also deliver an 'outward **manifest**' giving details of export cargo. Exporters of goods not controlled must give 'specifications' to the Customs authorities for statistical purposes.

Export house A general term applied to one of a number of services relating to exports. They are of various types. Some act as merchants, buying from manufacturers and exporting on their own account. Others effectively act as the export department of the manufacturers which they represent, putting the specialist knowledge which they have acquired over the years at the disposal of their clients and thereby facilitating selling in overseas markets. These latter generally offer financial services also, which enable the seller to obtain prompt payment and the buyer to obtain any credit facilities which might be appropriate.

Certain export houses also double as **confirming houses**, in which case they virtually act as agents for both vendor and overseas purchaser, often being instrumental in bringing the parties together initially and generally taking responsibility for financial arrangements on both sides.

Export houses are represented centrally by the **British Export Houses Association**, which will provide manufacturers with the names of houses most suited to their needs.

Export incentives Particular incentives given by the State to promote **exports**. They may be in the form of grants or subsidies to exporting industries or addi-

tional credit facilities or tax exemptions. Such incentives are discouraged by the **General Agreement on Tariffs and Trade** and are virtually excluded by the rules of the **European Union**. Perhaps the only surviving British incentive, apart from the aids offered by the **Export Credits Guarantee Department**, are the **Queen's Awards**, given annually – matters of prestige rather than cash.

Exports Goods and services supplied for reward to persons in other countries, for which payment is generally due in the currency of the supplier. This obliges the purchaser to arrange payment in that currency, to the immediate benefit of the vendor and the ultimate benefit of his country's **balance of payments**. Exports are classified as visible or invisible, the former being goods and the latter services, such as banking, shipping facilities, etc. The UK traditionally depends considerably on invisible exports in balancing international payments. ◊ **Accepting house** ◊ **Bill of exchange** ◊ **Discount (bills of exchange)** ◊ **Discount houses** ◊ **Documentary credit** ◊ **Export credit insurance** ◊ **Invisible trade**.

Express Delivery While **Datapost** and the **Royal Mail Special Delivery** service cater for fast delivery to inland areas in Great Britain and Northern Ireland, they do not cater for post directed to the Isle of Man, the Channel Islands and the Irish Republic. These areas are the preserve of the Express Delivery facility operated by the Post Office. This service covers all first-class letter post to the three areas and also parcels destined for the Irish Republic. Items sent by Express Delivery are treated in the same way as those sent by Royal Mail Special Delivery, being given priority treatment at the various stages en route and then sent on by Post Office messenger from the delivery office if this would be quicker than normal delivery schedules – and provided a messenger is available. Fees are paid by the sender in addition to the regular postage charge, though in the Irish Republic fees for distances above one mile are collected from the addressee. Fees are refundable on application if the service fails. Items sent in this way must be properly marked, e.g. with the word EXPRESS, and should preferably though not necessarily be handed in at a Post Office. Registered and recorded delivery mail may also be sent by Express Delivery.

Ex ship Ex ship **contracts** are similar to **free on board** ones, except that the seller is responsible for **freight** and **insur-**ance and does not pay them on behalf of the buyer. The **goods** are at the seller's **risk** until they reach the port of delivery. The seller's responsibility ceases as soon as the goods have left the slings of the ship – if barges are necessary the buyer must provide them. Such contracts are also known as 'free overside'.

Extended protest A captain's pro-test made before a **notary public** when there is damage to goods which may result in **insurance** claims.

Extractive industry Industry concerned with the extraction of raw materials from the soil or sea, such as mining, agriculture, fishing.

Extraordinary items ⬧ **Exceptional and extraordinary items**.

Face value Though used in the vernacular to mean the apparent value, commercially speaking the face value of an item is its nominal value, i.e. the value written on it or, as in the case of a share, contained in the normal description of it. This is a quite different thing from the **market value**, which is the price that a willing buyer is prepared to pay for it. A 200-year-old coin may be sold for £10 but its face value may be only 1d. Similarly the market value of a £1 ordinary share may be £68. Face value should also be distinguished from **intrinsic value**. The face value of a coin is often less than its intrinsic value, i.e. the worth of its metallic content. A useful instance is the modern gold **sovereign**, which has a face value of £1, an intrinsic value which varies with the price of gold but which will normally be greater than £50, and a market value which may be sixty times the face value. ⟡ **Shares, market value**.

Facsimile Fax or Facsimile machines are now standard office equipment. They are linked to the telephone system and by this means facsimile copies of documents, diagrams, orders, etc. can be despatched swiftly for no more than the cost of a telephone call – provided the business at the receiving end is equipped with a similar machine. Businesses with this facility normally print a **Fax** number alongside their telephone number. A document can be sent by **Fax** for a lesser cost than if the contents were read out over the same telephone line. A **Fax** machine will also serve as an internal office copier.

Factor A general mercantile **agent** dealing with a specified category or categories of **goods**. As an agent he is distinguished by the fact that, provided he has possession of the goods coming into these categories with the consent of the owner, he can sell and give a good **title** to an innocent purchaser for value, whether or not the true owner has given his permission to sell. An art dealer, for instance, could sell pictures lent to him for display, provided the buyer was not aware of this fact.

Factoring A factor in the financial world is different from a factor in the law of contract. Factoring is similar to **invoice discounting** except that a factor will normally accept responsibility for credit control, debt collection and credit risk, and of course will charge more correspondingly. There are two principal types of factoring, (1) with service and (2) with service plus finance. The service is the collection of debts and the assumption of credit risk (**invoices** are handed to the factor, who pays monies to the customer at stated intervals). When finance is offered as well, the customer receives up to 90 per cent of the invoice value at once from the factor, rather than 100 per cent, as it were in **arrears**, from the debtor. The debts are in fact purchased for cash; there is no question of repayment (provided of course that the goods are delivered and up to standard). The charge for this financing service might be $1\frac{1}{2}$ per cent over **bank rate**. Naturally, the factor chooses his debtors and customers carefully, and normally only deals with customers whose annual **turnover** is well over £100,000.

Facultative endorsement A special form of **endorsement** of **bills of exchange**, which waives certain duties towards the endorser; for instance it may say that no notice of dishonour is necessary.

Fair Trading Act 1973 This was passed with the aim of providing protection for the public against unfair trading practices and to provide for the proper implementation of prior legislation by the appointment of a Director General of Fair Trading with ancillary staff. The prior legislation included the **Monopolies and Mergers Act** 1965, the **Trade Descriptions Act** 1968, the Restrictive Trade Practices Act 1956, the Resale Prices Act 1964, the **Hire Purchase Acts**, the **Consumer Credit Act** 1974, the Unfair Contract Terms Act 1977, the Sale of Goods Act 1979, and the Consumer Protection Act 1987. The Director General, whose task is also to encourage fair competition, is neither a politician nor a civil servant but enjoys a quasi-autonomous status, with ultimate responsibility to the Secretary of State for Trade and Industry. Shortly after the first Director General was appointed the Office of Fair Trading was established; the former's role then became that of supervising the performance of this Office in carrying out the various duties and responsibilities initially given to him personally. ◊ **Resale price maintenance** ◊ **Restrictive trade practices**.

Farm subsidies At one time there were many and various grants and subsidies available to farmers for the production of meat and cereals and for farm improvement. The entry of the UK into the **Common Market** has entailed considerable revision of these policies, which were once in the hands of the Ministry of Agriculture and Fisheries but are now the province of the section of the **European Union**, which supervises the administration of the **Common Agricultural Policy**. ◊ **Common budget** ◊ **Green pound**.

Fax ◊ **Facsimile**.

Federal Reserve System The USA does not have one central bank. The function is filled by the federal reserve system. This consists of twelve regional central banks, each of which acts as lender of the last resort in a particular area. The Federal Reserve System is supervised by the Federal Reserve Board, appointed by and answerable to the Senate and the President as head of the Executive. These reserve central banks are owned jointly by the various member banks, the equivalent of the UK clearing banks, which receive a fixed divident – any surplus going to the US Treasury.

Federation of British Industries ◊ **Confederation of British Industry**.

Fellow subsidiaries Companies each of which is a subsidiary of the same holding company whether directly or indirectly, e.g. a subsidiary of a subsidiary, are referred to as fellow subsidiary companies. It is usual to show total indebtedness both to and from subsidiaries as a separate item in the holding company's accounts. ◊ **Annual accounts** ◊ **Group accounts**.

Feme covert A legal term for a married woman.

Feme sole A legal term for a spinster or widow.

Fictitious assets An accounting term for balances which are not strictly assets in the tangible, or even intangible, sense but are nevertheless shown on the asset side of a balance sheet because the rules of double-entry demand that they should be so shown. A good example of this would be a debit balance on a profit and loss account, or more precisely a loss carried forward with no accumulated profit or reserves against which it could be set.

Fidelity guarantee One person may **guarantee** the integrity or fidelity of another, e.g. in a **contract of employment**. Insurance companies also offer fidelity policies, agreeing to make good misappropriations by employees.

Fiduciary issue That part of the note issue of the **Bank of England** that is backed not by gold but by government and other **securities**. The total is controlled by Parliament. Any profits on sale of these securities go to the government, being paid into the **exchange equalization account**.

Final accounts This term normally refers to **annual accounts**, i.e. the presentation of the results of the financial year of an organization and the state of affairs at the year end to the members of that organization.

There are other meanings relating to particular circumstances. At the end of a **liquidation** the **liquidator** presents his final accounts to the person or persons for whom he acts – which, in a compulsory liquidation, could be the court dealing with the liquidation or the Department of Trade and Industry. It could also merely refer to the final settlement between the parties to a transaction or series of transactions. ⟡ **Annual accounts** ⟡ **Consolidated accounts** ⟡ **Group accounts**.

Finance Act An annual Act of Parliament which is primarily intended to give effect to the various proposals by the Chancellor of the Exchequer in his budget speech which have been debated, amended and passed by Parliament. The Finance Act also states the rates of taxation that will apply in the coming **fiscal year**.

Finance company ⟡ Finance house.

Finance Corporation for Industry Ltd Formed in 1945 by the **Bank of England**, London and Scottish **clearing banks** and many large **insurance** companies and **investment trusts**. Its **authorized capital** and **issued capital** was £25,000,000. The Corporation may borrow up to four times the nominal value of its issued capital. Most of its finance is by borrowed funds and these are obtained almost entirely from the banks. The object is to supplement other forms of finance with a view to rehabilitating industry. The minimum loan is £1m. The borrower must show that he cannot obtain funds elsewhere and that the loan is in the national interest. Loans tend to be large, and few. Rates of **interest** vary but are generally low.

Finance house A generic term covering finance companies, **merchant banks**, industry banks, etc. Many are owned by the **clearing banks** themselves. Their principal function is the finance of hire purchase transactions. Retailers and dealers offering hire purchase facilities do so through a finance house or finance company. The latter takes on the responsibility of collecting the instalments from the purchaser and handing over the purchase price less an agreed commission to the retailer. In this way the retailer is able to greatly increase the scale of his business without the attendant cash flow problems which rising turnover based on credit transactions must bring. ◊ **Factoring**.

The finance houses themselves obtain funds by borrowing from the clearing banks and the investing public, either directly or through the issue of **bills of exchange**. The operations of finance houses are supervised by the **Finance Houses Association.** ◊ **Hire purchase finance**.

Finance Houses Association Formed in 1945 by six large **finance houses** with the idea of presenting a united front in **hire purchase finance** *re* **interest** rates, **deposits**, etc. Membership is now much greater. It represents members' interests in discussions with the government and also acts as an information pool for members and the public.

Financial accountant A term, principally of convenience, to distinguish the accountant responsible for overseeing the financial structure and **liquidity** of a business as opposed to his counterparts who handle taxation matters (though in the smaller business these would be the concern of the financial accountant) and **internal audit** or costing and budgeting – the province of the **management accountant**. The financial accountant could also be described as the *ex officio* treasurer of the business – usually a **company** – with responsibility for ensuring that all cash resources are obtained on the best terms and used in a manner that will maximize advantage to the business.

Financial adviser This is a breed of investment consultant whose role has been highlighted by the provisions of the Financial Services Act 1986. Essentially any person who advertises as a financial adviser must specify whether he is in business as an independent adviser, whether he is the representative of a particular company, or whether he handles only a specific investment product which is marketed by an individual organization.

The independent financial adviser is one whose business lies in informing potential clients about the various investment products available, and in directing them towards those products most likely to fill the investor's needs. Such advisers must keep records which indicate the spread of investments placed on behalf of clients. These will substantiate their professed independence and show that there has been no undue preference shown towards the product of any one supplier. As independent financial advisers are, by the nature of their profession, obliged to offer 'best advice' they must be thoroughly familiar with the investment products of a wide range of competing providers. They come under the supervision of FIMBRA and must be registered with that Association. Membership of FIMBRA provides the authorization necessary to conduct business. Such membership brings with it the obligation to abide by the rule book of that SRO which, *inter alia*, requires them to obtain an adequate level of professional indemnity cover particularly if, in the course of business, they handle client's money.

The tied adviser is one who is concerned solely with marketing the investment products of a particular organization and this fact must be made clear to anyone seeking advice.

The organization whose products he sells must satisfy itself that he is a fit and proper person to act as its agent and that he is fully aware of the range of investment products which his employer offers. He must always give 'best advice' and must never seek to sell one product when he is aware of another product marketed by his employer which would be better suited to his client's needs.

Financial Futures ◊ **London International Financial Futures and Options Exchange.**

Financial Intermediaries, Managers and Brokers Regulatory Association (FIMBRA) FIMBRA is one of the **self-regulating organizations** currently authorized by the **Securities and Investment Board** under the Financial Services Act. It acts as the regulatory authority for firms whose principal activity lies in advising on, or making deals in, life assurance, pensions and units in authorized unit trusts and other similar collective investment schemes. Such firms include investment advisers and private investment portfolio managers.

To obtain FIMBRA membership applicants must submit audited accounts for the twelve months prior to application, agree to abide by the detailed rules set out by FIMBRA regarding the conduct of business, and show that every director or manager of the firm is a fit and proper person to undertake investment business. References must be supplied by individuals seeking registration as members. Members must, *inter alia*, hold adequate professional indemnity insurance, notify FIMBRA of any changes within the firm, and indicate FIMBRA membership in any advertisement or letterhead. From the consumer's point of view one of the more important rules laid down by FIMBRA is that members are not only required to offer investors 'best advice', but are also obliged to ensure that clients are aware of all risks involved in any investment transaction.

FIMBRA began life as a Trade Association in 1979 and became NASDIM – the National Association of Security Dealers and Investment Managers – in 1982. Its name was changed to FIMBRA in 1986 in anticipation of the requirements of the Financial Services Act of that year. There is presently a suggestion that it might be merged with LAUTRO to become one single SRO with the possible title of Personal Investment Authority.

Financial Reporting Council This was established in 1990 in response to the recommendations of the Dearing Committee set up to investigate and report on the adequacy of the accounting standard-setting process.

It is essentially an umbrella organization with three attendant bodies each with its own defined sphere of responsibilities. These are firstly the **Accounting Standards Board** which, as its name suggests, is charged with developing accounting standards of high quality and supervising their implementation; secondly the **Financial Reporting Review Panel** which has the power to look into the actual application of those standards in the published accounts of companies and, where necessary, refer those accounts back to the originating companies and require adjustments to be made; and thirdly the **Urgent Issues Task Force** (UITF) which exists to advise companies as to the proper interpretation of Standards when an ambiguity arises or where existing standards do not appear to provide for certain eventualities.

Financial Reporting Review Panel
One of three subsidiary bodies set up by the **Financial Reporting Council** to supervise the application of standards of good accounting practice established by the **Accounting Standards Board**. The panel draws attention to breaches of good practice by companies or other organizations to which ASB standards apply and insists on any rectification deemed necessary or desirable.

Financial Reporting Standards These are the statements of recommended accounting practice issued by the **Accounting Standards Board**. They replace the SSAPs previously issued by the Accounting Standards Committee.

Financial Services Act 1986 Though enacted in 1986 this statute did not come fully into force until 1988. It was the result of a detailed investigation into the need for investor protection carried out by a committee under Professor Gower which reported to the Department of Trade and Industry in 1984. The scope of the Act is immense and its provisions apply to all persons who wish to carry out investment business or allied services within the UK. It covers, *inter alia*, the activities of brokers, dealers, investment or unit trusts, traders in futures or options, financial advisers, and various aspects of the insurance business. All persons caught by the provisions of the Act are now required to obtain specific authorization either from the **Securities and Investment Board**, a private company set up under the Act and financed by levies on the investment industry, or from one of the bodies appointed by the SIB to regulate activities in specified areas. ◊ **Self-regulating organization** ◊ **Recognized investment exchange** ◊ **Recognized professional body**.

Financial Times Ordinary Share Index The *Financial Times* publishes many indexes of which, at one time, the most familiar was the *Financial Times* Ordinary Share Index, also known as the FT 30-Share Index. This began in 1935 with a base of 100, and is compiled by reference to the share prices of 30 leading British companies – originally major manufacturing and retailing companies but later including oil and financial stocks. It is substantially a **blue-chip** index calculated by geometric mean, and movements in it tend to reflect the general mood of the market. For specific portfolio needs other FT indexes might be more relevant, e.g. the FT-Actuaries indexes, of which there are many covering various sections of the market, plus the FT-Actuaries All-Share Index reflecting the movement of some 700 shares. One of the more recent and better-known FT indexes is the *Financial Times* Stock Exchange 100 Share Index (colloquially known as the Footsie or the FT-SE index). This began with a base of 1000 in 1983 reflecting movements in the share prices of the 100 largest companies, and is now considered the best contemporary guide to UK share price movements.

Financial year A fairly general term normally meaning the year of account, or **accounting period**. The Companies Act 1948 defined the term as any period in respect of which any **profit and loss account** was made up whether that period was a year or not. The 1985 Companies Act is more specific where the term is applied to limited companies. It states that a company's first financial year begins on the date of incorporation and ends, with certain stated exceptions, on its **accounting reference date** which is more than six, and less than eighteen, months after that date. Subsequent financial years begin on the day following the end of the previous year and run until the next accounting reference date. There is a provision to allow directors a slight leeway in fixing a financial year in order that it will always end on the same day of the week or always comprise exactly fifty-two weeks.

The 1989 Companies Act defines the financial year of undertakings which are not companies as being such periods for which a profit and loss account is required to be made up by whatever regulations govern such undertakings.

Financier A fairly vague term used to describe those persons with considerable private means or with access to large sums of money whose principal business it is to invest those funds in the energy and innovatory skills of others with the minimum risk and the maximum profit to themselves. ◊ **Corporate raider**.

Fine bill A **bill of exchange** discountable at the finest rate, i.e. where there is little or no risk.

Fine trade bill A **trade bill** with the backing of an established **bank** or **finance house**.

Fire insurance Insurance against losses due to fire. These **contracts** usually last for one year, with an option on renewal. Premiums may be changed from year to year. The policy holder should inform the insurance company of any change in the **value** of the property. He will never obtain more than the value of the actual loss, so it is pointless to over-insure, or to insure for the full amount with more than one company. If the property is under-insured, the policy holder will probably only receive a proportion of the actual loss. ◊ **Average clause**.

The insured must have an **insurable interest**. This must exist at the time of loss and, with buildings, also when the policy is issued. **Trustees** may insure trust property, and mortgagees mortgaged property. A **company**'s shareholders and **unsecured creditors** have no insurable interest in its property.

A policy may be assigned only with the consent of the insurance company. For this purpose a **mortgage** is not an **assignment**.

In the case of buildings, any interested party (i.e. the insurance company, a mortgagee, etc.) may insist that the policy money is used to reinstate the building (under the Fires Prevention (Metropolis) Act 1774). This is to dissuade people from letting their houses burn down and taking the money.

The insurer is entitled to take over the property (the wreckage) of the insured, when paying on a total loss. This is known as **subrogation**.

Firm Strictly the name given to a **partnership** business though often used more generally. In Scotland a 'partnership firm' is a separate legal person, though it does not have all the attributes of a corporate body. In England a partnership firm cannot contract in its own name: it has no separate identity.

First-class paper When **bills of exchange**, **government securities**, **consols**, etc., carry the signature of a well-known **bank, finance house** or

discount house, they are called first-class papers.

First in first out (FIFO) One of the many methods accepted by the accountancy profession and the taxation authorities for the valuation of **stock-in-trade** at a particular date. It adopts the proposition that items of stock are issued to factory or retail outlets in the same order as that in which they were purchased. Items in stock at any time will therefore be valued at the most recent prices at which purchased. Stocks will be priced for accounting purposes at the figure on the most recent purchase invoice, any surplus being priced according to the preceding invoice. This system should be carefully distinguished from the **last in first out** (LIFO) system, which presupposes that the most recently bought items will have been issued first and that stock-in-hand at any one time will therefore consist of goods bought at older, and usually lower, prices. ◊ **Stock valuation**.

Fiscal year The official government year of account ending on 5 April.

Fixed assets Those business **assets** which are purchased for continued use in earning profit (e.g. land, machinery, etc.). They are written off against profits over their anticipated life by charging an annual amount calculated so as to eliminate the original cost, less scrap value, over that period. ◊ **Current assets** ◊ **Depreciation**.

Fixed charge A term used to describe a **mortgage** of distinct assets against which a loan is made. The charge applies to assets specifically identified and is distinguished from a **floating charge**. These terms usually arise in connection with an issue by a company of **debentures**,

which are accordingly described as fixed, or floating, debentures. Occasionally the term fixed charges is also used as a synonym for **fixed costs**.

Fixed costs In the manufacturing process costs are incurred not only in the provision of the necessary labour and basic materials but also in a wide range of services and ancillary expenses, e.g. rent, rates, **depreciation** of machinery, interest on borrowed capital, etc. These costs tend, by tradition and for convenience, to be separated into two main categories: fixed costs and variable costs.

Fixed costs are those incurred irrespective of the volume of production. ◊ **Overhead expenses**. Variable costs fluctuate with the level of activity.

The latter category is often subdivided into further groups depending on the degree of variability. ◊ **Variable costs** ◊ **Semi-variable costs**. Even direct costs can be subdivided in so far as the unavoidable costs of keeping a factory closed may be less than those of keeping it at a low production level, e.g. a closed factory does not need any administrative staff. The distinction between fixed and variable costs is, of course, only relative. In the long term all costs are variable in so far as any productive process is optional. ◊ **Break-even chart**.

Fixed interest securities Those shares or **debentures** which carry a fixed rate of **interest**. The rate on a debenture is often lower than on a fixed interest share, e.g. **preference share**, because the fact that a debenture is secured makes it a less risky investment. Strictly, although preference shares are normally included in this group, they are not securities as, unlike debentures, **bonds**, etc., the capital outlay is not secured in any way. The price of fixed interest securities quoted on the **Stock Exchange** will mainly be determined by prevailing interest rates and will tend to settle at a level such that the actual interest or **dividend** paid will, when related to that price, approximate to the current rate ruling in the market. Variations that occur will be due to the extent of the risk attached to the capital itself and, in the case of preference shares, the probability of dividends actually being paid out. ◊ **Bank rate** ◊ **Minimum lending rate**.

Fixed trusts This term refers to **unit trusts** though it is no longer in common usage. It concerns the earlier trusts, where the portfolio of investments which formed the backing for units issued was confined to a selection from an initially defined list. Although such trusts minimized the risk of loss to small investors from poor **management** they also prevented good management from taking advantage of new investment opportunities which might prove highly beneficial to unit holders. ◊ **Investment portfolio** ◊ **Investment trusts**.

Fixtures, fittings, etc. An accounting term for immovable **assets** affixed to a building in some way though not strictly part of that building itself.

Flags of convenience All merchant ships must be registered with one country or another. Owners of ships registered in the UK are subject to taxation there and must abide by all the legislative requirements of that country regarding crew conditions, wages, etc. To avoid onerous taxes and employment regulations, there has been a strong tendency (particularly since 1945) for ship-owners to register their vessels in certain small countries where regulations and requirements are minimal. They must then fly the flag of

that country; such flags are known as 'flags of convenience'. The increasing influence of the trade union movement in the UK and other developed nations is already having an effect on reducing the advantages of this practice as far as conditions of employment are concerned. Parallel action by the Treasury and the Inland Revenue could eliminate it altogether. ◊ **Ship's certificate of registry**.

Flat yield The true **rate of interest** on a **fixed interest security**, found by relating actual income to present purchase price, without taking into account any benefit or detriment that might arise from the proximity of redemption date. ◊ **Yield** ◊ **Earnings yield** ◊ **Redemption yield**.

Fletcher A maker of or dealer in bows and arrows. Not in common use.

Flight coupon The portion of a passenger's air ticket which indicates particular places between which the coupon is good for carriage.

Floating assets Another term for **current assets**.

Floating charge When a loan to a business is secured on assets generally rather than on a particular item, there is said to be a floating charge. The lender has priority of repayment from the fund of assets that exist when, say, a **receiving order** is made against the business. At this time the charge is said to be frozen. ◊ **Debenture**.

Floating policy An **insurance** policy covering goods not all in the same place and not of constant **value**. ◊ **Open policy**.

Floor trading At one time most transactions on the major exchanges were effected through floor trading – members of the exchanges making deals verbally or by written contract on the floor of the exchange. This was particularly true in the Stock Exchange but recent developments in computer-generated price information systems ◊ **Topic** ◊ **SEAQ**, have led to trading being conducted by telephone from dealers' offices on the basis of information instantly available on screen.

The one area where floor trading still predominates is in the futures and options market, particularly financial futures and options. The bulk of LIFFE trading is still by Open Outcry from pits, each of which is dedicated to a particular type of financial instrument. ◊ **LIFFE**. This practice is not peculiar to London, but is common to most of the world's leading financial futures exchanges.

Flotation Traditionally and officially, the establishment of a **public company** and the raising of the necessary capital for it either by an open offer to the public or by **offer for sale** or by a **placing**. Modern usage has slightly altered this meaning, particularly when the **company** obtains its capital after and not at the same time as its formation – a practice now common. The term is now more often applied to the process of floating off capital, either by a new company or a **private company** which is 'going public', through the medium of a **merchant bank** or some other intermediary which will offer the shares to the public in the manner it considers most appropriate. The law concerning the need for a **prospectus** will, of course, always apply. ◊ **Company, formation of**.

Flotsam Goods or parts of a shipwrecked vessel found floating on the surface of the sea. If not claimed within a year and a day they belong to the Crown. ◊ **Jetsam**.

Flow chart A method of showing graphically the movement of cash or materials through a business or the manner in which various processes or levels of management are connected. ◊ **Critical path analysis**.

Foolscap A piece of paper measuring seventeen by thirteen and a half inches. The name originates from the water mark – once a fool's cap and bells. (It is suggested that this mark dates from Cromwellian times and replaced the royal arms.)

For the account A Stock Exchange term for dealings to be settled on the next **account day**.

Forbearance Forbearance to sue can be good **consideration** for an **offer** so as to constitute a **contract**. There must be a right to sue: if the claim is invalid then it is no consideration, provided the party knows it to be invalid. The claim must be based upon an enforceable contract and not on an illegal contract. ◊ **Contract, illegal**.

Foreclosure ◊ **Mortgagee, rights of**.

Foreign bills **Bills of exchange** other than those designated inland bills by the Bills of Exchange Act 1882. The Act defines an inland bill as one 'both drawn and payable within the British Islands, or drawn within the British Islands upon some person resident therein'. All other bills are foreign bills.

Foreign exchange market The market where dealings are made which, in the absence of controls, determine the **rate of exchange** of one **currency** with

Foreign judgments

another. The market is not in any particular place but consists of a web of dealings between banks and various dealers in **bills of exchange** and foreign currency. However, it is never quite free, particularly in the UK, where its operations are studied and manipulated by the **Bank of England**, which acts on behalf of the State through the **exchange equalization account** or on its own account, and by the operation of any prevailing system of **exchange control**. The **International Monetary Fund** also exists partly as a watchdog over the exchange markets of the world.

Dealings in currencies may be either 'spot' or 'forward'. Spot dealings are those made and completed at the current rate. Forward dealings are those where a person or a company agrees to buy or sell a given amount of another currency at a future date stated and at a rate fixed in the agreement. Whilst forward dealings can be purely speculative they can also be necessary, e.g. where an importer arranges a purchase for which he will not need the money until some future date, or where he anticipates making sales or purchases some time ahead and wishes to discount one of the two unknown factors – the future price and the future rate of exchange. Dealers in foreign exchange will usually quote both the spot rate and forward rate; the latter depends on the number of months required – usually limited to three. ◊ **Futures** ◊ **Sliding peg** ◊ **Snake** ◊ **Forward dealings** ◊ **European monetary system** ◊ **London International Financial Futures and Options Exchange**.

Foreign judgments Where a judgment is made in a foreign court and the **judgment creditor** wants to enforce it in this country, he must appeal to the High Court within six years to have the judgment registered. If registered, it is equal to a judgment in this country. If it is to be registered, it must be final and conclusive and must not involve payment of taxes, fines, penalties, etc.

Forfeiture of shares ◊ **Shares, forfeiture of**.

Forged transfer of shares Where a transfer is forged, registered, and a **share certificate** given to a transferee, the true owner is entitled to be reinstated on the register ◊ **Rectification of register**. The **company** cannot deny validity of the certificate issued and may be liable to pay damages to any innocent person who suffers loss by relying on it. Consequently a company will generally notify the transferor when it receives a transfer. The shareholder can ensure this by issuing a **notice in lieu of distringas**. Risks involved in transfers of shares in companies have been reduced since the installation of **Talisman**.

Forward dating The practice of dating commercial documents in advance. **Invoices** may be dated forward, perhaps to give the customer additional time to pay or where delivery has been delayed. **Cheques** may be forward dated where the drawer has no present funds but expects to be able to meet the cheque at the date specified. The bank should not cash the cheque before that date.

Forward dealings Agreements to buy or sell specific quantities in goods, currencies, etc., at a stated price and at a stated time in the future. Such dealings are common in international trade where, although both price and exchange rate are subject to frequent variations, contracts need to be made well in advance, particularly where a manufacturer wishes to secure raw materials for future delivery. In such an instance he may prefer to buy either at a fixed forward price or a fixed exchange rate and thereby eliminate at least one variable. Such forward contracts can be, and frequently are, bought or sold, but when entered into primarily for that purpose they are known as **futures**. ◊ **London International Financial Futures and Options Exchange**.

Forwarding agent A general agent who specializes in moving goods from a factory or port of entry to their proper destination. Such an agent normally owns the transport necessary for this work and often arranges **freight** and customs formalities for his principal. ◊ **Agent, general**.

Foul bill of lading A **bill of lading** which states that the **goods** have been put on board in a defective condition. The bill is usually endorsed to this effect by the master of the ship. It is also known as a dirty bill of lading.

Founders' shares **Shares** issued to the founders of a **company**. These shares usually have special **dividend** rights, etc. ◊ **Deferred shares**.

Fourth schedule The eighth schedule to the 1948 Companies Act laid down extensive requirements to which the annual accounts of limited companies had to comply both in form and content. It applied specifically to every **balance sheet** and every **profit and loss account** together with notes appertaining thereto which was laid before a company in general meeting and/or filed with the company's **annual return**. The matters to which it referred included both the manner of calculating and of stating various items of income and expenditure

and the method of computing the appropriate value of assets and liabilities. Separate parts of the eighth schedule applied to the preparation of group accounts and those of specialist companies.

This schedule was altered marginally by the 1967 Companies Act and extensively by the 1981 Companies Act, in which it was restated as Part I to the First Schedule to that Act. The 1981 Act also introduced the concept of standard formats for both balance sheets and profit and loss accounts, giving two alternatives for the former and four for the latter. All companies registered under the Act must adopt one of these given formats, as modified by the notes also contained in the Act, both as to the stated headings and the items listed under those headings. This requirement is, however, subject to the overall necessity of providing a true and fair view, and if the directors or auditors can show that in order to show such a view deviations from the formats are essential then such changes are admissible.

The Companies Act 1985, which repealed previous Companies Acts, reaffirmed the provisions of the 1981 Act and the legal regulations affecting company accounts are now contained in the fourth schedule to the 1985 Companies Act.

Franchise policy A **marine insurance** policy which disallows claims below a stated minimum unless the ship is stranded or sunk. The policy has the double purpose of avoiding petty claims and restricting liability on very risky cargo.

Franchises Licences given by manufacturers who wish to limit the distribution outlets of their products or who wish all their sales in one area to be handled by specified persons. The term also applies where a **patent** holder licenses a foreign manufacturer to produce the goods covered by the patent. The person giving the licence is known as the franchisor and the person receiving it is the franchisee. The latter is usually asked to make an advance down payment for the privilege of making or distributing the goods and also must often agree not to purchase from any manufacturer other than the franchisor and not to sell outside the area specified in the franchise. For these reasons alone the system is open to abuse. Innocent people often find themselves out of pocket by purchasing franchises which do not provide the profits they were led to expect. ◊ **Fair Trading Act** ◊ **Pyramid selling**.

Franco, rendu, or free contracts A variation of **ex ship** contracts where the exporter pays all expenses of delivery to the importer's warehouse. These contracts are unusual because the seller is not normally familiar with conditions in other countries.

They are very convenient for the importer however.

Franked investment income Investment income received by a **company** which has already been taxed at source. Provided certain conditions are fulfilled this income is not taxed again. ◊ **Corporation tax**.

Franking machines Businesses with a heavy outflow of mail often wish to bypass the necessity of buying and sticking on stamps. They apply to their nearest Head Post Office for permission to obtain a franking machine. This prints the value of the stamp on each letter, retaining the total cost within the machine. The machines are supplied by outside companies designated by the **Post Office** and must be maintained by those firms. The Post Office may inspect machines at any time and must be supplied with a weekly control card giving the details of use and amounts payable by the user. The user must pay the Post Office an advance sum of money before being allowed to operate a franking machine; the franked mail must be posted in the manner required by the Head Postmaster concerned. The machines can also be used for posting parcels, in which case the cost is printed on a strip of paper which is then affixed to the parcel. Franking machines often print the name of the business in addition to the mail charge. ◊ **Business reply service**.

Fraud If a **contract** is made as a result of fraud by one party, i.e. a fraudulent **misrepresentation**, the injured party may rescind the contract and also obtain **damages**. To be fraudulent, the misrepresentation must be made either with an attempt to deceive or without caring whether the statement was true or false. It should be a statement of fact (though in *Derry v. Peek* the judge commented that a man's opinion was as much a fact as the state of his digestion). Fraud is an offence in **tort** as well as in contract. Remedies of the injured party are: (1) to affirm the contract and sue for damages in tort for deceit; (2) to rescind with or without seeking damages in tort.

He may still be able to sue for damages if he has lost his right to rescind, due perhaps to the acquisition of rights by a third party.

Fraud, agreements to commit Agreements to commit a **fraud** are illegal and not enforceable at law. ◊ **Contract, illegal**.

Fraudulent conveyance A Bankruptcy offence. The debtor deliberately signs away part of his property with an intent to defeat **creditors**.

Fraudulent preference A **bankruptcy offence**. A deliberate (it must be deliberate) preference of one **creditor** or **surety** by an **insolvent** debtor.

Fraudulent preference: companies Rules similar to **bankruptcy** rules apply. If the **company** has preferred a **creditor** or a **surety** within six months of the commencement of the **winding-up**, the transfer or charge is void as against the liquidator, who can recover the property.

Fraudulent trading Where **directors** are considered responsible for fraudulent trading (i.e. carrying on business with an attempt to defraud **creditors**) they may become personally liable without limit for the debts of the **company**. The question of fraudulent trading will arise in a **winding-up**. ◊ **Insolvency Act 1986**.

Free alongside ship (fas) When an exporter delivers goods 'free alongside ship', he pays all charges involved up to that point. ◊ **Free on board**.

Free depreciation A term used in taxation where a business is allowed to depreciate fixed assets for **capital allowance** purposes at whatever rate it chooses; e.g. it could write off an asset in the accounts of the first year in which it is used, or it could stretch the writing-off period over a vast number of years, quite irrespective of the method of **depreciation** adopted for normal accounting purposes. The period chosen will depend on various factors but chiefly on the **liquidity** of the business and the current, and anticipated, rate of taxation. ◊ **Accelerated**

depreciation ◊ **Corporation tax** ◊ **Stock relief** ◊ **Taxation of profits**.

Free exchange rates Rates of exchange in the foreign market which are governed only by normal forces of supply and demand with no interference or supervision by State authorities, whether at a national or an international level. Free exchange rates are the opposite of fixed rates. When a country decides to abandon fixed rates of exchange in favour of a free market it is said to float the currency, i.e. leave the rate of exchange to float within the supply and demand market until its true level is determined. ◊ **Currency depreciation** ◊ **Exchange rates** ◊ **Foreign exchange** ◊ **Sliding peg**.

Free from particular average A **marine insurance** term meaning that the insurers are not responsible for anything other than total loss and **general average loss**. The clause may be qualified in various ways, i.e. the insurer may take responsibility for certain specified items of cargo.

Free of all average A marine insurance term for policies where the insurer takes no responsibility for general or **particular average losses**, and will only pay on a total loss.

Free of capture, etc A marine insurance term for policies which exclude liability from capture, seizure, detention by foreign powers or mutiny. It does not normally apply to a blockade.

Free on board (fob) When an exporter delivers **goods** 'free on board', he pays all charges involved in getting them actually on to the ship. His responsibilities include putting the goods in a condition for shipping, taking them to the ship and loading them (◊ **Free on board and trimmed**). The buyer must provide the ship, and the seller's responsibility ends when the goods are on board. The seller must notify the buyer to enable him to insure the goods, otherwise he may himself be liable for damage at sea. Property in the goods normally passes with risk, though the buyer may reserve the right to reject the goods if he has had no previous opportunity to examine them and they are not up to specification or quality when he receives them.

Free on board and trimmed A **free on board contract** peculiar to the coal trade. The seller, in addition to loading the coal, must see that it is properly stored.

Free overside ◊ **Ex ship**.

Free-port To facilitate the flow of international trade, and to help the balance of payments of the countries operating them, a number of free-ports have been established throughout the world and six have now been established within the UK. The advantage of a free-port is that goods can be moved through the area of the port without being subject to any customs or tariff charges or barriers. This is particularly significant in the context of **entrepôt trade**. The absence of customs barriers does not permit the landing of cargoes that are prohibited by the country operating the port, but the privileges afforded and the tendency to relax supervision are not infrequently abused by the more unscrupulous traders. ◊ **Single market**.

Free trade A condition where no restrictions by way of **tariffs** or quotas exist to limit the trade between countries. ◊ **Common Market** ◊ **Embargo** ◊ **European Free Trade Association** ◊

Free trade area ◊ **Single market**.

Free trade area A group of trading countries, normally inspired by geographical proximity, sometimes join to create an area of **free trade** by scrapping **tariff** barriers between themselves. By doing this they hope, through the pooling of knowledge and the growth in mutual understanding, to increase not only mutual trade but also the internal efficiency and economic expansion of each individual country. ◊ **European Free Trade Association** ◊ **Common Market**.

Freeboard The distance between the main deck and the waterline of a ship.

Freefone A facility operated through the telephone system whereby the caller asks the operator for a Freefone number. The charge for the call is borne by the person or service called. This is a system which, although available by arrangement to anyone, is made much use of by **British Telecom** itself as a means of supplying customers with details of special services available or with information relating to particular areas of operation.

Freehold land If a person has the freehold to land, he has the best possible **title**, being its absolute owner. There may, however, be encumbrances such as **easements**, etc. The term 'freehold land and buildings' is frequently used in accounts, and indicates freehold land owned by the business, and buildings on it. The freehold land is sometimes bracketed in company accounts with **leasehold land**.

Freepost Like the **business reply service** this is a facility offered by the Post Office whereby persons or organizations may have mail sent to them without any obligation on the sender to prepay postage. The word Freepost will be an integral part of the address. The Post Office charges the addressee normal postal dues plus an additional percentage which reduces as the quantity of mail increases. Freepost items will always be treated as second-class mail and will be delivered on second delivery each day, though there is a Priority Freepost service which will deliver with first delivery at an extra charge. Licences are necessary for Freepost facilities and the licensee will be asked to deposit a sum of money with the Post Office which will cover estimated charges for the following month; the fee will then be renewable at monthly intervals. Freepost mail cannot be redirected and the service does not extend to the Isle of Man or the Irish Republic. ◊ **Business reply service.**

Freight The money paid by a charterer to a shipowner in **consideration** of the latter letting the ship or space within the ship. The money is not payable until the goods are delivered to the ship. ◊ **Advance freight notes** ◊ **Lump sum freight** ◊ **Freight forward** ◊ **Pro rata freight** ◊ **Dead freight** ◊ **Back freight** ◊ **Shipowner's lien** ◊ **Baltic International Freight Futures Exchange.**

Freight forward A shipping term meaning **Freight** is payable at port of destination.

Freight notes Notes from shipowner to shipper, showing the amount of **Freight** due.

Freight release ◊ **Advance freight.**

Freightliner A door-to-door container service offered by **British Rail**. The emphasis is on speed and efficiency. Loaded containers are taken by road to a freight liner terminal, then transported speedily to another terminal. Space can be reserved in advance. The containers are delivered by road from the terminal. The containers (of a fixed size) are owned by the railway but packed by the user at his own premises. They conform with international standards. There are freightliner services between most major industrial centres. The containers are loaded on to British Rail vehicles free, but there is a charge for any delay over a stated limit, e.g. fifteen minutes per capacity ton. Containers must be returned within a specified time after use.

French companies Although there are many forms of business organization in France, the two which are probably of greatest relevance to UK citizens are the organizations most resembling British public and private companies. These are, respectively, the **société anonyme** and the **société à responsabilité limitée**. ◊ **European Union companies** ◊ **German companies.**

French gold francs An air transport term for francs consisting of 65.5 milligrams of gold with a fineness of nine hundred thousandths, i.e. 90 per cent pure.

Friendly Societies These grew out of the need of working people in the nineteenth century to provide some protection for themselves against financial problems arising from death or sickness when they could no longer provide for themselves or their dependants. This was before the State assumed the role of protector through the National Health Service with the provision of pensions, sick pay and later various other welfare benefits. The Friendly Societies began in a small way, usually catering for the particular area or trade which they were set up to serve. In time, some of these societies grew into nationwide mutual insurance corporations whilst others faded away for lack of either funds or purpose. The relevance of the Friendly Society today lies only in the fact that certain of the large insurance companies are still registered as Friendly Societies under the Act passed to control and protect them in 1846. ◊ **National insurance** ◊ **Supplementary benefits** ◊ **State earnings-related pension scheme**.

Fringe benefits Similar to **benefits in kind**, these are usually non-monetary benefits enjoyed by an employee which are not subject to tax. They are incentives to prospective employees or to existing employees where wage increases are not in view. They can also be used to indicate and reward marginal differentials in employment, e.g. at one time the provision of an umbrella stand was indicative of increased status in the civil service. Some of the more common fringe benefits today are staff discounts, social clubs financed by the employer, **luncheon vouchers,** etc. ◊ **Emoluments** ◊ **Company cars; directors and highly paid employees.**

Frozen assets **Assets** tied up so that transactions in them are restricted or impossible. Where a **company** has floating **debentures** and they become repayable, the assets of the company are frozen in favour of the debenture holders.

Frustration clause A **marine insurance** clause. The insurer takes no responsibility if the enterprise is completely frustrated.

Frustration of contract A **contract** is frustrated when it cannot be carried out, though neither party is to blame. Before the Fibrosa case (1942) the law took the view that the loss should lie where it fell; afterwards, that money paid could be recovered where the **consideration** had failed. The position was clarified by the Law Reform (Frustrated Contracts) Act 1943, which stated that monies paid could be recovered, but that the party from whom they were recovered might be allowed to deduct expenses and charge for the **value** of work done where the other party had received a benefit. (The Act does not apply to contracts for carriage of goods by sea, certain **charter parties**, **insurance** contracts and contracts for the sale of specific goods where the frustration arises from the perishing of the goods.)

Full employment In economic theory this term describes a situation where, within an economy, the total available labour force is being used in activities that contribute to the well-being of the nation and add to the gross national product — allowing for a measure of unemployment necessarily arising as persons move from one job to another. Alternatively, it can be defined as an economic situation where the demand for labour of all sorts equals or exceeds the supply.

Politically, the term is used in a more emotive sense as the goal towards which any aspiring political party must move. The fact that such an aim is totally inconsistent with the parallel drive towards increasing technology, automation and capital-intensive industry is ignored. The end result of such a policy must be economically disastrous in so far as the prices of goods made by **capital intensive** industry are inflated by the need to pay for labour that has, by the nature of the system, been rendered unnecessary. The resulting supernumerary national wage-bill makes the prices of goods uncompetitive with those of more efficient if less advanced countries which pay for only one factor of production. If **exports** cease to be competitive then countries relying on them to pay for essential **imports** will suffer considerably. ◊ **Balance of payments** ◊ **Competitive market** ◊ **Parkinson's law** ◊ **Prices and incomes policy**.

Fundamental terms Under the law of **contract**, these are terms in a contract which are so fundamental that breach of them would be considered to be complete non-performance, as opposed to breach of **conditions** or **warranties**. The distinction is important, for **exemption clauses** that apply to conditions or warranties do not apply to fundamental terms. ◊ **Contract, breach of**.

Funded debt That part of the **national debt** which the government is not obliged to repay at any particular time, e.g. **consols**.

Funded pension schemes These are pension schemes where contributions are put into a specific fund and invested to produce an income sufficient to pay all pension entitlements as and when they become due. In this way they are not dissimilar to investment companies, payments out to members being in the form of earned pensions rather than dividends.

All private **portable pension schemes** are funded schemes, as are many, if not most, occupational, contributory and trade union pension schemes. Because of the existence of so many self-financing schemes, pension funds are a major force in the investment market and offer a vast potential source for healthy companies looking for additional finance. Pension funds are likewise becoming the most ubiquitous of the institutional shareholders and their influence is continually increasing, particularly now that tax concessions encourage individuals to save through **pension schemes** out of untaxed income rather than to save through private investment out of taxed income.

The principal non-funded pension schemes are the **state earnings-related pension scheme** and most of those providing non-contributory or **ex gratia** pensions.

Funding A term used in connection with a variety of operations concerning the replacement of short-term loans by longer-term ones. Though normally associated with the management by the government (through the **Bank of England**) of the **national debt**, the term is often applied to companies which issue **debentures** or long-term securities with the intention of using the proceeds to pay off short-term debts and thereby strengthen the financial base of the company. ◊ **Capital gearing** ◊ **Loan capital**.

Fur auctions These take place at Beaver House, London, which is also the head office of the Hudson Bay Company. Sales of individual furs are held throughout the year and more general sales about four times a year. Buyers inspect the furs at the broker's warehouse (anyone may attend the sales). By tradition the wares of the Hudson Bay Company are sold first. **Settling day**, or prompt day, is usually thirty days after the first day of the sale. Brokers may refuse bids from undesirable buyers.

Future goods, sale of A contract for the sale of future goods is one where the goods contracted for are still to be manufactured. These contracts are governed by the **Sale of Goods** Act 1893. **Title** passes when the goods are available and the buyer notified.

Futures Although often used as a synonym for **forward dealings**, the term futures contract should be reserved for forward dealings where the person entering into the contract does so not with a specific future need in mind but more by way of a speculative investment. A person entering into a futures contract for goods, currency, freight or some other benefit will usually seek an opposite contract which, when set against the first, will leave him with a profit.

Alternatively, he may sell the original contract on one of the exchanges that deal in futures.

The futures market is complemented by that in **traded options**, where dealings are in options to buy or sell at a stated future date. Because an option is not a firm commitment to deal on the part of the holder, it can usually be secured by payment only of a premium, known as a **margin**. The option can be sold or purchased in the same way as can a futures contract and dealings in options are often referred to as margin dealings. ◊ **Options** ◊ **London International Financial Futures and Options Exchange** ◊ **Traded options**.

Gambling An agreement whereby one party pays a sum of money if an event occurs on **consideration** of the other party paying a fixed sum if it does not. Neither party has a personal interest in the event or stands to lose anything other than the money which is the subject matter of the agreement. For the legal position ◊ **Wagering contract** ◊ **Gaming contract**.

Gaming contract ◊ **Contract, gaming**.

Garnishee order A legal order made on a person owing money to a **judgment debtor** instructing him not to pay the debt until the debtor has made good the claims against him. It effectively (though not legally) gives the **judgment creditor** a **lien** on debts owed to the judgment debtor.

Gazetted ◊ **London Gazette**.

Gazumping A slang expression used in the context of buying and selling real property, particularly houses. It denotes a situation where, having made a legally unenforceable promise to sell property to a prospective customer, a person makes a quick cash sale at a higher price to another party. The gazumping relates to the initiative of a buyer with ready cash who wants to jump the queue. ◊ **Contract evidenced in writing** ◊ **Estate agent**.

Gearing ◊ **Capital gearing**.

GEMMS ◊ **Gilt-edged market-makers**.

General Agreement on Tariffs and Trade (GATT) An agreement signed in 1947 by more than forty countries, to campaign against the imposition of **tariff** barriers and quota restrictions and progressively to liberalize trade between the participant countries. There are provisions to discourage *blocs* within the group and to insist on **most-favoured-nation** treatment for all members if for any. In many instances, governments are expected to ask permission before making drastic alterations to tariffs. As the Agreement is a gentleman's agreement, its provisions have no legal force, though there is not usually any advantage in flouting them. Since the mid-sixties attention has been drawn to the economic plight of developing nations, and these have been excluded from the part of the agreement relating to most-favoured-nation status. They can be given this status without obligation on the donor's part to give it generally. GATT has been rather overshadowed in Western Europe by the growth of the **Common Market**.

General average loss A term used in **marine insurance**. When there is a partial loss of ship or cargo incurred for the benefit of parties other than the owner of the ship or that particular cargo, the loss is apportioned over all persons involved. For instance, if there is a fire in a ship and in putting out the fire cargo other than that which caught fire is damaged, then the loss is apportioned between owners of all the cargo, the freight and the ship. In order that a loss may be a general average loss there must be an extraordinary sacrifice or expenditure, voluntarily made at a time of necessity for the purpose of preserving all the property involved in the venture. The danger must be common to all those called on to contribute; **contributions** will be assessed at the port of discharge; the shipowners must collect contributions from the various parties and it is then up to them to claim from their respective **insurance** companies.

General average sacrifice A **marine insurance** term for a sacrifice made by the master of the ship for the benefit of the shipowner, charterer and cargo owners. ◊ **General average loss**.

General crossing ◊ **Crossing, general**.

General offer An **offer** to the public at large, acceptance usually being made by some act. Communication to the offeror is not always necessary. The offer may give rise to many **contracts**. For instance, if A advertises that he will pay £5 for every fifteenth-century coin submitted to him, he is bound to accept each coin offered and pay the money. On the other hand, the offer may give rise to only one contract. If A offers £5 for certain information, only the first person to provide the information is entitled to the £5.

General partner ◊ **Partnership** ◊ **Partnership, limited**.

Geometric mean A statistical term and a form of average, obtained by multiplying together _n_ numbers in a series and then finding the _n_th root. The geo-

metrical mean of the numbers 16, 8, 1 and 32, for example, is the fourth root of the product of those numbers. The product is 4,096 and the fourth root of 4,096 is 8. Geometric means are used statistically in the averaging of ratios and are usually calculated logarithmically. ◊ **Average** ◊ **Mean** ◊ **Arithmetic mean** ◊ **Median** ◊ **Mode**.

German companies Germany recognizes various forms of commercial organizations but the two most frequently encountered in international trade are the GmbH (Gesellschaft mit Beschränkter Haftung), roughly the equivalent of a UK private company (though without similar restrictions on the numbers of members), and the AG (Aktiengesellschaft) similar to a UK public company.

The AG is subject to strict legal requirements both in its organization and the conduct of its affairs, and these requirements tend to be more rigid and demanding than those applicable to British public companies. For example, founders of an AG must number five or more and be responsible for putting up at least one quarter of the minimum share capital (at present DM100,000) in cash before the company can be registered. Unlike their British counterparts, AG members cannot be called upon to contribute any more than their original investment when the number of shareholders falls below the specified minimum. There are also differences distinguishing the AG from the British counterpart, in the regulations governing management.

The GmbH is a more loosely knit organization and the lack of restrictions on the number of members can result in these companies becoming very large national or international businesses. Although there are no specific regulations relating to the audit of accounts, the larger the business becomes the stricter the rules regarding the need for an independent audit and the closer the GmbH becomes to the more rigidly controlled AG.

Unlike the case with an AG, a GmbH can be founded with only one member and there are, in fact, a great number of single-owner GmbHs in existence. The regulations require a minimum capital of DM50,000 of which at least DM25,000 must be subscribed in full.

Apart from these two categories of limited liability company there are many business organizations, some fairly large, with unlimited liability. Of these the principal types are the OHG (Offene Handels Gesellschaft) and the KG (Kommandit Gesellschaft). In addition there is another popular variety of business unit known as the GmbH & Co KG. At essence this is a partnership between a KG and a GmbH. Theoretically it is of the nature of a British limited partnership but as the GmbH, which is a company with limited liability, takes on the role of general partner so the effect is to transform the KG itself into a limited liability company. ◊ **French companies** ◊ **Partnership, limited**.

Gift A voluntary transfer of property, real or personal, by one person to another without that other being required to give any **consideration** whatever. Because of the absence of consideration, such transfers are not covered by the normal laws of contract and a promise, or offer, to give something in this manner is not binding unless it is made by deed. ◊ **Contracts by deed** ◊ **Covenants**.

Gifts, in cash or kind, may be subject to **inheritance tax**, where substantial, or treated as gifts *inter vivos*. ◊ **Estate duty**.

Gift cheques Decorative **cheques** sometimes made available by certain banks for use on festive occasions. Visual delights apart, the only real beneficiary is the **bank**, which will make a special charge to the account of the donor.

Gift token Can be of various kinds but is basically a means of giving another person a predetermined sum in the form of goods which the recipient may choose for himself.

Gift tokens are obtainable at many **chain stores** and can be exchanged for goods at any branch of that store in any part of the country. They are not exchangeable for cash nor can they be used at any shop other than a branch of the issuing store. It would not be an oversimplification to refer to them as IOUs for goods rather than for cash.

Gift tokens should not be confused with **book tokens**, which are issued, through bookshops, by a company known as Book Tokens Ltd. These can be exchanged at any bookshop which is a member of the Booksellers' Association, which covers most bookshops, though not newsagents who handle books, and they can technically be used only for the purchase of books even if the bookseller also sells other merchandise.

Gilt-edged market-makers (GEMMS) These are a new breed of primary dealers which grew out of the 1986 reorganization of the Stock Market – referred to as **Big Bang**. When the distinction between jobbers and brokers was abolished in favour of dual-capacity traders known as market-makers, the responsibility for dealing and trading in gilt-edged government securities was given to a new category of market-maker established for that purpose and known as gilt-edged market-makers or GEMMS. These GEMMS hold stocks of government securities and deal on their own account, both between themselves through the medium of **inter-dealer brokers** and with outside investors or their agents. In return for this virtually exclusive privilege given to them by the Bank of England they are subject to the strict supervision of that body. In addition to maintaining what the Bank deems an adequate capital base they are required to supply the Bank with details of their market positions at the end of each day. They cannot deal in equities, though equity dealers still retain the right to deal in gilts, and are obliged to make a market in all exsisting government securities including those that are index-linked. They are permitted to deal in other sterling fixed-interest securities and in derivatives of these such as gilt futures and options. Recently they have been afforded permission to deal additionally in ECU-denominated British Government bonds. They have access to a price information system through SEAQ, but this is more rudimentary than that available to dealers in equities.

Gilt-edged securities The term used to describe, somewhat euphemistically, **stocks** and **bonds** issued by the government of the UK and quoted on the **Stock Exchange**. Theoretically, they are non-risk investments, as it is assumed that the State will never renege on its debts. In fact, the low capital risk makes the market value of such securities totally dependent on prevailing interest rates and, consequently, an investor may be forced to sell them at a price lower than that which he paid for them initially. ◊ **Shares: market value**.

The **securities** in question may or may not be redeemable and the redeemable variety may be short-term, middle-term or long-term, depending on the monetary policy of the government at the date of issue and its forecast of its cash flow requirements. High-interest securities, because of the annual **interest** burden, are more likely to be short-term than are low-interest bonds. **Consols**, an abbreviation for Consolidated Annuities, issued by the UK government, are the best-known example of irredeemable securities. ◊ **Government securities** ◊ **Gilt-edged market-makers**.

Sales of UK gilt-edged securities are not subject to **capital gains tax**. This exemption applies not only to government securities but also to a wide range of fixed-interest financial instruments together with futures and options relating to them. ◊ **Blue-chip investments** ◊ **Short-term interest rates**.

Girobank plc Now one of the clearing banks, Girobank was established in 1968 as the National Girobank and was the banking arm of the Post Office. The original intention was to provide a public banking service with the advantage of it being more instantly available to the general public in post offices situated in virtually every town and village throughout the country which are open for longer hours. It offered services similar to those given by the High Street banks and also provided a means of transferring money to people who did not have a traditional bank account. Originally a public service with a head office in Bootle, Merseyside, it eventually joined the ranks of the other clearing banks as Girobank plc. In 1990 it was taken over by the Alliance and Leicester Building Society, though transactions are still routed through the Post Office.

GmbH ◊ German companies.

Gold Metals have long been internationally acceptable as a form of currency, partly because of their durability and partly because they are not easy to counterfeit. Of the many metals available, gold and silver, which are both particularly attractive, have proved to be the most popular; they are also very malleable, do not corrode and are fairly scarce, all of which accounts for their frequent use in the making of ornaments and jewellery. The predominance of gold over silver could be attributed to its colour and the consequent link with the many ancient cults of sun worship. Gold has been used as an almost universally accepted currency since the beginning of recorded history and has outlived silver, which, though equally iridescent, is no longer a major factor in international exchange.

An example of the unique standing of gold can be found in the time-honoured custom of mariners wearing gold earrings so that, whatever befell them, they would always possess on their person the price of a Christian burial.

Gold is found in many parts of the world but the major sources lie in South Africa. There are gold mines in the northern part of the USA, in the Russian Federation and even in the UK, where there is a tradition that the wedding ring of the reigning monarch is made from gold from the small mine in the Principality of Wales. ◊ **Gold and foreign exchange reserves** ◊ **Gold coins** ◊ **Gold standard** ◊ **Penny** ◊ **Sovereign** ◊ **Guinea** ◊ **Pound**.

Gold and dollar reserves ◊ **Gold and foreign exchange reserves**.

Gold and foreign exchange reserves

All nations have what might be called last-ditch reserves with which to pay their international debts. They tend to be accumulated in the natural course of foreign trade. However, when it comes to settling a particular debt it is obviously necessary to have the appropriate **currency**. A vast quantity of deutschmarks is not always acceptable to a creditor in Brazil or Russia. For this reason national reserves need to be held in a currency that is internationally recognized and the only commonly accepted currency is, traditionally, **gold**; thus, gold-producing countries have a valuable natural source of international exchange, though they have to take care not to devalue that asset by overproduction.

After 1945 and until relatively recently the American **dollar** was virtually on a par with gold in the international exchange market, as it was a currency that was always acceptable, particularly as its value in exchange was more likely to increase than to fall. In recent years the dollar has lost a great deal of its attraction due to lack of confidence in the stability of the American economy, and the emergence of other currencies backed by the economic strength of their countries of origin, e.g. Germany and Japan.

At one time the UK reserves were referred to as the gold and dollar reserves. The changing tides of fortune have led to this title being discarded in favour of gold and foreign exchange reserves. Considerable attention is paid to the level of these reserves and any tendency for them to fall calls for government action. The action taken must be such as to build up gold and currency reserves by attracting money from other countries. This can be done either by attempting to reverse an imbalance of payments by seeking means to bolster **exports** and discourage

imports or by attracting deposits on capital account by offering high interest rates to foreign investors. The first method is necessarily long-term only, barring abrupt **devaluation** of the pound when exchange rates are fixed, and the second has the disadvantage of involving the obligation to pay out higher sums by way of interest, thus making it even more difficult to balance payments in future years. This second method, then, is acceptable only as a stop-gap whilst the first is given time to take effect.

The international position has, in recent times, been much changed by the setting up of various supranational institutions which can offer help to particular nations over varying periods, and at a price. The primary source of aid is the **International Monetary Fund** (IMF), which can both sell or lend currency to a debtor country, within limits, and, more important, provide credit facilities over a stated period. This latter ability makes the IMF akin to an international bank, with power to grant **overdrafts** or make **loans** as the situation requires. The UK has on more than one occasion received loans and credit facilities from the IMF. These have not always been used up but can provide considerable assistance in both propping up and rebuilding a falling economy. Such facilities are not included in the stated figure of reserves.

Present moves within the **European Union** towards a single common European currency, though more apparent in theory than in practice, would have the obvious advantage to the UK of strengthening reserves, as present holdings of the various European currencies would merge into one fund acceptable throughout the EU, and a strong euro-currency might even become closer to gold in terms of worldwide acceptability than the dollar ever was. ◊ **Balance of payments** ◊ **Bank for International Settlements** ◊ **Bank rate** ◊ **Below the line** ◊ **Minimum lending rate** ◊ **European monetary system**.

Gold coins The use of **gold** in the making of coins for common currency is a practice dating back countless years. In more recent times the international exchange value of gold has increased so substantially, and paper currency has become so widely accepted, that the need to use precious metals in minting coins has virtually disappeared. Gold coins are now principally the province of investors and collectors. Some of those once in use and now collected are, in addition to the **sovereign**, the **guinea**, the noble, the angel, etc. Their worth is a combination of both intrinsic and scarcity value. At various times in recent history exchange controls have restricted the holding of gold coins to licensed dealers and banks. No restrictions apply in the UK at present.

Gold pool In 1961, eight countries (the United Kingdom, France, West Germany, Switzerland, Italy, the United States, Belgium and the Netherlands) informally agreed to intervene in the London Gold Market to prevent pressure on the **price** of gold and avoid too much **speculation** by preventing the price from rising above $35·19\frac{7}{8}$. This was done by forming the Gold Pool. In 1967 at the time of UK devaluation, France, for reasons best known to herself, opted out, and there was considerable speculation. This led to a crisis in the Gold Market, the creation of a two-tier price system, and the abandonment of the Gold Pool. ◊ **Gold and foreign exchange reserves**.

Gold standard A country on the gold standard agrees, by definition, to convert its **currency** freely into **Gold** through its central bank. At one time the UK currency was backed by gold and silver – a bimetallic standard. By the early nineteenth century silver had been discarded and the UK used only gold to back its currency. This state of affairs prevailed until the gold standard was abolished, provisionally in 1914 and finally in 1931 – though from 1925 to 1931 the standard was known as the gold bullion standard. Prior to the abolition of the gold standard in 1931 the note issue of the UK was backed by gold and the promise to pay on a £5 note meant that if such a note was presented at the Bank of England for payment in gold then that promise would be honoured. Since then the promise means only that the note will be treated as **legal tender** for the amount printed on it. ⟁ **Bank notes** ⟁ **Note circulation**.

Golden handcuffs A practice frequently adopted to deter competitors from poaching senior executives by devices such as **golden hello**s. Attractive remuneration packages are offered to senior management figures, particularly those with specialist knowledge, which make it more worthwhile for them to remain with present employers than to succumb to offers made by rival organizations. Generous but delayed share option schemes can form a helpful ingredient in preparing these inducements, known colloquially as golden handcuffs.

Golden handshake ⟁ **Compensation for loss of office**.

Golden hello A variation on the **golden handshake** theme, but to welcome the arriving executive rather than speed the departing one. When a major firm or company is looking for new and experienced executives it may try to poach those working for other companies by the offer of very attractive initial remuneration packages. In addition to high basic salaries, these might include special bonuses and valuable share options. Such a package is often referred to as a golden hello, and the practice was very common among market-makers attempting to establish themselves in the City after **Big Bang**.

Golden parachutes Esoteric jargon for the practice, more common in the USA, of providing package deals for senior company executives which give them various financial benefits and other privileges should their tenure of office be determined by virtue of a change in effective control of the company due to a takeover or major reshuffle of ownership. It can apply both where the executive loses his position or where circumstances make it desirable that he should relinquish it.

Good faith ⟁ **Bona fide**.

Goods The definition of 'goods' is important because of the obligations imposed and the protection offered by the Sale of Goods Act 1893. Goods are generally personal chattels, emblements, industrial growing crops and ships, but not **choses-in-action** or money. **Contracts** for the **sale of goods** should be distinguished from contracts for work and materials, which are not governed by the Sale of Goods Act. The test is, whether the payment was made for the work done rather than for the materials supplied. A contract for work done where the materials are incidental, e.g. the painting of pictures, will be a contract for work and materials.

Goods on approval A person may ask for **goods** on approval if he wishes to see them before deciding whether to buy, and the **vendor** will usually allow him a stated number of days in which to make a decision. Equally, a vendor may also send goods to a selected number of persons in the hope that they will purchase them. In the first instance, the purchaser is a voluntary bailee and has a duty to take care of the goods and to return them as directed. In the second instance, the person is a quite involuntary bailee and has no responsibility towards the goods, unless custom dictates otherwise. He may not destroy them, but may demand that the vendor retakes them immediately and at his own expense, or simply redirect them to the vendor, leaving him to pay. If the goods are in any way a nuisance, he may take necessary precautions. ◊ **Bailment**.

Goods on consignment Goods sent to an **agent** for sale. The agent has possession but not **title**, though he may be able to give a good title to a **bona fide** purchaser, even when acting outside his authority. The goods are usually returnable by the agent, who works for a **commission**. The venture is normally made for a limited period only.

Goodwill Dr Johnson defined goodwill when he said, 'We are not here to sell a parcel of boilers and vats but the potentiality of growing rich beyond the dreams of avarice.' It is a nebulous term for that part of the value of an asset or business arising from factors not directly associated with the assets or business as such. For instance, goodwill may arise from the good reputation of the business or the fact that it is making profits above the average due to some particular advantage of location.

When a business is purchased the price paid may include an amount for the goodwill created by the vendor. The purchaser will often show this as a separate item in the balance sheet. Until recently such items remained in the balance sheet unless it was decided by proprietors or auditors to write them off against profits. The 1981 Companies Act made it obligatory for limited companies to write off goodwill – by which it means goodwill purchased – by charges to the profit and loss account over a period not exceeding its economic life. The period chosen and the reasons for that choice must be indicated in a note to the accounts. Goodwill not arising from purchase but generated by the company itself must never be capitalized in a company's accounts, and if it has been, then the amount must be written off immediately.

Government bonds ◊ Bonds.

Government securities Fixed-interest securities issued by the government. They may be in the nature of **bonds** or other types of security and may or may not be redeemable. They may be issued to banks and other institutions in the **money market** or to the general public through banks or the **Post Office**. The **treasury bill** is a specific type of government security which is issued only within the money market, and particularly to **discount houses**, which tender for these bills each week. The rate of discount at which they are allotted is a pointer to the general health of the economy and can influence the current **minimum lending rate**. ◊ **Accepting house** ◊ **Consols** ◊ **Discount** (**bills of exchange**).

Graft US slang for money made in illicit dealings while employed on political or municipal business. Now sometimes applied more generally to monies made by taking illicit advantage of one's office.

Granny bonds A popular term for index-linked savings certificates. The name derives from the fact that these were originally only available to persons over retirement age. ◊ **National savings bonds** ◊ **National savings certificates** ◊ **Save as you earn**.

Gratuity Often referred to as a tip, this is a sum paid without obligation for services rendered. It is normally taxable in the hands of the recipient. In some industries, e.g. cab driving, catering or hairdressing, gratuities are an important source of income and basic salaries may be adjusted accordingly. The term is often used for lump-sum payments on the termination of employment, misleadingly in the case of the Armed Forces where such payments are actually contracted for. In the hotel industry, a charge may be added to the bill, supposedly in lieu of gratuities. This is known as a service charge, and is divided amongst the hotel staff much as **prize money** was divided in the romantic days of British naval supremacy.

Graving dock A dry dock where ships are taken for repairs and maintenance, particularly to the exterior of the ship below the waterline.

Green currencies The special arrangements which apply to agricultural products within the EU are dictated by the **Common Agricultural Policy** (CAP). By the terms of the CAP the prices of agricultural products traded within the EU are fixed in terms of the ECU so that, in effect, such prices are the same in all member countries.

These ECU prices have then, for settlement purposes, to be translated into the various national currencies. Because of the continual variation in intra-EU exchange rates the CAP introduced a special set of fixed exchange rates applicable to trade in agricultural products. These purpose-orientated currency values of the ECU are known as green currencies, e.g. the green pound. The green rate can vary between different products, but is fixed for that product unless and until a member country negotiates a new rate with fellow members. Because the green currency rates differ from the normal exchange rates there are opportunities for individuals to profit by re-routing goods or payments. To prevent this, the CAP imposes taxes or subsidies on dealings in farm products between EU members to counter the gap between the green exchange rates and those normally prevailing.

Green pound ◊ **Green currencies**.

Greengrocer Generally a retail trader in vegetables and fruit.

Grocer Generally a retail trader in provisions, particularly spices, sugar, dried fruit, etc. The name is derived from the fact that these traders originally purchased by the gross.

Gross profit Where the buying or selling of **goods** is concerned, it refers to the proceeds of **sale**, less the cost of putting the goods into a condition for sale. Where the goods are also manufactured, this cost will include part of the **overhead expenses**. Otherwise, overheads concerned with distributing or selling the goods and administering the business generally are charged after gross profit (also known as 'gross profit on trading') to produce **net profit** on trading. This will then be adjusted for exceptional items or items not connected with the major objects of the business, to produce the actual net profit.

Gross profit on trading ◊ **Gross profit**.

Ground rents **Rent** paid for land as opposed to rent paid for the buildings on the land. Rights to receive ground rents can be bought and sold. At one time, prior to April 1964, tax was deducted by the payer and the payment was treated as an **annual charge**. Payment is now made gross, i.e. no tax is deducted.

Group This generally refers to a group of interrelated companies (in fact one single business organization comprising many separate corporate parts). It normally consists of one **holding company** and a number of **subsidiary companies**, though there may be sub-subsidiaries and/or **associated companies**. For example if Company A and Company B each hold 50 per cent of Company C, then technically Company C is an associated company of both A and B; but if Company A has a controlling interest in Company B, then Company C is part of the Group while not strictly being a subsidiary of either Company A or Company B. Situations where Company A owns Company B, which owns Company C, which has a controlling interest in Company A are not permitted in law.

The 1989 Companies Act, in accordance with the seventh Directive of the European Council, widened the definition of a group by adding the category of 'associated undertaking'. This is one in which either the parent undertaking, or a subsidiary undertaking included in a group, has a participating stake and over whose operating and financial policy it excercises a significant interest. If a member of the group holds 20 per cent

or more of the voting rights in such an associated undertaking the assumption is that a significant interest does indeed exist. It should be noted that the substitution of the term 'undertaking' for the term 'company' in the provisions of the 1989 Act means that the legal definition of a **subsidiary company** has been widened to include businesses, other than limited companies, which are owned or controlled by the parent organization. When group accounts are prepared, all businesses caught by this wider definition of 'subsidiary' must now be included in the consolidated accounts that are required to be filed. Information regarding associated undertakings where the interest is classed as being 'significant' within the meaning of the Act, but which are not controlled by the parent, may be given by way of notes to the accounts.

Group accounts These are the additional accounts which a **holding company** is required to file with reference to the group which it controls. Prior to the 1989 Companies Act such accounts could be either in the format of **consolidated accounts** or in some other form more suited to the nature of the group and to the overriding duty of presenting a true and fair view of the state of affairs of the group and its profit or loss for the period concerned. The position was changed by the 1989 Act which, in giving effect to the directives of the European Council, provides that, with very limited exceptions, all group accounts must now be in the form of consolidated accounts. ◊ **Group accounts: omission of subsidiaries**.

There is also a blanket exception from the need to file group accounts at all in the case of groups of **small and medium-sized companies**, provided that no company in that group is a public company, a corporate body not being a company but empowered to issue shares or debentures, an authorized institution under the 1987 Banking Act, or an authorized body under the Financial Services Act 1986.

Where a parent company is itself a subsidiary of another company it need not file group accounts but must file prescribed information regarding the name and place of business both of its ultimate holding company and to any company in a group of which it is a member which is itself obliged to file group accounts.

Group accounts: omission of subsidiaries Until fairly recently it was legally permissible to exclude particular **subsidiary companies** from group accounts whether Consolidated or otherwise, provided certain relevant information was given, that is (1) reason for exclusion; (2) total value of shares held in those subsidiaries and amounts due either to or from them; (3) aggregate profits or losses attributable to the holding company for the particular year and since acquisition; and (4) any qualifications in auditors' reports of those subsidiaries.

The position has been changed by the 1989 Companies Act. All subsidiary undertakings must now be included in the **consolidated accounts**, filed by the parent undertaking, with very limited exceptions. These are (1) where the subsidiary company is too small to have any significant effect on group results; (2) where the problems involved in and the cost of obtaining the necessary information regarding any subsidiary outweighs the likely significance of including it in the consolidation; or (3) where the business of the subsidiary is so different from

that of the parent that consolidation would counter the overriding imperative of giving a true and fair view of the results of the group.

In this latter case, although the accounts of the subsidiary need not be fully consolidated into the accounts filed, the interest appertaining to the parent undertaking must be shown by way of equity accounting, that is by disclosure of the relevant portions of both profit (or loss) and net assets in the body of the group accounts and not merely by way of notes to those accounts as might previously have been permissible. ◊ **Group** ◊ **Group accounts** ◊ **Subsidiary company**.

Group of Seven (G7) This comprises the leading industrial countries outside what was once the Communist Bloc. Member nations are Japan, Germany, France, the United States, the United Kingdom, Italy and Canada. Ministers from each of these countries meet on a regular basis to discuss subjects of mutual importance, e.g. economic and financial policy coordination, and there is an annual meeting of heads of government. The group was born from an economic summit arranged in 1976.

Group of Ten Otherwise known as the Paris Club, this is a group of ten member countries of the **International Monetary Fund** which has been noted for its activity in innovating various schemes within the IMF, particularly the inauguration of **special drawing rights**. The countries are Belgium, Canada, France, Italy, Japan, the Netherlands, Sweden, the UK, the USA and Germany. Through the auspices of the **Bank for International Settlements**, these countries also play a major role in assisting countries with **balance of payments** problems.

Growth stocks Market jargon for **stocks** or **shares** which are judged, either on past performance or on future prospects, to be worth investing in over a period. The term is usually reserved for those without immediate income-earning capacity but which promise to be good long-term investments offering sustained capital growth. ◊ **Earnings yield** ◊ **Price-earnings ratio**.

Guarantee An agreement to be answerable for the debt, default or miscarriage of another. This is different from an **indemnity**, which is a **contract** where one party agrees to suffer the loss of the other (e.g. **fire insurance**). The indemnifier takes a primary liability: there may be only two persons concerned. A guarantor assumes secondary liability. He agrees to pay if the debtor defaults. He must have no interest in the contract between the debtor and **creditor**. He is sometimes called a surety. The contract of guarantee itself must be accompanied by a memorandum in writing. Normally, on default of the debtor, the creditor may take action against the guarantor without first having taken action against the debtor. If the guarantor pays he may then himself attempt to recover from the debtor. The liability of a guarantor may disappear if the contract between debtor and creditor is altered without his notice. The law on guarantees is fairly extensive.

Points to note are: (1) the guarantor in recovering from the debtor can take over a **security** previously held by the creditor; (2) he may also claim contribution from co-sureties. ◊ **Subrogation**.

Guinea An English gold coin first struck in 1661 in the reign of Charles II. It was so called because the coins were initially minted from gold that came from the Guinea Coast in West Africa, which was then a British colony. It continued in use until 1816, when it was replaced by the **sovereign**.

When first used it was worth twenty silver shillings but, as silver fell in value compared with gold, its worth increased until at one time it reached thirty shillings in exchange. In 1717 its value was fixed at twenty-one shillings. The sovereign that replaced it in 1816 was of a gold value of twenty shillings.

Although the guinea coin had not been in circulation since 1816, the term remained in use, representing twenty-one shillings, and was a unit in which many professional fees were fixed. Officially, this practice ceased when the introduction of decimalization discontinued the shilling, but there is a tendency for fees still to be expressed in the decimal equivalent of guineas.

Gunsmith A term usually reserved for describing a maker or repairer of sporting guns or small firearms generally.

Haberdasher Formerly a dealer in many different items, particularly caps, hats, etc. Now a dealer in clothing and dress-making accessories, such as ribbon, lace, thread, etc.

Haggle To cavil and wrangle when settling a bargain.

Half-commission man A **Stock Exchange** term for a person who, being neither a stockbroker nor a **Market-maker** introduces clients to either in return for a share in the **commission**.

Hallmark A mark made on precious metals after an **assay** test. At present there are two qualities of silver and four of gold. The British hallmark is accepted internationally as a guarantee of standard. There are four marks: the maker's mark, the hall or assay-office mark, the quality mark and the date letter. The hall or assay-office mark may be made at London (leopard), Chester (the arms of the city), Birmingham (anchor), Sheffield (crown), Edinburgh (castle), Glasgow (fish, tree, bell and bird) and Dublin (Irish harp with crown).

The quality of gold is indicated by the carat mark. The four recognized UK carat marks are 22 carat (i.e. twenty-two parts gold and two parts alloy), 18 carat, 14 carat and 9 carat. Dublin has an additional 12-carat mark. The quality marks for silver are a lion passant for England and a thistle or a lion rampant for Scotland. The date is indicated by a letter,

each year having a separate letter and the letters being changed at different times at different centres.

Every object made from gold or silver must bear a hallmark. There are some exceptions, which are briefly: (1) fine chains, e.g. dress chains, key chains, Alberts and other watch chains but the exemption does not necessarily apply to items suspended from the chains; (2) lockets; (3) the actual settings of precious stones; (4) imported items over 100 years old; (5) gold rings other than wedding rings, gold-jointed sleeper earrings, gold thimbles, gold pencil cases, gold items richly engraved or set with stones that could be damaged by marking and gold items too small to be marked (weighing less than ten dwts); (6) silver stamped medals and silver items which are very small in size or of negligible weight.

The penalties for selling gold or silver goods which are not hallmarked and are not exempt therefrom are severe.

Hammered A member of the **Stock Exchange** is hammered when he cannot meet his debts. The process was named from the three strokes of the hammer delivered by the **waiter** at the Stock Exchange as a prelude to the announcement of the name of the defaulter. It was once said to be the only effective way of producing silence in the Stock Exchange. Now that floor trading has virtually disappeared from the Stock Exchange the announcement that a member has defaulted is normally communicated to members via their **SEAQ** information screens.

Hard currency In the world of foreign trade this term is commonly used to describe any **currency** which is generally safe, i.e. in no apparent danger of losing its value by loss of confidence or by **devaluation**. The demand for a hard currency will, almost by definition, exceed the supply. At one time the **dollar** was looked upon as a hard currency, but its role has been partially usurped by others, e.g. the deutschmark and the yen. ◊ **Gold and foreign exchange reservers** ◊ **Soft currency**.

Haulage The charge made for carrying goods, though not usually for loading or unloading them.

Hawker A person who sells goods which he carries round with him; usually one who sells from a vehicle rather than from a pack or suitcase. ◊ **Pedlar** ◊ **Share hawking** ◊ **Street trader**.

Head lease When property is leased to one person and then sub-let in part or in whole to others, the original **lease** is known as the head lease.

Health and Safety Commission A statutory authority set up under the Health and Safety at Work Act 1974. It has partly taken over the responsibilities of inspectors appointed under the Factories Acts for the protection of people at work from employment hazards, particularly in industry. It oversees the provision of safeguards from accidents for both employees and the general public; in doing so it heeds the standards set by government. With the collaboration of employers, trade unions and local authorities it makes representations to the Secretary of State concerning the

maximization of safety precautions. ◊ **Employers' liability insurance**.

Hedging A trader, particularly if buying forward or selling forward in the **commodity exchanges**, may 'hedge' to protect himself from losses arising from variations in price. For instance, a dealer who has sold a large quantity of goods forward may want to insure against the possibility of heavy losses through a rise in price by buying forward to match all or part of the purchase. Alternatively, he may pass on some of his **forward sales** to other dealers (much as a bookmaker lays off bets). ◊ **Futures** ◊ **Traded options**.

Her Majesty's Customs and Excise Objectives are: (1) to control imports and exports and the manufacture of dutiable **goods**, and to assess and collect Customs duty, **excise duty** and/or VAT on them; (2) to administer the VAT system in the UK and collect the tax due and also levy betting and gaming duties, checking relevant statements of liability; and (3) to administer reliefs from, or repayments of, duties.

For collection of revenue, the United Kingdom is divided into thirty-four sections. The officials of the Customs and Excise fall into three categories: (1) officers of Customs and Excise (not uniformed), who control the landing and shipping of cargo and the manufacture of dutiable goods, and collect betting and gaming duties; (2) executive and clerical officials, who are concerned with all the background paper work, and with issuing **receipts** for duties paid; (3) the Customs Waterguard Service (uniformed), who are concerned with the prevention of smuggling, etc., are stationed at seaports and airports, and patrol the coast by land and sea, particularly the rivers, creeks, and harbours. They also patrol the land frontier in Ireland.

Hidden reserve ⟩ **Secret reserve**.

High seas The seas or oceans of the world which are not enclosed national waters, or what are known as **territorial waters** or the *'mare clausum'*. Any ship has the right to venture on the high seas.

Hire purchase Lord Greene MR once said that a great part of his time on the bench was concerned '. . . with people who are persuaded by persons whom they do not know to enter into **contracts** they do not understand to purchase **goods** they do not want with money they have not got'. Hire purchase was defined by the **Hire Purchase Act** 1965 as 'an agreement for the **bailment** of goods under which the bailee may buy the goods or under which the property of the goods will or may pass to the bailee'. That is, a hire purchase agreement is in effect an agreement to hire goods for a specified period, with an option for the hirer to purchase the goods at the end, usually for a nominal sum. The property in the goods does not normally pass to the hirer until the last payment is made. Both the seller and the hirer or buyer have certain rights and obligations defined by the Act. The hirer may terminate the agreement at any time by giving notice but must allow the seller to retake possession, and must also pay instalments due and the additional amount necessary to bring total payments up to 50 per cent of hire purchase price (unless a lesser sum is specified in the agreement).

The hirer may also be liable for any damage done to the goods due to his negligence. The agreement cannot restrict the hirer's right to terminate. The seller has certain rights. He may retake the goods if an instalment is not paid provided he serves a 'notice of default' requiring payment within seven days, and the payment is not made. This right is restricted in so far as after one-third of the hire purchase price is paid, the seller cannot recover the goods except by action in a county court. If he does otherwise, the agreement is terminated and the hirer may recover all sums paid. There must be a written agreement which must state the **cash price** of the goods, the hire purchase price, the true APR, the amount and date of the instalments, and a list of the goods. The agreement must be signed by the hirer and all other parties and must contain a notice of the right of the hirer to terminate the agreement and the restriction of the seller's right to recover the goods. A copy of the agreement must be sent to the hirer within seven days. ⟩ **Hire purchase contracts: conditions and warranties**.

Certain other regulations also apply. The principal legislation is the **Consumer Credit Act** 1974, which replaced the Hire Purchase Act 1965. Hire purchase sales are also, in so far as they involve goods, subject to the Sale of Goods Act 1893, the Supply of Goods (Implied Terms) Act 1973, the Unfair Contract Terms Act 1977, the Sale of Goods Act 1977 and the Consumer Protection Act 1987.

Most hire purchase contracts are financed by specialized finance companies which, by taking over the collection of instalments from him, enable the **vendor** to maintain his liquidity. The hire purchase contract will then be between the company and the purchaser, but the latter will retain rights against the vendor concerning conditions and warranties

applying to the goods themselves. ◊
Fair Trading Act ◊ **Factoring**.

Hire Purchase Act 1965 Formerly the
principal legislation governing hire purchase transactions; repealed and replaced
by the **Consumer Credit Act** 1974.

**Hire purchase contracts: conditions
and warranties** Certain **conditions**
and **warranties** exist by virtue of the
Consumer Credit Act 1974 and apply to
all **hire purchase** and **conditional sale
agreements**.

The conditions are, *inter alia*, that: (1)
the owner shall have a right to sell when
the time comes for the property to pass;
(2) the **goods** will be of merchantable
quality though if the hirer or buyer has
examined them he cannot complain of
defects he should have discovered; (3)
where the purpose is made known to the
supplier the goods will be reasonably fit
for that purpose; (4) where the goods are
sold by **sample**, that the bulk will correspond to the sample and the buyer or
hirer will have an opportunity to find
out that this is so; (5) if the goods are
sold by description, the goods will correspond to the description. None of these
conditions may be excluded in the **contract**, with the exception of (2) where
the goods are second-hand.

The warranties are: (1) the hirer or
buyer shall enjoy quiet possession of the
goods; (2) the goods shall be free from
any charge or encumbrance in favour of
a third party when the **title** passes.

Some of these conditions and warranties derive from **common law**.

Hire purchase finance Retailers selling **goods** on **hire purchase** or on
credit may need cash more quickly than
they receive it. They may therefore employ a finance company, which will make
agreements directly with the retailer's
customers, who will make their payments, including **interest**, direct to that
company. Interest is usually upwards of
10 per cent per annum, and the period of
repayment depends on government
policy. The finance company may require the retailer to **guarantee** the debt
or repurchase the goods if the customer
defaults. It will usually pay the retailer an
agreed proportion of the hire purchase
price when each contract is signed.

Alternatively, the retailer may sign
hire purchase agreements with his
customers and sell these agreements to
a finance company, which will immediately pay, say, 75 per cent of the hire
purchase price, which the retailer will
repay over the period of hire. The retailer
then collects the instalments on behalf of
the finance company. The charges for
this type of block discounting vary
according to the risk, and may be from
5 per cent upwards per annum.

Historical cost The original cost of an
asset as opposed to its saleable value,
replacement value or value in present or
alternative use.

Historical cost accounting The
traditional method of **book-keeping**
whereby all values, whether attributable
to assets and liabilities or income and expenditure, are expressed in terms of the
original amount expended. This means
that the monetary amounts featured
in published accounts are of historical
relevance only and do not represent the
real cost in terms of the contemporary
value of money or level of prices. In
times of inflation this practice can lead to
a misleading picture of the health of a
business.

Although the problem is recognized
within the accountancy profession, no

satisfactory solution has yet been found which will satisfy all concerned and which can be incorporated into the provisions of the various statutes dealing with the preparation of accounts. ◊ **Annual accounts** ◊ **Current cost accounting** ◊ **Current purchasing power accounting** ◊ **Fourth schedule** ◊ **Replacement cost accounting**.

HMSO (Her Majesty's Stationery Office). ◊ **Stationery Office**.

Hogshead A large cask. At one time it equalled sixty-three gallons of wine, or fifty-four gallons of ale. These measures are still in use in the United States.

Holder for value A term applying to **negotiable instruments**. 'Value' refers to **consideration** given, though this may take the form of antecedent debt. A holder for value is a holder of, e.g., a **bill of exchange**, for which value has been given at some time. He need not have given value himself. However, he can only claim from persons who were parties to the bill, up to the time value was last given; and cannot claim a better **title** than that of the person from whom he took the bill. ◊ **Endorsement**.

Holder in due course This concerns **bills of exchange**, including **cheques**. A holder in due course is a person who has taken a bill, complete and regular on the face of it, not overdue and without notice of any previous dishonour. He must have taken it in good faith for value and without notice of any defect in the **title** of the person from whom he took it. ◊ **Endorsement**.

The holder of a bill is presumed to be a holder in due course, unless the opposite is proved. If, however, **fraud** is proved at any stage, he must (to be recognized as holder in due course) prove that value

was given after that time (but ◊ **Cheques: protection of banker**). The advantage of being a holder in due course is that one has the best possible **title**, and can claim from all parties who have signed the bill.

Holding company ◊ **Subsidiary company**.

Holding company, identity of A **subsidiary company** must state in its accounts the name of its ultimate holding company and the country where this is incorporated, unless the subsidiary carries on business outside the United Kingdom and the **directors** and the Department of Trade and Industry are agreed that disclosure would be harmful.

Holding out This term has particular relevance to **partnerships**. If one partner leaves and his name is not deleted from the firm's name, whether on the business premises or on official documents (such as invoices, orders, etc.), he may remain liable for all subsequent **contracts** entered into by the partnership whether he is aware of them or not. This is known as 'holding out' and is the reason why changes in the composition of a partnership must be properly advertised both publicly and privately (i.e. to regular suppliers or customers). Needless to say, the liability does not arise if the person claiming **damages** or **indemnity** is aware of the change. It exists only for the protection of innocent third parties acting in good faith. ◊ **Bona fide** ◊ **Estoppel** ◊ **Partner, nominal**.

Honorary secretary A person who takes on the secretarial duties of a club or organization without payment or for a nominal *ex gratia* sum known as an honorarium.

Horizontal integration ◊ **Vertical integration**.

Hosier A dealer in stockings and socks.

Hot money Apart from its use in the world of crime to describe stolen or counterfeit money, hot money is a term sometimes used in the sphere of international finance to refer to funds that move quickly from one country to another in search of the highest rates of interest. ◊ **Balance of payments** ◊ **Below the line** ◊ **Rate of interest**.

Hotel ◊ **Inn**.

House journal A regular magazine or news-sheet circulated among the employees of an organization to keep them informed of developments within that organization; it is also intended to serve as a forum for discussion. ◊ **Personnel management**.

Hull insurance A **marine insurance** term for the **insurance** of the vessel itself and against liabilities arising from collision, etc.

Hyperinflation An inexact term applied to inflation when it is running at extremely high levels, e.g. in certain central European countries, particularly Germany, in the period following the end of the First World War. ◊ **Currency depreciation** ◊ **Paper profit**.

Hypermarket A popular name for the very large supermarkets sometimes known as superstores that are often found on low-rental land away from the main town or city shopping areas. The range of goods carried and the generally very competitive prices attract customers who prefer to accomplish a week's shopping at one time and in one place. As most customers tend to come by car, large car-parks are an important feature of such stores. Most hypermarkets are operated by large national retailing groups which make a business of trading through such units. Because they buy in bulk and can also make use of own-brand labelling, they are able to sell at prices far below those of the High Street trader. ◊ **Discount stores** ◊ **Cash and carry** ◊ **Quantity discount**.

Hypothecation, letter of Exporters may borrow from a **bank**, using the goods they are shipping as **security**. Until repaid, the banker has a **lien** on the goods, as they are listed in the **bill of lading**. The lien, which of course is not a **possessory lien**, is conveyed by a 'letter of hypothecation'.

Ignorantia juris neminem excusat A legal maxim stating 'Ignorance of the law is no excuse'. For example, if a person enters into an illegal contract, ◊ **Contract, illegal**, he cannot succeed by pleading that he was not aware of the illegality.

Illegal An illegal act is one forbidden by law. An unlawful act, on the other hand, is one which, though not forbidden by law, is not given the protection of the law.

Illegal partnerships Partnerships formed for illegal purposes are void *ab initio*. As a general rule, partnerships consisting of more than twenty persons are illegal: such businesses must be registered as companies. Larger partnerships of accountants, solicitors and stockbrokers are now permitted, provided certain conditions are satisfied.

Immediate annuity An **annuity** which is designed to provide immediate benefits. The **assurance** company commences payments as soon as the sum agreed as the cost of the annuity is paid over to it.

Immediate holding company A legal and accounting term for the **company** which actually holds the controlling interest in another company, even though the first company may itself be controlled by yet another company.

Imperial preference ◊ **Common Agricultural Policy** ◊ **Common Market** ◊ Commonwealth preference.

Imperial system The system of measurement used by the United Kingdom and certain other countries at one time colonized by the UK, including the USA. The imperial system is the product of many influences, including Roman and Anglo-Saxon. It is being phased out and will eventually be almost completely replaced by derivatives of the internationally acceptable **metric system**. At present the UK currency has been replaced by **decimal currency** and a **Metrication Board** exists to supervise the necessary changes in other measurements.

Impersonal accounts A term used in **double-entry book-keeping** to describe those accounts in the ledgers which are kept for recording capital, **assets**, expenses and income, i.e. impersonal accounts are all accounts other than those for debtors and creditors. ◊ **Accounts, nominal, real and personal**.

Implied terms Terms which are not included in a **contract** but which the law considers would have been included had the parties remembered or thought it necessary to do so, or which any reasonable man would have taken for granted. For instance, if a man builds a house for another, although the contract says nothing about it, it is taken for granted the house will be fit to live in. Terms may also be implied by custom or by statute (such as the Sale of Goods Act 1893 and the Supply of Goods (Implied Terms) Act 1973). Some terms may be excluded by an express clause to that effect in the contract.

Import specie point A term used in the **foreign exchange market** when referring to a country still on the **gold standard**. Depending on ruling exchange rates, it was often more advantageous to settle debts to that country in **Gold** rather than in any particular currency. The point at which this occurred was known as the import specie point. ◊ **Rate of exchange**.

Importers' entries of goods When a ship arrives in port, details of the **goods** on board must be entered on a special form by the importers involved, who then pay the appropriate duty. The form is sent to the Customs and Excise office and compared to the master's report, after which the goods may have to be examined. If the form is cleared it serves as a **warrant** allowing the goods out of Customs charge or to a bonded warehouse for duty-free storage. ◊ **Bonded goods** ◊ **Single market**.

Imports Goods or services purchased from other countries, involving the use of foreign exchange. Imports, like **exports**, may be visible or invisible. ◊ **Invisible trade**. Duty rates on goods vary according to the type of product and the nature of any existing agreement with the supplying country. ◊ **Single market**. Tendencies to impose restrictions are countered both by fear of reprisals by the other country, by particular trading treaties and by the **General Agreement on Tariffs and Trade**. Some goods may be the subject of quotas, i.e. only a certain quantity may be imported in any one year. All nations have a list of goods, the importing of which is prohibited. Such lists vary widely from country

to country and contain items ranging from nuclear weapons (USA) to gooseberry bushes (Eire). ◊ **Common Market**.

Impressed stamps Certain documents must be stamped at a stamping office. Duty is paid and the document is then impressed with the official stamp. Examples include the **memorandum of association** of a **company**, and conveyances. ◊ **Stamp duty**.

Imprest Originally the name for a loan paid over in cash by the State to be used for specified official purposes and for no other. The recipient accounted for each payment out of the fund and the loan might then be topped up according to the amount expended. The term now denotes a particular system of accounting for **petty cash** within a business. Under the imprest system, the petty cashier receives a fixed float for sundry expenses over a certain period. At the end of that period, or when the float is exhausted, vouchers for all expenses will be presented and the expenditure reimbursed, theoretically returning the float to its original level. The person responsible for petty cash has little opportunity for misappropriation because the reimbursement depends on the production of the vouchers; this gives the employer a reasonable degree of control over sundry disbursements.

Impulse buying A term used to describe the very human tendency to spend first and think afterwards. It is often heartlessly exploited by the owners of large stores and **supermarkets**, where goods are displayed in such a way as to tempt customers to buy them irrespective of a real need for the particular goods and regardless of their ability to afford such purchases. ◊ **Advertising, persuasive**. Traders at holiday resorts tend to rely greatly on impulse buying for the larger part of their **turnover** and **profit**.

Imputation system The imputation tax system was introduced in April 1973, when considerable changes in the methods of collecting personal and corporation tax were made. The imputation system refers to company taxation in general and to **corporation tax** in particular. Previously distributions of company income were discouraged by two factors: (1) corporation tax was payable on total profit and (2) in addition, income tax was payable on the part of profit distributed as dividend (◊ **Dividend restraint**). The imputation system replaced this old practice by abolishing the income tax payable on distributions of profit and introducing two-tier corporation tax, which distinguished between the corporation tax on dividends (known as **advance corporation tax** and payable immediately) and the mainstream corporation tax, payable on the balance of profit not distributed. The tax applies to all profits in a financial year. However, because dividends are paid at a different time and may be paid in a different tax year the rate on the dividends can differ from that on the mainstream profit. Although the abolition of the extra income tax removed the barrier to dividend declarations this was compensated for by the higher rate of corporation tax itself, which left less cash available for dividends. ◊ **Taxation of profits.**

In pari delicto 'Equally guilty', used with reference to illegal contracts. Where persons are not *in pari delicto*, the less-guilty party may be able to recover monies paid in spite of the fact that the contract was illegal ◊ **Contract, illegal**.

Incentive scheme A scheme, usually found in industry but not unknown in commerce, whereby employees are offered benefits (usually monetary) as a reward for increasing efficiency by their own efforts. Where the non-productive work-force is concerned, i.e. persons whose efficiency cannot be directly related to output, the incentive may take the form of a special bonus determined by overall profit. Most incentive payments are now covered by **Productivity deals** or agreements. ◊ **Piece-work** ◊ **Options to purchase shares**.

Inchmaree clause A marine insurance clause, so called after a ship of that name, covering risks which are not necessarily 'perils of the sea', e.g. damage to cargo while in harbour.

Inchoate instrument A term used with reference to **bills of exchange**. Where a blank signed piece of paper is given to another party to be made into a bill of exchange, that other party may fill in all necessary details, but he must do so within a reasonable time. Similarly, when a bill is in any way incomplete, the holder may make good the omissions, and provided this is done within a reasonable time the bill will be enforceable against prior signatories.

Income and expenditure account This, as its name suggests, is an account of income received and amounts expended by an organization or a person over a given period. It is similar in form to a **profit and loss account** but with the emphasis on cash, rather than credit, transactions. It would probably ignore such matters as **accrued charges**, **depreciation** and adjustments for that portion of **payments in advance** for which the benefit is outstanding.

The term also has a more exact meaning when applied to non-trading organizations which need, for official or other purposes, to produce a periodic statement of their various transactions but are not covered by the requirements of the Companies Act or the demands of the Inland Revenue to present audited statements of profit or loss.

Income bonds Bonds or investments in **unit trusts** where the prospect offered is a relatively high annual income, not merely capital growth. In contrast, certain investments are made with a view to the future realizable value (i.e. they look for capital growth rather than immediate income benefit). These are called capital bonds. ◊ **Capital gains tax** ◊ **Capital profit** ◊ **Paper profit** ◊ **Investment income surcharge** ◊ **Growth stocks**.

Income tax **Direct taxation** levied on all persons receiving an income above a minimum threshold. The threshold varies and is mainly determined by the current level of **personal relief**; the latter depends on the status of the taxpayer, i.e. whether married or single, or above a certain age. After all permissible deductions have been made the balance of income is taxed at a rate fixed by the Chancellor of the Exchequer. This rate is usually on a sliding scale with higher taxes for higher incomes.

The basic tax rate, i.e. that applying to the main section of the sliding scale, is known as the **standard rate** of tax. This is the rate frequently though not always used when tax is deducted by a payer at source. This can mean that the tax then paid is incorrect – the recipient may be liable at a different rate or, if below the threshold, may not be liable to tax at all.

The necessary adjustments are made by direct payment to the Inland Revenue or by a refund from them. The need for any adjustment will appear from the annual return of income that must be completed by all potential taxpayers. ◊ **Tax return, personal**.

Income tax does not apply to wealth or expenditure. These latter fields are covered by other forms of taxation. Expenditure is indirectly taxed in the form of **value added tax**, which replaced the old **purchase tax**. Wealth can also be taxed where a wealth tax exists. This is projected for the United Kingdom but not yet enacted. Instead levies may be made when wealth is transferred from one person to another by way of gift or legacy. ◊ **Inheritance tax**. Levies are also made on increases in wealth through **capital gains tax**. ◊ **Income tax allowances** ◊ **Tax avoidance** ◊ **Tax evasion** ◊ **Tax haven**.

Income tax allowances These are various deductions from income which can be claimed when calculating tax payable. The claim is made by taxpayers when completing their annual tax return. ◊ **Tax return, personal** ◊ **Allowance, mortgage interest** ◊ **Allowance, personal** ◊ **Allowances, sundry**.

Income tax: code number Employed persons taxed under PAYE each receive a tax code number. This is determined by the allowances against tax to which the person is entitled, those with more allowances receiving higher tax code numbers. When the tax payable is calculated by the employer, he first deducts from the gross wage or salary an amount known as free pay. This figure is taken from tables supplied by the Inland Revenue and the appropriate amount will be shown against the employee's code number. A second table provided then shows tax payable on the balance remaining after deduction of free pay. This tax will be at the prevailing rate.

Income tax, independent taxation Until 1990 husband and wife were treated as a single taxable unit, the **annual return** being the responsibility of the husband who in addition to claiming a marriage allowance could also, if his wife had her own earned income, claim an additional personal allowance against that income. In 1990 the system changed with the introduction of independent taxation. Each spouse is now entitled to a full **personal allowance** plus, of course, any other of the allowances specified in the **annual return** to which they are also entitled. There is additionally, where the man and wife are living together, a married couple's allowance. Though initially claimable by the husband it may, if he so agrees, be transferred to his wife, or alternatively it may be divided so that each takes a half. In calculating tax payable, income must be allocated between husband and wife by reference to whoever is beneficially entitled to that income. Where income derives from jointly-owned assets then it is divided either equally or, if a special declaration is made, according to the respective interest of each partner.

Income tax, reduced rates Taxable income is not always taxed in full at the **standard rate**. Prior to 1970–71 UK taxpayers could claim what was known as reduced rate relief. This in effect was taxation on a sliding scale and reduced the burden of taxation in the lower income brackets. Reduced rates were only applicable to a small portion of income, e.g. the first £360 of taxable income, after which all earnings were subject to tax at the standard (or higher) rate. For many years there were three levels of reduced rates of tax. In 1964–5 the number was lowered to two; in 1970–71 the scheme was abandoned and the benefits incorporated into personal allowances, which were increased. ↻ **Allowance, personal**. Reduced rate relief was reintroduced in 1978–9, when a lower rate of tax was applied to the first small slice of income. This was abolished in the 1980 budget.

A reduced rate band was again introduced in the tax year 91/92 being one lower band of 20 per cent which was extended in 92/93 and, according to present government policy, will continue to be extended until it effectively becomes the standard rate of tax. This may, however, prove to be more of a pious hope than a realistic expectation.

Income tax, repayment of If a person has over-paid tax he can claim repayment at any time within the following six years. Claim forms are available from the Inland Revenue. Persons who do not pay tax may need to claim repayment when they receive **dividends** or **interest** from which tax has already been deducted (tax is deducted from nearly all interest and dividend payments).

Income tax: self-assessment This is a system of collecting income tax whereby the onus is on the taxpayers to calculate the amount due in a particular financial year. It is intended to introduce this system for self-employed persons into the UK from 1996. It will replace the existing method of issuing taxation demands based on the income declared in the annual **tax return**. This latter system, known as the 'preceding year basis', has the effect that tax is accounted for in the year following that in which the income was earned.

Incorporation A company has no legal existence until properly incorporated according to provisions set out in the **Companies Act**. These include the filing of the prescribed documents (see **company, formation of**) and the payment of statutory fees and stamp duties. When the Registrar of Companies is satisfied that the legal requirements have been complied with he will issue a certificate of incorporation. The company then becomes a legal 'person' in its own right.

A **public company** must satisfy more stringent conditions than a private company and additionally cannot commence business until it has satisfied the Registrar that certain other requirements have been met, e.g. that share capital has been subscribed and paid for up to the minimum necessary for the company to qualify as a public company. ◊ **Company: commencement of business**.

Increase of capital A **company** may increase its **authorized capital** where the **articles of association** so permit. Additional **stamp duty** will be payable. Notice must be given to the Registrar of Companies within fourteen days. If the articles do not permit an increase, they themselves may be altered.

Indemnity An agreement whereby one person agrees to make good any loss suffered by a party to a **contract** to which he himself is a stranger. For example, A buys goods from B on credit, C states that he will see that B is paid. C indemnifies B – he takes primary liability, unlike a **guarantor**, who takes secondary liability, e.g. C pays B if A does not. The most common contracts of indem-

nity are found in the field of **insurance**. An insurer effectively indemnifies the person taking out a policy against loss of a specified asset. In this instance, however, the agreement is to reinstate the property insured, i.e. put the claimant in the same position, as far as possible, as he was before. No definite sum of cash is involved but the amount for which the asset is insured is usually the cost of replacing it. In a time of inflation it is necessary to increase the sum assured in line with rising **replacement costs** and some insurance companies provide for this in their policies. Whatever the total sum insured, the insurer will only make good the actual loss, provided there is no question of under-insurance; in that case only a proportion of the loss will be made good. ◊ **Average clause**.

Indent An order stating goods required. This term is not in common use in the United Kingdom but is sometimes applied to written orders in the international trade market.

Indenture A form of **deed**, but different from a deed poll in having serrated rather than straight edges. There were originally two parts of an indenture written on one piece of parchment, which was afterwards torn in half and one half given to each party. The impossibility of matching the tear was a guard against forgery.

Index-linked When attached to a recurring payment or receipt or to a fixed sum payable or receivable at some future date, this means that the payment or sum is to be adjusted when the time for payment arrives. The adjustment will accord with movements in a specified **index number** – usually the **retail price index** – in order that the real value of the sum originally agreed is maintained; e.g. an index-linked pension of £100 will rise to £120 if there is a 20 per cent rise in the index to retail prices.

Index-linked National Savings Certificates Nearly all **National Savings Certificates** are now index-linked. There are various issues still in circulation because if those now eligible for redemption are retained beyond the relevant date they continue to earn interest. The first to be issued was the Retirement Issue of 1975 which, as the name suggests, was available only to pensioners. From 1980 onwards index-linked issues have been available to everyone, although there is a limit to the number of certificates that may be purchased in each issue. The attraction of index-linking is that the capital value of the certificate is linked to the retail price index so that, on redemption, the amount paid back is, in real rather than nominal terms, the same as that invested.

More recent certificates carry the process of index-linking a stage further by adding interest earned to the capital sum at the end of each twelve months from the date of purchase and applying the indexing to the higher sum. As certificates must usually be retained for five years before redemption this means that each year's interest is automatically index-linked in the same manner as the capital sum. Both the interest earned and the capital gain are free of tax.

There is also a reinvestment facility by which, after the normal redemption date, certificates not redeemed can be transferred into Reinvestment Certificates which earn index-linked interest on a monthly basis. There is a maximum holding of Reinvestment Certificates.

Savings Certificates can be cashed in by application to the Department of Na-

tional Savings on forms supplied by post offices. Part only of a certificate may be redeemed and a balance certificate will be issued. Certificates cashed before redemption will earn a lower rate of interest, but receipts from wholly or partly cashed certificates are not subject to income or capital gains tax.

Index-linked policies Assurance policies which are specifically linked to a particular **index**, e.g. the **retail price index**. This means that the amount payable on maturity is continually revised so that the sum assured has a constant **real value**, e.g. if the assured sum is £2,000 index-linked then if, over the period covered, prices increase by 50 per cent, the sum assured automatically increases to £3,000. The principle of index-linking has particular application to certain **pension** plans. Civil service pensions, by being index-linked, assure the beneficiary of a pension constant in real terms, i.e. it will not be reduced because of a fall in the value of money.

Index of members In addition to the register of members (◊ **Share register**), every company with more than fifty members must keep an alphabetical index to that register. This must be maintained constantly and be kept at the same place as the register of members. If that register is already in alphabetical order, then the necessity of providing an index is waived.

Index number A number which measures relative changes. It may be used with reference to price or quantity or anything which can be stated numerically. One specified point of time or quantitative level will be taken as a base (usually given the value of 100) and each subsequent measurement will be expressed as a number above or below this figure, to be determined by the percentage change during the interval; e.g. the statement that the index of the price of barley is 158 (base year 1965) means that since that year barley has risen in price by 58 per cent.

In commercial practice the most common index is the **retail price index**, which is intended to show movements in the general cost of living. This particular index is a weighted index, i.e. attention is paid to the fact that the effect of a rise in the price of one item may be greater, or less, than a rise in the price of another. This is because the two items represent quite different proportions of total living expenses; e.g. in an economy where rice is the staple diet a rise in the price of rice will have a far greater effect on the cost of living than an equally steep rise in the price of jam. Other well-known indexes are the **Financial Times Ordinary Share Index**, the Wholesale Price Index, the Index of Wages and Salaries and various volume indexes connected with imports and exports. ◊ **Index-linked**.

Indirect expenses Expenses incurred in producing **goods** or services though not attributable to any particular item produced. The distinction between indirect and **direct expenses** is important in **costing**. ◊ **Overhead expenses**.

Indirect labour Labour needed in producing **goods** or services though not attributable to any particular item produced. The costs of administration are one example. The distinction between indirect and **direct labour** is important in **costing**.

Indirect taxation That part of total tax revenue collected by means of a levy attached to expenditure on goods or services. The present principal source of indirect taxation is **value added tax**, but others include duties payable on imports and certain home-produced goods. ◊ **Customs and excise** ◊ **Excise duty**. Prior to the introduction of VAT, indirect taxation included **purchase tax**, which was levied at varying rates depending on the nature of the goods. Purchase tax was levied on goods produced for the home market and was paid over by the manufacturer; VAT is levied on the value added at each stage in the provision of goods and services for the consumer and is collected from all parties concerned, from the manufacturer to the retailer. It is essentially a sales tax in that it is only payable when goods are sold and not, as with purchase tax, when the goods are made and passed to the retailer for sale; in the latter case the State receives the tax whether or not the goods are ever sold. ◊ **Cascade tax**.

Inducement to break a contract Generally speaking, if a person induces another to break a contract he is committing an actionable offence. In this context to induce is to bring pressure to bear or to offer a bribe to effect the breaking of the contract. There is nothing to prevent one person persuading another to terminate a contract in a lawful manner. The position when the party seeking to bring about the termination is a trade union has long been problematic, as trade unions have been virtually immune from legal action since the Taff Vale case. This immunity has been modified by recent **employment legislation** and unions who induce members to withdraw their labour without first having taken the steps required by law may now find themselves liable in a civil action for damages. ◊ **Duress** ◊ **Secondary picketing** ◊ **Closed-shops**.

Industrial and Commercial Finance Corporation ◊ **Investors in industry**.

Industrial artists and designers Designers involved with visual communication in industry: graphic artists, product and engineering designers or illustrators.

Industrial Artists and Designers, Society of This was formed in 1930, and is the only professional association of designers in Great Britain. Its objects are to preserve standards of performance and professional conduct and integrity, and also to provide educational facilities and information regarding the profession. There is a code of professional conduct.

Industrial bank ◊ **Finance company**.

Industrial espionage This has particular reference to the present age of increasing technology and the growth of the **multi-national corporations**. It is also a by-product of free competition. It concerns nefarious attempts by one company to obtain access to unpublished information regarding another. This may be in the form of specialized production techniques, money-saving innovations in plant or in manning levels, privately commissioned market surveys or financial information that is not required by law to be revealed. The techniques of espionage run through the whole gamut of intelligence work from telephone or computer tapping to infiltration of the other company's workforce. There is no easy way of preventing such espionage, barring simple precautions like careful personnel vetting, good security systems and the use of shredding machines to dispose of vital documents after use. ◊ **Insider dealings**.

Industrial estate ◊ **Trading estates**.

Industrial life assurance At one time one of the few methods available to ordinary people for providing against old age, permanent disability, premature death or sudden future monetary needs was by making use of the **assurance** facilities arranged on the basis of door-to-door collection by certain **insurance** companies or **friendly societies**. The payment of a few pence each week could assure a certain sum at a future date. The need for this type of assurance has been partly replaced by the provision of various State benefits and has also been countered by better education in the use of banks and other financial institutions. However, the habit of small saving in this manner dies hard and there are still many schemes in operation. The major disadvantage to the public of this form of assurance is that high collection costs inevitably reduce the ratio of the amount paid out to the premiums collected. ◊ **National insurance** ◊ **Supplementary benefits**.

Industry ◊ **Extractive industry** ◊ **Construction industry** ◊ **Manufacturing industry**.

Infant ◊ **minor** ◊ **Contract: infant's**.

Inherent vice A term used with reference to the carriage of **Goods**. The carrier may not be liable for the goods he carries, if their nature makes them an exceptional risk, which is not obvious, and has not been made known to him. ◊ **Common carrier**.

Inheritance tax This was introduced to take effect from 18 March 1986. It replaces the levy on gratuitous transfers of property effective on the death of the donor previously governed by the rules of **capital transfer tax**.

Capital transfer tax applied to all gratuitous transfers of property by one individual during his lifetime and, subject to the various exemptions available (e.g. transfers totalling less than a given amount in one year, transfers between spouses, etc.), became due once the gift had been made. It was levied on a sliding scale and the value of the gift made was measured by the diminution in the estate of the donor.

On 18 March 1986 the taxation of lifetime gifts was abolished. From that date genuine transfers of property by way of gift are only taxable when the donor dies within seven years of the transfer. When the donor dies after three years but within the seven year period the rates of tax are reduced year by year.

Such chargeable gifts, together with all property passing on the death of the donor, are now subject to inheritance tax, which is similar in both structure and effect to the estate duty levy, which was discontinued on the introduction of CTT in 1974.

Inheritance tax will also apply to all gifts made during the deceased's lifetime when he has retained some beneficial interest. In that case the value of the asset for tax purposes will be its value at the date on which the donor's interest ceases, not the value at the time the gift was originally made.

Generally speaking, the tax will be borne by the estate of the deceased and will not be levied on the beneficiaries or recipients of those gifts made within the seven year period, or otherwise brought into charge.

The tax will be charged on a sliding scale and is not payable on estates of a gross value less than a substantial minimum figure. This starting figure for the application of tax may be varied from year to year.

Initial allowances ◊ **Capital allowances**.

Injunction A court may order someone to perform or not perform some action. This order is called an 'injunction' in England, and an 'interdict' in Scotland. Injunctions are often issued to prevent someone from continuing to act in a certain way, or in a manner harmful to someone else. ◊ **Damages**.

Inland bill A **bill of exchange** drawn and made payable within the United Kingdom, or drawn within the United Kingdom upon a resident therein.

Inland post This service applies to all postal packets carried by the **Post Office** in the United Kingdom and to most packets sent to the Irish Republic, the Isle of Man and the Channel Islands. Inland post covers letters, cards, parcels, newspapers and articles for the blind. Subject to reservations contained in the **Post Office Guide**, it also covers postal services to HM Forces based in the UK and to ships in a UK port. If there is doubt as to whether the ship has sailed, inland post will be charged but an additional payment may be due if the item has to be redirected overseas. ◊ **Inland post, letter service** ◊ **Inland post, parcel service**.

Inland post, letter service This covers letters, cards, railway letters, newspapers, air letters, small parcels (below maximum letter weight), articles for the use of the blind, etc. The basic charge is determined by whether the sender wishes to use first-class or second-class post, though for packets that are to be given special treatment, e.g. **registered post**, airway letters, **Royal Mail Special Delivery** packets, the sender must pay the first class basic charge together with the amount payable for the particular service. Articles for the use of the blind are not charged, provided they are not over-heavy or over-large, and are treated automatically as first class. If an item is posted unstamped it will be treated as second class and the addressee will be charged twice the second class rate.

The Post Office does not guarantee delivery, nor does it promise that packets will be delivered at any specific time. As a general rule, however, second class mail will be delivered one day later than first class and the greater part of first class mail is delivered on the day following its posting. If senders wish to guarantee delivery they may use the **recorded delivery** service; if they wish to guard against loss through non-delivery or damage they may use one of the services offered for this purpose, e.g. registered post, compensation fee, etc. In all such cases an additional charge is made. Compensation is automatically afforded to recorded delivery packets and those sent by **express delivery** or **Datapost** provided the sender has complied with the conditions laid down about packing, sealing, addressing, etc.

Certain items cannot be sent by post. These include obviously risky packets, e.g. those containing fresh edible goods which quickly perish and those which are dangerous to health or liable to spontaneous combustion. The list of prohibited items is quite long but the greater part is dictated by common sense. It is hardly surprising that the Post Office is not willing to carry high explosives or radioactive material. Neither is it surprising that in many such cases the sender is liable to prosecution. ◊ **Air letters** ◊ **Bulk posting** ◊ **Business reply service** ◊ **Franking machines** ◊ **Freepost** ◊ **Post Office Guide** ◊ **Private boxes and bags** ◊ **Redirection of post.**

Inland post, parcel service Subject to limits to size and weight and to the rules regarding prohibited items the **Post Office** will accept any properly packed parcel for delivery to any address in the United Kingdom. Special rates apply to Eire and the Channel Islands. The inland charge depends on the weight of the parcel; reduced rates may apply to parcels addressed to a destination within the delivery zone of the Post Office from which it is sent. These are known as local parcels. There are special facilities for regular bulk postings of parcels and there is also a **compensation fee parcel service** for insuring against loss or damage.

Inland waterways A system of canals, rivers and lochs, used both for commerce and pleasure. Inland waterway transport is governed by the British Waterways Board. The Board provides (1) storage accommodation and up-to-date handling equipment, (2) road transport fleets from depots and trans-shipment points, (3) a container service and (4) three independent docks equipped as trans-shipment points between ocean-going vessels and inland transport. These are: Weston Point Docks, Sharpness Docks and Gloucester Docks.

Inland waterway traffic consists largely of raw materials in specialized vessels (e.g. bulk liquids in tankers or coal in compartment craft). Trains of barges may be towed by one motorized vessel. Canal transport may be slow, but the routes are usually more direct. For instance, on the Caledonian Canal, the speed limit is 6 mph on the canals (about twenty miles) though there is no limit on the lochs which make up the remaining forty miles. By using the canal, ships are saved the long and perhaps difficult voyage round the north coast of Scotland. Locks are the canals' main drawback.

Inland Waterways Amenity Advisory Council This was set up by the Transport Act 1968 to advise the Waterways Board and the relevant Minister on the use of **inland waterways** for recreational purposes.

Inn Traditionally a place where a jovial character known as an innkeeper offers hospitality. Originally subject to the Innkeepers Act 1878, he was bound to supply food and accommodation for 'genuine and proper' customers and their horses. The Hotel Proprietors Act 1956 has altered and clarified the position. Nowadays an establishment is either a hotel or not. Whether it is called an inn is irrelevant. A hotel is defined as 'an establishment held out by the proprietor as offering food, drink and, if so required, sleeping accommodation, without special **contract**, to any traveller presenting himself who appears able and willing to pay a reasonable sum for the services and facilities provided and who is in fit state to be received'. The proprietor cannot refuse accommodation without a reasonable excuse, for instance that he has no available rooms, or that the applicant is drunk or unclean (illness is no ground for refusal). If he does unlawfully refuse, he may be both civilly and criminally liable, as he may be if he charges excessive prices. He must provide food within a reasonable time and on payment, unless he has none in the house.

He is liable for the goods of his guests as if he were an insurer, unless the loss is due to an 'act of God, an act of the Queen's enemies, or negligence of the guest'. Proprietors often post notices to guests that goods of value should be deposited for safe keeping, but these notices have no legal effect and do not diminish the proprietor's responsibility. As far as damage is concerned, the innkeeper's liability once depended on his negligence. The 1956 Act increased his responsibility, but it may still be limited to a total of £100 per guest. This limitation only applies if the appropriate notice (as prescribed by the Act) is displayed. His liability is not limited when the notice is not displayed or when the loss or damage is occasioned by negligence of himself or his servants. The proprietor is not now liable for loss or damage except where the traveller was staying the night and the loss and damage occurred during the period beginning with the preceding and ending with the following midnight of the period for which the traveller was a guest. The proprietor is no longer liable for cars, bicycles, horses, etc. – except under the ordinary law of negligence.

The proprietor has a **lien** on the guest's goods for money owed.

Input tax In the VAT system, input tax is the tax charged to the person on whom a VAT claim is made; it can be deducted from **Output tax** by VAT-registered persons in arriving at the amount due to Her Majesty's **Customs and Excise**. ◊ **Value added tax**.

Inscribed stock Certain **stock**, usually government stock, may be 'inscribed'. This means that certificates are not issued to stockholders but their names are inscribed in a record book. When ownership is transferred, certain formalities must be completed before one name is erased and another put in its place. This type of stock is not very common, partly because it is so difficult to transfer.

Insider dealings These are dealings in stocks and shares by an individual who has access to special knowledge of facts which might influence the value of those shares. Such dealings have been expressly prohibited since the Companies Act 1980, the provisions of which were re-stated in the 1985 Companies Act and added to in both the 1936 Financial Services Act and the 1989 Companies Act.

Such knowledge may have been obtained by way of the individual's connection with the company or because he obtained information in the course of contemplating a take-over of the company. Dealings by individuals obtaining knowledge through persons in these two categories are also now prohibited.

Generally speaking, the ban on dealings by individuals connected with the company applies only to transactions within a period of six months after that connection has been terminated. The use of information obtained under other headings for dealings is banned for as long as that information remains unpublished, i.e. until the possession of the knowledge ceases to be confined solely to the individual originally obtaining it.

The prohibition on insider dealings extends not only to transactions on a recognized Stock Exchange but also to off-market trading. In addition to the statutory regulations the Stock Exchange itself operates a code of conduct to which directors of listed companies must ad-

here. A director must not deal in securities of his own company, or of any other company, when, by virtue of his office, he is privy to information of a price-sensitive nature. Furthermore a director should never deal in the shares of his own company without first giving notice, and obtaining the consent of, the company chairman; and should not buy or sell such shares within the period of two weeks preceding the announcement of annual or half-yearly results – unless personal financial circumstances of an exceptional nature make a sale necessary. A list of directors' dealings in the shares of their company must be circulated at board meetings. Restrictions applying to a director in the matter of share dealing extend to persons immediately connected to him, and, so far as is feasible, the board should ensure that the same code is observed by employees of the company generally.

The legislation imposes severe penalties on individuals contravening the sections concerned with insider dealing. Protection is, however, afforded to persons such as liquidators, trustees, jobbers, etc., acting in the normal course of business. It is also given to individuals who, though possessing sensitive information, buy or sell shares through necessity, i.e. without being motivated by prospect of gain, e.g. directors taking up qualification shares or holders selling to avoid financial embarrassment. The exceptions are strictly defined and any individual attempting to use them for personal profit will be liable to prosecution.

Insolvency A person or organization is insolvent when he or it is unable to pay debts when they become due. Insolvency is not the same as **bankruptcy** or **liquidation** of a **company** (though they may follow from it): a very rich man can be insolvent if his **assets** cannot be realized at the time he needs cash.

Insolvency Act 1986 This is essentially a consolidating Act which replaces the greater part of previous legislation relating both to the winding-up of companies, whether insolvent or not, and the administration of the affairs of individuals who become insolvent or bankrupt. In particular it replaces the Insolvency Act 1985 which itself replaced the Bankrupcy Act 1914 which had long been the principal Act relating to the bankruptcy of individuals and partnerships.

The new legislation, while generally tightening up the law as it applies to the insolvency of an individual or a company, also attempts to provide for less draconian alternatives to bankruptcy and liquidation. These include the **voluntary arrangement**, available to individuals and companies, and the **administration order** available to companies. Whatever procedure is selected, the Act provides that only an authorized **insolvency practitioner** can be appointed to supervise the necessary processes. In the case of companies the Act also makes available a greater range of sanctions against directors who by negligence, not necessarily fraudulent, may have contributed to the downfall of the company. Directors and ex-directors who can be shown to have acted negligently may find that not only do they face disqualification from participating in the management of companies for extended periods, but may also be called upon to give financial compensation for the losses arising from their negligence.

Insolvency Practitioner A person usually drawn from one of the professional bodies who has been authorized by the Department of Trade and Industry as a fit and proper person to conduct the winding-up of a limited company. Those so recognized tend to deal exclusively with company liquidations and also with other roles reserved to them, such as receivers, administrators under the Insolvency Act and trustees in bankruptcy. No person other than an authorized insolvency practitioner is permitted to act in any of these capacities.

Inspection of affairs ◊ **Investigations, company**.

Instalments, delivery and payment Where in a **contract** the promise is divisible, that is to say, delivery or payment is to be by instalments, problems arise from a failure to keep up these instalments. In the case of non-delivery, the court will generally look to the intention of the defaulting party. If it is obvious that he intends to continue to fail to deliver the instalments, then the case will be treated as one of breach of contract. If there is merely a failure on one instalment in part or whole then, other things being equal, the complaining party can only hope for **damages**. In the case of payment, the position has been clarified by various statutes. ◊ **Hire purchase** ◊ **Credit sale agreements** ◊ **Conditional sale agreements**.

Instant Term used in commerce, usually abbreviated to inst., referring to the present month.

Institute cargo clauses A **marine insurance** term for clauses included in policies to cover exceptional risks. The institute referred to is the Institute of London Underwriters.

Institute of Accounting Staff Founded in 1974, through the endeavours of its parent body the Chartered Association of **Certified Accountants**, this institute provides a recognized qualification and representative body for accounting staff employed in industry or in the offices of practising accountants. Membership is restricted to those who have passed, or been exempted from, the qualifying examination and who are not only judged suitable by the Institute but have also worked in the accounting field for at least three years. There is a membership fee and members may add the letters MIAS after their names.

Institutional investors A collective term for organizations which invest large sums of money in both **government securities** and the private sector, particularly through the **Stock Exchange**. The emergence in recent years of so many organizations representing other people's savings (e.g. pension funds, **unit trusts**, trade union funds) together with the steady increase in **insurance** companies has tended to make institutional investors a major force in the stock market; they own a high proportion of total available shares and securities. Very often it is their vote that determines the future of many a private or public enterprise. They normally employ specialists in the investment field to keep a careful eye on the market and the **portfolios** they hold with the object of maximizing benefits. Their effective power was considerably reinforced by the Trustee Investment Act 1961, which gave wider powers to trustees of other people's money to invest in quoted shares of **public companies**. ◊ **Investment portfolio** ◊ **Quoted investments**.

Insurable interest To insure any property or insure against any particular event, one must have an insurable interest, i.e. must stand to lose from the destruction of the property or from the event. In life **assurance** the interest must exist at the time the policy is made; in **marine insurance** it must exist at the time of the loss; in **fire insurance** and general **insurance**, it must exist at the time of the loss and usually also at the time of the policy, particularly where the insurance of buildings is concerned.

Insurance The payment of a sum of money by one person to another on the understanding that in specified circumstances the second person will make good any loss suffered by the first. ◊ **Fire insurance** ◊ **Marine insurance** ◊ **Average clause**.

Insurance broker This is a person employed to negotiate a contract of **insurance**. He is an agent for both parties but a principal for the purpose of receiving payment from the insured and may have a **lien** on the policy for unpaid premiums. The insurance broking profession has been restructured in recent years. The Insurance Brokers (Registration) Act 1977 led to the establishment of a supervisory body with statutory responsibilities, the **Insurance Brokers Registration Council**.

The Financial Services Act 1986 and the general reorganization of the market in financial services led to a number of substantial changes within the insurance industry. Any insurance agent, whether a broker or a more general financial advisor, must now make it apparent to all potential clients whether he acts in an independent capacity or as the tied agent of a particular company. If an independent advisor then he or she will be able to direct the client towards the provider who best serves the client's interests and may choose Company A for one type of insurance and Company B for another. As the scope of advice is likely to include life assurance and general financial recommendations the independent advisor is, by the provisions of the Financial Services Act, obliged to obtain recognition by one of the new self-regulatory organizations and abide by their rule books or, provided certain conditions obtain, become a member of the IBRC which, as a recognized professional body, will provide the authorization needed.

A tied adviser, one who sells the products of only one company may or may not belong to the IBRC and be bound by its rule book, but the fact that the adviser is an agent for one company only must be made abundantly clear to anybody with whom he or she transacts business. Whether or not the adviser needs to obtain authorization under the provisions of the Financial Services Act will depend on the nature of other services offered. Different rules apply to brokers registered at **Lloyd's**.

Insurance Brokers Registration Council A statutory body set up in consequence of the Insurance Brokers Registration Act 1977 with the object of providing a central register of insurance brokers, both individual and corporate, and generally acting as the supervisory body for the profession of insurance broking. Any person advertising himself as an insurance broker must be registered with the Council.

The role of the Council was broadened by the Insurance Brokers Registration Council (Conduct of Investment Business) Rules 1988. These were made necessary by the Council becoming a **recognized professional body** under the Financial Services Act. In addition to the initial code of conduct drawn up by the Council further rules have been made necessary by the provisions of that Act. Insurance brokers generally do not need to be registered with a self regulating organization or directly with the Securities and Investments Board if the amount of investment business in which they engage is incidental to their main activities; authorization by the IBRC as a recognized professional body suffices. Where, however, the investment business becomes a major contributor to turnover, the firm itself will need to become a member of FIMBRA or an equivalent SRO.

The code of conduct drawn up by the IBRC is comprehensive and, although it does not have the force of law, adherence to it on the part of brokers is demanded as a condition of continued membership. Members disregarding the code risk disciplinary action and, in serious cases, deletion from the register – which prevents them from advertising their services in insurance broking. To ensure compliance the Council operates an investigating committee to consider complaints received and a disciplinary committee to take appropriate action where investigation shows this to be necessary or desirable. Additionally members who, by the nature of their business, are also registered with FIMBRA will need to abide by the stringent requirements of that body and may be subject to periodic inspections by FIMBRA representatives.

The Council is also charged with ensuring that all members are covered by professional indemnity insurance sufficient to cover any claim that might be brought by an injured client. The Council discharges this obligation by insisting that members obtain cover up to a specified multiple of total brokerage. Each broker must provide evidence to the Council of adequate indemnity cover on each occasion such a policy is due for renewal. The Council may, if it so wishes, request sight of the policy or make direct inquiries of the relevant insurer.

In cases where indemnity cover proves insufficient, the Council has power to make such grants as it deems necessary.

Insurance premium What the insured agrees to pay to the insurer annually. It is payable on a stated date though a number of **days of grace** are normally allowed.

Intangible assets An accounting term for those unseen assets which have a value to the business and perhaps also a saleable value, e.g. **goodwill**, **patents**, **trademarks**, **copyright**, etc. These are sometimes called invisible assets, but should be distinguished from **fictitious assets**. ◊ **Brand values**.

Intelpost A high-speed method of transmitting facsimiles of documents electronically between various Intelpost centres, both in the UK and overseas. The service is operated by the Post Office but senders with their own facilities may transmit directly to PO Intelpost centres and will be billed accordingly by the Post Office. At the destination the document copy may be collected – notification of arrival having been given to the addressee by the Intelpost centre – or may be delivered by special messenger. Details of the service and the relevant charges can be obtained by telephoning Freefone Intelpost or by consulting the nearest post office. ◊ **Facsimile**.

Inter-dealer brokers With the reorganization of the Stock Exchange and the establishment of **market-markers**, **gilt-edged market-markers** and dual capacity firms to operate alongside the traditional dealers and stockbrokers, a further category of business has been introduced. This is the inter-dealer broker. An IDB is a company that may be admitted as a corporate member of the Stock Exchange. It is confined to providing dealing facilities between market-makers both in gilt-edged and other securities and is not permitted to deal directly with the public. All companies acting as IDBs are closely supervised by the Bank of England, which will need to approve any linking by merger or otherwise of an IDB with another type of business entity operating in the financial market.

Interdict Scottish term for **injunction**.

Interest The amount paid by a borrower to a lender in payment for a loan. Interest may be simple or compound. **Simple interest** is a fixed rate on a stated sum. The same amount is paid or accumulated each year irrespective of the amount borrowed, for instance £100 lent at 5 per cent simple interest would earn £5 a year. If the interest were not paid when due, it would not itself earn interest. But if a sum is invested at **compound interest** and the interest is allowed to accumulate, the interest is calculated each year on capital plus interest already accumulated.

Interest is normally stated at a fixed rate per cent per annun. If money is borrowed at 5 per cent interest, then the borrower must repay £5 for each year of the loan in addition to the capital sum. This is often stated as £5 per cent. In certain contracts there is an important difference between nominal interest and real interest. This always applies when repayment is to be made in instalments starting within a period of less than one year. Examples are **hire purchase** contracts and bank **personal loans**. If £1,000 is borrowed for one year at 10 per cent and the loan is repayable by monthly instalments beginning in one month's time, then the real interest is considerably more than 10 per cent. Although only £100 interest is to be paid, the average amount outstanding over the period will be not £1,000 but £500 and the true rate of interest is 100/500, i.e. 20 per cent. ◊ **Moneylender** ◊ **Consumer Credit Act 1974**.

Interest cover Similar to **dividend cover**, it relates to the number of times that the total fixed interest payable can be met out of the current income of a company or other organization. The 'break-even' point would be where income before tax is exactly equal to the total fixed interest payable before tax. ◊ **Capital gearing** ◊ **Fixed-interest securities** ◊ **Price-earnings ratio**.

Interest on calls Interest is payable on **calls in arrear**, though only if the **articles of association** of a **company** so provide.

Interest on debts ◊ **Moneylender**. The Law Reform (Miscellaneous Provisions) Act 1934 states that **interest** on debts recovered at law, or interest on **damages**, may be allowed by the court, over the period between the date when the cause of action arose and the judgment date. The Act does not apply to interest on interest, or to interest already agreed, or to the dishonour of **bills of exchange** (see the Bills of Exchange Act 1882). Where there is no agreement to pay interest, it may still be payable (1) where there is a trade custom that interest should be paid, (2) on bills of exchange – normally at 5 per cent, (3) in **contracts** of **indemnity**, and of **guarantee** where

the guarantor has paid the debt, (4) on **judgment debts** or **arbitration** awards – normally at 4 per cent, and (5) in any situation where the court thinks interest should be paid, over the period from cause of action to judgment.

Interest or no interest ◊ **Policy proof of interest**.

Interest out of capital The Companies Act 1948 prohibited distributions to members out of capital except in one limited instance: where subscribed capital was for the construction of works and no profit was being earned, then interest on that capital could be paid out of capital funds, provided that the articles so allowed and permission from the Department of Trade and Industry was obtained. This limited power was abolished by the Companies Act 1980.

Interest paid by companies The Companies Act 1967 stated that annual accounts must show details of **interest** payable by **companies**, distinguishing between (1) **bank loans** and **bank overdrafts**, and loans repayable within five years by instalments or otherwise, and (2) all other loans.

Interests in subsidiaries not consolidated An accounting term for the **value** of holdings in **subsidiary companies**, where the accounts of the subsidiaries are not consolidated when group accounts are presented. Subsidiaries may not be consolidated where, for example, the amounts involved are immaterial, or when the business of the subsidiary is quite different from that of the holding company. ◊ **Group accounts**.

Interim accounts Usually these are half-yearly accounts, probably unaudited, produced by a **company** or other association. ◊ **Final accounts** ◊ **Interim report**.

Interim dividend Dividends are paid on **shares** when the profits for the year are known. This may be some time after the end of the year. It is therefore common practice to declare part of the dividend, as it were on account, before the end of the year. This is known as an interim dividend. It will not normally be very large in relation to the total dividend, but it is an indication of the probable total dividend and the way business is going. The shareholder also receives some return earlier than he would otherwise do.

Interim receiver A person appointed by the court to protect the debtor's property until a **receiver** proper is appointed.

Interim report It is becoming increasingly common for **public companies** to issue interim reports to shareholders and the press with a view to keeping them informed of the progress of the business and preparing them for the final audited **annual report**. Such interim reports are normally small in format and give little more than the unaudited results of the first half-year, with comparative figures for the same period in the preceding year. Improvements over the comparative figures are, unless qualified, intended to suggest an upturn in the company's fortunes which will be revealed when the official annual report is eventually published. Interim reports are sometimes issued to support the declaration of an **interim dividend**. They could be necessary for such a purpose where lengthy **audits** delay the publication of the annual accounts until long after the end of the company's **financial year**. ◊ **Annual accounts**.

Internal audit The **audit** of a business conducted by the business itself on a continuous basis. This is part of the general system of **internal control**.

Internal check In-built systems of accounting control, part of the general system of **internal control**.

Internal control The agglomeration of systems and checking devices applied within a business organization to maximize accuracy in record keeping and minimize **fraud**.

International Air Transport Association (IATA) The aim of this association is to ensure that all international airline traffic moves with the maximum speed possible, consistent with both convenience and efficiency. It provides a means of expediting cooperation between various independent or national airlines by crossing language barriers and seeking to synchronize, as far as possible, the legal requirements of the various countries represented – as well as overcoming procedural differences. The latter has been approached by attempting to standardize documentation and handling procedures, particularly where hazardous cargo is involved. One innovation is the standard IATA **air waybill**. This makes the transfer of cargo between member countries far easier by enabling it to be routed from supplier to receiver without the difficulties that might otherwise be encountered in redocumentation during transfers from one airline to another. Problems have arisen, however, in the attempt of IATA to impose standard **tariffs** in that this is seen to be contrary to free competition. ◊ **Air freight** ◊ **Air traffic control** ◊ **Civil Aviation Authority**.

International Bank for Reconstruction and Development Often known as the World Bank, this was set up together with the **International Monetary Fund** by the **Bretton Woods Agreement** of 1944. Its purpose was to help finance post-war reconstruction by making loans to governments or guaranteeing outside loans. The loans are for fifteen- to twenty-five-year periods. The Bank is a specialized agency of the United Nations. About one-third of the funds come from Europe. Members must also be members of the International Monetary Fund. Two off-shoots of the Bank are the **International Finance Corporation** (1960) and the International Development Association (1961). Both of these place particular emphasis on aid to less-developed member countries, which have become more demanding in recent years.

International Finance Corporation (IFC) An offshoot of the **International Bank for Reconstruction and Development**, but whereas the latter tends to operate at government level the IFC was developed to provide aid for private investment projects, either by making or guaranteeing loans or by actual purchase of **equity**. Any equity involvement is, however, subject to a 25 per cent limit. Although its capital base is much smaller than that of the IBRD, it may borrow from that organization and reloan to private investors without the necessity of governmental approval. ◊ **Industrial and Commercial Finance Corporation**.

International Monetary Fund One of the fruits of the Bretton Woods Agreement in 1944. The Fund was formed in 1946 and began to operate in 1947. Its object is to maintain and stabilize **rates of exchange** and facilitate multilateral clearing systems, and also to eliminate unnecessary restrictions on foreign trade. It has the power to advance money to countries in **balance of payment** difficulties: it will supply a country with the currency it needs in return for that country's own currency. There is a repayment period of about five years. It also gives countries credit guarantees, that is, without actually lending, it agrees to lend, if asked. These facilities are obviously only available to member countries. Members finance the fund by making contributions according to an estimate of their means. The higher the contribution the higher the voting rights. The amount paid in is partly in gold and partly in the currency of the country. ◊ **Special drawing rights**.

Intervention price ◊ **Threshold price** ◊ **Common Agricultural Policy**.

Intrinsic value The **value** contained in the substance from which an article is produced as opposed to the stated value or price of the end product if put on sale in an open market. In commerce the term is often used in connection with metallic currency. ◊ **Face value** ◊ **Market value**.

Introduction A manner of offering new **shares** to the public through the machinery of the **Stock Exchange**. It is frequently used by existing companies which are issuing additional shares other than by a **rights issue** or a **bonus issue**, also by companies newly quoted on the Stock Exchange, where the object is to introduce the shares gradually into the market. The important factor is that the issue is made not by an open offer to the public but through the good offices of a respected **issuing house**, which agrees to introduce the shares as circumstances and the experience of that house dictate. In most instances it will still be necessary to issue a **prospectus**. ◊ **Offer for sale** ◊ **Placings**.

Inventory In US commercial usage an alternative name for **stock-in-trade** held by a business, whether in the form of raw materials or finished goods. ◊ **Stock control** ◊ **Stock valuation** ◊ **First in first out** ◊ **Last in first out**. It also has a more general meaning in as much as taking an inventory of a person's possessions involves the listing and valuing of them individually. This would be necessary on an intestacy or in a **bankruptcy**.

Inventory control ◊ **Stock control**.

Investigations, company The Department of Trade and Industry may carry out an investigation of a company for three quite distinct purposes. It may investigate the conduct of the company's business, it may look into the true ownership of shares and it may inquire into share dealings.

An inspection of affairs must be made by an inspector appointed by the Department if the court so orders. It may be made, at the discretion of the Department, if requested by a stated minimum proportion of members or by the company itself in general meeting. Such an inquiry is normally instigated if there is reason to believe that the business of the company is being carried out in a fraudulent or unlawful manner or that the company is behaving in a way prejudicial to any of its members.

In conducting the inquiry the inspector may call upon any officers of the company, including past officers, to give evidence upon oath and may have access

to all books and documents that appear relevant. When the investigation is complete a report will be made to the Department of Trade and Industry, which may publish that report in part or whole. The Department may, as a result of the report, order the company to be wound up and it may, where desirable, also instigate civil or criminal proceedings against officers of the company who have acted corruptly or abused the trust reposed in them by members.

The second type of investigation concerns the ownership of the company. If the Department believes there is good cause to do so, it may instigate an inquiry as to the true ownership of the company's shares. It must institute such an inquiry if required to do so by a stated minimum number of members. Prior to the 1981 Companies Act the company had a right to see any report on ownership arising from the inquiry, but that Act gave the Secretary of State power to withhold the report in part or in whole if he considers it to be in the interests of those concerned. Whilst the investigation is in progress the Secretary of State may impose restrictions on the transferability of shares.

The third type of investigation concerns dealings in shares. The Department of Trade and Industry has power to investigate dealings where it appears that directors have been entering into transactions in shares or options thereon prohibited by company law.

Investment allowance An allowance made to companies, for taxation purposes, in addition to the initial and annual **capital allowances**. It was not deducted from the **asset** in calculating these allowances and was used as an incentive to capital investment. It was discontinued in

1966 and was replaced by an **investment grant**.

Investment club A voluntary association of persons who pool their savings, or part of them, to build up an **investment portfolio**, which gives them a better return per person than each could expect separately. There is no fixed form for these organizations, and they vary considerably.

Investment company Any company which uses its funds to acquire **shares** or **securities** rather than engage in business on its own account. They are often referred to as **investment trusts**, but theoretically this is a misnomer, as **directors** of investment companies are not legally trustees and there is no trust instrument. True, securities are often held on trust for the benefit of others, but this is a different matter and takes the form of a trust proper rather than that of a company.

Investment grants Government grants which were available to industry for specified purposes, e.g. the purchase of machinery used for certain qualifying industrial processes. The grants were introduced by the Industrial Development Act 1966. They applied to the manufacturing industries but were also available for the purchase of computers, ships and hovercraft. The grants were of 20 per cent, but of 40 per cent in **development areas**. These rates were increased to 25 per cent and 45 per cent for expenditure between 1 January 1967 and 31 December 1968. Grants were discontinued on 27 October 1970.

Investment income In the context of business accounts this refers to income from outside investments, as opposed to income from normal trading operations.

Investment income surcharge This was introduced with the restructuring of personal taxation in 1973. Income from investments, if over a fixed minimum, was subjected to an additional tax of 15 per cent. This surcharge was abolished as and from the tax year 1983–4.

Investment Management Regulatory Organization (IMRO) This is one of the four **self-regulating organizations** currently recognized by the **Securities and Investments Board** as part of the necessary regulating system required to protect investors under the provisions of the Financial Services Act 1986. IMRO is particularly charged with regulating firms which are involved in the following activities: (1) managing the investments of others; (2) operating unit trusts and managing the assets of those trusts; (3) managing the investments of pension funds and investment trusts; (4) giving investment advice to institutional or corporate customers; or (5) acting as trustee of unit trusts.

Applicants for membership of IMRO must establish that they are, and will remain, fit and proper to undertake the business of the kind they propose. Once granted membership they must abide by the rulebook of IMRO and install systems within their own organization to ensure that all such rules are observed. They must also be prepared at all times to cooperate with any request from IMRO for any investigation it might wish to conduct. Each must also pay its share of the costs of IMRO through an annual subscription fee. No person or corporate body can engage in any of the activities overseen by IMRO without becoming a member of it, or of another SRO with equivalent authority, or by direct registration with the SIB itself. ▷

Life Assurance and Unit Trust Regulatory Organization ◊ Financial Intermediaries, Managers and Brokers Regulatory Association ◊ Securities and Futures Association.

Investment portfolio A collection of various **stocks**, **shares**, **bonds**, etc., held by persons or institutions investing money on behalf of others. They may be **unit trust** managers, **investment companies** or merely personal trustees. The spread of the investments contained in any particular portfolio will usually be determined by the deed or instrument appointing the managers or trustees or, in the latter instance, by trust law. The principal aim is to maximize the income of the fund on which the portfolio is based whilst at the same time preserving the initial value and attempting to increase it as far as possible without taking undue risks. Portfolio investment is the ideal form of group investment, because it enables investment to be spread over a number of different areas of risk, thereby hedging against possible losses; it also means that money can be frequently switched to take advantage of any profitable investment opportunity that arises in the short term. These advantages make it a good basis not only for unit trusts and **institutional investors** but also for humbler **investment clubs**. ◊ **Risk capital**.

Investment trusts Companies formed to invest the collected funds of shareholders. They invest in other companies, the spread of holdings being very wide. Investment trusts help small investors by giving them the benefit of spreading their risks and enjoying the advantages of experienced management. Investment is normally in quoted **securities**, but these companies will show interest in smaller or unquoted businesses where they are offered good security. They may also underwrite issues of shares or help to form specialist **finance companies**, perhaps with a view to investment in smaller businesses. Since the coming into force of the Financial Services Act 1986 all investment trusts are required to become members of the **Investment Management Regulatory Organization** (IMRO). ◊ **Investment company** ◊ **Unit trusts**.

Investments: in company accounts The 1981 Companies Act revised the treatment of investments held by a company in its published accounts. These accounts must now show, by way of note if not in the body of the accounts, (1) the total of listed investments, distinguishing between those listed on a recognized Stock Exchange and those listed elsewhere, (2) for investments listed on a recognized Stock Exchange, the current market value where this differs from book value and the aggregate Stock Exchange value where this differs from market value (e.g. where the company holds a controlling interest), and (3) unlisted investments – including those quoted on the **Unlisted Securities Market**. It is not necessary now, as it once was, to give the directors' estimate of the market value of unlisted investments.

There are additional rules requiring specified information where the company holds a **substantial shareholding** in another company by way of investment. For this purpose a substantial interest exists where the value of shares held exceeds 10 per cent of the equity. However, where it holds an interest that makes the second company an **associated company** or a **subsidiary company** of the first, then the disclosure provisions are more complex and reference should be made to the 1985 Companies Act, which has replaced that of 1981 and to ammendments contained in the 1989 Companies Act.

Investors' Compensation Scheme This scheme, set up in 1988 by the **Securities and Investments Board**, gives financial help to private investors who have lost money on the default of an investment firm fully authorized under the Financial Services Act, that is one which was a member of a self-regulatory organization or was otherwise authorized by the Securities and Investments Board.

If such a firm cannot meet its liabilities to investors and goes into liquidation, each investor is entitled to compensation from the Investors' Compensation Scheme. The amount recoverable on a validated claim is the whole amount up to £30,000 and 90 per cent of the next £20,000. This limits the amount of any claim to £50,000 and the amount recoverable to £48,000. Any difference, of course, can be claimed in the liquidation, though the scheme itself has first call upon the firm's assets.

Investors in Industry (3i) Originally the venture capital department of the Industrial and Commercial Finance Corporation set up in 1945 to aid small and medium-sized businesses in the UK, and owned and financed by the banks, including the **Bank of England**. Though this organization was allegedly independent of central government, the fact that the Bank of England was one of the principal members suggested that such independence might be more theoretical than factual. The same group, consisting of the central and clearing banks, now sponsors industrial investment through Investment in Industry, otherwise known as 3i.

Invisible assets ◊ Intangible assets.

Invisible trade The part of international trade which relates more to services rendered than to transactions in visible goods. Earnings from invisible trade are a very important factor in the UK **balance of payments**. This could be true of any other nation that relied heavily on other countries for both its food and raw materials. For many years the UK has covered a deficit on the visible portion of its international trading by earnings from services provided through its **insurance** companies, **shipping agents** and **banks**. These 'invisible exports' are effectively the bread and butter of the UK.

Invitation to treat This should be distinguished from an **offer**. When a person puts goods in his window or lists goods in a catalogue, with prices, he is not necessarily making an offer, but merely inviting the public to make offers to him. A shopkeeper is under no obligation to sell at the prices indicated in the window. Also, a person advertising an item for sale is obviously not bound to sell to every person who wishes to buy. He is in fact asking people to make him an offer even though he states a price.

Invoice The document tendered by a seller to a purchaser setting out details of goods or services supplied and the charge, together with any taxation applicable to the transaction. The invoice also usually indicates any discounts available to the purchaser, whether **trade discounts** or additional **cash discounts** for early settlement. It may also detail any particular **terms of trade** which apply to the transaction. ◊ **Advice note** ◊ **Pro-forma invoice**.

Invoice discounting The practice of obtaining money on the security of book debts (i.e. money to be received). A company which finds that it has too much **working capital** tied up in book debts may sell these debts to a **finance company**. This is known as invoice discounting. In a typical case, the finance company would agree to advance, say, 75 per cent of outstanding debts of a certain category. The security might be either **goods**, where the debtors are **hire purchase** debtors, or **bills of exchange** accepted by the borrower. The borrower would act as **agent** for the finance company, collecting the debts on its behalf and receiving the balance due on the debts purchased once the first 75 per cent has been repaid or the bill of exchange met.

The borrower is normally responsible for all bad debts and the finance company would charge a **commission**, depending on the financial state of the borrower. ⟡ **Factoring** ⟡ **Hire purchase finance**.

IOU This is a note indicating a debt owed by one party to another and has no other legal significance. It is normally a statement of liability signed by a debtor. It is not a **negotiable instrument**, needs no stamp and can be used as evidence of an **account stated** but not as proof of money lent.

Ironmonger A dealer in ironware and hardware, usually for domestic use.

Irredeemable debentures ⟡ Perpetual debentures.

Irrevocable and confirmed credit This is similar to an **irrevocable documentary acceptance credit**: it is a credit confirmed by a London bank, where the person opening the credit lives in a country that does not have a bank with an office in London. ⟡ **London acceptance credit**.

Irrevocable documentary acceptance credit A credit scheme to facilitate foreign trade. An overseas customer opens a credit in the London office of an overseas bank or with a London bank. The bank then gives the exporter an irrevocable **letter of credit**. The bank will then accept **bills of exchange** drawn on it by the exporter, when he presents his shipping documents. ⟡ **London acceptance credit**.

Issued capital The amount of **capital** actually issued by the **company**. ⟡ **Authorized capital**. Capital is issued normally in the form of shares. ⟡ **Share capital**. These may be **ordinary shares**, **preference shares**, etc. Issued capital is not the same thing as **called-up capital** or **paid-up capital**.

Issuing house A financial institution which acts as an intermediary between those seeking capital (usually industries) and those able to prove it. These houses handle issues of shares on behalf of companies, either by full **prospectus** or by an **introduction** or **placing**. They also often double as **underwriters** of share issues or as **merchant banks**. ⟡ **Share capital**.

Issuing Houses Association Formed in 1945, the Association has members not only in the City but also in other parts of London and in the provinces. It aims to represent the **issuing houses**' interests in dealings with other financial institutions and with government departments.

Jason clause A **marine insurance** clause covering risks undiscoverable even by proper diligence.

Jenkins Committee The committee set up to report on the state of the law relating to companies, and which published its findings in the Jenkins Report 1962. Its recommendations were many and various, and some were used as the basis of reforms contained in the Companies Acts from 1967 to 1985.

Jerque To jerque is to examine a ship's papers to ensure that the captain's list of any cargo agrees with that of the Customs house and to search for any unentered cargo. ◊ **Manifest**.

Jerque note A certificate issued by a Customs officer when he is satisfied the cargo is in order. ◊ **Jerque**.

Jerry building The construction of buildings, usually for habitation, with an eye for quick profit rather than durability. The term is usually associated with the quick speculative building of houses to accommodate the thousands of urban immigrants during the boom years of the Industrial Revolution in the UK. Jerry-built dwellings tended to be built of whatever materials were the easiest and cheapest to obtain and rarely outlived the constructor by any appreciable time. ◊ **Built-in obsolescence**.

Jetsam Goods thrown overboard to lighten a ship.

Jettisons A **marine insurance** term for objects thrown overboard to save a ship. ◊ **Flotsam** ◊ **General average loss**.

Job analysis Detailed analysis of a particular job leading to agreement on the best methods of carrying it out and the qualities needed by whoever is to do it. ◊ **Critical path analysis**.

Job Centre A government employment service agency with an emphasis on informality and personal attention. They exist in most urban areas and aim to supplant the 'situations vacant' columns in newspapers and to save job-seekers the necessity of touring the area looking for employment or asking to be put on waiting lists. They give advice on the various State aids available to those wishing to change either the location or nature of their employment, and offer occupational guidance and advice on retraining schemes. Although they are primarily intended to meet local needs, because they are organized on a country-wide basis they can also put applicants for jobs in touch with centres in other areas.

The centres are to some extent 'self-service' in that vacancies are posted up on cards for job-seekers to peruse, and, if there is a suitable one, the card can be referred to a receptionist who will contact the prospective employer. The importance of the job-centre scheme is that it provides a clearing house for both job-seekers, including the disabled, and job-providers in circumstances more attractive and less formal than the traditional employment exchanges (though these still remain). ◊ **Employment agencies** ◊ **Youth Training Scheme**.

Job enrichment A term used to describe devious methods of making a task seem more important, and the incumbent thereby deserving of greater respect, without involving the employer in parting with any additional cash. ◊ **Work study**.

Job evaluation ◊ **Job analysis**. The assessing of the relative worth of different jobs with reference to skills, responsibility, etc. It could form the basis for wage agreements. ◊ **Joint consultation**.

Jobber ◊ Stockjobber.

Jobber's turn A **stockjobber** always quoted two **prices** for **shares** or **securities**: a buying price and a selling price. The selling price was higher than the buying price and the difference was known as the jobber's turn. ◊ **Marketmaker**.

Jobbery Originally a term of abuse for sharp practice in **Stock Exchange** dealings only, but now used more generally.

Joint account In banking, an account opened in the names of more than one person, often a husband and wife. Each can draw on the account. Such accounts are becoming more frequent and they do fulfil a useful function as, with the ubiquity of the working wife, and the need for ready sources of funds by both parties to a marriage, it is becoming increasingly necessary for family budgets to be jointly controlled by husband and wife.

Joint and several A legal term referring particularly to partnerships. Partners are said to have joint and several liability for their firm's debts. This means that in addition to all partners being jointly responsible for debts incurred by the firm, each partner is individually, or separately, liable for all debts. This point is especially important when a partnership firm becomes bankrupt.

Joint consultation This refers to employer-employee discussion either within a single business entity or over many productive units within an industry.

In the former case it will comprise what are usually referred to as works councils or joint production committees in which shop stewards or other employee representatives can discuss organizational problems with representatives of **management**.

Joint consultation on a wider scale, embracing all or many of the firms within a particular industry, will generally take place within a more permanent organization, with perhaps a full-time secretarial staff, and will involve negotiations between trade unions and employers' organizations. They are often known as joint industrial councils and, in some instances, form the base for **Collective bargaining** on wages and conditions of employment. ◊ **Wages Council** ◊ **National Economic Development Council**.

The object of any form of joint consultation, whatever the level, is to provide a forum for the interchange of ideas and to enable management to outline future operations for comment or objection by those who will ultimately put them into practice.

Joint holders Where **shares** are held jointly, the holders may have them registered jointly, in which case only the first named receives notices. They may, however, split the holding and be registered separately.

Joint stock company The seventeenth-century forerunner of the present limited **company**. These companies grew out of ventures entered into by several people, usually on the agreement that the profits would be shared out in relation to each one's original investment. The ventures were generally connected with overseas trade and the regulations regarding the companies so set up were fairly informal.

These early attempts at company formation were abandoned, however, after the scandal of the **South Sea Bubble**, which none the less had one fortunate result in drawing attention to the need for effective control of companies by the law with protection for members and creditors.

The phrase 'joint stock' derives from the fact that these old unlimited 'companies' comprised a number of traders who pooled their stock of goods in selected ventures to exploit certain markets. The name continued in use for many years even when companies came within the law and the pooling was of knowledge, business acumen or skills rather than goods.

Joint stock companies should be distinguished from the still existing informal **partnerships** known as joint ventures where two or more persons get together, with no legally binding written contract, in a once only trading venture. Although the two types of enterprise have common roots, the joint venture proper is distinguished by the fact that it is limited to one objective and is not intended as a permanent association. ◊ **Partnership at will** ◊ **Partnership, limited** ◊ **Unlimited company**.

Joint tenants Persons who hold property jointly in such a way that should one tenant die the other takes the property. This is unlike a **tenancy in common**, where the representatives of the deceased tenant take his share.

Joint tenure A **partnership** for a limited period, usually without a written agreement. Not now in common use.

Journal A book-keeping term for the book or books where details of transactions are first entered. There are several, e.g. **purchase journal**, **sales journal**, private journal.

Judgment creditor ◊ County court judgments.

Judgment debt As a result of proceedings taken, a court may make an order that a sum of money is to be paid by one party to another. This may arise out of an action in **tort** or **contract** or from some other matter that has been the subject of a court hearing. The sum ordered to be paid is known as a judgment debt. Where such a debt is not paid after the prescribed period the creditor may apply again to the court for an alternative remedy, e.g. the compulsory seizure by bailiffs of such part of the debtor's property as will satisfy the debt. ◊ **Attachment** ◊ **Charging order** ◊ **County court judgments**.

Judgment debtor ◊ County court judgments, ◊ Judgment debt.

Junk bonds These are bonds of a company or corporation with a low credit rating which therefore carry a correspondingly high rate of interest which is part compensation for the high degree of risk attached to the capital subscribed. They became very popular in the US as a vehicle for raising funds in take-over bid situations and were frequently issued with that purpose in mind. The uncredit-worthiness of the issuer was often not known to those subscribing for the bonds, the investor being primarily attracted by the high rate of return offered. It was the lack of capital security which earned these investment products the soubriquet 'junk bonds'.

Kaffirs A group of **shares** in South African companies dealt with on the **Stock Exchange**.

Kangaroos A **Stock Exchange** term for **shares** or **securities** in Australian land, mining and tobacco **companies**.

Keelage Dues paid by a ship entering and resting in certain ports.

Kennedy Round An extensive renegotiation of multilateral tariff agreements, within the limits set by the **General Agreement on Tariffs and Trade**, instigated by the late President Kennedy. It was born of the American Trade Expansion Act 1962, which sought to increase the level of international trade by asking for major reductions in **tariff** levels around the world. Although other renegotiations had previously been attempted, this one was on a particularly large scale, and was further distinguished in that it tried to obtain general percentage reductions right across the board, rather than to renegotiate tariffs on various goods individually, with all the haggling that would involve.

Key money ◊ **Premium on a lease**.

Kite A slang term for an **accommodation bill**, particularly one raised with the express purpose of seeming affluent.

Kite flying ◊ **Kite**. The use of **accommodation bills** or other forms of raising money on credit, not supported by **assets**, in order to appear affluent or creditworthy.

Kite mark The symbol used by the **British Standards Institution** to indicate their official approval of a product being marketed. It gives the purchaser the satisfaction of knowing that the manufacturer has satisfied standards set by that institution. A manufacturer who has gained the right to use the kite mark on a product must accept the possibility of spot inspection by the BSI to ascertain that the quality is being maintained.

Knock-for-knock agreement A term used in automobile **insurance**. To save the time and cost of apportioning blame in an accident involving two or more cars the insurance companies concerned each pay out on the claim made by their own client. This does not apply, of course, when one party has, as a result of a court action in civil law, been deemed totally responsible for the accident, or has admitted liability, and the innocent party has successfully claimed from that party's insurers. ◊ **No claims bonus**.

Knot A term in measuring speed at sea and equivalent to one nautical mile per hour. The word itself incorporates 'miles per hour', i.e. one does not speak of 'knots per hour', merely of so many knots. Primitive methods of measuring the speed of a ship at sea derived from dropping a wooden log over the bow and noting the time it took to pass the known length of the ship. This led to the use of the log-line trailed behind the ship which was knotted at intervals so fixed that as the log-line was allowed to reel off then the number of knots in the line which passed a fixed point in twenty-eight seconds gave the ship's speed in nautical miles per hour.

Know-how A term used to describe saleable knowledge of techniques or special skills which have been developed within an industry for use on certain projects. This may be the result of many years of intensive research and development in the manufacture of a valuable product which **industrial espionage** has not succeeded in making available to competitors. An example might be the recipe for a unique beverage which cannot be sufficiently protected by the **patent** laws of the country of origin. ◊ **Goodwill** ◊ **Intangible assets**.

Krugerrand A South African **gold** piece in the shape and style of a **coin** but not intended to be used as **currency**. It contains one ounce of pure gold and was at one time looked upon in the UK as one of the best inflation-proof investments. The UK market in krugerrands was crippled by the British government in 1975, when it was decided that no more krugerrands could be imported into the country except under licence and even then only for re-export. Although restrictions have now been lifted by the UK government, the fact that VAT attaches to all sales of gold coins has, *inter alia*, somewhat reduced the appeal of krugerrands as an investment. ◊ **Gold coins**.

Laches A legal term for the delay sufficient to deprive a person of his right to **specific performance** of a **contract**, or to an **injunction**. The statute of limitations does not apply to equitable remedies – with these a person may lose the right to such a remedy by a short delay in seeking it. The length of time is decided by the court.

Laesio enormis The doctrine in certain continental legal systems that **consideration**, when a matter of **price**, must be fair and serious, otherwise the other party could rescind the contract. The doctrine is of Roman origin, and the cash offered has to bear some relation to the value of the object.

Lame duck Although this term was once reserved for members of the **Stock Exchange** who, not being able to meet their debts, were due to be **hammered**, it has recently been accorded a much wider use in the industrial sphere. The term 'lame duck company' or just 'lame duck' is now commonly applied to companies which can only be kept from complete ruin by being propped up by public funds. The State has interfered more than once in recent years to save public companies from the natural consequences of their inability to compete successfully with foreign manufacturers in both home and export markets. This may have been caused by bad planning, itself due to State interference, by overmanning due to trade union intransigence or merely by bad management. Whatever the cause of the impending collapse, it may be decided that rather than lose an industry which is considered vital to the country's image and/or create, or increase, considerable unemployment, it is in the public interest to prop up the company out of the taxpayers' money. Unfortunately, the matter is too often concerned with politics rather than with good economics and the real 'lame ducks' are often hidden under the cloak of **nationalized industries**, to which normal standards of efficiency cannot be applied.

Land waiter Also known as a landing officer or searcher, this is a Customs officer responsible for sampling and examining goods liable to duty. He makes out an account of landed goods for tax purposes, and ensures that goods for export are shipped in the prescribed manner.

Landed A term used in foreign trade **contracts**. It applies where the exporter, in addition to **ex ship** charges, sees to the landing of the **goods**. He is not normally responsible for dock charges.

Landing book A book kept by dock companies for noting details of all **goods** received off incoming ships. Landing accounts are made up from this book and sent to the relevant cargo owners. It gives them an indication of the state of the goods, and of when the **rent** due for, e.g., use of **warehouses** becomes payable.

Landing officer ◊ Land waiter.

Landing order ◊ Customs: landing cargo.

Lands Improvement Company A company formed by special Act of Parliament in 1853, to provide long-term loans for capital improvements to estates and farms. The improvements must be approved by the Ministry of Agriculture, Fisheries and Food. The loan is based on the rental value of the property, repaid by an **annuity** over a period of not more than forty years. Loans can be obtained on property already **mortgaged**. Capital cannot be called in and the **interest** is fixed.

Language laboratory As the need to communicate efficiently in more than one language becomes more important both commercially and socially, new methods of swift and effective teaching have been developed, and currently the language laboratory is much in use. Students are able to progress at their own pace using tape recordings of the language from which to develop familiarity with speech sounds and patterns. They can also repeat certain phrases into the tape and compare their own pronunciation with that of the speaker already on it. There is an overall instructor in the laboratory who can plug into any of the students' tapes and instruct and check on progress individually.

This method of language learning has become increasingly popular with business people.

Larboard The port or left-hand side of the ship (facing forward). The other side is called starboard.

Larceny Obtaining **goods** from another by trickery when that other had no intention of parting with them. Where the person intended parting with the

goods but the manner of obtaining them was fraudulent, this is obtaining goods on false pretences, not larceny. ◊ **Stolen goods**.

Last in first out (LIFO) ◊ First in first out.

Law Society A voluntary organization with over 19,000 members, the Society maintains the Roll of **Solicitors**, issues annual practising certificates, controls enrolment of students and supervises their education. It is the examining authority for the profession of solicitor. Although membership is voluntary, the Society has authority over all solicitors whether members or not *re* professional practice, conduct and discipline. It administers the Compensation Fund, keeps an appointments registry, library, etc., and offers advice on professional practice and procedure. It also administers legal aid and advice schemes. It is responsible for public relations.

The history of the Society is colourful – it began as the Society of Gentlemen Practisers in the Courts of Law and Equity in 1739, became the Metropolitan Law Association in 1819 and the Law Institution in 1825. When it received the first of five Royal Charters in 1831, its title was 'Society of Attorneys, Solicitors. Proctors and others not being Barristers practising in the Courts of Law and Equity of the United Kingdom'. The name Law Society was adopted in 1903.

Lawyer A member of the legal profession, usually a **solicitor** or **barrister**.

Lay days The days allowed by custom for loading or unloading a vessel. Failure to complete the job within these days may make the guilty party liable to pay **demurrage**. Lay days may be counted in **working days**, **running days**, or

weather working days. Where the number of lay days is not specified in the contract, the work must be done in a reasonable time (this might allow for delays due to strikes, etc.).

Laying-off A business which is in financial trouble may need to reduce its level of operations, perhaps substantially, and in doing so it may be necessary to reduce its workforce. This could also be brought about by a continual dislocation of production due, for example, to disruptions at the supplier's factory. Employees can be laid off either temporarily or permanently, and in the latter case it may be necessary to make statutory **redundancy payments**.

Lease An agreement whereby the legal owner of real property gives another person the possession of that property with freedom to use it as he wishes, though possibly under certain conditions, in return for a regular specified payment referred to as **rent**. Although personal, as opposed to real, property can also be lent to another, that type of transaction is normally referred to as an agreement to hire. ◊ **Hire purchase**.

The real property is freehold or leasehold land and/or buildings and is normally accompanied by such rights of way as are necessary for free access. ◊ **Easement**. The person obtaining possession, i.e. the holder of the lease, is said to be the owner of **leasehold property**, which can, unless the original agreement forbids, be sublet to another person, who in turn may sublet the property. Generally, subleases arise where the land contained in the first, or head, lease can be divided into various smaller portions each of which can command a price. For instance, a builder may obtain a lease of a fairly large area of land on which to build a number of separate houses. Each person buying a house becomes a subtenant of the true owner of the land (◊ **Ground rents**), and the house-owners themselves may go on to sublet part or all of their houses. Leases obtained for house building are usually very long, often ninety-nine years; the occupiers of each of the buildings now have a statutory right to a new lease when the old one expires – on condition that they are willing to pay a fair rent, which might be much higher than the old one, particularly when the value of money has fallen drastically during the term of the original lease. ◊ **Dilapidations**.

Lease-back ◊ **Sale and lease-back**.

Leasehold land Land rented from the true owner. The **lease** may be for a long or short period. At the end of the period it must be handed back, together with all buildings, whether these were on the land originally or not. The tenant may also be liable for **dilapidations**. It is possible to mortgage leasehold land, though the possibility will depend upon the term of the lease and any conditions imposed by the lease.

The Companies Act 1967 directs that published accounts shall show separately **freehold land**, land held on a long lease and land held on a short lease. A long lease for this purpose is one where there are at least fifty years to run.

Leasehold property Land and buildings or merely buildings in the possession of a person or a business and subject to the laws regarding a **lease** or **leasehold land**.

Ledger The book in which all the accounts of a business using **double-entry book-keeping** are contained. It is the ultimate record book, showing the consequences of all transactions entered into by the business. For practical purposes it is commonly split up into several books, e.g. the nominal ledger, the personal ledger, the private ledger and the cash book. ◊ **Book-keeping**.

Although ledgers are still maintained manually in small businesses, the records which comprise the ledger in larger companies are now more commonly kept by electronic means. These records are continually being updated and information referring to past periods will be stored on computer discs or in some form of computer databank or even on microfilm with facilities that enable such information to be brought on to a display screen for necessary and immediate access. ◊ **Accounts, nominal, real and personal** ◊ **Accounting records**.

Leeman's Act 1867 This deals with sales of **shares** in a joint stock **company**. The sale is void unless the numbers of the shares as given in the **share register** are stated in the **contract**. The **Stock Exchange** tends to ignore this provision, but a party to such a contract can still rely on the Act.

Leeward The side of the ship facing the quarter towards which the wind is blowing.

Legal tender Money which, if offered at a proper time and place in settlement of a due debt, must be accepted by the creditor in satisfaction of that debt. If the offer is refused then, although the debt is not extinguished, the creditor will lose his right of **lien** and will not be allowed to charge any further interest.

To constitute legal tender the offer of money must consist of legal currency, be unconditional and comprise the exact amount due. The offer of payment may

be either to the creditor himself or to his authorized agent. The debtor cannot demand change but if the creditor accepts the greater sum then he must provide change, which must itself be legal tender.

The currency that will constitute legal tender is determined by Act of Parliament, which imposes limits as to the amount of any type of coin that the creditor is obliged to accept. At present in the UK these are as follows: copper and bronze coins up to and including 20p; silver or cupro-nickel coins with a face value below 10p up to a maximum of £5; silver or cupro-nickel coins with a face value of 10p or more up to a maximum of £10; gold coins up to any amount. There is no limit at present on the £1 coin. Bank of England notes of current denominations are legal tender up to any amount in England and Wales but not in Scotland or Northern Ireland. Scottish and Irish notes, though generally acceptable throughout the UK, are not legal tender in any part of the UK.

It is important to remember that although one can enforce the rules of legal tender to the extent of refusing, say, ninety-five pennies in change on a bus, the conductor is not obliged to give change and the alternatives will be either to get off the bus or provide the conductor with a name and address to which the change may be despatched.

Lender of last resort Within the financial structure of any economy there are many institutions prepared to lend money. In order to lend, these institutions must first borrow, and those from whom they borrow must themselves have sources of funds on which to draw. There must then obviously be a lender who can, in the last resort, create or originate funds. This role is usually played by the central bank – in the UK, the **Bank of England** – and this central bank is often referred to as the lender of last resort. It must always make money available if called upon to do so, and in the UK such money is provided through the **discount houses**, either by repurchasing **treasury bills** or lending on other paper assets or, when amounts required are larger, by direct loans to the discount houses. In exercising this ultimate responsibility it will charge such **interest** rates as it judges sufficiently high to discourage borrowing, rates which will most certainly be in excess of those at which the borrowing houses are able to lend.

The particular rate charged by the Bank of England was, until recently, known as the **bank rate**. It then became known as **minimum lending rate** and afterwards as Bank of England **base rate**, which is effectively the same thing. Because the minimum lending rate must, by its very nature, be the highest of the current market interest rates for no-risk lending of money, it tends to influence all other interest rates in the country and an increase or fall in MLR will usually cause proportionate changes in other **rates of interest**. Because market prices of **securities** are governed by interest rates such prices will necessarily and promptly respond to changes in those rates. ⟡ **Mean price** ⟡ **Money market** ⟡ **Shares, market value**.

Lessee The person to whom a lease is granted.

Lessor The person granting a **lease**.

Letter of allotment ⟡ **Allotment of shares**.

Letter of attorney Similar to a **power of attorney**.

Letter of credit A document issued by a **bank** or other financial institution to a prospective borrower, for an agreed amount and for a definite or indefinite period. It allows the borrower to draw **bills of exchange** on the institution up to that amount – the bills will be accepted automatically. The purpose for which the money is required is stated initially and the bills drawn must conform to this. Letters of credit are also used in foreign trade. The buyer arranges with his bank to open a credit in the country of the seller, who may then obtain payment by presentation of the relevant documents when these have been accepted and returned by the buyer. When the seller is informed of the credit it becomes irrevocable.

Letter of hypothecation ⟡ **Hypothecation, letter of**.

Letter of indemnity When a manufacturer exports **goods** he sometimes sends a letter of indemnity agreeing to make good any loss due to faulty packing, short loading, etc. In doing this he ensures a **clean bill of lading**.

Letter of licence An insolvent debtor may come to some agreement with his **creditors** whereby they agree to give him some time to pay, and not to take any proceedings against him until that time has elapsed. This is known as a letter of licence.

Letter of mart and countermart An authority formerly issued to private adventurers in time of war, empowering them to seize the ships and goods of enemy subjects.

Letter of regret A letter sent to applicants for a new issue of shares, informing them that their application has not been accepted.

Letter of renunciation This applies to a **rights issue** of shares, where the holder who does not wish to take up the new shares may renounce his rights, either absolutely or in favour of another person, by means of a letter of renunciation.

Letters of administration ◊ **Administration, letters of**.

Letters patent These are granted to inventors once they have obtained a **patent**. Letters patent may be assigned according to the law on **assignment**. ◊ **Copyright** ◊ **Intangible assets**.

Leveraged buy-out A form of take-over engineered from within a company either by management or by a minority shareholding group, with or without the backing of institutional investors, banks and finance houses.

Control is sought by making an offer, conditional upon acceptance by sufficient shareholders, whereby high-interest stock is offered in exchange for existing equity shares – with the object of obtaining a controlling interest.

This stock may be underwritten by the financial institutions supporting the buy-out, but there is an increasingly popular technique of offering stock charged on the assets of the target company itself, assets which will not become the property of the offeror until the take-over is completed.

If the buy-out succeeds, then, whichever method has been used, the high gearing consequent upon the scheme will place a heavy burden on future profits. Those instigating the buy-out will usually have ensured that profits in the years immediately following the acquisition will suffice both to pay the interest charge and to protect the value of the equity.

The viability of the company in the more distant future will be the worry of those to whom the shares are subsequently and profitably sold.

The leveraged buy-out is a technique frequently employed when the object is to obtain control of a particular division of the company only. In that case, once the take-over has been effected the less attractive parts, which may comprise one or more distinct subsidiary companies, will be sold off. This procedure will often be initiated by those who see a prosperous future for the division to be acquired provided that it can be operated as a single unit, free from the encumbrances of the existing company structure. The proceeds from the sale of the unwanted sections of the old company will contribute towards this anticipated prosperity by providing necessary funds for expansion. These golden opportunities are, of course, not always apparent to the original holders of the equity, who will have exchanged their shares for fixed-interest stock, though as they now hold stock with a higher yield they are not expected to complain.

The newly generated funds may also be used to reduce the future interest burden by redeeming part of the recently issued loan stock. This will have the effect of reducing the long-term cost of obtaining control.

Liability A general term used to describe a debt. It may be cash or only a **chose-in-action**. ◊ **Long-term liabilities** ◊ **Current liabilities** ◊ **Contingent liabilities**.

Licence A document permitting its holder to do something otherwise forbidden, and usually obtainable by paying a fixed sum. Licences are a means of raising revenue and of controlling the use or abuse of certain rights. They are needed, *inter alia*, for driving or conducting a bus, carrying goods or passengers for money, selling wines, spirits, beer or tobacco, using a premises for dancing or singing and for hunting, shooting or fishing. Anyone in doubt as to whether or not he needs a licence should consult his local authority or the police. Conditions vary between parts of the country. Some licences are obtainable from post offices, e.g. television, CB radio, drivers', export, game, hounds and vehicle licences; others from magistrates, e.g. for the sale of alcohol; others from various other authorities. Members of the public can oppose the issue of particular licences by magistrates if they attend the court. Since the enforcement in 1978 of the licensing provisions of the Consumer Credit Act 1974, all businesses which grant credit or are connected with the granting of credit for goods must obtain a licence from the Director of the Office of Fair Trading.

Licence, motor vehicles In addition to the need for the driver of any motor vehicle on a public highway to hold a driving licence, the vehicle itself must be licensed. The provisions on the licensing of motorized vehicles are complex and depend considerably both on the nature of the vehicle and the purpose for which it is being used. Generally speaking, all vehicles must bear a current licence in a position from which it can be inspected from outside. Such licences are issued for fixed periods, usually one year, renewable at the end of that period. The date on which the licence expires is shown on the face of the licence, and, if the vehicle is driven or left upon a public highway after that date, whatever the intention of the owner may have been, the licence

renewal fee is payable. It is important to note that a licence must be held for a motor vehicle which is on a public highway even if the vehicle is not intended to be driven.

Particular licences must be obtained for any vehicles which carry passengers for hire, and it should be remembered that private cars are not normally licensed for this purpose. The licence duty on passenger-carrying vehicles is higher than on private cars, and higher rates are also payable for goods vehicles, increasing with the size and weight of the vehicle. Since the Transport Act 1968 road haulage firms which use vehicles over a certain weight need an 'operator's licence', which may not be granted if the licensing authority concerned considers that additional services in the area are not required.

There are certain concessions made for agricultural vehicles operated within closely defined limits, and also limited exemptions for invalid vehicles. For details of these it is best to consult the local licensing authorities. ◊ **Car tax** ◊ **Comprehensive insurance** ◊ **Knock-for-knock agreement**.

Licensed deposit taker (LDT) Prior to the Banking Act 1987 which reorganized the UK Banking System, there were a number of second-tier banks known as LDTs. The 1987 Act allowed these smaller concerns to operate as, and assume the name of, banks provided certain rigid provisions regarding capital adequacy and standards of fiscal prudence were observed. A Board of Banking Supervision was set up to ensure compliance with the requirements laid down in the Act.

Licensing laws: intoxicating liquors A complicated subject: reference should be made to the Licensing Act 1964. One or two points of general interest are: (1) licences are granted by local justices and can be revoked by them; (2) a licensee may refuse to serve any customer without giving his reason; (3) it is an offence to serve a drunken person with liquor or to buy a drink for one; (4) it is an offence to serve a person not yet eighteen years of age with liquor, or to buy a drink for one; (5) persons not yet fourteen years of age are not allowed in rooms where alcohol is being sold unless the sale is incidental to the provision of a meal; (6) persons under eighteen years of age may not be employed in rooms where alcoholic liquor is being served; (7) persons of sixteen and over can be supplied with beer, porter, cider or perry if it is consumed with a meal.

The regulations relating to opening hours contained in the 1964 Act have since been rendered more flexible in an attempt to bring conditions concerning the sale of alcohol more in line with those in Europe. While there are still restrictions on the times during which intoxicating liquor may be sold, these have shown signs of being extended and licencees now have a greater freedom in choosing the hours during which they open. Barring the granting of special licences by local magistrates, however, no sales are permitted after eleven pm. On weekdays public houses may remain open for twelve consecutive hours, but on Sundays, Good Friday and Christmas Day special restrictions on opening hours are still operative. The general licensing regulations do not apply to hotels, where residents and their guests may be served at any hour, and there are also more generous provisions applicable to licensed restaurants. The rules regarding clubs are complex and reference is best made to the Act.

Lien The right of a creditor to appropriate the debtor's property on non-payment of a **debt**, usually, but not always, where the property is legally in the possession of that creditor. The law pertaining to lien is complex and alters with circumstances. ◊ **Lien, possessory** ◊ **Lien, particular** ◊ **Lien on shares** ◊ **Lien, equitable** ◊ **Lien, general** ◊ **Lien, maritime** ◊ **Order and disposition**.

Lien, equitable This is not a **possessory lien**, although it could be. It is conferred by **equity** and is a right to have property disposed of in a certain way, e.g. the lien of a partner on the property of a **partnership**, or the lien of the **vendor** of land for the purchase money.

Lien, general Most **liens** which arise in commerce are particular liens. A general lien can sometimes occur and is much more far-reaching. It arises in certain specified circumstances and gives the holder the right to retain the goods of another not only until amounts due on account of those particular goods are paid but until other debts are also settled. General liens are sometimes accorded by the terms of a contract but can also arise through custom of trade. A **factor** has a general lien over the goods of his principal as does a solicitor over all his client's papers barring his will. The person exercising this right must, of course, have legal possession, i.e. they must have been freely entrusted to him by the debtor.

Lien, maritime In certain circumstances, persons have a lien attaching to a ship and/or its cargo which enables them to recover money owed to them. They are: **bottomry bond** holders; the master, for wages and disbursements; sailors, for work done; seamen, for wages; and the owner of another ship damaged in a collision. Possession is not necessary. $\lozenge$ **Hypothecation, letter of**.

Lien on shares The **articles of association** of a **company** usually provide that the company has first lien on the **shares** of a member for his debts or liabilities. The lien may also apply to **dividends**. It may be enforceable by **sale**, but cannot be enforced by forfeiture.

Lien, particular A **possessory lien** enabling the holder of **goods** to retain the goods until money due on those goods is paid. **Common law** affords such liens to unpaid carriers and unpaid sellers. The lien arises when goods are held for improvement rather than maintenance. The work must be completed. The fact that the goods do not belong to the person who deposited them does not always defeat the lien. $\lozenge$ **Uncollected goods, disposal of**.

Lien, possessory One person's right to retain possession of another person's **Goods** pending the payment of money due. The right varies according to the nature of the **Contract**. $\lozenge$ **Lien, general** $\lozenge$ **Lien, particular**.

Life assurance $\lozenge$ **Assurance**.

Life Assurance and Unit Trust Regulatory Organization (LAUTRO) LAUTRO is one of the **self-regulating organizations** currently recognized by the **Securities and Investments Board** as part of the regulatory network necessary for investor protection under the Financial Services Act 1986. LAUTRO is particularly charged with regulating the marketing (which includes follow-up services stemming from such marketing) of (1) long-term insurance contracts; (2) units in UK authorized unit trust schemes; (3) shares or units in overseas collective investment schemes so far as such schemes are recognized by the SIB; and (4) type A non-discretionary personal equity plans sold by unit trust managers.

LAUTRO's members are chiefly life assurance companies, unit trust managers and friendly societies. It regulates the activities of both the members themselves and their representatives. It does not regulate the activities of independent financial advisers. These are the responsibility of FIMBRA.

LAUTRO is charged with ensuring that its members are fit and proper to carry out the activities that they undertake and that they remain so. It operates through a system of committees, each of which is accountable for a particular aspect of responsibility. There is also a rolling programme of inspection by which each member's offices are visited on a regular basis in order that it can be satisfied that rules of the organization are being properly complied with and that instances of bad practice are identified and rectified without delay. Complaints against members from whatever source are investigated promptly and necessary disciplinary action taken.

Any person or organization which engages in activities which come within the remit of LAUTRO's regulatory responsibility must be a member of that body or obtain authorization either from another appropriate SRO or directly from the SIB itself. Without such authorization the person or organization cannot legally conduct business.

There is at present a suggestion that LAUTRO should be merged with FIMBRA to make one independent SRO, to be called perhaps the Personal Investment Authority. $\lozenge$ **Financial Intermediaries and Brokers Regulatory Authority** $\lozenge$

Investment Management Regulatory Organization ◊ **Securities and Futures Association**.

Light dues Levies payable by ships as contributions to the maintenance of lights, beacons, buoys or other navigational aids in rivers or roads. The dues are paid to Trinity House, through **Her Majesty's Customs and Excise**. The shipowner pays them on the basis of ten home trade voyages, eight foreign ones, or a combination of each.

Lighter This is a small flat-bottomed boat without the power of self-propulsion used for carrying cargo and generally towed by another craft. The sum charged for transporting goods by lighter is referred to as lighterage.

Limitation of actions The law holds that if an action is to be brought it must be brought within a reasonable time. The Limitation Acts 1939, 1954 and 1963 prescribe, *inter alia*, that an action should be brought within the following periods after the cause first arose: by **moneylenders** for the recovery of money and **interest**, within one year; by persons claiming **damages** in **contract** or in **tort** for personal injuries, within three years; actions generally in contract, tort or concerning trusts, etc., within six years; actions on certain **specialty contracts** or to recover land, or **mortgage** money secured on land, or personal property, or actions to do with claims on personal estates, within twelve years. The period normally runs from the date when the cause arose, or the date when the plaintiff was or could have been aware of the existence of the claim. **Part payment** of the debt or acknowledgement of the claim by the other party could start the time running again.

Limited Until the coming into force of the 1980 Companies Act every company which had limited liability was obliged to put the word 'limited' or a recognized abbreviation thereof after its name. Since 1976 Welsh companies, i.e those registered in Wales, have been able to use the Welsh equivalent. Since the 1980 Act the same rules have applied to all private limited companies, but a **public company** must, instead of the word limited, put the words 'public limited company' after its name and as part of its title. This may be, and usually is, abbreviated to PLC or plc.

There is one exception to this general requirement. A private company limited by guarantee may dispense with the limited if it is essentially a charitable organization and its memorandum prohibits any distribution of surpluses of either income or capital to its members. Such companies, which employ all income in furtherance of their charitable objects, are also released from the obligation to supply lists of members to the Registrar.

Limited company ◊ **Company.**

Limited liability This is a privilege extended to companies registered as limited companies under the Companies Acts. It means that members of those companies, i.e those providing the share capital, cannot be asked to contribute more than the nominal value of the shares registered in their names (but ◊ **'B' list of contributories**). In the case of companies limited by guarantee, the liability of members does not extend beyond the amounts initially guaranteed. The nominal value of the shares or the amount of the guarantee will appear in the **memorandum of association** and also in the **annual accounts**. The memorandum must also state that the liability of members is limited and the word 'limited' or, in the case of public companies, the words 'public limited company' or recognized abbreviations thereof must appear after the company's name. Failure to fulfil these requirements could revoke limitation of liability.

Limited partnership ◊ **Partnership, limited.**

Line management Line organization within industry is an arrangement wherein the roles of individual managers are related to the roles of those directly above and below them. Line management is, consequently, **management** where executives are directly responsible to the person above them in the management scale. It is, in effect, the organization of management by delegation. ◊ **Critical path analysis**.

Liquid assets In a general sense liquid assets refer to the immediate purchasing power of an individual. In a business context liquid assets are a subdivision of **current assets** and are sometimes referred to as quick current assets. They comprise that part of current assets which consists of cash or items that can be quickly converted into cash, e.g. **money at call**. The total of liquid assets is essential to the calculation of the **liquid ratio**.

Liquid ratio The ratio of **liquid assets** to **current liabilities**. Liquid assets are cash, and items readily convertible into cash, but not **stock** or **work in progress**, though stock could be included if it consisted of **goods** bought for resale for cash rather than credit. ◊ **Current ratio**.

The term 'liquid ratio' has a particular significance in the banking world.

Banks, by tradition, lend money which they do not possess, and usually a bank will only be called upon to pay over in cash to customers a small percentage of total credit balances. This means that the banks can invest customers' money at interest rates which are high, but where the profitability depends upon the money not being available for recall at short notice. Furthermore, banks lend monies deposited by one customer to another for a fixed period, and may also issue **bank notes**. These practices have evolved over many centuries and spring from the knowledge that a limited minimum amount of cash will support daily withdrawals, e.g. £10 cash may suffice to support a total of £100 in outstanding customer accounts. This minimum sum is expressed as a proportion of total debts and that ratio is known as the bank's liquidity ratio. In the case instanced, it is £10 or 10 per cent. If all customers called in their accounts at once a bank would be forced to close its doors and admit failure, and this has happened on various occasions in the history of banking – as recently as the nineteenth century. In present times the principal **clearing banks**, particularly in the UK, are protected by the willingness of the central bank of their country to support them in any crisis and also by the fact that no responsible government could afford the international ill-will that would necessarily flow from large-scale bank failures. ◊ **Bank of England** ◊ **Gold standard** ◊ **Lender of last resort**.

Liquidated damages ◊ **Damages, liquidated**.

Liquidation This term is applied to the winding-up of the affairs of a company when it ceases business. In most

publicized instances it indicates bankruptcy, but it is equally applicable to the winding-up of a company by its shareholders when the purpose for which it was initially founded has been completed.
◊ **Winding-up, voluntary**.

When a liquidation results from the effective bankruptcy of a company the rules that apply are set out in the Companies Acts as modified by the Insolvency Act 1986. These rules differ according to whether the winding-up of the company's affairs is instigated by shareholders or by creditors and, in the latter instance, whether it is voluntarily supported by the company or commanded by the court. ◊ **Declaration of solvency** ◊ **Winding-up, compulsory** ◊ **Insolvency Act 1986** ◊ **Administration order**.

Liquidation committee This committee consisting of both creditors and contributories may be created during the winding-up of a company to assist and supervise the person appointed as liquidator. Under the 1985 Companies Act, such a committee was referred to as a **committee of inspection**. The Insolvency Act 1985 provided for an equivalent committee and the 1986 Insolvency Act gave more form to its functions and directed that it be called a liquidation committee. In a creditors' voluntary winding-up, the decision whether or not to appoint such a committee is made by the creditors at their first or a later meeting. They may elect up to five persons to represent them and, should they do so, then the contributories may elect an equal number. Members' appointees may be rejected by the creditors and if such a rejection is not overruled by the court then the latter will appoint persons to represent members.

In a compulsory winding-up, a liquidation committee may be appointed at the same time as the liquidator himself. Otherwise he may call meetings of both creditors and contributories to establish whether such a committee is required, and must call such meetings if requested to do so by one tenth of creditors. If creditors cannot agree on whether a committee should be set up then, unless the court orders otherwise, a committee must be established. Where no liquidation committee exists its functions are fulfilled by the Department of Trade and Industry.

Liquidation: interest on debts While interest due up to the date of the commencement of a winding-up is included in the debt proved by a creditor, the Insolvency Acts introduced the concept of additional interest on debts covering the period between the beginning of the liquidation and the settlement of the debt. Such interest is calculated at a rate set by statutory instrument and is payable on all debts, *pari passu* – no distinction being made between kinds of debt – out of any surplus that remains after the debts proved have been settled in full.

Liquidation: preferential debts ◊ **Preferential debts**.

Liquidation: special manager ◊ **Special manager**.

Liquidator An official who supervises the **winding-up** of a **company**. He takes over the company's property, though it does not vest in him unless a court says so. He acts rather as a receiver and manager. Generally speaking, he does anything necessary to conduct the winding-up: *inter alia*, calling meetings where necessary, fixing a date for the proof of debts, admitting or rejecting proofs, settling lists of **contributories**, making calls and disclaiming property. If the company is **insolvent**, the **liquidation committee** settles his remuneration, otherwise the members of the company do. If the winding-up is compulsory, payment is usually a **commission** based on property realized and **dividends** paid.

The liquidator's powers and duties vary according to whether the winding-up is compulsory or voluntary. If compulsory, he is subject to court control and the court or the Department of Trade and Industry can remove him at any time, for instance if he becomes bankrupt, and can appoint additional liquidators if necessary. He is also subject to the control of the court or the liquidation committee on questions of (1) bringing or defending actions in the company's name, (2) carrying on the company's business, (3) paying any class of **creditors** in full, (4) compromising with debtors, creditors or contributories, or (5) appointing a **solicitor**. The liquidator must advertise his own appointment and that of the liquidation committee. He must report to the Registrar of Companies on the progress of liquidation, at the end of the first year and after each subsequent six months. If he carries on the business of the company, he must keep a separate trading account which is regularly audited by the **liquidation committee**. Creditors and contributories have certain rights to inspect books and receive summaries of accounts. The liquidator must give notice of winding-up to creditors, and tell them when proofs must be lodged if they are to receive a share in any distribution. The liquidator must pay all monies into the Insolvency Services account at the **Bank of England**, or else as directed by the Department of Trade

and Industry. When the liquidation is complete, he applies for his release. Various formalities must be observed. The liquidator must usually give security.

If the winding-up is voluntary, the liquidator is not controlled by the Department of Trade and Industry in quite the same way. He must advertise his appointment, deal with proof of debts and make statements to the Registrar of Companies. Monies, though, need not be paid into the Insolvency Services account unless they are retained for more than six months, or after the dissolution. The liquidator must generally submit some form of accounts for **audit** and his costs may be taxed.

The 1989 Companies Act provides that any person who seeks to act as the liquidator or provisional liquidator of a company must be a recognized **insolvency practitioner**.

Liquidators, appointment of In the case of a **voluntary winding-up**, the **liquidator** is appointed by the members of the **company** (or by the **creditors** in a creditors' voluntary winding-up). In the case of a winding-up by the court, the court appoints the **Official Receiver** as provisional liquidator or, if an administration order has been made, the person who was acting as administrator. He then calls meetings of creditors and contributories to decide whether to apply for a liquidator proper and/or a **liquidation committee**.

Liquidity A term for the ease with which funds can be raised by the sale of assets. In any business, cash is needed at various times for various purposes, but on the other hand idle cash earns no money. Cash may therefore be used to purchase assets, e.g. **bills of exchange**, **securities**, market investments, or may be deposited for short periods, so that **interest** is earned but the asset is quickly realizable. These funds are said to be near-liquid. ◊ **Liquid assets**.

List price Usually the manufacturer's recommended retail, or wholesale, selling price. Where price maintenance agreements do not apply, prices may sometimes be dropped below list price to encourage custom and/or increase turnover. This is a practice much favoured by **discount stores, supermarkets, hypermarkets and cash-and-carry warehouses**. ◊ **Cut-throat competition** ◊ **Loss leaders** ◊ **Manufacturer's recommended price** ◊ **Prices and incomes policy** ◊ **Resale price maintenance**.

Listed company A company of which the **shares** or other **securities** are listed on a recognized **Stock Exchange**. Such companies are always public companies and are also referred to as quoted companies. ◊ **Mean price** ◊ **Public company** ◊ **Quotations** ◊ **Quoted price** ◊ **Shares: market value**.

Listed investments This term has a particular meaning in relation to company accounts. The 1985 Companies Act provides that investments shown in the balance sheet should distinguish that part which comprises listed investments, and for that purpose defines these as investments which have been granted a listing either on a **Recognized Investment Exchange** (other than an overseas Investment Exchange within the meaning of the 1986 Financial Services Act), or on any Stock Exchange of repute outside the UK.

Livery companies The relics of the medieval craft guilds of the City of London – one of the oldest being the Merchant Taylors' Company. They are companies formed by Royal Charter – those that cannot produce their charters are assumed to have received them at one time or other. Today there are eighty-three, and the senior companies, referred to as the Great Twelve, are the Mercers', Grocers', Drapers', Fishmongers', Goldsmiths', Skinners', Merchant Taylors', Haberdashers', Salters', Ironmongers', Vintners' and Clothworkers'. Some of the guilds have formed their own schools, not necessarily for educating children into their own crafts, though that might have been the original intention. The Mercers' Company was prominent in this field. It formed the Mercers' School in 1542 and was also responsible for supporting St Paul's School. The guilds united to form the City and Guilds of London Institute in 1878, to help with technical education. In 1907 they helped form the Imperial College of Science and Technology. The Livery companies have elaborate dress for ceremonial occasions, and also some fine banqueting halls. Most of them are now little more than social organizations, but some still play an active part in their trade; for instance, the Fishmongers' Company still looks after Billingsgate and is responsible for seizing any bad fish.

Lloyd's The popular name for the Corporation of Lloyd's. It started in a coffee house in Tavern Street in 1689, and moved, via Lombard Street and Pope's Head Alley, to the Royal Exchange in 1774. Subsequently it moved into its own building, where it remains. Members are **brokers** or **underwriters**. The latter, known as 'Names', are sole traders although they normally operate in syndicates. The Corporation itself has no liability for the defaults of its members. However, a member must deposit a substantial sum of money before he is accepted. Premiums received by underwriters are placed in a trust fund. Claims are paid out of this fund. Annual **audits** are compulsory. The Corporation provides standardized documents, **shipping intelligence** services, a daily newspaper (**Lloyd's List and Shipping Gazette**), a claims bureau, and **Lloyd's agents** in nearly every important port in the world. **Lloyd's Register of Shipping** classifies vessels and gives comprehensive information regarding them. Lloyd's deals with a vast part of all annual **insurance** in this country, though not with **life assurance**. Its main business has been, is, and probably always will be, **marine insurance**.

Regulation is vested in the Council of Lloyd's set up by the Lloyd's Act 1982 which enhanced existing self-regulatory powers. The Council comprises twelve representatives elected from and by working members of Lloyd's; eight representatives elected from and by non-working members; and eight representatives from outside Lloyd's nominated by the Council and approved by the Governor of the Bank of England. The Council has overall responsibility for the control and supervision of both the members and of the market itself, and draws up rules for the proper conduct of affairs with powers to discipline members who contravene such rules. A further cog in the regulatory regime, which applies to Lloyd's, is the requirement that it satisfies an annual solvency test whereby it is obliged to demonstrate to the Secretary of State for Trade and Industry that solvency requirements in respect of individual members and the market as a whole have been met.

Lloyd's agents Agents throughout the world appointed by **Lloyd's**. They supply information regarding shipping,

aviation, etc., to Lloyd's, and also appoint surveyors to report on damage or loss. They may also be authorized to settle claims.

Lloyd's: High Level Stop Loss Scheme
A scheme drawn up by the Task Force appointed by Lloyd's to review its capital structure in view of the escalation of claims on underwriters in recent years – a phenomenon which seemed to threaten the stability of the market. In an attempt to provide a more attractive balance between risk and reward the Task Force, reporting in 1992, proposed the establishment of a High Level Stop Loss Scheme which was accordingly introduced to take effect as from 1 January 1993. It will provide protection when net losses over a four-year period exceed 80 per cent of a Name's overall premium limit. Losses up to that figure of 80 per cent will be the responsibility of the Names concerned. Any balance over that limit will be met by a fund financed by levies on all Names.

Lloyd's List and Shipping Gazette
Founded in 1734 and at one time *Lloyd's List*, this is a daily paper providing extensive shipping information, particularly on the movement of ships.

Lloyd's medals These are awarded for extraordinary exertions in saving life at sea or preserving vessels or cargoes. There is also a Lloyd's War Medal for exceptional gallantry at sea, and a medal awarded for outstanding service to **Lloyd's** itself.

Lloyd's Register of Shipping A society formed to survey and classify ships for the benefit of insurers and other interested parties. If a ship is constructed under the supervision of Lloyd's surveyors it is marked with a Maltese cross. Ships are generally given periodic surveys. The society is responsible for an annual publication known as *Lloyd's Register of British and Foreign Shipping*. This contains details of all vessels afloat of 100 tons or more. ◊ **A1.**

Load line This refers to one of a series of lines inscribed on the hull of a steamship and indicating the maximum depth to which that ship may be safely loaded, thus guarding against the possibility of accidents caused by overloading. The reason for more than one load line is that the danger level differs slightly according to whether it be summer or winter or sea water or fresh water.

All British merchant ships plus those of other countries using British ports also carry a general reference load line, known as the Plimsoll line. This was introduced and made obligatory by the Merchant Shipping Act 1874 as the result of the efforts of Samuel Plimsoll towards ensuring the safety of ships at sea. The line, represented by a circle with a line drawn through it, was the precursor of the grid of load lines appearing on the ships of virtually all merchant lines today. The load lines are determined by **Lloyd's** in respect of all ships registered in the UK and any vessel loaded to a degree that defies these lines can incur heavy penalties in any part of the world where the regulations are accepted and enforced. ◊ **Marine insurance** ◊ **Freight.**

Loading broker An **agent** acting for a ship-owner with a view to obtaining cargo.

Loan capital That part of the **capital** of a **company** or other organization subscribed for a fixed period or for a period determinable by either party or on the happening of a stated event. It is entitled to fixed **interest** and may be secured on the property of the business or on a **guarantee** by a third party. It must be distinguished from **share capital**. The most common form of loan capital is a **debenture**.

Loans to directors Companies may not normally make loans, other than a temporary advance of less than £5000, to directors or to persons connected with those directors. There are limited exceptions laid down in the 1980, 1985 and 1989 Companies Acts. These fall into two main categories. Moneylending companies may make loans in the normal course of business to directors, provided they are made on terms no more favourable than those available to borrowers generally. The second category is more tightly drawn and reference should be made to the relevant provisions of the Acts. Generally speaking, loans or quasi-loans may be made to a holding company which is listed as a director, and loans may be made to directors for the purpose of the proper carrying on of their duties, provided that such loans are approved by the company in general meeting.

Lock-out Action by employers equivalent to a strike by employees. It occurs when an employer refuses to allow employees entry to their place of work unless they agree to certain terms that have been put to them. Nowadays lockouts are infrequent due to both the power of the trade unions and the increasing involvement of the State in industrial disputes. ◊ **Advisory Conciliation and Arbitration Service** ◊ **Central Arbitration Committee** ◊ **Redundancy.**

Locus poenitentiae A legal term applying to illegal contracts. Where money is paid for an **illegal** purpose the parties may be allowed a '*locus poenitentiae*' – an opportunity to change their minds. Once the illegal purpose is carried out no action at law can be maintained. ◊ **Contract, illegal**.

Lombard Rate The Bundesbank, Germany's central bank, carries the responsibility of maintaining both the internal and external value of the German currency, the deutschmark. In doing this it is responsible for domestic interest rates. In addition to the key rate, which is the equivalent of the British **base rate**, there are other relevant, if less important, rates, the best known being the Lombard Rate. This is the rate set by the Bundesbank at which it will lend, on the security of first-class paper, to other banks within the German banking system. Its nearest British equivalent is probably the LIBOR rate.

London acceptance credit An exporter's credit with a London **accepting house** or **bank**, which enables him to draw **bills of exchange** on them conditionally, e.g. payable within three months and up to a stated amount. Credits may be indefinite or for a fixed period. If the latter, maturing bills will often be replaced by others, and this is known as a revolving credit. **Security** is usually though not always necessary, and may take the form of **letters of hypothecation**, tender of shipping documents, etc. By this means the exporter obtains cash immediately, perhaps before the **goods** are made, or when they are shipped. He is obliged to put funds at the disposal of the **acceptor** when the bills are due for payment.

London bank export credit Similar to **London acceptance credit**, except that the UK exporter draws **bills of exchange** on the overseas buyer and the **bank** collects these bills.

London Bankers' Clearing House Until automated clearing was introduced in 1984 this was the central organization initiated by member banks to settle inter-bank indebtedness arising from daily cheque clearings. Settlement was effected through accounts held by the various banks at the Bank of England. Bank Clearings are now handled by APACS.

London Clearing House (LCH) This is an independent clearing house which clears trades on various **Recognized Investment Exchanges** namely, **London Fox, London Metal Exchange, London International Financial Futures Exchange** and the International Petroleum Exchange. The LCH is owned by six leading banks, Barclays, Lloyds, Natwest, Midland, Royal Bank of Scotland and Standard Chartered. When the LCH registers a trade for a member of one of the Exchanges it becomes, by novation, the central counterparty. While not a party to any contract entered into by such members, it ensures that those contracts will be financially performed. It covers the risks inherent in such an obligation by calling for margins to be deposited on all open contracts margins which are adjusted daily.

London Commodity Exchange ◊ **London Fox**.

London Fox (London Futures and Options Exchange) This is the name by which the London Commodity Exchange became known in 1987 to reflect the fact that, in addition to its function as an umbrella organization for various soft commodity futures market exchanges, it had embraced the hitherto separate Traded Options Market. It offers futures and options contracts in a list of defined commodities by both open outcry (**Open Outcry market**) and electronic screen trading.

In 1991 BIFFEX, the **Baltic International Freight Futures Exchange**, was also merged with London Fox. All contracts made on London Fox are registered with the **London Clearing House** which becomes the central counterparty by novation and acts as guarantor to the transaction – covering its risk by demanding a margin, by way of deposit, from each member on all their open positions and varying with the estimated risks on particular contracts. The margins are reviewed daily with reference to market prices, and differences are settled between members and the Clearing House.

London Gazette A weekly bulletin enjoying the unique distinction of being 'published by authority'. Any information published in the *London Gazette* (or in Scotland, the **Edinburgh Gazette**) is notice to the world, or rather to the nation, and no one can deny knowledge of it, even though he has neither heard of, nor seen, the publication. Matters included in the *Gazette*, apart from certain traditional items, are notification of public appointments, etc., details of winding-up orders, **bankruptcies**, meetings of **creditors**, changes of names of **companies**, **partnerships** and individuals, changes in the consititution of partnerships, and all other matters which the law requires to be 'gazetted'.

London Inter-Bank Offered Rate (LIBOR) This is the rate of interest at which banks will lend to each other in the inter-bank market. It is a benchmark rate for wholesale money transfers and is quoted for both sterling and other currencies. As a constantly changing measure of the cost of money in large quantities as it moves between banks themselves, it is a more exact indicator of current interest rate movements than the bank base rate.

Unlike minimum lending or base rate it is not the subject of relatively infrequent publicized changes but fluctuates on a daily basis and is quoted at differing rates for differing time scales, e.g. from seven days to six or twelve months.

London International Financial Futures and Options Exchange (LIFFE)
This was created in 1991 by the merger of the London International Financial Futures Exchange with the London Trade Options Market. It has been given the status of a **recognized investment exchange** by the Securities and Investment Board which is charged with implementing the provisions of the Financial Services Act 1986.

Forward buying of currency in anticipation of future needs has long been common practice within the context of international trade. If, say, a manufacturer needs to obtain a given quantity of a raw material in nine months' time he may arrange delivery with a seller in another country, but neither party can be certain of what the market price of the goods will be at the time of completion. By that time the prevailing market price may have moved up or down and the exchange rate for the currency needed to effect payment may have changed, perhaps dramatically. In seeking to minimize the risk the buyer might wish to insure against one or both of these variables. By fixing the price nine months in advance he ties himself into a fixed cost.

In doing this he guards against an unfavourable rise in the spot price but at the same time accepts the possibility of paying too much if the price falls before the date of completion. Likewise he can insure against fluctuation in the exchange rate of the necessary currency by purchasing a right to obtain that currency at a given rate but in nine months time. He now holds two futures contracts, one for the goods and another for the currency.

Both these contracts can be sold on through LIFFE which provides a market for trading such contracts. Indeed the importer, rather than set up those contracts, may actually be able to purchase similar contracts already in existence through the Exchange.

Such contracts in goods and currency form only a small part of the transactions passing through LIFFE, which also provides a market for futures in short- or long-term bonds denominated in a variety of currencies, interest rate futures which provide a facility for locking in to a particular interest rate, various other financial derivatives and, particularly since the merger with the London Traded Options Market, a range of financial options contracts. The attraction of options dealing in a futures market is that, rather than be tied into a specific purchase of say a particular currency at a given date, a trader can buy an option to purchase such a currency contract and secure that option by putting down only the required margin. That option itself can then be traded perhaps at a profit. In fact, many traders buy and sell futures and options on LIFFE having no underlying interest in the product they represent but as a business in itself. All LIFFE dealings are cleared through the **London Clearing House** which operates in respect to LIFFE much as it does to **London Fox**.

Trading on LIFFE is by Open Outcry in pits, each being specific to a particular financial product and in which set times for trading are allocated by LIFFE. Members of the Exchange may be individual persons and organizations or subsidiaries of financial institutions such as banks, discount houses, broker-dealers etc., and all may be operating either on behalf of clients or merely on their own account. Although LIFFE is a recognized investment exchange the provisions of the Financial Services Act make it necessary for members to obtain authority to conduct investment business either directly from the SIB or indirectly by registering with an SRO, usually the Securities and Futures Authority, by whose rule book they must then abide.

London Metal Exchange (LME) First established in 1877 the LME is now an internationally recognized market for the buying and selling of the metals – principally copper, aluminium, nickel, lead, zinc and tin – in which it trades. Silver was traded on the LME at various times in its history but such a market ceased in 1989. The LME is ultimately a physical market where delivery is in the form of a warrant enabling the buyer to take possession of a specified tonnage of a particular grade of metal at a stated date from an LME-approved warehouse. At one time delivery was confined to sites within the UK, but the broadening of the LME market has led to the establishment of delivery points throughout Europe and in various other international locations. Although a physical market handling spot transactions, which are by the nature of the market normally represented by forward contracts, it also deals in futures and options, as well as offering hedging facilities. Under the terms of the Financial Services Act it has become a **recognized investment exchange** and all transactions are now settled through the **London Clearing House** which, in guaranteeing all trades, operates a margin system similar to that which is in place at **London Fox**. The international nature of the LME is evidenced by the fact that more than 80 per cent of its dealing members are fully or partly owned by overseas companies.

London Stock Exchange ◊ **Stock Exchange**.

Long-term liabilities An accounting term for amounts borrowed by a business and not repayable within the next **accounting period**.

Loss leaders Goods deliberately offered at prices well below normal and usually at a loss to the vendor, to attract customers into the premises in the belief that they will more than make up the initial loss by boosting the sales of other lines. The offer of very low-price butter in a **supermarket** may, for instance, attract the eye of the average housewife, who, once inside, may then complete the rest of her food purchases for the week. Certain curbs were put on the use of loss leaders by the Resale Prices Act 1964 (◊ **Resale price maintenance**) but the vendors are not so easily deterred and the practice is still very common. ◊ **Advertising, persuasive** ◊ **Impulse buying** ◊ **List price** ◊ **Sale of goods**.

Loss of profit insurance ◊ **Consequential loss**.

Loss of capital ◊ **Capital: serious loss** ◊ **Companies: reduction of capital**.

Lost share certificates Articles of

association generally provide that where **members of companies** lose a **share** certificate the **company** will replace it but will be indemnified by that member.

Lump sum freight Freight payable irrespective of the amount of **goods** loaded.

Lump system This refers to the employment of labour in the construction industry where separate contracts of employment are not drawn up for employees, who are often skilled workers, on the grounds that they are self-employed subcontractors entitled to an agreed lump sum for the work contracted to be done. In the past this method of payment has enabled the persons so employed to escape taxation and **National Insurance**, but steps have been taken by the State to make this less easy by insisting on all sub-contractors being named by the main contractor. ◊ **Tax avoidance** ◊ **Taxation schedules**.

Luncheon vouchers Vouchers or slips of paper (issued, for instance, by employers to their staff) which are exchangeable for meals but not for cash. The employer purchases the vouchers from an organization specializing in this kind of business. This organization later repurchases them from the restaurant, making its profit from the discount offered by the restaurant and the **commission** paid by the employers. Luncheon vouchers are a means of giving employees additional benefits in kind and are tax-free up to a fixed amount per day. Not all restaurants accept them.

Lutine bell In 1799, the *Lutine*, insured at **Lloyd's**, went down in the North Sea with a large cargo of bullion, much of which was never recovered. The Lutine bell is the ship's bell taken from the

Maastricht Treaty This agreement was reached in 1991 by heads of government of the EU countries. The Treaty was intended to agree certain policies already discussed and delineated at earlier meetings. It clarified various steps towards the ultimate goal of monetary unity within the EU – the implementation of which depended on the ratification of the Treaty by the individual countries. Central to the Treaty is the intent that all citizens of member States shall be *ipso facto* citizens of the EU which would initially enjoy permanently fixed exchange rates and eventually a common currency. This would necessarily lead to an independent European Central Bank which would engineer a communal monetary policy and subsequently common European policies attaching to education, transport, telecommunications, health and energy. Greater powers will be accorded to the European Parliament which itself would be given a greater role in formulating the policies initiated by the European Commission together with the right to veto measures in the field of consumer protection, environmental policy and the Single Market. Again, a Cohesion Fund will be established to finance environmental and transport projects in the poorer countries, together with an effective Court of Auditors and a Committee of the Regions to advise on topics relating to specific regions within the EU. There is also a clause, from which the UK obtained exclusion, enabling the EU to lay down more stringent rules regarding social and employment matters than those contained within the Treaty of Rome.

Mail order firm A firm selling a wide variety of customer goods but operating through post or parcel service rather than through retail premises. Comprehensive catalogues are made available to interested parties who either act as agents or purchase on their own account. Goods are sold at competitive prices and can normally be returned free of charge if unsuitable. Economies in marketing enable the mail-order firm to offer attractive introductory gifts and provide easy payment terms to customers. Commission is paid on all purchases and this goes either to the direct purchaser or to the agent depending on who files the order.

Mainstream corporation tax Under the imputation system introduced in 1973 **corporation tax** collected from companies was divided into two parts. **Advance corporation tax** is deducted in the form of income tax from dividends paid. Undistributed profits are taxed once those profits have been agreed with the Inland Revenue and the tax, collected at a different date and often at a different rate due to budget changes, is known as mainstream corporation tax.

Maintenance This term has several quite distinct meanings. (1) It refers to the cost of maintaining something. Considerable expense may be incurred within a business through the continual maintenance of items of plant and machinery.

Costs of maintaining equipment are normally treated as expenses incurred in earning the profit for any given period. They are allowable as deductions for tax purposes. (2) The term has an equivalent meaning when applied to persons rather than objects. A man divorced from his wife may be ordered by the court to pay both her and their children, if any, fixed sums each week or month for their maintenance, i.e. living expenses. Amounts payable on a court order are taxable in the hands of the recipient and are tax deductible for the person making the payment. (3) Maintenance has a specific meaning in the law of **contract**. It is applied to payments made to the plaintiff (or agreements to make such payments) by third parties, where the particular third party has no legal or moral interest in the action or insufficient interest to satisfy the court that his offer of financial backing is justified. Where payments of this type are not seen as representing a justified interest they are illegal, and any contract connected with their payment would be treated as illegal. ◊ **Champerty**.

Making a price This is primarily a **Stock Exchange** term referring to the obligation of a **market-maker**, at one time a jobber, to quote a 'double' price applying to any security in which he deals. The market-maker does not know when asked by a broker, or other party permitted to trade with him, whether the inquirer wishes to buy or to sell, nor has he the right to know in advance. He therefore quotes a two-part price, being on the one hand the price at which he will buy and on the other hand the price at which he will sell. This is known as making a price and the dealer is bound to deal at the price

he makes if the other party so wishes.

Making up day A Stock Exchange term for the first settlement day. ◊ **Account days** ◊ **Pay day** ◊ **Making up price**.

Making up price A Stock Exchange term for the price at which bargains are carried over from one account to another. ◊ **Account days**. It is normally the market price at noon on that day.

Mala fide ◊ Bona fide.

Management Those people who, collectively or individually, are responsible for running a business or organization. Management is usually broken down into specific parts, e.g. works management, **personnel management**, sales management, etc. The **British Institute of Management**, established by the Board of Trade in 1964, is an overall body which claims to represent all the various elements; it promotes courses and is involved in the dissemination of information. The Institute offers membership to (1) those who have achieved a position of respect in the world of management – these are made fellows (FBIM); (2) those who have a diploma in management studies – these are made associate members (AMBIM). Other members are known as MBIM. Members are often colloquially referred to as the 'BIM boys'. In recent years, the role of the British Institute of Management has been somewhat overshadowed by the establishment of specialist **Business Schools** which teach and offer qualifications in management. These range from the Diploma to the increasingly sought after Master of Business Administration – awarded upon completion of a comprehensive and intensive course in a variety of management skills. ◊ **Line management** ◊ **Management company** ◊ **Management consultant**.

Management accountant The term usually employed to distinguish the accountant in industry who is primarily concerned with presenting information on which cost-conscious **management** decisions will be made from the purely **financial accountant**, concerned with the overall financing of a business. Management accountants must decide, through analysis of the cost variances concerned, the precise amount of funding necessary for a given project. They are also concerned with **budgetary control** (it is upon the figures which they supply that budgets are ultimately agreed) and **standard costing**. Management accountancy has evolved as a profession from cost accounting. Its governing body is now known as the Chartered Institute of Management Accountants.

Management Accountants, Chartered Institute of This is the professional institute and governing body for **management accountants**. It began life as the Institute of Cost and Works Accountants then changed its name to the Institute of Cost and Management accountants to emphasize the greater role that members were playing in industry. The present title is more consistent with its present pre-eminence in the field of management accounting within the UK. As a governing body it seeks to promote the use of scientific methods in preparing accounts for management purposes, and to establish minimum standards of expertise and skill by the issue of certificates only to those who satisfy stringent membership requirements including the passing of professional examinations.

Within its remit is also the supervision of the conduct of members, the taking of disciplinary measures to uphold standards, and the provision of education facilities for members and prospective members. Those admitted to the Institute are entitled to use the initials ACMA if associate members, or FCMA if fellows of the Institute.

Management buy-outs The management buy-out is a relatively new phenomenon in the UK. When a company is in difficulty or when it faces the possibility of a take-over bid by another company, senior executives of the first company may obtain substantial institutional backing with a view to taking over the company themselves. Apart from a natural disinclination to see control pass to other hands, they may believe that reorganizing the company's affairs along lines which they have devised will offer a prosperous future. Provided that banks and institutional investors will back their ideas, then they will obtain funds to bid for the equity shares of the company. They will then hope that the restructuring, when implemented, will make the outlook sufficiently attractive for the shares they have purchased to be resold on the market, often at a substantial profit to themselves.

A management buy-out should be carefully distinguished from an **employee buy-out**, where the object is to give control to a shareholding workforce. It should equally be distinguished from a **leveraged buy-out**, though it does occasionally take that form.

Management company A relatively new phenomenon in the financial world, it is the name accorded to companies that are responsible for managing, i.e. deciding, the content of the investment portfolio of a **unit trust**. The management company is generally paid a fee, based on the services it provides, by the unit holders; normally this fee is incorporated in the agreement setting up the trust.

Management consultant A person whose business is to advise on management problems, on making more effective use of resources employed, and also on problems involving basic organization, administration and reorientation. Consultants advertise their range of services as (1) overall policy and planning, (2) cost reduction and utilization of resources, (3) personnel function and industrial relations, (4) management techniques and (5) overseas services. ◊ **Management Consultants' Association**.

Management Consultants' Association An association founded in 1956 to establish high standards of ethical conduct and technical competence throughout the management consultancy profession in this country.

Management game Often synonymous with 'business game', this is an educative exercise beamed at schools, colleges, etc. The participant students are those who may intend to make a career in **management**. The 'games' attempt to simulate real-life theoretical situations which present management problems or business situations requiring one of a variety of decisions. Contenders attempt to maximize real profits by the solutions or decisions they choose. Any number of variables may be introduced into the situations and the problem may be complicated by new factors being introduced after each of a series of separate decisions. Although the true value of these 'games' is possibly as nebulous as any of the

situations imagined, they do afford a useful introduction to the processes involved in decision-making at management level. ◊ **Variable costs** ◊ **Semivariable costs**.

Managing director The director of a company who generally ranks first in seniority under the chairperson or president and, being normally the **chief executive**, he will be the key figure in the running of the business with ultimate responsibility for all decisions that are made in the area of **management**. Any change in the control of the company arising from share dealings may well cost this director his job. In the smaller company the managing director is often also the chairperson. ◊ **Chairman of a company** ◊ **Executive director** ◊ **Line management**.

Manchester Ship Canal A very important canal linking Manchester with the sea and making Manchester in effect a port.

Mandate A document giving one person authority to act on another person's behalf with the backing of the law. Mandates may be given to directors, or others, to sign cheques on behalf of a company. In this instance, the banker must possess a specimen signature of the person holding the mandate. Mandates may also be given to responsible persons who will act and contract on behalf of another person who is, as a result of a court order, deemed unable to act on his own behalf, e.g. a person of unsound mind or a **bankrupt** or deceased person. Any change in a mandate must be authorized by those initially responsible for granting it. ◊ **Power of attorney** ◊ **Proxy**.

Manifest A detailed list of a ship's cargo

which must be sent to agents abroad, and to Customs authorities, within six days of clearance outwards. ◊ **Exporters' declarations**.

Man-of-war Any ship commanded by a person in a nation's recognized armed navy. For instance, any ship commanded by an officer of the Royal Navy would theoretically be a man-of-war.

Manufacturer's agent An **agent** who obtains **contracts** for manufacturers. He works within a specified area for a **commission**, and probably has the sole agency for a manufacturer within that area.

Manufacturer's recommended price ◊ **Recommended retail price**.

Manufacturing industry That branch of industry concerned with the manufacture of **goods** by the application of labour to raw materials supplied by the **extractive industries**.

Margin A margin is strictly the difference between the cost of an asset or investment and the amount that a lender of money is willing to advance for its purchase; or (and this is much the same thing) the amount of money a **speculator** puts down in **futures** dealings. Where a person wishes to buy or speculate in a property he may not intend to take it up, but the margin or deposit is an earnest of his intentions. The term is particularly used with reference to futures dealings in commodities or currencies. Dealings in margins occur when a speculator, having secured a certain quantity to be taken up in the future at a fixed price, sells the contract to another person, who pays only a competitive price for the margin. ◊ **London International Financial Futures and Op-**tions Exchange ◊ **Baltic International Freight Futures Exchange**.

Margin dealing ◊ **Margin**.

Marginal cost The extra cost of producing an item above and beyond the agreed output level. The figure for this cost (usually **direct expenses** only) is used to decide whether the additional production is justified. Other considerations such as **goodwill** apart, the additional sales revenue should equal or exceed the marginal cost. ◊ **Average cost**.

Marginal relief Where many income tax bands existed this was an option open to taxpayers whose income just took them into a higher bracket. It entitled them to pay tax at the rate in the lower bracket provided they handed over the amount by which their income exceeded the limit for that bracket (e.g. if tax rises from 30 to 40 per cent on incomes above £5,000, a person who earns £5,008 could pay 30 per cent tax on £5,000 and then add to this sum the amount by which income exceeded £5,000, i.e. £8). ◊ **Income tax** ◊ **Standard rate**.

Marine insurance A marine insurance contract is concerned with a marine adventure: with insuring ships, cargo, passengers, etc. Marine insurance is rather a complex matter. Policies are long and couched in language both colourful and obscure. The relevant act is the Marine Insurance Act 1906.

The risks insured against include damage by fire, storm and tempest, detention by foreign princes, seizure under legal process and dangers occasioned by 'men-of-war, fire, enemies, pirates, rovers, thieves, jettisons, **letters of mart and countermart**, surprisals, takings at sea, arrests, restraints, and detainments of all kings, princes, and people of what nation, condition, quality so ever, **barratry** of the master and mariners, and of all other perils, losses, and misfortunes, that have or shall come to the hurt, detriment or damage of the said goods and merchandises, and ship, etc., or any part thereof'. 'Pirates' includes passengers who mutiny and rioters who attack the ship from the shore, but 'thieves' does not include clandestine thefts by one of the crew or a passenger. This is a general list; any particular policy may exclude some of them or include others.

The insurer must have an **insurable interest**, i.e. he must personally stand to suffer from the loss insured against. The interest must exist at the time of the loss, though it need not when the policy is signed. Gambling policies where the insured has no interest at any time are likely to be void. The policy holder may even be prosecuted. ◊ **Policy proof of interest**.

Marine insurance policies are policies **uberrimae fidei**. The contract must take the specific form of a marine insurance policy and must be signed by the insurers. It must state: (1) the name of the insured; (2) the subject matter; (3) the risk; (4) the voyage or period; (5) the sum insured; (6) the name of the insurers. Policies may be **voyage policies**, time policies or a mixture of the two. They may also be valued or unvalued. A valued policy specifies the agreed **value** of the subject matter, an unvalued policy does not. On a total loss the holder of an unvalued policy would receive a sum related to the value of the subject matter at the time of the loss. The holder of a valued policy receives the sum insured irrespective of the value at time of loss. A floating policy is a general policy leaving the name of the ship or ships, etc., to

be given subsequently. There are various express and implied **warranties** and if these are not complied with by the insured, the policy may be ineffective, e.g. the ship must be seaworthy at the commencement of each part of the voyage, and also fit to carry the goods. With voyage policies the ship must sail from the place specified. It must not deviate from the course nor delay unduly. (This does not apply to **deviations** or delays due to factors outside the master's control or deviations to help ships in distress, where human life is in danger.) There are other deviations allowed (these are specified in the Act), e.g. for the safety of the ship or other insured matter, or for obtaining medical aid. Marine policies can be assigned by **endorsement**, unless this is prohibited by the policy. The assignee must have an interest. It is immaterial whether or not the loss has occurred. There are different forms of loss, and liability varies accordingly. ◊ **General average loss** ◊ **Particular average loss**.

Marine insurance: third-party risk
Although the doctrine on **privity of contract** is fairly sacrosanct, there are certain exceptions. Road **insurance** is one, **marine insurance** is another. The **consignee** of goods named in a **bill of lading** and an endorsee of the bill have the same rights and liabilities as the original party to the **contract** of carriage.

Market capitalization A term more popular with journalists than with economists, this refers to the total market value, at current Stock Exchange **list price**, of a specified category of issued shares in a particular company. The shares in question are usually the ordinary voting shares, i.e. **equity capital**. When the **quoted price** of a £1 share in a very large company falls or rises by a relatively small amount the individual shareholder may not react noticeably. If, however, this fall or rise is multiplied by the total number of shares in issue the resultant figure can make good headline material. An apparently startling financial statement that the **Stock Exchange** records fifty million pounds knocked off a company in one day may mean only that the ordinary shares of the company have fallen by a mere two per cent; but when this is related to a **share capital** running into nine figures the change in total market worth, or capitalization, can be immense. This type of shock tactic is also sometimes employed on a wider scale; a short-term rise in general stock market prices, brought about by nothing more than an unfounded budget rumour, can be expanded into a multi-million stock-market paper explosion as the rise is reflected in the market capitalization of all quoted shares. ◊ **Paper profit** ◊ **Shares: market value**.

Market forces The underlying forces in an economy, which affect the levels of prices through exerting pressures on the demand for or the supply of various goods and services. In a completely free market these forces will be regulated ultimately by fluctuations in public taste and the availability of both raw materials and finished goods. Free market conditions are nowadays infrequent and levels of supply and demand are very much at the mercy of government policy: e.g. supply can be manipulated by quotas and **tariffs** on imported goods, while demand is at the mercy of **indirect taxation**; both can also be much affected by vacillating rates of exchange. ◊ **Balance of payments** ◊ **Free trade** ◊ **Imports** ◊ **Minimum**

lending rate ◊ **Value added tax**.

Market leader The firm or company which has the biggest share of the available market for a specified product. The phrase is normally used in the context of sales in one country, e.g. the market leader for product B in the UK may be an American or German company which, in its home market, is merely another competitor ranked no higher than an 'also ran'. ◊ **Branded goods** ◊ **Market share** ◊ **Marketing**.

Market-maker A term with specific reference to dealings in stocks, shares, bonds and securities generally within the UK and emerging from the restructuring of the Stock Market at the time of **Big Bang** in 1986. The market-maker is the person, or organization, who undertakes to make an ongoing market in the securities in which he elects to deal either with investors or other dealers. He must retain stocks of those securities and must make a two-way price on a continuous basis in each, at which price he is then committed to deal. This price will be made available to any enquirer and will additionally feature on SEAQ screens.

Prior to the changes in 1986 the role of market-maker was the exclusive preserve of the **stockjobber** who bought and sold on behalf of a **stockbroker** acting for the outside investor and also dealt with other jobbers on his own account. There was also another category of operatives within the market known as licensed dealers. These were authorized by the Department of Trade to buy and sell certain shares, usually those traded in the Over-the-Counter Market which, due principally to the provisions of the Financial Services Act, has now ceased to exist – a fate shared by the licensed dealers themselves.

Market overt

When the jobbers' monopoly was abolished, members of the Stock Exchange could either opt to become full market-makers with the obligations attached to that role or, alternatively, could become broker-dealers who supplied clients with shares they had on their books but were under no obligation to maintain a continuous market in such shares. Both market-makers and broker-dealers can also act as agency brokers executing orders on behalf of private clients who pay them a commission for the service – in this they are reverting to the pre-1986 role of stockbroker.

The creation of market-makers led to a considerable opening up of the stock market. Merchant banks and other financial houses either bought up existing firms of stockbrokers and stock-jobbers, a procedure made possible by the relaxation of Stock Exchange rules which had hitherto prohibited ownership of Stock Exchange firms by outside interests, or alternatively set up market-making arms which would apply for and obtain Stock Exchange membership. The entry of the big financial institutions, including the clearing banks, introduced a much-needed source of funds into the market and it was this upsurge in liquidity which was so instrumental in expanding the London Stock Market and re-establishing it as a major international dealing centre.

Market overt An antique term with a rather specialized meaning. Generally speaking, a person who has not a **title** to **goods** cannot pass a title (i.e. cannot sell them). If, however, the sale is made between sunrise and sunset in market overt, when the goods are exposed publicly, in bulk (a **sample** is insufficient) and are of the class usually dealt in by the seller, then a good title can be passed to the purchaser in good faith, irrespective of the title of the seller. In the City of London, market overt is held daily (except on Sunday) in all shops and markets. In the country, it is held on special days in special places according to charter, custom or statute. ⟡ **Stolen goods**.

Market research ⟡ **Marketing research**.

Market Research Society A professional association for persons using survey techniques in market, social and economic research. Founded in 1947, it seeks to promote and protect the interests of its members and those employing their services. It also attempts to publicize the profession. Members are bound to observe a standard code of practice in conducting scientific sample surveys and reporting results. Various conferences are held to exchange information, and liaison with government departments, universities, scientific institutions, etc., is preserved. Members may be full members (MMRS) or associates (AMMRS), the former having obtained full professional standing.

Market share The proportion of the total supply of a product (usually in terms of value rather than quantity) controlled by any one particular firm or company. ⟡ **Market leader** ⟡ **Marketing**.

Market value A term (often used in published accounts) for the amount that an **asset** would realize if sold in a completely free market. (⟡ **Shares: market value** ⟡ **Stock-in-trade**). Distinction should always be made between value in present use and value in alternative use. The latter may be very much greater, for instance where factory land could profitably be developed for housing. The Companies Act 1967 states that where the market value of land held by a company is substantially higher than its book value, the directors should draw attention to this fact. However, the Act does not say whether 'market value' means value in present or alternative use and so allows directors to equivocate.

Marketing A term defined by the **Institute of Marketing** as 'the management function which organizes and directs all those business activities involved in assessing and converting customer purchasing power into effective demand for a specific product or service to the final consumer or user so as to achieve the profit, target or other objectives set by a company' (that is, the presentation and distribution of goods and services in the manner best designed to benefit the producer, the distributor and the public). ◊ **Advertising**.

Marketing, Institute of This was incorporated in 1911 as the Institute of Marketing and Sales Management (◊ Marketing) in order to provide its members with opportunities to develop their skill and judgement and to educate their successors in marketing theory and practice. Members may be fellows (F Inst MSM), members (M Inst MSM), associates (A Inst MSM) or graduates (G Inst MSM), and are elected by the Council of the Institute at its absolute discretion.

Marketing research Marketing research is distinguished from market research in that, while the latter deals with the pattern of a market, the former deals with problems involved in marketing a particular product. It starts with market research and then studies practical difficulties in selling and deciding, for instance, what lines might be pushed in particular areas and what special problems might be met in any particular region. It is concerned with the problems attached to selling a particular product for a particular manufacturer, while market research on the other hand would tend to study the state of consumers' demand in relation to perhaps a group of products of a very similar kind. Thus market research might be used by a group of manufacturers to obtain a field study whereas marketing research would be used by a particular manufacturer to discover the best way of selling his own particular **goods**.

Marriage brokage contracts Some persons offer for reward to provide a partner in marriage. These **contracts** are **illegal**. The **locus poenitentiae** rule does not apply and money may be recovered even after part performance or marriage itself.

Marzipan layer A colloquial term for senior personnel in City broking and dealing firms who, though expert in technical knowledge, are not partners in those firms and can be often lured away by competitors for higher salaries.

Master porter A dock company employee responsible for supervising the unloading of a ship.

Matched-bargains A technique sometimes applied in the field of share trading and particularly common among licensed dealers in the days of the OTC. When an investor wished to buy a given number of shares in a particular company the dealer would look for a would-be seller of the same quantity and put the two parties in touch with each other. In such instances the dealer himself does not take a position in the shares, i.e., he does not hold any shares on his own account.

Mate's receipt

Mate's receipt ◊ **Shipping notes**.

Maturity date The date when a debt, for which an extended time for payment has been given, must be settled. ◊ **Bills of exchange**. Also the date on which a debenture, bond or other **security** originally taken out for a fixed time becomes due for payment or renewal. The maturity date for an **endowment** policy is the date when the capital sum, with or without accumulated profits, must be paid out by the **assurance** company.

Mean A form of **average** used in statistics. It is a weighted **arithmetic mean** where each digit included in the summation is multiplied first by a factor representing its relative frequency or statistical importance. The weighting of individual items to find the true mean is similar to the process used in calculating the **retail price index** ◊ **Arithmetic mean** ◊ **Geometric mean** ◊ **Median** ◊ **Mode** ◊ **Index** ◊ **Weighted average**.

Mean deviation A simple and easy measurement of dispersion used in elementary statistics. When considering a series of values, the **arithmetic mean** is first determined. Then the differences between the actual and that mean value are added together and divided by the number of items in the series. The result is the mean deviation. ◊ **Standard deviation**.

Mean price Often referred to as the middle-market price, it is the arithmetic mean of two given prices, e.g. the buying and selling price quoted by a **unit trust** or a market-maker or (more frequently in the context of annual accounts and market value of investments) the average of the high and low price quoted on the daily listing of the **Stock Exchange**.

Median Another form of statistical average used where the **mean** does not give a fair picture, due to the presence of a few extreme values in a series, the inclusion of which gives an unrepresentative average. The median is arrived at by putting the series in an ascending scale and taking the middle one as the average or median. If the number of items is even, the two middle items are taken, added together and halved. ◊ **Mode**.

Medium-term capital Funds raised for a stated and limited period, not repayable at call. The period is normally less than five years. Funds raised for longer periods are classed as **long-term capital**.

Meeting, notice of Members of com-panies must receive notice of every meeting (the **articles of association** normally state that notice may be sent by post and need not be sent to anyone not resident in the United Kingdom). The notice must contain details of any special business to be transacted. For the **annual general meeting** twenty-one days' notice is required, for other meetings (but see below) fourteen days. Where the meeting is to remove a **director** or authorize a director of seventy to act, or to remove the **auditor**, the company must receive twenty-eight days' notice of intent to move the resolution, and must pass this notice on to the members, with the notice of the meeting. The director and the auditor have a right to make representations at the meeting. If wrong notice is given the meeting is invalid, unless: (1) at the annual general meeting all members who are entitled to attend and vote do so; (2) at other meetings members holding 95 per cent or more of the **nominal value** of the relevant shares agree otherwise.

Meeting, ordinary The **annual gen-**

eral meeting as opposed to an extra-ordinary meeting.

Members of companies A person becomes a member of a **company** when his name is entered in its register of members. Subscribers to the **memorandum of association** become members automatically. Other persons are entitled to registration when allotted **shares** on application, or when shares are transferred to them. Strictly speaking, anyone whose name does not appear on the register is not entitled to the rights of membership. A court may order **rectification of the register** if a person's name is wrongly omitted. On the other hand, entries in the register are not conclusive, and a person may have his name removed if it has been wrongly entered, though application to the court may be necessary first. Similarly should he allow his name to remain on the register he may be estopped from denying his membership. ◊ **Contributory**.

Members' voluntary winding-up ◊ **Winding-up, voluntary**.

Memorandum of agreement ◊ **Hire purchase**.

Memorandum of association Every limited company when formed must file with the Registrar of Companies a document known as its memorandum of association, which is open to public inspection. It must contain certain statutory clauses, though others may be added to suit the whim of individual companies. The clauses which are obligatory are those giving: (1) the name of the company (◊ **Company, name of**); (2) the UK country where the **registered office** is situated; (3) the objects of the company; (4) if a **public company**, the statement that the company is to be formed as a public company; (5) a statement that the liability of members is **limited** either by shares or by guarantee; (6) the number and amount of the shares authorized to be issued or, in the case of a company limited by guarantee, the amount of the guarantee.

These details should be accompanied by what is referred to as the association clause, signed by the subscribers to the company, who must number at least two, must give their names, addresses and occupations and must state the number of shares each takes. Their signatures must be properly witnessed.

A company is strictly bound by its memorandum and for that reason the objects clause is usually made very wide, so as to enable it to conduct a variety of businesses. It is possible to alter the memorandum, but only by **special resolution**, and any alteration must be immediately notified to the Registrar of Companies. ◊ **Company, objects of**.

Memorandum of satisfaction A document stating that a **mortgage** or charge on property has been discharged by repayment of the money lent. It should be signed by all parties concerned. A copy should be sent to the Registrar of Companies, if the mortgage has been made by a **company**, and registered.

Mercantile agent ◊ **Factor**.

Mercer Traditionally, a dealer in fine cloths and fabrics.

Merchant banks These, unlike the clearing or **commercial banks**, evolved from the need to finance foreign trade. They tended, historically, to trade on their specialized knowledge of overseas financial organizations and institutions and their contacts with them. Their major concern has always been with the facilitation of international trade; also with the problems of exporters seeking assurance of payment for goods delivered abroad and importers looking for convenient methods of settling indebtedness to overseas suppliers. They are the principal brokers for international trade though much of their business in this sphere is connected with the acceptance or negotiation of **bills of exchange**. ◊ **Export credit insurance** ◊ **Export house** ◊ **Foreign bills** ◊ **Foreign exchange market**.

In more recent times they have broadened the spectrum of their activities by involving themselves in the raising of finance for industry both at home and overseas. This includes the high-risk area of **hire purchase finance** and the slightly less risky area of the floating of new **share** or **debenture** issues by UK companies. To this extent they tend to duplicate, or overlap, the services offered by **accepting houses** and **issuing houses**. They are also increasingly involved in such matters as **take-over bids** and **mergers**, offering specialized advice to the parties initiating such ventures. They also offer normal banking facilities and are fast becoming used to the role of 'jack-of-all-trades' in the world of finance. ◊ **Flotation** ◊ **Introduction** ◊ **Offers for sale** ◊ **Placings**.

Merchant shipper A person who buys directly from manufacturers with a view to selling overseas. These merchants are also known as export merchants and most belong to the **British Export Houses Association**.

Merchantable quality A term used with reference to the **sale of goods**. There is an implied **condition** that **goods** are of merchantable quality, which means that

a reasonable person, after full examination, would accept them in satisfaction of his **contract**. Where there is more than one use of the goods, and the buyer has not made his intentions known, it might be sufficient that they are suitable for one of the purposes.

Merchantman A ship engaged in trade or commerce, not for war-like purposes. ◊ **Man-of-war**.

Merger The combining of two or more business organizations into one unit with a view to increasing overall efficiency. Mergers occur mainly in the world of **limited companies**, where the owners or directors of separate companies agree that the creation of one single company to carry out the objectives of each will be to the greatest interest of all concerned. The average merger is rather different from a **take-over bid**, where one company buys up another, often against the wishes of the latter's **board of directors**. Mergers are generally amicable and arranged for the mutual benefit of the companies concerned, though they may still need to be approved by the **Monopolies and Mergers Commission** and survive the scrutiny of the panel supervising the **City Code on Take-overs and Mergers**. When companies merge the owners tend to remain much the same and members of the old companies are usually offered equivalent holdings in the new company. ◊ **Amalgamation** ◊ **Anti-trust laws** ◊ **Cartel** ◊ **Consortium** ◊ **Group** ◊ **Monopoly** ◊ **Multinational** ◊ **Syndicate**.

Metric system The system of measurement in multiples of ten. In use in most developed countries, it is gradually being adopted by the UK and the USA. The system was proposed for international use at a conference in 1960. It is derived from the French metric system and is known as the SI (Système Internationale d'Unités). It creates a common language covering a wide range of scientific and technological uses: size, weight, mass, length, etc. There are marginal variations for specialized products. Trimmed paper is an example. **Paper sizes** are based on a basic rectangle with an area of one square metre and with sides in the proportion 1:1.4. This size is referred to as A0; other sizes are divisions thereof, e.g. A4 is one-sixteenth the size of A0. ◊ **Avoir-dupois** ◊ **Decimalization** ◊ **Decimal currency** ◊ **Imperial system** ◊ **Metrication Board**.

Metrication Board An advisory body set up by the government and responsible to the Secretary of State for Trade and Industry. It has no compulsory powers but exists to oversee the adoption of the **metric system** in the United Kingdom and coordinate various efforts being made to that end.

Middle market price ◊ **Mean price**.

Middle market value ◊ **Closing price**.

Middleman In commerce, a person who puts producers in touch with consumers. In the sale of goods, both wholesalers and retailers are middle-men. So also, in other fields, are **stockbrokers**, **solicitors** and **agents** of various categories.

Milliner At one time a dealer in fancy wares and apparel, particularly from Milan (hence the name), but now a dealer in or maker of women's hats or trimmings.

Minimum lending rate In 1974 **bank rate** was replaced by MLR as the official

minimum **rate of interest** charged by the **Bank of England** in discounting **fine bills** of exchange; it is also the minimum rate charged to **commercial banks** should they need to borrow money from the Bank of England. In 1981 MLR ceased to be publicly announced each week, but as the base rate of the Bank of England it still has a major say in fixing interest rates generally, as those charged to the general public will necessarily be affected by the price of borrowing from the central bank. For this reason it can be used as an instrument of government policy even if changes in the rate do not have the mandatory effect of changes in the old bank rate. There may be no obligation to follow the MLR, but the consequences of not doing so could be financially disastrous. Consequently, a watchful eye is kept on this rate by those bodies acting or dealing in the **money market**. ◊ **Discount houses** ◊ **Lender of last resort**.

Although MLR is no longer directly linked to the **Treasury bill** rate the two rates tend to move in concert. It also plays a leading role in international monetary movements, for as it moves up or down (particularly where in so doing it underlines expectations of foreign investors) so money flows in or out of the country. Fluctuations in the MLR, especially long-term trends, thus have a very considerable effect on the UK **balance of payments** and the size of the country's **gold and foreign exchange reserves**. ◊ **Tight money**.

Minimum subscription The amount stated in the **prospectus** which the **directors** consider the minimum that must be raised for the **company** to be launched successfully.

Minor A person under the age of eighteen. Minors are normally referred to, for legal purposes, as infants. In commerce the matter of infancy is, for the most part, relevant only to the law of contract. ◊ **Contract, infant's**.

Minority shareholders Members of a company in which the controlling interest, i.e. the majority of the **equity share capital**, is held by another company – a **holding company**. Minority shareholders have little or no say in the conduct of the affairs of the company, but the law does provide safeguards against their exploitation although these safeguards are somewhat diluted by the **Rule in Foss v. Harbottle**. Generally speaking, the courts will interfere when it can be shown that a particular decision of the company constitutes a fraud on the minority. In **take-over bid** situations where the bidding company or person has already acquired more than 90 per cent of the shares of a particular class (◊ **Shares, ordinary** ◊ **Shares, preference**), minority shareholders can insist that their shares be purchased at a price decided by the court.

Mint The organization authorized by the State to manufacture and issue, on a monopoly basis, the **bank notes** and **coin** which make up the **legal tender** of a nation. ◊ **Royal Mint**.

Misfeasance summons A summons which may be taken out against any **director**, **promoter**, **liquidator** or **officer of a company** in a **winding-up**, where it is believed that he has misapplied or retained money or property, or has been guilty of misfeasance or breach of trust. He may be publicly examined and ordered to repay the money.

Misrepresentation If a person induces another to enter into a **contract** by providing false information, he is guilty of misrepresentation. This may be innocent or fraudulent. If the person who made the representations can show that he believed them correct, the misrepresentation is innocent. In this case the injured party cannot always claim **damages**, though he can rescind the contract if he can show (1) that he has not implicitly accepted the misrepresentation, (2) that he has acted promptly, (3) that no innocent third parties have obtained rights in the subject matter for value (i.e. some kind of payment, and (4) that the parties can be restored to their former positions. The injured party can claim damages for innocent misrepresentation if (1) an **agent** has misrepresented his authority, (2) misrepresentations have been made in a **prospectus**, (3) misrepresentation is in the form of a **condition** or **warranty** or (4) there is a special relationship between the parties (a **solicitor** or banker, for instance, has a legal duty to take care), though in this case there would have to be negligence. The **Misrepresentation Act** 1967 gives additional aid to victims of innocent misrepresentation in certain cases.

Fraudulent misrepresentation entitles the injured party to damages and rescission. ◊ **Fraud**.

Misrepresentation Act 1967 The law dealing with innocent **misrepresentation** in **contract** has been altered by the Misrepresentation Act 1967, which states, *inter alia*: (1) **damages** may be obtained even for innocent misrepresentation, unless the person making the representation proves that he had reasonable grounds to believe, and did believe up to the time the contract was made, that the facts represented were correct (representation must be of a fact and not an opinion); (2) where a contract could be rescinded for innocent misrepresentation and the court thinks **rescission** would cause hardship, it may award damages in lieu; (3) in certain circumstances, contracts can be rescinded on the grounds of innocent misrepresentation, even though they have been performed; (4) in the case of contracts for the sale of specific goods, the Sale of Goods Act 1893 has been amended so that the contract may be rescinded, on grounds of breach of condition, even though property has strictly passed to the buyer. Provisions in a contract which attempt to avoid this Act may be treated as void by the court.

Mistake Generally speaking, when two persons enter into a **contract** it is taken for granted that they know what they are doing. The law will therefore not interfere, and if one party fails to perform his part he will be liable for breach of contract. Mistakes nevertheless do happen. They may be mutual or unilateral; they may be mistakes of fact or of law. If there is mutual mistake fundamental to the contract, whether about the existence or the nature of its subject matter, or about some other matter material to the contract, the contract will be void *ab initio*, for it does not represent the intention of either party and the court will not enforce it. This will not apply where the mistake is superficial, where the parties are getting substantially what they bargained for – though there may be grounds for an action for **damages**.

Where the mistake is **unilateral** the position is rather difficult. Where there has been **misrepresentation** on the part of one party, whether fraudulent or innocent, particular rules apply. Where there has been no misrepresentation the doc-

trine of **caveat emptor** will probably apply. However, even where no representations have been made, there are situations where unilateral mistakes can invalidate contracts. For instance, if one party is mistaken on something material to the contract, whether the person with whom he is contracting, or a term in the contract, or the nature of the document, and if the fact that he is mistaken is known to the other party (who need not have contributed to the mistake himself), the contract will not be enforced.

Mistakes of law are usually irrelevant as everybody is expected to know the law: '*Ignorantia juris neminem excusat*'. However, money paid where there is a mistake of law can sometimes be recovered if it would be inequitable for the other party to retain it, e.g. if the payee knew of the mistake.

Mitigation of damage In an action for breach of contract, where the plaintiff is claiming **damages**, the court will consider whether he has taken all steps necessary to minimize damage. For example, a seller must dispose of **goods** if there is an available market. The court will not award damages that could have been avoided by reasonable action, though the plaintiff is not expected to go out of his way to help the defendant. None of this applies to anticipatory breach of **contract**. ◊ **Contract, anticipatory breach of**.

Mixed economy A convenient term used to describe national economies which contain both publicly owned enterprises (e.g. in the UK, the coal industry, the Post Office, etc.) and businesses run as private enterprises. Most national economies, even those predominantly socialist or communist, contain a certain degree of mixing. ◊ **Competitive**

market ◊ **Nationalized industries** ◊ **Public corporation**.

Mobile shop A retail outlet which takes goods to potential customers rather than wait for them to come to the shop. A few retailers use this type of outlet alone. It normally consists of a large van stocked with a variety of consumer goods, mostly food. Mobile shops are valuable to both vendor and customer in rural areas where the population is too widely scattered to support an ordinary counter shop. Such a method of selling can increase the **turnover** of a business by extending the area served and by supplying a regular clientele of consumers who would otherwise spread their purchases over a wider number of shops. The idea has been taken up on an increasingly large scale by milk roundsmen, who now offer many other products, dairy and general, to their daily customers. ◊ **Consumer loyalty** ◊ **Goodwill**.

Mock auction Under the Mock Auctions Act 1961, a mock **auction** is one where during the course of **sale** (1) any lot to which the Act applies is sold at a **price** lower than bid, or any part of the price is repaid or credited to the bidder, (2) the right to buy is restricted to those who have bought or agreed to buy one or more articles, or (3) any articles are given away or offered in the form of **gifts**. Anyone running or helping to run a mock auction could be fined £1,000, imprisoned for not more than two years or both. ◊ **Cheap jack**.

Mode Another form of **average** used in statistics, though not as common as the **mean** or the **median** as its application is of only limited use. It is the value which occurs most frequently in a given series. It might, for instance, be relevant in assessing a set of examination marks. Where the pass mark is 54 the fact that 40 per cent of examinees achieve exactly 53 marks while the marks of the remainder are widely distributed may call into question the state of mind of the examiner or the agreed pass mark, or both.

Money That which is generally acceptable either as a medium of exchange or in the settlement of a debt. In the developed countries, money usually consists of **coins** and **bank notes**. Only these can be said to be **legal tender**, although the quantity of money within the economy at any given date would also include amounts standing to the credit of customers' accounts at banks and other depositories ◊ **Money at call and at short notice** ◊ **Money supply**.

Money at call and at short notice An item on a **balance sheet** of a **bank**. Money at call is money that must be repaid on demand. Money at short notice may be money borrowed for, say, twenty-four hours, at a very low **interest** rate. There is a great deal of money at short notice circulating in the City. When more money is offered than required, money is said to be 'easy' – when the reverse is true, money is said to be 'tight' in Lombard Street. ◊ **Overnight loan**.

Money broker A person who puts **banks**, etc., with money to lend from day to day in touch with persons or institutions wishing to borrow on such terms, e.g. a **discount house** looking for an **overnight loan**. The broker neither lends nor borrows – he is an intermediary receiving a **commission**. ◊ **Middleman**.

Money had and received A particular form of legal action where money paid by one party to another is claimed, not so much because the second party has failed to perform his part of the **contract** properly, but rather because there has been total failure of **consideration**, or because the money was obtained under false pretences or under duress and it would be unconscionable for the second party to retain it.

Money: M0, M1, M2, M3 Terms of convenience developed in monetarism. ◊ **Money supply**.

Money market This consists of institutions, such as **discount houses**, **banks** and even the government itself, which deal in very short-term loans. The principal commodities dealt with in the money market are **bills of exchange** in the shape of **Treasury bills** which are offered for tender each week. Other organizations often included in the term 'money market' are **accepting houses**, **finance houses**, **merchant banks** and the **Bank of England**. ◊ **Money at call and at short notice**.

Money supply Present monetarist economic policies are geared to what are referred to as money targets, which are various measures of total money in the economy. The underlying assumption is that price levels, i.e. inflation and the general level of economic activity, are closely related to the quantity of money in circulation. That quantity is consequently controlled by the Treasury, both directly through government financial policy and indirectly through the banking system.

There are various measures of the money supply, known as M_0, M_1, M_3, the last sometimes referred to as sterling M_3 or SM_3. At the risk of oversimplification, it can be said that M_0 consists of the total of circulating currency, i.e. coin and notes; M_1 is M_0 plus the total of

private sector current accounts with clearing banks; SM_3 is M_1 plus both public sector current accounts and all deposit accounts; M_3 as opposed to SM_3 also brings in foreign currency bank deposits in the UK; M_2 was a definition somewhere between M_1 and M_3 but was abandoned some time ago.

These distinctions broadly represent the view that both price levels and economic activity are essentially functions of total demand, which itself is geared to the amount of money in circulation. M_0 and M_1 are considered to determine short-term demand whereas in the longer term M_3 must be more relevant. As all these definitions of money supply have defects, modifications have been introduced, both in an attempt to eliminate deficiencies and because they are more relevant to certain economic circumstances. The more common of these are PSL_1 and PSL_2, where PSL stands for private sector liquidity. These modified definitions distinguish between long- and short-term deposits and exclude public sector accounts.

At present these money measures fail to take account of the potential demand represented by **credit cards** in circulation though attempts are being made to remedy this fault.

Moneylender One of those persons whose business is lending money. They are bound by strict regulations, *inter alia*, that they: (1) must not carry on business except in their own names, (2) must hold a moneylender's certificate and annual Excise licence, and (3) must not charge **compound interest**.

Rates of **interest** may vary, but a court may not allow recovery of interest that it considers excessive. A rate of interest over 48 per cent is *prima facie* excessive. Moneylending **contracts** and **securities** relating to them are unenforceable unless a note in writing is made and signed personally by the borrower. The note must be made before the loan. It must include the date, the amount of the loan and the rate of interest. ◊ **Bank loans** ◊ **Pawnbroker**.

Monger Once just a dealer or trafficker in **goods**; now a person carrying on some disreputable trade.

Monopolies and Mergers Act 1965 This Act created the Monopolies Commission. It has been superseded by the **Fair Trading Act** 1973, which established the wider **Monopolies and Mergers Commission**.

Monopolies and Mergers Commission This was created under the **Fair Trading Act** 1973 and replaced the old Monopolies Commission. It has full powers to investigate any potential monopoly situation referred to it by the Department of Trade and Industry or the Director of Fair Trading, and report back its findings. If the business investigated appears to operate against the public interest, an order may be made terminating the existing business agreement or ordering that the organization be broken down into separate competing parts. The only acceptable manner of avoiding such investigation is in a case where the apparently monopolistic agreements have been accepted and registered under the **Restrictive Trade Practices** Act 1956. The reason for the inclusion of the word **merger** in the Commission's title is that monopoly situations very often result from the merging of separate companies. Thus, any companies wishing to merge may first find it advisable to clear the merger with the Commission

rather than proceed with it only to find that it has to be abrogated.

Special rules apply to the merger of newspaper companies. Any such merger which will result in a proprietor obtaining a daily circulation of over 500,000 copies must, with very limited exceptions, be referred to the Commission and will be void and illegal until written consent has been obtained from the Department of Trade and Industry.

Monopoly A situation where a producer of particular goods or services controls the market, having eliminated all potential or real competitors, or is in possession of a **patent** to which no other producer has access. The elimination of competition can enable the producer to dictate prices and thereby earn excessive or monopoly profits. The fact that the producer is the major customer for the raw materials often means that potential competitors can be prevented from obtaining supplies of those materials; this strengthens the producer's control. Monopolies are usually unacceptable in democratic societies and legislation generally exists to keep them in check. The USA has its **anti-trust laws**, Germany has legislation against **cartels** and in the UK the system is regulated by the **Monopolies and Mergers Commission**. ◊ **Competitive market** ◊ **Consortium** ◊ **Fair Trading Act** ◊ **Merger** ◊ **Syndicate**.

Monopsony The reverse of a **monopoly**, it is an industry in which there are many willing sellers but only one buyer. The buyer can therefore set each seller against the others and obtain supplies at the lowest possible price. By being able to obtain raw materials at an unrealistically low price the buyer may in certain circumstances (e.g. competing in a world market) be able to sell his end products at a price which will produce an excess profit. The supposition behind this is that foreign competitors will not share the buyer's advantages in purchasing cheaply. ◊ **Competitive market**.

Moonlighting Working in two distinct jobs in any single employment period where the second job is carried on after apparent full-time employment in the other. This habit is quite common nowadays as shorter working hours, or shift work, provide an individual with sufficient spare time to take an additional occupation and so increase earnings. Very often the additional job is of the **self-employed** type and income is not declared for tax purposes. ◊ **Tax avoidance** ◊ **Tax evasion** ◊ **Black economy**.

Moral obligation Acts or payments arising from feelings of moral obligation do not constitute good **consideration** for the formation of a **contract**.

Mortgage Any transaction by which land is given as **security** for repayment of a loan. The rules are governed by the Law of Property Act 1925. Mortgages may be legal or equitable. A legal mortgage may be of two kinds. (1) A **deed** granting a lease for a stated number of years to the mortgagee – the lease to end on repayment of the money at or before the end of that period, with the possibility of a **second mortgage** granting a lease for the same number of years plus one day. The mortgage is usually accompanied by the deposit of title deeds. The mortgagee may insist on this. Possession of title deeds means that the mortgage need not be registered as a land charge. (2) A charge by way of legal mortgage. This dates from the

1925 Act. It is similar to (1), but not strictly a **lease**, and can therefore be used for mortgaging leasehold land and when the lessee is not allowed to sublet.

In both types of mortgage the mortgagor always has a right to redeem – this cannot be taken from him by clauses in the deed (◊ **Equity of redemption**). It may however not be possible until the term of the mortgage (or some lesser time) has run.

Equitable mortgages may be made by deposit of title deeds or written charge. No strict form is necessary. Possession of title deeds is good security, but if there is a charge then this should be registered at the Land Registry, or else it will not be valid against a **purchaser for value** in good faith. Equitable mortgages rank in the order of their registration and not in the order in which they were made.

Mortgagee, rights of The rights of the mortgagee where the mortgagor has defaulted are: (1) to sue on the personal covenant to repay; (2) to enter and take possession – though this is dangerous as a mortgagee must account scrupulously for income and expenses; (3) to foreclose, which involves asking the court to order repayment within a specified time, with a view to obtaining permanent ownership of the property; (4) to sell the property. There is an implied power of sale in all mortgages by **deed** – unless anything is said to the contrary. Sale can only take place after the date of repayment and with three months' notice, or when **interest** is two months in **arrears** or some other covenant is breached. The mortgagee, after paying expenses and himself, holds the **balance** on trust for the mortgagor, or other lenders; (5) to appoint a **receiver**. This is an alternative to selling. The receiver is the **agent** of the mortgagor although appointed by the mortgagee. He pays charges on the property, interest on loans, etc., and applies the balance of income to reducing the loan.

Most-favoured-nation clause This concerns international bilateral trade agreements where each country offers 'most-favoured-nation' status to the other and a clause is inserted to this effect in the trading agreement. To give such status is to agree that each will afford the other best available **tariff** and quota terms in the course of international trade. The importance of this status was emphasized in the **General Agreement on Tariffs and Trade**. However, exceptions were at one time made where **Commonwealth preference** applied; they are also to be found in customs unions, particularly the **European Union**. ◊ **Common Market** ◊ **Multilateral trade**.

Motor Insurers' Bureau A bureau set up by various **insurance** offices for the protection of the general public, when a motorist involved in an accident is not properly insured against third-party risks. All insurers handling motor insurance must belong to the Bureau and the responsibility for covering uninsured third-party risks is assigned to each on a rota basis by the Bureau. The Bureau also handles claims arising from accidents involving foreign motorists and their vehicles, and is responsible for supervising the green card scheme which applies to motorists travelling overseas.

Mountain This word now has a particular commercial meaning in the **Common Market**, e.g. butter mountain, apple mountain; liquids are referred

to as lakes, e.g. wine lake. These represent surpluses of particular farm products in the EU. They are a direct result of the implementation of the **Common Agricultural Policy**, under which farmers in all member countries must adhere to minimum selling prices set by the Union. If world prices are below this minimum, the EU will buy produce offered at a guaranteed intervention price slightly below the minimum selling price. This policy benefits farmers, who can now plan ahead with the knowledge of a floor price, but it has led to the accumulation of vast quantities of particular agricultural products. ◊ **Threshold price**. The Common Agricultural Policy prevents their being sold within the Community, and so they are destroyed, given away to low-income groups or sold at a loss to countries outside the EU.

Moving average A statistical term used to show trends in a series of figures. It attempts to iron out casual fluctuation by showing the movement in an n year average: for example, if total assets are shown for fifty years, the average for the first, say, five years would be taken. The next figure would be the average after dropping the first year and adding in the sixth, the process continuing until the fiftieth year is included. This type of average is rather rudimentary and tends to be of value only when the series is particularly long. In any event the initial figures are not true averages.

Multilateral trade Whereas bilateral trade describes trading agreements between two countries, multilateral trade is international trade carried on with many different countries and involving many currencies, which often benefits from the setting up of international clearing houses for mutual indebtedness. ◊ **European Payments Union** ◊ **General Agreement on Tariffs and Trade** ◊ **International Bank** ◊ **International Monetary Fund**.

Multilateralism The carrying on of indiscriminate **multilateral trade**.

Multinational An abbreviation for a **multinational corporation**.

Multinational corporations Often called international corporations, these are very large business enterprises, normally of a corporate nature, with interests (e.g. **subsidiary companies**) in businesses situated throughout the world. They are structured on a global basis and although they may originate from, or be registered in, a particular country, they rarely acknowledge allegiance to any one country – unless it is convenient to do so. For this reason, such companies tend to provoke discussion among academics and suspicion among governments as it is felt that they see themselves almost as sovereign states responsible to no one and often unable to avoid mixing business with politics.

Multiple store A shop which carries a wide range of both consumable and durable goods, rather than specializing in a specific type of product. It should not be confused with a **chain store** even though many chain stores are also multiple stores, e.g. Woolworths. ◊ **Hypermarket** ◊ **Supermarket**.

Muster roll A book kept to record details of all persons on board a ship.

Mutual life assurance company A mutual **company** is one where there are no shareholders. These companies developed from **friendly societies**, and were formed by large numbers joining together for their mutual interest. The **capital** of the company is made up of premiums paid in and profits are ploughed back for the benefit of policy-holders.

Mutuality This concerns actions for **breach of contract**. The court will not give a decree of **specific performance** unless there is mutuality, that is to say, unless the remedy would be available to both parties. For instance, a **minor** will never obtain specific performance of **contracts** which cannot be enforced against him because of his infancy.

Name day ◊ Ticket day.

National Association of Securities Dealers Automated Quotation (NASDAQ) The United States version of the UK SEAQ. A computerized price information system used by competing American dealers, who are the equivalent of UK **market-makers**, in the securities in which they agree to deal. They show bid-and-offer prices on NASDAQ screens. Originally set up to operate alongside the New York Stock Exchange and concentrate on the OTC market, it is now the second largest exchange in the USA.

NASDAQ has been present in London since 1987. In 1988 it was accorded the status of a **recognized investment exchange** under the Financial Services Act, putting it in a similar trading position to that of the London Stock Exchange. NASDAQ's role in London, and in Europe generally, is to provide UK and European companies with information relating to the US securities industry, and also provide support for those companies whose shares trade on NASDAQ markets, usually in the form of **American depositary receipts** (ADRs). It will, in addition, hope to promote the advantages of investment in NASDAQ-listed securities and advise on raising capital in US markets. Through its international service it also offers facilities for trading across time zones so that traders in London or in the US can continue to deal from the opening of the London markets to the close of the US markets.

National Bus Company Before deregulation in October 1986, bus services in England and Wales were the responsibility of the National Bus Company, established in 1968 as a public authority (Scotland was the preserve of the Scottish Transport Group). The company supervised the provision of adequate bus services within the UK, cooperating with the Scottish Board, the London Board, the Railways Board and local authorities.

It was authorized to carry passengers by road in or outside England and Wales and also by ship or hovercraft. It could hire out vehicles for carriage of goods and could act as a travel agent. It took over existing privately operated bus companies previously providing bus transport.

National Chamber of Trade ◊ Chamber of trade.

National Coal Board The NCB was set up as a **public corporation** to supervise the coal industry after its nationalization in 1946. The Coal Mines Nationalization Act 1946 brought almost the whole of the coal industry into public ownership, though certain mines which employed less than a given number of persons were left to be worked independently.

British Coal acts as the governing body for coal production throughout the UK and manages the industry through regional groupings which each have a degree of local autonomy. It is charged with maximizing the use of the nation's coal resources and with selling coal at competitive prices both at home and overseas. It is also charged with the promotion of economy in the use of solid fuel generally, to which end it operates various advisory services. In conjunction with the Department of the Environment it attempts to minimize the effect of its operations on the localities in which it operates and helps restore sites to a condition user-friendly to alternative activities when mining operations cease. ◊ **Nationalized industries**.

National debt A term used to describe the estimated total indebtedness of the UK central government to its own nationals and, to a lesser extent, persons or bodies overseas. Although the greater part of the debt is permanent and irredeemable, the identity of the persons to whom it is owed is by no means constant as the slips of paper which comprise it are constantly being bought and sold in the market. ◊ **Deadweight debt** ◊ **Government bonds** ◊ **Government securities**.

National Development Bonds These were government **bonds** obtainable from the **Post office** or **Trustee Savings Banks** and were introduced in 1964. All issues have now matured and interest is no longer paid on them.

National Economic Development Council (NEDC or 'Neddie') This was set up by the UK government in 1962 with the overall aims of encouraging economic growth and keeping a watch on industrial development generally. It consists of representatives of government, employers and trade unions, and is chaired by a leading government minister. In order to achieve greater coverage of national industrial problems sub-committees were set up in 1964, with responsibilities for particular industries and with power to make representations to the Council. These sub-committees became known as 'Little Neddies'. Their number varied according to the needs of the moment, and whilst new ones were sometimes created others were disbanded when they were no longer relevant. From 1981 the NEDC became part of the **British Technology Group**. ◊ **Development areas** ◊ **Industrial and Commercial Finance Corporation** ◊ **Trade and Industry, Department of**.

National Freight Consortium PLC This organization, owned principally by its employees, was set up in 1982 to purchase from the state the National Freight Corporation. With well-known companies such as British Road Services, National Carriers, Pickfords and the National Freight Company itself as subsidiaries, this consortium is now the largest and most diverse British road transport organization. In addition to transporting goods of all shapes, sizes, weights and bulk, it also offers facilities for storage, contract hire, factory and home removals, truck and trailer rental, travel services, export packing and freight shipping and forwarding. It also has locations overseas and operates transport businesses in Australia and the USA. It is now known as the NFC plc, and is listed as such on the Stock Exchange.

National Insurance This encompasses all the various aspects of insurance benefits for which the State is responsible, including sickness benefits, unemployment pay, maternity benefits and other money payable to cover known contingencies, e.g. retirement and widows' pensions. It is ultimately the responsibility of the Department of Social Security, which also pays other **supplementary benefits**

as ordained by current legislation. The central fund is financed principally by contributions paid by employed persons earning over a fixed minimum and partly by the Exchequer out of general taxation. These contributions are in two parts, the smaller being deducted from wages through PAYE, and the larger paid directly, on behalf of the employee, by his employer. Self-employed persons contribute by purchase of National Insurance stamps from the **Post Office**. Now, all contributions are earnings related, as are retirement pensions, though where an employer can demonstrate that he can provide a private scheme equal to, or better than, the State scheme, he has the option of contracting out of the latter. In an **occupational pensions scheme**, the contributions payable by the employers and employees to the State, through National Insurance contributions, will be much lower than in the State scheme. The fact that they still must contribute to the State fund, even though they have obtained a contracting-out certificate, is explained by the fact that the State scheme covers not only retirement benefits but also the running of the National Health Service. It also provides a basic pension to all retired persons. ◊ **Pay As You Earn**.

National Insurance should be distinguished from what was once known as National Assistance and is now referred to as supplementary benefits. These are semi-gratuitous payments paid to persons for whom ordinary National Insurance benefits are inadequate, due to exceptional circumstances of distress. In fact, if not in theory, supplementary benefits are available for multifarious reasons and anyone who considers that they suffer particular hardship, irrespective of the reasons, can apply for them. The system which allows these benefits to be paid

has evolved from the application of successive and, to a large extent, arbitrary Acts of Parliament; in view of the abuses which it tolerates, it is in dire need of reform by some type of consolidating legislation.

National Research Development Corporation (NRDC) Now part of the British Technology Group, this was first set up in 1949 by the then **Board of Trade** to develop and exploit inventions and new ideas arising from research in government laboratories, universities and other public bodies. It may also help in independent research within the private industrial sector, though only where such investment is deemed to be in the public interest.

National Savings Bank Once known as the Post Office Savings Bank it is now the responsibility of the Department of National Savings, though most of its business is still conducted through post offices. Anyone of seven years of age or over may open an ordinary account, and younger persons may have an account opened on their behalf. Accounts can also be opened in joint names and by clubs or trustees, but not by **limited companies**. The minimum deposit required for opening an account is at present £5, and there is an upper ceiling of £10,000 which can only be exceeded in certain defined circumstances. Monies may be deposited or withdrawn at any time without notice at any post office with NSB facilities, though there is a limit on the amount that can be withdrawn at any one time. When an account is opened, depositors receive a book in which all transactions are recorded. The NSB may, through the Post Office, call in the book at any time and must do so when the book is full. Interest is payable at a fixed rate and, up to a stated amount, is tax-free.

Investment accounts are also available and if less commonly used this is because they were not primarily intended for the small saver for whom the National Savings Bank was originally designed. Investment accounts carry a higher interest rate, but there is no tax exemption and the amount that any one person can retain in such an account is at present limited to £25,000.

National Savings Bond The Department of National Savings offers long-term investment through the issue of National Savings Bonds. While these carry higher interest rates than those available at the National Savings Bank, the money is tied up for longer periods. Also if it becomes necessary to cash the bond earlier than initially agreed, the interest earned may be substantially reduced.

The Bonds available at any time vary as to nomenclature but are generally either Capital Bonds intended for the long-term saver, or Income Bonds where the capital invested is tied up for a certain period but the interest is paid to the holder on a monthly or yearly basis depending on choice. In all cases the security of the sum invested is guaranteed. For Capital Bonds the interest rate is normally guaranteed for the period of the investment, say five years, but for Income Bonds the rate is subject to change.

The bonds are available from the National Savings centre in Glasgow but purchase can be effected either directly or indirectly through the Post Office. Whether the bonds are capital or income there is a minimum that must be invested at any one time and an overall maximum that may be invested by any one person.

National Savings Certificates A government **security** introduced in 1916 (when it was called a War Savings Certificate) and obtainable at post offices. No **income tax** is payable on **interest** from these Certificates (it need not be specified in a UK tax return); nor does **capital gains tax** apply to an increase in their **value**.

Certificates are available in multiple units and now tend to be index-linked as to capital. ◊ **Index-linked National Savings Certificates**. They may be bought by anyone in his own name or that of another. There is a limit to the number any one person may hold at one time. Each holder has a number. A signature is necessary except for children under seven, for whom the date of birth suffices instead. Repayment follows from written application to the Director of National Savings. Forms are obtainable at most post offices and normally eight working days' notice is necessary.

Nationalized industries These are industries owned by the public, i.e. in the control of the government through a semi-autonomous Board of Management. There are no shareholders apart from the government, though to raise money to buy the **shares** (or just to provide additional finance) the government has sometimes issued **bonds** at fixed **interest**. Certain industries may be acquired by the back door, by purchasing shares gradually, and sometimes, rather than purchase an industry outright, the government acquires a sufficient stake to enable it to direct policy – a modified form of nationalization. ◊ **Public corporation**.

Nautical mile ◊ **Admiralty measured mile**.

Near money Not quite cash in the **bank** or in hand but nevertheless near liquid, such as **money at call and at short notice**.

Necessaries Articles reasonably needed and suitable to the station in life and standard of living of the person wanting them. The word is significant in **infants' contracts**. A married woman has an implied authority to pledge her husband's credit for necessaries. He can only escape liability by showing that he has forbidden his wife to do so and has given notice to those persons whose bills he has paid in the past. If the husband had already supplied the wife with sufficient goods, then naturally she cannot claim the goods purchased to be 'necessaries'.

Negligence of auditor An **auditor**, in the performance of his duty, may be negligent and so liable for **breach of contract**. This **contract** is with the audited **company** and it is the company which has the course of action. Difficulties arise when third parties rely on audited accounts and suffer loss. In the past it has been held that auditors have no liability to third parties. Now the attitude of the courts seems to be changing and, in any event, when the auditor knows, or can infer, that the accounts are to be shown to another person who may, on the strength of those accounts, lend money to the company, he may be liable for negligence.

Negligence of directors Generally speaking, **directors** are not liable for **contracts** made on behalf of the **company** where they are not acting **ultra vires**. They have, however, a duty to take care, and this could involve them in a charge of negligence. A director may be liable for the acts of his fellow directors if he habitually abstains from attending board meetings. He is not liable, when he acts in good faith, for errors of judgement. Also, provided he acts honestly and reasonably, the court can relieve him from responsibility for *ultra vires* transactions. ◊ **Insolvency Act** 1986.

Negotiable instrument A document of **title** that can be freely negotiated. It usually concerns **choses-in-action**. Title can be transferred by delivery, and no particular form is necessary. **Bills of exchange**, **cheques**, **promissory notes**, are all negotiable instruments. It should, however, be noted that holders of a negotiable instrument cannot pass on a better title than they themselves possess. This would be relevant in instances of **theft**. ◊ **Cheque crossing** ◊ **Not negotiable**.

Net assets A term often used in published accounts for the total of fixed plus net **current assets**, or fixed plus current assets less current liabilities. ('Fixed assets' means here all **assets** which are not current assets.) The significance of this total may be somewhat doubtful depending on whether or not one considers it equal to **capital employed**. It is often described as this.

Net book agreement One of the few ostensibly restrictive practices in the retail trade accepted for registration, as being in the public interest, under the **Restrictive Trade Practices** Act 1956 and the Resale Prices Act 1964. It is an agreement between publishers and the Booksellers' Association which precludes the offer of books for sale below the price marked by the publishers. There are some exceptions, including a category made up largely of school textbooks, books which have been in stock with a bookseller for a long period and books which are offered for sale as publisher's remainders or in an official national book sale. ◊ **Recommended retail price** ◊ **Resale price maintenance** ◊ **Restrictive practices court**.

Net book amount This is a phrase often used as a synonym for the **written down value** of fixed assets belonging to a company or other business unit. When businesses are sold or companies are taken over, then fixed assets are often said to be acquired at net book amount, i.e. they are technically acquired at that value and it is at that figure – the net book amount – that they appear in the books and accounts of the new owner. Any premium paid over the net book value is then treated as having been paid for goodwill, and is shown as that by the acquirer; it is usually a lump sum which is the difference between the total assets at the agreed net book amounts and the actual purchase price.

There was also, however, a specialized sense in which the phrase net book amount was used, arising from the passing of the 1948 Companies Act. This Act made it necessary for all companies to show fixed assets at cost, with the amount written off for depreciation given as a separate figure. In certain cases it was impossible or severely impractical to ascertain the original cost, and where this could be shown to be so, the companies were permitted to show the assets concerned at their net book amount in July 1948. Thereafter, companies continued to show fixed assets in published accounts at a figure described as 'historical cost or net book amount at July 1948'. Older companies may still retain assets in this category.

Net present value A term used with particular reference to investment control. When a project is being considered, various devices are employed to discover whether it is profitable. One method is to take the projected value of expected net receipts for the years the plant will be productive. This is discounted back at a rate of **interest** consistent with the risk involved, to the date of investment. There will be a figure for each year. If the total of these figures exceeds the **capital** to be invested, the project may be profitable. Another similar method is to find the rate of interest that would produce the anticipated net income on the amount invested. The project is then assessed according to the adequacy of that interest rate. The first method is known as the net present value technique. The second is more appropriate where the income is concentrated at one point in the future. Both methods are in common use. There are also other more sophisticated techniques, but they are basically variations of these two, i.e. worked on the theory of **compound interest**. ◊ **Discounted cash flow**.

Net price The amount a buyer pays after all discounts, etc., have been deducted. This is also called 'net cost'.

Net profit Strictly speaking, this is the business profit accruing to the owners of capital after all costs have been provided for and all other factors of production have received their due. It is used in accounting to describe the amount remaining from **gross profit** after all charges in respect of overheads and any other costs, often referred to as **extraordinary items**, have been deducted. Though this is technically the same as the first definition given, the net profit so calculated will, in the case of companies, be divided between various providers of capital in proportions determined by the conditions on which this capital was subscribed. If the fixed dividend falling to holders of preference shares absorbs all the current net profit, then the ordinary shareholders, who might be described as the true owners, will not receive any part of that net profit. Net profits per accounts may also differ from net profit for purposes of taxation due to the special rules set out by the Inland Revenue, both as to allowable and non-allowable costs and as to methods of calculating certain **variable costs**. For this reason the phrase net profit cannot be considered in practice as having a precise meaning.

Net weight The actual weight of **goods**, after deducting the weight of all packing materials.

Net worth An accounting term for the total of **share capital** and **reserves** or rather the difference between total **assets** and outside liabilities. ◊ **Capital employed**.

Night safe A facility offered by **banks** (and available at most branches) whereby money can be dropped into the bank strong-room through a form of letterbox after banking hours. The money is in a bag containing details of the customer's name, etc. Customers using a night safe do not legally bank the money and it is left there at their own risk. They collect it the following morning and bank it officially.

No-claims bonus Motor **insurance** policies usually incorporate a substantial no-claims bonus which is set against the annual **premium** where the insured has satisfied the conditions written into the insurance contract. This normally applies where no claim has been made on the

insurer for a specified number of years. The principal reason for such bonuses is to dissuade motorists from making frequent claims for minor damage. If a no-claims bonus is lost then the premium payable will increase considerably and it may take some five years or so for the reduction afforded by the bonus to be progressively reinstated. ◊ **Comprehensive insurance** ◊ **Third-party insurance**.

Nominal accounts ◊ **Accounts, nominal, real, and personal**.

Nominal capital Generally speaking, the same as **authorized capital**, as opposed to issued or called-up capital. ◊ **Share capital**.

Nominal value The **face value** of a share in a company is usually referred to as its nominal value. In a more general sense the term is used to describe the current exchange value of an item, as opposed to its **real value**. ◊ **List price** ◊ **Mean price** ◊ **Shares, market value**.

Nominee shareholders Shares need not be registered in the name of their beneficial owner. They may be registered in the name of a nominee or **trustee**. In this way the true ownership of perhaps substantial holdings may be concealed. The Companies Act 1948 gave the Department of Trade and Industry drastic powers to investigate true ownership where necessary. It could appoint inspectors to investigate the membership of a **company** and discover who was financially interested in its success or who was able to control it. The Companies Act 1967 made it necessary for **directors** to give full details of shares held by themselves, or by other persons for their benefit, or by persons closely related to them, such as wives and children. ◊ **Directors' shareholdings**.

There were also provisions in the 1967 Act regarding official notification to a public company by any person, whether or not a registered member of that company, of any interest of 10 per cent or more which that person had in shares carrying unrestricted voting rights. The 1985 Companies Act broadened this requirement and made it obligatory for anyone having an interest (this word is afforded a fairly wide compass) amounting to 3 per cent or more in any class of shares in a public company to notify the company of that interest and also of any subsequent change in that interest. ◊ **Company: disclosure of interest in shares**.

Non-contributory pensions Certain types of employment provide employees with pensions on their retirement without requiring contributions from pay from those employees during their employment. Such arrangements, which usually accompany slightly lower rates of pay, are becoming increasingly less common and such pensions are obviously non-portable. In the same category are the *ex gratia* pensions which are sometimes paid to retiring employees who, although they have served many years in a business, have not belonged to the relevant contributory pension scheme for a sufficiently long period to entitle them to an adequate pension. ◊ **Pension schemes**◊ **State Earnings-Related Pension Scheme** ◊ **Occupational pensions scheme**.

Non-executive directors As the name implies these are directors who, although they have seats on the Board, are not working or executive directors. In earlier times (and sometimes even now) they were little more than well-known names whose appearance on the published list of directors gave an aura of respectibility. This was particularly useful when the company was looking to raise capital from an often reluctant public, and also gilded the image of the company to an extent that it was given an edge over its competitors. In the present industrial climate, however, non-executive directors tend to be brought on to the Board either because they have specialist knowledge or because of their contacts and experience in certain aspects of the company's business. Though they take no part in the running of the company, their presence at Board meetings where planning and policy-making come to the fore can be very valuable.

There have been moves recently towards giving non-executive directors a more positive and distinctive role in two areas where management responsibility and public interest show indications of colliding. On the one hand, it has been suggested that they might take a greater part in determining the remuneration packages awarded to senior executives. Lately these have been showing a tendency towards escalation beyond the bounds of prudence. On the other hand, there have been suggestions that they could play a major role in the establishment of audit committees. These could be charged with keeping a weather eye on the running of the company by those entrusted with various executive responsibilities and would be empowered, if necessary, to report back directly to shareholders.

Non-taxable income Incomes not liable to **income tax** include wounds pensions and disability pensions, bounty payments to army volunteers, widows' war pensions regarding children, the

Korea gratuity, annuities paid to Victoria Cross and George Cross holders, **interest on National Savings Certificates**, certain interest on **National Savings Bank** accounts, interest from SAYE schemes, scholarship income, payments regarding unemployment, sickness benefits, etc., and various lump sum payments to retiring or redundant employees. Certain incomes earned abroad may not be taxable if not remitted to this country. ◊ **Golden hand shake**.

Non-voting shares ◊ **'A' ordinary shares**.

Normal market size (NMS) This method of classifying shares was introduced by the Stock Exchange in 1991 to replace the old alpha/beta/gamma/delta method by which shares were previously classified to reflect their perceived importance in terms of market turnover. The NMS for a share is found by dividing the value of the previous twelve-month turnover of a share by its closing price on the last day of the quarter. The appropriate NMS band is then found by reference to a published table which gives the number of SEAQ shares in that band. The NMS of a share will determine the speed at which transactions in it are reported. For example, details of transactions in shares with an NMS of 2000 or more are published immediately, while those with an NMS of 1000 or less are published in the next day's official list.

Not negotiable If the words 'not negotiable' are written across a **bill of exchange**, a person taking the bill cannot get a better **title** than the person from whom he took it. This does not prevent the bill from being negotiated, but the bill is no longer a **negotiable instrument** proper. ◊ **Crossings: not negotiable**.

Notary public Usually a **solicitor** and someone specifically appointed to deal with such matters as the **noting and protest** of **bills of exchange**, attesting **deeds**, etc. A notary's word is acceptable as evidence in most foreign courts.

Note circulation ◊ **Bank of England**. Note issue is controlled by Parliament, through the Issuing Department of the Bank of England. The Bank of England has a monopoly of note issue in England and Wales. At one time notes were backed by gold; this is no longer so. The note issue is now almost entirely a **fiduciary issue**. The gold held by the Issue Department was transferred to the **Exchange equalization account**. Profits on note issue, and any surpluses or deficiencies on weekly revaluation of **securities**, etc., which are held by the Issue Department, are also put to this account.

Bank of England notes now in circulation are in the denominations £50, £20, £10 and £5; the £1 note has been phased out and replaced by the **pound** coin, first issued in 1983.

Notes of £2 and £1 were first issued by the Bank of England in 1797 but were discontinued in 1821. With the outbreak of war in 1914 the sovereign began to disappear from circulation and a £1 note was issued by the Treasury to fill the gap. These Treasury notes continued to be issued until responsibility for the £1 note was passed back to the Bank of England in 1928. Otherwise, the Bank's notes, until 1928, were limited to £5 and upwards, Bank of England notes having been **legal tender** since the year 1833. The £5 note dates from 1793, the £10 note from 1759. Notes of £50, £100, £500 and £1,000 were discontinued in 1943 for political reasons though the £50 note was reintroduced in 1981. Other denominations issued at one time were £15, £25, £30, £40, £60, £70, £80, £90, £200, £300 and £400. Only the £200 note survived the nineteenth century, and this was abolished in 1928. The number of notes in circulation at any time, though limited by the fiduciary issue, depends upon conditions of supply and demand. Banks in Scotland and Northern Ireland issue their own notes, though all but a very small number of these must be fully covered by holdings of Bank of England notes, gold, or silver coin. ◊ **Bradburys**.

Notes to accounts The various Companies Acts direct that certain information which must be divulged in annual accounts of companies may be given by way of notes to either the balance sheet or the profit and loss account if not included in the accounts themselves. The 1987, 1985 and 1989 Companies Acts added to the information that must be so given. Among other things, the notes must give details of accounting policies that have been followed in preparing the accounts themselves. Notes to accounts necessarily form part of the accounts, and information which these Acts permitted to be given by way of note rather than in the body of the accounts cannot be given in the directors' report. With one or two very limited exceptions, comparative figures for the previous year must also be given alongside amounts stated in the notes.

Notice in lieu of distringas This is used in company law to prevent the wrongful transfer of **shares**. The notice is issued by the shareholder to the **company**, which must then inform him of any attempt to transfer his shares. ◊ **Share transfer**.

Notice of abandonment Notice must be given to the insurer when a ship is abandoned as a **constructive total loss**. ◊ **Abandonment**.

Noting and protest Where a **bill of exchange** is not accepted or paid when presented, the holder, to protect himself and prove that the rules regarding presentment have been observed, should take the bill to a **notary public**, who, either himself or through an **agent**, re-presents it on the day of dishonour or the next successive business day. He also makes an entry in his register and 'notes' on the bill, or a document attached to the bill, various particulars including the reason for dishonour. This is known as noting.

The protest is a document containing (1) an exact copy of the bill, (2) details of the persons protesting and protested against, (3) the time and place of the protest, (4) a statement that acceptance or payment was refused and the reasons given. The signature and seal of the notary appear on the document.

If a notary public is not available, the bill may be protested by any householder or substantial resident in the presence of two witnesses. Protest should be at the place of dishonour, unless the bill has been presented and returned by post, or is payable at some place other than the place of acceptance, when the protest should be made at the place of payment. Noting and protest are only legally necessary with (1) **foreign bills**, (2) **inland bills** as a preliminary to an **acceptance supra protest**.

Novation ◊ **Contract of novation**.

Numbered account The term used to describe a bank account which is identified by a number only – and where the bank is not free to give the name of the account holder to anyone. These accounts are usually in Switzerland, where the laws governing banking allow the high degree of secrecy necessarily involved, and are frequently used by those who wish, for reasons ranging from **tax evasion** to shady or plainly crooked dealing, to hide the existence of large sums of money. The Swiss banker is not necessarily thereby willing to become an accessory to crime, but tradition precludes asking a customer the source of the money which that customer wishes to deposit, or disclosing either the names of specific depositors holding numbered accounts, or the amounts in them at any time, except in very strictly defined circumstances. This practice should be carefully distinguished from that existing in the UK, where concealment of doubtfully or illegally acquired funds through banks is considerably more difficult. ◊ **Banker, disclosure of information by**.

NV An abbreviation attached to the title of a corporation registered in the Netherlands. The letters stand for Naamloze Vennootschap and an NV is similar to the British **public company**, the French SA and the Geman AG. ◊ **European Union companies** ◊ **French companies** ◊ **German companies**.

Objects clause ◊ **Memorandum of association**.

Obsolescence In the business world obsolescence can be a major constraint in the employment of plant and machinery. It relates to situations where the useful life of fixed assets is prematurely terminated, not by deterioration but by the fact that technological advances have necessitated their replacement by more up-to-date equipment. In times such as now, when the development of new techniques is constantly accelerating, the problems posed by the obsolescence factor can be very serious and keeping a competitive edge can therefore become a costly process. ◊ **Built-in obsolescence**

Occupational pensions scheme A **pension** scheme devised by a business organization for the benefit of employees which has satisfied the conditions which allow the employers to contract out of the **State Earnings-Related Pension Scheme**. Such schemes must obtain the approval both of the Inland Revenue and the state examining body known as the Occupational Pensions Board. ◊ **Pensions** ◊ **Non-contributory pensions**.

Off-licence A shop licensed to sell intoxicating liquor for consumption off the premises.

OFFER This is an acronym for Office of Electricity Regulation, the regulatory body for the electricity industry set up in 1990 when the 1989 Electricity Act came into force. OFFER is responsible for licensing both generating and supply companies, the latter temporarily operating under franchises granted by the regulatory body. It is charged with ensuring that the various companies operating within the industry offer a fair and efficient service, and with investigating and resolving complaints from electricity users. It also sets maximum prices at which power may be sold and, where necessary, settles the terms by which other suppliers can have access to the public distribution system. With these objectives in mind, it has established offices in each of the individual supply regions.

Offer A term used in the law of **contract**. The offer is the first step. Other things being equal, **acceptance** of the offer can bind the offeror. The offer may be conditional or unconditional. The acceptance must be in the same terms as the offer. An offer is not operative until communicated to the other party. Posting a letter, for instance, is not sufficient. An offer should not be confused with an invitation to make an offer. A shopkeeper who marks his goods with a price in the window is not offering to sell at that price, or to sell at all; he is inviting persons to come into the shop and offer to purchase the goods.

An offer does not necessarily have to be in writing. ◊ **Invitation to treat**.

Offer and acceptance by post An **offer** by post is not final until communicated to the offeree and therefore can be revoked until that time. Acceptance is complete when the letter is posted, and proof of posting is proof of acceptance. (Delivery to a postman is not posting – the letter must be placed in the post box.) The offeror may be bound even though the acceptance does not reach him.

Offer by tender ◊ **Tender: capital issues**.

Offer for sale Instead of making a formal issue through a prospectus, a company may sell all the shares to an **issuing house**, which will then offer the shares to the public. This offer must be in the form of a prospectus.

Offer price ◊ **Bid price** ◊ **Unit trust**.

Office Management, Institute of The institute was established over sixty years ago to cater for specialists in office management, full-time office managers and persons with senior office responsibilities. Members may be Fellows (FIOM), Ordinary Members (MIOM) or Associates (AIOM). An ordinary member must be over twenty-seven and either have a Diploma awarded by the Institute, be responsible for at least a large section of his **company**'s office, be a specialist in office management or teach the subject. Associate Members must be over twenty-three, be engaged in responsible work in office management or hold the Institute's Certificate. Fellows must have been ordinary members for five years and occupy senior positions in general or office management, or have rendered outstanding service to the Institute. Companies can become patrons.

Office of Fair Trading ◊ **Fair Trading Act**.

Officer of a company In **liquidation** proceedings it is sometimes important to know who are the officers of a company. The Companies Act 1985 allows the court to investigate the conduct of officers with a view to their being compelled to repay money or property by means of a **misfeasance summons** (which can be made against any **director**, **promoter** or officer of a company). The term 'officer' includes directors, managers, secretaries and, in some cases, when they are acting on behalf of the company, **auditors** and **solicitors**. The 1980 Companies Act provided that when loans, quasi-loans or guarantees are afforded by a company or its subsidiary to officers of that company, then aggregate details of such benefits must be given in the accounts.

Official List The list published by the **Stock Exchange** at the end of each day's dealings, giving current prices of **shares**, **bonds**, etc.

Official Petitioner When a criminal bankruptcy order has been made the Official Petitioner, a role taken by the Director of Public Prosecutions by virtue of his office, must decide whether the public interest is best served by instituting civil bankruptcy proceedings. If he does so petition, then he is allowed to reimburse the expenses incurred by other persons in connection with the pursuance of that petition.

Official Receiver A person appointed to conduct either directly, or in a supervisory capacity, the winding-up of a bankrupt's estate or the affairs of a company which has gone into liquidation. Initially appointed by the court, he must, where circumstances dictate, report to the Department of Trade and Industry. This latter occasion will arise where, in course of a **compulsory winding-up** of a company, the Official Receiver decides that further investigation into the conduct of the company's affairs is desirable and mentions this fact in a report to the Department of Trade and Industry. In the report the Receiver may also state whether it is likely that any fraud on the company has been perpetrated by its officers. In a company liquidation the Official Receiver may also be appointed as the provisional liquidator until an official **liquidator** has been named. ◊ **Investigations, company**.

Where put in charge of winding up the affairs of a bankrupt and acting as the trustee in **bankruptcy**, the Receiver is similarly charged with reporting to the court any findings which appear to suggest that the bankrupt has committed misdemeanours or in any manner contributed to his own bankruptcy. ◊ **Bankruptcy, trustee in**.

Official reserves ◊ **Gold and foreign exchange reserves** ◊ **Gold and dollar reserves**.

OFGAS The popular acronym for the Office of Gas Supply, a regulatory body set up by the government under the Gas Act 1986 which effectively privatized the UK gas industry. The Director-General of OFGAS is independent of ministerial control. The Office's function is to regulate the gas industry and monitor its behaviour as a supplier of gas to industry and private consumer alike, to ensure that existing pipelines are available to competitors of British Gas, which began as a monopoly provider, and to fix and publish maximum prices at which gas can be resold to the public. It is further briefed to act as mediator in any disputes between rival suppliers of gas within the UK.

OFTEL This is the popular acronym for the Office of Telecommunications. Headed by a director-general and set up by the Government it is an independent body which oversees the telecommunications industry within the UK. It is charged with maintaining competition within the industry and with ensuring that those licensed to provide telecommunication services comply with the terms of the licences. It is also responsible for promoting the interests of consumers as to quality of service and prices charged, and has the power to investigate any complaints brought by corporations or private individuals.

OFWAT An acronym for the Office of Water Services headed by a director-general and set up by the government as an independent body to oversee the privatized water industry in England and Wales. The director-general operates through ten regional customer service committees in ensuring that the different water companies, set up by the Water Act 1989, abide by the terms of their licences. He is additionally responsible for investigating all complaints.

Old Lady of Threadneedle Street A traditional and vernacular name for the **Bank of England**, which is situated in that London street. The nickname dates from the early nineteenth century and the time of the Napoleonic wars when the famous caricaturist, James Gilray, published a cartoon in which the Bank of England was portrayed as an old lady being attacked by certain politicians who wished to obtain her gold in order to further prosecute the war. It has been suggested that Gilray was obliquely referring to Sheridan's description of the Bank as 'an elderly lady in the City' during a speech in the Commons.

Oligopoly Control of a market by a few independent organizations. ◊ **Cartel**.

Ombudsman Common parlance for a Parliamentary Commissioner for Administration. This office was created under the Parliamentary Commissioner Act 1967 and is modelled on Swedish practice which for many years has provided for an independent **arbitrator** where government bureaucracy clashes with public interest. In theory the UK ombudsman is available to inquire into any complaints that a member of the public may make about apparent victimization by a person acting on behalf of the government. In fact, the ombudsman's powers are very limited and, in dealing with complaints, he relies on the disinclination of government departments to invite adverse publicity rather than on any ability to force the government to act differently.

Originally, the ombudsman's role was restricted by his inability to inquire into areas outside those of central government departments. The position has since been partly improved by giving him authority to investigate complaints relating to the Health Service other than those which arise from the use of clinical judgement.

Additionally, complaints against local authorities are now possible since the establishment of a number of local commissioners who are effectively ombudsmen, with powers of investigation into complaints against abuse of authority by local government bodies in the areas to which they are attached. Booklets describing the remit of local ombudsmen are available from the Office of the Parliamentary Commissioner.

Independent ombudsmen have recently been established to handle complaints arising from within the various branches of the financial services industry. There now exist separate ombudsmen in the fields of banking, building societies, insurance, investment products and pensions.

On demand A **bill of exchange** is payable on demand when it is payable on presentation. An uncrossed **cheque** is a bill payable on demand.

On stream A term commonly used nowadays to refer to the fact that a particular asset acquired or investment made has begun to earn its keep either, in the case of plant, by being made fully operative or, in the case of some other investment, by being finalized and beginning to bring in an income. The phrase is borrowed from the electrical energy generating world, particularly nuclear energy, where a power plant is said to be brought on stream when it has been linked in with the national grid system.

On the berth In shipping terminology, a vessel loading, unloading or waiting to do either.

Oncost ◊ **Overhead expenses**.

Open cheque A **cheque** that is not crossed and therefore does not need to be paid into an account but may be cashed over the counter. A crossed cheque can be opened (by the drawer) by writing 'pay cash' over the **crossing** and signing the alteration.

Open cover ◊ **Open policy**.

Open credit Prior to the common use of the **cheque card** or **credit card**, open credit facilities were the most effective way in which people could obtain cash from a bank other than at the branch where their own account was kept. By prior arrangement, open credit facilities up to a predetermined amount could be given at a particular bank in another town by a customer's own bank. ◊ **Bank: open credit facilities**.

Open general licence Importers must obtain **licences**. There are usually restrictions on some goods imported from certain areas, but where no restrictions apply, open general licences are available.

Open indent When someone in another country wishes to purchase UK goods, he may use an export **agent** in the United Kingdom. The export order is known as an indent; an open indent gives the agent *carte blanche* in selecting the manufacturer. A closed indent indicates the manufacturer.

Open-jaw trip An air-transport term for a (usually long-distance) wide-ranging tour whose starting and finishing points do not coincide.

Open market Open markets are those where **offers** to buy or sell are made to the public at large and not to a restricted number or behind closed doors. ◊ **Market overt**.

Open-market operations Operations by the central bank intended to stabilize **interest** rates or adjust the quantity of **money** in circulation. For example, the **Bank of England** may increase the quantity of money enormously by buying **securities** on a large scale in the **open market**. The money it spends will increase the **balances** of the **clearing banks**, and this will enable them to lend an even greater amount to the public.

Open policy A **marine insurance** term used where **goods** are insured though the **value** of the goods is not known or not fixed when the policy is effected. A provisional sum is agreed and the premium adjusted when the value of the goods is known.

Operating profit or loss An accounting term that has been given more significance by the terminology adopted in the formats for the profit and loss accounts of limited companies first provided in Schedule I of the 1981 Companies Act and now contained in Part I of Schedule 4 of the Companies Act 1985. These suggested formats refer to 'operating income' and 'operating charges', being the items of income and expenditure appropriate to the principal activity of the company, i.e. before items of an extraordinary nature are dealt with. The difference between operating income and charges would be the operating profit, or loss, for the period.

Operating statement An imprecise term for a statement showing the cost of running a business and the profit earned by a business or one of its departments.

Operation of law A **contract** may be discharged by operation of law. A judgment obtained by a party to a contract discharges the contract – the contract becomes merged in the judgment. Again, a contract, or the obligations of a contract, may be discharged by the lapse of time. ◊ **Limitation of actions**.

Operational (operations) research This concerns the development of procedures in the various disciplines that co-exist within industry with the object of maximizing efficiency in the use of resources and time available. It is necessarily much concerned with management techniques and is, to this extent, a tool of management. A fair example of ends to which such research is directed lies in the precise control of stock levels. This includes minimum quantities and schedules relating to both the time and quantity of repurchasing, geared to various levels of output. ◊ **Critical path analysis** ◊ **Inventory control** ◊ **Work study**.

Operator's licence Under the Transport Act 1968, an operator's licence (obtainable from a local licensing authority) must be held by any person using a goods vehicle on a road for carrying goods either for hire or reward or in connection with any trade or business carried on by the owner. This only applies to vehicles of more than thirty cwt unladen weight. Others do not now need any additional licence. The provisions of the Act are rather complex and users of goods vehicles are advised to study them.

Opportunity cost A hypothetical measure of the monies forfeited when an **asset** is put to one out of two possible uses. It is the amount that, in theory, that asset would have earned in the other use. Income so forfeited should, ideally, be less than that earned or be outweighed by other benefits gained and thus justify the particular investment made. ◊ **Cost benefit analysis** ◊ **Discounted cash flow** ◊ **Pay-back period**.

Options An option is essentially an agreement giving one person the right to buy or sell a given quantity of specified goods, services or choses-in-action at an agreed price at any time within a stated period. Options are usually concerned with dealings on the **Stock Exchange**, **London Fox**, the **London Metal Exchange** or the **London International Financial Futures and Options Exchange**. They arose out of the need to hedge against certain variables in trading situations and tend to be bracketed with **futures**, both being of the type of Financial Instrument

known as a **Derivative**. ◊ **Traded options**.

Options to sell are known as deals for the 'put' or 'put options', and options to buy are likewise referred to as 'call options'. It is a criminal offence for a director, or anyone connected with him, to deal in options to buy or sell shares in the company of which he is a director or in any associated company.

Options to purchase shares A person may be given an **option** to take up **shares** in a **company** at a stated **price** provided he does so before a given date. Whether he does so or not depends on how the market price has moved or is moving. He could make a large profit immediately by selling the shares as soon as he takes them up. For this reason, options often have to be paid for.

The larger companies frequently grant options to employees as a way of increasing their effective remuneration whilst at the same time reinforcing loyalty to the company that employs them. Although most of these options have in the past been afforded to directors and senior executives, there is an increasing tendency to offer them to more junior employees, sometimes through an employee shareholding trust.

Options to purchase shares given to company promoters must be stated in the **prospectus** and those given to directors may be subject to the various constraints contained in the 1985 Companies Act regarding transactions between the company and directors. They must also be taken into account when computing **directors' emoluments**.

Oral evidence Evidence given by word of mouth in court. Generally speaking, oral evidence cannot be admitted to change a written agreement, though there are certain exceptions to this rule. These are: (1) where the whole **contract** is not in writing and oral evidence may be allowed to supply additional terms; (2) where it is necessary to show trade usage or custom or that a subcontract was subject to a condition precedent; or (3) to explain that words are used with a meaning other than their everyday meaning (trade usage perhaps).

Order and disposition A clause in **bankruptcy** which establishes the right of a bankrupt's creditors to take and sell goods to which the bankrupt has no title. This has in effect provided that: (1) it is not obvious that the goods belong to someone else; (2) the bankrupt has behaved so as to suggest to an innocent third party giving him credit that the goods are not only in his possession but also his by legal ownership. The true owner can only recover the property if it can be shown that the trustee or creditors concerned were not acting in good faith. ◊ **Bankruptcy: debtor's property**.

Ordinary resolution A resolution passed at a meeting of the shareholders of a company usually at the **annual general meeting**. A simple majority of those present is sufficient for the passing of such a resolution, unless the **articles of association** of the company say otherwise. Also, barring any provision to the contrary in those articles, no special notice of the resolution need be given to members other than that necessary for calling the meeting (usually twenty-one days in advance) and stating the reasons for it. ◊ **Meeting, notice of** ◊ **Special resolution**.

Ordinary shares ◊ **Shares, ordinary**.

Organization for Economic Cooperation and Development ◊ **Organ-**ization for European Economic Cooperation.

Organization for European Economic Cooperation (OEEC) The parent body of the many organizations set up within Europe after the Second World War to facilitate and coordinate the national and international attempts to promote the full recovery of the European economy. The primary driving force behind this body was the Marshall Plan, whereby American aid was to be equitably distributed among the various nations. One of the first tasks was to set up and police the **European Payments Union**, which aimed to speed up the rate of trade between the different European countries both amongst themselves and with the United States. The OEEC was indirectly to promote the establishment of many other bodies including, ultimately, the **European Union**. In 1961 its role was taken over by the larger Organization for Economic Cooperation and Development (OECD), which included, in addition to the original European countries, the USA, Canada, Australia, New Zealand and Japan.

Originating bank A term used in foreign trade. Where a system of **documentary credit** is used and/or a foreign buyer works through the London branch, say, of an overseas **bank**, the overseas bank is the originating bank and the London branch is known as the correspondent bank.

Outcry market A term used with reference to financial futures exchanges. In an outcry market dealings are by private **contract**, but every deal must be shouted out so that it can be recorded.

Output tax In the VAT system this is the tax collected by a supplier of goods or services, who is registered for VAT purposes, and which must be accounted for to **Her Majesty's Customs and Excise** after relevant **input tax** has been deducted. ◊ **Value added tax**.

Outside brokers Stockbrokers who are not members of the **Stock Exchange**.

Outward manifest ◊ Exporters' declarations.

Outwork Part of a particular industrial process which is given out to persons working at home. This practice was more prevalent during the earlier years of the Industrial Revolution, particularly within the textile industry.

Over-capitalized A business is over-capitalized when it has more **capital** than it can profitably use. ◊ **Capital gearing** ◊ **Overtrading**.

Over entry certificate A Customs term used with reference to importing. Duty is paid initially on the basis of **prime entry**. It is sometimes found that too much duty has been paid and an over entry certificate is issued. If the duty paid was insufficient, a post entry is paid.

Over-the-Counter Market (OTC) This was a market in unlisted shares operated by licensed dealers – persons authorized by the Department of Trade to deal in shares. The OTC was never, at any time, part of the Stock Exchange and was not popular with that august body. Dealings were usually conducted by telephone and frequently on a **matched-bargain** basis. With the advent of the Financial Services Act and the regulations on investment trading that it incorporated the Over-the-Counter Market disappeared.

Overdrafts ◊ **Bank overdrafts**.

Overhead expenses Sometimes known as on-cost, these are expenses incurred in manufacture, though not directly identified with any particular item produced. Examples are administrative expenses, selling expenses, etc. ◊ **Direct labour** ◊ **Direct expenses** ◊ **Indirect expenses**.

Overinsurance Property is overinsured if insured for more than it is worth. There is no advantage in this as an insurer will never pay more than the true value of the property, which is normally the replacement cost.

Overnight loan A loan made by a bank to a bill **broker** enabling him to take up **bills of exchange**, the loan being repayable on the following day. It is usually renewed; if not, the broker must turn to the **Bank of England** and would then be forced to pay **minimum lending rate**. As this is higher than that charged by the clearing banks, general discount rates may be affected by the broker's assessment of this possibility.

Overriding commission A **commission** paid to **brokers** who find persons willing to **underwrite** the issue of **shares**.

Overseas companies Companies incorporated outside the UK but with a place of business in the United Kingdom. They must deliver to the Registrar of Companies: (1) a certified copy of their charter or **memorandum of association** and **articles of association**; (2) particulars of **directors** and **secretary**; (3) the name and address of person or persons resident in the United Kingdom authorized to accept service of process and notices; (4) an annual statement in the form of a **balance sheet** and **profit and loss**

account, conforming with the provisions applicable to UK companies.

These companies must mention their country of origin in all prospectuses and all official publications. They must also register charges on English property. If liability of the members is **limited**, this must be stated.

Overseas post Letters and parcels from the UK to destinations overseas are accepted by post offices subject to various conditions being observed and the appropriate pre-payment being made. Facilities for **insurance** are also available, as is the registration of parcels and letters. It is not possible to list the various conditions applicable as these vary according to the country of destination, e.g. certain goods may be completely prohibited in one country but quite welcome in another. There are also customs duties, levies and surcharges that vary from country to country, as does the length of time needed to effect delivery. Some remote areas depend on irregular calls by ships for their communication with the outside world and, for this reason alone, mail may be a considerable time in transit. The annual **Post Office Guide** gives all the relevant information country by country.

There are two basic overseas postal services: airmail and surface mail. The former is by far the swifter but is also much more expensive than surface mail. Because weight is a deciding factor in the method of delivery, the greater part of the airmail service deals with letters, and special lightweight paper is available to minimize the charge. The Post Office also sells air letters (preprinted on blue paper with space allocated for addresses, destination and source, and message). These **airmail letters** fold into the shape

required for posting and the postal charge printed on them is included in their original cost. Overseas editions of newspapers are also often printed on special light paper.

European letters are covered by what is referred to as the 'all up service'. This means that genuine letters, as opposed to printed papers and small packets, are always sent by air from the United Kingdom unless surface mail would be quicker. In this instance no additional airmail charge is made but an airmail label should still be attached. There is also an 'all up service' available for newspapers and periodicals, which are registered at the Post Office for this purpose. An 'all up service' operates on incoming mail from certain European countries. Mail to other parts of the world must be deliberately marked 'airmail' and the proper charge paid, otherwise it will automatically go surface mail. Packets and letters should be marked with the sender's name and address; any contents must be declared prior to sending in order that Customs dues may be assessed. Packets must be easily openable for examination and, where a cheap small-packet rate is being paid, the packet must not contain personal correspondence. The cheap small-packet rate is available to most countries for packets below a certain maximum weight. Cheap rates are also available for genuine printed papers, e.g. advertising material, books, newspapers, etc. Again, this rate only applies if the contents are easily inspected and do not include personal correspondence. Literature in Braille for the blind may be sent without charge by surface mail and at greatly reduced rates by airmail.

Oversubscribed **Shares** are said to be oversubscribed when more are applied for than are offered. In these cases, applications are usually scaled down pro rata, though sometimes small applications are met in full and only large ones (above a stated limit) are scaled down.

Overtime request Customs officers are sometimes requested to supervise cargo outside ordinary hours, in which case special charges must be paid.

Overtrading A business is said to be overtrading when it tries to do more business than its **working capital** will allow, i.e. when too much money is tied up in **stocks** and debts, and cash is not coming in quickly enough to pay **creditors**, or the normal expenses of running a business, like wages, **rent**, etc. The term also applies where large increases in **turnover** are not matched by appropriate increases in capital employed. ◊ **Liquidity**.

Own brand Some retailers, particularly those who operate on a large scale, often sell goods which would normally come under the heading of **branded goods** under their own private brand name – referred to as 'own brand'. In fact, many so-called 'own brand' **supermarkets** and **chain stores** buy on a large scale from the producers of reputable branded goods but use their own labels rather than the brand labels. By doing so their private brand name can achieve an independent reputation quite distinct from the original. Again, the use of 'own brand' labels is a useful way of avoiding manufacturers' listed or recommended prices. ◊ **Advertising, competitive** ◊ **Recommended retail price** ◊ **Packaging** ◊ **Prestige advertising** ◊ **Brand values**.

Packaging A **marketing** term for the presentation of **goods**, i.e. the manner in which they are wrapped or displayed. The wrapper can be a vital selling factor, apart from being a platform for **advertising**. Where the weight of the goods must be stated, the weight of the wrapping should not normally be included. **Net weight** means the weight of the goods without the packaging.

Adequacy of packaging may be important when goods are to be sent by post, and the Post Office has set certain standards. These are explained in the **Post Office Guide**.

Paid-up capital That part of the **capital** of a **company**, both called-up and paid-up. The difference between called-up capital and paid-up capital will represent calls in arrears.

Paid-up policies In the world of life or endowment **assurance**, the insured may sometimes find it necessary or desirable to cease paying premiums but may not wish to terminate his interest completely by surrendering the policy for cash. Provided the premiums have been paid for a stipulated minimum number of years – the period may vary with the policy and the insurer – there is usually an option to treat the policy as 'paid-up'. The premiums then cease to be payable and the insured retains a limited interest. This interest will not be realized until the time at which the policy would have normally terminated; the insured will then receive such a portion of the total sum assured as the number of premiums paid by him bears to the total number that would have been paid had the policy run its full term. In practice the proportion he receives will not be so exact, as the insurer will tend to attribute a greater portion of the administrative charges to the early years of the policy than to the later ones. With-profits policies may also be treated as paid-up, but whether or not the sum accumulated at that date will still be eligible for further bonuses depends on the insurer. ◊ **Life assurance**.

Paper money Documents being **legal tender** with a **value** stated on them but having no value in themselves, e.g. a five-pound note.

Paper profit Strictly speaking, increases in value of unrealized investments or assets not sold. A company may know that certain property in its possession has a **market value** well above the price originally paid for it and still recorded as the value in its books. However, since the company has no intention of parting with the property, because it needs it to continue business, the fact that it could be sold at a profit is of interest only on paper. ◊ **Value** ◊ **Value in use**.

The phrase is applied rather more loosely in inflationary times when businesses announce large **profits** which are the consequence not of increases in efficiency but merely of the fall in the value of money. In terms of purchasing power, the profit may be comparatively small: e.g. a reported increase of £50 million may, when adjusted to take account of price inflation, all but disappear. The announced profit may then be dismissed as a mere paper profit. ◊ **Current cost accounting** ◊ **Historical cost accounting** ◊ **Secret reserves**.

Paper sizes ◊ **Metric system**.

Par value A share's **nominal value**.

Parent company ◊ **Subsidiary company**.

Pari passu A legal term meaning 'ranking equally'. For instance, all shares of one class in a **company** rank *pari passu* as to receipt of **dividends** and return of **capital**.

Paris Club ◊ **Group of Ten**.

Parkinson's Law An unofficial law, proposed by C. Northcote Parkinson in his book entitled *Parkinson's Law*, which has been generally accepted as a very relevant half-truth. It claims that work expands according to the time available in which to perform it. ◊ **Quangos** ◊ **Work study**.

Part load A term used with reference to transport, normally road transport. Rather than hire a vehicle, someone wishing to send goods may buy space in a vehicle already going to a particular area without a full load.

This can be the most economical way of sending those goods.

Part payment Part payment of monies due under a contract or a debt is a not infrequent practice on the part of debtors, but it has no legal significance except that, in acknowledging the existence of a debt, it could extend the period before it would become statute-barred under the Statute of Limitations. There is one instance when part payment can extinguish the whole debt and that is when a lesser amount is accepted by the creditor in consideration of some fresh promise by the debtor: e.g. early payment but of a lesser sum might constitute good consideration for the cancelling of the whole debt.

Part payment should be distinguished from payment on account. This is a procedure whereby the creditor allows the debtor to pay in irregular instalments as the best way of assuring eventual settlement of the debt in full.

Part performance Some **contracts** need to be evidenced in writing before either party is able to enforce them, but this evidence may be waived where one party has by his actions indicated that the contract actually exists. This is known as part performance. It must be proved by the party claiming redress or **specific performance**.

Partial loss Most **insurance** policies are intended to cover partial loss as well as total loss and the majority of claims refer to repair rather than complete replacement. It is important, however, to remember the **average clause** which appears in most policies. It is included to prevent insured people deliberately under-insuring property on the supposition that they will never need to claim for its complete destruction. The average clause means that, if the property is only insured for 10 per cent of its value, only 10 per cent of any particular loss will be covered.

Partial loss has another more specific meaning in **marine insurance**. ◊ **Particular average loss**.

Participating preference shares ◊ **Shares, preference**.

Particular average loss A marine insurance term for a loss which is not a **general average loss** but one caused by damage to a particular cargo, borne by the insurers of that cargo, not shared by the insurers of the rest of the cargo. Certain policies are free of particular average, i.e. do not cover particular average losses.

Partner, active A partner in a **firm** who works for the firm and is not merely a sleeping partner.

Partner, general A partner in the full sense of the word, without restrictions on his liability. ◊ **Partnership** ◊ **Partnership, limited**.

Partner, infant An infant partner is bound by the **partnership** deed until he repudiates it. Repudiation must take place before coming of age or soon after. He cannot be made bankrupt. Regarding his relations with the public, his liability is that of an **infant**.

Partner, limited A partner whose liability is limited by law. ◊ **Partnership, limited**.

Partner, nominal Anyone who allows their name to be used in the advertised name of a **partnership** is nominally a member of that partnership. This situation can arise when a person's name is used in order to enhance the reputation of a **firm** even though the person concerned has no intention of participating actively in the business. Use of their name automatically makes the person liable, along with the other partners, for any debts incurred. The liabilities of nominal partnership also apply to people who, although retired or resigned from the firm, do nothing to prevent their names continuing to be used as part of the firm's name or in a list of partners published on partnership notepaper. In both instances the person involved will be unable to deny liability for debts. ◊ **Partner, sleeping** ◊ **Holding out**.

Partner, sleeping A partner who provides money but takes no active part in the management or organization of the business. He may or may not be a **limited partner**. The term has no legal significance.

Partners, incoming and outgoing Incoming partners are not liable for debts incurred before they become partners, though they could be liable if they agreed to be. Outgoing partners are liable for all debts incurred when they were partners. They could also be liable for subsequent debts if they have not given proper notice that they are no longer partners. They can avoid liability for past debts by a **contract of novation**.

Partnership Two or more people involved in the ownership and control of a business. This form of organization is governed by the Partnership Act 1890. The relationship between partners and their individual rights and duties are governed by the agreement that they draw up. In the absence of an agreement all partners are equal as regards profits and losses: each partner may act on behalf of the **firm** and bind the firm, providing that he is acting within his apparent authority, and each partner must indemnify every other partner doing so. (This obviously does not apply to matters outside the normal business of the firm.) A partner is not entitled to **interest** on his **capital** nor to remuneration (in addition to his share of the profits). Each partner may take part in the management and differences are decided by a majority. No changes may be made in the nature of the partnership without the consent of all the existing partners. A partnership **contract** is a contract **uberrimae fidei**: partners must account for private profit and must not compete with the firm. Subject to agreement, partnership is automatically dissolved on the death or **bankruptcy** of any partner.

Partnership may be construed where it does not officially exist, when persons act together so as to give an impression that they are in partnership. ◊ **Holding out**.

Partnership, assignment of share in
There is nothing to prevent a partner assigning his share in profits to another person, though that other person has no right to interfere in the business.

Partnership at will A partnership where there is no particular written agreement. If a **partnership**'s written agreement expires and the partners continue to act, they are partners at will. Relationships of this kind are governed by the Partnership Act 1890.

Partnership, limited A **partnership** governed by the Limited Partnership Act 1907. Intended originally as an alternative to a limited **company**, it is similar to an ordinary partnership except that certain partners have a **limited liability**. The liability is limited to the amount the limited partner contributes on becoming a partner. He cannot dispose of his share or withdraw it, take part in the general management of the business or bind the **firm**. He cannot dissolve the partnership or object to the introduction of another partner. The limitation of his actions is obviously a considerable price to pay for the limitation of liability. The general partners have the last word in just about everything. There must be at least one

general partner with unlimited liability. A limited partnership must be registered with the Registrar of Companies and the registration must be accompanied by certain particulars. These are (1) the firm's name, (2) the general nature of the business, (3) the principal place of business, (4) the full names of the partners, (5) the term of the partnership, (6) the date of commencement, (7) a statement that the partnership is limited, which also names the limited partners, (8) the amount paid in by each limited partner, and the manner of payment (cash or otherwise).

Passenger coupon That part of an air-passenger's ticket which constitutes the passenger's written evidence of the **contract** of travel.

Passengers' luggage Passengers on railways may normally take a reasonable amount of luggage free of charge. The railways will be responsible for the loss of this luggage up to £50 where the loss is due to their negligence, but certain valuables must be declared before they will be liable. These are specified in the Carriers Act 1830 and include, for example, precious stones, watches, and furs. There is no liability if the passenger himself is negligent. A passenger is not negligent if he leaves his luggage to go to the restaurant car.

The luggage must be personal luggage, not merchandise or items connected with the passenger's work. It has been held that a **solicitor**'s briefcase is not personal luggage, nor is an instrument carried by a professional musician.

Passing a name A Stock Exchange term for stating the name of a buyer on **account days**.

Patent A patent gives the patentee the sole right to make, use or sell his invention during the period the patent remains in force. This period is sixteen years from the date of filing, subject to the payment of fees. These fees are an initial fee when the patent is registered and renewal fees payable annually. British patents only apply to the United Kingdom. Protection in other countries can only be obtained by applying for patents in those countries.

When a person wishes to apply for a patent, he must apply to the **Patent Office**. Before an invention will be patented it must be proved to contain an element of novelty. Patents are not given if the invention, or its use, is contrary to law or morality, or if it consists of foodstuffs or medicine with no other properties than the ingredients are already known to contain. No financial assistance or advice is given. Information on whether patents are still in force, and in whose name they are registered, may be obtained on application to the Patent Office.

When applying for patent it is often advisable to employ a patent agent – a list of registered patent agents can be obtained for a fee from the Chartered Institute of Patent Agents (CIPA).

An International Convention for the Protection of Industrial Property helps to obtain patent rights abroad by giving the holder of the patent in a member country priority in obtaining similar patents in another country. Most well-known countries belong to this Convention, including the UK, the USA and most Commonwealth and European countries.

Patent Office A central department responsible for the grant of **patents** and the registration of **trade marks** and designs.

Pawnbroker A dealer in pledges, licensed to carry on a moneylending business on the **security** of **goods** taken into pawn. The loans are governed by the Pawnbrokers Acts 1872 and 1960, now replaced by the Consumer Credit Act 1974, provided the money involved is less than £50. If the amount is over £50, the Acts do not apply and **common law** rules prevail. For loans over £5 a special pawn ticket must be given and signed, and a duplicate signed by the pledgor. **Interest** on loans below £5 is limited. The goods pledged are redeemable within six months, with seven days' grace. After this, the pawnbroker may then dispose of the goods at a public **auction**. Until he does so the goods are still redeemable. In the case of pledges for more than £2 the pawnbroker must retain any money the goods make (beyond what he is owed) for three years and hand it over. Pledges of less than £2 he can take absolutely at the end of the six months and seven days. Tickets must always be issued – if lost they may be renewed by a magistrate (the old ticket then becomes void). The pawnbroker must not deliver the goods to any person other than the one with the ticket. When the pawnbroker sells goods pawned, he may on no account buy them himself.

Pay As You Earn (PAYE) An **income tax** collection system whereby tax is deducted from wages or salaries by the employer before payment. This saves the employee the trouble of saving money to make tax payments at regular intervals. It only applies to regular employees. When a person terminates his employment, he will receive a form from his ex-employer which will state his gross pay to date in the tax year, tax deducted to date and his code number.

Pay-back period The period over

which the discounted net income from an investment amounts in total to its original cost. The calculation of this period is used in the course of deciding whether or not to make any given investment, particularly in industry. ◊ **Discounted cash flow** ◊ **Net present value** ◊ **Opportunity cost**.

Pay day A vernacular rendering of the **Stock Exchange** day when settlements are due, better known as **account day**. The term has an equally loose commercial meaning, viz. the day employees receive their wages or salaries.

Payroll The list prepared by a firm each week or month, giving details of wages and salaries. It states the name or number, or both, of the employee and the amounts paid. It may also give information on how the net pay is calculated. For instance: basic pay, plus overtime, minus lost time, gross pay, insurance and other deductions, tax paid and net pay. When prepared on a machine, pay slips for inclusion in wage packets may be prepared at the same time – the one being a carbon copy of the other. The term 'payroll' is normally reserved for the list of weekly wages and the pay of those who have not achieved what might be called an executive status. The salaries of the latter are normally closely guarded secrets, and the equivalent payroll is compiled quietly, separately and privately.

Payroll tax A form of business taxation levied on the payroll on a pro rata basis, thereby penalizing the over-employment of labour. It is favoured as an economic weapon in **capital-intensive** economies for this very reason. However, in so far as it can increase the level of unemployment, its value as a constraint in maintaining overall competitiveness internationally is

rather doubtful. The cost of supporting the people made redundant may be as damaging, if met indirectly out of increased taxes, as if met by over-employment. Consequently such a tax is valuable only in so far as labour released from one sector can be usefully absorbed into another. ◊ **Redundancy**.

There is no payroll tax as such in operation in the United Kingdom at present, though a modified form, known as Selective Employment Tax, was introduced from September 1966 until April 1973.

Pay slip A slip of paper included in a pay packet, giving details of how the net pay has been calculated. ◊ **Payroll**.

Payable to bearer A bill of exchange is payable to bearer when no particular payee is named, or where it is endorsed in blank. (◊ **Endorsement**.) A holder, by adding his name, could make the bill **payable to order**.

Payable to order A bill of exchange is payable to order when the name of a payee is stated, and where there are no restrictions on transfer. ◊ **Endorsement**.

Paying-in book A book used by a **bank** customer, recording details of cash, **cheques**, etc., paid in to his account at the bank, over the counter.

Payment for honour supra protest Where a **bill of exchange** is not paid and is protested (◊ **Noting and protest**) it may be taken up to be honoured by a party whose name is not on the bill.

Payment in advance An accounting term for money paid for goods or services not yet received and where the cash normally cannot be recovered. Examples are rates and **rents** paid for a period ending after the date to which the accounts are made up. Payments in advance are usually included with debtors in balance sheets.

Payment in kind Remuneration for work done or for services rendered can, theoretically, take the form of goods and services supplied rather than cash. This form of remuneration was much in evidence during the unregulated years of the Industrial Revolution in the United Kingdom. ◊ **Tommy shops** ◊ **Truck**. The Truck Acts attempted to put an end to this practice. It was much favoured by employers, who could gain an additional monetary advantage by paying wages in goods cheaply acquired rather than in cash. Although official wages must now be available in cash form, reminders of the past still exist in certain areas, e.g. miners can obtain coal at concessionary rates or even without payment; this is considered a relevant factor when wage claims are being considered. So also are the concessionary fare rates available to employees of British Rail and **British Airways**. ◊ **Benefits in kind** ◊ **Directors' emoluments** ◊ **Gratuity**.

Payment on account Part payment of a debt. This should be distinguished from a **deposit**.

P/E ratio ◊ **Price-earnings ratio**.

Peculation Embezzlement of money or **goods**, particularly public money or goods, by a person to whose care they have been entrusted.

Pedlar Someone who sells from door to door for cash. He needs a **licence**, which he can obtain from the police if he has been resident in the district for one month and can provide two testimonials. Once he has a licence, the pedlar can sell anywhere. The licence is renewable annually. ◊ **Hawker**.

Pegging the exchanges Dealings on the foreign exchange market by, say, the **exchange equalization account**, intended to stabilize **rates of exchange**. ◊ **Sliding peg**.

Penalty clause A clause in a contract stating that a certain sum should be paid by any party breaching the contract. If the figure stated is not a genuine attempt to estimate the possible level of damage, but merely a penalty imposed by one party on the other it is generally unenforceable. Where, however, damages are very difficult to assess in advance, it may be customary to include lump-sum payments by way of compensation. The court will uphold these where, in the circumstances, they appear reasonable, for example **Demurrage**. ◊ **Damages, liquidated**.

Penny Possibly the oldest, in name, of British coins. The origin of the name 'penny' is uncertain but probably Germanic. In medieval times it was known as a sterling and was made of pure silver to the weight of twenty-four grains in Troy measure. The grain is traditionally derived from the weight of one grain of wheat used in paying dues to feudal overlords. As the penny was of twenty-four grains its weight gave its name to the pennyweight. After the British coinage had been, at various times, debased the penny was no longer made of pure silver, but its name was retained.

In more recent years the penny was made of bronze and was a twelfth part of one shilling. Prior to decimalization of the British coinage, the penny was denoted by the symbol 'd'. This derived from the Roman 'denarius', which was the lowest in value of Roman coins. In Anglo-Saxon times, the penny had a cross on the reverse. It was often cut into two or four pieces, along the lines of the cross. In this way the terms 'half-penny' and 'farthing' (four things) derived. Subsequently, these divisions were superseded by smaller coins which retained those names. With the decimalization of the UK currency the penny was redefined, becoming one hundredth part of a pound sterling, and a new coin was struck to replace the old. This new coin was given the symbol 'p' instead of the old 'd' and was originally known as the new penny. The adjective new has since been dropped, both on the face of the coin and in general usage. Other coins were obviously needed in the metric system and, to make the changeover simpler, and until new 5p and 10p coins had been minted, the old shilling became the five-pence piece and the old florin became the ten-pence piece. A new denomination of coin, the fifty-pence piece, was introduced to replace the ten-shilling note. Although the old half-penny was replaced by a new half-penny, much smaller in size, this has now been discontinued, as has the old sixpence, which for a time was used as a two-and-a-half-penny piece. ◊ **Currency** ◊ **Troy weight**.

Pennyweight A unit in the **Troy weight** scale. The name derives from the silver pennies, another name for 'sterlings', by which the fine silver coins introduced in the reign of Edward I were known. One pound sterling was equal to 240 of these pennies, the pound originally meaning one pound troy weight. This explains the imperial coinage of 240 pennies to the pound. ◊ **Penny** ◊ **Sterling**.

Pension A regular payment paid to a retired person. It may be paid by the government or by the person's ex-employer. In the United Kingdom retirement pensions are paid by the state and are due to the recipient by virtue of **National Insurance** contributions. State pensions are continually being reviewed as the cost of living increases, and the system has been considerably improved by the introduction of the **State Earnings-Related Pension Scheme**.

In the private sector many businesses tend to adopt certain responsibilities for long-serving employees on their retirement, particularly where insufficient provision is made by the government. Pensions paid in the private sector may be based on contributions made during the claimant's working life or may be **non-contributory pensions**. In the latter category one may include **ex gratia** pensions awarded occasionally by business organizations to selected employees. ◊ **Occupational pension scheme**.

Pensions are also awarded to widows. These are called widows' pensions and are payable through the National Insurance Fund. Such widows' pensions are also often paid by businesses in the private sector.

Pension schemes Most people seek to make some provision for a continuing income after they retire from full-time employment. Many are able to effect this through pension schemes provided by employers, whether that employment be in the public or the private sector. Almost all public-sector employers make membership of a contributory pension scheme obligatory for every full-time employee. The Civil Service is an excellent example. Such a compulsory scheme exists here and members continue to belong to it even when they have moved, whether to a different department or another location within the Service. The same applies in the education system, where teachers, irrespective of movement between schools, belong to a state pension scheme which will provide them with a regular pension on retirement. Some schemes, particularly the Civil Service's, offer the considerable additional benefit of index-linking the pensions earned so that they automatically increase with the cost of living. In all these schemes initial pensions are linked to the salaries or wages previously earned – usually the salary or wage received during the years immediately preceding retirement.

Employers in the private sector often provide contributory pension schemes where, as in the public sector, contributions made by the employee are matched by equal or greater contributions made by the employer. An additional advantage of all such schemes is that both sets of contributions are tax-deductible. Pensions eventually paid are normally taxable, but in most instances an option exists to take a lump sum payment on retirement in place of a regular pension, or sometimes a smaller lump sum plus a modified pension. Such lump sums are tax-free. These schemes are known as **occupational pension schemes**.

The one disadvantage of these contributory schemes is that should the employee leave the public sector to work in the private sector or, being in the private sector, move to another employer, then the pension rights will cease. If he or she has been many years in that employment an entitlement to an appropriate pro rata pension on retirement may be frozen according to contributions paid. In many instances, however, all that happens is that the contributions paid to date by the

employee are returned and any future pension rights must then be re-earned. ◊ **Portable pensions**.

Because of such occurrences and for the benefit of the vast number of self-employed persons to whom no pension scheme applies, many finance or insurance companies have instituted personal pension schemes which take the form of contracts whereby future pension rights can be accumulated by the payment out of earnings of regular amounts, which can be varied from year to year according to the means of the payer. The contributor can often choose between alternative funds, each of which invests contributions in a different type of security, e.g. property funds, equity funds, gilt-edged funds, etc. What is more, he can also, in certain instances, opt to split his contributions between selected funds. As with the employment-related schemes, contributions are tax-deductible (within fixed limits) and there is an option to take a tax-free lump sum on retirement in place of all or part of the pension.

All these pension plans, whether employment-related or privately funded, provide pensions which are in addition to the basic State pension, which is paid out under the National Insurance scheme.

Peppercorn rent A nominal rent intended merely to indicate that property is not freehold but leasehold. The peppercorn is the dried berry of the pepper plant. As a spice, pepper was at one time much sought after and quite valuable. During the Middle Ages feudal rents were frequently paid in pepper or peppercorns. When pepper became plentiful its price dropped so much that rents expressed in terms of peppercorn were virtually nil. The phrase peppercorn rent was retained, however, for use in what is in effect a derisory sense.

Per contra A book-keeping term meaning 'on the other side'.

Perfecting the sight ◊ Bill of sight.

Performance bond A **surety** given by, say, a **bank**, on behalf of a person doing **contract** work for, for instance, a government department. It is a **guarantee** that the work will be done properly.

Period bill A **bill of exchange** not payable **at sight** but on a particular date.

Perishable goods Goods which deteriorate if not used within a specified time, e.g. food.

Perishing of goods In a **contract** for the **sale of goods**, it happens sometimes that the **goods** perish either before the contract is made, or before delivery. Goods 'perish' when they cease to be substantially the goods contracted for or described. The perishing of unspecified goods is unimportant, because then the seller must provide some from another source. Where the sale is of specific goods, if they have perished before the contract was made, the contract is void; if they perish after the contract is made but before the **risk** passes to the buyer, the contract may still be avoided. The perishing must be the fault of neither party.

Permission to deal When a **company** issues a **prospectus** it often states that permission has been obtained, or is to be sought, for the **shares** to be dealt with on a recognized **Stock Exchange**. Any **allotment of shares** is void if either permission has not been applied for before the opening of the subscription lists or permission is refused before three

weeks after the closing of those lists. The monies must then be returned.

Perpetual debentures Debentures which the holder cannot redeem by demanding repayment are called perpetual debentures. When they cannot be redeemed in any event, they are called irredeemable debentures.

Perpetual inventory A method of continuous stock-taking. Businesses with large quantities of raw materials awaiting use in manufacturing processes or of goods purchased for resale need to be constantly aware of the amount of capital tied up in this manner and must also be continually on guard against loss from pilfering. Perpetual inventory systems go some way towards achieving these objects. Various categories of stocks or materials are identified, and bin cards or some equivalent thereof are used to record daily movements and running totals within the stores building itself. A similar set of records will be maintained in a separate part of the business, e.g. the accounting section. Both sets of records should be regularly compared, as should physical quantities with figures on bin cards. If these processes are maintained, then a reliable figure for total stock will always be available for accounting and management purposes.

Perpetual succession One of the attributes of a corporation. Any corporate body, whether a **corporation sole** or a **corporation aggregate**, has a legal existence quite distinct from the person or persons of which it is composed. For this reason its lifespan is not limited by that of its member(s) and it is therefore said to have perpetual succession. It continues to exist until wound up in the manner prescribed by law. Each incumbent of an office which comprises a corporation sole and all members of a corporation aggregate, a limited company being a prime example, assume responsibility for all acts of predecessors.

Personal accounts ◊ **Accounts, nominal, real and personal**.

Personal allowance Every person paying income tax may deduct from his, or her, gross taxable income an amount, varying from one year to another, known as a personal allowance. Since the introduction of independent taxation in 1990 this allowance may be claimed by both husband and wife as well as by single persons. ◊ **Income tax** ◊ **Independent taxation** ◊ **Additional personal allowance**.

Personal calls For a fixed charge a telephone call may be made to a particular person or named substitute(s), at the same time giving the caller's own name and number. If the person is not available a message can be left for them to ring the operator at the originating exchange as soon as possible. Alternatively, the original caller can ask that further attempts to establish contact be made at stated intervals by the originating operator. Such instructions will be automatically cancelled after twenty-four hours. The fixed charge is always payable whether or not the call is successful. If a connection is made, the ordinary charges apply in addition to the personal call charge; however, the timed charge does not begin until the person required comes to the telephone. ◊ **Telephone**.

Personal equity plans (PEPs) A government-sponsored scheme whereby individuals can obtain tax benefits on a type of savings scheme geared to investment for at least one calendar year in quoted companies. The proposals were introduced in the 1986 budget and PEPs, as they have become known, were launched early in 1987. Anyone can invest in one PEP in each year and there is a stated maximum in that year – originally £2,400 but now £6,000 and rising. The PEP however must be managed by a professional fund manager – an individual cannot manage his own PEP – and while the investment remains intact, then any income reinvested or capital gain is tax-free. A new PEP can be created each year and in this way an individual can build up quite an extensive portfolio.

Investments were originally restricted to UK companies but recently the range has been widened to include any EU companies. Investment in unit trusts or investment companies is restricted to 50 per cent of any one PEP. Investments may be realized at any time but on realization the tax benefits will cease. In 1992 the scheme was broadened again to allow the additional investment of up to £3,000 in a single-company PEP. This can be promoted by the company itself, and shares forming part of an employee share incentive scheme, can be put directly into a PEP with no capital gains liability.

Personal loan This phrase entered commercial language with the willingness of the **clearing banks** to make unsecured advances to customers. The applicant approaches the bank manager and, if the latter is satisfied with the applicant's creditworthiness, is advanced a specified sum. Interest is added to the loan and the total is normally repayable in instalments over an agreed period. The rate of interest charged is usually higher than for **overdrafts**, because no security is demanded. ◊ **Bank advance** ◊ **Bank loan** ◊ **Interest**.

Personnel management Defined by the Institute of Personnel Management as 'that part of management concerned with people at work and with their relationships within an enterprise. Its aim is to bring together and develop into an effective organization the men and women who make up an enterprise and, having regard for the well-being of the individual and of working groups, to enable them to make their best contribution to its success.' It is concerned, *inter alia*, with manpower planning, recruitment and selection, education and training, terms of employment, standards of pay, working conditions, consultation at and between all levels, wage negotiations, etc.

Petties A term sometimes used on **invoices**, etc., for minor charges not enumerated separately.

Petty cash This refers to ready money kept within a business for the purpose of meeting small incidental expenses on a day-to-day basis, and also perhaps for reimbursing staff for minor costs incurred on behalf of the business. Details of money allocated for this purpose and the manner in which it is spent are usually recorded in a book known as the petty cash book, sometimes on the **imprest** system. The petty cash float should be kept apart from money taken in the course of conducting business.

Petty cashier A person responsible for keeping **petty cash** and the petty cash book. ◊ **Imprest**.

Pie-chart A popular manner of presenting statistical information to the general public. A circle is drawn representing a pie or cake and slices are cut in the 'cake'

to represent the contribution of various ingredients to the whole. A company may use a pie chart to illustrate portions of total costs taken up, or value added by, labour, materials, taxation, etc. The emphasis of the exercise is intended to be on the very small slice representing **dividends** or **profits**. ◊ **Public relations**.

Piece-work Wages are often paid on a piece-work principle. It means that a person's pay is directly related to the number of units produced in the period covered by that pay. It is an alternative to payment on a time basis, i.e. a fixed weekly wage for a defined number of hours. Occasionally the two methods of payment are combined, particularly in connection with a productivity bonus, and the employee receives a fixed wage plus an additional amount related to production above a fixed minimum. ◊ **Productivity bargaining** ◊ **Productivity deal**.

Placings A method of issuing **shares**, normally used where small amounts are involved. The shares are placed by an **issuing house** or a **broker** with investors who may be interested. The broker makes a profit from the difference between the buying and selling **price** of the shares. This form of issuing shares is common with **private companies** converting to **public companies**. It is like an **introduction**, except than in that case the broker or issuing house does not purchase a stated number of shares, but agrees to introduce them gradually on to the market.

Planned obsolescence Another term for **built-in obsolescence**.

Plant hire ◊ **Equipment leasing**. The Companies Acts 1967 and 1985 provide that the amount paid for plant hire should, where material, be shown in the accounts.

Plant registers A business's register giving details of all items of plant and machinery. There is usually one card or page for each item, giving date and details of purchase, annual **depreciation** and date and details of **sale** or realized scrap value.

Plimsoll line ↻ **Load line**.

Ploughed-back profit That part of the profit for the year not distributed but retained in the business, normally for development by reinvestment.

Point of sale The point where the property in goods passes from seller to purchaser. The term has assumed greater importance in the context of **indirect taxation**, particularly **value added tax**, as the tax becomes payable at the point of sale. ↻ **Purchase tax** ↻ **Sale of goods, title**.

Poison pill tactics In recent years company directors have been increasingly anxious to establish lines of defence against unwelcome take-over bids, particularly those by the new breed of **corporate raiders** whose unenlightened self-interest often outweighs the good of the target companies. One useful defence mechanism is known as the poison pill tactic, whereby the acquisitor automatically triggers a process which can render the acquired company not a little indigestible.

The poison pill tactic operates by giving the present holders of certain categories of shares the right to purchase a quantity of loan, or preferred, stock as soon as the invading bidder has acquired more than a stated minimum percentage of the equity. If these rights were to be exercised, the unwelcome raider would

find that upon acquiring control not only would his anticipated profit flow be seriously diminished but the revised capital gearing would have so reduced the marketable value of the equity that it could now be resold only at a loss.

Those preparing the poison pill naturally protect their own position by providing that should the rights serve to deter the predator, then they may be bought back in by the company at a nominal price, before being exercised.

Policy proof of interest In **marine insurance**, PPI policies are those where the insured has not the necessary **insurable interest** in the subject matter or a **bona fide** expectation of acquiring one by the time of loss. Strictly speaking, these are void under the Marine Insurance (Gambling Policies) Act 1909, which inflicts both fines and imprisonment on offenders. However, they are used in commerce quite frequently and are treated by insurers as **contracts** of honour.

Political and charitable contributions The Companies Act 1967 made it necessary for companies to give details in accounts of any such contributions made by themselves or their **subsidiaries**. Total political or total charitable contributions, if above a particular figure, must be shown. Also, if a political contribution amounts to more than a minimum stated amount the name of the political party must be given.

Poll A vote at a shareholders' meeting. It is usually taken by ballot and **members** have votes in proportion to the number of **shares** they hold. Preliminary voting is by show of hands, but the **articles of association** may provide that a certain minimum number of members can demand a poll on any matter except the election of **chairman** or adjournment. A member with several shares may vote one way with some shares and another with others. A **proxy** can vote in a poll but not on a show of hands unless the articles provide otherwise. The Companies Act 1980 provided that at a class meeting of shareholders any member of that class present personally or by proxy may demand a poll.

Port ◊ **Larboard**.

Port clearance ◊ **Exporters' declarations** ◊ **Her Majesty's Customs and Excise** ◊ **Customs: final clearance inwards and entry outwards**.

Portable pensions This term is used with reference to **pension schemes** which do not terminate when the beneficiary changes employment. All privately funded schemes are essentially portable and occupational schemes within the public sector are portable within that sector, e.g. pension entitlements earned by teachers in State schools are portable provided that the person to whom they apply remains a teacher within the State system. ◊ **Occupational pension schemes** ◊ **State Earnings-Related Pension Scheme**.

Portfolio ◊ **Investment portfolio**.

Post entry ◊ **Over entry certificate**.

Post Office Once a government department, the Post Office became a public corporation in 1969. Although it had traditionally been responsible for both postal and telecommunications matters throughout the UK, over both of which it enjoyed a monopoly, in 1981 the structure was changed and all telecommunications business was transferred to a new corporation known as **British Telecom**. Since that date the Post Office has been concerned with the transmission of letters, packets and parcels by Royal Mail, both at home and to countries overseas, together with certain other specialized services, mostly on behalf of government.

In providing these various services, and with a view to future privatization, the Post Office has now been divided into Royal Mail, Parcelforce and Post Office Counters plc., the latter being a limited company. Post Office Counters handles many agency services for government, particularly for the Departments of Health and Social Security on behalf of which it pays out old-age pensions, child benefit etc., on the production of the requisite documents. It acts as a licence issuing body for motor taxation, TV and radio, game etc., and as a collection agency for the gas, water, electricity and telecommunication supply companies. It also handles transactions for the **National Savings Bank** and as agent in issuing **National Savings Certificates** and **Premium Bonds**.

For a comprehensive list of services and charges concerning all aspects of the Post Office, reference should be made to the **Post Office Guide**. ◊ **Inland post** ◊ **Overseas post** ◊ **Postage stamps** ◊ **Postal orders** ◊ **Postmarks** ◊ **Poste restante** ◊ **Postcode** ◊ **Franking machines** ◊ **Express delivery** ◊ **Datapost** ◊ **Royal Mail Special Delivery** ◊ **Railway letters** ◊ **Airways letters** ◊ **Airmail letters** ◊ **Post Office: licences**.

Post Office: evasion of postage It is not permissible to evade postage by enclosing one letter inside another, unless they are both addressed to the same person. If this happens and is detected, the Post Office may take out the second letter and send it separately, charging postage.

Post Office Guide A substantial book-let issued annually by the **Post Office** giving details of all services available with accompanying charges including a consid-erable amount of information regarding the terms of carriage by post both inland and to various destinations overseas. Sup-plements are issued as necessary through-out the year to keep the information up to date.

Post Office: HM Forces There are special rates for and regulations concern-ing mail to servicemen at home and abroad. Consult the **Post Office Guide**.

Post Office: licences Certain **licences** are obtained from the Post Office. These are:

(1) Broadcast receiving licences for monochrome or colour TV. Separate li-cences are necessary for sound transmis-sion to the public. These licences are all renewable annually. There are special sav-ings schemes. ◊ **Licences**.

(2) Vehicle licences. These licences, and their cost, vary according to the class of vehicle. They are all renewable annually.

(3) Miscellaneous. CB radio licences, game licences (red, green, blue), game licences (occasional) for fourteen days, game dealer licences, gamekeeper li-cences, hounds licences.

Post Office: pensions and allow-ances Certain pensions and allowances are payable at a post office: for instance, child benefit, and old-age pension. The relevant order book should be presented on the due date or within a certain period afterwards.

Post Office Savings Bank ◊ **Na-tional Savings Bank**.

Post town A town with a head Post Office.

Post-war credits During the years 1941–6 additional tax was levied, with a promise that it would ultimately be paid back. So far, it has only partly been paid, but since October 1959 the government has paid **interest** on the amount still due. On application to a local tax inspec-tor, repayment in full can be obtained, but only by men over sixty, women over fifty-five, those who can prove special hardship or the successors of a holder who has died.

Postage stamps Current postage stamps are ordinarily available from any Post Office. They can be purchased either in rolls, for first- and second-class stamps, books (containing either a fixed number of one denomination or a variety, the book price being the sum of the stamps contained therein) or from stamp vend-ing machines which are often situated outside post offices for people wishing to obtain stamps outside opening hours. Recently franchises for selling postage stamps have been given to various re-tailers who sell stamps either singly or in book form on behalf of the Post Office.

Current stamps are those bearing the head of the reigning monarch. Those which though bearing this head have been discontinued will be repurchased at the face value by the **Post Office**. Em-bossed stamps cut off from unused pack-ets are admissible for repurchase if not defaced in any way, though this conces-sion does not extend to impressed Inland Revenue or other government depart-ment stamps.

Postal orders These enable the transfer of money otherwise than in cash. Postal orders cater for the smaller amounts and can be obtained at any post office branch on payment of the amount represented by the order, which can be from 50p to £20, plus a fee known as poundage. Poundage is chargeable at fixed amounts on a sliding scale. At present there are only two steps on that scale, referring to orders for less than £2 and to those for more. Although postal orders are in denominations representing round sums at fixed intervals their values can be increased marginally by the addition of postage stamps in the space provided.

A postal order is **not negotiable** and the sum stated must only be paid to the person whose name appears thereon, though if no name is inserted by the sender then anyone can cash it. If an order is paid to a person other than the named payee, the sender has a right of action against that person though, in the absence of negligence, not against the **Post Office**; the Post Office will, however, help trace missing orders on production of the counterfoil detached by the sender and other relevant details.

Postal orders are valid for six months after the date of issue. After that time the authority of the Head Postmaster or some other official is required before payment can be made. If a postal order is crossed, it can only be realized through a bank account.

Postal orders can also be sent abroad for approved purposes and to specified countries, generally those that are, or were, colonies.

Postcode A combination of letters and figures appended to every address within the UK which identifies the position of that address within a post office grid system. The first part indicates the particular location and the second part the relevant delivery area. Postcode addresses are converted into a machine-readable language at post office sorting depart-

ments to enable mail to be electronically sorted and thus to facilitate distribution.

Poste restante overseas Incoming post from abroad is similar to poste restante UK. Outgoing post varies. The packet must give the name of the addressee (initials, figures, forenames only, are disallowed). Some countries charge an additional fee. In Belgium, France and Spain, the parcels service is operated by the railways and not the post office, so the words '*en gare*' should be used instead of 'poste restante'.

Poste restante UK Letters, parcels, telegrams, etc., may be addressed to any post office (except sub-post offices) to be called for by the addressee. The words 'poste restante' or 'to be called for' must be written on the packet as part of the address. The person calling for the letter or parcel is expected to furnish some evidence of identity. The poste restante service is mainly for the benefit of travellers and a poste restante address cannot normally be used in the same town for more than three months.

Inland packets are normally retained for two weeks, overseas packets for one month, before being returned or treated as undeliverable. There is an exception for poste restante items at ports for persons arriving by sea – in this case they are retained for two months.

Postmarks These have three principal objects: (1) they cancel the stamps affixed; (2) they form part of the **Post Office** internal control system; (3) they can be used for advertising – this may be for services offered by the Post Office itself, for public events or festivals or, by arrangement, for private projects or businesses. In the latter case the advertiser will pay to have his slogan incorporated in the postmark without any right to recompense if the slogan is smudged or unreadable in some instances.

Pound The word 'pound' derives from the Latin *pondo*, a pound weight, the abbreviations 'lb', (pound weight) and '£' (pound sterling) from *libra*, also Latin for a pound.

The pound weight is a basic unit of weight under the British Imperial system of measurement and was also adopted in the USA and certain other English-speaking countries. The pound referred to is the pound **avoirdupois**, though there was also a pound in the **Troy weight** system. Troy weights, like apothecaries' weights, are traditionally used for measuring small quantities of very light materials and, generally speaking, the largest weight necessary in both systems is the ounce. As the avoirdupois system of weights gives way to the metric system, the pound weight will gradually fall into disuse.

The pound is also the basic unit in UK currency, in which it is technically referred to as the pound **sterling**. The currency pound was also a measure of weight. In the reign of Edward I a common unit of money was the silver penny, introduced by Germanic merchants. These pennies were also known as sterlings and 240 of them weighed one Troy pound. That sum became known as the pound sterling. It was equivalent to twenty shillings and coins of that value appeared during various reigns, sometimes in gold, sometimes in silver. In the reigns of Charles I and Charles II they were actually called pounds, but in other reigns they rejoiced in such names as 'unite', 'broad', 'sovereign' and 'laurel'. During the 500 years up until 1816, when the currency was restructured and the Mint moved out of the Tower of London, the number of coins in circulation and their value were almost totally determined by fluctuations in the prices of gold and silver and the whim of the reigning monarch. In 1816 the British coinage was officially linked to a gold standard, the guinea was abolished and the twenty-shilling gold sovereign became the basic unit. At the same time, a new range of silver coins of a token value was introduced, their face value being independent of intrinsic worth.

The sovereign remained a basic currency unit in Britain throughout the remainder of the nineteenth century and up to 1914, when it went out of general circulation. This was principally because, on the outbreak of the First World War, the convertibility of the Bank of England notes, which had been legal tender since 1833, was suspended and the consequent rise in the demand for and price of gold made the sovereign worth more than its twenty-shilling value in exchange, thus causing it to be saved rather than spent.

Although convertibility was restored in 1925, the sovereign never again assumed its role as a unit of currency, and although it is still technically legal tender for one pound, its intrinsic and collector's value has remained well above its face value. Today, with the gold price no longer artificially fixed, sovereigns can fetch up to seventy times their token value, as can half-sovereigns. No sovereigns were minted after 1975.

In 1914 the Treasury issued new one-pound and ten-shilling notes, which were colloquially referred to as **Bradburys**. After the 1914–18 War, note issue became the sole prerogative of the Bank of England and the one-pound note took over the role of the basic British unit of currency. This situation continued until 1982, when the pound coin was introduced. Of little intrinsic value, it is the only official pound sterling now that the notes have been withdrawn.

Power of attorney An instrument in writing empowering the holder to represent the person issuing that instrument in the matters contained therein. A general power of attorney gives the holder fairly exclusive rights to act for another person, e.g. sign deeds on his or her behalf. This often happens where the holder is acting for a person totally incapacitated or abroad. A special power of attorney is of a more limited kind, perhaps for acting on one occasion only. ◊ **Proxy**.

Precedent, rule of ◊ **Common law**.

Pre-emption Before an **offer** is made generally, a prior right to purchase may be given to a person or an organization. This is called a pre-emption. ◊ **Shares, pre-emptive right of purchase**.

Preference shares ◊ **Shares, preference**.

Preferential debts In a bankruptcy or a company liquidation there will be various categories of creditor and a strict order of precedence among such categories, all debts in one category being paid in full before any monies are given to creditors in the next. Secured creditors are entitled to be repaid out of the property on which the debt was secured, though if such security fails to cover the whole debt any balance remaining will rank with debts of unsecured creditors. Once the entitlements of secured creditors have been satisfied and any **pre-preferential debts** settled, then whatever funds remain will be distributed among unsecured creditors. However, within that class of creditor there are some who can legally claim preferential treatment.

The 1986 Insolvency Act lists those debts which are to be regarded as preferential debts to be paid in full before any monies are handed over to other unsecured creditors. Briefly these are as follows, the phrase 'relevant date' being a reference to either the date of the making of an administration order, the date of the appointment of a provisional liquidator or, if none appointed, the date of the winding-up order, the date of approval of a voluntary arrangement or, in the case of a bankruptcy, the date of the appointment of an Interim Receiver or, if none then the date of the bankruptcy order. (1) Sums due at the relevant date to the Inland Revenue on account of PAYE deducted during the previous twelve months; (2) any VAT due with reference to the period of six months prior to the relevant date; (3) any sums due in respect of car tax or betting or gaming tax during the twelve months preceding the relevant date; (4) any sums due in respect of Social Security contributions and becoming due within the preceding twelve months, but not exceeding one year's assessment; (5) any sums due by way of remuneration to employees or ex-employees for a period of at least four months prior to the relevant date plus accrued holiday pay or sickness pay to which an employee may be entitled. Where there are insufficient monies available to pay all preferential debts then the creditors concerned will rank equally.

Preliminary expenses These are the expenses necessarily incurred in the formation of a **company**; for instance, the expenses of promoting the company, publishing a **prospectus**, issuing **shares**, obtaining the **statutory books**, etc.

Premium Though generally thought of as the term used to describe the annual amount payable on an **insurance policy**, it also has other commercial connotations. ◊ **Share premium** ◊ **Premium on a lease** ◊ **Premium savings bonds**. A further usage occurs in the area of the purchase and sale of **securities**. A bond may be issued at a par value of £100 and, when dealings begin, immediately be quoted at £110. It is then said to be available at a premium of £10. ◊ **Stag**.

Premium on a lease Very often when property is leased, the lessee, in addition to paying a **rent** for an agreed period, pays a lump sum. This is known as a premium, or sometimes as 'key money' and was once intended to avoid taxation and disguise the true rent. Premiums for leases granted for fifty years or less are now taxable. For tax purposes the premium is reduced by 2 per cent for every complete twelve months of the lease's length after the first twelve months.

Premium put ◊ **Convertible capital bond**.

Premium savings bonds A government lottery, under the guise of a **security**, first introduced in 1956. It is a security in that interest accrues on each bond; it is a lottery in that the total interest is pooled and distributed to a random few, determined by a computer known as 'Ernie' (Electronic Random Number Indicator Equipment). The amount of interest, totalled and fed into the pool, is based on a periodically fixed percentage of total funds invested and may be changed at any time by three months' notice given in the London, Edinburgh or Belfast *Gazette*. The bonds may be purchased in £1 units at most post offices and **clearing banks**, in minimum quantities of one hundred units initially and thereafter in quantities of

ten units up to a maximum holding of £10,000. They are available to persons aged sixteen or over and to younger persons on trust through a parent or guardian. They cannot be bought by clubs or corporate bodies. There are prize draws, the prizes being divisions of total accumulated interest, at weekly and monthly intervals. Prizewinners are notified at their last recorded address; any change of address should be registered. Unclaimed prizes are retained until winners notify the **Post Office** of their new address.

Bond holders may cash in their bonds at any time, provided that notice of intent is given, but the amount received will be no more than the **face value** of the bond. On the other hand, those persons lucky enough to win prizes are not subject to any UK taxation on their prize money. At present weekly prizes range from £25,000 to £100,000 and monthly prizes from £50 to £250,000.

Prepayments ◊ **Payments in advance**.

Pre-preferential debts In a **bankruptcy** or company **liquidation** there are a very few creditors who rank even before preferential creditors. These are persons on whose behalf the bankrupt or company holds monies on trust or as an officer of a registered **friendly society**, etc. ◊ **Preferential debt**.

Present value ◊ **Discounting back** ◊ **Net present value**.

President In commercial parlance, the title 'president' is sometimes accorded to the most senior executive in a public company. This is most common in the USA and is occasionally found among UK companies, where it is more often a title of honour rather than an indication of responsibility or rank. ◊ **Chairman** ◊ **Chief executive**.

Prestel A 'viewdata' system developed and operated by **British Telecom**. In so far as the television screen in the home is used to display data, there is an incidental similarity to **Teletext** services operated by the BBC and IBA. However, whereas the data provided by the latter comes through a television signal, Prestel is linked both with the national and international telephone systems and with regional BT computers plus electronic data terminals rented from BT by the users. In addition, certain information providers have private computer links which can both transmit and receive messages to and from users.

Prestel is essentially a two-way facility through which users can obtain access not only to general facts and features of the type made available through Teletext but also to specialized information made available by private parties – information providers – being businesses with goods or services to sell. The Prestel user can thereby enter into transactions with such businesses. Each Prestel user is registered with BT and is given a personal account number for customer identity and a personal password, both of which are peculiar to the particular user and neither of which will be revealed to any third party.

Every query, message, etc. passed through Prestel is preceded by this identity number and password and the particular user is then debited by BT with the charge for using the system, a charge related to the cost and time of equivalent telephone calls to the nearest Prestel computer, which will, in the majority of cases, be within the local charge band. In addition to the charge related to usage of the system, there is a quarterly standing charge plus, in certain instances, a charge made by the information provider. All these charges appear on quarterly BT telephone bills.

If charges are incurred as a result of transactions entered into through the information provider's own computer by means of a private gateway, then the user will be accountable to the particular provider, though the actual transmission cost will, of course, be recouped by BT.

British Telecom provides an extensive and comprehensive directory to all Prestel users with a regular supplement updating the available services. These are mailed free to all registered customers.

Prestige advertising Increasingly common among the larger **public companies** – particularly those that offer services rather than sell goods – this is a form of advertising that associates the name of the company with a particular sporting activity or competition which the company sponsors by providing prize monies. ◊ **Advertising, persuasive**.

Prevention of Fraud (Investments) Act 1939 ◊ **Share pushing**.

Price Very generally, the total amount of money that must be handed over in exchange for an article or service that is being purchased. This does not necessarily have anything to do with the **value** of the item. ◊ **Market value** ◊ **Cost price** ◊ **Hire purchase** ◊ **Middle market price** ◊ **Closing price** ◊ **Cash price**.

Price control Direct intervention by the government to keep prices stable during an emergency situation. There was an extensive and complex system of price control in the United Kingdom during the Second World War. Intervention may also be made necessary by runaway inflation. Price control is a remedy rather than a cure and is used normally on a short-term basis only. ◊ **Prices and incomes policy**.

Price–earnings ratio A term in investment analysis for the ratio between the **market value** of **share capital** and the profit for the year. The taxed profit is divided theoretically between the number of **ordinary shares**; the result is called earnings-per-share. This is then divided into the market price as quoted by the **official list**. The result is known as the price–earnings ratio. The figure is high when the **yield** is low, i.e. when the demand for the shares has forced the price up, relative to the profits being made, and possibly also to the **dividends** being paid. This happens when the prospects of the organization are highly rated, rightly or wrongly, by the investing public.

Prices and incomes policy A longer-term and less precise form of **price control** with a similar restraint on incomes. The principal object of such a policy, favoured by successive governments in recent years, is to attempt to keep inflation in check by holding down both prices and wages. It is seen mostly in the sphere of wages, where any agreement to minimize wage increases is made ultimately with the trade unions individually and the TUC overall. The assumption is that if wage levels are kept in check then, in so far as prices are determined by them, the overall cost of living will also be controlled. ◊ **Fair Trading Act** ◊ **Retail price index** ◊ **Wage freeze** ◊ **Wage restraint**.

Primage Part of the cost of loading or unloading a ship. This varies from port to port and is included in the **freight** charge.

Primary dealer A term used in the United States bond market for a firm acting in much the same capacity as a **market-maker** in the UK. Similarity of roles often causes the term to be used in the UK as a synonym for market-maker. Since the changes brought about by **Big Bang** the title of primary dealer has been applied to **Gilt-edged market-makers** within the UK.

Prime costs The prime costs of production are direct materials, direct labour and direct expenses, i.e. materials, labour, and expenses that can be directly associated with the cost of producing a specific item.

Prime entry ◊ **Customs entry**.

Prime entry, books of In double-entry book-keeping detailed records of transactions or transfers between accounts are first recorded in day books or journals, which may be kept in book-form or in some other suitable manner. These records are known as books of prime entry. Good examples are the **purchase journal** and the **sales journal**. From these initial records the ledgers can be written up at leisure. In contemporary electronic or machine accounting systems all relevant records are effectively written up simultaneously, ledger entry, customer invoice and sales journal summary being created by one electronic or mechanical process, thus virtually eliminating the function of the traditional books of prime entry.

Prime lending rate This is the American equivalent of the British banker's **base rate**, though the term is creeping into UK commercial jargon.

Private bank Rather a vague term carrying echoes of past centuries when most banks were privately owned. In more recent years it has been applied to those banks which are not clearing banks or, more specifically, not members of APACS.

Private boxes and bags These are rented privately from the **Post Office**, usually by business customers. The box is a means of collecting mail addressed to a box number. The mail is retained in the locked box pending collection by the addressee, who may collect in advance of normal delivery times. The rental for a private box will be doubled where the renter wishes to collect between 6 am and the time the Post Office opens or the (earlier) start of the first delivery. There is a substantial additional fee if the renter wants a normal delivery in addition to the box facility. This fee is paid for each delivery. Bags, which must be provided by the user, are intended for making deliveries to him and are locked by the Post Office beforehand.

Private carrier A private carrier is a carrier making no general **offer** to the public but carrying goods on specific contracts. He is subject to the general law relating to **bailments**, etc. ◊ **Common carrier**.

Private company ◊ **Company, private**.

Privateer A ship and its crew authorized by its government to attack and loot the ships of certain other nations. These were common in the sixteenth and seventeenth centuries.

Prize money The proceeds of the sale of property, particularly of ships, seized in war, and distributed among the captors in proportions that at sea seem to have favoured the senior members of the crew considerably.

Pro forma invoice Where a vendor requires payment before delivery of goods, he issues to the prospective purchaser a pro forma invoice giving details of the payment necessary to obtain them. This will be the selling price of the goods plus, where applicable, additional charges for postage and packing or, in some industries, surcharges applicable to small orders. In trading situations the pro forma invoice will also show the **trade discount** that is applicable.

Pro rata freight A proportion of the agreed **freight** payable when **goods** are delivered at a port, short of the agreed port of discharge, with the consent of the owner of the goods.

Procuration The power given to another person to sign documents and act on behalf of the person giving it. Hence 'pp' (*per procurationem*). **Power of attorney** is strictly necessary but not always given.

Productivity bargaining The process of negotiating productivity deals as part of a particular wage claim. ◊ **Prices and incomes policy** ◊ **Productivity deal**.

Productivity deal A term used with increasing frequency within industry to describe agreements between employers and employees where the latter agree to changes in working practices aimed at increasing productivity, i.e. value added per man hour worked. In this way wage increase can be self-generating in so far as the agreed increase in remuneration is matched by the increase in value of the work completed in a given period. In such manner, during periods of government demands for pay restraint, it is possible to raise wages without increasing unit costs as the larger wage bill is spread over a corresponding increase in the number of units produced.

In fact, although theoretically sound, such deals often do little more than nudge output up to the level that should have been achieved without them. This fact, amongst others, explains why union negotiators frequently seek productivity deals when claiming an increase in basic remuneration. A seemingly low percentage wage increase with a productivity deal attached can often be more beneficial financially to the employee than an ostensibly higher basic wage increase. ◊ **Prices and incomes policy** ◊ **Wage restraint** ◊ **Wages and salaries**.

Professional indemnity insurance A form of **third-party insurance** not dissimilar to the one compulsory under the Road Traffic Act. It is frequently taken out by persons working in a professional capacity on their own account, e.g. solicitors, accountants, estate agents. It is intended to cover any liability to third parties arising from negligence by the policyholder in the course of carrying out his professional duties. Any person who suffers loss because of such negligence and can prove it in court may be entitled to damages, which could be substantial. Apart from an unwillingness to be bankrupted by such a claim, professional advisers prefer to retain adequate insurance cover in order to preserve both their good name and their practice. It is particularly relevant to partnerships where each partner is jointly and severally liable for the negligence of the other. ◊ **Negligence of auditor** ◊ **Negligence of directors**.

Professional valuation A term sometimes used in **balance sheets** or **prospectuses**. **Assets** are said to be at professional valuation, which means that they have been valued by a person who professes to have the expertise necessary to value them, or whose profession or job suggests that he is competent to do so. The valuation is usually written and signed, and the valuer could be guilty of negligence if it is not made properly.

Profit and loss account The results of all trading organizations and businesses operated for profit are usually shown in a profit and loss account. By tradition this account tends to be in three parts: the trading account, the profit and loss account proper and the profit and loss appropriation account. Such an account is usually, though not necessarily, prepared on an annual basis.

The trading account shows the turnover for the period and, when the cost of sales is deducted therefrom, the **gross profit** to be transferred to the next section. This, the true profit and loss account, shows additional income not directly connected with trading, and after deducting all expenses necessarily incurred in marketing and administration it gives the **net profit** for the period under review. This figure is adjusted for any extraordinary items of expenditure and against it is set the tax charged on profit, which leaves net profit after taxation to be carried down into the appropriation account, where the division of the spoils is detailed, i.e. the net profit after tax is either apportioned to the proprietors or transferred into reserves to be ploughed back into the business as an investment in future years.

The profit and loss account of a limited company is governed by the provisions

Profit sharing

of the Companies Acts, particularly the **fourth schedule** to the 1985 Companies Act which replaced the **eighth schedule** to the 1948 Act. The Schedule to the 1985 Act provides a choice of four specific formats, one of which must be used by all companies governed by that Act, though this obligation is modified by the overriding requirement to provide a true and fair view of the profit or loss of the company during the financial year. This requirement may make deviation from the standard format necessary in exceptional circumstances, though the onus is on the directors and auditors to demonstrate the necessity.

Profit sharing The concept of offering employees a share in the **net profits** of a business. ◊ **Incentive scheme** ◊ **Productivity agreements**.

Profits policy ◊ **Assurance**.

Profits tax This was a tax levied in addition to **income tax** on **companies** but not on individuals or **partnerships**. It was a flat-rate tax on profits after adjustments in addition to those necessary for income tax purposes. It was abolished when **corporation tax** was introduced.

Program The set of linked instructions given to a computer in order that it may systematically perform a given task. Errors attributed to computers almost invariably arise from faults in the form or content of the program and are therefore more properly ascribed to the fallibility of the human programmer.

Programme evaluation and review technique (PERT) Closely related to **critical path analysis**, this is a continual review of the procedures developed by critical path analysis, with a view to maximizing efficiency and making necessary alterations at the earliest opportunity.

Programming A fairly general term concerning data processing by computers. A computer will only do what it is told to do. The instructions given to a computer are known as a program, and devising these instructions as programming.

Promissory note Defined by the Bill of Exchange Act 1882 as an 'unconditional promise in writing made by one person to another, signed by the maker, engaging to pay, on demand or at a fixed or determinable future time, a sum certain in money to, or to the order of, a specified person, or to bearer'. The note must be delivered to the payee or bearer. The person signing the note must pay it to a **holder in due course**; he has no right to deny the existence of the payee or the capacity of the payee to endorse.

Notes payable on demand should be presented within a reasonable time – how long that is depends on the custom of the particular trade.

Promoter The person responsible for the formation of a **company**.

Promotion A word with several meanings: (1) increasing **sales** of specific **goods** or services by means of **marketing research**, **advertising**, etc.; (2) upgrading an individual in his employment; (3) forming a limited **company**. ◊ **Promoter**.

Proposed dividends Dividends proposed to be paid. When the **annual accounts** of a **company** are printed they usually contain an item for dividend on **ordinary shares**. This is the amount recommended by the **directors**, but it does not become payable until it has been approved by the shareholders at the **annual general meeting**.

Proprietary insurance company An **insurance** company organized in the same manner as an ordinary limited **company**, i.e. not a **mutual** company.

Prosecution, agreements to stifle Generally speaking, agreements to stifle prosecution are illegal, being against public policy. There are one or two exceptions: for instance, a man may not disclose a fraud if he hopes that by doing so he will enable other frauds to be detected; or where there are both civil and criminal remedies, an innocent party may sometimes go for the civil action where this is to his benefit. The threat to bring legal proceedings, or give evidence leading to prosecution, could constitute **duress** in equity, where the purpose of the threat is not to serve the purposes of the law but rather those of the threatener.

Prospectus Whenever an offer of shares or debentures for sale to the public is made, the offering company must issue a prospectus and file this with the Registrar of Companies. Such offers include circulars, advertisements, etc., which can be construed as invitations to the reader of them to subscribe for shares or debentures. The only offers excluded from this requirement are those made to existing shareholders to subscribe for shares of a class already issued or invitations extended to employees or their families.

The prospectus is a detailed and lengthy document which must conform to the provisions of the Third Schedule to the Companies Act 1985. Apart from describing the aims, objects and capital structure of the company together with any past history of operation, it may also contain statistical information and projections as to future profits. Any statements by 'experts' in a prospectus must be published with the approval of those experts and the fact that this approval has been given must be stated.

Companies cannot avoid the issue of a prospectus by offering shares through a third party, e.g. an **issuing house** or a **merchant bank**, as shares and debentures so issued are considered to be issued by the company itself.

There are substantial penalties for knowingly making false statements in a prospectus and persons doing so may incur additional costs by way of compensating third parties who have suffered losses by relying on those statements.

Foreign companies inviting subscription for shares or debentures within the UK must comply with the regulations contained in sections 72–79 of the 1985 Act.

Protected transactions ◊ **Relation back, doctrine of**.

Protest ◊ **Noting and protest**.

Provision An accounting term originally defined in the Companies Act 1948 as 'any amount written off or retained by way of providing for **depreciation**, renewals, or diminution in **value** of **assets**, or retained by way of providing for any known liability of which the amount cannot be determined with substantial accuracy'. If the amount is more than the **directors** consider strictly necessary, the difference should be treated as a **reserve** and not as a provision. The 1981 Companies Act provided that in the accounts of limited companies notes must be supplied showing the amount of every material provision for liabilities or charges and distinguishing between the figure at the commencement of the period to which those accounts relate and the closing figure. Details of transfers to and from those provisions must also be given.

Provision for renewals An accounting term for the replacement of minor items of the fixed assets variety. Instead of charging each year's replacement costs as they fall due, a company may include in its accounts an average year's expenses. These charges will be reconciled with actual costs in an appropriate equalization account.

Provisional liquidator When a winding-up order is made the court appoints the **Official Receiver** as provisional **liquidator** pending the appointment of a liquidator proper.

Proxy A person acting in place of another. A **member of a company** can nominate another person (who need not be a member) to attend a meeting and if necessary vote. The proxy can only vote if the member has power to vote, and only on a **poll**, not a show of hands, unless the articles provide otherwise. Notices calling meetings must state that a member may appoint a proxy. The appointment is usually made in writing on a form provided by the **company**. It must be deposited with the company before the meeting, but the company cannot insist that it be deposited more than forty-eight hours before.

There are various forms of proxy: a general proxy with power to vote at any meeting, and a special proxy (for a particular meeting). Special proxy forms may be: (1) at the discretion of the proxy holder – he may vote as he thinks fit; (2) two-way proxies – these are printed so that the member can state whether he wants the proxy to vote for or against the resolution; and (3) three-way proxies, basically a combination of the first two. The **Stock Exchange** insists that companies wanting **quotations** must provide for the issue of two-way proxies. If the member attends the meeting as well as the proxy, the proxy might just as well not be there. It is common practice for **directors** to issue proxy forms offering themselves as proxies for the members.

Public company ◊ **Company, public**.

Public corporation A quasi-autonomous body similar in function to a company but set up by the State to run either public services such as the BBC or an industry which is in the hands of the State either by tradition, such as the Post Office, or by the process of nationalization, such as British Coal.

Although the ultimate control of a public corporation rests with the minister responsible for the relevant department of government, the day-to-day management of the corporation is delegated to ministerial appointees who, subject to the broad policy lines established by the State, are expected to run its affairs in a manner beneficial to the public which it is intended to serve.

Inasmuch as public finance is provided for the proper operation of the corporation its management is expected to operate the business of the corporation not with a view to the maximization of profits, as would be the case were it in the private sector, but in such a way that will best serve to provide the income that will cover expenditure necessarily incurred.

Public holidays ◊ **Bank holidays**.

Public house A house licensed to sell intoxicating liquor for consumption on the premises, and differing from a hotel or **inn** in that it does not offer accommodation. A pub offering accommodation to casual customers will probably be a hotel within the definition of the Hotel

Proprietors Act 1956 and the various Innkeepers Acts.

Public lending right (PLR) Authors and illustrators of books are normally remunerated by **royalties** on the number of copies sold. Because sales are very much reduced by the loaning of books from public libraries, some compensation is given to authors and illustrators through the public lending right system. Legislation was introduced in 1979 and the system came into force in 1983; the first payments were made in February 1984. Under the scheme an approximation of the number of times a book is borrowed is arrived at on the basis of a sample of sixteen public libraries throughout the United Kingdom. Payments are made to authors, etc., in proportion to the number of times their books are borrowed, the amount paid being dependent on the total made available by parliament for distribution under the scheme. There is a lower payment limit of £1 and an upper limit of £5,000. In the first year over 60 per cent of authors received less than £100 each.

Public liability insurance This form of **insurance** is compulsory for business organizations whose operations bring them directly, or indirectly, into contact with the general public. The law insists that they obtain insurance cover for any loss suffered by members of the public whilst on their premises. ◊ **Employers' liability insurance**. ◊ **Third-party insurance**.

Public relations (PR) This concerns the relationship existing between a business or an individual and the general public, and relates specifically to the image of that company or individual in the mind of the public. Public relations firms exist to project and protect that image and the role of PR consultant has been described as his, or her, 'being accountable for ensuring that organizations or people enjoy the reputation they deserve and, at the same time, helping them to deserve a good reputation'.

Public utilities These organizations, sometimes in the form of public corporations, are essentially managed or supervised by central or local government to supply fundamental services to the public in cases where a natural monopoly usually exists. At one time power and transport within the UK were the province of public utilities, so were the supply of water and the postal service. In recent years most of these have been sold off to the private sector. ◊ **British Gas** ◊ **Electricity supply**.

Public trustee A government official who is appointed to act as **trustee** in any instance where a **trust** exists and a specific trustee has not been appointed.

Puisne mortgage A legal **mortgage** without the deposit of **title** deeds. It is registerable at the Land Charges Registry. If there are other mortgages, priority will be given to those first registered.

Punched cards Cards used for recording information. This is done by punching holes in the cards at positions determined by various ciphers, which are numbers or letters. When the cards are fed into a machine, it will then reproduce the information in full. The cards are punched perhaps twice to avoid error. They can be automatically sorted, e.g. if each card represents a sales **invoice**, the cards may be automatically sorted into numerical or alphabetical order according to customer. The cards are usually small and easily handled and can contain a great deal of information. Their uses depend upon the sophistication of the equipment with which they are used. Though once common in industry, their role has now been taken over by the computer.

Puncheon A liquid measure of eighty-four gallons.

Pupil The word used in Scottish law for **infant**.

Purchase journal A book-keeping term for the book in which details of all purchases are first entered. Under the **double-entry book-keeping** system, the information is afterwards transferred to the personal and general **ledgers**. The journal gives the name of the **purchaser**, a description of the **goods**, the date of purchase, the **price** charged, **trade discounts**, etc. This method of recording purchases has virtually disappeared in the contemporary business world where most accounting systems are electronically based, and the various accounting records which must necessarily flow from any purchase are virtually effected simultaneously and automatically. Whatever the sophistication of the system in use there must always be safeguards to ensure that the original data is correctly recorded – a requirement that demands an inbuilt verification procedure to provide insurance against the ubiquitous risk of human error.

Purchase tax A tax once levied on certain **goods** manufactured in this country, either to raise revenue or to restrict the manufacture of the goods. It was not payable on goods exported. Manufactur-

ers needed to keep special records and these were open to the inspection of Customs officials at any time. Persons manufacturing goods subject to tax had to be registered with the Customs and Excise authorities and received a **licence** from them. ◊ **Value added tax**.

Purchaser In common usage a person who buys **goods** from another, but legally any person taking a **title** to goods from another person, whether cash passes or not.

Purchaser for value A person who has purchased **goods** and given **value** for them, i.e. paid for them either in cash or in kind.

Purser A person on board ship who keeps the cash account and is responsible for cash payments.

Pyramid selling A practice of selling goods which has fallen into much disrepute and invited direct legislation to prohibit its use. The basic system is tied up with the selling of **franchises**. The 'promoter' invites applications for the sole rights to sell certain products. These rights are in turn hived off to subsidiary franchisees at a predetermined price. Again, these franchisees sub-let their franchises at a price and the process ends up in door-to-door selling by the last in the line. Generally speaking, the only person to profit is the original instigator of the system; the persons down the scale earn little but bad will and indebtedness to those above them. ◊ **Consumer Credit Act** ◊ **Factor** ◊ **Fair Trading Act** ◊ **Sale of goods**.

Qualified acceptance This is an **acceptance** of a **bill of exchange** which varies the effect of the bill as drawn. It only affects the rights of those previously liable on the bill. Normally the drawer presents the bill for acceptance and need not accept the qualification. If the bill has been negotiated before acceptance, the holder is not bound to take a qualified acceptance when he presents the bill, and may treat the bill as dishonoured. If he takes a qualified acceptance he releases from liability all previous signatories who did not assent. Partial acceptance, i.e. only part of the sum specified, does not release the previous signatories providing they are notified.

Qualified report When an **auditor** is not satisfied with the books of account, records, etc., of the business whose accounts are being audited or when unhappy about explanations given by the proprietor or staff, the report written as an accompaniment to the audited profit and loss account and balance sheet may be qualified. This is obviously only important where the auditor is reporting to persons other than those who keep the books and, for that reason, qualified reports are generally associated with limited companies. ◊ **Annual report** ◊ **Annual return** ◊ **Auditor's report**.

Quality control When a product is being manufactured in quantity it is necessary to ensure that each item is up to the specified quality. In order to keep a check on this standard it is common to introduce a statistical method of quality control which relies on the taking of random samples from the production line and subjecting them to intense scrutiny. The results of such tests (allowing for a predetermined margin of failure) will determine whether or not the total output is of an acceptable quality.

Quality of bills of exchange In the **money market**, **bills of exchange** are graded into various qualities according to their reliability. There are three principal qualities: (1) **trade bills**; (2) **agency bills**; and (3) **bank bills**.

Quango Popular acronym for one of a large number of semi-permanent public commissions or agencies usually in the gift of ministers of the Crown. Though many such bodies fill a useful role (e.g. **Advisory Conciliation and Arbitration Service** and the NEDC), others do little more than add to the already excessive numbers of bureaucrats paid out of the public purse. These 'Quasi-Autonomous Non-Governmental Organizations' tend to be excellent examples of **Parkinson's Law**, with members expanding in a geometrical progression and the chairmanship often little more than a sinecure. The main objection to the emergence and growth of the quango lies less in the fact that they are funded from the public purse than in the power they often possess to dispose of large amounts of public money.

Quantity discount Additional discount

obtained in bulk-buying. It is partly the ability to obtain these discounts that enables **supermarkets** and **hypermarkets** to offer goods at prices below those of the smaller High Street shop. ◊ **Discount store** ◊ **Trade discount**.

Quantity rebate ◊ **Quantity discount** ◊ **Rebate**.

Quantity surveyor Among various definitions are 'the economist of the construction industry' and 'one who advises on all cost and contractual arrangements and acts as the accountant of the project'. A quantity surveyor is concerned with construction and provides a link between the **architect** and the contractor. He is consulted by the architect or engineer responsible for the design and advises on probable costs, perhaps considering alternative possibilities of structure, lay-out or materials. When the design is complete, he prepares a bill of quantities concerning labour and material required. This is concerned with quantity and not **price**. A copy is sent to each contractor tendering for the work, who then quotes a price. The quantity surveyor may also be required to assess progress payments made to contractors and final settlements. Quantity surveying can be specialized, particularly in the case of civil engineering, or work done for government departments and local authorities. The quantity surveyor may work in a private capacity or for a contractor. Specialization may concern both type and sphere of work. A quantity surveyor will belong to one of the recognized institutes, either the **Royal Institution of Chartered Surveyors** or the **Institute of Quantity Surveyors**.

Quantity Surveyors, Institute of This was founded in 1938 and aims: (1) to develop the science and techniques of

quantity surveying ◊ **Quantity surveyor**; (2) to recruit suitable persons to the profession; (3) to help members in the performance of their task; (4) to give them recognized status; (5) to protect the public by ensuring that only suitable persons should be allowed to use their distinguishing letters and designation; (6) to maintain satisfactory standards of professional etiquette. Membership is open only to quantity surveyors proper and not to general surveyors. Members must pass the examination set out in its regulations and syllabus.

Quantum meruit This applies when someone does not complete work he is contracted to do and may perhaps claim payment *quantum meruit*, that is, 'as much as he has earned'. For instance, someone supplying the wrong quantity of goods can claim payment in proportion, if the purchaser does not decide to refuse delivery altogether.

Quarter days The four days taken by custom to mark the quarters of the year. On these days, tenancies begin and end, and rents and other quarterly charges become due. In England and Ireland the quarter days are: 25 March, 24 June, 29 September and 25 December – namely, Lady Day (the Feast of the Annunciation), Midsummer Day, Michaelmas (the Feast of St Michael) and Christmas Day. In Scotland they are: 2 February, 15 May, 1 August and 11 November – namely, Candlemas Day (the Feast of Purification), Whitsuntide, Lammas (Loaf Mass – harvest festival) and Martinmas (the Feast of St Martin).

Quasi-contracts These occur when, although no proper **contract** exists, a court considers that one person has an obligation to another. One could arise for instance from an illegal contract, where the court allows one party to recover money paid even though the contract was void. ◊ **Contract, illegal**.

Quasi-loan The Companies Act 1980 introduced the legal term 'quasi-loan' in sections concerning the restrictions on companies making loans to directors. A quasi-loan arises when the company incurs a liability or agrees to incur such a liability in circumstances when the director is under an obligation to reimburse the company for the amount involved. An example would be where the company holds a credit card and that card is used in a transaction for the sole benefit of a director personally. The company has assumed a liability through use of the card and the director, as beneficiary of the transaction, must reimburse the company.

Queen's Awards The first Queen's Award to Industry was instituted in 1962. There are now three Queen's Awards given to business or industrial units in recognition of outstanding achievement in the fields to which they apply. The awards are respectively, the Queen's Award for Export Achievement, the Queen's Award for Technological Achievement and the Queen's Award for Environmental Achievement. The awards are given to the unit itself rather than to an individual and recognize the accomplishments of the group, managers and employees jointly, in the area in which they work. They may be applied for by any organization, working within the UK and the Channel Isles, which meets the necessary criteria irrespective of size or location and whether it is engaged in production, research, commerce, education or is part of local or national government. All that is necessary

is to demonstrate a degree of efficiency that merits the award. Awards are held for five years. During this period the holders may display the appropriate award emblem on both stationery and products.

Quick assets Another name for **liquid assets**.

Quintal A term used in Liverpool and the USA for 100 lb avoirdupois.

Quorum The number of persons who must be present at a meeting in order that the meeting can officially take place. Absence of a quorum will nullify any decisions made at that meeting. For public and private companies the number of members attending which constitutes a quorum may be stated in the articles. If no number is stipulated then two persons personally present constitute a quorum.

At a class meeting of shareholders the required quorum is two persons holding either personally or by proxy at least one third of the nominal value of the issued shares of that class. The number is reduced to one at an adjourned meeting. Also, any person present holding shares or proxies may demand a **poll**.

Quotation Shares of public companies cannot be dealt with officially on the **Stock Exchange** unless they have been granted a quotation. This is applied for on formation of a company, but before it is granted, stringent conditions laid down by the Stock Exchange and the Companies Acts must be satisfied. A company must also supply regular information regarding **meetings**, **dividends**, **directors' emoluments**, half-yearly profit statements, etc. Even when a quotation has been granted, it can always be withdrawn again if the company ceases

Quoted investments

to satisfy the conditions or if the Exchange becomes dissatisfied with its integrity. Shares may be subscribed for on condition that a quotation is obtained. The monies would be repayable if it were not. ◊ **Permission to deal**. In certain circumstances permission to deal on the Exchange may be given without a quotation, but of course the shares would not feature in the **official list**. ◊ **Unlisted Securities Market** ◊ **Listed company**.

Quoted investments An accounting term for investments in **shares** or **debentures** which are quoted on a recognized Stock Exchange. The amount at which the quoted investments are shown in accounts is normally their cost at the time of their acquisition. However company law requires that the **market value** be given, and also the Stock Exchange value where this is different. ◊ **Investments in company accounts** ◊ **Listed investments** ◊ **Listed company**.

Quoted price Usually, the **price** of a **share**, etc., as stated in the **official list**. ◊ **Mean price**.

Rack rent Property is said to be let at a rack rent when the **rent** is equal to the total income from the property and is therefore only just worth paying.

Racking A Customs term for the drawing off of wines and spirits from casks.

Radiotelegrams It is possible to send radiotelegrams through coastal stations to ships at sea, both Royal and Merchant Navy, and to aircraft in flight. The service is provided by British Telecom and relevant information can be obtained therefrom.

Radio-telephone This is a service provided by **British Telecom** for the provision of telephonic communication between persons aboard ships or aircraft and persons on shore. Much depends on the equipment available on the ship or the aircraft and reference should be made to the current situation by inquiry either on the vessel or to British Telecom. Generally speaking, the service does not cover coin-operated call boxes.

Railway advice A document issued by British Rail indicating that **goods** are waiting for collection and stating **demurrage** terms.

Railway letters The Post Office operates an agreement with certain railway companies for transmission of first-class letters by those railways to a specified station where the addressees may collect them or alternatively where they will be transferred to the post. The railway companies involved in this service are listed in the **Post Office Guide** and tend to be the rural, privately operated lines. The facility is available only within the UK. A fee is payable to the railway at the station where the letter is handed in, in addition to normal postal charges, and the letter must be properly marked, i.e. with details of the station of destination and whether it will be called for.

Railways ⟡ **British Rail**.

Rate capping In an attempt to restrain extravagent spending by local authorities the Rates Act 1984 empowered the Secretary of State for the Environment to subject allegedly delinquent authorities to a process known as rate capping. This reduced the amount those authorities were able to charge rate-payers, thus denying them the income by which the so-called excess expenditure could be funded.

Rate of exchange The price of the **currency** of one country in terms of the currency of another. In international trade, decisions to buy from abroad will be influenced not only by the prices ruling in another country but also by the cost of buying the amount of that country's currency necessary to make the purchase. Traditional economic theory, based on the argument that exchange rates were dictated by comparative costs and would settle at a point that made prices in competing countries equal, has tended, despite alterations in the facts that supported that theory, to create the impression that international trade and exchange rates are each functions of the other. This is no longer so, for many reasons that range from the blatantly political to the everyday complications of practical economics.

The creation of the **International monetary fund**, with powers to interfere with the customary processes of fixing or changing rates of exchange in the interests of international harmony, was but one quasi-political decision that upset natural economic forces. Others were the creation of other organizations from the GATT to the **Common Market** and its **green currencies**. An example of more blatant political interference lay in the imposition of the **dollar premium**.

Disregarding bilateral agreements and special circumstances, exchange rates are traditionally either fixed or floating. At the time of the Bretton Woods Agreements which set up the International Monetary Fund and the **International Bank for Reconstruction and Development** in 1944, exchange rates were fixed in terms of the dollar. By the 1970s most rates of exchange had been allowed to float, that is to find their own level in terms of one currency against another in the world market. This situation was modified considerably within Western Europe by the introduction of the **European exchange rate mechanism** in 1978. This replaced the **Snake** in attempting to bring some form of order to exchange rates within the EU. ◊ **European Monetary System**.

The question of rates of exchange is necessarily tied up with the **balance of payments** of any country and, perhaps even more, with the movements of foreign capital from weak to hard curren-

cies. In the long term the price of **gold** tends to be the deciding factor, though lately even this has created confusion for although the **dollar** price of gold may fluctuate the UK price does not vary in tandem, because of unrelated changes in the dollar price of **sterling**. ◊ **European Payments Union** ◊ **General Agreement on Tariffs and Trade** ◊ **Gold and foreign exchange reserves** ◊ **Gold standard** ◊ **Special drawing rights** ◊ **European Monetary System**.

Rate of interest ◊ **Interest**.

Rate of return ◊ **Discounting back** ◊ **Net present value** ◊ **Return on capital** ◊ **Yield** ◊ **Earnings yield**.

Rate of turnover An accounting term for the speed with which stock is turned over. In a retail business, for instance, if stock averaged £10,000 and annual sales were £75,000, the stock would be turned over seven and a half times per annum.

Rateable value In collecting business rates the rating authority – now the Inland Revenue – imposes a levy on all property owners. The rate is expressed as so much in the pound on the rateable value of a property. This value, although it appears to be arbitrarily assessed, is, in fact, directly based on the estimated rent that the property might be expected to command in the **open market** and with vacant possession.

Rates This refers to a tax levied at one time on all properties, both residential and commercial, within the UK, the charge on commercial properties being considerably higher than that on domestic properties. It was set and collected by the responsible authorities at both district and county level and was expected, together with the aid of government

grants, to cover the cost of lighting, libraries, road maintenance etc., not to mention the provision of education and
leisure facilities.

In an effort to control local expenditure and make the population more
aware of its continual escalation, the
rating system in the UK was scrapped in
1990 in favour of the Community
Charge or Poll tax which was levied as a
flat rate on all adults. Each local authority established the required rate for the
area for which it was responsible and
consequently rates of charge varied considerably throughout the country, depending partly on the profligacy or otherwise
of the authority concerned. This experiment in local taxation was universally
unpopular and has now been scrapped in
favour of the **council tax**. The Community Charge never applied to commercial
enterprises which, from the time of introduction of that levy, became subject to
the **uniform business rate**. ◊ **Rebate**.

Ratification of agent's contracts If an
agent acts outside his actual authority,
the principal can ratify the **contract** and
become bound by it. That is, if A purports
to act for B without B's knowledge, then
providing A states himself to be an agent
for B, B can ratify and adopt the contract.
But ratification cannot be used to introduce a stranger to a contract: if A contracts
with C on a private basis, B cannot claim
afterwards that A was acting as his agent.

When a contract is ratified, rights and
obligations are related back to when the
contract was made.

If the agent is acting within his apparent authority and has been held out
by the principal as his agent, ratification
is not necessary.

Real accounts ◊ **Accounts, nominal,
real and personal**.

Real property Property consisting of
freehold land or certain rights over freehold land. The term derives from a very
old tradition in English law which divided property according to the manner
in which recompense could be made to a
person wrongly deprived of it. Land
could always be recovered by an
action *in rem*, a real action. Other property was not recoverable by such an
action and the only remedy available
to the plaintiff was an action *in
personam*. Hence the division of property
into real and personal. The distinction
between real and personal property
has ceased to be of great importance,
since various statutes passed in the
twentieth century abolished most of the
privileges and special rules on inheritance
which applied only to real property. The
term is still, however, used frequently
in published accounts. ◊ **Annual
accounts**.

Real value In general, the term 'real', as
used to describe value or price, refers to
value excluding fluctuations brought
about by inflation or deflation. It is
mostly used in making comparisons over
a period when prices have reacted to
arbitrary and artificial pressures which do
not reflect genuine worth. This concept
is very important in published figures,
e.g. **profits**, **dividends**, wages, etc.,
when it is necessary to restate current
figures in terms of prices ruling at the
time when the figures with which they
are being compared were compiled. This
is done by applying an appropriate **index
number**. Real value may also be applied
to money itself, e.g. the real value of a
1985 pound sterling may be only 50
pence at 1977 prices. ◊ **Current cost
accounting** ◊ **Current purchasing
power accounting** ◊ **Market value**

◊ **Nominal value** ◊ **Retail price index** ◊ **Stock-in-trade**.

Realization account An account opened for convenience when a business is being wound up. **Assets** are debited to it, liabilities and proceeds of **sale** are credited, and the **balance** after paying debts is called the profit (or loss) on realization.

Rebate A rebate is similar to a discount in so far as it reduces an amount payable. Sometimes it is used as a synonym for discount in a trading situation. However, a discount is strictly a reduction allowed by the payee, whereas a rebate is an amount returned to the payer – often at a later date. The term rebate is frequently associated with rent and rates, as certain people who are considered to be of limited means are given back portions of rent or rates paid to a local authority. These repayments are known as rent or rate rebates. ◊ **Cash discount** ◊ **Quantity discount** ◊ **Trade discount**.

Receipt A document issued by a **creditor** to acknowledge payment of a debt. At one time a stamped receipt was demanded as proof of payment. Now, if payment is by **cheque** made out to the creditor and paid into his account, no other receipt is legally necessary.

Received for shipment A **bill of lading** containing these words indicates that the **goods** have been received alongside, but not that they have been shipped. Such bills are not popular, though they can be sent to a third party more quickly than a **shipped bill**.

Receiver A person appointed by the court, or some other competent authority, to take over the property of a debtor, whether a person or a corporation, and to supervise the collection of income and its distribution to creditors

until debts are paid in full. In company law, **debenture** holders often have the right to appoint a receiver where the company has acted in a manner prejudicial to their interests. A receiver does not normally have power to manage the business of the debtor but the court may consider that the best interests of creditors would be served by appointing a manager to carry on the business and may combine the role of receiver and manager in one person. ◊ **Administration order** ◊ **Official Receiver** ◊ **Special manager** ◊ **Insolvency Act 1986**.

Recognizance A form of contract made between an individual and the Crown or a court of law. It frequently involves an agreement to stand bail, i.e. to forefeit a fixed sum of money deposited with the court, if a named person does not either attend a hearing on a fixed date or, at a court's request, desist from certain activities which may cause a breach of the peace. ◊ **Contract of record**.

Recognized investment exchange (RIE) The Financial Services Act which requires persons involved in financial or investment business to register with a relevant self-regulating organization does not impose the same requirement on the markets in which investments are traded. These may apply instead to the Securities and Investments Board for the status of Recognized Investment Exchange – though their members will still need to obtain individual authorization to carry out investment business, either independently with the SIB or through an SRO. The London Stock Exchange is a RIE within the purposes of the Act. Others are **London International Financial Futures and Options Exchange** ◊ **London Fox**, ◊ **London Metal Exchange**.

Recognized Professional Body (RPB) Under the rules of the Financial Services Act the requirement by the Securities and Investment Board to belong to designated SROs is relaxed in the case of certain professional bodies, such as the Institute of Chartered Accountants in England and Wales, whose members engage in investment activities in a manner which is quite incidental to their main area of business. Such organizations can apply to the SIB for recognition as registered professional bodies. This relieves their members from each being obliged to register separately with an SRO.

Recommended retail price Producers or manufacturers of consumer goods do not, unless an agreement has been registered under the **Restrictive Trade Practices** Act, have the power to control the price charged by an independent retailer. They do, however, attempt to circumvent this by recommending a price at which the product should be sold and by advertising this price as 'recommended'. If goods are introduced to the public by a manufacturer's advertisement which gives a suggested price, it will be difficult for the retailer to sell at a figure above that stated, although he can always sell below it. The advertised price is referred to commercially as the recommended retail price or the manufacturer's recommended price (MRP). ◊ **Resale price maintenance** ◊ **Own brand**.

Recorded delivery A service offered by the **Post Office** to customers who want to be completely sure that a letter or package is received at the address stated on it. The service basically provides a record of postage and delivery.

Recorded delivery items have to be handed in at a post office, where a form is completed. A fee is payable in addition to normal first-class postage. Although the Post Office agrees to deliver to the address stated it will not undertake to deliver to any particular person at that address, and the recipient rather than the addressee signs for it. For an additional fee the customer can have specific 'advice of delivery', which will be signed by the postal officer making the delivery, not by the recipient.

There is an automatic limited compensation for recorded delivery items lost or damaged in transit – provided the contents are not on the prohibited list – but no special treatment is afforded to them. The service is inland only and does not extend to Eire. ◊ **Inland post** ◊ **Registered post**.

Recourse agreement In **hire purchase** transactions, this is an agreement the seller makes with the hire purchase company to repurchase the goods from the company if the hirer defaults and the company repossesses.

Rectification of the register Where a person convinces a court that his name should be on the register of members of a **company** but is not, the court may order the register to be rectified at the cost of the person responsible for the error. Similarly, when the court thinks a person's name should be removed from the register it may order that to be done. ◊ **Share register**.

Redeemable preference shares Preference **shares** which the **company** reserves the right to redeem. The fact that the shares are redeemable must be stated in the **balance sheet**, together with the earliest and latest dates for redemption and any premium payable. The shares may only be redeemed out of distributable profits or the proceeds of a further issue of shares. Where redemption is made out of profits, a sum equal to the amount redeemed must be put into a capital reserve, and this cannot be distributed. ◊ **Capital redemption reserve fund** ◊ **Companies: purchase of own shares** ◊ **Companies: redeemable shares**.

Redemption date The date at which a certain category of **security** becomes due for repayment by the borrower. Also referred to as the 'maturity date'. Where the securities are long-term, particularly where they are State-issued, the borrower may have reserved an option to convert them into another security; and even where no such right has been reserved, an attempt may be made, where the borrower is short of cash, to persuade the holders to accept a substitute security in place of cash. ◊ **Redemption yield** ◊ **Rescheduling debts**.

Redemption yield Similar to the **earnings yield** or **dividend yield**, except that this concerns **bonds** with a fixed **redemption date**, or more particularly with a premium on redemption, and takes these factors into account: e.g. rate of **interest** acceptable 10 per cent; bonds earning 5 per cent on £100 nominal value; market price would tend to be £50 on dividend yield. However, were the bonds redeemable at par in, say, a year, the gain on the redemption of £50 over the dividend yield price has to be taken into account before a market price can be established. The yield shown by relating the dividend plus the capital gain to the market price would be the redemption yield.

Redirection of post Letters may be redirected by the recipient to the addressee at another address without charge, provided the redirection is made on the same day or the next working day. **Business reply** post and **Freepost** can only be redirected by the **Post Office**. Redirected post will be carried on the original terms, i.e. first-class letters will continue to be treated as first-class. If the time for redirection has expired or the letter has been tampered with, postage will be charged at normal rates. ◊ **Inland post**.

Parcels can only be freely redirected within the same postal delivery area. In any other case they will be recharged at usual rates.

When a person changes his address he can apply to the Post Office for automatic redirection of all his mail. He will be charged on a sliding scale determined by the length of time the redirection service is to be continued – charges are higher for longer periods.

Reducing balance depreciation ◊ **Depreciation**.

Redundancy Employers are legally obliged to make payments on a scale set down by statute to all employees leaving employment by reason of being made redundant. Redundancy involves being dismissed by an employer with or without notice when the employee has not been guilty of any breach of the contract of employment – whether that be express or implied – and has not been offered reasonable alternative employment by the same employer. Constructive dismissal will be inferred where the employer acts in a manner which precludes continuation of employment.

The sum payable on redundancy will vary with the length of time that the person has been employed, starting from between one and one-and-a-half weeks' pay for each year of continuous employment, depending on the age of the recipient. A large part of this sum can be reclaimed by the employer from the State.

Refinance credits Credit facilities obtainable by an overseas buyer, where the exporter cannot provide credit and the buyer does not wish to pay cash. A credit is opened at the branch of an overseas **bank** in London in favour of the exporter. The exporter is paid on a **sight draft** drawn on the buyer's credit; the advising bank in London (this being a recognized London bank) accepts a **bill of exchange** on the buyer; the bill is discounted and the proceeds put to the account of the foreign bank that issued the credit, thus offsetting the amount paid to the exporter. The buyer pays nothing until the bill drawn on the London bank matures.

Register of charges All charges on the property of a **company** by way of **mortgages**, fixed or floating **debentures**, **bills of sale**, etc., must be registered with the Registrar of Companies. If not, they will be void and so not enforceable against **liquidators** or **creditors**. The company itself also keeps a register containing full details of each charge: the property, the persons involved and the amount of the charge. This must be kept at the offices of the company and must be open for free inspection by **members of the company** and creditors.

Certain charges must also be registered with the Land Registry. ◊ **Mortgage**.

Register of companies A register kept at Companies House. All **companies** must file certain documents with the Registrar of Companies before they can obtain a certificate of incorporation. Companies may be struck off the register if the Registrar has reasonable cause for

believing that they are not in business. He ascertains this by sending a letter. If he receives no reply within a month, he sends a registered letter. After another month, if there is still no reply, or if the company replies that it is not in business, he may notify it that it is to be struck off the register, unless good reason can be given why this should not be done. The company will then be dissolved after three months. Notice that the company has been struck off must be published in the **London Gazette** or, where applicable, the *Edinburgh* or *Belfast Gazette*. ◊ **Defunct companies**.

Register of debentures ◊ **Register of charges**. Each **company** must keep a register of all **mortgages** and charges affecting its property. It must also keep copies of all mortgages and charges that must be registered with the Registrar of Companies. It need not keep a register of **debenture** holders but will usually do so.

Register of directors Every **company** must keep a register of **directors** giving names, former names, addresses, nationalities, business occupations, dates of birth and other directorships held. A copy of this register is sent to the Registrar of Companies, who must also be notified of any alterations.

The 1981 Companies Act included an additional requirement that the register should contain, in relation to each director named, all previous directorships held during the preceding five years unless those directorships were in dormant companies or within the same group as the present company.

Register of directors' interests Under the Companies Act 1985 every **company** must keep a register showing the number, description and amount of **shares** and **debentures** of the company or its **subsidiary companies** held by its **directors**, or held in trust for them, or of which they have some right to be holders. Directors are obliged to notify the company in writing of all shares and debentures, and interest in shares and debentures, that they hold, cease to hold or acquire the right to purchase in the company or a subsidiary. A person in accordance with whose instructions a director is accustomed to act is considered to be a director for these purposes. Interest in shares and debentures is construed fairly widely. If the shares are held by a body corporate, the director is interested if he holds a third or more of the voting power at a general meeting of that body. He is also interested if he can at any time require the shares to be registered in his name or to call for delivery of the shares to himself. Interests of wife or infant sons and daughters are interests of the director.

It is the responsibility of the director to inform the company of all relevant facts within a very short period. There are very heavy penalties for failing to comply with the Act. The register must be kept at the **registered office**, or wherever the **register of members** is kept, and shall, during business hours, be open to the inspection of any member without charge and any other person for a small fee. It need not be open all day but must be so for at least two hours. If the register is not in alphabetical form then an index must also be provided.

Register of interests in shares Anyone who alone or jointly has an interest of 3 per cent or more in the nominal value of any class of shares in a public company must notify the company both when such an interest is acquired and when it ceases

to be held. ◊ **Company: disclosure of interest in shares**. For its part the company is obliged to keep a register of such interests, with a separate index if necessary, and to make this register available for inspection by any person without charge for at least two hours in each working day.

Register of members ◊ **Share register**.

Registered land certificate Certain land in the country is registered with the Land Registry. The title deeds can be exchanged for a certificate, which facilitates transfers, as any **charge** not registered at the Land Registry will be void, and so not enforceable against a **purchaser for value**. The certificate will give details of the land, the owner and any charges.

Registered office The official residence of a **company**. Any document which the law requires to be delivered to the company must be delivered to the registered office. The Registrar of Companies must be notified of any change of address.

Registered post A service offered by the **Post Office** for the sending of articles of value which ensures that they will be handled with additional security. It is an inland service only. ◊ **Inland post**.

Items which are to be sent by registered post must be securely packed, sealed and handed in at a post office. A registration fee is payable in addition to normal postal charges, which will be at the first class rate. The fee will vary according to the value on the packet and delivery will be recorded, i.e. the signature of the recipient at the address shown will be obtained. Unlike the **recorded delivery** service it is possible to have the signature of the person accepting the packet on an 'advice of delivery', though an additional fee is again payable. ◊ **Compensation fee parcel service**.

Registered stock This is (1) similar to **inscribed stock** or (2) ordinary **stock**, converted from **shares**. A stock register may be kept, just as a **share register** is.

Regulated companies These were companies formed for the regulation of particular trades and professions. Their function has now been taken over by trade unions and professional associations and this type of company has become obsolete.

Reinsurance An insurer may frequently find it expedient to spread the risk he takes. A particular example of such spreading of risk may be found at Lloyd's, where insurers known as underwriters operate through syndicates wherein each member assumes only a fixed proportion of any liability. This is very necessary, as the possible claims under a Lloyd's policy could be far beyond the ability of a single insurer to cover.

The principle applies in most types of insurance, albeit in a minor way, and it is not uncommon for any insurer to hedge his liability by reinsuring, i.e. passing on part of the risk to another party much as a bookmaker hedges his bets by laying part of them off with other bookmakers. Needless to say, unless the reinsurance is agreed with the insured, the original insurer remains primarily liable for any claim under the policy.

Relation back, doctrine of In cases of **bankruptcy** and **liquidation**, the power of a trustee or **liquidator** relates back to the commencement of the bankruptcy or liquidation. This means that he can ignore all transactions that are made

between the commencement and his appointment and recover monies paid. He is entitled to all the property that existed at the commencement. There are, however, certain protected transactions. These are generally transactions made by the debtor in good faith and for value.

Rendu ◊ **Franco, rendu, or free contracts**.

Rent The sum received by a person who hires his property out to another.

Rent roll A list of all **rents** receivable from an estate.

Renting back ◊ **Sale and lease back**.

Reorder levels ◊ **Inventory control**.

Replacement cost An accounting term for the cost of replacing an **asset**, as opposed to **historical cost**. Assets are sometimes valued at replacement cost, perhaps to show **fixed assets** at a more realistic **value** in a **balance sheet** or perhaps to charge the true cost of materials or goods against **sales** in the manufacturing or trading account. ◊ **Stock valuation**.

Replacement cost accounting A simple form of **current cost accounting** where the adjustments are largely concerned with fixed and current assets which are brought into account not at their **historical cost** but in terms of their **replacement cost**. This type of inflation accounting is partly in use already where stocks are charged to production on a LIFO basis and where **fixed assets** are frequently revalued and depreciation charged accordingly. ◊ **Accounting for inflation** ◊ **Revaluation of assets**.

Replevin The restoration of **goods** to an owner after the goods have been distrained and while the court is deciding whether the **distraint** was right and proper.

Repudiation A **contract** is repudiated when one party makes known to the other his intention not to fulfil his part.

Reputation, loss of Generally speaking, in the law of **contract**, **damages** are not available for loss of reputation. However, a banker may be sued by an account holder for loss of reputation if he returns to drawer a **cheque** when there are funds to meet it. There is also the question of the reputation a contract itself would have brought: an actor suing for breach of a contract for a leading part may obtain damages for the loss of the prospective reputation.

Reputed owner The person who appears to be the owner of property even though it may in fact belong to some other party. The phrase has a particular meaning in **bankruptcy**: if A has allowed B possession of **goods** knowing that third parties might assume B to be the true owner of them, then A may be estopped from denying this if B were to go bankrupt. ◊ **Estoppel** ◊ **Order and disposition**.

Resale price maintenance Attempts by the manufacturers or suppliers of goods to dictate the price at which, or the conditions on which, goods are to be sold by the retailer. Although common at one time in the UK, and during wartime actually compulsory for goods subject to price control, the practice has now been made virtually illegal. Manufacturers can now fix and enforce prices only where an agreement has been entered into and registered under the **Restrictive Trade Practices** Act 1956. Registration will only be accepted if the

restrictive practices court considers that price maintenance is in the public interest, and only in very few cases has it been deemed to be so. The best-known agreement is the **net book agreement** between publishers and booksellers, but the prices of certain pharmaceutical products are also maintained.

The abolition of price maintenance was underlined again with the Resale Prices Act 1964, and suppliers are now not only prevented from fixing prices but also from witholding supplies from traders who sell at low prices – though they can interfere if the trader is using the goods as **loss leaders**. The withholding of supplies is taken to mean not only cutting them completely but also refusing to supply on customary terms or terms available to dealers generally.

Although price maintenance by suppliers has been all but eliminated, the practice of publishing a manufacturer's **recommended retail price** has tended to take its place in giving back some control over retail prices to the suppliers.

Rescheduling debts This is a practice more commonly met with in international finance but it can also occur, albeit on a smaller scale, within a trading corporation. In the latter case it would almost certainly be part of a reconstruction. It happens when the country or business entity has serious liquidity problems which it convinces creditors are a temporary phenomenon only. Creditors for loans due for payment in the near or immediate future agree to convert the outstanding loans into others which are not repayable until some more distant date. In return they may obtain better interest rates or repayment in the form of stated instalments at staggered dates. Such agreements are usually backed by a guarantee from a third party. In practice such rescheduling may often be acceptable to creditors, as it provides a more reasonable chance of eventual repayment, the alternative being to force the debtor into bankruptcy, thus possibly losing the money altogether. On the international scene such rescheduling arrangements are often set up and supervised by the **International Monetary Fund**.

Rescission This is what happens when a **contract** is, as it were, wound up and both parties are restored to their original position. It is the usual remedy in cases of **misrepresentation**. It is only allowed, though, where the parties *can* be restored to their original position, where no third parties are involved and where the claimant has acted within a reasonable time.

Research and development expenditure This is often referred to by the abbreviation R & D expenditure. Most companies, particularly the larger ones, are continually researching into and developing better ways of achieving their stated objectives. They may be looking for new methods of producing old lines, or discovering and elaborating techniques for the production of new items either to replace or to compete with products already marketed by others. R & D is, therefore, an integral part of the world of competition and enterprise – whether free or State-controlled.

Much R & D expenditure is targeted to future production and in the past, as the benefits were expected to accrue in subsequent periods, it was often the practice to capitalize such costs and write them off over future periods. In 1978 this method of deferring costs was reversed by the Accounting Standards Committee, and the views of this body were reinforced by the 1981 Companies Act. Companies can no longer capitalize research costs, and development expenses can only be capitalized in strictly defined circumstances. These, taken along with the relevant accounting standard, are that the expenses must be geared to a clearly defined project and that future profits and resources can be reasonably expected to be sufficient to cover these expenses. Additionally, notes to published accounts must indicate both the reason for capitalization and the period over which the expenditure is to be written off.

Reserve capital A **company** may pass a **special resolution** stating that a portion of its **capital** not already called up shall not be capable of being called up except in the event of the company being wound up. This capital is called the reserve capital and sometimes reserve liability. It cannot be turned into ordinary capital without permission of a court and it cannot be charged by the **directors**.

Reserve currency A **currency** which governments or international finance agencies are prepared to hold as part of their **gold and foreign exchange reserves**. A good reserve currency is both stable and convertible. At one time both the US **dollar** and the pound sterling were recognized as excellent reserve currencies, but economic trends over recent decades have ousted **sterling** from this role and tended to replace the US dollar with the deutschmark and the yen. ◊ **Official reserves** ◊ **Rate of exchange** ◊ **Special drawing rights**.

Reserve for bad debts A misnomer for the provision for doubtful debts. ◊ **Bad debts** ◊ **Doubtful debts, provision for**.

Reserve for obsolescence A sum of money set aside by a business out of profits to guard against the possibility of sudden **obsolescence** of fixed assets. In accounting, an asset becomes obsolete when a new model or a new method is invented which renders the old asset uneconomic. ◊ **Built-in obsolescence**.

Reserve liability ◊ Reserve capital.

Reserve price A term used with reference to **auctions**. A lot which is subject to a reserve price is one which the owner does not wish sold below this price. If the **auctioneer** sells below this figure, the **sale** is void provided that the catalogue does indeed state that there is a reserve price (it need not, of course, say what the price is). If there is no indication in the catalogue, then where the auctioneer has signed the memorandum (which he does if the **contract** must be evidenced in writing), the **title** will pass to the purchaser. The owner's remedies are to stop the sale before the memorandum is signed or to sue for **breach of warranty of authority**.

Reserves The capital available to a business at any time during its existence consists basically of (1) capital subscribed by proprietors, be they entrepreneurs, partners or shareholders, (2) amounts loaned for varying periods and (3) additions to capital resulting from profits made and retained or funds otherwise acquired in the normal course of business. Such additions are generally shown in the **balance sheet** of that business as reserves. Whether these reserves are available for distribution to the owners of the capital will depend on the circumstances of the business, the manner in which the reserves were acquired and the nature of the business organization. Special rules apply to limited companies. Reserves are often divided into **capital reserves** and revenue reserves. ◊ **Reserves, revenue** ◊ **General reserves** ◊ **Provisions** ◊ **Distributable reserves**.

Reserves, gold and dollar ◊ Gold and foreign exchange reserves.

Reserves, movements on The Companies Act 1967 made it necessary for **companies** to show details of movements on all reserve accounts which are not **depreciation** reserves, giving reasons for increases and decreases.

Reserves, revenue A general heading for all reserves which are not **capital reserves**. They are monies available for distribution but for various reasons not yet distributed, e.g. balance on a **profit and loss account**. ◊ **Distributable reserves**.

Resolution, notice of intended Members of companies who represent one-twentieth of the total voting rights of those entitled to vote at the meeting, or 100 or more members holding **shares** on which a minimum of £100 has been paid, can claim at their own expense to have notice of an intended resolution sent to members, together with a statement of not more than 1,000 words. The requisition must be deposited at the registered office not less than six weeks before the meeting.

Resolution of members ◊ Ordinary resolution ◊ Special resolution.

Respondentia bond A shipping term for a loan raised by the master of a ship on the **security** of the cargo.

Restitution A remedy that does not play a large part in English contractual law though it does feature to a limited extent in **equity** – but then only when the parties to a contract can be restored to their previous condition. Occasions when it is applied as a remedy include actions for **money had and received** and in infants' contracts, where although the infant may avoid the contract by pleading his minority the law will not allow him to profit by it and will insist that benefits received are restored by him to the other party.

Restraint of trade, contracts in These, unless there are special circumstances, are contrary to public policy and so void. Restraints are only reasonable if they are in the interests of the contracting parties and also of the public. ◊ **Restrictive covenants**.

Restrictive covenants Terms in a **contract** which restrict the right of one party to contract freely after determination of the contract or during its continuance. They occur in contracts of employment where the employee agrees not to compete with the employer or practise his trade within a given area or time after leaving his employment. They may also appear in the contract for the **sale** of a business where the **vendor** agrees not to compete with the purchaser, perhaps within a given area, or in any way diminish the value of the **goodwill**. Another instance would be a contract for the sale of goods which restricts the rights of the buyer to purchase elsewhere. Such covenants are disliked by the law and are generally only enforceable when they are thought necessary for the protection of the party concerned and are not against the public interest. ◊ **Restrictive trade practices**.

Restrictive endorsement Bills of exchange may be endorsed in a way which restricts the freedom of the endorsee to negotiate them.

Restrictive Practices Court This was set up in 1956 to deal with matters arising from the **Restrictive Trade Practices** Act, i.e. to investigate trading agreements. Since 1964 it has also had responsibility for matters arising from the Resale Prices Act.

Restrictive trade practices At one time these were the province of the **common law** (◊ **Restraint of trade contracts in**), but under the Restrictive Trade Practices Act 1956 and Resale Prices Act 1964 a great number of trading agreements must now be registered with the Director-General of Fair Trading. These are those between two or more persons carrying on business in the United Kingdom, concerning goods, prices, conditions of sale or supply, the way in which the goods are to be manufactured, restrictions on quantities to be sold, processed or manufactured, or restrictions as to areas where goods are to be sold or supplied. The 1956 Act does not apply to agreements dealing with exports. Particulars to be registered are names of persons or parties involved and details of the agreement. It is irrelevant whether or not the agreement is in writing. Any person may apply to the Restrictive Practices Court to investigate these agreements. Where the agreement is considered to be against the public interest the court may prohibit it or order it to be rectified. The court may also, when prohibiting an agreement, prevent further agreements being substituted for the prohibited one. The 1964 Act also provides for the enforcement of certain agreements that are in the public interest. Very often what are known as sole distributor agreements are allowed. The matter is somewhat complicated and the Act very detailed. ◊ **Resale price maintenance**.

Retail price index The **index number** which attempts to measure changes in the cost of living. It is frequently quoted with reference to inflation and can be used to evaluate real as opposed to nominal changes in prices. The current price can be restated in terms of the value of money in another chosen year by the use of the two relevant index numbers. When this is done the purely inflationary increase can be eliminated and the real change in price over the period can be seen. This process is slowly coming to be accepted by accountants as a method of eliminating the often dangerously misleading trading results inherent in traditional **historical cost accounting** and annual reports based on them. ◊ **Current cost accounting** ◊ **Current purchasing power accounting** ◊ **Paper profit**.

Partly for convenience and partly because of changes in consumer spending patterns, the official retail price index is sometimes scrapped and restated in terms of a later base year. This is not merely a matter of changes in weighting, which are made annually, but relates to more fundamental changes in such things as quality and public taste. Such changes occurred in the UK and were reflected in the alteration of the base year in 1956, 1962, 1974, etc. Although the new indexes can still be mathematically related to the old, fundamental 'basket', changes may make comparisons inexact.

Retail trade The provision of goods and services directly to the consumer. Retailers obtain goods from either **wholesalers**, or directly, from a manufacturer. They are essentially 'middlemen' who provide the link between supply and demand, and obtain their income from the margin between the price at which they buy and that at which they sell. Although certain organizations, e.g. **cash and carry** warehouses, attempt to bypass them, the retailers' strength lies in **after-sales service** and advice, which those other concerns are frequently not prepared to give, and for this reason they are perhaps most important in the service industries themselves. ◊ **Middleman** ◊ **Resale price maintenance**.

Retained profits That part of the earnings or net profit of a business not distributed to the owners – shareholders in the case of a company – but reinvested in the business. Until 1973 the UK tax system penalized the distribution of profits by companies by imposing additional tax on dividends, thus encouraging reinvestment. ◊ **Distributable reserves** ◊ **Reserves, movements on** ◊ **Reserves** ◊ **Reserves, revenue**.

Retention money In certain types of **contract**, particularly building contracts, part of the **price** is kept back for a period after the contract is complete in order to give the purchaser time to inspect the work done and discover any bad workmanship.

Retiring a bill A **bill of exchange** is said to be retired when it is withdrawn from circulation by being paid by the acceptor on the due date or earlier.

Return load When a vehicle is hired to carry **goods** to a particular area, the haulier, rather than bring the vehicle back empty, will advertise for return loads. ◊ **Part load**.

Return on capital A rather nebulous phrase. In the terminology of investment analysis and accounting it means the profit earned by **capital**. If the profit were £10 and the capital £150, the return would be $\frac{10}{150}$, i.e. $6\frac{2}{3}$ per cent. However, there are so many ways of defining both capital and profits, and so many difficulties involved in each definition, that it is doubtful if the phrase has any valuable meaning. It is often stated as return on **capital employed**. In company accounts the quoted return on capital may be the ratio that the profit bears to the total **equity** funds or shareholders' funds employed, but because definitions vary so widely, it is better to read the wording in the accounts rather carefully. The phrase 'return on capital' is frequently used when what is really meant is **dividend yield** or **earnings yield**.

Revaluation of assets The **fixed assets** of a business are frequently subject to change in value, both real and nominal. **Real value** can change where the asset is of a durable type, e.g. land, the demand for which has forced up the **market price**. Nominal values rise continually in times of inflation, where the fall in the value of money is reflected in higher **replacement costs**. Some increases in value are often acknowledged in the published accounts of the business, where the asset value is restated in terms of current prices. In such instances the words 'at cost or valuation' after the assets will appear in the balance sheet, and the relevant **accumulated depreciation** totals will also be revised.

In company accounts specific rules which were extended by the 1980 Companies Act apply. Where any fixed assets have been the subject of revaluation, certain additional information must be given by way of note to the accounts if not contained therein. Each revalued asset must be shown at its revalued amount,

distinguishing between opening and closing figures. If the revaluation has been made in the year to which the accounts relate, then both the names of the valuers and the basis of the revaluation must be supplied. In addition to the opening and closing figures, the notes must contain details of any acquisitions and disposals plus depreciation provided for the year and the accumulated total of depreciation provisions. Any other transfers to or from fixed asset balances must also be detailed, as must the effect of any application of **alternative accounting rules**.

The 1967 Companies Act included a provision to the effect that where directors are of the opinion that the value of fixed assets, comprising land or interest therein, differs materially from the value shown in the accounts, then that fact must be stated in the **directors' report**. This provision is confirmed by the 1985 Companies Act. ◊ **Accounting standards** ◊ **Accounting for inflation** ◊ **Current cost accounting**.

Revaluation reserve The 1981 Companies Act provided that where assets are revalued by application of the alternative accounting rules, then any surplus on revaluation must be shown as a separate figure in the accounts. This surplus need not be described as a revaluation reserve but it must be retained as such and is subject to certain regulations. These are, *inter alia*, that it cannot be reduced except where the value of the assets which gave it birth are themselves reduced and it cannot be distributed other than in the form of bonus shares unless those assets are realized.

Revenue account Another term for **profit and loss account** or **income and expenditure account**.

Reverse take-over A **take-over** in which normal conditions are reversed, i.e. a small **public company** or a **private company** takes over a large one. This is not common and where it occurs the reasons will often be found to be in a prior agreement between the two companies that, for complex legal or taxation purposes, a reverse take-over is in the best interests of both companies – the reality is an agreed **amalgamation** best served by the instigating company being the smaller of the two.

Reversible lay days If **lay days** are reversible, then if a shipper loads his cargo in a shorter time than agreed he may be allowed to add the time saved on to the days allowed for unloading.

Revocable credit A term used in foreign trade. It refers to credit facilities given by a banker willing to accept **bills of exchange** up to a certain value and which is revocable at any time without notice. ◊ **Documentary credit**.

Revolving credit ◊ **London acceptance credit**.

Rigging the market Operations designed to create an artificial market to benefit the operator. Everyday examples are **bull** and **bear** activities on a large scale.

A **company** may, by increasing **dividends**, etc., raise the market price of its **shares** prior to a new issue. This issue may then be put out at a **premium**, but unless the dividend is maintained the issue price will be artificially high. The Treasury is often accused of 'rigging the market' when, prior to a new issue of **bonds**, it instructs the **Bank of England** to buy heavily, thus creating an artificial demand and enabling the new issue to be made at more favourable terms.

Right of resale In certain circumstances a seller of **goods** may resell, for instance after **stoppage in transitu** or because of a **lien**. Neither stoppage nor lien rescinds the **contract**, but the seller can, if the goods are likely to perish, resell the goods and give a good **title**. He may also resell if the buyer does not pay within a reasonable time after the seller has announced his intention to resell. If the title has passed to the buyer the surplus on resale belongs to him, after the seller has reclaimed any expenses.

The above does not apply where in the contract the seller reserves the right of resale; then the contract *is* rescinded.

Rights issue An invitation to existing shareholders to acquire additional **shares** in the **company**. The right will be, e.g. one new share for each two shares previously held. The price is usually lower than it would be in the **open market** and the shareholder can normally sell the right to buy to a third party, thus making a profit for himself. From the point of view of the company it is an easy way of raising new **capital**. ◊ **Shares: pre-emptive rights of purchase**.

Ring trading A term used with reference to dealings in commodities. Dealers come together around what is known as a ring, and bids and offers are called and prices paid recorded.

Risk ◊ **Sale of goods: risk**.

Risk capital Often referred to as **venture capital**, this is capital invested in a project which contains an element of risk. It is the opposite of fixed-interest capital and is often identified with **equity capital** in companies, though it is equally applicable to money invested in a hazardous joint venture. Excellent examples of high-risk investments were supplied by the companies that brought about the bursting of the **South Sea Bubble**.

River dues Amounts payable for use of rivers by vessels.

Road haulage Road haulage in the United Kingdom is partly in the hands of the **National Freight Consortium PLC** and partly in the hands of smaller **road hauliers**. There is no definite distinction between the work done by the National Freight Consortium and the others. The services offered are various and are generally a matter of private negotiations.

The principal advantage of road transport appears to lie in the fact that **goods** are taken directly from the sender to the recipient without needing to move the goods from one vehicle to another, as is the case with rail or water transport. Express services are available for long distance transport. There is an organization, the Road Haulage Association, which supplies details of reliable road hauliers in any particular area who are members of the Association.

Road transport is governed by general laws relating to the carriage of goods, e.g. the Carriers Act 1830, and the liability of a road haulier depends on whether he is a **common carrier** or **private carrier**. The Road Transport Act 1964 relates to carriage of goods by road between two separate countries and lays down regulations on compensation for losses, etc.

Road haulier A person offering to carry goods by road. ◊ **Road haulage**. He may be a **common carrier** or a **private carrier**.

Rolling settlement system This has been proposed as an alternative to the existing fourteen-day Stock Exchange account system, where dealings for the particular account and settlements are effected at the end of that particular account period. Under the rolling settlement system shares would be taken up and paid for at a specified number of days after the deal was struck. It was suggested that there could even be a two-tier rolling settlement system with institutional investors being expected to settle in a shorter time-period than private investors. Most of the planning connected with this new system was tied in with **Taurus** and the abandonment, at least for the foreseeable future, of Taurus has put the accompanying rolling settlement system idea on hold.

Rolling stock A general term for railway engines, carriages, trucks, etc.

Roll-over relief A term used in the jargon surrounding **corporation tax**, and particularly **deferred taxation**. It is a system which enables a company to defer payment of tax on gains from the disposal of a **fixed asset** where the proceeds are used to purchase a replacement for that asset. ◊ **Capital allowances**.

Rotation of directors A number of **directors** normally retire each year and offer themselves for re-election (the number or proportion is usually stated in the **articles of association**). This is to give shareholders an opportunity of changing the directors without going through the procedure necessary to dismiss them. Table A as at present constituted requires that at a **company**'s first **annual general meeting** all directors retire and at subsequent annual general meetings one-third of them do.

Roup The Scottish term for **auction**.

Royal Commission Technically, this describes an investigatory body set up by royal warrant to look into a matter of public importance and report back on it. In fact, it is usually set up by the government of the day as a prelude to legislation on a subject which is beset by controversy or complexity. It is composed of unpaid appointees of various occupations – academics, MPs, union leaders, representatives of special interest groups, peers of the realm and laymen – with an official independent chairman, after whom the report which the Commission will eventually produce is usually named. Although Royal Commissions are often necessary to the proper appreciation by Parliament of the problems surrounding an area of proposed legislation, they can equally provide a useful method of deferring legislation on a sensitive issue *sine die*.

Royal Mail Special Delivery This service is offered by the Post Office within the United Kingdom; it does not cover the Isle of Man, the Irish Republic or the Channel Islands. It consists of an undertaking to deliver a first-class letter packet on the next working day after posting and the repayment of the special fee charged should the service fail. Letter packets are processed through normal channels but are given priority at each sorting or post office; they are delivered specially at the receiving end if they arrive within working hours but too late for normal delivery, subject to availability of staff. There is a 'latest posting time' for such packets, which must always be sent from a post office, where the fee will be charged in addition to normal postage and a special RMSD label will be attached. This service can also be used for registered and recorded delivery mail. Where delivery is not made on the day agreed, the fee will be returned without any need for the sender to apply for a refund.

Royal Mint The organization within the UK which has the sole authority to manufacture the **coin** and note-issue of the realm. Once situated in London, but now in Llantrisant in Wales, it is under the control of the Chancellor of the Exchequer and has had the sole right to make legal coinage since the sixteenth century. Besides being the sole provider of the official UK coinage and notes it also manufactures currency for other nations and is often charged with the making and supply of commemorative medals. ◊ **Bank-notes** ◊ **Mint**.

Royalties The sum paid for the right to use another person's property for productive purposes. For instance, royalties may be paid for working mines to the owner of the land, or by a publisher to an author. There are special taxation rules for dealing with royalties where they apply to books, the object being to spread the income over the period of expenditure. Thus the income may be spread back over the time the book was written. ◊ **Public lending right**.

Rule in Foss v. Harbottle This is a rule observed by the court *re* limited **companies**. It will not interfere with the running of a company at the instance of any particular shareholder if it considers that the shareholder has his own redress within the rules of the company itself. Generally speaking, majority decisions within a company are upheld, assuming there is no **fraud** on the **minority shareholder**.

Rule in Hadley v. Baxendale In **breach of contract** cases, a court will only award **damages** for a loss which arises out of the breach itself and which might have been contemplated by the parties at the time at which the **contract** was made.

Rule in Royal British Bank v. Turquand This was a common law decision protecting third parties who relied on the propriety of a transaction which was within the powers of a company but happened to be outside those of the directors exercising them. If the third party had acted in good faith then the company would be bound. This protection afforded to innocent third parties has now become part of statute law through the provisions contained in the 1989 Companies Act. ◊ **Ultra vires**.

Rummage HM Customs preventive officers rummage a ship (i.e. search it) for all contraband and dutiable or prohibited **goods**. There are often a number of unannounced searches.

Running broker A **bill broker** who acts as an intermediary.

Running days Consecutive days including Sundays – not only **working days**.

Running down clause A **marine insurance** clause whereby the insurers agree to indemnify the shipowner against **damages** arising from a collision where the insured ship is in some way to blame.

Rural Development Commission A statutory body set up in 1988 merging the Development Commission for Rural England with the Council for Small Industries in Rural Areas. It is funded by government aid and charged with stimulating job creation in rural areas and ensuring the provision of essential services in those areas and in the countryside generally. It also acts in an advisory capacity to the government on the economic and social needs of such areas.

SA An abbreviation for **Société anonyme**, following the title of many European companies. Though normally French, companies bearing these letters may also be registered in Belgium or Luxemburg. ◊ **European companies** ◊ **French Companies**.

SAEF ◊ **SEAQ Automatic Execution Facility**.

Safe custody This is a service offered by most clearing and commercial banks. They volunteer to accept deeds, documents, jewellery and other items of property for storage in safe custody on behalf of customers. The property may be tendered in sealed boxes or packages, or the bank itself may provide deed boxes which may be sealed in the presence of both the customer and a bank official. Items so deposited are entered in a special register kept by the bank for this purpose. In accepting the property the bank becomes voluntary **bailee** and the extent of the bank's liability will usually be specified in advance and may vary, as with any **bailment**, according to whether or not any payment is made by the customer.

Sale In the Sale of Goods Act 1893, a **contract** of sale is defined as 'a contract whereby the seller transfers, or agrees to transfer, the property in goods to the buyer, for a money **consideration** called the **price**'.

Sale and lease-back An increasingly common commercial phenomenon whereby a company, or other business organization, which needs the cash tied up in its land and buildings to fund everyday activities makes a contract with a property investor, usually an insurance company, to sell the relevant land and buildings thereon to that investor on condition that the sale is accompanied by a document leasing the same property back to the business for an agreed term. Sale and lease-back agreements feature prominently in such nefarious activities as **asset stripping**. ◊ **Liquidity**.

Sale of goods Subject to the overriding doctrine of **caveat emptor**, contracts for the sale of goods have, like all contracts, always been covered by **common law**. However, the then state of common law was codified by the Sale of Goods Act 1893 and, from that time, sales were governed by that statute. There were many occasions when the courts were called upon to interpret and decide upon various aspects of the statute, not least with the growth of credit trading and the popularization of **hire purchase** contracts. As case law accumulated, further statutes came into being, each covering particular aspects of contracts of **sale**. Acts were also passed for the additional protection of the innocent purchaser, e.g. the **Misrepresentation Act** 1976, the **Trade Descriptions Act** 1968, the various Hire Purchase Acts, particularly the Hire Purchase Act 1965, the **Fair Trading Act** 1973 and the important **Consumer Credit Act** 1974. The **Supply**

of Goods (Implied Terms) Act 1973 was directly intended to tidy up certain parts of the Sale of Goods Act 1893, but, subject to the slight changes this made, the 1893 Act is still the principal legislative instrument governing any contract for the sale or transfer of goods or personal property, covering not only straight sales for cash or credit but also sales by description or by sample. ◊ **Credit sale agreement**.

Unless specifically, and legally, excluded, there are certain **conditions** and **warranties** which by virtue of statute law apply automatically to any sale. Firstly, there is an implied condition that the seller of goods has a good title to those goods, or will do so when the sale is to take effect. There is also an implied condition where the sale is by description that the goods shall conform to the description. Specific conditions apply to sales by **sample**.

There are no general conditions or warranties governing the quality of goods sold or their fitness for any special purpose except that:

1. Where the sale is in the normal course of business, there is an implied condition that the goods are of a **merchantable quality**, except where faults have been pointed out to the purchaser or the goods have been sufficiently examined prior to purchase for any defect or flaw to be apparent.

2. Where the purchaser has asked for goods for a specific purpose and has, reasonably, relied on the seller's advice on their fitness for that purpose, then there is an implied condition that the goods are fit for that purpose. This condition only applies to sales in the normal course of business.

There are also two principal warranties implied by the Sale of Goods Act. One is

that the buyer shall enjoy quiet possession and the other is that the goods shall be free of any **charge** in favour of a third party unknown to the purchaser.

The position of the purchaser has nowadays been improved by the growth of such independent organizations as the **Consumers' Association**, which examines and compares various goods on offer, publishing its findings in a magazine called *Which?*. Other forms of protection are afforded by the **British Standards Institution**, with its **kite mark** signal of approval of certain categories of goods. ◊ **Hire purchase** ◊ **Sale of goods: risk** ◊ **Sale of goods: title**.

Sale of goods: risk Generally speaking, risk passes with **title**. If there is a delay in delivering the **goods** themselves, the risk will remain with the party responsible for delay. In marine contracts, the seller must also give the buyer sufficient information to enable him to **insure** the goods. If he does not, they will remain at the seller's risk.

Sale of goods: sub-sales When **goods** are sold by a purchaser to a third party, this is known as a sub-sale. In an action for damages for breach of (the original) **contract**, the claimant may hold that valuable subcontracts have been lost and that this has increased his monetary loss. Whether or not an action will lie for the recovery of these losses will depend on the circumstances and the loss that might have been anticipated when the original contract was made. It was decided in *Victoria Laundry (Windsor) Ltd* v. *Newman Industries Ltd* that as the defendants knew that failure to deliver certain machinery must result in loss of profits, they were responsible for loss of normal profits, but not for particular losses arising from some particularly lucrative contract that they could not have foreseen. ◊ **Contract, breach of**.

Sale of goods: title It is often important to know when the title of **goods** passes. When the **sale** is of ascertained goods, title will normally pass according to the intention of the parties. The **Sale of Goods** Act 1893 states that where the contrary is not defined in the contract, if specific goods are named and are in a deliverable state, then the property passes immediately the contract is made. When the contract is for specific goods and something remains to be done to them before they can be delivered, then title passes when that something is done and the buyer is notified of it. Goods are in a deliverable state when they are in such a state that the buyer would be bound to accept them.

Where goods are unascertained, e.g. where an order is made for a quantity of goods, and the specific goods are not named, the intention of the parties is still relevant, but generally speaking title passes when goods are appropriated to the contract with the assent of the buyer and the buyer has been notified. The assent may be implied and may even be given before goods are appropriated. Where goods are on sale or return, title passes when the buyer either signifies his assent to the contract or retains the goods for an unreasonable length of time.

So far as the title of the seller is concerned, there is an implied **condition** in the Sale of Goods Act that the seller is entitled to the goods and is able to sell them, or will be when the time of sale comes.

Generally speaking, a person without a title to goods cannot pass a title to a third party. There are exceptions to this rule. For instance: (1) where, in a contract for sale, the buyer has possession of the documents of title, or the goods, with the assent of the true owner, the buyer is able to give a good title to an innocent third party. Also, where the seller retains the documents of title or the goods, after the ownership has passed to the buyer, the seller can give a good title to an innocent third party; (2) sales by **factors**; (3) sales in **market overt**; (4) sales of certain goods which are still subject to hire purchase agreements.

Sales agent A **marketing** term for the person employed by a **company** or manufacturer to control or supervise the distribution of his goods in a particular area. The sales agent strictly negotiates **contracts** between the manufacturer and a third party and is not himself a contracting party. It is, however, a vague term and often used very much more widely to describe persons selling a particular manufacturer's goods, regardless of whether they act as principal or **agent**. ◊ **Factor** ◊ **Manufacturer's agent**.

Sales journal In book-keeping terminology this is the book, or other record, in which details of a sale are first entered. In form it is similar to the purchase journal. It is also referred to as a sales **day book**.

Sales representative A **marketing** term for a person employed by an organization to sell its **goods** and to make **contracts** on its behalf concerning these sales.

Sales tax ◊ **Value added tax**.

Salvage The reward given to persons who save, in part or whole, a ship or its cargo from shipwreck. The person rendering assistance must show that he did so voluntarily, that there was danger involved and that he showed enterprise, that the ship was in need of help and that some benefit did arise from what he did. Salvage money cannot be claimed by those already responsible for the care of the ship. The reward is given by the owners of the ship and cargo.

Sample A proportion of bulk sent to a prospective customer so that he may decide whether to make a purchase. If he purchases on the basis of the sample, the bulk that he receives must correspond to it. If it does not he may return it, but he must do so promptly or he will be presumed to have accepted it. The Sale of Goods Act 1893 imposes three conditions on a **contract** for the **sale of goods** by sample: (1) the buyer must have a reasonable chance of comparing the bulk with the sample; (2) the bulk must correspond with the sample in quality; (3) the goods must be free from any defect not apparent in the sample but making them unmerchantable. ◊ **Merchantable quality**.

Sandilands Report ◊ **Current cost accounting**.

Sandwich courses Courses run at technical colleges, etc., based on the idea that practical experience and theoretical knowledge should be obtained at the same time but that part-time day-release and evening classes are not a satisfactory method of education. The student spends a period of three or six months in college followed by a similar period with the business for which he works. The course is planned so that he may take the various exams leading to the qualifications he wants. The student usually receives full pay while at the college but generally must agree to work for his sponsor for a certain period after qualifying.

Sans recours ◊ **Without recourse**.

Save As You Earn (SAYE) A method of saving introduced in 1969 whereby employees could arrange for deductions from their pay, equivalent to a fixed monthly amount, to be invested automatically in National Savings; it constituted a contract for a five- or seven-year period at the end of which the amount saved would be repaid together with a prearranged bonus.

From 1975 the savings became index-linked and after the five-year period the amount repaid was equal to the index-linked equivalent of each contribution. If the savings were to be left invested for a further two years, then further index-linking would apply and a bonus of two additional monthly payments would accrue. Amounts not then withdrawn would still be index-linked and a nominal rate of interest would also be paid. This would be tax-free.

After 1980 the scheme changed in nature and became available to any person qualified for the purchase of shares under a share option scheme approved by the Inland Revenue. Contracts were again for five or seven years, with a tax-free bonus equal to eighteen or thirty-six monthly payments.

In 1983 another scheme was introduced to operate concurrently with the 1980 scheme. In this share option series B scheme, bonuses were fourteen and twenty-four monthly payments after five and seven years respectively. There is an additional provision to cater for employees who change or leave employment during the progress of the scheme. Proposal forms are supplied by participating employers.

Under all SAYE schemes there is provision for persons unable to complete the

SAYE contract. Generally speaking, they are entitled to the return of their contributions and, if they have been paying in for more than one year, they will receive in addition a nominal amount of interest, which is at present 6 per cent. All benefits under SAYE schemes are free of income tax and capital gains tax.

Savings bank ◊ National Savings Bank.

Scheduled territories ◊ Sterling area.

Scotland: company law Generally speaking Scottish company law and English company law correspond. There are, however, differences in terminology. For instance, the word 'interdict' is used instead of '**Injunction**', 'pledge' or 'bond and disposition in security' instead of '**mortgage**', 'heritable property' instead of 'real property', etc. Again, the *Edinburgh Gazette* takes the place of the **London Gazette** in publishing official notices.

Other differences in Scotland arising from both common law and statute include:

(1) Companies which have their registered offices in Scotland are responsible to the Registrar of Companies in Scotland, who is quite distinct from the Registrar of Companies in England and Wales.

(2) The register of members may contain notice of a trust. The trustee may be the registered holder, but the fact that he is a trustee only can be indicated as can the name of the holder of the beneficial interest. However, any trustee so registered is personally liable for amounts due on the shares.

(3) There is no such thing as a **notice in lieu of distringas**.

(4) Shares cannot be pledged as security either with or without a blank transfer. They must be transferred with a provision for retransfer when the debt is settled.

(5) The Limitation Act 1939 does not apply to Scotland but certain debts, e.g. unclaimed dividends, become barred by the long negative prescription after twenty years.

(6) Although winding-up rules are similar to those in England and Wales there is no Official Receiver for Scotland, though a person may be appointed Interim Liquidator in his place.

(7) Until relatively recently the fact that movable property could not in Scottish law be pledged to secure a debt meant that Scottish companies were unable to issue debentures carrying a floating charge. The Companies (Floating Charges and Receivers) (Scotland) Act 1972 gave Scottish companies power to issue debentures secured on a floating charge and gave the debenture holders powers similar to those of their counterparts in England and Wales to appoint a Receiver if their security was threatened.

Scrip issue An issue of **shares** to existing shareholders made possible by the **capitalization** of **reserves**. No payment is necessary, so it is often called a bonus issue. In cases where one new share was issued for every two previously held, the shareholder would be receiving an acknowledgement that his capital had increased by 50 per cent. However, if the old rate of **dividend** were not maintained, the share **prices** would be depressed and the shareholder might not find himself financially better off. If the dividend were maintained, he would have received something that he could sell. It may be good policy to capitalize profits rather than distribute them in the form of dividends, but unless profits are increasing, it will not be possible to maintain dividend rates on an expanding capital.

Scrivener Historically similar to a scribe, being a person who writes letters or other documents at the behest of another and for a fee. Such practitioners are common in countries where illiteracy is high and where their skills are required by unlettered people who wish to communicate in writing for private or business reasons. In commerce, the term scrivener is sometimes used for a money broker.

Seal Documents and other items can be secured by a seal. A small pool of soft wax is run over the join and before it hardens this is impressed with a metal design, which should be peculiar to the sealer (signet rings were originally meant for this purpose). When the seal is hard, the document cannot be opened without breaking it. **Deeds** which are sealed are effective even though no **consideration** has been given. Various other legal documents, for instance conveyances, also require seals. Sometimes a thin wafer of wax is still used, but today it is more common to find that documents are simply impressed with the mark of the sealer. ◊ **Company seal**.

SEAQ Automated Execution Facility (SAEF) A facility offered by the London Stock Exchange which enables small trades in UK securities to be executed automatically by special SAEF terminals set up for this purpose. The deal is automatically effected at the best available price with the relevant market-maker and a trading document is passed automatically into the **Talisman** settlement system. The SAEF system is not extensively used, partly because it is only available for small trades, and partly because it is very impersonal.

SEAQ: ◊ **Stock Exchange Automated Quotation System**.

SEAQ International This was set up at the same time as SEAQ itself to serve the London market in international securities. It operates similarly to SEAQ with individual market-makers feeding their quotations into a screen-based price information system, but details of trades, which tend to be by professionals and in large quantities, are not made available until the following day.

Searching the register Various official registers have to be kept in a form specified by Statute. Within the UK there are hundreds of different official registers and records dealing with such diverse matters as births, marriages, deaths and local land charges. In the world of commerce the more relevant are those which limited companies are bound to keep. ◊ **Charge** ◊ **Register of charges** ◊ **Register of Companies** ◊ **Register of directors'** ◊ **Register of directors' interests** ◊ **Registered land certificate** ◊ **Share register**.

Members of companies and the general public have certain rights to inspect these registers, sometimes on the payment of a nominal fee. They also have limited rights to take copies of items registered. Various businesses exist to inspect registers, particularly company registers, on behalf of third parties.

Seasonal variations In compiling statistical tables results are often distorted by variations which are directly attributable to seasonal influences. Retail sales figures will tend to show substantial increases in the month prior to Christmas; employment figures will also tend to rise at that time, as they will at other periods of peak demand, e.g. in the tourist industry during the summer.

These seasonal peaks, or troughs, are not representative of real trends, and in providing fair and comparative figures statistical techniques are used to eliminate the effect of these seasonal variations.

Second mortgages The remortgaging of property already mortgaged. This is the province of the fringe **finance companies**. As the original mortgagee holds the security, usually the title-deeds, the second mortgage carries a high risk, which is reflected in high, sometimes very high, interest rates. Such mortgages should be registered with the Land Registry, but the holder of the original first **mortgage** will have the greater security. However, registration does protect the second mortgagee from the claims of subsequent creditors, secured on the same property. ◊ **Charge** ◊ **Register of charges**.

Second via A copy of a **bill of exchange** sent by a different route in case the original is mislaid.

Secondary banking Secondary banking is not, as is other banking, primarily concerned with offering a banking service to the public, complete with current and deposit accounts. It is more concerned with transacting the type of business that **clearing banks** prefer not to dabble in, such as the granting of **second mortgages** and other high-risk operations. This area of banking has tended to fall into a certain disrepute in the UK and the **Bank of England** is charged

with keeping a watchful eye upon it. ◊ **Finance company**.

Secret profits Profits made by a person who is in a fiduciary relationship with another, and makes the profits by reason of the relationship, or arising out of it, without disclosing them to the other person. When they are discovered, they must be accounted for and in certain circumstances the guilty party may also be sued by the innocent party. Examples of secret profits are profits made by an **agent** while working for his principal, profits made by one partner while about **partnership** business, profits made by **directors** of companies from contracts with other organizations in which they have an interest.

Secret reserves An accounting term for **reserves** kept by a **company** or business but not disclosed to the public in the **balance sheet**, being hidden in the wrongful valuation of **assets** or liabilities. For instance, a company may overdepreciate assets or refrain from revaluing them when they increase in **value**, thus showing them at a value far less than their true one. Were these assets to be realized, the company would make a profit not apparent from the accounts. Limited companies may not have secret reserves, although **banks** are given favourable treatment and allowed them, as it is thought that this may increase public confidence by providing an additional hedge against possible adversity. Although it is technically illegal to keep secret reserves in limited companies, the law appears to refer to those kept deliberately rather than those effectively contained in the failure to account for inflationary increases in the values of assets. ◊ **Revaluation of assets**.

Secretary The person who deals with the general administration of an organization, particularly with clerical work such as correspondence, taking minutes at meetings and keeping records. It is often a full-time occupation. ◊ **Company secretary**.

Secretary, personal A person employed as an assistant to deal with correspondence and other matters not needing the employer's personal attention.

Secretary, private A **personal secretary**, but acting for one person only instead of many people within an organization.

Secretary, private confidential A **private secretary** with greater responsibility than normal and so allowed to deal with confidential matters.

Secured creditor A creditor whose debt is secured, e.g. by a **charge** on the property of the debtor; this may take the form of a **debenture** where a company is concerned. The charge may be a fixed or a floating charge. A **fixed charge** is one where the actual property is specified; a **floating charge** is one which attaches to the property of the debtor generally – the actual property only becomes known when the debt is payable, when it is said to crystallize.

Securities At one time a security was essentially something given or guaranteed by a borrower to safeguard a loan. In banking and moneylending this remains the case, a security being given in the form of property or rights over that property, e.g. a charge by way of mortgage, to the lender as **collateral** for the money lent.

In more recent times the term securities has become the generic term for virtually all stocks, shares, bonds, etc., traded on the Stock Exchange including **derivatives** such as futures and options. Government issues are afforded the accolade of **gilt-edged securities** as they are supposedly risk free – a quality which tends to ignore the real losses that can result from the ravages of inflation.

Securities and Exchange Commission An official body set up in the USA to oversee the behaviour of the American Stock Exchange and the financial scene generally. It has considerable powers, even if they are rarely used, to regulate public offers of shares and securities and to keep a watch on such matters as **insider dealings**. Although there is no equivalent body in the UK, the possibility of one emerging in a similar form should not be discounted as the size and power of companies increase. ◊ **Multinational** ◊ **Securities and Investments Board**.

Securities and Futures Association (SFA) The merger of the Stock Exchange with its counterpart dealing with London-traded international bonds to create a body known as the International Stock Exchange of the UK and the Republic of Ireland was one of the first consequences of the coming into force of the **Financial Services Act** 1986. This new body was accorded the status of a **self-regulating organization** under the title of The Securities Association (TSA). In 1991 this SRO merged with the Association of Futures Brokers and Dealers to form the Securities and Futures Authority (SFA). In the same year the Stock Exchange reverted to the shorter name of the London Stock Exchange and the SFA is the regulatory body for its members. The Stock Market itself, as opposed to the members, is a

Recognized Investment Exchange registered with the SIB.

Securities and Investments Board (SIB) The SIB is not a government agency but a private company charged with the overall regulation of the investment industry according to the provisions of the Financial Services Act 1986. Anyone, whether an individual or a corporate body, operating or involved in an investment business, must now obtain authorization to do so. All authorization comes ultimately from the SIB which must ensure that those seeking such authorization are fit and proper persons to conduct investment business; that they have adequate financial resources; keep proper records; employ strict safeguards to protect assets or monies of clients which are entrusted to them; observe high standards of integrity and fair dealing; avoid conflicts of interest; and exercise all due care and skill in handling clients' affairs.

Although the SIB itself has established core rules, the mechanics of day-to-day regulation have been allocated to certain **self-regulating organizations**. These are now four in number: (1) the **Securities and Futures Association** (SFA); (2) the **Financial Intermediaries, Managers and Brokers Regulatory Association** (FIMBRA); (3) the **Life Assurance and Unit Trust Regulatory Organization** (LAUTRO); (4) the **Investment Management Regulatory Organization** (IMRO). These SROs play a leading role in the regulation of those whom they represent and each publishes an elaborate rulebook to which members must conform.

The rulebook is based on the overriding core rules of the SIB which are updated in order to fit the regulatory requirements appropriate to the investment and financial products offered by members of the particular SRO.

Certain professional bodies whose members engage in investment business, but only such as is incidental to their main activities, can apply to the SIB for the status of **Recognized Professional Body**. This then makes it unnecessary for their members to seek individual authorization for the investment business that they undertake. Again any market in which investment business is transacted can apply for the status of **Recognized Investment Exchange**. This covers the transactions conducted in that market though, in this instance, members themselves will need personal authorization to carry out investment business. Examples of RIEs are the London **Stock Exchange**, the **London Metal Exchange**, **London Fox** and LIFFE. These RIEs are responsible for ensuring that business is carried out in an orderly manner and that information that will enable them to provide the best service to clients is available to dealers.

Individuals or organizations which are outside the remit of the various SROs, but which carry out investment business to which the Financial Services Act relates, must obtain separate and individual authorization directly from the SIB.

Although the SIB was set up in 1985 it is still feeling its way forward as it seeks to define its role of regulator. Its many rules have been subject to criticism which has, over a period, led to a degree of reappraisal and a move towards a reduction in complexity. Another cause for complaint has been the cost which compliance has imposed on the various branches of the investment industry. Some critics accuse it of being too powerful and overintrusive, others complain that it is insufficiently armed to look after the needs of the small investor in real need of protection from the many predators that frequent the financial world. Suggestions are made that a watchdog has been provided where an armed guard would have been more appropriate. Should such fears be heeded then the alternative to the SIB would be something akin to the US Securities and Exchange Commission – a solution hardly likely to please those who complain of over-regulation.

Securities Association ◊ **Securities and Futures Association**.

Seed Capital A term applied to the minimum amount considered necessary to set up a new business, sufficient to conduct some preliminary research and fund initial equipment required. The Enterprise Allowance, made available to unemployed people wishing to start up in business, was effectively conditional on the recipient himself being able to raise such seed capital. The Enterprise Allowance, in the form of weekly payments, was intended to provide support during the gestation period of the new business.

Self-balancing ledger An accounting term for a personal **ledger** containing a **control account**.

Self-employed Those who are in business on their own account. The distinction between 'employed' and 'self-employed' is of particular significance in taxation as the self-employed are not subject to PAYE. The tax they pay depends on an income figure agreed with the Inland Revenue and they are able to claim all expenses incurred in securing that income. They are, however, obliged to keep careful records of their dealings to rebuff 'estimated earnings' assessments,

which, in the absence of proper accounts submitted, might be issued by the tax inspector. ◊ **Pay As You Earn** ◊ **Lump system**.

Self-liquidating An **asset** is said to be self-liquidating where its original cost is paid for out of its earnings over a fixed interval.

Self-regulating organizations The Financial Services Act 1986 inaugurated a complex system by which the UK financial markets were to be regulated. The corner-stone of this system is the **Securities and Investments Board** (SIB). Below this central organizing authority there are a series of bodies known as self-regulating organizations, each responsible for a particular type of financial activity. Each SRO must produce a rulebook for members and ensure that it is followed. The rulebooks are approved by the SIB which is charged with monitoring the manner in which the SROs operate and ensuring that they adhere to the rulebook by which they profess to be governed. Originally there were five SROs. With the merger of the Securities Association and the Association of Futures Brokers and Dealers the number has been reduced to four. These are the Securities and Futures Authority (SFA); The Life Assurance and Unit Trust Regulatory Organization (LAUTRO); the Investment Management Regulatory Organization (IMRO), and the Financial Intermediaries, Managers and Brokers Regulatory Association (FIMBRA).

Self-service Many retail outlets, from supermarkets to petrol stations, now adopt the principle of self-service. Under such a system, the customer takes such goods as he requires and pays for them in total on leaving the premises. This eliminates the need for counter staff in shops and is particularly useful where **branded goods** are being sold and the retailer's advice is not necessary – or even desirable. Goods are generally displayed with the aim of making shopping easier and prices are marked upon them. Shops often supply wire baskets or trollies and a great deal of persuasive advertising. Although such a system increases the possible loss from **shoplifting**, such a risk is generally outweighed by quicker service, greater returns and considerably reduced staffing levels. ◊ **Hypermarket** ◊ **Loss leaders** ◊ **Supermarket** ◊ **Superstore**.

Sellers' market A situation where market conditions are favourable to sellers, usually because demand is running ahead of supply.

Sellers over A term used in the Stock Exchange for market conditions when there are more sellers than buyers.

Selling out A **Stock Exchange** term covering the situation that arises when a buyer cannot take up the shares tendered for and the owner, or broker, sells for the best price he can get. The original buyer is liable for both the difference between the price obtained and the price originally contracted and any expenses incurred in the selling out.

Selling price Generally, the cash **price** which a customer must pay for an article. ◊ **Sale** ◊ **Sale of goods**.

Selling short A term used in the **Stock Exchange** where stocks or shares are sold which a person does not own but anticipates acquiring at a favourable price prior to the date for **settlement**. This is effectively a **bear** situation. ◊ **Bear market** ◊ **Account days** ◊ **Backwardation**.

Semi-variable costs Costs which are fixed for a given level of output and vary as different output levels are reached; for example, while one overseer may be adequate when output is below a certain number of units, an additional overseer may be needed when it exceeds that number. The overseers' wages are semi-variable costs. Pricing according to **two-part tariffs** is a reflection of the incidence of semi-variable costs within certain industries. ◊ **Variable costs**.

Sequestration The legal appropriation of property by a third party pending the settlement of a dispute.

Service charge ◊ **Gratuity**.

Service contracts ◊ **Directors' service contracts**.

Service industry An organization offering services to **extractive industries**, **constructive industries** or **manufacturing industries** or to the public: for instance, **plant hire**, **car hire** or catering. These organizations do not actually make anything; they provide a service by putting producers in touch with consumers. ◊ **Middle man** ◊ **Invisible trade**.

Set-off A right of set-off can occur when two parties are indebted one to the other. One debt can only be set off against another when the parties concerned are acting in the same capacity. For instance, a personal debt from A to B cannot be set off by B against monies he owes to A acting as **trustee** for a third party.

Settlement On the **Stock Exchange** the date on which various transactions made during one period, known as an account, are settled, with the various provisions for contango and backwardation taken into the reckoning. ◊ **Account days**.

Settlement discount Another term for **cash discount**.

Settling days ◊ **Account days**.

Severable contracts This phrase often occurs in **contracts** for the **sale of goods**, particularly where the goods are to be delivered in instalments. It may be possible to treat separate instalments as separate contracts, and in a breach of contract case the court would look to the intention of the parties. Failure to deliver, or pay for, one instalment might be a breach of the whole contract. On the other hand, the contract might be treated as severable, and an action may lie for only the one particular failure to deliver or pay. ◊ **Instalments: delivery and payment**.

Severance pay Payments made on termination of a contract of employment, usually of an executive. ◊ **Compensation for loss of office** ◊ **Redundancy**.

Shadow director A person or body who is not a named director of a company but who is, for certain purposes specified in the Companies Act, and in defining close companies for taxation purposes, treated as a director if the board tends to act upon his directions or instructions. This does not apply where those views are given in a separate professional capacity. Such a person is known as a shadow director.

Share broker ◊ **Stockbroker** ◊ **Market-maker**.

Share capital The total of **shares** issued, or authorized to be issued, by the **company**. The **capital** stated in the **memorandum of association** is the **authorized capital**. The company cannot issue more than this amount unless it first passes a resolution at a general meeting.

The amount of capital usually appears in the company's **balance sheet**, followed by a list of shares of various categories actually issued, under the heading 'issued capital', as opposed to **paid-up capital**, which is the amount called up and paid on shares issued.

Share certificate This is evidence of ownership of shares but not a **negotiable instrument** nor strictly a document of title. Ownership is determined by the entry in the company's **share register**.

If a person is in possession of a certificate properly issued, a company may be estopped from denying that he is the owner of the relevant shares. ◊ **Share transfer**.

Share hawking At one time it was possible to hawk **shares** from door to door, but nowadays nobody may deal in **securities** or shares unless they are exempt dealers. Exempt dealers are e.g.: (1) members of recognized Stock Exchanges or recognized associations of dealers in securities; (2) the **Bank of England**; (3) statutory or municipal corporations; (4) **trustees** of authorized unit trusts.

Share index An **index number** based on the **prices** of a particular parcel of **shares** supposed to be representative and intended as a guide to overall market fluctuations. It may refer to share prices generally or to one particular group of shares. Among the better-known share indexes are the **Financial Times Ordinary Share Index** and the **Dow Jones Index**.

Share option ◊ **Options to purchase shares**.

Share premium A sum over and above the nominal **value** may be charged on an issue of **shares** if their profitability indicates that their real value is in excess of their **nominal value**. Share premiums are put to a special account (the share premium account), which is a **capital reserve** and cannot be distributed to members. It can, however, be capitalized and form the basis of a **scrip issue**.

Share pushing Shares were once touted, sometimes from door to door, by share pushers who made unsubstantiated statements regarding the shares. The matter was dealt with by the Prevention of Fraud (Investments) Act 1939. Now no one can deal in shares without a licence, except for members of the **Stock Exchange**, etc. (◊ **Share hawking**). Misleading statements, etc., may be an offence, and circulars inviting persons to purchase shares must comply with the provisions of the Companies Act 1985, i.e. they must take the form of a **prospectus**.

Share register The register kept by a limited **company** giving the names and addresses of **members** and particulars of their share holdings. Where shares are held jointly, both names are entered. Where there is a trust, the names of the **trustees** only are entered (other than under Scottish law the company is not bound to take any notice of the fact that they are in fact acting as trustees: ◊ **Notice in lieu of distringas**).

The register also records the dates of the beginning and ending of membership, and the amounts paid up on shares (◊ **Paid-up capital**). Entry in the register is *prima facie* evidence of membership or liability if the shares are not fully paid. The share register must normally be kept at the **registered office** and it must be open, to members gratis and to non-members on payment of a nominal sum. ◊ **Index of members**.

Share transfer When a company share is sold or otherwise disposed of to another person it is necessary to transfer formally the right of ownership. This is effected by the completion of a transfer form which is then sent, together with the **share certificate**, to the **registered office** of the company. Such business is normally conducted by a bank or a broker. On receiving the transfer form, signed by the seller, the company will enter the buyer's name in its **share register** and delete that of the seller. It will then issue a new certificate to the buyer. If the seller is disposing of part only of the holding then the company will make out two new certificates but, to speed up the transfer process, will initially return the old certificate to the seller marked with a **certification of transfer**. Companies tend to charge transfer fees payable by the buyer. The latter is liable also for any **stamp duty** payable on the transfer though this is due to be abolished. **Brokerage** fees are also normally payable by both buyer and seller where a broker has been employed.

The introduction of the Talisman system in the early 1980s revolutionized the share transfer process for shares quoted on the Stock Exchange and, by simplifying the procedure, allowed a greater volume of business to be accommodated in the Stock Market. ◊ **Talisman** ◊ **Stockbroker** ◊ **Marketmaker**.

Share warrant A **share certificate** that does not contain the name of the member, so that title is transferable by delivery. It is not a **negotiable instrument**. Warrants can only be issued when shares are fully paid. The member's name is struck off the register when the warrant is issued. The **articles of association**

usually allow the warrant holder to vote at meetings on presentation of the warrant. **Coupons** are usually attached.

Shares The owners of a **company** are its shareholders, that is, the people who have promised to subscribe a sum of money to the company's **capital** in return for a portion of the profit. The **share capital** is divided into shares of, say, £1 each. These shares are transferable, freely in public companies though private companies normally restrict the right to transfer. Transfers are usually effected through a stockbroker. There is no limit to the number of shares an individual or organization can hold in a company. A company must have at least two shareholders. ◊ **Stock**. Each company keeps a **share register**, which members of the company may inspect. A copy is kept at the Companies Registration office and is available for inspection by members of the public. However, as shares are often held in the names of nominees, it is not always possible to ascertain true ownership this way, though, in the case of public companies, since the Companies Act 1981 any interest representing more than 3 per cent of any class of shares with unrestricted voting rights must be made known to the company and is recorded in a separate register of interests in shares. This could make known the names of nominees with substantial interests, as also could the provision in the Act that directors must disclose their true holding of shares including any held for them by nominees. ◊ **Register of directors' shareholdings**.

Shares: cross-holding This situation occurs when Company A holds shares in Company B, which itself holds shares in Company A. Such cross-holdings are permissible except where one company is a subsidiary company of the other. A **subsidiary company** is barred from owning shares in its parent company. There are very limited exceptions to this rule which concern shares held prior to the 1948 Companies Act, shares held in the role of personal representative or trustee (unless the parent company is a beneficiary) and shares held by a subsidiary in its role as market-maker. In all such cases, while the shares may continue to be held the holder cannot vote at meetings.

Shares, deferred ordinary A special category of **share**, often issued to the founders of a company. These shares normally give the owner special **dividend** rights, and often entitle him to all profits after a certain percentage has been paid on the other classes of shares. This type of share is not very common in public companies as it tends to arouse suspicion.

Shares, forfeiture of When a shareholder does not pay the **calls** due on his shares, they may be declared forfeit by the **directors**, provided that the **articles of association** of the **company** allow. Forfeited shares may be reissued.

Shares in trust Shares held in trust for another person are usually registered in the name of the trustees, who have full power to deal with them subject to the provisions of the trust deed. As no indication of the trust can appear in the company's share register, the company cannot prevent wrongful dealing by the trustees, but ◊ **Notice in lieu of distringas**.

Shares issued at a discount The Companies Act 1980 specifically prohibited the issue of shares at a discount. Prior to the coming into force of this Act, it was possible under Section 57 of the 1948 Companies Act to issue such shares under specified conditions, which included court approval. The 1980 Companies Act did not have a retrospective effect in this matter and shares already issued under the old rules were not affected.

Shares: lien The **articles of association** of a **company** normally give a first **lien** on the **shares** of each member, for debts and liabilities, to the company. The lien usually applies to **dividends** due; the company cannot enforce it by forfeiting the shares.

Shares: market value The **price** at which **shares** are available on the **open market**. The price of Quoted Shares will be found in the **official list**, published daily. For other shares it is a matter of negotiation. Any restrictions on the transferability of shares could influence the price. ◊ **Mean price** ◊ **Unlisted Securities Market**.

Shares: no par value These are **shares** having no **nominal value**. All monies payable are similar to **share premiums** and would be put into a stated capital account. These shares are not permitted in this country at present.

Shares: nominal value The nominal value of a **share** is the value stated in the **memorandum of association** and on the **share certificate**. The market value of the share may be quite different. ◊ **Shares: market value**.

Shares: ordinary These have no particular right to **dividend** but are entitled to all the profits after prior demands, such as loan **interest** or preference dividends. However, whether and when they receive the profits is at the discretion of the **directors**, who may if they wish put all profits into **reserve**. The ordinary shareholders are the true owners of a **company**. The directors are, strictly speaking, stewards. The shareholders meet at least once a year and may put forward any resolution that they wish, provided that certain legal conditions are complied with. ◊ **'A' ordinary shares**.

Shares: pre-emptive rights of purchase When a company seeks additional capital by the issue of a new block of equity shares, existing shareholders stand to suffer by having the value of their holdings diluted (◊ **Equity dilution**). To prevent this they were in the past frequently given pre-emptive rights to purchase the new shares, usually by means of a **rights issue**. The Companies Act 1980 made the granting of pre-emptive rights obligatory for all companies, whether public or private. It stated that no equity securities, which could be other than ordinary shares, should be issued for cash unless each existing holder of such securities was given the right to apply for and obtain such a proportion of the issue as corresponded to his existing holding, and on no less favourable terms than those available to subscribers generally.

A private company may exclude the need to offer pre-emptive rights in its memorandum or articles and public companies may also give directors power to modify these requirements of the Act.

Shares, preference These **shares** have a preferential right to **dividend**, i.e. they are entitled to a fixed sum before anything is paid to holders of **ordinary shares**. The dividend may or may not be cumulative. In any event, dividends are paid at the discretion of the **directors** and the shareholders cannot insist on them.

The voting rights of preference shareholders are normally strictly limited: they can usually only vote when their dividends are in arrears.

Shares are occasionally also preferential as to return of capital, and are also sometimes redeemable at the company's option. Occasionally one finds preference shares with additional dividend rights (e.g. a right to a further share in profits after ordinary shareholders have received a certain percentage). These are usually known as participating preference shares. The rights of preference shareholders can vary considerably and will be detailed in the company's **articles of association**. ◊ **Redeemable preference shares**.

Shares, preferred ordinary Ordinary **shares** with additional rights. They rank before other ordinary shares when it comes to payment of **dividends** or repayment of **capital**, but are not common.

Shares, qualification Shares taken up by the **directors** of a **company** as a qualification for directorship. The Companies Act 1985 does not insist on a director holding shares but the **articles of association** often provide that he should. The shares must be paid for.

Shares, surrender of Where **shares** could have been forfeited, a **company**, if its **articles of association** permit, may accept a surrender if this is more convenient. A surrender, like a forfeiture, is void if its intention is to relieve the shareholder of his liabilities. ◊ **Shares, forfeiture of**.

Shares: variation of rights Registration of rights appertaining to classes of shares and variations in those rights are regulated by the Companies Act 1985 with provisions first introduced in the 1980 Companies Act. Alterations to rights attaching to particular classes of shares, being those detailed in the **memorandum of association** or **articles of asso-**

ciation or in any resolution that has been filed, must be notified to the Registrar of Companies, who will then gazette such information. If a company wishes to vary the rights attaching to any class of shares, then the procedure differs according to whether or not a provision for variation is included in the memorandum or the articles.

If no provision is contained, then (1) where the rights are set out in the memorandum, any variation requires the consent of all shareholders in that class, and (2) where the rights are specified in the articles or elsewhere, then the consent of 75 per cent of class members or an extraordinary resolution of that class must be obtained before any variation is possible.

Where a provision for variation is contained in the memorandum or the articles, then with certain reservations that provision must be adhered to, with the proviso that if an alteration is effected, then holders of 15 per cent or more of the shares in that class may apply to the court for the variation to be cancelled.

Alterations to the articles directed at changing the rules regarding variation of class rights are treated in the same way as the variation itself. These regulations, contained in the 1985 Companies Act, allow for variations previously only possible under a scheme of arrangement.

Shell company A company that exists only in name. Occasionally, after a company has ceased to trade and has disposed of all assets and liabilities, it defers the ultimate step of applying to be struck off the register and sells its name to another business, which can thereby minimize the cost of setting up a new company. Shell companies are also formed and registered by organizations which sell ready-made companies with all the necessary statutory books, etc., to persons who are unfamiliar with all the procedures involved. This type of company is also referred to as a skeleton company. ◊ **Company, formation of**.

Ship-broker An **agent** acting for the shipowners to obtain cargo and sell cargo space. He also deals with passengers, **insurance**, **freight**, **bills of lading**, **charter parties**, etc.

Shipowner's lien The **lien** that a shipowner has for **freight** and other charges attaching to the **goods** that he carries. This lien may even exist when the goods have been warehoused if notice has been given to this effect. The lien for freight or general average contributions is a possessory lien. The lien for other expenses in protecting the goods is a maritime lien. ◊ **Lien, maritime** ◊ **Lien, possessory**.

Shipped bill A **bill of lading** beginning 'shipped in apparent good order and condition'. It merely attests that the goods have been loaded on the ship. ◊ **Received for shipment**.

Shipping agent A general agent specializing in the export or import of goods by sea. He deals with shipping documents, **insurance** and Customs, and sees that cargo space is available as needed. Some are connected with particular steamship companies and these often circulate information about available space. ◊ **Agent, general**.

Shipping bill A document used for claiming **drawback** from the Customs authorities. ◊ **Exporters' declarations**.

Shipping Claims Tribunal Established in 1939 to deal with compensation for requisitioned ships, the Tribunal was never really active. It exists now only theoretically. Each year the Registrar checks that entries in reference books are correct.

Shipping intelligence Shipping intelligence received at **Lloyd's** from the **Lloyd's agents**, coast radio stations, shipowners, etc., is collated and distributed to newspapers, etc. Within Lloyd's the intelligence is edited and published, by various departments, in **Lloyd's List and Shipping Gazette**, *Lloyd's Shipping Index*, *Lloyd's Shipping Index Supplement*, *Lloyd's Weekly Casualty Reports* and *Lloyd's Loading List*. There are also other publications, such as *Lloyd's Maritime Atlas*, *Lloyd's Calendar*, *Lloyd's Survey Handbook* and *Lloyd's List Law Reports*.

Shipping notes The various documents that are involved in exporting goods. ◊ **Exporters' declarations**. One of these documents is the mate's receipt – signed by the mate when the goods are received on board.

Ship's articles The **contract** signed by seamen when taking up employment on a ship.

Ship's certificate of registry A document giving all the relevant details of a ship: its name, owner, tonnage, master and country of registration.

Ship's chandler At one time a chandler was a dealer in candles. Later it was a term used to describe various types of suppliers, with an explanatory noun attached, e.g. corn chandler, ship's chandler. Nowadays, the term chandler is virtually synonymous with ship's chandler, meaning a person or business supplying ships with necessary provisions. ◊ **Custom: ship's stores**.

Ship's clearance inwards and

outwards ◊ **Customs: final clearance inwards and entry outwards**.

Ship's husband An **agent** acting for the owner of a ship and taking care of it when in port.

Ship's master The captain of a merchant vessel.

Ship's papers Various documents carried by a ship, including its **ship's certificate of registry**, **manifest**, charter agreement, **ship's articles** and log book.

Ship's passport A document carried by the master of a neutral merchant vessel in time of war to prove nationality.

Ship's protest A declaration on oath made by the master and crew of a damaged ship or cargo concerning the damage and how it arose, etc.

Ship's report The captain of a ship or his representative must give a report of his ship and its voyage, cargo, etc., to the collector of Customs at a port. The report contains details of the cargo and where it was loaded, of the ship's stores and of unusual objects encountered on the voyage, such as shipwrecks or icebergs.

Ship's store bond ◊ **Customs: ship's stores**.

Shop assistant A person selling **goods** from behind a shop counter, as **agent** for the shop owner. He can **contract** on the owner's behalf, for instance in selling on credit, provided he is acting within the scope of his apparent authority.

Shoplifting Taking goods from a shop without intending to pay for them. This is a major problem with which shopkeepers have to contend and the larger stores, which rely greatly on **impulse buying** and put or display goods within easy reach of customers, accept shoplifting as something which can be controlled but not eliminated and 'budget' for it accordingly. The gains from the high turnover are considered a reasonable price to pay for losses by shoplifting. ◊ **Self-service**.

Stores which deal in expensive goods, such as jewellery, will find that **insurance** companies lay down fairly stringent conditions on security before giving cover for theft. Many stores employ house detectives whose job it is to mingle with shoppers, looking for lawbreakers. A more recent innovation, and one which is increasing in popularity, is the use of closed-circuit television. Although such a system may be costly to install or rent, the gain from reducing losses from shoplifting may exceed the cost.

Shop's closing-hours: general Shops must be closed for the serving of customers after a certain time in the evening, e.g. not later than 9 pm on a late day or 8 pm on any other day. Local authorities can vary these hours within limits, but they cannot force shops to close before 7 pm. Customers may be served after hours if they were in the shop before closing time. There are special regulations allowing the **sale of goods** after the specified hours where the goods are: (1) meals or refreshments for consumption on the premises; (2) newly cooked provisions to be consumed off the premises; (3) alcohol to be consumed on or off the premises; (4) tobacco, table waters or matches sold on licensed premises; (5) tobacco, table waters, confectionery sold in theatres, cinemas, etc.; (6) medicine or medical appliances; (7) newspapers, periodicals and books on station bookstalls; (8) transactions of Post Office business.

The provisions of the Shops Act 1950 may be modified with regard to holiday resorts and sea fishing centres. Local authorities may dictate hours of opening suitable to local conditions if asked to do so by a majority of shopkeepers.

Until recently shops were not allowed to open on Sunday except for the supply of certain defined goods or where, in holiday centres, local authorities decreed otherwise. This legislation is at present in dispute as not being consistent with traditions common to other countries within the EU. In future it seems likely that the prohibitions against Sunday trading will be relaxed if not abandoned.

Short bill A **bill of exchange** payable on demand, **at sight** or within a very short period (less than ten days).

Short interest A **marine insurance** term for the difference between the value of the goods and the amount for which they are insured. Where the latter is greater the difference is known as short **interest** and the excess premium may be reclaimed.

Short ton A measure used infrequently, being 2000 lb and not 2240 lb.

Shorthand One of various recognized forms of abbreviated writing. Shorthand is, *inter alia*, used in business, to take notes in court and to take records of parliamentary proceedings.

Shorthand typist A person trained to write **shorthand** and use a typewriter, and so able to take down dictation and type; 120 words per minute is a good shorthand speed, fifty a good typing speed. Of course, there are other qualities to be considered. A well-trained shorthand typist will have had tuition in other commercial subjects and may act as a private secretary. ◊ **Audio-typist** ◊ **Wordprocessor**.

Shorthand writer A person who makes a profession of writing in **shorthand**. He may be permanently employed in a court or in Parliament, or wherever verbatim accounts of any legal or other proceedings are necessary.

Short-term capital **Capital** raised for short periods, perhaps to cover temporary fluctuations in fortune. **Bank overdrafts** are an example.

Short-term capital gains ◊ **Capital gains tax**.

Short-term deposits Monies deposited with **banks**, **finance houses**, etc., on terms which allow them to be withdrawn at short notice. Generally speaking, the shorter the loan, the lower the **interest** rate and the greater the **liquidity**. ◊ **Short-term interest rates**.

Short-term interest rates Whereas in the **money market** short-term interest rates tend to be close to **base rates** or **minimum lending rates**, they can be higher in certain banking situations. Banks will often offer very high rates for large sums lent for a fixed but short period. These rates may be very much higher than normal deposit account rates, since they are determined not by the prevalent minimum lending rate but by the fact that the monies are deposited as a loan for a fixed period, in which withdrawals are not permitted, and are in the nature of specific loans to a bank rather than being accepted as on deposit. ◊ **Account, deposit** ◊ **Rate of interest**.

Shorts A colloquialism for short-dated securities, usually **Government securities** with less than five years to run before repayment. ◊ **Bond** ◊ **Treasury bills**.

Shunter A person in provincial Stock Exchanges who marries transactions in those exchanges with transactions in the London Stock Exchange.

SI system ◊ **Metric system**.

Sight draft A name give to a **bill of exchange** payable **at sight**, i.e. payable when presented irrespective of when it was drawn.

Silence A seller does not have to make any representations with reference to his goods. Silence does not constitute **misrepresentation** unless the circumstances are exceptional. When a person makes an offer, he cannot state that silence will be taken as an acceptance. However, in **contracts** which are **uberrimae fidei** there is a duty to make all relevant facts known.

Simple interest Interest calculated on the original **capital** sum and not including interest on unpaid or accumulated interest.

Single European Act This Act, which passed into the law of each EU member in 1987, was the enabling Act to bring about the European **single market** by 1 January 1993.

Single market In a European context this is a concept which dates back to the Treaty of Rome which established the European Economic Community. In 1985 heads of government within the EU committed themselves to completing a single market, wherein trade between member nations would be as free and unencumbered as that between two cities in any one nation, by the end of 1992. It was envisaged that a genuine barrier-free market for goods and services within the EU would, by reducing business costs and increasing efficiency, encourage the creation of both wealth and employment. Since 1985 obstacles to a free and unrestricted single market have been progressively addressed and in great part resolved. This has involved changes in many areas of business such as the synchronizing of company law and product standards, and the near elimination of public purchasing and subsidy policies which have been shown to be contrary to the aim of true competition. Needless to say the single market which officially came into being is still far from perfect. There are still certain national divergences in quality and safety standards which need to be resolved and levels of VAT, together with the range of products to which various rates apply, have yet to be aligned. Despite these continuing obstacles to unfettered trade there is a general and genuine determination on the part of all members of the Common Market to work towards their progressive elimination and create a true single and unrestricted market across the whole of the EU. In everyday intra-EU trade, customs forms which were so time-consuming have become a thing of the past. Customs posts at borders between EU states have virtually disappeared, although certain limits are imposed on the importing into the UK of goods to which excise duties apply.

Sinking fund An accounting term for cash set aside for a particular purpose and invested so that the correct amount of money will be available when it is needed.

Sister-ship clause A marine insurance clause covering claims for damages following a ship's collision with another ship belonging to the same owner. Without this clause, an owner might not have any claim, as he cannot sue himself.

Sliding scale

Sliding scale ◊ **Ad valorem**.

Sliding peg ◊ **Exchange control** ◊ **Rate of exchange**.

Slip A slip can be attached to an **insurance**, particularly a **marine insurance**, policy and each **underwriter** then writes on this slip the amount for which he agrees to be liable until the amount of the insurance is reached.

Slump The point in the **trade cycle** when prices and employment are at their lowest. To escape from a slump and move towards **boom** conditions is not easy. It is a gradual process and depends, among other things, upon the slow return of confidence.

Small claims in the county court Whilst there is no small claims court as such, small claims can be brought by creditors through the county courts without the need to employ solicitors, barristers, etc., and thereby incur further expense, as claims for legal costs are not generally allowed where the debt is less than £500. Such small claims are usually settled by reference to arbitration after a preliminary court hearing. A booklet giving details of the necessary procedure can be obtained from the local county court offices.

Small and medium-sized companies A company which qualifies as being small or medium sized enjoys certain advantages when it comes to the statutory requirements regarding the filing of accounts and other documents with the Registrar of Companies. Briefly, small companies need not file a profit and loss account and need only file an abbreviated balance sheet. The benefits afforded to medium-sized companies concern the contents of the accounts to be filed and allow such companies merely to show in total certain categories of expense which companies in general are obliged to give in detail. They are also relieved from the obligation of giving a breakdown of turnover. Both small and medium-sized companies must also file a special auditor's report. To qualify as either small or medium-sized, a company must show that at no time in the period was it a public company, a banking or insurance company, or an authorized person under the Financial Services Act. It must also show that it is not a member of a group in which any member falls into one of those categories.

By the 1989 Companies Act a small company is one which can satisfy two out of three requirements. These are (1) turnover £2m or less; (2) balance sheet total £970,000 or less; (3) employees fifty or less. A medium-sized company must satisfy two out of three similar requirements: (1) turnover £8m or less; (2) balance sheet total £3.9m or less; (3) employees 250 or less. In both cases the requirements must be met for the year for which exemption is claimed and for the preceding year.

Similar provisions apply to small and medium-sized groups, though in this case the figures are the aggregate figures for the group.

Small firms: loan guarantee scheme As part of a package aimed at assisting small businesses the government has introduced a loan guarantee scheme. Qualifying businesses are those in the manufacturing and engineering sector with expansion plans for which finance is needed. The government will guarantee bank loans made expressly for such projects up to 70 per cent of the amount of the loan. It charges the borrower a premium of 5 per cent (originally 3 per cent), which is payable in addition to normal bank interest. When interest rates are high, as they have been since the scheme was introduced, this premium makes the total interest charge on the loan much higher than many projects can support – which accounts for the high business failure rate among borrowers and the noticeable lack of enthusiasm which the scheme has generated.

Small Firms Information Centres Information centres set up nationwide by the Department of Trade and Industry, intended to help smaller businesses, particularly sole traders, with day-to-day problems. They either give free guidance or direct the inquirer to the appropriate source of information.

Snake Originally called the 'snake in the tunnel' principle. Methods adopted by the then **European Community** to control day-to-day fluctuations in the rates of exchange of member currencies against the dollar. It was a somewhat unsteady concept but, basically, it was agreed that rates would be able to vary to within $2\frac{1}{4}$ per cent on either side of the dollar without interference by the central banks. It was also agreed that $2\frac{1}{4}$ per cent should be the maximum difference between the strongest and the weakest of the EC currencies and that, within this limit, the currencies could be allowed to wander freely or to 'snake'. In 1979 the Snake was replaced by the **European Monetary System**. ◊ **Currency** ◊ **Exchange control** ◊ **European currency unit** ◊ **European exchange rate mechanism**.

Société Anonyme (SA) The nearest equivalent to the UK public company in France, Belgium and Luxemburg. The

SA needs at least seven founder members, who must draft and sign 'articles of association', which are filed at a commercial court. The contents of these 'articles' are many but amount effectively to the British memorandum, articles and prerequisites for starting trading in one document. The founders must also obtain subscriptions for all the company's capital and, in the case of a public subscription, i.e. a company, the shares of which are offered to the general public, a summary of the contents of the articles must be published in a state publication known as the *Bulletin des annonces légales obligatoires*.

Shareholders of an SA are known as **actionnaires** and fully paid shares are usually in bearer form. Management is by either (1) a board of directors similar to the UK board but with fewer powers and more restrictions (e.g. a director cannot be appointed for longer than six years and employees are not eligible as directors until they have been with the business at least two years) or (2) a directorate and a committee of supervision based on the German AG (◊ **German companies**).

Employees are not, at present, entitled to appoint members of the board of directors, but if employees number more than fifty, they must form a works council, which in turn elects observers to sit in at board meetings or meetings of the committee of supervision. ◊ **European Union companies** ◊ **Société à Responsabilité Limitée**.

Société à Responsabilité Limitée (SRL) A small French company similar to the UK **private company** in that membership must be more than one and less than fifty – all members signing the 'articles', which serve much the same purpose as in a **Société Anonyme**. An SRL, can only issue fully paid shares and, unlike the SA, cannot issue bearer shares. Management is handled by appointees of the members. They need not be members themselves and there is no restriction on the term for which they may be appointed. ◊ **European Union companies** ◊ **French companies**.

Soft currency The opposite of a hard or **scarce currency**. Soft currencies are those which are falling in value, usually due to continual **balance of payments** problems in the countries they represent. They are, by nature, not welcome within any nation's **gold and foreign exchange reserves**.

Sola A **bill of exchange** with no other copies in circulation.

Sold note ◊ **Contract note**.

Sole trader A person who trades on his own account rather than in **partnership** or as a member of a **company**.

Solicitor A person working within the precincts of the law. Basically, he is the intermediary between the public and the dispensers of justice. His work consists for the greater part in advising clients on their legal rights, dealing personally with smaller matters from conveyancing to proceedings in magistrates' courts, and putting the client in touch with a **barrister** where legal action is to be taken at a higher level. The charges made by a solicitor, e.g. for conveyancing, are dictated by the **Law Society**, which keeps a watchful eye over the profession. A solicitor who engages in nefarious activities, offends against accepted modes of conduct or misuses his client's monies may be subjected to severe penalties.

A solicitor must be articled to a firm of solicitors for a defined period and pass certain examinations set by the Law Society.

Solicitor's letter Colloquially, a letter sent by a **solicitor** – usually for a fixed charge – to a debtor who has not paid his debt within a reasonable period of time. It is usually a last resort before taking the matter to court. In a subsequent court action the cost of the letter will be claimed from the debtor.

Solvent ◊ **Insolvency**.

Source and disposition of funds A statement often included with published accounts showing the cash coming in and the cash going out during the financial year, or alternatively, explaining in a slightly different way the alteration in the **working capital**.

South Sea Bubble Towards the end of the seventeenth century **companies** were formed in vast numbers and for quite bizarre purposes, such as importing jackasses from Spain or in one case for 'purposes to be revealed at a later date'. It was a get-rich-quick period. There was little legal control over companies and no **limited liability**. The climax came when the famous South Sea Company, originally formed to explore the South Seas, essayed to buy the **national debt** and issued **shares** for this purpose. To do this cheaply it attempted to increase the **value** of its own shares by creating a fictitious market. For a long period it did nothing but lend money for the purchase of its own shares (which were issued at frequent intervals). Very soon the whole country became involved, and large fortunes were both made and lost. Thomas Guy built Guy's Hospital with the profit he made. Little was done to stop the process, as both Parliament and the king were involved financially. The company failed in 1720 when public confidence suddenly disappeared, because money lent out and private profits made, rather than coming back in for the acquisition of shares, were used for the purchase of land. This company, formed in 1711, the biggest the country has ever seen, suddenly disappeared from the scene (as did the **secretary**), leaving behind financial chaos and a great deal of misery. It was over a hundred years later that Parliament allowed the formation of companies again and then only on very strict conditions.

Sovereign When first minted, in the reign of Henry VII, it had a value in exchange of twenty-two shillings and sixpence. This fell in subsequent years, but was legally fixed at twenty shillings in 1817. It ceased to be circulated in 1914, even though sovereigns and half-sovereigns continued to be minted until 1975. Their disappearance is understandable, for commercial if for no other reasons, as the **intrinsic value** of the sovereign is now far greater than its **face value** and its **market value** considerably higher again. Half-sovereigns, which are more difficult to obtain than full sovereigns, may have a greater market value than the latter. ◊ **Gold coins**.

Special buyer Bank of England official responsible for **open market operations** in **Treasury bills**. The Bank does not itself enter the market but works through a **discount house**. The special buyer is an agent of the discount house.

Special crossings ◊ **Crossings, special**.

Special delivery ◊ **Royal Mail Special Delivery**.

Special deposits These are deposits made by the **clearing banks** at the **Bank of England**, usually by order of the government through the Treasury. They are used as a means of restricting credit generally. Bank lending is directly related to available cash and the request for special deposits, which are quite distinct from the balances which those banks hold at the Bank of England as part of their general cash resources, forces them to tie up cash resources on a semi-permanent basis. This reduces cash available as the base for granting credit to the business world, the volume of which depends on that base. ◊ **Liquid ratio**.

Special drawing rights (SDRs) SDRs are, in effect, an international **reserve currency** sponsored by the **International Monetary Fund** (IMF), through the **Group of Ten**. The idea was originally put forward by J. M. Keynes, who had suggested an international **currency** to be known as 'Bancor'. This idea was dropped, but in 1969 the Group of Ten persuaded the IMF to introduce special drawing rights, which were similar to Keynes's currency but consisted of 'paper gold'. Members of the IMF were automatically allocated SDRs when the original issue was made and these became part of their **official reserves**. The original allocation was made proportionally to the quotas of currency originally subscribed by the various countries to the IMF on its formation, though since then additional allocations have been made on bases determined by the directors of the IMF. The drawings are 'special' in that they are additional to the credit facilities already existing for member countries of the IMF and, unlike the latter, are not repayable. SDRs can be used in settlement of international trade balances, and a member country must, if asked by the

Special endorsement

IMF, supply its own currency to another member country in exchange for SDRs, unless it already holds more than three times its original allocation. There is also a requirement that each recipient member must retain at least 30 per cent of its original allocation in its official reserves. SDRs can also, as demonstrated by the UK, be used to repay debts to the IMF itself.

The money value of the SDR was originally expressed in gold, which had a fixed dollar price. Since 1974 member countries have had to agree the value of the SDR in terms of their own separate currencies and it has become, itself, the standard unit of account of the IMF.

Special endorsement Bills of exchange are sometimes endorsed to a named person.

Special manager For the **liquidation** of a company, the **Official Receiver**, with the approval of the court, may appoint a special manager, if the nature of the business calls for specialized knowledge or the **creditors** or **contributories** require protection. His remuneration is fixed by the court and he must give security. He must account to the Official Receiver. He has the powers of an ordinary **receiver** and manager, or other powers that the court decides. A special manager may also be appointed by the Official Receiver or by the trustee in a **bankruptcy** where a creditor asks him to do so and can show that it is necessary to the carrying on of the business. His remuneration is fixed by the creditors. He can be removed by the Official Receiver or by a special resolution of the creditors. ◊ **Insolvency Act** 1986.

Special resolution This features in company law. It is similar in form to an extraordinary resolution but, in addition, twenty-one days' notice of the meeting at which it is to be proposed is necessary. Special resolutions are normally reserved for important changes in the constitution of a company, e.g. alteration (where permissible) of the **memorandum of association**, changes in the company's **articles of association**, reduction of capital, etc. ◊ **Resolution, notice of intended**.

As with an extraordinary resolution the majority needed is three-quarters of those voting, whether present or not. This means that a resolution, where no **poll** is asked for, could effectively be passed by a small number of members present at the meeting, despite the fact that the motion would have been rejected had all those entitled to vote done so either personally or by **proxy**. ◊ **Members of companies**.

Specialty contract ◊ **Contract, specialty**.

Specialty debt A debt which is not barred until twelve years have elapsed, e.g. a **dividend** or a call on shares.

Specie Term used for coins as opposed to **bullion** or **bank notes**.

Specific performance A court may order a **contract** to be completed rather than award **damages** to the party who has claimed that he has suffered loss. This is an equitable remedy and will only be awarded where the contract is fair between the parties, enforceable by both and capable of supervision by the court.

Speculation Although effectively a sophisticated form of gambling, speculation is recognized in business as a necessary constituent of a healthy free-enterprise economy. In the commodity market particularly, the willingness of dealers to speculate on future prices can serve to maintain a fairly stable price level. The speculator sells forward at a price acceptable to the purchaser and with no certain knowledge of the price he will have to pay for the commodity when the time comes to fulfil the contract. If supplies are plentiful and prices low, he stands to make a more than adequate profit, but if supplies are scarce, due perhaps to a poor harvest, he may be forced to buy in at prices far above those at which he has contracted to sell and may thereby incur considerable losses. Dealings in more than one commodity can provide a safeguard, as gains in one may be able to compensate for losses in another. Because of the risks involved in such dealings, speculation nowadays is principally in **options**. ◊ **Traded options** ◊ **Bear** ◊ **Bull** ◊ **Forward dealings**.

Split-level trust A form of organization occasionally adopted by an **investment trust** or **investment company**. The capital of the company is divided into income shares and capital shares, the former being entitled to the income from the investments held and the latter to any increases in the capital value of those investments.

Spot Market This refers to dealings at spot prices as opposed to **forward dealings**. 'Spot' is effectively a synonym for 'immediate'. In the Spot Market goods, options, currencies, etc., are bought and sold for immediate delivery, which, in practice, may be two days' time. In the forward market they are bought and sold for future delivery. Tables of prices in commodity and financial markets usually distinguish between spot and forward price, the latter perhaps further divided

into one month, three months, a year, etc.

Spit A weapon used by Customs authorities to discover whether dutiable **goods** are hidden in other cargo.

Spot transactions Dealings for cash rather than for credit or in **futures**, particularly on the **Commodity Exchange**.

Stag A **Stock Exchange** term for an individual who buys heavily on a new issue of **stocks** or **shares** in the expectation that the price will rise very quickly, earning him a worthwhile profit. He normally holds shares only for a very short time.

Stakeholder A person involved in a **wagering contract** or **gaming contract** who holds the money pending the outcome of the wager with the view to paying it over to the winner. Generally speaking, these contracts are void and no legal action can be taken to recover money on a bet, but it is possible to recover money from a stakeholder before he has paid over the winnings.

Stale cheque A cheque drawn a long time previously which a bank will no longer accept. A bank will rarely take a cheque over three months old.

Stamp duty Various documents have to be impressed with an official stamp indicating that the duty payable to the State to validate the instrument has been paid. The rate of duty varies with the nature of the document and may be fixed or charged on an *ad valorem* basis. There is, for instance, a fixed rate applying to contracts under seal, but an *ad valorem* rate on transfers by way of the sale of land where the consideration exceeds a given sum. There is duty payable on the sale of shares, though an intent to abolish this was declared in the 1990 Finance Act and the duty has been waived pending the date of abolition being fixed. There are various minor duties such as the fixed sum payable on the filing of a company's annual return, and that applying to a Declaration of Trust, or the granting of a **power of attorney**. Transactions relating to charities are generally exempt from any stamp duty which might otherwise have been payable.

Stamped stationery The Post Office sells, through branch offices, a variety of prepaid letterpost items. These include registered letter envelopes, ordinary envelopes preprinted with the appropriate postal charge, air letter forms in different sizes, lettercards and Forces' air letter forms. Where necessary, the price of any item of stationery includes the relevant **value added tax** charge. ◊ **Airmail letters**.

Standard and Poor ◊ **Credit rating**.

Standard costing A costing technique which uses predetermined standards. A product is costed on the basis of a budgeted output. Where the output has been fixed, the amount of material then needed is known, as is the amount of labour. The amount of **overheads** is taken as a constant. Each product then has a fixed material cost, a fixed **direct labour** cost and an overhead charge, probably stated as a fixed percentage of **direct expenses**. There is therefore a standard profit for the period. Actual cost will not correspond to budgeted cost, but the differences are handled through accounts known as variance accounts and the amount charged to any particular job or product is not altered until the standards are altered.

Standard deviation This should be distinguished from **mean deviation**; it is a rather more exact statistical measurement of dispersion. It is found by listing deviations from the **mean**, squaring these values, adding them, dividing the total by the number of items and finding the square root of the resultant value. Although similar to the mean deviation as a statistical measure of dispersion, the manner in which it is calculated gives proportional significance to extreme values in the series being examined. It is also important to more complex statistical analysis, whereas the mean deviation has a very limited use. ◊ **Median** ◊ **Mode**.

Standard error A statistical term used in production control indicating the possible degree of error that could occur in a sample taken at random. ◊ **Quantity control**.

Standard industrial classification A convenient method of classifying various industries for producing industrial statistical information.

Standard rate of income tax ◊ **Income tax**.

Standing order An instruction to a **Bank** to pay a certain sum at certain intervals, for instance subscriptions or **Hire purchase** instalments. ◊ **Direct debits**.

Starboard ◊ **Larboard**.

State Earnings-Related Pensions Scheme (SERPS) Introduced by the Social Security Pensions Act 1975 this scheme, which came into force in 1978, aims to provide earnings-related pensions in place of the existing flat-rate pensions payable on retirement, widowhood or invalidity. The new retirement pension will comprise a basic minimum plus an additional earnings-related premium. Eventually, retirement pensions will be based on the contributor's twenty best years' earnings during his or her normal working life. This full entitlement will not materialize until the contributor has been paying the new income-related national insurance contributions, which were introduced as part of the scheme, for more than twenty years. Until then, entitlement to the earnings-related part of the ultimate pension will be restricted to $1\frac{1}{4}$ per cent of average annual earnings for each year the new contributions have been paid, building up to 25 per cent after twenty years.

Although this graduated pension scheme has only recently been introduced, it is already in danger of being abolished. It is considered unworkable on the grounds that, not being a **funded pension scheme**, contributions in future years may fall so far behind pension dues that an intolerable burden is put on the government, which will have to make up the difference.

At present many persons do not belong to the scheme, being in the employ of companies or other organizations which, in view of their operating an approved **occupational pension scheme** of their own, have been permitted to opt out of the State scheme. Employees belonging to opted-out schemes retain their entitlement to the basic state pension; they only opt out of the earnings-related increment.

Statement of account This should be distinguished from the more precise and binding **account stated**. A statement of account is basically a document issued by a creditor to a debtor, or occasionally vice versa, detailing the transactions entered into to date. It will itemize invoices

issued, cash received, credits allowed, etc. The balance will be the amount due from the receiving party at the date of issue, subject to any agreed terms of credit.

When statements are not paid at the time agreed, they will normally be followed by further demands in the form of statements on which only the amount due is stated, assuming further transactions have not been entered into in the interim. If the latter is the case, then it is common for the amount owing to be broken down into the relevant trading periods. ◊ **Appropriation of payments**.

When money is tight, i.e. when interest rates are high, the creditor will be more eager for payment and may bring greater pressure to bear. This will often take the form of attaching severe reminders about credit terms to statements and may eventually lead to more direct action such as cutting off supplies, or, in the last resort, taking legal action or hiring professional debt collectors.

Statement of affairs Any statement of accounts which shows the financial position of a person or organization at a particular time. A **balance sheet** is a good example.

Stationery Office (HMSO) The organization which both publishes and sells (through retail outlets in most cities) books and papers which come under the heading of 'official publications'. These take various forms and include: White Papers. Acts of Parliament, reports of parliamentary and **Royal Commissions**, international treaties, information provided by the **Central Statistical Office**, directives and recommendations issued by government departments to industry. **Annual reports** of some public bodies and **nationalized industries**, the **London Gazette** and other periodicals, Hansard (the continuous record of parliamentary business), guides to historic monuments, etc. It also publishes a variety of books of both specialized and general interest on subjects ranging from brass rubbings to meteorites. Perhaps its most important function, however, lies in its role as official publisher to the Crown.

Statistics A collection of figures arranged to illustrate a particular point.

Status inquiry An inquiry addressed to, for example, a **bank** by a person who wishes to discover the creditworthiness of a prospective customer. ◊ **Credit rating**.

Statute law That part of the law which owes its origin to Acts of Parliament. It should be distinguished from **common law**, which is built on custom and precedent.

Statute-barred debt A debt that cannot be recovered at law because its time limit has elapsed. The time limit within which action must be taken is set out in the Limitation Act 1939: it is six years for an ordinary debt or twelve years for a debt under seal, or a **specialty debt**. The time runs from the end of the credit period. ◊ **Limitations of actions** ◊ **Scotland: company law**.

The time can begin to run again if the debtor acknowledges the debt. This may be by making a part payment or by acknowledging the debt in writing. The debt may also be revived if the debtor does anything which admits the continuing existence of the debt.

Statutory books The books which a **company** is bound by law to keep.

These are, *inter alia*, (1) a **register of members**, (2) a **register of directors** and secretaries, (3) a **register of charges** and (4) minute books.

The company must also keep proper **books of account**, where all its transactions are recorded and which, generally speaking, must be sufficient to enable **annual accounts** to be properly prepared.

Failure to keep these books in the manner directed can lead to heavy fines on the **officers of the company** who happen to be in default.

Statutory companies Companies set up by an Act of Parliament for some specific public purpose such as the provision of gas, electricity or communications which, when operated under private enterprise before nationalization, needed certain statutory rights to cross the property of other people. The powers of statutory companies were contained in the Acts by which they were created and an additional Act would be needed to change them. This made them particularly rigid and inflexible bodies, something which contributed to their now being very rare. ◊ **Public corporation** ◊ **Public utility**.

Statutory companies: transfer of shares ◊ **Contract by deed**.

Statutory instruments Effective legislation initiated by a minister of the Crown under powers conferred by an Act of Parliament.

Statutory sick pay (SSP) The National Insurance scheme provides, among other things, sickness benefit to contributors when they are obliged to be absent from work due to ill health. The way in which the scheme operates has been changed in recent years to alleviate the workload of the Department of Social Security and increase that of individual employers.

Since April 1983 the onus of paying SSP has been on the employer, provided that the period of sickness does not exceed eight weeks in any tax year. After eight weeks responsibility reverts to the DSS. Employers will pay the statutory rates to sick employees on normal pay dates, though if the business already pays employees during periods of sickness, then no additional payment need be made provided that the amount paid is above SSP. SSP is only payable for periods of absence above three days. It is subject to tax and National Insurance and any payments made by the employer are recoverable from the DSS, provided that the records prescribed are maintained. The employer's National Insurance contribution is also recoverable. Employees not paying National Insurance contributions are not entitled to SSP, i.e. those of pensionable age or earning less than the weekly wage at which NI contributions are payable.

Stay of proceedings During the **winding-up** of a **company**, the court may suspend proceedings pending against the company after a petition has been presented. ◊ **Cesser of action**.

Stepped costs Another name for **semi-variable costs**.

Sterling Money of a defined standard weight or fineness. Although usually associated with silver, it applies equally to gold. The gold pound sterling which took the place of the silver pound sterling in 1816 is 22 carat or 91·66 per cent fine gold. The word 'sterling' is traditionally derived from the term 'easterling', which was the name given to North German merchants who settled in London under Edward I. Their money was considered particularly good and 240 of their silver pennies, or 'sterlings', came to be known as the pound sterling, as in Troy measure they weighed one pound. This silver was of a standard of 92.5 per cent pure, and silver goods are still of this standard fineness even though the silver coinage was debased in 1920. ◊ **Troy weight**.

The commercial importance of the term 'pound sterling' is merely to distinguish that unit of **currency** from others, particularly pound units in other currencies.

Sterling area A number of countries, known as the scheduled territories, most of them past members of the British empire, whose currencies used to be linked to **sterling** and which retained sterling as their official **reserve currency**. For many years members of the sterling area enjoyed certain privileges, the principal ones being freedom from **exchange controls** and the right to draw at will on that part of their national currency reserve represented by **sterling balances** held at the **Bank of England**. The abandonment of sterling as a safe currency on the international scene, the emergence of the **European Union** and British membership of it have all, however, diminished the importance of the sterling area, and the sterling balances in particular, and its role in international trade is no longer of any major significance.

Sterling balances There are, of course, other sterling balances besides those held by **sterling area** member countries as part of their official reserves, these being brought about in the normal course of international trade and through the attractiveness of investment in sterling to other nations. Before the 1939–45 war sterling was a currency much sought after, but in recent times, as the role of sterling as a **hard currency** or a good **reserve currency** has virtually disappeared, the importance of sterling balances has considerably diminished; however, the UK government may need to bolster or diminish them, depending on the state of the **balance of payments**.

Sterling Transferable Accruing Government Securities (STAGS) Sterling bonds which are a repackaging of gilt-edged government stock. The dealer, having acquired gilt-edged stock, issues the capital part in zero-interest bonds. The purchaser can therefore acquire parcels of stock with a fixed maturity date. By forgoing the annual income on the stock, he obtains an interest in the capital value at a price much lower than that obtaining on the current gilt-edge market. These bonds are aimed at investors solely concerned with capital gain and are new to the UK market. ◊ **Zero bonds**.

Steward One who manages the provisions on board ship, or one who manages an estate on behalf of another.

Stipend Remuneration paid on a regular basis to a person holding a particular office. The term is normally used with reference to the monies paid to a clergyman.

Stock When used in connection with the capital of a company, stock is similar to, but not synonymous with, share capital. Shares may be converted into stock only when they are fully paid. Being so converted, they lose their identity as individual units and become merged into an aliquot part of total equity capital. The advantage of converting shares into stock

is that transferability is made easier, in so far as capital can then be bought or sold in monetary quantities not bound by the nominal value of individual shares.

The term 'stock' is also used with reference to interest-bearing government securities, frequently described as loan stock, and to any capital issued in parcels rather than defined units. Distinguish from **stock-in-trade**.

Stock control The system operated by a business whereby **stock-in-trade** of goods and materials is kept at necessary levels. This may involve the use of **bin cards** or other records on which movements in stock are noted in such a way that the storekeeper is automatically warned to reorder, though there is a growing tendency for both the stock levels and the reordering to be managed electronically. There may also be mathematical forms of stock analysis which indicate not only minimum and maximum stock levels but also quantities which need to be ordered to cover projected production levels. The efficiency of the system of stock control within a business can determine its resilience to change in trading patterns and, ultimately, its chances of survival. ◊ **Overtrading** ◊ **Reorder levels**.

Stock Exchange The familiar name of the London Stock Exchange, founded in 1773 at the corner of Threadneedle Street and Sweetings Alley by brokers who were looking for somewhere more permanent to conduct business than the coffee taverns they normally frequented. Other stock exchanges subsequently appeared in provincial centres such as Manchester and Birmingham, but they, with the Scottish exchange in Glasgow, merged with the London Stock Exchange in 1973, and now the trading 'floors' still operative in those cities are an integral part of the main administrative centre in London, the second largest Exchange in the world. The coffee house origin is still preserved in the use of the term 'waiters' for attendants who carry messages about the floor.

The Stock Exchange is the central market for dealing in freely transferable stocks, shares and securities of all types – government and other. It publishes daily an **official list** of buying and selling prices of the securities which are quoted. These include the shares of public companies that have fulfilled the requirements demanded by the Exchange as a condition for an official **quotation**, and prices are listed under categories of industry or service which those companies represent. In addition to shares of public companies, the list contains government securities, local authority loan stocks and the stocks, bonds and securities of various foreign companies and governments admitted to listing.

Traditionally, the members of the Stock Exchange were either **stockjobbers** or **stockbrokers**. The former were stockists, or wholesalers, of stocks and shares who sold on their own account, but only to the stockbrokers, and quoted a double price in doing so – the price at which they would buy and the price at which they would sell. Stockbrokers, on the other hand, were intermediaries between the general investing public and the jobbers. Any investor wishing to purchase shares would approach a broker who would shop around jobbing firms on the Exchange looking for the best price. The broker would then obtain the shares on behalf of the client, complete the paperwork necessary to the purchase and ensure that the shares bought were registered in the name of the new owner.

For this, the investor would pay him a commission.

The distinction between jobbers and brokers was peculiar to the British trading system and the strict division of roles, something that had already been eroded in dealings in certain foreign securities, has recently been abolished. Under the new system, which became official in 1986, the predominant trader in the Exchange is likely to be a member firm which combines the roles of jobber and broker and is a **market-maker** who deals directly with the outside investor. Many of these firms will probably be part of large companies, both domestic and international, and will often be connected to, if not owned by, the bigger banking groups. Under the new rules it will still be possible for firms to opt for the single capacity role of either stockbroker or broker-dealer, but they will no longer enjoy any monopoly privileges and are more likely to deal in specialist securities.

The Stock Exchange has always offered protection to the public against members who are **hammered** and unable to meet their obligations to outside investors. The current system will continue the compensation arrangements, though non-member holders of substantial interests in member firms, e.g. owning more than 29·9 per cent, will not be eligible for compensation on the failure of that firm, nor will the associates of that holder. The compensation fund is administered by the **Stock Exchange Council**.

After its merger with the International Securities Regulatory Organization (ISRO) in 1986 the official title of the Stock Exchange became the International Stock Exchange of Great Britain and the Republic of Ireland. In 1991 it reverted to the more familiar title of the London Stock Exchange. Shortly after this the regulatory structure underwent a further change when the original regulatory body for the Stock Exchange, The Securities Association, merged with the Association of Futures Brokers and Dealers, previously a separate SRO, to form the Securities and Futures Authority.

Stock Exchange Automated Quotations System (SEAQ) This is a system, based on the American NASDAQ, which was introduced by the Stock Exchange in 1986. The computer-based visual display system, known as TOPIC, was already in place and SEAQ built upon this system by allowing market-makers and broker-dealers who possessed the necessary equipment to enter their quotes directly on to the screen. There are three levels at which SEAQ operates. There is the investor service which provides, for the benefit of potential investors, the best quotes currently available on a range of high-profile UK securities. There is the dealer service which shows the two-way prices offered by all market-makers in the UK securities in which they deal, plus the prices quoted by broker-dealers. The third service, offered by SEAQ, is that referred to previously which allows UK market-makers direct access to the screens and enables them to input current prices and to update information on a continuous basis.

In addition to current quotes for all securities in which a market exists, SEAQ also offers to dealers running information on deals made and, on a daily basis, the highest and lowest prices recorded together with details of the last six trades in any one stock. ◊ **SEAQ international**.

Stock Exchange Council The govern-ing body of the London Stock Exchange. Its primary concern is to see that the rules of the Exchange are observed in line with its motto, 'Dictum meum pactum' – 'My word is my bond'. Any member acting in breach of the rules or in any way threatening the overriding interests of the investing public will be liable to disciplinary action by the Council. Such action can range from a fine to suspension of membership. Since the establishment of the **Securities and Investments Board** these functions are now shared with the official regulatory body for the Exchange, the Securities and Futures Authority.

The Council is also the body which is responsible for acceptance of securities for listing and will scrutinize closely the affairs of any company applying for a quotation.

Through the Council the Exchange offers guided tours to the public and provides a visitors' gallery open daily with no charge for admission. There is also a cinema which shows colour films on the activities of the Stock Exchange.

Stock Exchange: default of members Members of the London **Stock Exchange** occasionally find themselves insolvent and may then be **hammered**. For the protection of clients who might otherwise suffer, the Stock Exchange has established a central fund, subscribed to by members, from which compensation may be paid.

Stock Exchange money brokers ◊ Stock lending.

Stock-in-trade An accounting term which appears in many **balance sheets**, sometimes abbreviated to 'stocks'. It applies to the quantities of raw materials or finished goods in hand, and is often coupled with **work in progress**. ◊ **Stock valuation**.

Stock lending This facility is available generally, but particularly useful to market-makers both in the equity and in the gilt-edged market. It fulfils a doubly useful function. Firstly it enables market-makers to obtain stock of which they are short when the time comes to complete a bargain. Secondly it enables them to sell short in the knowledge that stock will be forthcoming should they need it. This also enables them to quote more competitively when dealing in large amounts of stock. Stock borrowing must, by the current rules of the Stock Exchange, be effected through money brokers who act as principals to both the market-makers and the institutional lenders who make the stock available. All loans are made on the collateral of cash or other securities, and the fee paid by the borrower is split between the money broker and the lender.

Stock option The US equivalent to a UK **option** to take or apply for shares.

Stock relief For tax purposes this referred to the allowance given by the Inland Revenue against taxable profits of a company or sole trader to offset the inflationary increase in the value of closing stocks of saleable goods. When inflation was running at a high level profits would be artificially swollen by the inclusion of closing stocks which, though constant in quantity, would have a considerably higher money value. The tax on this increase, being a levy on a non-existent profit, would have a painful effect on the cash-flow position of the business. ◊ **Liquid ratio** ◊ **Stock-in-trade** ◊ **Stock valuation**.

The Inland Revenue attempted to minimize this problem by granting a temporary relief which was intended not to remove the tax burden but to defer it. The relief was abolished in the 1984 budget and liability for tax deferred was cancelled.

Stock turnover The total sales **turnover** for a stated period, divided by the total average stock carried during that period. It is one of many ratios used in assessing the health of a business and is intended as a guard against the holding of excessive **stock-in-trade**. The argument is that money tied up in stocks is money idle unless those stocks are continually being sold and replaced. ◊ **Current ratio** ◊ **Liquid ratio** ◊ **Return on capital**.

Stock valuation Valuation of **stock-in-trade** for accounting purposes. Where any one business is concerned, the most important thing is consistency. There are various methods of valuation, among them: (1) unit-cost: the fundamental method – each item is priced at its actual cost; (2) FIFO ('first in first out'): **goods** are priced on the assumption that the first goods purchased are the first goods used and therefore that stock-in-hand should be valued at current **prices**; (3) average cost: goods are valued by averaging the cost of goods brought forward, with the cost of goods purchased during the **accounting period**; (4) **standard cost**: a predetermined or budgeted cost per unit; (5) LIFO ('last in first out'): goods are valued on the assumption that those purchased most recently are the first to be used, and that the goods in stock are likely to be old and so will not be valued at the current buying price, but at the first recorded cost of purchase; (6) base stock: often used in retail businesses – the assumption is that stock is constant in quantity and therefore given a fixed value, based on its original cost, this **value** being used for all accounting purposes; (7) adjusted selling price: sometimes used in retail businesses – stock is valued at selling price less expected profit and selling expenses. ◊ **Stock control**.

None of these methods is entirely satisfactory. Where the present selling price of the stock is less than the figure any valuation method reveals, the selling price should be used instead.

Stockbroker This is a broker specializing in stocks and shares. Since the reorganization of the Stock Market, known as **Big Bang**, stockbrokers have become better known by the title of either **market-maker** or broker-dealer. Their function as intermediaries between the general public and the Stock Market has not fundamentally changed and they still buy and sell shares on behalf of private and institutional investors. The difference now is that as market-makers they can hold shares on their own account and no longer need to circulate jobbers looking for the best price. When acting for a member of the public the broker becomes the agent of that person and charges a commission for the service he provides. If he is in business within the UK he must be a member of the **Stock Exchange**, and lists of market-makers and broker-dealers may be obtained from that body.

Stockist A **marketing** term for a person who agrees to hold certain minimum stocks of a specified manufactured product in return for special buying terms, entitling him perhaps to a particularly favourable discount.

Stockjobber Originally a trader in stocks and shares. Stockjobbers started transacting business in coffee house and later used the Royal Exchange. In 1773 the Stock Exchange replaced these venues and stockjobbers were differentiated from stockbrokers in so far as the jobber was made effectively a wholesaler in stocks and shares. He bought from and sold to stockbrokers only, and they then acted as agents for the general public. ◊ **Jobber's turn**. The distinction between jobbers and brokers in Stock Market dealings was a peculiarly British phenomenon. Since the changes brought about by the revolution in 1986, known as **Big Bang**, the role of the stockjobber has been taken over by the **market-maker**.

Stolen goods Generally speaking, if goods are obtained by **larceny** then the thief has no **title** to pass to a subsequent purchaser for value in good faith and the true owner can recover them. At one time this also applied even if the goods were sold in **market overt**, but since the Theft Act 1968 goods, though stolen, which are bought for value and in good faith in market overt cannot be recovered; this applies even if the thief is convicted. Where, on the other hand, the goods have been obtained under false pretences, rather than by theft, e.g. where a seller has been misled as to the identity of a purchaser, that purchaser can always pass on a good title to an innocent third party. ◊ **Misrepresentation**.

Stop for freight Orders given to a dock authority by a shipowner or broker, not to allow delivery of goods until **freight** has been paid.

Stop order Made by a customer giving a **stockbroker** instructions to sell should **prices** fall below a certain level.

Stopover A break in a journey agreed to in advance by the carrier.

Stoppage in transitu The seller of goods or documents of **title** therein may retake them from the carrier, before the buyer has taken possession, though only if the buyer has become **insolvent**.

Straight line method In calculating **depreciation**, the cost or agreed value of an **asset** is written off over its expected life by charging equal amounts against profit each year.

Stranding A **marine insurance** term once defined as 'a taking of the ground by the vessel, which does not happen solely from those natural causes which are necessarily incident to the ordinary course of the navigation in which the ship is engaged either wholly or in part, but from some accidental or extraneous causes'.

Street trader A person who sells out of a suitcase in a street, usually with a delightful line of patter. His main object is to dispose of his goods (whose quality he rarely guarantees) before being asked to move on. He may need a **licence** – this will depend on local by-laws. ◊ **Cheap jack** ◊ **Hawker** ◊ **Pedlar**.

Structural unemployment A contemporary term for an economic phenomenon which, though it first appeared and received comment in the 1920s, has only recently been officially recognized. It refers to the inevitability in highly industrialized **capital-intensive** countries, bent on increasing automation in industry, of a continually lessening need for labour of almost all kinds. This indicates an acceptance of the economic inevitability of a permanently high level of unemployment which is known euphemistically as structural unemployment. ◊ **Built-in obsolescence**.

Sub-agent ◊ **Agent** ◊ **Delegatus non potest delegare**.

Subdivision of capital ◊ **Consolidation of capital**.

Subpoena A court order to appear at a specific place at a specific time.

Subrogation A term used in **contracts** of **insurance**, **guarantee**, etc. It refers to the right of the insurer, etc., to stand in the shoes of the person whose claim he has paid and to take over not only what is left of the property, but all the legal and equitable rights of the insured person, including the right to sue a third party for damages. If an insurer pays for a total loss he may take over the subject matter and rights attaching to it; in a partial loss he may take over the rights but not the subject matter.

Subscriber A person who puts his name to the **memorandum of association** of a **company**. Subscribers must be named and described (they may be **minors** or aliens) and their signatures must be witnessed. Their duties are to pay for their shares, to sign the **articles of association**, to appoint the first **directors** and to act for the directors until they are appointed. The subscriber becomes a member by signing; neither allotment nor registration is necessary. He must take his share directly from the company and not from another subscriber.

Subscriber capital ◊ **Authorized capital** ◊ **Issued capital**.

Subscriber trunk dialling (STD) One of the fundamental results of the automation of telecommunications has been the gradual introduction of direct dialling of long-distance telephone calls. This facility is also available for most overseas calls. Charges for calls are based on standard units of time. e.g. *x*p for each ten seconds. For inland calls there are three charge scales determined by distance and two others applying specifically to mobile phones and premium rate lines. The charge scale is indicated in the STD code list by a letter before the exchange. Scales for overseas calls vary considerably but can be ascertained by contacting the Telephone Area Office or the international operator. ⇩ **Telephone** ⇩ **British Telecom**.

Subsidiary company Prior to the 1989 Companies Act, which incorporated certain company law directives of the EU, a subsidiary was defined as one controlled by another, known as its **holding company** by virtue of that other controlling either more than half of its equity capital or being able to dictate the composition of its Board of Directors.

In the 1989 Act the terms 'subsidiary company' and 'holding company' have been replaced by the terms 'subsidiary undertaking' and 'parent undertaking'. The use of the word 'undertaking' has the effect of bringing the provisions of the Act to bear on businesses which are not necessarily limited companies in the UK sense of the term. It defines the relationship of parent and subsidiary as existing where either (1) the 'parent' holds a majority of the voting rights in the subsidiary Board of Directors; or (2) it has the right to direct the operating and financial policies of the subsidiary either by virtue of provisions in the memorandum or articles or by virtue of a contract giving it control; or (3) being a member of the subsidiary it controls, either alone or pursuant to an agreement with other members, a majority of the voting rights.

The change to the definition of a sub-

sidiary was partly intended to put a stop to the use of 'off-balance sheet' financing by purpose-built organizations controlled by the parent company but falling outside the net spread by previous Companies Acts.

Subsidy Effectively, a method of supporting a **price**. The government subsidizes prices when it allows **goods** to be sold at a price lower than the market price, by giving the seller the difference between the **selling price** and a viable one. The term subsidy is also used for a sum of money given by one person to another to help him over a difficult period.

Substantial shareholdings: details of This applies to holdings by one company in the shares of another and is additional to the requirement to notify the latter company itself of certain interests ⇩ **Company: disclosure of interest in shares**. The 1967 Companies Act, as amended by subsequent Acts, requires any company holding 10 per cent or more of the nominal value of any class of shares of another company (or where the amount of the holding as shown in the accounts exceeds one tenth of its assets) to give certain information about that holding in the notes to published accounts. This information must include (a) the name of the company and the country in which it is incorporated; (b) if incorporated in the UK then whether registered in England and Wales or Scotland; (c) if unincorporated then the address of its principal place of business; and (d) the name of each class of shares held and the proportion of the nominal value of each.

If the substantial holding extends to 20 per cent or more then additional information must be supplied being (a) the profit, or loss, for the year; and (b) the aggregate capital and reserves at the end of the particular year. Even more information is required where the company is a listed company. Again, special rules apply where the company in which the interest is held qualifies as an **associated undertaking**.

Subvention payments Ex gratia payments made by one **company** in a group to another intended to offset losses in the payee company. At one time these were important for tax avoidance purposes, but their importance is now very much less.

Sue and labour clause A **marine insurance** clause allowing the insured to take any steps necessary to mitigate a loss.

Suez Canal clause A **marine insurance** clause stipulating that taking ground in the canal is not stranding. However, the insurers will be responsible for loss resulting directly from doing this.

Summary administration ◊ **Bankruptcy: small bankruptcy**.

Summary Financial Statements (SFS) If certain conditions laid down in the Companies (Summary Financial Statements) Regulations 1990 are satisfied, a public company whose shares are listed on the London Stock Exchange may send to members Summary Financial Statements rather than the full accounts and reports normally required. The latter, however, must still be sent to those members who wish to have them. The SFS must contain a notice prominently displayed informing members both of the limitations of the SFS and of their right to receive the full report and accounts.

The regulations specify the information to be given in the SFS and the order in which the necessary figures must be shown, an order which roughly corresponds to the account formats contained in the Fourth Schedule to the 1985 Companies Act. It is further specified that comparative figures for the previous year must be given in all cases. Provided the regulations concerning minimum details are complied with, the company is free to add whatever further material it thinks fit or helpful.

The directors' report, which accompanies the SFS, must be either the full report or a fair summary and must include: (a) the review of developments; (b) relevant post-balance sheet events and developments; and (c) full details regarding the directors. The SFS must also be accompanied by an auditor's statement that they are consistent with the full accounts and comply with the regulations. Any qualification in the full auditor's report must be featured in full. Finally, with the SFS there must be a pre-paid postcard on which the member may indicate that he wishes to receive a full set of accounts and reports.

The option to substitute an SFS for the full report and accounts does not apply to financial years commencing prior to 23 December 1989.

Supercargo A person travelling with a merchant ship to look after the cargo and perhaps obtain additional cargo *en voyage*.

Supermarket In general usage this term now denotes any large **self-service** retail outlet. The emphasis is on ease of selection, persuasive advertising, high turnover and equally high profits. Costs are kept at a minimum by economizing on staff, customers serving themselves with little or no supervision, bulk-buying to match the high turnover and often, due to the location of the premises away from town centres, low rents and rates. ◊ **Quantity discount** ◊ **Quantity rebate**.

Originally, a supermarket described a collection of traders, each operating on their own account but sharing common facilities under one roof. When this meaning was abandoned for the more general usage described above, theoretical distinctions were still made according to the size of the business. Those of less than 186 square metres in floor space were strictly 'superettes', those with a larger area were supermarkets proper and those which were very large and carried vast quantities of goods (often specializing in either durables or household furniture) were to be known as **hypermarkets**. These distinctions have become blurred in usage.

Superstores ◊ **Hypermarket**.

Supervening impossibility ◊ **Frustration of contract**.

Supplementary benefits A generic term for gratuitous payments made by the Department of Social Security, to persons who by reason of unemployment, retirement, sickness or any other social deprivation are in need of aid in addition to the statutory payments made under the **National Insurance** Acts. The benefits are usually in cash but may take the form of free travel, domestic aid, free dental treatment, free prescriptions, subsidies towards household furniture or special rent and **rate rebates**. The system of supplementary benefits supplanted the old National Assistance Board.

Supply of Goods (Implied Terms) Act 1973 ◊ **Sale of Goods**.

Surety ◊ **Guarantee**.

Surrender value An **assurance** term for the amount a person will receive if he cashes in his policy before the date of its maturity. In life assurance policies that have not run for a very long time, it will often be less than the amount actually paid over in premiums.

Surtax An additional levy on higher incomes and for many years part of the UK taxation system. It was essentially a penal tax and was abolished in 1973.

Surveyor of Customs The superintending officer of a Customs house station or **warehouse**.

Swaps The swap is a fairly recent financial innovation but is essentially a natural extension of back-to-back loans. A German national raises a loan in his own country at fairly low interest rates. A French national does likewise in his country. The reality is the desire of the French national to raise a loan in deutschmarks. Because the German national will obtain better terms than the Frenchman, the latter raises the loan through a German counterpart with a collateral agreement by which the Frenchman will take over the loan in exchange for the German accepting responsibility for servicing a similar loan taken out by the French citizen in his own country. Each then pays the more favourable interest rate available to the other. This system allows companies operating abroad to obtain cheaper finance by exploiting their comparative advantage in their own credit markets.

This fundamental concept has been refined and extended in its scope to the point where one party will pay a premium to another if that other will raise a loan on the first party's behalf. The latter will find that taking over the payment of the interest on the loan raised on favourable terms by the other party will reduce the cost of servicing that loan by an amount which more than covers the premium paid.

Swaps are of two distinct types, the interest rate swap and the currency swap. The first enables the instigating party to raise capital on more favourable terms or to exchange a fixed interest rate for a floating one. The currency swap is rather different as it involves an agreement to exchange both interest and capital payments (or repayments). A German company, for example, raises a deutschmark loan in Germany for the benefit of a French company which raises an equivalent loan in francs. By swapping these loans the German company accepts the responsibility of repaying the French loan in francs, while the French company takes over and agrees to service and repay the deutschmark loan in that currency.

Swaps wholly within one country have increased in popularity as useful instruments in recent years, particularly where a party tied into a fixed rate loan wishes to enjoy the cash-flow benefits of a floating rate to such an extent that it

may be willing to pay a premium for this advantage. Conversely where a borrower tied into a floating-rate loan is apprehensive as to the cash-flow problems attaching to an anticipated rise in interest rates, it may be preferable to effect a swap into a fixed rate loan. Markets in swaps have emerged to provide such facilities, though circumstances where swap agreements have been found unenforceable in law have created serious problems in the UK between banks and local authorities where the voidability of the agreement has created serious financial difficulties.

Syndicate A group of people, not necessarily **partners**, working together towards a common objective – usually profit. Each member of a syndicate is essentially in business on his own account even though the cooperation of the other members is essential if individual aims are to be achieved. A good example is provided by Lloyd's underwriters who form syndicates to cover large risks which one person on his own could not take on. ◊ **Slip** ◊ **Underwriter at Lloyd's**.

Table A The First Schedule to the 1948 Companies Act contained a model set of **articles of association** which could be adopted by a company limited by shares. It was in two parts, Part I referring to public companies and Part II to private companies.

The 1980 Companies Act, in redefining categories of limited company, repealed Part II of Table A. All limited companies are now assumed to have adopted the provisions of Table A Part I, which is now Table A of the 1985 Companies Act Section 8, except where any of those provisions are expressly or implicitly excluded by the particular set of articles filed by the company on registration. A company is not obliged to file articles, but if it does not do so it will be bound by Table A.

Take-over bid An **offer** made to the shareholders of a **company** by a person or organization to gain control of the company. If the company is quoted on the **Stock Exchange** the bidder is expected to observe certain recommendations. ⟡ **City Code on Take-overs and Mergers**. There is a similarity with the highway code in that though the recommendations have no legal force they cannot be flouted with impunity. They are backed up by the listing requirements of the Stock Exchange which are, if anything, more rigorous and by which companies who wish to retain their listing are effectively bound. Additionally it must be a term of any take-over bid that the offer will lapse should it be referred to the **Monopolies and Mergers Commission** or be subsequently deemed to infringe EU regulations, though in this latter case the original offer may be expressed as conditional on EU approval.

Although take-over bids are in most instances voluntary, attempts by one company, or by a financier acting alone, or in concert with others, to obtain control of another company, there are circumstances set out in the City Code where a bid may be mandatory. This occurs when the bidding party has already acquired 30 per cent or more of the voting rights of the target company, or where holding between 30 per cent and 50 per cent it acquires another 2 per cent within a twelve-month period. In such cases an offer must be made to all holders of shares in the class concerned. This must be made in cash and at a price no less than the highest price paid for such shares in the preceding twelve months.

If a person owns a certain proportion of the **shares** of the company, a minimum of 90 per cent, he can apply to the court for an order entitling him to purchase the shares he does not already hold at a **price** approved by the court. Similarly the shareholders may insist that their shares are purchased. ⟡ **Minority shareholders**.

Bids may be conditional or unconditional: the bidder may offer a price for the shares but make the offer conditional upon receiving a sufficient number of acceptances to give him control. When

he is satisfied that he has received sufficient acceptances, he may then make the
offer unconditional.

Take-over panel The panel responsible
for seeing that the **City Code on Take-
overs and Mergers** is honoured both in
fact and in spirit. This code is extra-statu-
tory and the panel is not responsible to,
or governed by, the State; however, all
companies are expected to conform to it
or incur the wrath of the **Stock Exchange** which could mean suspending
the quotation of the shares of offending
companies. ◊ **Official list**.

Takers-in Persons prepared to carry
over commitments for **bulls** by taking up
the **stock** that the bull does not wish to,
or cannot, pay for at that particular time.

Talisman An acronym for Transfer Accounting Lodgement for Investors. Talisman is a facility set up by the Stock
Exchange to handle the steadily increasing number of share transfers arising
from market dealings and to smooth out
some of the complex problems which
frequently cling to such dealings, e.g.
those arising when the seller is parting
with only part of his holding or when
the buyer is receiving a block of shares
made up of purchases from a number of
different sellers.

Talisman operates through a special
company set up by the Stock Exchange
and known as Sepon, which is another
acronym, this time for Stock Exchange
Pool Nominees. All shares and stocks to
be sold are initially transferred to Sepon
Ltd, which receives the Talisman transfer
form signed by the seller together with
the necessary share certificates. These
documents are checked for title and,
where the sale is an **ex div** or **cum div**
transaction, Sepon ensures that the par-

ticular dividend is credited to the party
entitled. Individual companies deal,
through their registrar's department, only
with Sepon, for which they maintain an
account in their share register. On
account day Sepon retransfers the
shares to buyers in the proportions indicated by the dealer concerned. If only
part of a holding is being sold, Sepon
will arrange for the seller to receive a
certificate for the balance of shares remaining. ◊ **Balance ticket**.

Because it possesses all the latest electronic equipment and makes extensive
use of computer systems, Sepon can
retain details of all transactions notified
to it by the various registered dealers and
use this information to speed up and
smooth the way for settlements. It also
collects any stamp duty payable by the
buyer and passes it on to the Inland
Revenue.

At present Talisman handles all dealings in UK stocks and shares barring
those in government and local authority
gilt-edged and those in new issues. It is
also gradually beginning to handle dealings in certain Commonwealth and US
securities, though indigenous complexities militate against too rapid an expansion in these areas.

Tally Historically, a tally was a strip of
wood, usually notched, split down the
middle to record a transaction. Each
party took one half and the fact that the
two halves matched was evidence of the
contract. Tallies were also used as receipts
for loans made to a sovereign or to the
Exchequer. The word is also used to
describe a distinguishing mark on an item
or bale of merchandise.

Tallyman This could be (1) one who
sells goods on credit to be paid for by
instalments, (2) a type of **accountant** or

(3) a person who checks off a ship's cargo against a list.

Talon This concerns **share warrants** or loan certificates. It is a slip of paper to be sent to the **company** or other authority to obtain new dividend **coupons** when the supply of them has been exhausted.

Tangible assets Physical objects in the legal ownership of the person or business to which they are ascribed. Though the term technically applies to all those assets recognizable by the senses, it is often used in business jargon to describe fixed, as opposed to current, assets which are not **intangible assets**. ◊ **Current assets** ◊ **Fixed assets**.

Tap issue The issue of securities by the Treasury directly to government departments or other chosen recipients as opposed to being placed on the market or put up for tender. ◊ **Government securities** ◊ **Tender for bills** ◊ **Treasury bill**.

Tap stock Readily available securities, particularly gilt-edged government stock, which can always be obtained on demand – much as water from a tap. Tap stocks should be distinguished from **Tap issues**. ◊ **Government securities**.

Tare An allowance for packing, etc., made in establishing the weight of goods. Tares may be actual, agreed by custom or estimated.

Target price A term used in **Common Market** trading for the theoretical price that has been set as the norm for the sale of farm products under the **Common Agricultural Policy**. It is fixed annually on the basis of what is a fair return for economic and efficient farmers in each of the member countries. It may therefore vary from one member state to another

and is the basis for the formulation of the annual **threshold price** and **intervention price**.

Tariff Generally a list of charges, established by an organization for services or goods. For instance, a hotel tariff is the list of charges for various rooms, meals, accommodation over a period, etc.

The word also has specialized meanings:

(1) The Customs authorities issue a tariff showing dutiable goods together with the amount of duty payable. ◊ **General Agreement on Tariffs and Trade**.

(2) There are what are known as two-part tariffs, where a set basic charge is made together with an additional charge which varies with the contract. For instance, a subscriber pays a set rental for a telephone, plus an additional charge which varies with the number of calls.

(3) The term two-part tariff is also applied where one rate is charged up to a certain maximum and a higher or lower rate for purchases or orders above this level.

Tariff offices **Insurance** companies or offices which charge rates set by an organization to which they belong, for instance, the Accident Offices Association. Non-tariff offices are free to quote their own rates of **insurance premium**.

Tasting order An order given to a specified person to taste wines, spirits, etc., stored in dock **warehouses** before making any purchase or sale.

Taurus An acronym for Transfer and Automated Registration of Uncertified Stocks, it represented a technological leap forward in the execution of Stock Exchange bargains by the electronic transfer of shares between the parties to a transaction. This, it was hoped, would eliminate a considerable amount of paperwork and, theoretically, would reduce the cost of trading in equities to the particular benefit of the small investor – the more so as the government had indicated that, upon the introduction of Taurus, stamp duty would be abolished. This system was due to be inaugurated in 1993, but the problems of implementing it have been so increased by obstruction from interests coinciding with the existing system that Taurus has been temporarily abandoned.

Tax avoidance A legal, if complex, system of minimizing total taxation liabilities. Most Finance Acts, whilst attempting to cover all contingencies, inevitably leave loopholes which may legitimately be explored and used by persons wishing to minimize the amount of tax to which they could be liable. Tax avoidance should always be distinguished from **Tax evasion** – a serious offence for which the penalties can be heavy. ◊ **Back duty**.

Tax deduction card This is concerned with PAYE (◊ **Pay As You Earn**). When an employer deducts tax from wages or salaries, details of gross pay, tax deducted, net pay and **National Insurance** contributions are entered on a tax deduction card or form. A summary of these is submitted to the Inland Revenue at the end of each tax year.

Tax deposit certificate A certificate issued to a company which has deposited a fixed minimum sum with the Commissioners of Inland Revenue. It can be used in paying **corporation tax** and, if used for that purpose, attracts interest for the period of deposit.

Tax equalization account ◊ **Deferred taxation**.

Tax evasion The deliberate defrauding of the Inland Revenue by making false tax returns or withholding relevant information regarding taxable income, whether revenue or capital. A criminal offence. ◊ **Tax avoidance** ◊ **Back duty**.

Tax Exempt Special Savings Accounts (TESSA) These were a new savings product of the 1990s, introduced by the government as from January 1991, allowing individuals to hold special tax-free savings accounts at banks or building societies. The maximum amount permitted in a TESSA account was fixed at £9,000 over five years – with £3,000 allowed in the first year and £1,800 in subsequent years up to the £9,000 maximum. The intention was to give the smaller saver similar advantages to those enjoyed by people with **personal equity plans**.

Tax haven An independent country, usually small, which specializes in providing sanctuary for high-income earners and the immensely wealthy of other nations who wish to escape losing a large part of their income or wealth to their mother country through tax laws. Legally aiding other nationals to avoid tax is the basic industry of a tax haven. The tax may be **income tax**, **capital gains tax** or **inheritance tax**. The haven gains by the spending of those to whom it offers refuge and through the industry that those persons, or companies, attract by the very fact of their riches. The best-known tax havens are the Bahamas, the smaller European republics such as Liechtenstein and Andorra, the Channel Islands and, on a different scale, Switzerland. The latter is able to offer the often essential inducement of banking secrecy through **numbered accounts**, in addition to a low rate of national income tax for certain categories of residents.

Although usually associated with individual tax-dodgers such as pop stars and property tycoons, tax havens are also used by international and **multinational corporations**, which can frequently make substantial tax savings by siting their registered office or by opening selected branches there.

Two major snags attach to tax havens. The first is that the less-known variety may be politically unstable and the person making use of attractive facilities may find that he loses everything in a political upheaval. The second is that the more secure tax havens are often very expensive places in which to live and much of the gain from **tax avoidance** may be swallowed up in a considerable increase in the cost of living.

Tax loss A term much misused and abused. A tax loss is strictly a loss, as opposed to a profit, agreed with the Inspector of Taxes, which may or may not be carried forward and charged against future profits from the same source or set off against income from other sources in calculating annual tax liability. It is frequently referred to in the media as if it were an asset, but, barring exceptional circumstances, e.g. the tax law applying to new businesses prior to the introduction of the 1973 tax reforms, the only benefit that a tax loss provides is that it reduces the income on which tax is payable. Less tax is paid but less income is, in the long run, earned.

The only sense in which a tax loss can be an asset is when a profit in a healthy business is reduced by a tax loss in another venture where that loss exists on paper, to the detriment of other investors, but the business concerned has a favour-

able (i.e. positive) cash flow. This applies particularly to companies where an associated or **subsidiary company**, which has a positive cash flow even though it is unprofitable, can show a paper loss which, when set off against paper profits of other companies in the same ownership, reduces overall tax payable. ◊ **Taxation of profits**.

Tax point Any stage in the distribution of goods at which **value added tax** becomes payable to the collector, i.e. **Her Majesty's Customs and Excise**. Generally, this occurs when goods are handed over or services are given in the course of a genuine transaction for value. However, Customs and Excise reserves the right to direct that the tax point should be earlier than that date if circumstances merit: such directions are not common. ◊ **Indirect taxation** ◊ **Input tax** ◊ **Output tax**.

Tax reserve certificates These are no longer issued, although some may still remain from the periods in which they were available. The object of a tax reserve certificate was to help taxpayers to accumulate funds for the payment of taxes due. They were a form of interest-bearing government bond with the proviso that interest was conditional upon the surrender of certificates in paying taxes. If they were redeemed for cash no interest would be given. They have been replaced by **tax deposit certificates** with a similar but more limited purpose.

Tax return, personal Within the United Kingdom it is the duty of every adult person to prepare a return of his or her income, however earned, including capital and revenue earnings, and submit it each year to the Inland Revenue. Detailed forms intended for use in giving this information are circulated by the Inland Revenue, but this is gratuitous, as the fact that a person receives no form in no way absolves them from the duty to declare their income. It is on the basis of completed and agreed returns that various reliefs and allowances are fixed and PAYE code numbers allocated. ◊ **Pay As You Earn** ◊ **Taxation schedules**.

Taxation: net United Kingdom rate UK tax paid by a company where, due to the fact that it is paying overseas tax plus UK tax, the net or average rate is less than the UK **standard rate**.

Taxation of profits ◊ **Income tax** ◊ **Corporation tax** ◊ **Unified tax system** ◊ **Capital gains tax** ◊ **Tax loss**.

Taxation schedules Headings used to facilitate the administration of the tax system and the proper collection of taxes. The schedules are:

(A) This was, prior to the Finance Act 1963, a straight property tax levied on persons owning land and buildings thereon and was based on what was known as the **annual value** of the property. The 1963 Act abolished schedule (A) but it was reintroduced by the Income and Corporation Taxes Act 1970 in a different form. It now applies to income earned solely through ownership of land, e.g. rents, rent charges, etc., and **premiums on leases**.

(B) This schedule has been abolished. It applied to the taxation of commercial woodlands where the income did not fall under any other schedule. Such income is no longer subject to income tax.

(C) This covers interest and dividends paid by the government and public authorities, usually taxed at source.

(D) This contains six parts known as cases which are concerned with income from (1) trades and businesses; (2) professions and vocations; (3) interest on securities where tax is not deducted at source, annuities, etc.; (4) income from securities – not shares – held overseas; (5) other income, including **dividends** on shares, from overseas; (6) profits or income not captured by any other case or schedule.

(E) Income received in the form of wages and salaries arising out of a contract of employment. This tax is usually collected through PAYE.

(F) Dividends and other payments made by companies by way of distribution of profits amongst members. ◊ **Tax return, personal**.

Taxation: separate assessment Prior to the introduction of independent taxation in 1990 a married couple could elect to be assessed separately rather than have all their income treated as if accruing to the husband. If separate assessment was chosen then the various relevant allowances were apportioned between the husband and wife, and each was responsible for payment of their own tax. Independent taxation has made separate assessment obsolete as from 6 April 1990.

Taxation: taxable income All income arising in the United Kingdom is taxable; income from abroad received by persons considered resident in the United Kingdom is also taxable. Where a person is not resident in the United Kingdom but domiciled abroad or, being British, is ordinarily resident abroad, only overseas income actually remitted to the United Kingdom is taxed. A visitor to the United Kingdom is considered resident if present there for more than six months. Persons may also be considered resident if, although they spend less than six months per annum in the United

Kingdom, they make frequent visits or maintain a place of residence there.

Taxi A vehicle licensed to ply for hire, that is, to roam the streets looking for passengers wishing to be conveyed privately to destinations previously unspecified. A taxi normally has a meter showing the cost of the journey.

Taxis should be distinguished from vehicles operated by **car hire** firms. Certain firms have vehicles licensed to carry passengers which can be ordered (e.g. by telephone) for a specific journey, but these are not allowed to ply for hire. They may often be called taxis but it is illegal for them to stop in the street at the request of a passer-by.

Tea auctions Auctions held at Plantation House. Tea is sampled by selling **brokers** and buyers – the buyers making notes on their catalogues. Buying brokers must give the names of their principals within twenty-four hours of any purchase and the seller must approve the name. Brokers sometimes act as both selling and buying brokers. Payment consists of a deposit paid to the selling broker in exchange for a weight note, plus the balance paid on prompt day, three months after the sale. Indian tea is auctioned on Monday and Wednesday and Ceylon tea on Tuesday.

Telecommunications ◊ **Confravision** ◊ **Datel services** ◊ **Radiotelephone** ◊ **Radiotelegrams** ◊ **Telemessage** ◊ **Telegraphic address** ◊ **Telephone directories** ◊ **Telephone** ◊ **Telex**.

Telegrams ◊ **Telemessage**.

Telegraphic address Because telemessages are paid for according to the number of words, including the address

of the recipient, it is customary for organizations, particulary the larger ones, to apply to **British Telecom** for a telegraphic address. This may consist of one word and is sufficient to identify the organization. A fee is payable.

Telegraphic transfer A swift method of transferring monies abroad, operated by a bank at the customer's request and risk. The bank cables the relevant instructions to its overseas agent, usually another bank or the overseas branch of the UK bank. The agent then effects the necessary credits or debits, usually in the currency of the transferee. Needless to say, such transfers must conform to any **exchange control** regulations.

Telemessage The telemessage service was introduced in October 1982 to replace inland telegrams. Far more expensive than first-class letter post, the telemessage is transmitted through telephone or telex systems, thus ensuring swift delivery. It is a service operated by **British Telecom** and messages may be telephoned or telexed on a **freefone** basis to the Telemessage Service before 10 pm or before 7 pm on Sundays, to be delivered on the next working day. For special occasions there is a range of greetings cards in which BT will insert the message. BT also offers facilities for multiple addressing of telemessages and a reply service.

It is possible to send telemessages to the United States. For other countries there is an international telegram service.

Telephone With the odd exception, e.g. the city of Kingston upon Hull, which traditionally runs its own system, the telephone network of the whole United Kingdom is owned and operated by

British Telecom, which took over from the Post Office in 1981.

As the entire system of telecommunications, of which the telephone is but a part, moves towards complete automation, the need to route calls through a telephone operator is disappearing. **Subscriber Trunk Dialling** (STD), which enables one caller to establish direct contact with another not only within the inland network but also for over 90 per cent of international calls, has left the telephone operator to deal more or less exclusively with inquiries and individual problems.

Although the traditional method of transmission by wire or coaxial cable is still maintained for the majority of inland calls, increasing use is being made of optical fibre cables, which transmit by means of pulses of light rather than electrically. International communications are steadily becoming the preserve of microwave and satellite transmissions rather than submarine cables, though the latter are still being both used and installed. The new technologies, particularly the use of fibre optics, greatly increase both the quality of transmission and the carrying capacity of individual cables, the latter advantage being particularly significant with the increasing use of the network for the transmission of computer data, etc.

Telephone users pay both a fixed rental and a charge on what are referred to as units consumed. Each unit of *x* pence buys calling times, which will vary according to the distance and the time of day. Generally speaking, there are three rate bands for inland calls; these relate to distance and are, in order of cost, local, up to 56 km and over 56 km, with a reduction for calls connected over low cost routes. There are a further three rate bands for time of day or week. Daytime rates operate from 8 am to 6 pm Monday to Friday; cheap rates run from 6 pm to 8 am. Weekend rates are cheaper still. Higher charges apply to mobile phones and to 'premium rate' numbers. Charges for international calls are naturally much higher but are based on similar principles, so that a short call to the United States at a time when cheap rates apply need not be prohibitively expensive.

Although British Telecom initially had a monopoly on the supply of first telephones to customers, this right ceased on 1 January 1985. BT still, however, retains its effective monopoly of the communications network itself, and although it must legally allow competitors to use the existing network, at a price, the capital cost of the complex systems of exchanges and lines is so great that the appearance of much truly independent competition is unlikely. At present only Mercury offers competition but to do so it must use the BT Network. ◊ **Freefone** ◊ **Personal calls** ◊ **Alarm calls** ◊ **Transferred charge calls**.

Telephone bills At present these are submitted by British Telecom on a quarterly basis and consist of two parts, a rental charge payable in advance and a charge for all calls made. Call charges are based on a unit system, a unit being the amount of time allowed for a fixed basic sum, e.g. 4.2p. This time allocation varies according to whether calls are made during the day or at cheap periods. Where an exchange is fully automated subscribers can, if they wish, obtain details of all calls of more than a minimum number of units. These details show time of call, number called and price. Differing systems of billing apply where the supplier is not British Telecom.

Telephone directories

Telephone directories Directories covering local telephone areas are issued without charge by **British Telecom** to all telephone subscribers. The principal directory for private users is the residential directory, in which all subscribers, other than those who have opted to remain ex-directory, are listed alphabetically. In addition to this residential directory, each subscriber receives a business directory in similar format plus the **Yellow Pages**. The business directory lists businesses situated in the area in alphabetical order whereas Yellow Pages lists them by classification. There is a fourth directory, known as Business Pages. Aimed at businesses, this contains both classified and alphabetical lists of organizations offering services or supplies to businesses rather than to the general public.

Telephone: private circuits Constant telecommunications between two points can be made less costly by using a direct private line, which is obtainable from British Telecom, between those points. A rental will then be payable on a quarterly basis but communications will be completely free of charge. The rental cost of a private circuit will obviously vary with the distance covered, and whether or not it is an economic proposition in any particular case can be judged only by comparing the expected charge for frequent calls with the once-and-for-all cost of installing the direct line, represented by the resultant rental.

Teletext The provision of general information to the home through the medium of the television set. The information is presented under various headings listed in a directory provided for user reference and is contained in 'pages', each of which can be summoned to the screen by the viewer. The basic teletext services are Ceefax and Teletext UK provided by the BBC and ITV respectively. Apart from such obvious subjects as current TV programmes there are sections for national and local news items and details of various leisure activities. ▷ **Prestel**.

Telex The telex service operated by **British Telecom** in the United Kingdom provides a swift and efficient means of sending and receiving printed information. The process is fully automated and printouts of the message are made by both the sending and the receiving telex machine. Telex messages can be sent even when the receiving machine is not attended. This can be of considerable commercial importance both nationally and internationally where hours of business do not coincide – particularly when, in the overseas area, there is a distinct time difference. In the United Kingdom the telex service is in operation on a twenty-four-hour basis.

Telex machines are not cheap to rent but the amount paid covers all the necessary equipment and full maintenance service. Each telex call is charged on a tariff basis similar to that for **telephone** calls and subscribers receive a free copy of the UK telex directory. Overseas directories must be paid for.

Telex calls are made by direct dialling where possible: this covers the United Kingdom and many countries overseas, particularly in Europe. The twenty-four-hour service applies to Europe but not necessarily to all other countries. Where direct dialling is not possible calls may be routed through the London switchboard. In addition to the telex service, there is a growing phototelegraphic service for sending facsimile copies of documents, photographs, pictures, plans, etc. Information regarding the availability of this service can be obtained from British Telecom. ◊ **Datel service** ◊ **Facsimile**.

Teller A **bank** clerk who gives and takes money across the counter.

Temporary exports Certain **goods** to be used as **samples** or exhibits and to be reimported may be initially exported free of duty if certain Customs procedures are observed.

Tenancy in common A situation where persons held land in common, but could deal separately with their shares. Tenancies in common have been virtually abolished by the Law of Property Act 1925, but they are still possible in one instance. Where land is to belong to a number of persons in common, it is vested in, say, the first four persons mentioned in the **deed**, and these hold it in trust for all the persons interested. Those four persons are legally tenants in common. This does not apply to charities.

Tender: capital issues Shares are occasionally issued by tender. The **company** issuing the shares asks for tenders for them, at **prices** above a certain minimum. Tenders will be made at various prices. If an **offer** is made for all the shares at the highest price, this will be accepted. Othewise the shares will be issued at the highest practicable price, so that all shares will be disposed of. This means that persons offering the highest prices may receive the shares for less. This method of share issue has a certain popularity as it minimizes the possibility of **stag** dealings. ◊ **Capital issues**.

Tender for bills The government covers its short-term finance requirements through the weekly issue of **Treasury bills** of differing denominations. These are tendered for by **discount houses** and other financial institutions. The amount tendered for is not revealed before the bills are issued, nor is the discount demanded. The government then allots the bills to the highest bidder. The total issue is, however, underwritten by the discount houses *en bloc*, and if they need funds to take up excess bills, then the **Bank of England** supplies those funds in its role as **lender of last resort**. Where the discount houses are 'forced into the Bank' in this way and have to pay the Bank of England the current **minimum lending rate**, the repercussions may tend to affect interest rates generally. ◊ **Tap issue**.

Tenor A **bill of exchange** may be payable sometime in the future. The length of this time is known as the tenor of the bill.

Term assurance This refers to a **life assurance** policy taken out for a limited term only. It may cover as small a period as an air or train journey, or a period which runs for the length of a twenty-year loan. The intention is to protect dependents against the death of the assured over what may be considered a critical period – a journey involving danger or the duration of an outstanding loan. It is also a form of life assurance which, particularly in the case of, say, plane journeys, offers substantial benefits to dependents at a very low cost in the event of the accidental death of the insured. If the insured survives the term nothing is of course paid out on the policy. There are variations on term assurance. The renewable term allows the insured to pay for a further term at the end of the specified period without having to provide further evidence of health, though this does not apply to persons over sixty-five years of age.

Other forms of term assurance include 'decreasing term' where the sum assured falls each year, or even more frequently, until it reaches zero – a policy frequently tied in with a house mortgage, 'increasing term' where the sum assured rises each year to keep pace with changing circumstances, and 'convertible term' giving an option to convert to full life or endowment.

Terminal loss A taxation term referring to a business loss which cannot be carried forward in the normal way, because the business is closing down or being wound up. If no other relief is available, e.g. there is no other source of income against which the loss can be set off in that year, then the Inland Revenue may allow the loss in the ultimate year to be 'carried back', i.e. reclaimed against profits of prior years. Terminal losses cannot be carried back more than three years. ◊ **Tax loss**.

Terms of trade A term used in international trade to describe the current trading prospects of a particular country. Terms of trade are said to be good where import prices are generally low compared with the prices commanded by exports. When terms of trade are bad, export prices have to be kept low, perhaps artificially, in order to finance the import requirements of that country. ◊ **Balance of payments** ◊ **Balance of trade** ◊ **Visible imports and exports**.

Territorial waters The area of seawater surrounding a nation over which it claims jurisdiction. Traditionally, this area was three miles, a distance determined by the average range of a cannon-ball. With the advent of more sophisticated weapons and international squabbles over fishing rights, the extent of territorial waters has become a matter for high-level negotiations and, in the last resort, gunboat diplomacy. The position has been further exacerbated by the exploitation of offshore oil discoveries. Fifteen miles has become common but some countries claim up to 200 miles. Different distances are frequently claimed for different purposes, e.g. one distance for oil exploration and another for fishing rights. The UK Territorial Sea Act 1987 fixed a general limit of twelve nautical miles, though this does not extend to fishing rights where the UK claims jurisdiction extending to 200 miles.

Third-class paper Bills of exchange, particularly commercial bills, tend to be graded. The grades vary with the reputation of the acceptors, so that there are first-class, second-class and third-class bills.

Third-party insurance This is a contract of **insurance** taken out by an individual, or by a company, which covers injury not to the person or company itself but to other persons or their property which might arise from the actions of the insured. Some forms of third-party insurance are compulsory by statute law, e.g. motorists must have third-party cover whether or not they wish to insure their cars or themselves. So also must employers have third-party insurance for injury to employees in the course of work. Owners or tenants of property must have a form of third-party insurance, known as **public liability insurance**, which protects the interests of persons invited on to their premises. Optional third-party insurance would include such policies as **professional indemnity insurance**. Where compulsory third-party insurance exists, the injured party may sue the insurance company directly for **damages** if the insured fails to do so. This is an exception to the general rule that a person not a party to a contract cannot obtain rights under it. ◊ **Contract, privity of** ◊ **Damages, unliquidated** ◊ **Employers' liability insurance**.

Threshold agreement Part of a **contract of employment** whereby the employer agrees to grant a fixed percentage increase in wages when the cost of living, as measured by, e.g. the **retail price index**, moves above a predetermined level. The increases may be tied to successive movements in the index and become payable, say, every time there is an upward movement of so many points. This type of agreement, though theoretically sensible, is not popular in the United Kingdom because of its built-in inflationary pressures. ◊ **Productivity deal**.

Threshold price This is the minimum price under the **Common Agricultural Policy** for imports within the **European Union** of agricultural products. Levies are exacted on any goods imported at a price lower than this minimum, which is fixed for a stated period by agreement between the member countries. The fixed threshold may vary from one trading year to another according to the state of the market. Below the threshold price there is an **intervention price** at which individual surpluses are bought up by the Community through the Common Agricultural Fund (CAF) or **common budget** to compensate farmers within the community who have been unable to dispose of all their produce because of the minimum price rule. Alternatively,

these surpluses, or any produce, may be sold outside the community at a lower price; CAF will then compensate the seller by paying over a 'subsidy' to cover the difference between the actual sale proceeds and the intervention price. ◊ **Common Market**.

Ticket A ticket should be distinguished from a **receipt**. Tickets are issued (for cash) particularly for transport or entertainment. They are usually an essential part of the **contract** and contain conditions of the **offer** or else refer to the existence of these conditions and state where they are to be found. The contract is not closed until the customer accepts the ticket and hands over the money.

A **receipt** on the other hand is an acknowledgement of payment of a debt already due and cannot contain further conditions applicable to the contract.

Ticket day A **Stock Exchange** term for the day when the **stockbrokers** give the names of the buyers to the sellers for the purpose of settling transactions. The slip of paper on which the name is given is known as a ticket. This is also sometimes called name day. ◊ **Account days**.

Tied loan In the field of international trade one country often lends money to another on condition that the loan is spent in buying goods or services in the lending country. Such a loan is known as a tied loan.

Tight money Money is said to be tight when credit can only be obtained at very high interest rates. This may be the result of deliberate governmental interference, e.g. increasing the **minimum lending rate**, calling for substantial **special deposits** by the banks or imposing controls on the granting of credit – particularly in the **hire purchase** field. By acting thus the government may hope to restrict spending and check the rate of inflation without pushing the economy into a **slump**. Such monetary measures are very common, though they are heavily criticized by whichever political party is in opposition as meddlesome stop-go politics. ◊ **Prices and incomes policy**.

Time and motion study This is one part of **work study**.

Time bargain A **Stock Exchange** term for dealings in **futures**.

Time card A card used to record hours worked by an employee who is paid on a time basis. ◊ **Clock card**.

Time charter The hiring of a ship, or space in it, for a particular time. The ship might make any number of voyages within that time.

Time office That office in a factory concerned principally with recording the hours worked by employees who are paid on a time basis.

Time sharing A term in computer jargon referring to the practice of two or more businesses using a computer at the same time but for different purposes. This type of sharing is an additional help in maximizing the use of very expensive computer equipment and thus reducing the cost to the individual who wishes to buy time on it.

Tip Either slang for information passed by one person to another, enabling him to profit financially, or a **gratuity**.

Tithe Strictly 'a tenth part'. At one time people were expected to give a tenth part of their income to the Church for the upkeep of their parish church and priest. These tithes were the principal means of support of the clergy and a living was often judged by the tithes attached to it. In course of time they have tended to become fixed payments made at regular intervals and unrelated to the income of the payer.

Title ◊ **Sale of goods: title**.

Token coins Coins with an intrinsic value less than their face value.

Tolerance The degree, dictated either by contract or custom, by which a finished item may differ from the original specification without giving grounds for rejection. ◊ **Quality control** ◊ **Standard error**.

Tolls Charges made for using certain roads, bridges, canal locks, etc. The monies collected are intended to pay for their building and upkeep.

Tommy shops At one time it was the practice for wages to be paid partly in kind and partly in tokens. These tokens could only be used at the company's or factory's shop and good value was not normally given. These shops became known as tommy shops. It was a much abused practice and abolished by the Truck Act 1831. This is probably the origin of the phrase 'tommy rot'.

Tonnage The cubic capacity of a ship, not necessarily related to its carrying capacity. A ton is 100 cubic feet. Tonnage dues are payable when a ship enters or leaves port. ◊ **Burden**.

TOPIC Acronym for Teletext Output Price Information Computer which preceded SEAQ within the Stock Exchange as an electronic means of making price information available to market-makers. The computer-based visual display system has considerably speeded up the dealing operations of the Stock Exchange. This, plus the additional information provided through SEAQ, a price information service based on the American NASDAQ system, means that most dealing activities have moved away from the floor of the Stock Exchange to the premises of market-makers themselves where trading is effected on the basis of screen data by telephonic means.

Tort That branch of the law dealing with civil actions arising from breach of a duty imposed by common law or statute and dealing with injuries to the person or his property. It should be distinguished from the law of contract which deals with breaches of duties arising out of transactions entered into by mutual consent. Examples of offences in tort would be trespass, deceit and libel.

Total assets The total of all the **assets** employed in a business. This must be distinguished from **net assets**. ◊ **Capital employed**.

Towage The charge made for towing a ship.

Trade, Department of This government department, set up in 1974 under the Secretary of State for Trade, replaced the old **Board of Trade** as the State body responsible for supervising and ultimately controlling the regulations governing both public and private industry and commercial enterprises, with particular reference to **limited** companies. Among other activities it promoted international trade and, where circumstances permitted, offered aid through such channels as the **Export Credits Guarantee Department**. It also organized worldwide trade fairs and, in other ways, advertised the services and products offered by British businesses. In certain instances it negoti-

ated and allocated large international contracts, though this was more common in cases that concerned the **nationalized industries**. It controlled the **British Overseas Trade Board**, the president of which was the Secretary of State for Trade himself. The latter was also the President of the Board of Trade, an office which pre-dated the Department of Trade and was that of the head of the old Board of Trade. The Department of Trade has now become part of the Department of Trade and Industry, which has assumed all its functions. The Secretary of that Department has reserved for himself the title of President of the Board of Trade.

Trade and Industry, Department of A government department with overall responsibility for matters appertaining to industrial activity and commerce both domestic and in the context of international trade. It is charged with supervision of competition policy and protection of consumers and in this connection it acts closely with the Office of Fair Trading and the **Monopolies and Mergers Commission**. It is also responsible for the implementation and administration of legislation relating to companies. The Registrar of Companies is accountable to the DTI, which has taken over all functions previously appertaining to the Department of Trade. ◊ **Trade, department of**.

Trade bill A **bill of exchange** drawn on and accepted by traders. Whether these bills are marketable depends on the standing of the **acceptor**. Such bills are normally discounted with **banks** rather than **discount houses** and **interest** rates may vary.

Trade creditor An accounting term

for a person to whom money is owed in the course of trade.

Trade cycle Prices and employment do not remain stable but tend to move upwards (◊ **Boom**) and downwards (◊ **Slump**) in an irregular pattern. This movement is known as the trade cycle.

Trade Descriptions Act 1968 This replaces the Merchandise Marks Acts 1887 and 1953. The Act contains various provisions prohibiting, *inter alia*, 'misdescriptions of goods, services, accommodation and facilities provided in the course of trade' and 'false or misleading indications as to the **price** of goods'. A trade description may refer, *inter alia*, to quantity, size, gauge, history of ownership, fitness for purpose, performance, accuracy testing, approval by some other organization or authority, method or place of manufacture. The trade description may be attached to the goods in fact, by implication or may be contained in an advertisement. It may be in writing or oral. It is false if false to a material degree, or misleading. It is also an offence to imply royal approval without having it. Penalties for offences are (1) on summary conviction a fine and (2) on conviction on indictment a term of imprisonment in addition to a fine.

Trade discount The profit margin which a retailer of goods obtains from his supplier, i.e. the percentage the supplier deducts from the **recommended retail price**. The size often depends considerably on the total amount of the order. **Supermarkets** can often obtain additional trade discounts by buying in exceptionally large quantities. ◊ **Quantity discount**.

Trade-in offer In selling certain consumer **durable goods** vendors often offer what are referred to as trade-in terms. This means that they will make an allowance for an old model handed over as part of the contract. Most trade-in offers are a form of price-cutting in so far as the vendor cuts his profit for a quick sale, not expecting to gain anything for the model taken in part exchange except its scrap value. In the motor industry models taken in part exchange are, however, often dressed up and resold at a price that may either extinguish the loss of profit on the new car sold or, in some instances, actually increase the gain on the whole transaction.

Trade Investments Generically these are investments by one business organization in another with a view to furthering the interests of the investor. This might lie in obtaining control of sources of raw materials or in broadening the potential for sales by securing a greater range of outlets. The essential attribute of a trade investment is that it is not a temporary measure for the employment of idle funds, but an investment made with the aim of securing a permanent business advantage to the investor.

Trade mark A particular mark or motif employed by a manufacturer to identify and often to advertise his **goods**. Trade marks may be registered at the **Patent Office**. There is a registration fee and an annual renewal fee, but registration protects the manufacturer against wrongful use of the mark by competitors.

Trade price The **price** paid by a retailer to a wholesaler for **goods** to be resold. ◊ **Trade discount**.

Trade references When a business wishes to open an account with a new supplier the latter will usually ask for trade references, i.e. the names of other firms supplying that business which can be contacted in order to establish the creditworthiness of the applicant. ◊ **Banker, disclosure of information by** ◊ **Credit rating**.

Traded options An extension of the **option** market whereby the options, rather than the contracts to which they relate, are bought or sold before they expire. There are specific and regulated markets for dealing in traded options.

The principal advantage of the traded option over the traditional option within the futures market is that the link between the person taking the option and the ultimate vendor or purchaser of the commodity is dispensed with and the option itself is traded as if it were a commodity. The person acquiring the option needs only to pay a predetermined premium on it and, when that option is afterwards resold, any resultant profit or loss is restricted to the movement in the premium, which will be a function of the current state of the market. Each traded option market is governed by a central authority which exists partly to buy in options when no other purchaser can be found.

This role is currently played by the **London Clearing House** which guarantees all contracts in futures and options taken out on various **recognized investment exchanges** such as the **London Metal Exchange**, the **London International Financial Futures and Options Exchange**, and **London Fox**. The RIE for traded options was the London Traded Options Market but this has now become part of the London International Financial Futures and Options Exchange. The London Clearing House, owned by the major UK clearing banks, is financed both by subscriptions from the members

of the exchanges which it supervises and by the 'margins' which all dealer members are obliged to deposit with the LCH on contracts made: each member taking out of, or paying into, the margin fund according to their open positions at the end of each day's trading. In line with the provisions of the Financial Services Act, the self-regulating organization for the traded options market was the **Association of Futures Brokers and Dealers**, but after this SRO merged with the **Securities Association** it became the **Securities and Futures Authority**.

Traded options can be contrasted with traditional options where the holder can only profit from his position by hedging, e.g. a person holding an option to buy might seek out an option to sell at a price which would give a profit if both options were exercised.

Trading associations Central organizations formed by persons or companies in the same line of business with the object of furthering the aims of the members and providing a common, often influential voice in representing the interests of the trade and its members in the media and in dealings with the government. ◊ **Chamber of commerce** ◊ **Chamber of trade** ◊ **Confederation of British Industry** ◊ **Export assistance register**.

Trading certificate Under the 1948 Companies Act a public company could not commence trading until it had satisfied the Registrar that the conditions entitling it to receive a trading certificate had been fulfilled. The 1980 Companies Act did not specifically refer to a trading certificate but, while repealing the relevant section of the 1948 Companies Act, it again set out the conditions that must be fulfilled before a new public company can either borrow or commence business. ◊ **Company: commencement of business**.

Trading estates At times of economic crisis the government may step in and provide cheap factory space with other incentives. The years of depression experienced in the United Kingdom in the late 1920s provide a good example. There are two ways in which this can be done. The first in time, if not in importance, was evidenced during the late nineteenth century, when the government alloted land, to be developed by commercial and private interests, at a subsidized cost, to be offered to new industries wishing to establish factories at a low rental. The second and more relevant case was when the government itself established what were often called trading estates. These were buildings offered at low rentals, with or without additional capital subsidies for the purchase of plant, in depressed areas. In these instances the government acted as both dispenser and controller. The favoured industries were usually light industries and the factories were often of a standard design. ◊ **Development areas** ◊ **Small Firms Information Centres** ◊ **Subsidy** ◊ **Assisted areas**.

Trading profit or loss In the annual accounts of a trading organization the first part of the profit and loss account is commonly referred to as the trading account. The balance brought down from this account to the next section of the profit and loss account is known as the trading profit or trading loss. These terms are used in general accounting practice but have no application to the financial statements of limited companies required by statute. The closest equiva-

lent in that context to the trading profit would be the **operating profit**.

Trading stamps A method of inducing increased **turnover**, less common in recent years, is the use of trading stamps as a means of giving very small discounts to customers. These discounts can appear more attractive because they are in stamp form rather than cash – the same stamps can come from many sources and be accumulated by purchasers until they have enough to exchange for a consumer gift. Trading stamp companies sell stamps to **retailers**, who issue them to customers on a *pro rata* basis according to purchases made. Customers accumulate stamps in books provided and can exchange these books of stamps for goods at special shops set up by the stamp companies – or through the post. The goods available are normally of a wide variety and of the quality associated with the better department stores. The customary retail price is restated in terms of stamp values. The issue and exchange of trading stamps is governed by the Trading Stamps Act 1964, which provides certain protective clauses, including the insistence that the cash value of the stamp should appear on its face and that shops should display notices which enable customers to ascertain the number of stamps to which they are entitled. It also introduced the requirement that customers should be offered the option by the stamp issuing company of obtaining cash for stamps collected. In fact, due partly to the ability of the stamp companies to buy goods cheaply by bulk-buying, the cash value of the stamps tends to be much lower than their value in terms of the retail price of the goods offered. The stamp companies make their **profits** partly by having the use of cash paid for the stamps prior to their eventual exchange for goods and partly from the high profit margin on goods supplied due to bulk-buying and low distribution costs. ⟱ **Quantity discount**.

Training Agency This was set up by the government in 1989 to oversee various schemes for providing both training and retraining in a variety of skills with a view to helping those unemployed as well as persons entering the labour market for the first time. It was given responsibility for supervising the **Training and Enterprise Councils** and through them the **Youth Training Scheme**. It is not a government department, but is responsible to the Secretary of State for Employment and is government-funded. The Training Agency replaced the Training Commission which itself assumed the role of the Manpower Services Commission.

Training and Enterprise Councils (TECs) These were established by government on the basis of a prospectus issued in 1989 to restructure Britain's approach to training and enterprise development. They take the form of independent companies which are under contract with the **Training Agency** to actively promote training by employers and individuals in their area with the aim of regenerating local economies. The directors of individual TECs, usually drawn from the senior management of major industrial companies established in the area, are charged with providing effective and relevant training programmes, which will include the Youth Training Scheme. In doing so, they draw up and develop a business plan which defines the role of the particular TEC in terms of the specific social and economic needs of the area. In the words of the White Paper which gave birth to the TECs, 'each community must shape a clear vision . . . and place education, training and enterprise in the broader context of economic and industrial development'. They also have been given a key role in ensuring that training and education, supplemented by work experience, will provide the workforce that the nation requires for sustained economic growth.

Tramp steamer A ship carrying **goods** and offering itself for general hire, not belonging to any particular shipping organization.

Tranche When large sums of money are to be raised through fixed-interest securities issued by governments or major corporations, it is often to the benefit of both the issuer, who does not require the full amount authorized immediately, and the market, which needs time to absorb new issues, that the process is staggered over perhaps quite an extended period. Each proportion of the total is, at the time it is introduced, referred to as a tranche.

Transfer pricing A term referring to the transfer of goods or services between different sectors of one multinational corporation, or between individual subsidiaries within a group of companies. The transfer price is the charge made, effectively on paper only, by the transferrer to the transferee. It may be the normal market price or, at another extreme, it may represent merely the cost of production. Where each party is a separate profit centre the transfer price may be dictated by overall policy within the whole corporation or group. This price might be influenced by the tax applicable to the declared profits of each sector, particularly when each is in a separate country or subject to a different tax regime.

Transferred charge calls Telephone calls can be made at the expense of the persons called provided they agree to accept the call. In addition to the normal call charge, an additional 'transfer charge' is payable. For inland calls the fee is not excessive, but if a person accepts a call from overseas the cost can be quite high. As for the transfer of charges for calls made *to* an overseas number, this depends on whether such a service is operated in the other country. If it is and the other party refuses to accept, no charge is made. ◊ **Freefone**.

Transire A shipping document used by coasting vessels listing the **goods** carried and signed by the master of the ship. There are two copies: one is given up to the Customs authorities as a clearance certificate on leaving port; the other is used as a certificate of entry at the next port.

Transmission of shares Effectively, the automatic transfer of **shares** not by transfer deed but by what might be called operation of law. Executors, for instance, have a right to be registered as shareholders on production of probate; the Trustee in **bankruptcy** may have a right to be registered instead of the bankrupt.

Trans-shipment This occurs where **goods** are moved from one ship to another. Certain Customs regulations must be observed and these vary according to whether the goods are dutiable or not.

Traveller's cheques These are specialized cheques which are made available to persons travelling overseas and which can be converted into the currency of the country visited at the traveller's convenience. They are normally issued by the clearing banks but are also available from the **building societies** and indirectly through some travel agencies.

They are issued in various denominations and may be obtained either in sterling or in the currency of the country of destination. Unused traveller's cheques can be re-exchanged for cash, either at the place of purchase or through the Post Office. There is usually a small commission charged when cheques are exchanged, whether abroad or on return to country of origin.

Treasure trove Gold and silver found in some hiding place. The word 'trove' derives from Anglo-French *trover* (find). Treasure trove must be reported to the police, the Director of the British Museum or the nearest coroner; failure to do so is a criminal offence. The finder is awarded the saleable **value** of the find, but the treasure itself goes to the legal owner, if traceable.

A jury meets to decide whether the find is really treasure trove, who found it and to whom it legally belongs. If the owner cannot be traced it belongs to the Crown. In Scotland, all treasure trove belongs to the Crown.

Treasury bill A bill of exchange issued by the government and payable in three months. They are issued by tender every week in very large amounts and **discount houses** make offers, quoting prices. Rates of **interest** are usually very low. By far the greatest amount of bills dealt with by discount houses are treasury bills; discount houses sometimes sell to the **clearing banks**, but the banks never tender directly. Treasury bills are sometimes allotted to central banks of other countries.

In recent times there has been a move towards issuing Treasury bills denominated in ECUs. This has the twin objectives of firstly assisting the management of the UK foreign exchange reserves, and secondly encouraging the development within the UK of an active market in ECU-denominated instruments.

Treasury notes Known colloquially as **Bradburys**, these were the notes issued by the Treasury in place of gold coin, which was starting to disappear from circulation in 1914. They ranked along with, and were eventually amalgamated with, Bank of England notes in 1928. ◊ **Bank notes** ◊ **Note circulation**.

Trial balance A list of all balances contained in the **ledger** (or ledgers, including the cash book). It is a two-column list, **debit** balances and credit balances being listed separately. The purpose is to check that the totals of each column agree and therefore show that the rules of **double-entry book-keeping** have been observed. It does not indicate any error arising from a total omission or an incorrect amount recorded correctly.

Trial of the Pyx Coins are tested annually at the Royal Mint to ensure they contain the correct ingredients. The test is made by a jury of the Goldsmiths' Company and is known as the Trial of the Pyx.

Trigger Point When one company builds up a stake in another it must be on the alert lest its holding reaches the level at which a **take-over bid** becomes mandatory. The precise level at which this occurs is known as the Trigger Point. The term is also applied to the point at which the size of a shareholding by one individual acting alone, or in concert, must be declared to the company in which the shares are held. The present level of a shareholding, which necessitates disclosure to the company, is one that

consists of 3 per cent of the voting rights in any particular category of share.

Trinity House An organization superintending navigation in British waters. It is responsible for beacons and lighthouses and for appointing pilots. It also conducts the examinations of mariners and is responsible generally for supervising the marine interests of the country.

Troy weights Though in the distant past a measure of bread, these have long been used for the weighing of precious metals. Troy measure should be distinguished from the more common **avoirdupois**, though both feature in commercial usage. The name 'Troy' derives from the fairs held at Troyes in France during medieval times, but the terms for the names of the individual weights themselves are of even older derivation. The smallest is the grain, which was once literally the average weight of a grain of wheat. Twenty-four grains are represented by one pennyweight, ◊ **Penny**, and twenty pennyweight is equal to one Troy ounce. This is nowadays the largest denomination in use, but there is a Troy pound which comprises twelve Troy ounces. On the avoirdupois scale one pound is the equivalent of 7000 Troy grains.

Truck An old term for trading by exchange of goods. It came back into more general usage during the bad days of the industrial revolution in nineteenth-century Britain. Factory-owners would often insist that workers accept goods in lieu of cash wages or give cash or tokens to be spent only in the factory-owner's own shop, situated on the factory site. These shops were known as **Tommy shops**. The practice was abolished over a long period by a series of Truck Acts, beginning in 1831. Reminders of this system, though now in favour of employees, are the miners' coal allowances and the air and railway employees' free travel vouchers.

Truckage A charge made for the use of railway trucks, apart from carriage charges.

True and fair A term with particular relevance to audited company accounts. Generally speaking, any accounts prepared for proprietors by third parties acting as accountants or auditors would be expected to give a true and fair view of the state of affairs of the business or organization to which they relate. The 1981 Companies Act, following the obligations first imposed by the 1948 Companies Act, specifically required that auditors of companies should ensure that any balance sheet presents a true and fair view of the state of affairs of that company at the relevant date and that any profit and loss account should similarly give a true and fair view of the profit or loss appropriate to the period to which it relates. The provisions contained in the Act as to the proper contents of these accounts must be seen as subject to the overriding requirement to present a true and fair view and should be added to or detracted from as necessary to this purpose, the onus being on directors and auditors to prove that the necessity does exist.

Trust In commerce the term applies to a combination of companies which decides that the best interests of each will be served by a merging of interests. This usually takes the form of the creation of a **monopoly**. The term is in wider use within the USA, where the companies concerned are subject to the **anti-trust laws**.

In the law of **equity** trust has a very specialized meaning which has been adapted commercially in the creation of **investment trusts** and **unit trusts**, common in both the UK and the USA.

Trust deed ◊ **Debentures**.

Trustee A person who handles monies or property on behalf of another in a trust. He usually has the **title** to the property but in fact acts merely as a **steward**, all the benefits belonging to persons known as the beneficiaries. Because he has the legal title, he can dispose of the property to an innocent third party without the consent of the true owner; this would be known as a breach of trust. It is therefore essential that a trustee is one whose integrity is undisputed. ◊ **Bankruptcy: Trustee in**.

Trustee in bankruptcy ◊ **Bankruptcy: Trustee In**.

Trustee investments Persons holding monies on trust are not completely free to invest those monies in any manner they choose, unless the trust deed states so. At one time they had no choice but to invest in safe, government securities. Since the Trustee Investments Act 1961, trustees have been allowed a little more latitude in that they can now invest up to one half of the fund in the shares of well-established companies. ◊ **Investment portfolio** ◊ **Trustee**.

Trustee Savings Bank (TSB) The first trustee savings bank was established in 1810 in Scotland. It was followed by many others throughout the UK, all of them with the intention of encouraging thrift amongst industrial and rural workers. These small savings banks were a product of the nineteenth-century movement which also pioneered the growth of **building societies** and **friendly Societies**. They all began as small organizations catering for local needs or particular groups within the working community. In time, by processes of growth and merger, the numbers of each decreased and those remaining became large national entities.

The trustee savings banks, managed by boards of trustees, were no exception, and during the first seventy years of the twentieth century they became, along with the Post Office Savings Bank, now the **National Savings Bank**, the principal repository of the small savings of the nation, with the advantage to the small saver of offering tax-free interest.

In 1976 the number of individual trustee savings banks was reduced from seventy to four: one for England and Wales and one each for Scotland, Northern Ireland and the Channel Islands. The concept of management by a board of trustees was maintained for each, with all four being answerable to a Central Board.

In the same year the TSB was given a different image. It relinquished its right to offer tax-free interest, which it had shared with the National Savings Bank, and was granted full banking status, thus making it a national commercial bank in competition with the 'big four' **clearing banks** – though the emphasis was still on personal and small-business customers.

In 1986 the Central Board, having restructured the TSB as a public company registered in Scotland and known as the TSB Group PLC, applied for Stock Exchange listing and coincidentally made an Offer for Sale of 1,500 million ordinary shares, thus firmly establishing the TSB both as a major clearing bank and as a public company answerable to its shareholders. This was only possible after extensive litigation had established that the existing assets of the TSB belonged not to the depositors but to the community at large.

Turnkey contract A contract, usually on a large scale, where the person paying leaves the contractor, usually a specialist organization, to see to all details and settle all problems that may occur during the period of the contract. Payment is due on completion, i.e. when the contractee, if satisfied, can merely turn the key and take over an operational unit.

Turnover An accountancy term for gross takings or total **sales** before any deductions.

Turnover, disclosure of The Companies Act 1967 made it necessary for a **company** to disclose its annual turnover. The notes to the accounts or the accounts themselves must show how the turnover is distributed between various classes of business. These provisions do not apply to **small and medium-sized companies** as defined in the 1985 Companies Act.

Turnover tax A form of sales tax levied at each stage in the distribution process. ◊ **Cascade tax** ◊ **Value added tax**. The latter, introduced in the UK in 1973, is a form of turnover tax.

Two-part tariff ◊ **Tariff**.

Tycoon Slang expression for a person who has accumulated a large sum of money in industry or commerce.

Uberrimae fidei 'Of the utmost good faith' (contrast with **bona fide**). Certain **contracts** may be void or voidable unless the party complained of has acted in the utmost good faith, i.e. has disclosed all facts relevant to the contract whether or not he has been asked to do so. The most common are contracts of **insurance** and **partnership**: a party to be insured must tell the insurer everything that may affect his decision in issuing a contract. Again, a partner must be quite open in his dealings and must not make **secret profits**, etc.

Ullage This word is used in two senses. Originally, it meant the difference between the capacity of a cask and its actual contents; in Customs terminology it is now used for the actual contents (the difference is called the vacuity). In **marine insurance** the difference is still known as 'ullage', is not usually considered a loss and is not covered by the **insurance** policy.

Ultimo 'Of the previous month.' This word is common in correspondence, where it is normally abbreviated to 'ult'.

Ultra vires 'Beyond the powers of', used mostly with reference to limited **companies**, which are bound by the powers set out in their **memorandum of association**. Until 1989 any act not consistent with these powers would be void as being *ultra vires*, i.e., outside the powers of the company, acting through the directors, to so order and the public

would be deemed to know of such limitations. The position has been changed by the 1989 Companies Act. While members still retain the power to seek a court injunction against an *ultra vires* act, third parties are now protected by a provision introduced by that Act which gives security to those who enter into a commercial transaction with a company in a matter which proves to be outside the powers given in the memorandum. Provided the third party acted in good faith, then the company will be bound by the agreement – though this leaves open the possibility of members bringing action against directors for exceeding their authority.

The provisions of the Act also cover the situation where directors act within the company's powers but outside their own authority. This was the situation which previously brought into play the **Rule in Royal British Bank v. Turquand**, where it was decided that an innocent third party should not be obliged to ascertain whether a director was actually exceeding the powers given to him by the company. This example of case law has now been given legal effect. The third party must still have acted in good faith, but the presumption now is that he did so unless it can be proved otherwise.

Umpire ◊ **Arbitration**.

Unabsorbed cost Where **overhead expenses** are allocated according to a budgeted output, each unit produced has a fixed overhead charge – perhaps a percentage of its direct cost. When the output aimed at is not reached, then not all of the overheads are charged to production. The **balance** remaining is known as unabsorbed cost.

Unappropriated profits That part of the profit of a business not paid out in **dividends** or allocated to any particular use.

Unauthorized acts by directors ◊ Rule in **Royal British Bank v. Turquand**.

Uncalled capital That part of the issued **share capital** of a **company** not yet called-up. ◊ **Called-up capital**.

Uncollected goods, disposal of Where **goods** left for repair are not collected, the repairer has certain powers either by custom or by statute. The most important statute is the Disposal of Uncollected Goods Act 1952, which states that if the goods are not collected or paid for within a reasonable time, the **bailee** may give notice that the goods are ready for collection. If he receives no reply to his notice after twelve months, he may give another notice stating his intention to sell. If no reply is received within two weeks, he may sell the goods, but only by public **auction**. The proceeds of the **sale** must be retained and after deduction of costs, including storage, etc., the monies must be handed over to the bailor. A notice that the provisions of the Act apply must be prominently displayed on the bailee's premises. ◊ **Bailment**.

Unconscionable bargains The law in **equity** affords protection to poor and ignorant persons who are taken advantage of in an unconscionable way when they have no opportunity of taking or using competent advice. For instance, a person who buys valuable land from a poor and ignorant man for a song may find that the transaction is set aside in equity. ◊ **Duress** ◊ **Undue influence**.

Undated stocks Government **stock** with no stated date for redemption. They may be permanent funds the government has no intention of ever redeeming, such as consolidated stock. Because they are undated, they are often the best indication of the movement of **interest** rates, as their **price** is influenced only by the prevailing rate of interest on risk-free investments. ◊ **Consols**.

Undertaking A term introduced into UK Company law by the 1989 Companies Act with particular reference to groups of companies in which the **holding company** is now referred to as the parent undertaking and the **subsidiary companies** as subsidiary undertakings. The change in terminology was necessary partly to counter off-balance-sheet accounting where organizations or business entities might be used or set up for particular purposes but, not being companies, were not caught by the legal requirements of the older company legislation, and partly to accommodate the relevant EU Directives. By the provisions of the 1989 Companies Act a **Group** is now defined as a parent undertaking and its subsidiary undertakings. ◊ **Group accounts** ◊ **Group accounts, omission of subsidiaries**.

Underwriter A person (or more often a **merchant bank** or **issuing house**) who agrees to underwrite an issue of **shares** by a **company**. This means that in return for a **commission** he (or they) agree to take up a certain proportion of the shares if those shares are not subscribed by the public. The amount they agree to take up is very often related to the **minimum subscription** stated in the **prospectus**.

Underwriter at Lloyd's A member of the Corporation of **Lloyd's** concerned mainly with **marine insurance**, but also with car **insurance**, etc. Members have unlimited liability and come under the heading of **tariff offices**. The name originates from the fact that when a **contract** of insurance for a marine adventure is required, various persons agree to take liability for a certain proportion of the total insurance required. They will write their name under the details of the contract in question on what is known as a **slip**. As an example: A wishes to insure two ships for £6,000,000, and applies to Lloyd's, where B signs for £200,000, C for £50,000, etc. Losses would be apportioned accordingly.

Although theoretically **sole traders**, the underwriters tend to work in **syndicates**.

Undischarged bankrupt ◊ **Bankruptcy: application for discharge**.

Undisclosed factoring A type of **factoring** used by a trader who prefers that the public, or those with whom he deals, are not aware that he is making use of such facilities. Technically, the distinction is that the factor, rather than buy the debts, buys the goods and appoints the seller to resell and collect payment on his behalf. The trader is the **agent** and the factor the **undisclosed principal**. The factor is responsible for bad debts; the commission charged will vary.

Undisclosed principal If an **agent** acts without indicating that he is acting as agent, third parties, on discovering the true state of affairs, may elect to treat the principal or the agent as the contracting party, i.e. they may treat the agent as principal. If the identity of the principal is sufficiently important to him, the third party may be able to avoid the **contract**.

Undistributed profits ◊ **Distributable reserves**.

Undue influence A form of moral pressure. A **contract** will not be enforced by a court if it can be shown that the defendant was in a position that prevented him forming a free and unfettered judgement. Undue influence will not be presumed unless certain relations, e.g. parental or confidential, exist between the parties.

Unearned income Income which does not arise from employment. At one time unearned income was taxed quite differently from earned income. Subsequently, the major penalty incurred by recipients of unearned income lay in the **investment income surcharge**. This has now been abolished. ◊ **Investment income**.

Unenforceable contracts These are strictly speaking not **contracts** at all, either because they are promises not supported by **consideration** or because the formalities of the law have not been observed. ◊ **Contract in writing** ◊ **Contract evidenced in writing**.

Unfair dismissal ◊ **Redundancy** ◊ **Severance pay**.

Unfunded debt Various short-term government loans, e.g. **ways and means advances**, **Treasury bills**, etc. It is also known as floating debt.

Unified tax system The tax system introduced in April 1973, when the old system of collecting **direct taxation**

through **income tax** and **surtax** was abolished in favour of a single graduated personal tax plus an additional levy known as the **investment income surcharge**, now discontinued. The system also abolished **earned-income relief** and the categories of **reduced rate relief** which had previously existed. The introduction of the unified tax system was accompanied, so far as companies were concerned, by the **imputation system**, which affected **corporation tax** payments and introduced the concept of **Advance corporation tax** (ACT). ◊ **Taxation schedules**.

Uniform business rate When the general rating system was replaced by the **poll tax** the rating of businesses, which had been a part of the old system administered by local authorities, was passed to the Inland Revenue. The old rating valuations were retained pending a general revaluation, and a uniform business rate was set which was to be applied on a nationwide basis. Although the proceeds accrue to the Inland Revenue the local authorities still collect the rates, but they now do so as agents of the Revenue.

Unilateral 'One-sided'. A unilateral agreement is a promise to do something, the promise not being supported by any **consideration**. A unilateral mistake is a **mistake** by only one party to a **contract**.

Unilateral contracts Strictly speaking, these are not **contracts** at all but promises. If someone promises to do something provided something else is done, no other person being named or put under obligation, he is only bound if the condition is fulfilled. For instance, if someone contracts to pay £12,000 to anyone who will build a new ward for a hospital,

he is only bound if the ward is built. ◊ **General offer**.

Unit cost ◊ **Stock valuation**.

Unit trust An organization for the collective purchase of **shares**, **securities**, etc. By spreading the investment risk over a large **portfolio** of investments, this risk is minimized; and by appointing experienced managers, profit, by way of **dividend**, **interest** or profit on sale, may be maximized for each individual member or unit holder. A unit trust is different from an **investment** company, because it is a mutual organization where the amount of capital can be varied according to the number of units in circulation, and because the shares or securities are held on trust for members and not as income-earning **assets** of a **company**. For this reason unit trusts are said to be an open-ended investment vehicle as opposed to an investment trust which, being limited by its subscribed capital, is referred to as close-ended.

Units are purchased initially in multiples of, say, 25p, an invitation being made to the public to take up units. The shares or securities are registered in the names of **trustees**, perhaps **banks**. There is a special **management company** responsible for buying and selling the shares and managing the affairs of the trust. This company makes its money from a percentage of annual income plus a percentage of the capital value of units issued. The company will normally belong to the Association of Unit Trust Managers. Every day it will state a buying and selling price for units. Units can be bought and sold by the management company itself. Prices of units are usually quoted in the daily papers. Some unit trusts specialize in seeking high income, others are more interested in capital **appreciation**, others again deal only in, say, **preference shares**, thereby hoping for a steady average high return. There are also differences in choice of industry, e.g. some trusts may specialize in certain types of manufacturer or producer, some may restrict themselves to Commonwealth countries or some may look to the **European Union**. The relative value of each to the investor depends on his point of view. There is a new development in the unit trust movement aimed at attracting wider membership and also at competing with **life assurance** companies. Units are offered at prices which include life cover for the whole time that the units are held. The Finance Act 1968 made these schemes somewhat more complicated as far as tax saving is concerned. The regulatory body for unit trusts required by the Financial Services Act is the **Investment Management Regulatory Organization** (IMRO).

Unitary tax Taxation of companies operating within the USA is levied on a regional basis. In certain states assessments are made under what is known as a unitary tax system. Such a system directs that tax is payable not merely on the profit arising from operations within that state but on the basis of total corporate income irrespective of where it is generated.

Despite relief that may be available through double-taxation agreements, such a tax regime can be financially crippling to the companies concerned and can act as a serious disincentive to multinationals who might wish to open a place of business within that state. There has been much lobbying at federal level by both domestic and foreign corporate bodies for the introduction in those states

of what is referred to as the 'water's edge' principle, whereby whatever the rate of corporate tax chargeable by a particular state, it can only be applied to income generated within the borders of that state.

Universal Postal Union An international intergovernmental agency which is responsible to the United Nations. Its role is to supervise international postal services and attempt to ensure adherence to the parcel and letter-post regulations of the Universal Postal Convention. The latter sets the standards to be observed for postal services between member countries (of which the UK is one). Details can be found in the **Post Office Guide**.

Unlawful This describes an act or contract not in itself illegal but which the law does not recognize and on which no legal action can be based. Most contracts involving wagering are unlawful.

Unlimited companies These are companies in which the members are liable for all debts without limitation. As the main attraction of incorporation is to obtain limited liability such companies are not common. They do, however, enjoy the advantages of separate identity and perpetual succession, and being exempt from *ad valorem* stamp duty on capital they are less costly to form. They need not have a share capital and, by virtue of the 1985 Companies Act, are always private companies.

To obtain the legal status of unlimited company an organization must be registered as such with the Registrar of Companies. The fact that a business adds the words '& Co.' to its name does not necessarily mean that it is incorporated as an unlimited company – the addition may be merely descriptive or indicative of a **limited partnership**.

Unliquidated damages ◊ **Damages, unliquidated**.

Unlisted Securities Market (USM) This was launched by the Stock Exchange in 1980 to cater for the many companies which needed facilities for raising capital and marketing their shares but were unable or unwilling to apply for an official Stock Exchange listing. Until this market was opened, such companies were obliged to seek necessary facilities by private negotiation, and the Stock Exchange therefore did not get the business. Since the USM was established, well over 200 companies have entered it and obtained quotations for their shares.

In the case of smaller companies, the USM is often preferable to an official listing, for various reasons. It caters for companies with a market capitalization below the £500,000 minimum insisted upon by the Stock Exchange as a prerequisite for an official listing, and a company can gain admission to the USM with only 10 per cent of its equity in public hands as against the 25 per cent necessary for entry to the **official list**. Other attractions lie in the shorter trading record demanded, the less stringent preconditions to entry and the considerably lower initial costs by way of both advertising and fees, thus giving the benefits of a quotation at a lower cost.

Against the obvious advantages of a listing on the USM must be set the attendant duties and obligations to provide a considerable body of facts regarding trading and results on a regular basis to the Stock Exchange, individual shareholders and the general public. Disclosure requirements are almost as comprehensive as those applying to officially quoted shares.

Unload A slang term in commerce for dumping a large quantity of **goods** on the market at a low **price** to make a quick **sale**. The supplier is prepared to accept a low profit margin – this gives him competitive advantage. ◊ **Dumping**.

Unquoted investments An accounting term for investments in **shares** or **debentures** which are not quoted or dealt with on a recognized stock exchange. The value at which these are shown in published accounts is normally cost at time of acquisition, less any amount written off (this being stated separately). ◊ **Unlisted Securities Market** ◊ **Investments: in company accounts**.

Unsecured creditors **Creditors** of a **company** or other business whose debts are not secured. In a **winding-up** or **bankruptcy** they are paid **pari passu** after **secured creditors** and the settlement of preferential debts.

Unsecured debentures ◊ **Unsecured loan stock**.

Unsecured loan stock An accounting term for loan **capital** raised without **security**, e.g. **unsecured debentures**.

Upset price An auctioneering term for the lowest **price** at which the **vendor** would allow bidding to begin or the object to be sold. ◊ **Auction** ◊ **Reserve price**.

Urgent Issues Task Force (UITF) The third of the bodies set up by the **Financial Reporting Council** in its role of initiating and supervising the general upgrading of accounting and auditing practices within the UK. The UITF

447

exists to employ swift action where accounting standards are in danger of being abused either because of lack of clarity in the wording of such standards, or because of misunderstandings of the law relating to the contents and presentation of published accounts. In grey areas, companies or their auditors can consult the UITF for a ruling as to whether the proposed accounting treatment is consistent with existing standards. In doing so they may avoid the embarrassment of a confrontation with the **Financial Reporting Review Panel**.

Uruguay Round A further comprehensive round of trade negotiations under the aegis of the **General Agreement on Tariffs and Trade** (GATT) which commenced in Uruguay in 1986 and was concluded in December 1993 after a series of compromises, chiefly between the USA and the EU, were accepted. As with other rounds, e.g. the **Kennedy Round**, the aim was to extend the boundaries of free trade and encourage further reductions in tariffs and other obstacles to the unimpeded flow of international trade on a multilateral basis. Some of the more intractable problems centred on agricultural produce, particularly on the apparent inability to reconcile the US search for wider markets for its grain exports with the mutually protective stance of the EU reflected in its Common Agricultural Policy.

In completing the round it was agreed to establish a new body to be provisionally known as the Multilateral Trading Organization, which would be charged with supervising the implementation of tariff cuts and with the overall regulation of international trade.

Usance Bills of exchange may be drawn as usance; these will be bills between two foreign countries with separate currencies. They are short-term bills and 'usance' means the time allowed by custom for payment. For instance, usance for bills drawn in New York upon Europe is sixty days.

Usufruct The right to use the property of another person for profit but without enjoying either the rights attaching to ownership or the right to diminish its value.

Vacuity ◊ Ullage.

Value The **price** which an item would fetch in an **open market**. Distinction should be made between value in present use and value in alternative use. For instance, a factory building may be worth £500 to a person wishing to use it as a factory but £50,000 to a person wishing to redevelop the land. Value is also determined by various other factors, ranging from sentiment to long-term **speculation**; so it is in fact a rather imprecise term. ◊ **Market value** ◊ **Value in use**.

Value added A term for the increment added by each person or organization involved in the manufacture of a particular item, becoming part of its price. As an example, A provides raw materials at 25p, B works on the materials and passes them on to C at 37p, so B has added 12p to the value. ◊ **Value added tax**.

Value added tax (**VAT**) This tax, already applied in other European countries, was introduced to the United Kingdom in 1973. Although a novelty by name, its effect was not dissimilar, from the viewpoint of the ultimate consumer, to the **purchase tax** which it replaced. However, in so far as it does not have to be paid to the Customs and Excise until goods or services on which it is levied are exchanged for cash by the consumer, the **retailer** is theoretically in a better position than under purchase tax, which, being levied on the **manufacturer**, was automatically included in the value of goods bought by the retailer, whether sold or not. However, the amount of additional paperwork involved has virtually extinguished the advantages.

The underlying principle of VAT is that tax is levied at each stage of the production of goods or services and on the value added at each stage; e.g. tax is paid by manufacturers on the cost of making an item, by **wholesalers** on the price they charge the retailer and by retailers on the price they charge the consumer. Each party in this process must account to the Customs and Excise for the tax on their output but may deduct from this figure the amount of tax already paid by the party supplying them. If we look at it in reverse and take an article priced at £11 in a shop, then, assuming a VAT rate of 10 per cent, the tax is £1, i.e. one eleventh of the total price. Although the Customs and Excise are entitled to £1 they will receive it in stages determined by the number of hands through which the article passes on its way to the consumer's pocket. Part will be paid by the manufacturer, part by the wholesaler and part by the retailer, and all these portions will be handed over at different times. Apart from the paperwork involved, additional problems are posed by differing rates of tax and distinctions between taxable and non-taxable goods and services. ◊ **Output tax** ◊ **Input tax** ◊ **Zero-rated**.

Manufacturers and distributors must

keep adequate records to show how the various VAT regulations have been applied and must produce such records on demand. They must also complete a quarterly return showing tax due and how the amount is calculated. Needless to say, the tax is not popular but was part of the price paid for entry into the **Common Market**. There are VAT centres in most cities and many explanatory books and pamphlets available on inquiry. Businesses with a small **turnover** may apply for total exemption from VAT. ◊ **Her Majesty's Customs and Excise**.

Value in use The **value** of an item to the person using it. This may be quite different from the sale **price**. A piece of equipment or machinery might have no saleable value, due to the difficulty of dismantling it, but to the person currently using it, it may have considerable value, producing **goods** for sale.

Valued policy A **marine insurance** term for a policy which contains a stated sum insured. ◊ **Open policy**.

Variable costs An accounting term for costs that vary according to the level of output. ◊ **Fixed costs** ◊ **Semi-variable costs**.

Variation of written contracts ◊ **Oral evidence** ◊ **Rectification of contract**.

Vendor A person selling **goods**.

Vendue Another name for a public **auction**.

Venture capital ◊ **Risk capital**.

Verba chartarum fortius accipiuntur contra proferentem A legal maxim which points out that where any doubt arises as to the precise meaning of a written **contract**, it will be construed more strongly against the person who drew up the contract. This can be quite important where **exemption clauses** are concerned.

Vertical integration A term used with reference to the amalgamation of business organizations each of which is concerned with a different stage in the production of specific goods or services. The merger of companies involved respectively in sheep farming, spinning of wool, weaving, dyeing, clothing design and manufacture, and the operation of both wholesale and retail clothing outlets would constitute a fairly comprehensive instance of vertical integration.

The merging of businesses involved at the same level in the production or distribution of a particular article or service is known as lateral or horizontal integration. ◊ **Merger**.

Vested interest Interest now in being as opposed to interest anticipated. It is a term frequently used in law with regard to the **Title** to goods or land. Property is said to vest when the absolute owner is finally established and his interest is in no way capable of being terminated by anyone but himself.

Vicarious performance Generally speaking, when one person **contracts** with another, he anticipates that that other will perform the contract. Where the contract relies on the particular skill of the other person, that person cannot delegate the work: an artist if asked to paint a portrait must paint it personally and paint the whole of it personally. In certain types of contract, however, delegation of all or part of the work must be anticipated, particularly in building contracts, where a great part of the work is subcontracted. Subcontracting should be distinguished from **assignment** of contract. The liability for breach of contract still remains with the original contracting party. ◊ **Delegatus non potest delegare**.

Victualling bill A list of all bonded or **drawback** goods that a ship takes on for use during the voyage. It must be presented to the Customs authorities for clearance. ◊ **Bonded stores**.

Viewdata ◊ **Teletext** ◊ **Prestel**.

Vigilantibus non dormientibus jura subveniunt Equitable maxim stating that if anyone has, or thinks he has, a claim, he should proceed with it without delay. Delay can result in the loss of certain remedies. ◊ **Laches**.

Vintner A wine-dealer.

Visible imports and exports Goods actually shipped or otherwise sold – as opposed to invisible exports or imports, which are services earning or costing foreign exchange, e.g. shipping, **insurance**, etc. The United Kingdom has thrived for many years on invisible earnings and very rarely has a favourable balance on visible trade. ◊ **Invisible trade**.

Voluntary arrangement The Insolvency Act 1986 provides for a procedure known as a voluntary arrangement, short of a winding-up, in the case of companies or a bankruptcy order, in the case of individuals, by which a composition in satisfaction of outstanding debts or a scheme of arrangement in relation to them under the supervision of an appointed nominee, who must be qualified as an **insolvency practitioner**, is approved and so ordered by the court. An application for a voluntary arrangement will be made by the debtor where it is an alternative to a bankruptcy, or by

the directors of a company when it is sought to avoid a winding-up.

If such a voluntary arrangement is ordered then all further proceedings against the defendant are stayed, unless the court rules otherwise, while the order is in force. The appointed supervisor will within a stated period (fourteen days in the case of an individual or twenty-eight days in the case of a company) obtain from the person proposing the voluntary arrangement details of its application and a statement of the affairs of the debtor or company, and subsequently shall report to the court whether and when a meeting of creditors should be called to discuss the proposals submitted by the debtor or company.

The creditors' meeting, if called, will discuss the proposals and may accept them with or without modifications, which must be agreed with the proposer, or may reject them. If the proposals are accepted and the voluntary arrangement is approved by the court then it is binding on all creditors. The Act contains certain provisions protecting the rights of secured creditors from being diluted without their express approval. ◊ **Administration order**.

Voluntary winding-up ◊ **Winding-up, voluntary**.

Volunteer In law, this is a person who performs some act without any obligation to do so. Generally speaking, if he suffers loss through this he can obtain no redress. Claims cannot be followed even in **equity**: 'Equity does not assist a volunteer.'

Voting rights These must be stated in the **prospectus** of a company. The rights of various shareholders to vote will also be contained in the **articles of associa-tion**. ◊ **Proxy** ◊ **Poll**.

Voucher In accounting, this is a docu-ment supporting entries in a **journal** or other book of prime entry. ◊ **Prime entry, books of**.

Voyage charter A charter agreement which applies to a particular voyage. The charter may be of the ship or of space in it, but ceases on completion of the voyage. There are various obligations im-posed on both shipowner and charterer. The owner must bring the ship to the agreed port at the agreed time and the charterer must deliver the goods at the specified port at the specified time. The shipowner **warrants** that the ship will be seaworthy at the commencement of the voyage though not necessarily during the continuation of the voyage. Where the ship calls at a number of ports, it must be seaworthy on leaving each port. The ship must also be properly equipped and must be ready to proceed with due dispatch. It must not deviate from its course (for exceptions ◊ **Marine insur-ance**). The charterer must load or unload within the specified **lay days**. The ship-owner does not usually accept liability for losses such as arrest and restraint of princes, rulers and people, fire, **barratry**, gales, **stranding**, other damages of navi-gation (i.e. those most applicable to voyage by sea), or acts of God or the Queen's enemies. The liability of the ship-owner is, apart from this, that of a **common carrier**.

Voyage policy A **marine insurance** term for a policy insuring cargo and ship on a particular voyage.

Wage freeze An attempt by government to hold wages and salaries at a certain level, usually as part of a general policy aimed at stemming inflation. It is based on the premise that prices and wages are so closely linked that the freezing of the one will have a similar effect upon the other. ◊ **Price control** ◊ **Prices and incomes policy** ◊ **Productivity deal** ◊ **Wage restraint**.

Wage restraint An alternative to a **wage freeze** commonly used by the government in combating inflation. Knowing that an attempt to freeze wages will be unlikely to succeed, because it is seen as an infringement of the democratic right to negotiate rates of pay, the government may opt for a policy of wage restraint whereby it obtains trade union support for modification of wage increases in the interests of the general health of the economy. One of its faults is that it tends only to apply to nationally negotiated wage and salary scales and leaves the higher-paid executives and the sole traders free from any really effective control over the salaries they negotiate for themselves. Unlike the factory worker, they have a greater mobility, as do employees of professional firms, and can obtain higher salaries merely by re-signing from one firm and joining another. ◊ **Productivity deal** ◊ **Wages council**.

Wagering contract A **contract** between two parties whereby either may win or lose a sum of money, or other valuable **asset**, dependent on the outcome of some investigation or on the happening of some future event in which neither has any personal interest except in so far as he stands to win or lose. Each party is pitting his own skill or luck against the other's. Wagering contracts should be distinguished from contracts of **insurance**, for the insured must always have an **insurable interest**. All wagers were made void by the Gaming Act 1845 – this covers wagering contracts and **gaming contracts**. It makes it impossible to regain money paid or **securities** given. Wagering contracts are void but not illegal; a fresh promise to pay for a fresh **consideration** is also caught by the statute. If a person who has lost money in a wager attempts to recover it, he cannot succeed even though by law he has no obligation to pay it. Where money is lent by one person to another to enable that other to enter into a wagering contract, he may or may not recover the loan. If the loan was to enable the debtor to pay, e.g. betting debts, he may be able to recover. He will not recover if he pays the debt himself. Money lent for gaming is never recoverable unless the gaming takes place in a country where it is lawful.

Wagering policy A marine insurance policy where the insurer has no acceptable **insurable interest**. These **contracts** are **gambling** contracts and are technically illegal. ◊ **Policy proof of interest**.

Wages and salaries A generic term for remuneration paid to employees of a business or other organization. Both are fixed by contract and are usually determined by a trade union or national agreement. The distinction between a wage and a salary is fairly nebulous but, generally speaking, wages are paid weekly and salaries monthly, or wages apply to manual workers and salaries to clerical workers. When references are made to a **wage freeze** or to **wage restraint**, the term wage includes both wages and salaries. ◊ **Contract of Employment Act** ◊ **Wages council**.

Wages council An independent body appointed by the Secretary of State for Employment consisting of equal numbers of representatives from employees and employers in a particular industry and three or more independent persons, one of whom chairs the council. The purpose of the council is to negotiate and fix wages and conditions of employment in the industry that it represents. Wages councils are only found within industries which do not have their own **collective bargaining** arrangements through trade unions. There have been moves afoot to abolish wages councils but so far the only step has been the removal of the power to institute new wages councils by the Wages Act 1986.

Waiters Attendants at the **Stock Exchange** who take messages, run errands and generally take care of the details of the day-to-day running of the Exchange. The term is a relic of the days when dealings took place in coffee houses and the waiters took messages.

Waiting time In business parlance, time which an employee spends idle, though not through his own fault, e.g. time spent waiting for a machine to be repaired or set up ready for use. It is obviously worthwhile to minimize this time.

In some services, for example **taxi** driving, a charge may be made for waiting time.

Waiver Where one person waives his rights in a **contract**, this is known as a waiver. Though an alteration of an existing contract, it is in effect a new agreement and requires **consideration** if it is to be enforceable at law. ◊ **Discharge of contract**.

Waiver clause The clause in **marine insurance** policies allowing either party to take steps to minimize a loss without thereby prejudicing rights.

Wall Street The location of the New York **Stock Exchange**.

Warehouse Generally speaking, a place where **goods** are stored prior to their being sold or used. The word is more restricted in shipping terminology, where it means a public warehouse where goods are stored on being landed from a ship. These warehouses are often responsible for sorting, examining and delivering goods as well as storing them. The goods may be for home consumption or re-export. Some warehouses are bonded warehouses, where duty need not be paid on the goods until they are actually removed from the warehouse. ◊ **Bonded goods**.

Goods are released on production of a **warehouse keeper**'s order issued by the Customs.

Warehouse keeper A person in charge of a **warehouse**. If it is a bonded warehouse, he will need to give **security** for the duty that may become due on the goods in his charge.

Warehouse keeper's order ◊ Warehouse.

Warehouse officer Bonded warehouses are controlled by a warehouse officer employed by the Customs and Excise in addition to a **warehouse keeper**. He inspects many of the **goods** on receipt and on delivery; delivery is only allowed when proper documents (e.g. the warehouse keeper's order) are produced. The documents must have been countersigned by a Customs officer.

Warrant A receipt for **goods** deposited in a public **warehouse**. The receipt identifies the goods and may be transferred by **endorsement**.

Warranty A statement of fact in a **contract**, either express or implied. If it is unfulfilled, the injured party cannot repudiate the contract but may be able to claim damages. The difference between a warranty and a **condition** is that a condition is fundamental to a contract whereas a warranty is not.

Warranty, floating A **warranty** which may be enforceable by a third party, i.e. by a person not a party to the **contract** when the warranty is given. If A asks B to contract with C, C may have an enforceable warranty against A. For instance, suppose A asks B to paint his house and obtain the paint from C (A having obtained C's advice as to suitability). If B buys the paint from C and it proves faulty, A may be able to sue C even though he was not party to the contract as C has in fact warranted the paint to A. The principle is important in **hire purchase** contracts when the **vendor** sells through a hire purchase company. The buyer buys from the company but may enforce warranties against the vendor.

Warranty of attorney A type of **power of attorney** given to a **solicitor**, whereby the solicitor attends court and pleads on behalf of an accused person.

Warranty of authority ◊ Breach of warranty of authority.

Wasting assets An accounting term for **assets** which are used up gradually in producing goods. It is sometimes applied to **fixed assets** generally, but is perhaps better applied to assets which are exhausted after a certain period of time, such as quarries, mines, etc.

Watering stock The issue of additional **shares** of a certain class without any expectation of being able to maintain the old **dividend** on the new total **share capital**. ◊ Equity dilution ◊ Stock.

Water's edge principle ◊ Unitary tax.

Waybill A traditional document issued in the course of the carriage of goods by road, rail, air or water. It is usually prepared by the carrier and, in addition to a description of the goods and the name of the parties concerned, normally gives the conditions of the contract of carriage. ◊ Air waybill ◊ Common carrier.

Ways and means advances Short-term loans made to the government by the **Bank of England**, to supplement money raised on **Treasury bills**.

Wear and tear Another term for depreciation. ◊ **Depreciation** ◊ **Capital allowances**.

Weather working days Working days, particularly at a port, when the weather allows work to be done.

Weighted averages ◊ Index number.

Weights and Measures Act 1963 This established a national network of government inspectors who now act within the framework of the Consumer Affairs section of the Department of Trade and Industry to ensure that goods are sold in proper weights and measures and to instigate proceedings against offenders. They may make random investigations of scales used in shops and measures used in public houses, etc. The inspectors work in close collaboration with other consumer protection agencies and may direct the attention of other departments to apparent abuses under, e.g. the **Trade Descriptions Act** 1968.

Wharfage The charge made by the owner or manager of a wharf, which is another name for the quay where goods are deposited after being unloaded from a ship or before being loaded thereon. A wharf is frequently combined with a **warehouse** and the wharfinger, the person controlling the wharf, will then double as **warehouse keeper**. The wharfinger or, if doubling as such, the warehouse keeper, will give a receipt known as the wharfinger's receipt for goods awaiting collection from him. The goods will be handed over on production of this receipt, which is *de facto* a negotiable instrument. This receipt is also known as a wharfinger's warrant.

Wharfinger ◊ **Wharfage**.

Wharfinger's receipt ◊ **Wharfage**.

Wharfinger's warrant ◊ **Wharfage**.

Whole life assurance A contract of **life assurance** only, i.e. without any endowment option. ◊ **Assurance**. ◊ **Term assurance**.

Wholesaler The middle man between manufacturer and **retailer**. He is able to buy in large quantities and then break these into smaller parcels for the benefit of the retailers. The wholesaler takes a profit either by adding to the manufacturer's price or by charging a **commission** to the retailer. Where **selling prices** are fixed by the manufacturer, the manufacturer in effect gives a share of his profit by way of discount to the wholesaler, who passes on a share to the retailer. This is often referred to as a **trade discount**. The wholesaler's justification is that without him it would be necessary for the manufacturer himself to set up depots in various parts of the country to facilitate distribution and keep careful track of local demand.

Wildcat strike A common term for a sudden unofficial strike, usually by a group of key workers in an industry, with the object of causing maximum disruption of production and obtaining some additional non-negotiated benefit either in pay or conditions of employment. ◊ **Employment legislation**.

Windfall profit A profit not anticipated. It might arise perhaps from changes in legislation. An increase in tax or duty might result in the manufacturer making additional profit on stock whereon the lower rate of duty has already been paid. Windfall profits, being exceptional, should be shown separately in **company** accounts.

Winding-up ◊ **Liquidation**.

Winding-up, alternatives to The Insolvency Act 1986 introduced two possible alternatives to the somewhat drastic and often expensive process of winding-up a company in difficulties. These are (a) the granting of an **administration order**; and (b) company **voluntary arrangements**. The latter are similar to the remedies now available as an alternative to bankruptcy. ◊ **Insolvency Act** 1986.

Winding-up by a court: reasons therefor A company may be wound up by a court where (1) it passes a special resolution to the effect, (2) it does not commence business within a year of incorporation or suspends business for a year, (3) it is unable to pay its debts, (4) the number of members has fallen below two, (5) it has not received a trading certificate within one year of incorporation if it is a public company, (6) the court considers it 'just and equitable' that the company be wound up because, for example, its *raison d'être* has gone or the company is a bubble or the number of members are reduced to two and those two cannot agree and/or are unable to carry on business amicably. ◊ **Bubble** ◊ **Insolvency Act** 1986.

Winding-up, commencement of In voluntary liquidation the winding-up is deemed to commence with the passing of the resolution. In a compulsory winding-up the relevant date is that on which the petition was presented unless a voluntary winding-up was already in progress when the date of the resolution becomes the appropriate date. In the matter of establishing preferential debts, the relevant date is that on which the court appoints a provisional liquidator or, when no such person is appointed, then the date of the winding-up order or, where applicable, the date on which an administration order was granted.

Winding-up, compulsory: early dissolution Where the Official Receiver is acting as liquidator and is of the opinion that (1) the assets of the company are not sufficient to justify the cost of an extended winding-up and (2) no further

investigation into the company's affairs seems necessary, then he may pursue the early dissolution procedure provided for in Section 202 of the 1986 Insolvency Act. Having given twenty-eight days' notice of his intention to do so to all creditors and contributories he applies to the Registrar of Companies for a dissolution order and, provided no objection is registered by those to whom he has given notice, then the company is automatically dissolved three months from the registration of his application.

Winding-up, compulsory: petition A petition for the compulsory winding-up of a company may be presented by (1) the company itself, by special resolution; (2) the directors, all acting jointly; (3) any creditor including a contingent or prospective creditor; (4) a contributory but only in specified circumstances; (5) the personal representative of a deceased contributory subject to similar conditions; (6) the Secretary of State for Trade and Industry; and (7) the Official Receiver where the company is already in voluntary liquidation.

On hearing the petition the court may either dismiss it, grant a winding-up order, adjourn the hearing or make such other order as seems fit in the circumstances. On hearing a creditor's petition the court may wish to consult the wishes of other creditors in deciding whether or not to make any particular order.

Winding-up, compulsory: powers of court In addition to the powers and duties of a **liquidator** in a compulsory winding-up certain powers are reserved to the court unless they are specifically delegated to the liquidator as an officer of the court. These are briefly (1) to settle the list of contributories; (2) establish a date by which creditors must prove their debts or relinquish any right to share in a distribution; (3) state when and where creditors and contributories may inspect the company's books and records; (4) realize the company's assets and apply them in payment of its debts, recognizing the priority of preferential debts.

The court may also stay winding-up proceedings if it decides that such is necessary on the application of the liquidator or any creditor or contributory, and can make calls on contributories or, where necessary, rectify the register of members. Other powers of the court include the holding of a public examination of any officer of the company where asked to do so by one-half in value of creditors or three-quarters in value of contributories, and the right to arrest an absconding contributory and seize his movable personal property.

Winding-up, public examination In a compulsory winding-up the **liquidator** may apply to the court for permission to call for the public examination of any past or present officer of the company. This will include not only directors but also prior liquidators or administrators, or any person who has taken part in promoting or forming the company. He must apply for public examination, at the discretion of the court, if required to do so by either one half in value of creditors or three-quarters in value of contributories.

Winding-up, voluntary A **company** may be wound up voluntarily in the following ways: (1) by **ordinary resolution** (unless the **articles of association** specify otherwise) when the company has achieved what it intended, or has reached the end of its anticipated life; (2) by **special resolution** – for any reason; (3) by **extraordinary resolution**, when by

reason of its liabilities it cannot continue in business and ought to be wound up. Voluntary winding-up commences on the date of the resolution. The resolution must be published in the **London Gazette**. The results of the winding-up are: (1) that a company ceases to carry on business except for the purpose of winding-up; (2) that transfers of **shares** and alterations in the status of members are prohibited, although the **liquidator** may allow a transfer of shares.

There are two kinds of voluntary winding-up – members' voluntary winding-up and **creditors'** voluntary winding-up. The conduct of a members' voluntary winding-up will depend on whether the **directors** have been able to make a successful **declaration of solvency**. This is a statutory declaration that the company will be able to pay its debts in full within twelve months. It must be made within five weeks before the resolution and must contain a statement of **assets** and **liabilities**. A liquidator is appointed by the company. If he is not satisfied that the declaration was properly made, he must call meetings of creditors and the winding-up will then in effect become a creditors' voluntary winding-up. Where he is happy with the statement he takes over completely and the powers of the directors cease except where he or the company in general meeting states otherwise. He must call annual meetings of members and account to them, and also a final meeting where **final accounts** are presented. He then notifies the Registrar of Companies, sending him a copy of the accounts, and after three months the company is dissolved. (The final meeting has to be advertised in the *London Gazette*.) Where the voluntary winding-up is a creditors' voluntary winding-up, no declaration of solvency having been made, the company must call a meeting of creditors on the same day as, or on the day after, the resolution. The meeting must be gazetted and the creditors given a statement of affairs and a list of creditors. The creditors may appoint a liquidator as well as the members, but the creditors' appointee will take preference. The creditors may also appoint a **liquidation committee**. The company can appoint members to the committee with the creditors' approval. Everything is then as in a members' voluntary winding-up except that a final meeting of creditors must be held as well as a final meeting of members. Additional matters applicable to both methods are: (1) that the liquidator must establish the debts of the company; (2) that he may carry on business for the purpose of winding-up but does not become personally liable; (3) that after payment of costs of liquidation, monies are applied first in payment of creditors (◊ **Preferential creditors**) and anything remaining is distributed to members; (4) that the liquidator settles the list of contributories – this list is *prima facie* evidence of liability; (5) that dissolution can be deferred where this is thought necessary; (6) that during the course of a voluntary winding-up, a creditor may petition for a **compulsory winding-up**; a contributory may also petition but the court will not grant it unless there are serious grounds for believing that the winding-up is being carried on fraudulently.

Window dressing Apart from its literal meaning of displaying goods in a shop window in a manner that maximizes the chances of passers-by being tempted to buy them or at least to enter the shop, this term has certain specialized commercial meanings.

Traditionally, in banking it refers to the now defunct practice of calling in short loans and postponing payments in order to show a handsome cash ratio in the annual accounts. In the world of accounting it describes the somewhat dubious practice indulged in by some companies of manipulating (lawfully) their published accounts in order to give a reassuring overall picture to both members and the public. One easy way of doing this is by revamping the style of presentation to members so that comparisons, particularly of ratios that have to be calculated by the reader, are more difficult to make. ◊ **Annual accounts** ◊ **Annual report** ◊ **Fourth schedule**.

Window shopping Parading up and down a shopping street with intent to covet rather than to buy.

With profits policy ◊ **Assurance**.

Withholding tax This refers to tax deducted from dividend or other payments to persons in other countries. The relevant tax is 'withheld' when the payment is made, but the recipient can frequently set this tax against his liability in his own country in the form of **double taxation relief** where the necessary agreement has been effected between the countries concerned.

Without recourse These words added to a **bill of exchange** indicate that the holder has no recourse to the person from whom he took the bill should it not be paid. It is often written as 'sans recours', and may appear after an **endorsement**.

Woodlands, taxation of Since the abolition of land tax as such, the occupation of woodlands does not give rise to a liability for tax unless they are managed on a commercial basis and with a view to profit.

Wordprocessor An electronic device that is fast supplanting the traditional typewriter. It consists of a computer unit which is tied in with a keyboard, display screen and printer. The keyboard is used much as that on a typewriter and the words keyed appear on a display screen where they can be amended or moved from one position to another. When the operator is satisfied with the text it can be automatically transferred to paper by means of the printer. Wordprocessors are becoming increasingly sophisticated, and the number of functions incorporated into them is being continually expanded. Some are even programmed to correct spelling errors automatically. Others are merged with stored information so that specific details, such as names and addresses are automatically added to, or incorporated within the text.

Work and materials, contracts for ◊ Goods.

Work in progress A term usually found alongside **stock-in-trade** in a **balance sheet**: i.e. 'stocks and work in progress'. It represents the **value** of work commenced but not completed. In a manufacturing business this will be in partly finished **goods**. In a contracting business it will be in the form of uncompleted contracts. Difficulties arise in valuation, one problem, particularly on a long-term contract, being whether to include part of the anticipated profit and how to deal with cash paid in advance. The traditional method is to take profit into account in the same proportion as the amount paid is to the work certified.

This applies to contractors' accounts and profit is normally reduced by any anticipated losses.

The valuation is important as often a large proportion of total assets is represented by 'stocks and work in progress'. ◊ **Stock valuation**.

Work study A study concerned with reviewing working methods and deciding how long particular jobs should take. Its aim is to reduce effort involved in various operations, to organize labour in the most economical manner and to provide data for planning, estimating and financial incentive schemes. ◊ **Job enrichment**.

Worker cooperative A form of business organization particularly associated with Communist countries but common throughout the world in those areas of industry which are essentially labour-intensive. It is particularly suitable to agriculture, where individual farmers find that considerable advantages can arise when they arrange to pool available land in order to gain the benefits of large-scale crop cultivation. In such instances expensive agricultural machinery is acquired on a collective basis, thus saving each individual the considerable capital investment involved in purchasing it solely for his own limited use.

Worker cooperatives also emerge in other industries where, rather than see a factory close down with resultant loss of jobs, the factory employees arrange to run it themselves. This is more common in circumstances in which the employees have specialist skills that are a major factor in the production of the relevant goods or services. As such enterprises normally begin with only the pooled savings of the workers, the State will sometimes candidate's own choosing. These NVQs are awarded at four levels and are intended to be an indication of competence and skill for presentation to a prospective employer.

Yankees Stock Exchange slang for US securities.

Year's purchase A term used in calculating the purchase price of a business or of land where that price is related to the estimated average annual profits or **rent** and is stated to be x years' purchase of the profit or rent.

Yellow Pages The colloquial name for the official classified telephone directories issued by British Telecom. There are individual directories for each designated business area and a copy is issued free to every subscriber in that area. All entries are listed under the appropriate trade or business and no charge is made for the simple line entry. Many businesses opt to buy block entries or some special display form which advertises their services more prominently. The sale of space in this manner helps recoup the cost of making the directories freely available.

In addition to the Yellow Pages, British Telecom now provides (1) a business directory to match the residential directory, giving business entries in strict alphabetical order, and (2) Business Pages, a direct companion to Yellow Pages, listing services and suppliers to businesses themselves by classification.

Yield The return earned on an investment, taking into account the annual income and its present **capital** value. It also has other, more particular, meanings – perhaps as many as there are financial

editors. ◊ **Earnings yield** ◊ **Dividend yield** ◊ **Redemption yield**.

York–Antwerp rules Optional rules drawn up in 1877 to help those engaged in the carriage of **goods** by sea, with **general average clauses** in **bills of lading**, **marine chartering** and **marine insurance** policies.

Youth Training Scheme (**YTS**) Originally established by the Manpower Services Commission which acted through appointed training agents to provide a bridge between leaving school and entering full-time employment for young unemployed people, usually sixteen- and seventeen-year-olds. Employers were encouraged by the offer of cash incentives to find placements for these newcomers to the labour market. The theory was to give the youngsters experience of workplace conditions and combine this with taught courses at local colleges of further education. At the end of the agreed period, normally two years, the candidates would receive a certificate indicating the level of their achievement. The YTS scheme has now become the responsibility of the **Training and Enterprise Councils** which, in administering the scheme, encourage entrants to work towards obtaining one of the various vocational qualifications which are being made available through the TECs themselves and through other examining bodies such as the RSA. The aim is to achieve a National Vocational Qualification (NVQ) in a field of activity of the

Xerography Now the most widely used method in photocopying, this process, invented in the USA in the late 1930s, was first developed commercially in the 1950s. Although once the province of a single supplier it has since come into general use and is notable for the extra fine resolution in the copies it produces. Since the 1970s the xerographic process has been so refined that it can now produce coloured images with equally fine resolution and clarity. It can print on both sides of the duplicating paper and has the facility to vary the size of the image produced without detracting from the clarity of that image.

make a grant or provide a repayable loan to help with initial capital requirements and the employment of managerial skills. The overall management of such cooperatives is usually vested in a committee of the employee-owners.

Working capital An accounting term usually defined as the difference between **Current assets** and **current liabilities**. It is also sometimes referred to as circulating capital as such assets and liabilities are continually circulated or turned over in the normal course of business. ◊ **Current ratio** ◊ **Liquid ratio** ◊ **Quick assets**.

Working days A common commercial term but with a specialized meaning in certain trades, particularly the shipping industry. ◊ **Lay days**. Working days are generally calculated as being each day of the week except Sunday and excluding **bank holidays**. Custom of trade sometimes also excludes Saturday as a working day, i.e. where a five-day week is normal.

Working director A company director who is employed on company affairs in a full-time capacity as opposed to a person who agrees to be named as a director for the experienced advice he can offer or because his connection with the company will give it a greater degree of respectability ◊ **Non-executive directors**.

Workmen's wages in winding-up ◊ **Preferential debts**.

World Bank ◊ **International Bank for Reconstruction and Development**.

Writ A legal document summoning a person to attend at a certain place or to perform a certain act. There are penalties for failure to comply. ◊ **Subpoena**.

Writer to the signet A person acting in the Supreme Court of Scotland as a **solicitor** does in England.

Written down value An accounting term for the cost or valuation of an **asset**, less depreciation written off. It is no indication of the present selling price of that asset.

Zero-rated In the field of **value added tax** certain goods and services are zero-rated, i.e. although they are taxable the tax charge is at a nil rate. There is an important distinction between items that are zero-rated and those defined as exempt. The latter, which are contained in the Exemption Schedule to the Finance Act 1972, as amended, include many public services such as health and postal services. The relevance of the distinction between exempt and zero-rated is that the former covers goods and services which are outside the VAT system while the latter covers those that are inside but not taxed. This means that people paying zero-rated tax can reclaim **input tax** but exempt people cannot. ⟡ **Output tax**.

Zero bonds Bonds which carry no interest and are issued at a discount to attract investors who are more attracted by a capital profit on redemption than a regular income flow. ⟡ **Sterling Transferable Accruing Government Securities**.

Zip code American equivalent of the British **post code**. The word 'zip' is derived from the initial letters of the Zone Improvement Plan.

READ MORE IN PENGUIN

In every corner of the world, on every subject under the sun, Penguin represents quality and variety – the very best in publishing today.

For complete information about books available from Penguin – including Puffins, Penguin Classics and Arkana – and how to order them, write to us at the appropriate address below. Please note that for copyright reasons the selection of books varies from country to country.

In the United Kingdom: Please write to *Dept. EP, Penguin Books Ltd, Bath Road, Harmondsworth, West Drayton, Middlesex UB7 0DA*

In the United States: Please write to *Consumer Sales, Penguin USA, P.O. Box 999, Dept. 17109, Bergenfield, New Jersey 07621-0120.* VISA and MasterCard holders call 1-800-253-6476 to order Penguin titles

In Canada: Please write to *Penguin Books Canada Ltd, 10 Alcorn Avenue, Suite 300, Toronto, Ontario M4V 3B2*

In Australia: Please write to *Penguin Books Australia Ltd, P.O. Box 257, Ringwood, Victoria 3134*

In New Zealand: Please write to *Penguin Books (NZ) Ltd, Private Bag 102902, North Shore Mail Centre, Auckland 10*

In India: Please write to *Penguin Books India Pvt Ltd, 706 Eros Apartments, 56 Nehru Place, New Delhi 110 019*

In the Netherlands: Please write to *Penguin Books Netherlands bv, Postbus 3507, NL-1001 AH Amsterdam*

In Germany: Please write to *Penguin Books Deutschland GmbH, Metzlerstrasse 26, 60594 Frankfurt am Main*

In Spain: Please write to *Penguin Books S. A., Bravo Murillo 19, 1° B, 28015 Madrid*

In Italy: Please write to *Penguin Italia s.r.l., Via Felice Casati 20, I–20124 Milano*

In France: Please write to *Penguin France S. A., 17 rue Lejeune, F–31000 Toulouse*

In Japan: Please write to *Penguin Books Japan, Ishikiribashi Building, 2–5–4, Suido, Bunkyo-ku, Tokyo 112*

In South Africa: Please write to *Longman Penguin Southern Africa (Pty) Ltd, Private Bag X08, Bertsham 2013*

READ MORE IN PENGUIN

BUSINESS AND ECONOMICS

North and South David Smith

'This authoritative study ... gives a very effective account of the incredible centralization of decision-making in London, not just in government and administration, but in the press, communications and the management of every major company' – *New Statesman & Society*

I am Right – You are Wrong Edward de Bono

Edward de Bono expects his ideas to outrage conventional thinkers, yet time has been on his side, and the ideas that he first put forward twenty years ago are now accepted mainstream thinking. Here, in this brilliantly argued assault on outmoded thought patterns, he calls for nothing less than a New Renaissance.

Lloyds Bank Small Business Guide Sara Williams

This long-running guide to making a success of your small business deals with real issues in a practical way. 'As comprehensive an introduction to setting up a business as anyone could need' – *Daily Telegraph*

The *Economist* Economics Rupert Pennant-Rea and Clive Crook

Based on a series of 'briefs' published in the *Economist* , this is a clear and accessible guide to the key issues of today's economics for the general reader.

The Rise and Fall of Monetarism David Smith

Now that even Conservatives have consigned monetarism to the scrap heap of history, David Smith draws out the unhappy lessons of a fundamentally flawed economic experiment, driven by a doctrine that for years had been regarded as outmoded and irrelevant.

Understanding Organizations Charles B. Handy

Of practical as well as theoretical interest, this book shows how general concepts can help solve specific organizational problems.

READ MORE IN PENGUIN

BUSINESS AND ECONOMICS

The Affluent Society   John Kenneth Galbraith

Classical economics was born in a harsh world of mass poverty, and it has left us with a set of preoccupations hard to adapt to the realities of our own richer age. Our unfamiliar problems need a new approach, and the reception given to this famous book has shown the value of its fresh, lively ideas.

Lloyds Bank Tax Guide   Sara Williams and John Willman

An average employee tax bill is over £4,000 a year. But how much time do you spend checking it? Four out of ten never check the bill – and most spend less than an hour. Mistakes happen. This guide can save YOU money. 'An unstuffy read, packed with sound information' – *Observer*

Trouble Shooter II   John Harvey-Jones

The former chairman of ICI and Britain's best-known businessman resumes his role as consultant to six British companies facing a variety of problems – and sharing a new one: the recession.

Managing on the Edge   Richard Pascale

Nothing fails like success: companies flourish, then lose their edge through a process that is both relentless and largely invisible. 'Pascale's analysis and prescription for "managing on the edge" are unusually subtle for such a readable business book' – *Financial Times*

The Money Machine: How the City Works   Philip Coggan

How are the big deals made? Which are the institutions that really matter? What causes the pound to rise or interest rates to fall? This book provides clear and concise answers to a huge variety of money-related questions.

READ MORE IN PENGUIN

DICTIONARIES

Abbreviations
Archaeology
Architecture
Art and Artists
Astronomy
Biology
Botany
Building
Business
Challenging Words
Chemistry
Civil Engineering
Classical Mythology
Computers
Curious and Interesting Numbers
Curious and Interesting Words
Design and Designers
Economics
Electronics
English and European History
English Idioms
Foreign Terms and Phrases
French
Geography
Historical Slang

Human Geography
Information Technology
Literary Terms and Literary Theory
Mathematics
Modern History 1789–1945
Modern Quotations
Music
Musical Performers
Physical Geography
Physics
Politics
Proverbs
Psychology
Quotations
Religions
Rhyming Dictionary
Saints
Science
Sociology
Spanish
Surnames
Telecommunications
Troublesome Words
Twentieth-Century History